Mass Culture
Revisited

Mass Culture Revisited

Edited by

Bernard Rosenberg
Professor of Sociology
City University of New York

David Manning White
Chairman, Division of Journalism
School of Public Communication
Boston University

▣ Van Nostrand Reinhold Company
New York / Cincinnati / Toronto / London / Melbourne

Van Nostrand Reinhold Company Regional Offices:
New York / Cincinnati / Chicago / Millbrae / Dallas

Van Nostrand Reinhold Company International Offices:
London / Toronto / Melbourne

Manufactured in the United States of America

Published by Van Nostrand Reinhold Company
450 West 33rd Street, New York, N.Y. 10001

Published simultaneously in Canada by
Van Nostrand Reinhold Ltd.

15 14 13 12 11 10 9 8 7 6 5 4 3 2 1

To Daniel

for Max,

who would probably agree with the Mad Queen, that
it takes all the running you can do to keep in the
same place, and that if you want to get somewhere
else, you must run at least twice as fast as that.

Introduction

Plato has Socrates lament the discovery of writing. It will create forgetfulness in the learner's soul, and people will have the appearance of wisdom without the reality. Ever since then innovations in media of communications have been met with doleful predictions. The dime novel, the rental library, the early movies, all were considered bound to destroy culture.

Concern with the danger seems to vary with the historical situation, however. In this country we attained a peak of discussions about mass culture between 1935 and 1955. I think there were two reasons for this. The extension of radio and the advent of television brought about great changes in daily habits of the broad masses. This, in turn, made the intellectual sector of the community especially aware that the issue merits attention. Secondly, there was need for a burning issue. New Deal legislation had at least temporarily taken care of some of the early controversial topics: child labor, recognition of unions, minimum wages, etc. As a matter of fact, a somewhat ironical situation had developed. Progressive leadership had greatly increased the time and financial resources available to the working man. But instead of going to Columbia University for intellectual uplifting, he went to Columbia Broadcasting for entertainment.

When concrete studies provided more specific information, a striking fact became apparent, which wasn't really new but had never been so visible. This is the sharp social stratification in taste. The correlations between level of education on the one hand and interest in good music, serious drama, or competent discussion of news were much greater than any class difference studied before, including political affiliations. Perhaps the most disturbing finding was the fact that the large majority of the lower social strata liked the "detestable" commercial. Probably the broadest summary of the positions that had crystallized after World War II was expressed in a symposium characteristically sponsored jointly by the Academy of Arts and Sciences and the Tamiment Institute, a center for labor education. The report on the two-day confrontation of artists and philosophers, scientists and managers of mass media had a question mark in its title: Culture for the Millions?

It is my impression that since the time of this symposium, broad concern with mass culture has perhaps only temporarily abated. Two reasons seem to account for what at least became a plateau. For one, large new social issues came to the fore: McCarthyism, race relations, and the beginning of the Vietnamese war. But also the role of the mass media had become more complex from the point of view of the social critics. By and large, the media were on the liberal side. With some exaggeration one can say that the civic record of television improved as the cultural level of its entertainment programs deteriorated. This, incidentally, is not altogether surprising. Originally "the Press" was considered the spokesman of the citizenry against the danger of a tyrannical government. But slowly this changed to what is now a three-cornered situation: the citizen, the government, and the communications industry. Constantly shifting coalitions have formed. The progressive citizen in particular will sometimes call on the government to improve the level of broadcasting and sometimes enjoy the help of the mass media in finding out all the government is up to. The mass media too try to reach an optimum balance in this system. The civic courage of television in the last few years for instance, is quite impressive; as a matter of fact, foreign observers often ask me for an explanation. Somewhat facetiously I once put it this way: the networks continue their bad programs because this makes for larger audiences and therefore more profit from advertising. But they appease the social critic by supporting the liberal side of major social issues, since this does not cost much money, is consistent with a strong tradition of American constitutional guarantees, and is not too dangerous.

The present volume probably appears at just the right moment. A number of technological innovations in mass communications are on the horizon and that always elicits increased discussion of their cultural implications. When FM radio was introduced, Siepman talked of radio's second chance, because the larger number of available channels would permit diversification and attention to more specified tastes. Actually it did not turn out this way, because shortly thereafter television drowned out everything. Without the Xerox machine the spread of the underground press would not be possible. Now massive devices, such as cable television, satellites, and casettes are coming up. And, for the first time some public funds have been made available to support educational broadcasting. No one really can foresee the consquences of all this, but it will be interesting and important to watch these developments. To make us better observers a book such as the present one will be a great help indeed.

Debates about mass culture have a tantalizing way of ending in a draw. Sesame Street cleverly uses advertising techniques to teach children the alphabet; but does it not thereby make them more generally susceptible to commercial influences? Broadcasting has vastly increased the spread of classical music; but does it not degrade its structural qualities into lines one can whistle? Or inversely, women use television as a baby-sitter, but this may be the beginning of a type of family life in which day-care centers or kibbutz kinds of living will liberate both mother and child from a coercive isolation. Violence in movies is often in bad taste, but it may provide for many people a catharsis which keeps them from acting out their violent fantasies. The wit and insight invested in these arguments is impressive in its own right; of course, the balance is somewhat uneven. The communications industry has few defenders but it has the power of decision; the opposition has a better chance of being included in a book on mass culture. But there always are some situations where public opinion, through the moral strength of criticism or through political pressure, makes its influence felt. The reformer should be prepared to act when his opportunity arrives.

Herein lies the second merit of a collection such as the present one. It includes the report of insiders who relate in retrospect what they regret having done. Specific performances are carefully analyzed to reveal manipulation or unconscious biases by the producer. Efforts are made to explain the appearance or persistence of special eddies in the sea of cultural mass consumptions. Some empirical information is provided on the net of feedbacks relating the producer and the consumer; and there is some imaginative speculation linking this net with the broader social and economic system, although on this point an interlocutor should ask what is cause and what is just an indicator.

The amount of concrete knowledge we have on all these matters is still very meager, for a variety of reasons. It is technically difficult to study empirically how the supply in the mass culture market really affects the "consumer," what motivates him, and how open he would be to new ideas. Even if good research designs are available, they are expensive to carry out. And when it comes to the industry itself, secrecy veils many of its decisions.

One more handicap blocks the quest for factual information. In the last analysis what we do or hope for in regard to mass culture is based on value judgments. The prejudice is abroad that facts have no bearing on values. But this is a mistaken notion. The range of feasibility, the role of at first unanticipated consequences, the availability of alternatives, the emergence of effects concomitant to previous decisions—all these are topics which the empirical social scientist can handle. It is true that the contributions of such empirical work depend upon how well formulated a specific research problem is and how significantly it fits into the total picture. Here a third merit of the present publication appears. It can provide guidance for all those who feel it important to reduce, whenever possible, the gap between knowledge and social action.

Paul F. Lazarsfeld

July 1971

Contents

FILM

MAGAZINES AND NEWSPAPERS

SPY FICTION

ADVERTISING

ALTERNATIVES

Mass Culture
Revisited

The Issues

Mass Culture Revisited*

By Bernard Rosenberg

"If . . . Othello is absolutely better than Bonanza, then the Nielsen ratings are not so much a justification as an indictment. . . ."

Is mass culture an abomination, a harmless anodyne, a blessing? These are the real, if too often merely implicit, questions in an interminable and ferocious debate. No one yields. (Like travel, disputation very often narrows one—causing a man to confirm his old biases.) Even now, when most of us are sick of each other's polemics, the issue will not go away. And why should it? Could anything matter more than our manhood, and is anything less than that at stake?

Protagonists lambaste antagonists—who clobber neutralists—in an arena littered with faulty logic, shopworn analogies, dubious data and, over all, the unappetizing remains of a stale argument. I was once chided by an eminent art critic for sullying myself with this subject matter. He said to me and people of my captious disposition, as though addressing himself to sex censors who privately revel in the pornography they publicly condemn, "If you don't like the goods, stop handling them." (Days after his printed attack, we met by chance at Amos Vogel's Cinema 16 where he and I had gone, for our delectation, to view *Gold Diggers of 1936*.) Of course you can stop handling the stuff, but it won't stop handling you. Or has someone discovered a way not to hear Muzak, not to see billboards, not to be touched by propaganda? We are all deeply and equally implicated in a phenomenon which continues to revolt some of us as much as it pleases others. Many, like Marshall McLuhan and his followers, have managed to swallow the nausea they once felt. At peace in the electric wonderland, they celebrate what used to sicken them. After years of courtship, and growing but unrequited love, McLuhan married the Mechanical Bride whose every gesture used to repel him. He moves and anachronistically writes in a psychedelic delirium comparable only

* Reprinted from John G. Kirk, ed., *America Now*, 1968, by permission of the author and publisher (copyright 1968 by Atheneum Publishers).

to that of Timothy Leary. (Will they collide and embrace as inner and outer space converge?) Whole pages from that dated medium of Gutenberg's by which they so often go on expressing themselves, could be transposed from one author's work to the other's.

Here then we confront the champions of two debilitating and medically hazardous drugs: TV and LSD. TV, which probably does much to derange the nervous system through constant interruption and certainly hastens the onset of glaucoma, also turns out to be radioactive (and not just from cultural fallout). Color adds to the danger, and color sets multiply like cancer cells. LSD in good solid cubes can induce psychosis. Each is hallucinogenic in its own way. These are the media we are asked to exalt, complete with their appalling "massage" that "works us all over."

To what end? To the end that we should have a transcendental experience hitherto denied the species, to the end that we should explore previously unknown realms—and find God. Can anyone in possession of his senses, a human being who despite Leary's advice has not fully "blown his mind," help squirming and resisting when the Ad Alley physiotherapists lay their hands on him?

So, although I hesitate a spilt second on account of Harold Rosenberg's admonition (maybe I unconsciously love the thing I profess to hate, but if so, then like Oscar Wilde, I wish to kill that thing), allow me to reenter the fray. Back we go, and damn the opposition. Above all, damn that part of the opposition according to which mass or so-called popular culture does not even constitute a problem. My strongest criticism I therefore reserve for a friend and fellow sociologist, Herbert J. Gans—but solely in his role as culture critic. Gans does excellent community studies, and only now and then, but always disastrously, ventures outside his field.

It is a little thing if in California he lectures Hollywood screenwriters by telling them that they never had it so good. Such talk simply makes his auditors marvel at the staggering naïveté of an apparently sophisticated man, Gans, however, does a bigger and sillier thing when he covers popular culture in prose. His lengthy contribution to a widely disseminated textbook called *Social Problems* bears a subtitle which asks a nearly unintelligible question: "Popular Culture in America: Social Problem in a Mass Society or Social Asset in a Pluralist Society?" Reams of prose follow, all designed to answer that rhetorical question by insisting that his chosen social problem is really not a problem. One can only tell him, "All right, already. If you like the goods so much, go on handling them, but do not trouble your mind with Social Assets. Let the White House compute them. Find Liabilities, possibly a few lying around in some neglected community, uncounted, unweighed. Study them. If not, cease and desist."

Typical of those who attempt to dispose of the problem either by denying it or embracing it is the pose of objectivity. Rational discourse cannot take place when one group of passionate defenders claims scientific detachment for itself and dismisses every detractor as hopelessly subjective and emotional. Facts must be gathered and analyzed, but every one of us is, at bottom, engaged in a battle over values. Literary intellectuals are licensed to express their preferences; social scientists, if governed by positivist dogma, must remain disinterested. Whether there are more television sets than bathtubs in the land (there are) can be statistically determined. Whether this ratio is desirable or not is a question social science can neither answer nor evade. Moral judgment comes into play, always and necessarily, and certainly not as the exclusive concern of sociologists.

Auguste Comte, that brilliant neologist, coined two durable terms, and unnaturally conjoined one to the other. They are: sociology and positivism. Comte's first publication was *A Program of Scientific Work Required for the Reorganization of Society.* The founder of sociology saw a world out of kilter, and quixotically proposed to set it aright. Here and abroad, Comte's successors have followed in his footsteps. Social scientists, hip-deep in the values they ritually forswear, a majority of them genuinely concerned about the malaise of modern man, cannot help being "problem centered." Given something like race prejudice, overpopulation, suicide, international tension, or juvenile delinquency, they commit themselves to studying the problem in hand, with a view to ameliorating or abolishing it. Many practitioners apply the pretense of utter detachment to mass communications but surely, on this topic, everyone is prejudiced.

We had better own up to that simple truth: you tend to be for mass culture or against it *tout court.* If not, you have mixed feelings, strong or bland, but in neither case are they to be confounded with Olympian indifference. Dwight Macdonald, say, or Ernest van den Haag and I, for rather different reasons, abhor the whole business. Do evidence and reason support our revulsion? The question is discussable, and it might even be answerable. By the same token, when Gilbert Seldes or David Manning White or Frank Stanton is in the mood to offer qualified, reasoned praise for mass culture, one can come to grips with their case. But apparitions are not so easy to combat. Beware therefore the disguised apologist who hides his ghostly "objective" presence behind a smoke screen of jargon and gibberish. In other words, gentlemen, come on out and fight.

If sham objectivity is inadmissible, so is the contention that critics of mass culture are ipso facto critics of "the masses." Some are, and they speak from an aristocratic point of view best elucidated over a century ago by Alexis de Tocqueville. But there are other bases for criticism. I side with that earlier Macdonald who saw the masses (which is to say, everybody) as victims of a merciless technological invasion that threatened to destroy their humanity.

To reject "mass-cult" and "mid-cult" is to espouse high culture—and to do that is to be put down in certain circles as a snob. Very well, there are worse epithets. Shakespeare really does seem to me to be a better playwright than Arthur Miller and a better writer than Mickey Spillane. That they—and Homer and Faith Baldwin—are all popular is as incontrovertible as it is irrelevant. Such enormous qualitative differences separate them that no common frame of reference is broad enough to encompass their works. If to hold such a view is proof of snobbery, so be it.

But there is an attitude far more vicious than snobbery which converts the term "masses" into "slobs." Mad Avenue chefs "know" that finer fare, which they themselves prefer, should not be wasted on ordinary men and women. The communications industry drips with this contempt. Tough executives crudely and brutally assert the complete disdain they feel for their audiences. When a Dr. Frank Stanton or a Dr. Leo Rosten phrases these feelings with elegance, we are only slightly shocked. Intellectuals inside the business world may even deserve a measure of compassion: the late Gilbert Seldes of CBS had to walk more softly than Professor Gilbert Seldes of the academic world. But it is really distressing that so many philosophers, historians, psychologists, and other academics should also be irremediably contemptuous of the people at large. They form a sonorous and gratuitous echo of the noises made for money by manipulators and managers who at least have the goodness to hate themselves for bamboozling the rest of us.

All this talk of culture snobbery and bamboozling brings us at last to that central, unavoidable question that makes the cynical purveyors of and apologists for mass-cult so uneasy. It is a question, incidentally, that also makes Millsian democrats and utilitarians uneasy and probably should make all the rest of us uneasy as well. Quite simply, it is: by what right do we call high culture "high"?

If, as Jeremy Bentham insisted, pushpin (that is, pinball) brings greater happiness to a greater number of people than does poetry, and if there is no other way to compare poetry and pushpin, it follows that the slaves of the Nielsen ratings are home free. Then by any objective standard *The Beverly Hillbillies* are as good as—in fact, demonstrably better than—Mr. Leinsdorf and the Boston Symphony. To prefer Shakespeare to Spillane becomes mere eccentricity, and to publish *Valley of the Dolls* in contravention of one's own better taste becomes a sort of philanthropy—a little self-interested, perhaps, but plainly benign.

If, on the other hand, *Othello* is asolutely better than *Bonanza,* then the Nielsen ratings are not so much a justification as an indictment, and it makes no difference how many people at any given moment think otherwise. In that case there have to be persuasive arguments for describing *The Beverly Hillbillies*—without apology—as cultural garbage and the people who present the *Hillbillies,* as cultural garbagemen.

Does this sound offensively absolutist—a matter of elevating the prejudices of a minority to the level of categorical imperatives? Are cultural standards really exempt from that most cherished American method of extracting decisions from imponderables: majority rule?

Certainly standards of cultural excellence are created by people, and certainly, in the end, they are products of a consensus. But the important thing to remember is that the process has meaning only in a dimension of time. The judgment of one generation is merely a fragment of the consensus of many generations, one vote in the parliament of history. And about some cultural matters, the verdict of history seems reasonably clear. For example, it seems reasonably clear that for human beings everywhere art has always been a fairly serious and central preoccupation and that the most affecting and enduring art has related most closely to what is essential in the human condition. Conrad once summed up the elementary stuff of the novel by saying simply, "Men were born, they suffered, they died." There is more to it than that, of course—men also enjoy, love, wonder about their place in the universe—but Conrad was talking about priorities, and his point was that all these matters are high-priority concerns of art. Presumably he would have felt that showing for the ten-thousandth time what an amiable boob dear old Dad is would rate fairly low in the aesthetic sweepstakes.

Hardly anyone is unaware—at least viscerally—that ninety-nine percent of the material conveyed to us by the mass communications media is aesthetically and intellectually trivial. Why, then, do we put up with it? Worse, why do we vote for it, paying good money for kitsch magazines, elevating worthless books to best-sellerdom, and endorsing television imbecilities via the rating polls? It is not—as too many of my colleagues and all mass communicators insist—that the average man is no better than what he votes for. To a truly shocking degree, his vote is the product of communications-induced anesthesia. He is a victim, and his victimized voting tells us nothing about the thing in him on which the future of our culture and, no doubt, our democratic system absolutely depends. I am talking about his *potential*.

I mean to come back to this, for it is the core of my argument. But first I want to say a little more about the ways that mass communications can and do anesthetize us.

Do you doubt that they are capable of anesthetizing us? Competitive, if basically indistinguishable products—like variously packaged and skillfully projected political candidates—are said to be bought on the basis of personal influence. Those who propound this theory, when they are not subverting it (the same distingiushed social scientist who acts as prime consultant to the ad racket is capable of writing a book which purports to demonstrate that ads have no appreciable effect whatsoever) —those who propound this theory believe that direct face-to-face confrontation is really decisive: parishioners look to their priests, wives to their husbands, an army of susceptible followers respond to the "influentials" in their midst. Only small children and total amnesiacs could mistake this grotesque picture for reality, but it is not, therefore, a total falsehood.[1]

Let us not overtax our memories. You will recall in the year 1942 Japanese-American citizens and noncitizens were herded into concentration camps, their rights ruthlessly abrogated by an executive order straight from President Franklin D. Roosevelt. Why? Because the only good Jap was a dead one. China was, meanwhile, our noble Far Eastern ally. Now the only good Chinaman (unless resident on the island of Formosa) is a dead one, and Japan is our noble Far Eastern ally. Suppose the year is 1938: Stalin is a butcher, the USSR is a police state, its people are slaves. By 1943, "Uncle Joe" was an amiable autocrat and the USSR was economically democratic and getting to be politically democratic. By 1948 it was okay, or rather, it was mandatory to repeat what had been said in 1938. Later, as President Eisenhower made a move toward rapprochement with Russia soon after settling the Korean War, it looked for a moment as if the infinitely flexible media would be mobilized yet again.

We have learned as well as any people on earth that vice and virtue are interchangeable terms. Pollsters recently discovered that twenty-five percent of the American public believe Chiang Kai-shek still holds sway over mainland China. Thirty million Americans represent a large reservoir of superfluous goodwill: Red China could as easily be glorified tomorrow as it is reviled today. The trick consists of turning on the faucets of influence, of mobilizing the media.

Tyranny plus technology is the formula for totalitarianism. In this context, technology usually refers to modern mechanical means of produc-

---

[1] A friendly critic objects that I have been less than fair in presenting Paul Lazarsfeld's famous thesis. But no one protested in 1963 when Joseph Bensman and I put the matter as follows: "The public is unequally exposed to mass communications, and quite often, as the sociologist Paul Lazarsfeld has shown, those more exposed influence others who have trouble deciding between candidates and commodities. A personal element is present in what Lazarsfeld and Elihu Katz call 'the two-step flow' of mass communications. A heavy consumer of mass culture watches Ben Casey, listens to Chet Huntley, or vibrates via old movies to Clark Gable, and perhaps influences others to smoke Camels, buy EverReady Batteries, prize dimpled masculinity and abandon the undershirt. That messages originating in television, radio and films circulate this way—in a kind of aquatic mazurka, taking two steps instead of one—has misled some students into believing that personal influence is more powerful than the mass media. Yet, on the evidence so far adduced, opinion leaders who learn what to think from *Time* magazine, from *The Defenders,* from David Brinkley, merely magnify the power of these institutions by incorporating and transmitting their judgments to a still wider circle. I may buy Richard Nixon as my candidate at your suggestion, but if your suggestion comes from the firm of Batten, Barton, Durstine and Osborne, the advertising agency for the Republican National Committee, *there,* and not in your persuasive skill, lies the locus of power."

tion, but it should also refer to modern mechanical means of communication. I do not mean to divagate further into the relationship between mass communications and political tyranny. Suffice it to say that mass communications have demonstrated such a distressing ability to promote tyranny in the cultural realm that we can only tremble at the implications of their political misuse. Tremble, and fortify ourselves.

How? I think the answer, simply, is to take a more respectful attitude toward our fellow man. My position is that the antidote to mass culture is high culture, that high culture means art and learning and that these goods are potentially accessible to every person not suffering from severe brain damage.

I have never heard the disrespectful attitude more offensively presented than at a conference, some years ago, on mass culture, to which a wide assortment of scholars and artists were invited. A truncated version of what they said may be found in a back issue of the magazine *Daedalus* (Spring, 1960) and in a book called *Culture for the Millions.* The conference was rigged in favor of intellectuals who support mass culture. Its centerpiece was a paper by Edward W. Shils who had long contended that "brutal culture" perfectly suited the masses. He repeated his thesis with the utmost gentility, thereafter lapsing into merciful silence. Others took up the cudgels; but as a peripheral participant, I had no opportunity to deal with Shils' peculiar system of classifying his opponents. As an anti-anti-mass-culturalist, Shils had some while before explained that writers upset about mass culture are mostly disillusioned Marxists, angry at the masses they foolishly idealized in the thirties. Now I realize there are many more ex-Trotskyites than there ever were Trotskyites; but as a case in point I, who beginning with my first "scholarly" article in 1948 have consistently found fault with Karl Marx's thought, really did not then, or ever, belong to a school of German sociologists into which Mr. Shils squeezed me. Anyhow, my target—like that of most anti-mass-cultists—was not the masses, but those who gull and dehumanize them.

To the fore of the conference stepped Arthur Schlesinger, Jr. He pointed out—with no mention of their notorious inadequacies—that IQ tests show an unequal distribution of intelligence in the population. Additionally, he suggested the existence of an AQ, or aesthetic quotient. Some few people are naturally responsive to art; the masses are not; everyone gets exactly what he is capable of absorbing. Neat, equitable, democratic—provided only that most people are natural inhabitants of Slobbovia. Are they? I would suggest several lines of evidence which indicate that they are not.

Almost all introductions to sociology contain a brief list of "universals," or institutions found everywhere. Religion and the family nearly exhaust the list. Anthropologists are likely to add art. From Frazer to Kroeber and beyond, anthropologists have been fascinated with primitive art. Few sociologists are expert in primitive art, and even fewer display interest in its civilized manifestation. Nevertheless, art is universal. No human society, however oppressive its circumstances, is devoid of art. This singular datum merits some socioligical consideration. At present, it receives hardly any.

Since art is universal, the aesthetic impulse may be an integral part of human nature. I have argued elsewhere that it is. The individual needs food and shelter simply to survive; I would contend that he needs art about as much as he needs sex. Either drive can be extinguished, and he will go on living, but not without paying a heavy price in the diminution of his being. Small children in the United States spontaneously express themselves with whatever art materials they find. Youngsters react to pictures and to music with a measure of authenticity rarely attainable later on in their lives. What happens? It is like what happens to American taste buds. Frozen and packaged foods, above all bread (the staff of life —that compost of air and glue), those oats which only horses ate until Mr. Kellogg sold them as dry cereal: a diet like this from infancy onward can deaden anybody's palate. With gruel today and gruel tomorrow, who can savor gourmet meals? Similarly, extended pseudosexual behavior produces fixation at that level, virtually barring "the real thing," true sexual fulfillment. In precisely the same way, kitsch and instant education, if ingested for long enough, lead to cultural and intellectual dyspepsia or anesthesia.

In *The Theater of the Absurd,* Martin Esslin describes an unusual presentation of *Waiting for Godot,* a play that flopped on Broadway after the daily reviewers declared it to be excessively obscure. The production mentioned by Esslin took place in a maximum-security prison before a truly captive audience—which was enthralled by a play it found perfectly intelligible. The Freedom Southern Theater does vanguard drama successfully before rural Negroes who dig the message that a meaningful contemporary play somehow cannot convey to jaded middle-class theatergoers seeking expensive entertainment. The Théâtre Nationale Populaire performs in tents outside Paris; proletarian theatrical enterprises have been revived in England; Shakespeare clicks in the park or on the street. What does this enthusiasm signify if not the capacity of common men to surmount the trash that is heaped upon them? They too are able to have aesthetic experiences. One percent of the public views living drama with any regularity on the stages of North America. An ambitious, and no doubt unrealizable, goal is to double that number, all the way to two percent. Those who go are homogeneous: overwhelmingly upper middle class, professional, disproportionately Jewish. Blue-collar workers shun theaters and bookstores all over the Western world—which does not prove that they are constitutionally unresponsive to the drama or incapable of reading good books. Workers in Buenos Aires buy Argentine classics (deliberately priced low on an experimental basis) at kiosks instead of book-stores, which they would never dream of entering. A change of locus—for instance, theater in union halls and not in ever more lavish "cultural centers"—is frequently all that we need to reanimate the aesthetic im-pulse which lies dormant in every man.

Dedicated artists and teachers realize all this. The custodians of mass culture and their academic satraps do not. By their gross underestimation of human potentialities, they drug us beyond any hope of redemption. We must continue to do battle with them or become willing accomplices in the creation of "joyous serfdom." For, to withdraw from that battle out of fatigue, boredom, or despair, is in large measure to be morally accountable for losing it.

If Godard can do three or four low-budget films a year and make money producing art, albeit not necessarily great art; if Pacifica can operate a network of FM stations, broadcasting views that may be politically repug-nant, but are usually dissident and provocative, and all this on a shoe-string; if even Hollywood, after destroying much of its best talent (Welles and Huston in our time, Griffith, Von Stroheim, and Keaton long ago), can offer directors enough leeway to be creative without forcing them into exile or into obsequious submission, and Warsaw or Budapest can do the same; if little magazines with limited circulation can survive; and if subscription TV finally emerges as something less than a disaster—then, the direction in which we must try to move is clear.

Art does not have to be swamped by machines—provided the machines are used to foster pluralism, diversity, and decentralization. However Sisyphean a job it may be, the present process which involves deperson-alization, concentration, and deracination must be reversed, and as rap-idly as possible. For, just as only the young can effortlessly learn a second language, so there is a chronological point after which generations bred on TV cannot assimilate the best that has been written and said. Sub-art systematically unfits a person for art, and vice versa. They really are incompatible. Not mere dabbling, but heavy consumption of one eventually obviates the other. You cannot have a lot of both.

If art is long, sub-art is longer and life remains incredibly short. I would rather miss a flower in the jungle of mass culture (possibly the Beatles are such a flower) than lose myself in that jungle. "Liberalized" totalitarianism isn't good enough for most of us who still reject any op-pressive system. Similarly, a thaw in the arts, here or elsewhere, does not produce that rich and wonderfully varied garden we have every right to demand.

The artist is basically an anarchist who should have as much solitude and tranquillity and as much withdrawal from commercial or political clamor as society can provide. He and we desperately need his creations. The human spirit will perish without them. As things stand, I can only agree with Herbert Read that Shelley chose his epithet well in calling poets *unacknowledged* legislators of the world. Read goes on, "The catalyst is unchanged, unabsorbed; its activity therefore not acknowledged. It is peculiarly difficult for the artist in society to accept this thankless task: to stand apart, and yet to mediate, to communicate something to society as essential as bread and water, and yet to be able to do so from a position of insulation, of disaffection. Society will never understand or love the artist because it will never appreciate his indifference, his so-called objectivity. But the artist must learn to love and understand the society that renounces him. He must accept the contrary experience, and drink, with Socrates, the deadly cup." Perhaps not forever. Surely now.

Mass Culture Revisited*

By David Manning White

That astute and perceptive historian, Tacitus, once referred to Petronius as an *elegentiae arbiter.* After reading Bernard Rosenberg's eloquent discourse of the preceding pages one must concede that he, too, is a sincere arbiter of the public taste. Since by nature I am an acquiescent person, all of my preacquiescent dispositions are to avoid yet one more confrontation on mass culture. Like Ferdinand the Bull I would prefer to smell the flowers rather than tangle with a brilliant matador, except for one nagging, unrelenting conclusion: Mr. Rosenberg is still mistaking *cause* for *effect,* shadow for substance, especially when he proclaims that we must continue to debate mass culture with "nothing less than our manhood" at stake.

Although I deplore some of the blatantly dehumanizing aspects of mass culture as much as he does, I also realize that *Homo sapiens* has always found ways in which to confound and corrupt the fabric of his society. I am no more repelled or distressed by the obnoxious blight of a peepshow on Broadway and 42nd Street in 1971 than by the recollection of that ingenious pander who fashioned pornographic snuff boxes in early 19th century England and who was apprehended hawking his wares in a convent school.

The mass culture critic always insinuates that in some previous era the bulk of men were rational, pacific, and learned.[1] The good old days— like the Roman Empire during Nero? Admittedly, the Romans didn't have a television set to watch the lions massacre the various unwilling guests

---

* Published for the first time in this volume.
[1] Karl Jaspers quotes an Egyptian chronicler of 4000 years ago: "Robbers abound. . . . No one ploughs the land. People are saying: 'We do not know what will happen from day to day. . .' The country is spinning round and round like a potter's wheel. No more do we hear anyone laugh. Great men and small agree in saying: 'Would that I had never been born.' The masses are like timid sheep without a shepherd . . . Impudence is rife."

during the Colosseum half-time show. If I seem to have a penchant for Nero, forgive me, but few characters in history hold as much fascination for me.

One might blame Nero's subsequent psychopathia on poor schooling, except that his main tutor was Seneca, the renowned Stoic philosopher, who later became a powerful advisor when his pupil became Emperor. Steeped in the classic tradition, Nero had a greater passion for high art (poetry, drama, and music) than any ruler in history. For example, he practiced the harp so assiduously that in 64 AD (the same year that Rome burned down) he gave a public concert in Naples. The auditorium was so overcrowded for his recital that it collapsed shortly after the performance. In his various recitals, Nero also sang poems he had composed, and he even tried the boards as an actor, playing at various times the roles of Oedipus, Heracles, and the matricide, Orestes.

So here was Nero, the classic culturist *par excellence,* who never in his life had been corrupted by a comic book, Mickey Spillane, the Untouchables, Harold Robbins, Guy Lombardo and the Royal Canadiens, or an ad for Alka-Seltzer. Still he proceeded to have his mother murdered, not to mention his first wife, Octavia (whom he dispatched so that he could marry Poppaea). Not that Poppaea fared much better, for she died during advanced pregnancy from a kick in the stomach by Nero. He subsequently found a youth, Sporus, who closely resembled Poppaea, had him castrated, and married him in a formal ceremony that led a local Art Buchwald to quip that it was too bad Nero's father hadn't had such a wife.

Inevitably, this black comedy had to come to an end, but not before Nero had his old teacher, Seneca, killed, as well as the poet, Lucan, who opened his veins and died reciting his own poetry. As the Senate's soldiers finally tracked Nero down, he mourned a doleful "Qualis artifex pereo" and slashed his throat. Granted history has few to match Nero, but if we are going to make a great *megillah* on how the mass media are dehumanizing us, all I ask is that we remember the Robespierres, Caligulas, Napoleons, Jack the Rippers, etc., who "did their thing" long before the technology-engendered mass media.

The dangerous fallacy in Mr. Rosenberg's well-intentioned argument lies in its implication that many of our worst troubles in this anxiety-ridden century stem from the proliferation of mass communication entertainment. It's like blaming John Wayne for creating the Green Berets and the Vietnam war. Incidentally, despite Mr. Rosenberg's belief in the overwhelming propaganda valence of the mass media, the movie of the Green Berets was hardly a blockbuster at the box office.

There is a distinct danger that if we make the mass media the scapegoat for the miasmic lives we have given ourselves during this century, we may be insulating ourselves from more basic problems. As Lazarsfeld and Merton so aptly put it, "Many make the mass media targets for hostile criticism because they feel themselves duped by the turn of events."

Suppose we were able to go back by a time machine to 19th century Russia, or 17th century Egypt, or to the bear-baiting pits of 15th century England, which amused the public long before Thomas Kyd's initial attempts to create dramas. If we took a probability sample of the population of those periods, I believe we would find people less aware, less concerned about the pressing problems of their day than the 20th century American.

It is feckless to speculate whether the "average" Englishman during the reign of Charles II was more vulgar and less knowledgeable than a peasant living under Ivan the Terrible, or the kind of silent-majority American who voted for Warren Gamaliel Harding in the election of 1920. Each age, each people, each culture has its own brand of coarseness, vulgarity, and stupidity, and always enough to suffice unto itself.

Mr. Rosenberg is deeply troubled because so much of the content of the mass media is trivial. I have yet to find any hard evidence that the average man of 100 years ago spent his leisure hours reading Spinoza or listening to symphony orchestras or partaking of other cultural pursuits. As Henry David Thoreau wrote about life a century ago, "The mass of men lead lives of quiet desperation."

Men in Thoreau's time worked seventy hours or more each week, and only the most wealthy and privileged knew that a world of art and music and drama existed. The six-day week of seventy-two hours prevailed in 1900; by 1950 the work week in most industrial countries decreased to about forty-four hours, and today is forty hours or less.

The average worker today has about 2750 hours of leisure each year (after we subtract his work week, his eight hours sleep each night, his eating, and commuting). Mr. Rosenberg's argument implies that if it were not for the "abominable" mass media influencing the public taste, the majority of men would devote most of these 2750 hours of leisure in pursuit of "high culture." He says that "high culture means art and learning, and that these goods are potentially accessible to every person not suffering from severe brain damage."

I agree that today high culture is accessible, in fact more so than in any previous period of history. So why doesn't the average man avail himself of his ever-increasing leisure to study Bach's two-part inventions or attend lectures on the Postimpressionists at his local museum of fine arts? Why, in other words, does he choose to sit passively in front of the television set night after night? Why are the mass media so seductive of his hard-won leisure hours? Perhaps, because the seductee is getting what he has always craved—a partial, palatable answer to the questions all men ask themselves, whether they are philosophers or coal-miners: Who am I, why am I here, what is the meaning of my life vis-à-vis the universe? Tough questions, seldom-come-to-grips-with questions, for most men, long before the mass media served them as an anodyne.

Participating in the activities of "high" culture is not simply a matter of having more leisure hours, or having a much higher standard of living than our fathers had, or the availability of museums, libraries, great musical organizations, and educational television stations. In reality, "high" culture is not so easily attained, and it is a canard to suggest that the major impediments to an almost universal involvement are the seductive, venal, trivializing mass media.

We partake of "high art" via great novels and drama, timeless painting and sculpture, profoundly conceived symphonies—all of which have a common thrust, a demand that the reader or viewer has developed a sensibility that enables him to understand and accept the enigmatic nature of man's existence. This sensibility does not come with the privileges of birth or class, but depends on whether an individual is motivated toward a fuller understanding of his life experience, realized only through encounter with "high art." It doesn't make any difference whether that individual is Robert Lowell, descendant of the bluest blood of New England, or James Baldwin, expatriate from the rat-infested estaminets of Harlem. Why one person elects to find his *raison d'être* in a life of high art is clearly not a matter of mere sociocultural variables.

Two kids grew up in the same decrepit block in Brooklyn in the early 1900s, both of them sons of immigrant Jewish families. One of them gave us the opera *Porgy and Bess;* his peer became "Lepke," the boss of Murder, Inc. Throughout recorded history most men have sought anodynes from the deepest anxieties about their existence. They did so before any aspects of mass culture pervaded society; they would continue to do so if every vestige of mass culture were to disintegrate and disappear tomorrow.

Because "high art" demands, of both creators and audiences, motivation and years of dedicated interest, I cannot believe that it is *solely* mass entertainment that stands in the way of high culture on the part of the majority. Nor can I accept the Swiftian picture that emerges from Professor Rosenberg's essay suggesting that the Yahoos became that way because some casuistrous Houyhnhms on Madison Avenue, Radio City, and Hollywood have plotted to lobotomize their artistic sensibilities.

There is, without doubt, a great deal of "escapist" fare in our mass media diet. Yet every day all of our media are also telling us of the almost insuperable problems of overpopulation, poverty, the rape of the earth's resources, and the ever-present potentiality of atomic apocalypse. To single out *The Beverly Hillbillies* as the hallmark of television is to misrepresent how the mass media *in general* reflect and survey the state of contemporary life for the great majority of Americans.

It is fairly easy to find enough sleazy and banal offerings foisted by meretricious entrepreneurs on some members of the Great Audience. But these are not the whole audience. It is therefore wrong to underestimate the mass media's contribution to a more general awareness of social problems, and, perhaps, to their solutions.[2] Learned scientists may wearily prognosticate an ecological doomsday at an M.I.T. or Harvard symposium. Yet how much more urgent the problem of pollution becomes for twenty or thirty million Americans when Walter Cronkite, during his daily television news program, asks, "Can the world be saved?"

As the noted director of the Max Planck Institute for Physiology of Behavior, Dr. Konrad Lorenz, observed: "Despite the drawbacks of television, there are great blessings coming from the mass media. For instance, the whole antagonism against the war in Vietnam which you find in America —the very just antagonism—is largely based on the fact that people actually see the atrocities."

Or as educational reformer, John Holt, put it: "Students do not find out from the S.D.S. alone in what desperate shape our society and civilization find themselves, and how little idea anyone in the older generation has of how they may be saved. They find this out in our TV, newspapers, and mass media."

Are we Americans the only people who turn to the mass media for surcease from the too immediate realities of our external worlds? Only eighteen months after it was introduced into Israel (in mid-1968), television became the most pervasive form of entertainment. In a country surrounded by enemies who daily threatened total destruction, ten percent of the Israelis have each invested about $400 to buy an old-fashioned black-and-white TV receiver. This is a lot of money in Israel, where the Director of Television for the country's Broadcasting Authority earns a monthly salary of only $400.

What were the Israelis watching in 1970? Mostly syndicated reruns of *Bonanza, Mission Impossible, I Spy, The Defenders, Robin Hood,* and that sophisticated soap-opera equally popular in England and the United States, *The Forsythe Saga.* Television is hardly the Trojan Horse craftily placed in Tel Aviv by some Egyptian Ulysses. The latest news reports from Israel belie any suspicion that television has narcotized the will or the ability of these people to defend their homeland.

---

[2] Dr. Karl Menninger writes, "We are all transfixed by the extraordinary fact of witnessing history as it occurs—the space flights, the death of a President, the Middle East crisis. These are the hours when the television set becomes a tie that unites us with people all over the Nation, even the world. For a time we are experiencing the same scenes and sounds as thousands or millions of other concerned persons. There is comfort and growth in such experiences. Our sympathies are engaged, our thoughts are excited and our horizons are expanded through sharing sorrow and tension and acts of courage. We need to know how other people live and strive, succeed and fail, meet disaster and tragedy and success."

Professor Rosenberg continually asserts that the mass media have the ability to tyrannize, propagandize, and narcotize the whole so-called mass audience indiscriminately. One might ask that *if* the media can have such collective negative effects, why can't the same mass media have collective positive effects?

But any discussion of mass-media audiences as nameless, homogeneous collectivities is naïve. First of all, this notion of a vast, undifferentiated audience is a generalization employed too glibly by some social scientists as well as some advertising agencies, both intent on "selling" us something. Audiences consist of individuals, who even when they share common viewing or reading experiences, use the media to satisfy their own particular purposes. A so-called "audience of fifty million" is a statistical amalgam that indiscriminately lumps together fifty million distinct individuals, each concerned with fulfilling his own needs, goals, and expectations.

At one particular hour a viewer may be part of the Great Audience watching the puerile antics of the Beverly Hillbillies; this doesn't preclude the possibility that he watches many other kinds of programs. Indeed, he might have been watching the forementioned Cronkite report, and for psychological equanimity was impelled to seek relief sans challenge. Personally, if I couldn't read Charles Schulz's *Peanuts* every morning in my newspaper, I don't know if I could tolerate the grim tidings of the front page. But that doesn't mean that I read only comic books all the day long.

Television seems to disturb Professor Rosenberg more than the other mass media, perhaps because it has become the most pervasive and time-consuming leisure activity of this generation. But even the evaluation of television depends to a large extent on a critic's expectations. For example, in February 1969, on a Sunday evening, the Columbia Broadcasting System televised the Royal Shakespeare Company's production of *A Midsummer Night's Dream*. It competed at the same hour with NBC's *Bonanza* and ABC's movie of the week *Spartacus,* starring Kirk Douglas. Shakespeare got an ostensibly measly 13.7 Arbitron rating, or about a 23% share of those watching television at that hour, as compared to ABC's 37% and NBC's 40% of the audience. Granted that *Midsummer* is a relatively minor gem in the Shakespearean jewel box, the production was delightfully performed for an audience of some twenty million men, women, and children. This figure can be interpreted two ways, depending on one's expectations. It can be compared invidiously with the thirty-five million who elected to watch the simplistic homilies of *Bonanza;* but I prefer the observation that more individuals saw this particular Shakespearean comedy than the Globe Theater could seat in 10,000 performances.

Is television really, as Mr. Rosenberg asserts, a "cancerous growth that systematically unfits a person for art, and vice versa?" Although television is hardly more than a quarter of a century old as a mass medium, one could still point to hundreds of television programs that quite conceivably have ameliorated an individual's capacity to enjoy high art. Certainly, one example is Leonard Bernstein's Young People's Concerts, widely seen over the past fifteen years on the CBS Television Network by an aggregate audience approaching a billion Americans. To such fine music programs we might add the television documentaries that deal with artists and cultural artifacts, such as those done by Lucy Jarvis and John Secondari, the National Geographic and Jacques Cousteau discovery programs, and the consistently excellent Hallmark Hall of Fame drama series.

Mass culture does not and cannot remain static in our society, primarily because it follows the needs of the people rather than fashioning them. A good example of this has happened to Hollywood, the erstwhile dream factory. The big studios are closing down and selling their costumes, Roman galley ships, and iron horse choo-choos to curio buyers. In 1969, MGM lost $53 million, Twentieth-Century Fox lost more than $70 million, and comparable losses beset Paramount and Warners. The explanation was stated succinctly by Martin S. Davis, senior vice president of Gulf and Western, the large conglomerate which owns Paramount. "These kids," he said, "aren't going to the movies to take home dreams." By "these kids" he meant that 75% of today's movie audience is between sixteen and twenty-five years old. Raised in a crisis society, "these kids" are involved and voluble individuals who are beginning to demand relevant movies reflecting reality as *they* perceive it. As Pauline Kael so aptly put it in her review of an excellent 1970 film, Irving Kershner's *Loving,* "It is no longer true that no one ever went broke underestimating the intelligence of the American public; look at the figures on *Doctor Doolittle.*" The European moviemakers who became popular at the art houses helped to break down the acceptance of predigested entertainment, and during the last year talented Americans, who in the past were frustrated and crushed by the studio heads, have finally been making contact with the audiences who are willing to work out their own responses.

Today, the kinds of films that young people are willing to plunk down the $2.50 to see are Costa-Gravas' *Z* and the brilliant *The Confession,* *M.A.S.H.,* and *They Shoot Horses, Don't They?* They aren't paying that kind of money to see Kirk Douglas go skinny-dipping with Faye Dunaway in an atrocious Elia Kazan film based on his novel *The Arrangement,* or to watch an over-plump, aging Elizabeth Taylor shack up with beautiful Warren Beatty in a film which showed the heavy hand of a once resourceful director, George Stevens.

This is the same young generation that is the first to be brought up entirely on television, and just as they are now beginning to influence the cinema, they will inevitably demand more challenging television fare. Gore Vidal believes that television has had a major role in developing the social consciousness of our troubled youth. "On Vietnam, on the race issue," he says, "youth is probably the only group in the United States which is behaving well, and much of their rebellion is positive . . . . they're acting as if the principles we say we believe in and they should believe in are true."

One is encouraged to think that today's films are creatively more relevant, too, than those of even a dozen years ago, when MGM's *Gigi* got nine Oscars at the annual publicity extravanganza known as the Academy Awards. By 1969, *Z* was a strong contender for Hollywood's highest award, competing with an American film of such artistic calibre as *They Shoot Horses, Don't They?*

What is not open to question is a changing audience and films that reflect that changing audience's taste. We will see even more changes in films, hopefully in the direction of high art. There are hundreds of college campuses in the United States offering courses in film as a contemporary art form, and it is a truism that among college students, "film is in."[3]

As the college enrollments have continued to increase enormously in the past two decades, we see other indicators of their impact on the mass media. For example, in 1960 the number of paperback books in print was 6800, and in 1970 the number had increased nearly *twelve times* to 81,000. Granted that several thousand were kitsch of no conceivable value, still one is skeptical about the old saw that bad art drives out good when we note seventeen different paperback editions of Jane Austen's *Pride and Prejudice.* Or take another indicator of what is happening to our popular culture, the redoubtable Schwann catalogue of recordings, and compare the 1970 edition with its counterpart of even a decade ago.

It is time to draw this debate to a close (unless in 1984 Mr. Rosenberg and I decide to have another go at it in yet one more volume, undoubtedly to be titled "The Son of Mass Culture."). Clearly, he will never convince me that the mass media *per se* are the bêtes noires that have poisoned the sources of our artistic creativity. We really can't blame the mass media because our culture has not produced an artist of Shakespeare's magnitude since his death in 1616. For nearly 300 years, sans television and motion pictures, *Playboy* magazines, and Madison Avenue, there still wasn't another Shakespeare. Might it not be that a genius of his dimensions emerges only every 400 years? Mr. Rosenberg finds it impossible to consider that the next Bard of Avon might find himself working for

---

[3] Robert Windeler observed in the *New York Times,* April 18, 1968, that "Mike Nichols and Jean Luc-Godard have become the heroes of many college campuses. The American director and the French movie-maker are the Pied Pipers of a movement that has 60,000 graduate and undergraduate students enrolled in 1,500 film courses at 120 colleges."

David Lean or as a resident dramatist for the Columbia Broadcasting System; I do not discount that possibility.

The measurement of cultural level in any particular society at any given time is, of course, extremely difficult, if not impossible. My feeling (which Professor Rosenberg obviously does not share) is that slowly the level of our cultural life in the United States is rising. There are, naturally, many millions who will continue to extract from the media the least demanding aspects of artistic rewards. Middle America, with its "silent majority," influences the mass media far more than the mass media influence it. Note, if you will, that the four "most admired men" in a 1970 Gallup Poll were Richard Nixon, Billy Graham, Spiro Agnew, and Lyndon Johnson.

We are not going to return to the time when men worked seventy hours a week. Rather there will be a proliferation of mass leisure in the years ahead. My major hope for an amelioration of our cultural life lies in the rapidly increasing number of our young people who attend college, for as they enter the mainstream of American life they are effecting changes in our mass culture. The emerging pattern of motion pictures, the paperback book revolution, the hundreds of cultural television programs (scores of them on network programming), all attest to the quality of this growing audience.

As Alfred North Whitehead once clearly observed, "There are no whole truths; all truths are half-truths. It is trying to treat them as whole truths that plays the devil." Yet, Mr. Rosenberg and I are seeking the same qualities in American life, even though we differ on the ways an Augustinean City of Culture may be realized. My side of the half-truth says: there are more opportunities for an individual in America today to partake of the best of the past and to demand the best of today's artistic works than any previous time in history. For those who believe in Whitehead's words, "art is the imposing of a pattern on experience, and our esthetic enjoyment is recognition of the pattern," it is the task to enlist the help of educators and media-managers—all who believe this credo—for the enrichment of our collective lives.

The Overview

We begin with a little galaxy of selections, each brilliant in its own way, all suggesting how little and how much the discussion has shifted since our first anthology appeared. Plato looms large. John Stuart Mill appears and reappears. And so inescapably does Matthew Arnold. Our authors ring new variations on old themes, and then subtly introduce new themes as well.

Sebastian de Grazia, an American political scientist and philosopher, offers us the fruits of his reflections on leisure, exploding several myths as he goes along. After his analysis of data painstakingly gathered by the Twentieth Century Fund, it is difficult to believe that Americans have much free time, and impossible to equate that time with leisure in any historically meaningful sense. So to put the matter is to challenge widely accepted suppositions, and to provide a more appropriate theoretical setting for the study of mass culture.

Edward Shils, an exceptionally sophisticated sociologist, plunges us once again into a timeless controversy. His paper is probably the most powerful defense yet written of how things are and the ostensibly positive direction in which they are moving. For all his force and logic, Shils is apparently not unassailable. Ernest van den Haag, a social scientist, and Hannah Arendt, the political philosopher, provide incisive rebuttals and different perspectives. Their exchange took place originally within the context of a three-day symposium on mass culture which for the first time included not social scientists but representatives of the mass media, critics, historians, and philosophers. This mixture had a generally leavening effect, partly reflected in the material that follows.

With Allan Trachtenberg, a professor of English and American Studies, we are on the same ground, and yet radically removed from it. Trachtenberg transports us from a relatively quiescent period—the early sixties—into what seems another time, another place, our own more tempestuous present. No one clearly foresaw the transition from a silent to a strident generation. Trachtenberg causes the reader to consider some paradoxes that have arisen in a situation which fosters militant but mostly expressive political action, with maximum publicity provided by the establishment.

To the widely abused "counter culture," Kingsley Widmer adds such richly connotative terminology as "populist culture," "sub-establishment," and "underculture." These concepts complicate, even as they illuminate, certain significant currents and crosscurrents of our time. His own variegated intellectual background makes possible a most suggestive distinction between *power-preservative culture* and *post-industrial mass culture*. It also equips this author for the task of meeting Marshall McLuhan's delirious celebration of the mass media: he undertakes to demolish it with a much more subtle dialectic of his own. If Widmer as a broadgaged literary man, is merciless in his critique of McLuhanism (dubbed McLunacy by even more savage detractors), he is hardly gentle in dealing with "mainstream mass culture and its technocratic ideology" or with traditional but diluted estheticism or with problematic populism. Nuances are of the essence, and Widmer's polemic stance notwithstanding, they are abundant in this seminal essay.

Finally, to round out our introductory overview, two gifted sociologists, Joseph Bensman and Robert Lilienfeld, address themselves to "the journalistic attitude," its indispensable uses and frequent abuses.

All in all, and at the very least, a mixed picture, which convinces us more than ever that we urgently need the best possible interpretations.

Transforming Free Time[*]

By Sebastian de Grazia

What kind of rule is this? The more timesaving machinery there is, the more pressed a person is for time. Take modern home appliances, an electric beater or whipper, for example. Cuisine has not improved over the last hundred years because of the superiority of one beater over another. A soufflé today is no better than it was a hundred years ago. In fact, the gourmet would argue the contrary: a motorized beater is of no use in making a good soufflé, or even a good mayonnaise. If time is saved, then, it may be at the expense of the culinary art, but is time really saved?

Note that the time counted consists only of those one and a half minutes less it takes to whip the egg whites. The electric beater costs more; whatever costs more has taken somebody's time to earn the money to buy it. This time is not counted. Money is not exchanged for labor and skill alone, but also, as current phraseology might put it, for labor and skill through time. The worker, we mustn't forget, sells his time. Furthermore, of the one and a half minutes saved, how many are depreciated? Once cookbook authors recognized that some things are easy to do, their recipes began to call for beating, whipping, chopping, and mixing without prudent limits. So the same one and a half minutes saved, repeated unnecessarily, are no longer saved but added. How often was the grass cut before the lawnmower (now motorized) was invented? In sight of grass mowed to the quick the American may be happier for his success in keeping nature under control, but he is no healthier, the grounds no cleaner, the landscape no lovelier. Still this is not the point. Rather, how much time does he save as a result of the timesaving lawnmower? Let us hope such tools and appliances save some minutes; if not, who would find time to keep them in repair? Motorized appliances are harder to

* Reprinted from *Of Time, Work and Leisure*, 1962, pp. 330–380, by permission of the Twentieth Century Fund. Copyright, 1962, by the Twentieth Century Fund.

repair by oneself, so the housewife gets on the telephone—and so on, until she reaches the time-money it costs the breadwinner to pay the repairman.

Let us move on from the level of the lowly household to the wide plane of diplomatic action. In the Vatican until recently vacations have been brief for the *curia romana*. A hundred years ago, though, it took so long to send a message to Spain, say, and to get an answer back, that the custom was to take off the months from mid-August to mid-October. Or we can use a transportation sequence from the pages of modern history: A man has to walk one hour to work. He doesn't think much about it until he learns that there are ways within his reach to do it in less time. A horse was always too expensive; a bicycle, though, called for but a small capital outlay and an almost negligible upkeep. As yet, neither horse nor bicycle, as means of transport, brings about a time and space revolution, although the bicycle begins to extend the city's limits. Then comes public transportation, followed by automobiles. Though at first a man can get to work in ten minutes instead of his former one hour, it isn't long before he is spending one hour riding or driving to work. Some might point out regretfully that he lacks the healthy exercise of a morning walk. Yes, but usually he can still walk if he wants to. (Most bridges still have pedestrian runways.) From home to the job would take about five hours. Others might point out that the air he breathes in the roar of rush hour traffic is not so pure as it used to be—but you can't have everything.

In big-city rush hours people push and cram into bus and subway: they must get to work on time. On the way out it's the same thing: rush. Dinners and families are waiting (why is home on such a strict time schedule?), or a courting is on, which means get home, eat, clean up, change, and back to make the date. Wherever time-saving appliances, communications, and transport abound, time-harried faces appear at every turn.

TODAY'S FREE TIME

To save time through machines is not easy. To transform free time into leisure is not going to be easy either. The modern idea of free time and the classic ideal of leisure revolve about different axes. Off-center to one another, they cannot be called opposites. Were it not for this, they would be poles apart.

Let us consider at some length and afresh the various components of the contemporary idea of free time, often said to be leisure. In the absence of other tradition it lives, as we have seen, in the shadow of work and commerce. Since the world of industry runs on quantitative time, free time runs to the same rhythm. Because of this, free time exists in fragments—off-work hours, weekends, vacations. Sunday, the hoary, ineradicable day snatched from work week by religion, makes the lone exception. On the other days the job picks free time to pieces. By saying that free time is time off the job, one may forget momentarily that the job comes first, and that unless one has a job he has no free time: he is unemployed. The positive is employment; the negative is formed by the prefix "un-." We have no word for un-leisure like the Greek *ascholia* or the Roman *negotium.*

Work influences the drive for betterment that often appears in free-time activities. To improve one's position and increase one's skill, to be always on the lookout for something better, to pursue happiness, to be ever anxious (as the Puritan saying urged) to "do yᵉ nexte thynge," to let up never—much of this constellation of habits grows out of striving for greater skill and status at work.

Before improving himself, a man must be able physically and mentally to do work. Rest is needed. The uncritical and immobile way free time is spent—at home in the evenings in unthinking or unchallenging activities, chiefly as an armchair spectator—seems related to the pacing and concentration of work, especially in factories, within a span of hours. Of course it also seems related, for all classes of workers, to the tenseness and discomfort of the long ride home, which often tires a man out more than the job. Increasingly, free time is being consumed in predominantly ocular activities, and, within that category, in the pictorial variety—picture magazines and film screens—rather than in the kind that involves an intermediate step of deciphering, like reading. Cicero once sent a friend at Stabiae a letter touching on the difference. "I don't doubt that you in your lovely bedroom with its lovely loggia overlooking the Gulf are spending the morning hours these days with edifying reading while we unfortunates who had to return to the city are sitting sleepily in the theater."

Unthinking is perhaps a better word than passive to describe these activities. One could apply passive to not getting up to go out of the house, and certainly to that part of the Roman repertoire that was putting Cicero to sleep. If one dozes off before a stage or screen, the activity is passive in the ordinary sense of the word. But there are subtleties that bear watching: the whole question of passivity as characteristic of free time today warrants fuller attention at this point.

A man lies down on a bed and closes his eyes and remains that way breathing regularly for eight hours. If his breathing becomes imperceptible and other signs used to distinguish life from nonlife have vanished, the man is usually judged dead. If we assume he does no more than breathe in this period—a most unreal assumption—is the man active? What he is doing is called sleeping. In fact, we may either say that he is *doing* something ("he's sleeping") or that he *is* something ("he's asleep"). If we admit he can have dreams, then we can picture a veritable turmoil of activity going on in his head and muscles. Actually, we have but to think of his circulatory system to visualize other kinds of incessant activity. Let us imagine the same man in a chair, still breathing, his eyes open or closed. He sits there for an hour. Is there activity going on apart from his breathing and the transformation of cells in his body? We do admit he may be thinking or reflecting or meditating. So there is the possibility that a man is always somehow in action.

Now let us suppose he faces a wall or a screen. Is he more active if he imagines moving figures on the wall, or if moving figures are projected there, or if legitimately alive actors are performing on a stage? The question is not easily answered. We should note that in the second and third instances the representation was made by others, while the first instance was a self-production. The second and third examples interest us most, for the key to the passivity of mind of today's free-time activity lies there. Most critics of the cultural scene hold that sitting before a TV set is passive, whereas going to the theater is not. Clearly they are not objecting to the lack of exercise in sitting before the TV. Nor are they complaining that at the theater the spectators number a relative few, while in TV the viewers constitute a mass audience. Previously, TV critics complained in the same way about the movies, for which one had to go out of the house. What they object to is not so open-and-shut. It is not the caliber of the representation, nor the play—for someday on TV one may find good actors playing Marlowe. The real objection touches all modern mass communication. For the movie or TV screen, the newspaper or magazine, the viewer or reader has no way of making his reactions known directly to the writer, producer, or performer of the story. In conversation one can praise or condemn another's views, and in the theater or opera one can hiss, boo, whistle, stir nervously, or stand and clap for eleven curtain calls. Human beings, except for rare pathological cases, are influenced by other human beings. Such active attention cannot be given to communication systems. One can write or telephone to an office; who knows where the message will go and who, if anyone, will ever look at it? Or else wait to be counted in a rating survey—which will not be likely to ask what you really wanted to say anyway. The rating, like the program itself, allows no backtalk. Nor can you influence the program by buying or not buying the product it advertises. The product has qualities of its own. For this reason, it is misleading to call these systems mass media of communication. The word communicable signifies a common lot, a sharing. These media don't share; they convey or transmit. They could better be called conveyors or transmitters. The older words used for radio—transmit, receive, broadcast—are closer to fact.

These considerations stand apart from another important one: that the possibility of active attention or communication builds up a critical audience which in time raises the level at which artists or communicators present their story or play to the public.

But here I wish to concentrate on the so-called passivity of free-time activities in the United States. The same supineness is part of listening to music on disks. As with books, there is a variety to choose from; the setting for listening, though, is not so rigid as that for reading. In order to read, good light, immobility of the reader, and the absence of need to do any but the most routine tasks are required. Today the setting for music can be ignored. Chamber music can be listened to in the kitchen. The organ's ringing out of *Sleepers Awake* fails to keep anyone from taking a bath, answering the phone, scolding the children, or making a ham sandwich. Music, chosen to suit the mood, has become an accompaniment to other activities and largely a tranquilizer or relaxer, a soother of the tense breast. The musical skill required to play, read, or compose music oneself has given way to the mechanical skill required to assemble excellent turntables, tuners, amplifiers, and speakers. Except for technicalities of reception, listening to the music is uncritical. You can buy better speakers but not clap, boo, or shout "bravo" at the end of the composition and hope it reaches the musician's or composer's ears.

A certain refrain recurs when the mass media are criticized: If people don't like what they hear or see, they won't buy the things that are publicized; sales are the best index to popular approval. Sales, to be sure, have always been an indication of how much a product is liked. How good an indication it is, is hard to say. We have seen that a person may be forced to buy something he wants less than something that has vanished from the market. A restaurant may have a menu two feet long but if nothing on it meets your fancy, you have no choice but to eat something you don't want . . . or not eat at all. Moreover, there are many extraneous factors that enter into a purchase. Just what is being approved when a record is bought? Are people buying the music, the performance, the attractive wrapper, the love life of the maestro, the prestige of the orchestra, or the low price put on for the after-Christmas season? Whether sales are heavy or light has little bearing on the main point anyway, which is that the mass media of transmission develop an uncritical audience. This result, I suggest, is causally related to the previous point. An uncritical audience develops because the media *transmit* rather than *communicate.* They offer no chance of real response.

Evidently, the present world has given us a new way of being spectators or listeners. This discussion of passivity is not based on participation on one side and spectatorship on the other. I should not contrast the activeness of the workingman's watching television today with the passivity in which he once used to sit on the porch and brush away flies; nor would I cite the substitution in the clerk's backyard of a badminton set for the old hammock (which, incidentally, still decorates many of Charleston's gardens). Perhaps Americans are indeed participating less in sports, music, and the theater than they did once. Existing figures give no clear answer. Many critics do base their complaints about passivity on this: the lack of participation in activities requiring movement. Defenders in reply utter the words, "the new active leisure," an advertising phrase that exploited the "improvement" bent of Americans and their vulnerability to youth-and-motion ideas of themselves. America's oldest tradition is youth, said that disreputable Englishman, Oscar Wilde. As with kittens and pups, energetic play everywhere characterizes the young. With slight variations the rule must be universal. Full-grown cats and dogs, when they have nothing to do, curl up and go to sleep.

Man is not a beast who just sleeps and feeds. In fact it would be ungenerous to call beasts mere sleepers and feeders. They even have some of man's pleasures—lying in the sun, courting, fighting, maneuvering, striving in concert, playing. Yet man has pleasures beasts don't have. Rarely do animals watch other animals except as direct objects of love, fear, play, rivalry, or help. They are not capable of representation. They know neither the drama nor the story. This alone would distinguish man's free time from the beast's. He has his stories and plays, and beyond them the whole world of imagination and ideas. Only man is so lucky.

Unfortunately, modern devices for recording and projecting sound and images have removed people from direct contact and thus lowered their critical attention to the point where they are almost in the state of the older cats and dogs. What good does it do for a man to yell, "Kill the umpire!" to a TV set? He might as well doze off.

In sum, the charge the free-time activities are passive should be founded on the split in spectatorship, between the old kind, in which any man in the audience could make himself heard on the spot, and the new kind, in which the word "uncritical" or "unthinking" fits better than "passive."

Give the individual worker not just a few evening hours but a few days to play with and he may show another side of himself, and another characteristic of free time today. He needs rest and undemanding distraction or somnifacients, but to bring himself each day to the round of disciplined work and timing he seems also to need periods of letting go of himself in noise, boisterousness, and violence. Other times have recognized a need to let loose by providing a carnival season—to which our New Year's Eve is closest in spirit. Other times also provided for physical contests between various quarters of the city. By comparison, our intercity baseball is a pallid rivalry. Peasant life, too, needs relief from the myopia of the daily backbreak, to get away in the color and alcohol of fiestas.

In part perhaps because there is so little of festive relief; in part also because the demands of work are less physically exhausting and yet more confining than they used to be, Friday and specially Saturday night are nights that fill up the volumes of the police blotter. The pleasure in doing what one was unable to do during the work week—stay up late, sleep late, get drunk, fight, whirl away at one's own crazy speed, act the boss, give way to the Dionysian rhythm of the dance, spend like a sailor— this is called fun. Some would call it puerility because it seems as if adults were acting the child, or, as is often the case, the adolescent. It is true: children are notable for play, and the pleasure they get from it they call fun. Adults have fun, too, and without being puerile, their fun comes from play and games less energetic and more refined than the child's. The pleasure of having fun is a recognizable part of spending weekend free time properly. For this reason political and religious activities are not considered free-time activities proper: they are not fun. Nothing serious is free time either, unless it is of the kind that leads to success. Political and religious activities are in neither the fun nor the success category. The fun pattern, for all its orgiastic flare, is well under control. Sunday is a quiet day and the evening ends early. On Monday, back to work.

Similarly with still longer free-time periods. Only the retired don't have to worry about getting back to work. Often that is what worries them most —that they will never go back to work. The others, the younger in years if not in spirit, obey the clock, whether they go off for one free week or four, whether to a lakeside cottage or to Palm Springs.

There is no such thing as prison leisure. By contrast with ordinary life, however, prison may offer the chance for unhurried thinking, reading, writing, and conversation. In his autobiography Trotsky pointed out that prison life developed political thinking and provided, for those who never had it, a kind of general education. In more recent times Adriano Olivetti, the late industrialist and philanthropist, attributed his increased interest in political theory to time spent in political asylum. All this applies principally to political prisoners, and those around them. The list of political and literary figures who have composed works while in prison or exile includes such luminaries as Thucydides, Polybius, Dante, Marco Polo, Machiavelli, Tommaso Campanella, San Juan de la Cruz, André Chénier, Lenin, Louis Aragon.

Recreation, certainly, can be had even in jail. Prisoners have recreation programs and directors; they are given exercise and recreation so that they will stay in their cells more docilely and keep in better health. We would be justified in saying that all the activities mentioned above as common to today's free time are recreation. They are dominated by work because they are either influenced by work scheduling or done to improve skill or status at work; or, also, because they make it possible, through rest, distraction, and release, for men to keep on working.

The commercial and industrial world we live in further affects the modern idea of leisure. First of all free time is spent generally in the company of commodities, sometimes called leisure equipment, facilities, products, or items—a TV set or a juke box. This characteristic is sometimes labeled a part of "American materialism." The term is not common in Europe, except in applying the word to America. The sense possibly takes its origin from socialist language, wherein materialism is directly related to the means of production, referring essentially, in a system based on capital and industry, to factories and mills. Perhaps, since machines were and still are made principally of iron or steel, and since many early assembly-line products like cars used steel in large quantities, materialism and metals were associated. The result is that today the charge of materialism reflects a shiny steel and chromium culture. In Europe a materialist is generally thought of as a person who thinks chiefly of his carnal appetites, and since this involves flesh, metals can play only a subsidiary role. Metals, however, are as good an indication as any of the commodity-acquiring habit in the United States. The per capita consumption of metals, steel, copper, lead, zinc, aluminum, magnesium, chromium, nickel, and tin is about one ton, easily the highest in the world. We also use up hundreds of pounds of nonmetallic minerals, but, except in stone, sand, and gravel (which we consume in tons again for highways and dams), our margin over the rest of the world is not great.

The commercialization of free time, insures that free time is spent collectively or uniformly. Whatever free-time accessories are offered to the consumer must be marketable. The work-oriented education and specialized training Americans receive, combined with their lack of a leisure tradition, leaves them open to suggestion from advertising, or, on a local scale, from recreation directors, counselors, or coordinators, however they may be called. Moreover, to be marketable in an industrial world means to be salable to many people, whether they are counted by the busload or by the millions in a TV audience.

True, not in every case does a product have to seek out the lowest common denominator of taste, intelligence, and pocketbook to become marketable. There are markets and submarkets, big ones and little ones. Yet a product needn't be something-for-everybody to be spread widely enough to give the impression of uniformity. American "detached" homes are much alike, cheap little houses. Inside there is the usual assortment of household electrical appliances, radio, and TV; outside, the same little lawn and alongside or in front the automobile in shiny colors and chromium. The department stores sell thousands of identical ladies' hats, suits, and dresses for each age group, and myriad perfumes and soaps. The supermarkets bulge with things done up in series, weighed, packed, wrapped, packaged, and stacked in rows. From one end of the country to the other we see the same small towns and bigger towns, the same new products, the same new cars, the same new houses, and the same new food. (Other countries like France and Italy may have the same *old* food, but it is good food and varies from region to region.) Apart from being rich, there is no escape, and even then it is difficult. If everything must be marketable on a large scale, as we saw before, things that are no longer marketable—skills like marble cutting—go out, and can no longer be found at any price. Hence, the impression of a country filled with nothing but sameness.

Free time, then, is spent in company with accessories in a similar manner. People, further, have similar amounts of free time and expect that they will profit from it as much as the next fellow. Equality of free time and its activities and benefits seems to flow naturally from the universality of work in the United States. Everyone is influenced in free time by the context of work time. Equality flows, too, from the rapid leveling of income in the last thirty years, and from the doctrine of equality in general, not only political but economic—the notion that one dollar is one vote. Thus, if before the French Revolution rich and poor alike had time, today they both have free time and they fill it alike, with more or less the same activities and kinds of products. The poor man's rowboat is the next one up's sailboat or outboard motor, and the next one's motorboat, and for the one who doesn't have to worry about upkeep, a yacht.

Of the rich men we have (and we still have a few), how many keep a trio or a string quartet on an annual basis in order to have good music when they want it? It wouldn't cost much more than $50,000 a year, and some of it could be charged off to business entertainment expenses. (You can well imagine the incredulous look on the tax agent's face.) Like marble cutters and regional handicrafts, good musicians are becoming hard to find; recordings have driven them out into more lucrative and steadier jobs. That is only part of the problem. The much larger part is that the rich man would get no fun out of having a chamber-music quartet around, and neither would the poor man. To get even the former to like such music, you have to organize a program for him somewhere and then get him to attend by hook or crook, generally by stressing its publicity and uplifting aspects.

This is not the place to think of the things people could do if only they were influenced in their free time by something other than this month's advertising campaign. Nor need I spend much time pointing out that the uniformity is not confined to possessions or commodities, but extends to thought, or to a uniform lack of thought in the meditative, reflective, or contemplative sense. Constant low-level attention to the movies, TV, radio, and print prevent a person from ever being alone with himself. Whenever he is giving attention to other persons, he is influenced by them, and within limits this is both natural and desirable, but of course he is not alone with his thoughts then; whenever he is alone and awake, he puts himself into a fireside sleep, absorbed by the screen. As a result he has not heard from himself in a long time. The moment for being inwardly attentive is never allowed to come. Perhaps you can judge the inner health of a land by the capacity of its people to do nothing—to lie abed musing, to amble about aimlessly, to sit having a coffee—because whoever can do nothing, letting his thoughts go where they may, must be at peace with himself. If he isn't, disturbing thoughts cut in and he will run to escape into alcohol or the flurry of activity called work.

Perhaps it's just as well, though some persons think it abominable that everyone walks, talks, hurries, smiles, and smokes alike, and is as odorless as a TV image.

We say everyone. This is an exaggeration, and like the others just preceding it, to be taken in the spirit of the French *tout le monde*. It is hardly necessary to remind ourselves that the United States is filled with many kinds of people, that they all have their differences, large and small, that the South and North, East, West, and Midwest, and north Midwest differ; that tomorrow's Americans are not today's nor yesterday's. Yet there are uniformities among them, some obvious, some unknown to them. If we can recognize some, perhaps even tomorrow's Americans will be more understandable. "Everyone" and "the American," then, refer to many Americans and sometimes to almost all of them, as in the statement, "Everyone in the United States works." Custom, soil, climate, thought, continental position affect us all.

Right now, we are concerned with those uniformities brought by our kind of work and industry and their effect on leisure. Is it polite in the United States to ask someone you have just met what he does for a living? Do men shave in the morning for work or in the evening for their "leisure hours"? Are love affairs tailored to the business pattern—no frills, few flowers, no time wasted in elaborate compliments, verses, and lengthy seductions, no complications and no scenes, please—and do they constitute no excuse for being late to work? Is the country well-known for its "casual dress," a phrase that could refer to "sloppy dress," one that has been proudly associated with comfort and leisure, but of both the comfort and the leisure time spent in such dress, work (including work around the house) is a clear beneficiary. An American business suit and sport coat are equally loose about the muscles. Baggy pants are useful in any kind of sedentary pursuit, be it on a horse or in a swivel chair. On the distaff side, short skirts and short hair emanate efficiency and visible activity, too. And are the parks and squares filled by anyone except bums and foreigners? Central Park and Washington Square are examples. Perhaps everybody is at work, or people nowadays want more excitement than a stroll in the park, or the advertisements do not recommend stretching the legs, or perhaps people want to avoid the wondering that wandering brings. The promenade used to be part of the American scene from New Orleans to Brooklyn. Now it is disappearing even in Europe.

RESISTANCE TO CHANGE

All these qualities, then, whatever their causes may be, describe the current idea of free time, or leisure. Set off from yet mesmerized by work, it is limited by the clock and available in only small fragments. At times busily active; then at others passive and uncritical; and in most cases uniform or collective. Supposedly beneficial for everyone who has done his work and has a few dollars in his pocket, it appears flanked by commodities and bent for fun. Matters like religion and politics and education it tries to avoid. The modern idea is what it is, today. And tomorrow? It will be the same.

Democracy has not changed the idea much. We are so used to thinking of free time as accompanied with accessories that cost more than a jackknife or a pack of cards or wooden balls to bowl on the green that we conclude the poor and rural people of the past had no free time or had less variety in it. The prejudice affects the questions that are put in freetime questionnaires and interviews, so that if the person doesn't own a radio or TV set, or has no cinema or public library within ten miles, owns no sailboat, saxophone, gramophone, do-it-yourself kits, or power tools, he is, poor chap, out of the swim of things. Indeed he may be. But this doesn't mean he has no free time. Has industry changed the characteristics of free time much? Yes, by making things worse by expropriating time and space. Has universal education changed the idea? Everyone reads today, but the bulk of what they read would not stand up literarily to the tales and songs of storytellers and storysingers of preliterary times.

Reading and writing have become an index of educational progress. Doubtless they help increase the size of the community and enable a man to serve in the factory and army and to know what's on sale today, and what's going on in town tonight. Is this the knowledge that philosophers of democracy were interested in? Socrates was against writing; Plato expressed a similar aversion. Sicilian ·noblemen for a long time refused to learn to read, holding that, as with numerals, the job is one for servants. Does reading serve as anything today but a bulletin board, a function largely reduced by radio and television, which do not call for reading? At one time a writer wrote a book for readers he knew almost personally and on whom he could count to read the book with care and thought. Today, and a hundred years ago too, a large proportion of Americans read, but few read anything better than the newspaper, that daily letter from the world to which they never write back. At one time poor people read well enough to read the Bible. Today the

Bible is read by priests, students in theology, and some in archaeology. Other people read books about the Bible (in which they learn that the Bible is great literature), and in overwhelming numbers all the newspapers, books, and magazines that these days come hot off the presses.

Like the other mass media, print today is used at the uncritical low attention level as a kind of drug to kill the dull hours of public transportation or sitting at home with nothing better to do. The more pictures in it, the better. Eighteenth-century America had few readers and few writers, but they were good readers and good writers. The Revolutionary soldier, reputedly a good soldier, could not read or write. The favorite reading matter of the United States Armed Forces today, reputedly a democratic military institution, is comic books. And the most easily digested fare for millions of civilians seems to be the illustrated weeklies. In most cases of comic books and the others sold in drugstores and supermarkets, the author does not matter. He has too many "readers." Only a minuscule percentage of readers ever wishes to talk to or dreams of talking to the author. But he who addresses a prologue to *"Buveurs très illustres"* announces that wondrous things are to come . . . and is a different kind of author.

If democracy, industry, and universal education have not improved the quality of free time, what about the prosperity they have brought? No one can say that this is not the right moment to take stock. It is true that the military budget is large; still we lack nothing. Democracy reigns, industry flourishes, everyone's son and daughter not only know how to read but will soon be college graduated, and pockets are jangling everywhere. Certainly the abundance of things has helped persuade the American that he's on top of the heap, that his way of life is the best in the world, that he has the proof (as long as he can buy appliances and things) that he is enjoying life and giving his family what it needs in order to be happy. The face of a suburban woman who knows she is dressed and made up like an advertisement in the slick fashion magazines, the smugness written on it, is a lesson in containment. The New York girl, the high-school senior, is a better sight to see, the one who knows, too, she is made up like the ads (different ones). At least here the smugness is naturally uncontained. Progress is still riding high; American physicists and businessmen are expansive, the first about the universe, the second about the economy. If a new throughway is financed to save workers ten precious minutes, the event is heralded as a triumph for business, government, and foresight. In the next year the ten minutes plus ten more will be lost to increased traffic.

This progress resembles the change from legs to bicycles to cars. Those in favor of technology consider it progress if technology manages to repair some of the damage it has done. The time and space Englishmen had at the coming of industry are lost. Englishmen and Americans pay up for it every day. Yet wherever a park is opened up, it is unblushingly heralded as a triumph of good government or philanthropy, and progress in any case. The partial recovery of lost ground becomes progress.

The common man's free time still has not become what J. S. Mill hoped. If anything, the cultural efforts of the nineteenth century, the Chautauquas, crude though they were, showed more of a will to learn than anything that can be seen in TV programs and audiences. Although the American's free time has not at all increased in the magnitude broadcast, he could have chosen more time. To Aristotle it seemed childish to work for the sake of fun. Today, with plenty of money in his pocket, the American is not, if he can help it, choosing more free time over more money. He prefers to exert himself so he can buy the leisure equipment, facilities, items, products, commodities, and consumption goods he and his family need, at least need more than they do free time.

Perhaps people won't have a choice. Perhaps, with the spread of automatic machinery, free time will increase even against their will. The number of jobs should not decrease so long as people continue the circle of buying whatever they and the machines produce. More and more is produced? Then more and more will be bought. There are two possibilities, though, that might change the sequence. The kind of jobs automated machines provide are those only a limited number of persons have the wit to fill. Intelligence is not equally distributed among all men. Secondly, the market may not expand as far as machine production can. The businessman may believe in an eternally expanding economy but he too has the idea that automation can cut down the number of workers on a job. The direction is the same in both cases—toward more free time. There will either be the same number of jobs—but with their hours cut down drastically and legislation to prevent overtime and moonlighting—or, more likely in view of the first possibility, a relative few will work, and the rest will live on Easy Street.

Easy Street might be something like ancient Rome at the time of the rise of the *plebs urbana.* The workers were a dedicated and skilled few—administrators, lawyers, artisans, merchants, inventors, and military officers. The *plebs* were those who had free time and the vote to insure their bread and circuses. The circuses, like TV, went on at all times of the day. We are the Romans of the modern world, boasted Oliver Wendell Holmes. Today, we can see another Roman side to us moderns. The interesting jobs are held by executives and managers. They comprise the group that works the longest hours. They include the advertisers. The rest like their job not so much for the part that is written up in the job-description but for the social and status elements in it. If they were paid for not working wouldn't they gladly drop the work and, all together with their friends and their votes, raise the cry for bigger and better circuses?

Before I let you formulate your own answer, let me recall one thing. This kind of free time, and that of the *plebs,* is not leisure. Point by point the characteristic of free time today as an idea or an activity differ from the classical ideal, the exact opposite in some places, total irrelevance in others. To start, the measurement of leisure by time is out of the question. Time has its stop in leisure. In free time, it becomes an obsession, leading some writers to define leisure as disposable (uncommitted or unobligated) time. For leisure the idea simply does not apply. Even for free time the notion is as awkward to handle as its economic counterpart, disposable income. If free time were the blocks of time one could dispose at any given moment, and one were to be asked, "Can you spare me ten minutes?" or "Can you come with me on a three-week trip tomorrow?," the answer might be yes or no or maybe, but none of them necessarily expresses free time. The obligation or commitment or power to dispose merely shifts scenery: The issue becomes, who is asking and why? How obligatory or committing is the request when asked by one's boss, one's husband, or a co-worker? Leisure remains a concept outside of time. Anything framed in time shorter than a lifetime is not leisure. *Hay mas tiempo que vida,* the Mexican saying goes. There is more time than life. And it is true. If you look at life instead of time you will see.

Not being divided up by time, leisure does not suffer the fragmentation that free time does. Any stopping or shrinking of an activity in leisure is intrinsic, done for the doer's own interest. The self-improvement, the always pursuing-something and bettering-oneself aspects of present free time are negative qualities as far as leisure is concerned. Life is not on a vertical incline, nor is truth. It comes not to him who is always on the run after something that tickles his senses. Neither busily active to some end nor supremely uncritical of whatever passes by, the activity of leisure refers chiefly to the activity of the mind.

Free time is opposed to work, is temporary absence from work, but leisure has as little to do with work as with time. If someone has to work it means he has to do something not for its own sake but for money or something else. Therefore it is not leisure. A man of leisure, however, may be intensely engaged in something which an innocent observer might call hard work. The difference is that its end or pursuit was chosen for its own sake.

Fellows, and friends too, are those chosen for their own sake, not for some ulterior end like business or party. In no case can leisure be collective or organized. It does not depend on other people. If one is alone, he can be at leisure by himself. Commodities are irrelevant. A walk outdoors will do. As the *Republic* opens, Socrates goes to the house of a rich old man named Cephalus. It took no show of commodities to get him to make the visit. To lure Socrates all you needed was the promise of conversation. How Cephalus's house looked or was furnished had little importance (although Socrates notes that his host's head bears a festive garland of flowers). In most of antiquity there was little furniture anyway. The Etruscan house, for instance, would have a bed, blankets and bolsters, armchairs and chests. The rooms were illuminated by oil lamps hanging from the ceilings. The classic ideal of leisure was indifferent to what we would call materialism. It was even more indifferent to the idea that leisure was everyone's right and that everyone could benefit from it equally. Only men brought up as free men *should* be brought up could benefit from leisure. For a proper education, as Pindar says, book learning is not enough. Persons who are themselves free of necessity must surround you from birth. Hoi polloi are not free; they are dragged along by any sensation, they itch after things, are prey to fears and anxieties. Book learning will never help them out. Pindar does not swerve from an aristocratic position. Though one considers his views extreme, the Greek philosophers who developed the concept of leisure—Plato, Aristotle, and Epicurus—all held little esteem for hoi polloi. The people would not know what to do with leisure was the consensus.

A man of leisure, according to Aristotle and Plato, was a man who devoted the best of himself to the state, and who believed that cultivating the mind, so important for the state, was the brightest of all activities, the single one in which man was revealed as related to the gods, and in the exercise of which he celebrated the gods. Politics and religion were at the heart of leisure. Fun never dominated the picture. This element, which some writers today maintain is a characteristic of leisure or free time—its mood of the anticipation of pleasure, its having-a-good-time-ness—is not a necessary part of leisure. What a man does when he does not have to do anything he does for its own sake, but he does not think of it as fun or having a good time. It may be difficult or easy, pleasant or unpleasant, and look suspiciously like hard work, but it is something he wants to do. That is all.

So the ideal of leisure differs on every score from today's and tomorrow's free time. The classic tradition exists in the United States only in attenuated form, and for the most part in the oldest universities. The ideal of leisure, however, has been deformed almost everywhere, even there. Perhaps only among classical scholars can we meet and recognize the pure thing, and by no means in all or even most of them. The point at which the deformation is most obvious is in the idea that leisure is owed everyone and everyone can benefit from it in equal measure. The educators try to say that leisure and democracy were destined for each other. To the Greeks, who were more liberal than we in the matter of bedfellows, these two would still be strange partners. First of all, contemporary educators, like so many others, have confused free time and leisure. Their predecessors in the nineteenth century were unable to resist the model of the German trade schools which made a clean sweep of the country. Possibly to oppose this movement, taking allies wherever possible, the educators have absorbed strong strains of radical democracy and European socialism.

The main ideas of Jacksonian democracy are familiar. The socialist position is also familiar, whether one thinks one knows it or not. As far as this subject goes, there is little noteworthy difference between the two. One has merely to read old socialist writers, or look at the statements of contemporary socialists or communists or at the program of so-called socialistic or communistic governments. They are and have always been in favor of a shorter work week and leisure for the working classes. So familiar are the ideas that I shall not go into them. Whenever anyone talks of "socialist" or "communist" ideas of leisure, all we have to do is substitute "democratic" and the notion is clear to us. But saying "socialist" or "communist" is not the same thing as saying "Marxist," and even less is it the same as saying "Marx's ideas."

Marx, whose ideas influenced the whole Western world more than it thinks or is willing to admit, is one of the rare thinkers who expressly noted a relation between the ideals of leisure and freedom. With the growth and expansion of technology, he believed, capitalism in spite of itself would create disposable or non-work time, thus reducing work time to a minimum and giving everyone free time for his own development. Up to this point, he does not differ much from J. S. Mill, save in degree. Human freedom, he states, has as its fundamental premise the shortening of the working day. He goes further, in generalizing that the realm of freedom is beyond the realm of material production. Free time, he says in his notebooks, which means both leisure time and the time for higher activity, naturally transforms those who dispose of it into a different type of agent. Marx, too, confuses free time and leisure, of course—he even has them upside down—but he recognizes a higher type of activity, and this we may take to mean the activity of men of leisure.

The interesting thing is that Marx seems to have been groping for a fresh expression of the classical concept. (This should not surprise us too much: Marx's doctoral thesis was on Epicurus.) He maintained that only as one passes into the realm beyond work and production does one become free; in leisure one is transformed into a different kind of person. But *who* is transformed—anyone at all? Here Marx goes back again to the democratic ideal, or rather here Marx is one of the precursors and advocates of the ideal. Some former societies gave leisure to a few. Capitalism and technology (unwittingly) and socialism (consciously) will give it to all, eventually. Then the free development of individuality will correspond to the artistic and scientific education of all individuals, thanks to the free time made available. And in the future communist society, he writes in the *German Ideology,* he, Marx (who spent his life in libraries), will do "this today, and that tomorrow, hunting in the morning, fishing in the afternoon, raising cattle in the evening, and even be a critic after dinner . . . just following my fancy." So, even though Marx has subtleties in his writing that do not appear among the doctrinaires, for all practical respects the ideals of democracy and socialism in regard to free time are twins, similar if not identical.

Let us set apart for the time being the historical evidence on the fate of leisure under democracy and socialism. Instead, let us ask ourselves a central question, a dangerous question, outright. Few writers seem to want to tackle it in the affirmative. Most think it prudent not to raise it, not even obliquely. The question: Are democracy and leisure compatible? The answer: No. In democracy today free time does exist, though in less quantity than is thought; of leisure, there is none.

Swiftly the train of discourse has again moved over onto the terrain of the political. Most people find it difficult to realize that leisure and politics are related. The reaction stems naturally from the idea that leisure is fun and political matters are not. The political bearing that they can see more easily appears in legislation affecting free time and its activities. A government agency exercises powers over radio and TV—clear enough. Government subsidies go to farmers and agricultural schools, but not to musicians and music schools—another clear case. The government controls passports, which in turn determine where or whether one can travel abroad; Congress appoints committees to study recreation—all these are clear instances of politics. Clear, surely, but minor instances. Politics and religion, too, stand in a more fundamental position to leisure. Their significance appears upon asking a single question, logical and simple enough. Why can't the present idea of free time be modified so that it comes closer, at least, to the classical concept?

Suppose we take any one of the eight or ten characteristics of free time discussed above and try to transform them. What would be necessary to carry out the change? In every case, democracy, as it is conceived today, would have to retreat.

To take the time-ridden quality out of free time one would have to take it away from work and machinery. It would be equivalent to saying to people: You can come to work or not and at whatever time you please; it really doesn't matter; we assure you enough to live on. Who has the authority to say this in a democracy? An ideology not based on time and work could not support an industrial system. If in certain quarters we can find a different time schedule—say, restaurants open all night—the reason is usually that there are night shifts at work in the vicinity. Greenwich Village in New York makes one of a few exceptions: many shops are closed on Monday and normally open from noon to 9 or 10 PM or midnight. Elsewhere we may find a few little islands supported by small groups of persons, artists and writers, some of them in good faith living off the margins of the business world while ideologically revolted by it. The millions of other Americans cannot afford this luxury.

To take the improvement, the ethicizing, the busily active, the always-chasing-something quality out of free time would mean stealing the doctrine of progress away from democracy, of melioration, of optimism, of the very mobility it prides itself on: that anyone can rise from bottom to top (and, less proudly, skid from top to bottom). A second's reflection would make it appear doubtful that social climbing and the struggle for status can lie down peacefully with leisure. Striving means you want something badly, that you are in a state of necessity, the state opposed to leisure.

To take the passivity or uncritical spirit out of free time would be as difficult as to take away its craving for fun too. If they are essentially relief reactions to a workaday life, they apply to Americans universally, for in America work is universal. In the old days of sociology, when a scholar wanted to determine whether a given species showed instinctive behavior, he would ask himself, what activities do all members of the species do without exception? Using such logic, he might have been led to believe that job-holding is an instinct of *Homo americanensis*. The only way to rid the race of its free-time traits would be to relieve workers of work, something that no one can do unless another way of acquiring a livelihood is given in return. The same applies to free time's base of operations—commodities. To keep Americans away from things one would have to eliminate advertising and offer them another authority to guide their free time. Advertising interests are formidable in themselves. And, of course, in back of them stands business.

Industry had found advertising and marketing techniques necessary to keep a capricious market from playing hop, skip, and jump. As more and more production is based on so-called leisure items, industry's dependence on advertising (for all that advertising cannot completely cure its marketing troubles) becomes greater and greater. The American economy has as its ultimate purpose to produce more commodities. It would come as no surprise to hear an economist say that this is the goal, the object of everything that we are working at: producing things for consumers. To try even to put a tax on advertising would raise fears of the economy's collapse, as well as make an issue of the extent to which a democratic, professedly antisocialistic government can itself operate in restraint of trade. The luxury taxes the United States now has exist only because World War II made it possible to push them through.

CONTENDERS FOR AUTHORITY

Whatever measures are tried to break the grip of commercialism implicate the substitution of authority, of government direction for commercial direction. Immediately some would say that this would then be socialism, not direction. Others, however, will be reminded that J. S. Mill, too, thought of the government as a teacher, and he by now is no longer regarded as a socialist by anybody. Still others might remember that Venice passed sumptuary edicts, and she was never regarded as socialist by anybody. In that magnificent commercial power, you could have a gondola of any color you wished, as long as it was black. Of course it wasn't long before Venetians took to brightening their colorless vehicles with fine silks and satins profusely displayed. The gondola today is still black and retains the same height and length, but an expression from a gayer epoch survives also. As applied to a woman—"She's all decked out like a gondola!"

We are again at the impasse common to educators and democratic theorists. The government as educator has been an ineffective teacher, evidently. Mill thought it couldn't help teaching men about politics and, by giving them a sense of participation, make them feel a solidifying common interest. It is doubtful, though, that the ordinary citizen knows any more about politics than any of Shakespeare's characters from the lower ranks, and doubtful that he is better informed or feels a deeper sense of participation in national events.

Mill didn't go much further than believing that political participation would bring about better government. Since the original government had to be good enough to enact the laws permitting people to participate, it had to be good to start with. Mill's problem of authority was easy. He believed implicitly in a superior class, a class of taste, education, wealth, and breeding. So if he never got much beyond the problems of suffrage, representation, and administration, it was because he took for granted that if things began to look up, and workers had free time on their hands, they would follow the guidance of their betters. To a limited extent, and for England, not the United States, he was right. One can see the slight difference by comparing private radio and TV programs in the United States with those of the BBC. To the new democracy in the United States after the eighteenth century this kind of authority was unacceptable. For this very reason educators have always had to insist that one man's taste in anything was as good as another's and that everyone is entitled to leisure.

What makes anyone think that if the government instead of business set up entertainment programs they would be any better than they are? Can the government find men of better taste than industry can, or artists of greater stature? The trouble is that such men are not to be found in any camp. A national shortage of them exists, has existed for a century and a half or more. Government officials on the whole have had a more general education than business executives, but not enough to raise hopes. Remember that the schools, apart from those few older universities, have done an efficient job in denying the leisure tradition. Suppose everyone by the next generation has a college education. Will they spend their free time differently from that described by the contemporary free-time ideal? Not at all. Indeed advertisers and marketing men are only too glad that college enrollments are on the increase. It's a kind of audience they like to get: one with the itch for status and things. They buy commodities as fast as anyone else, and usually faster.

So far, in the tension between government and private industry, the government's role in free time has been restricted to supplying certain facilities gratis, or at a nominal price, without giving them enough publicity to compete with commercial facilities. The government confines itself (with the exception of museums) chiefly to the outdoors, through parks, forests, and playgrounds, offerings that are not accessible on a daily basis to working adults and that require enough energy to get up out of the armchair. The health and morale of the poorer classes of children has often guided the government in providing outdoor recreation; by the same token such efforts are noncontentious because noncompetitive. These children have little to spend on private facilities. Criticism that the government has not done enough has always existed, and alongside it the criticism that it does too much. Recently critics have taken to comparing expenditures for education and other services with those of private industry for advertising. One of the points they make is that by looking at advertising costs one can see that the country needs to spend more money on education. The logic, of course, is far from invulnerable. Why must advertising and education have a seesaw relation to each other?

On the other hand, of course, government and business work together in many ways and hold the same beliefs. Without what I have described as its allies, advertising's influence would go down almost to the level of a peddler; the on-foot salesman, the advertiser before the days of mass media, would again come into his own as in the days of Babbitt. These quiet allies—consumer credit, installment purchasing, obsolescence and disappearance of commodities, and so on—are not only part of business, but also by now part of government legislation. The government, too, acts as an ally. The whole scene has given rise to economic theories that if the consumer does not continue to buy commodities, the economy will soon give the healthy appearance of weeds growing high in abandoned railroad tracks. Until a new economics comes along basing itself on new facts, every government is at the mercy of economists who tell it that without consumption the end is near. Actually with the economics that exists (it is surprising that no one has noticed it) free time in quantity is unhealthy and would quickly lead to ruin.

The maze may have an earlier exit, that is, government support of recreation. Since the person is hit on all sides by shrapnel, striking him with contradictory fragments—one, that he should buy things; two, that he should enjoy them in his free time—and since he can't work to buy and have free time simultaneously, he is left dissatisfied no matter what he does. His recourse is to use his other vote, the ballot. If the only way to enjoy life is to have these things, and if everybody should have them —these are both themes of advertising—then the government should make them part of its services. Indeed, another of the claims of the critics mentioned above is that the vast amounts spent on advertising could be better spent by government in services to the public. So, curiously enough, advertising, which at first leads to greater spending and a less capricious market, eventually leads to government support of recreation facilities. The role of advertising in laying the basis for the welfare state would be a study well worth doing.

Once the government enters the field a number of different things may happen. If it dips into the pool with but its little toe, which it has done so far, the situation is one of the tension already described as existing between government and business. If the government is in a stronger position and moves in more confidently, as it did during the depression, then advertising has less to advertise, titillation of the consumer decreases, the demand for commodities goes down and free time increases. At the same time, if the government sinks money into longer-range expenditures, such as buildings for the arts, then the less material kinds of free time may show a spurt of activity. The problem of government interference in the arts is just as serious as business interference, since there is no difference in the education of their personnel, but the government is not interested in selling things commercially. If anything, it is interested in selling programs wrapped, at the present rate, in two- to four-year packages. The electoral term gives it a slight edge over the shorter-run approach of advertising. Government can allow a wider margin in the recreation area than immediate popular approval on sales charts. If, furthermore, it confines itself to grants of permanent character, like buildings, squares, and city planning, the possibility of its interference in recreational and cultural activities is cut down. The same would be true if business made grants through foundations. Once the money is in foundations the control of business diminishes; once the foundation puts the money in bricks and mortar, then its control possibilities diminish too. All to the good. Architecture then seems to be a key to the kind of government or foundation intervention that would lead to a break in advertising and business control of free time and yet would not involve excessive direct control over choice. Still every step is a step affecting choice, this cannot be denied.

Undoubtedly the government's entry into recreation, as in all welfare and service functions, means more technical government, which in turn means more bureaucracy.

Contemporary practices in state welfare took shape at the beginning of the twentieth century, in England perhaps in Parliament's National Insurance Act of 1911, in the United States about 1913 with the national revenue made possible by Federal income tax law. Ever since the Beveridge report of 1945 (where the phrase does not occur) English, American, and Scandinavian governments have sometimes been dubbed with the ambiguously flavored title of "welfare state." Such a government arranges by law for insurance, medical care, pensions, and other bureaucratic services for the citizenry. Doubtless these services can be increased, and commodity spending can be decreased, by taxes on consumer goods or on advertising or on incomes generally. Apart from the effects, calculable and incalculable, that this would have on the economy, the reduction of commodities and advertising and the increase in government services would not solve the problem of what citizens are supposed to do in their free time. They all work and have need of recreation. As part of its services the government would have to go into the entertainment industry. The problem of who chooses what entertainment shall be offered in the evening hours remains the same, except that the authority to choose has been shifted from business and advertising executives to government officials. Since the need for recreation comes from work, and work will not have changed character, the public's tastes (in so far as they can be expressed) will remain the same.

Thus, no sooner does one begin to think of changing the present idea of free time than the charge arises that democracy is being undermined. At first "socialism" is the charge, but only because to eliminate advertising and substitute government for business influence is the first solution many persons think of. They believe that the government has or can have something different in mind with which to entertain the people. Actually, the change counts for little. Work and its consequences remain: therefore the people will need their recreation. We cannot believe that work will be eliminated, for then how should we live? The solution, let some work, some not, runs against both the democratic and socialistic grain.

The charge now becomes aristocracy, and this strikes closer to the core. For in both cases above, that is, the advertiser versus the government official, the people were considered as the arbiter of taste.

Or rather, the question of taste did not appear on stage. What the people like in entertainment—as in services, as in commodities, as in free time—whatever they like is what they shall have. The businessmen and advertisers count dollar-sales as votes; the government official counts ballots. The authority, the shaper of choice, remains the people. In theory. And one step removed. If we say that this one step removed makes all the difference, we are wrong. It merely replaces an advertising account executive with a bureaucrat. There is no evidence that in the United States the one has notably better taste than the other. Besides, the public will be no more communicative of its preferences than before, since the mass media of entertainment will remain in force, still holding their audience in uncritical attention. The argument for leisure belongs on another plane. One barrier is work. The other is equality. The plane is aristocracy.

Educators take their sides, as they have since the last century, some insisting that everyone should have an emphatically liberal education, some wanting everyone to have a chiefly vocational or technical or scientific education. To see that ideological barriers dictate the sides they take, we need simply note that both say "everyone" and neither says "impossible." With their horns thus locked, it is empty rhetoric for them to say, as a respectable report on American education does say, that there must be a rigorous re-examination of our present methods, and bold experiments with new ones. The reappraisal will try to put education more in tune with the latest technological and military requirements. The "bold experiments" will amount essentially to suggesting the use of the latest technological methods again, like TV, to reach new masses of students and adults, thereby reducing education to a lower level of critical attention than that to which it has hitherto sunk.

Do those educators who talk about liberal education ever advise the methods of Socrates or the Academy or the Peripatetic School or the Kepos? The siesta in the country, walking or stretched out on the grass, under a tree, near fountain or stream—these are the particulars of the *beata solitudo* that reach us from Plato's *Phaedrus,* after the seduction, or the way of uncounted poets and philosophers. A liberal education cannot be given over TV or in lecture halls seating hundreds. Education is the discovery and drawing out of the best that is in a person. How can it be done in crowds? Mass education is a contradiction in terms. There must be a one-to-one or at least one-to-a-few relationship. Out of Socrates came one Plato, and out of Plato one Aristotle. If we are willing to assign such a man-power ratio to education, then we can have a liberal education right here. But how can we? We have to work (work, again) and we cannot discriminate, can we, by selecting a few (equality, again)? Is it any surprise that advertisers greet the prospect of a college-graduate population of 100 percent as good news?

Far from being unrelated to politics, the issue for anyone interested in leisure today is political. The way in which leisure and the political got separated is instructive. It bears, for one thing, on the tension between government and business. For political theory, the event is of interest, for in much the same manner the political sphere, which for the Greeks embraced all of life, dried up to a shriveled pea called government.

In the breaking away from the feudal, monarchical, and aristocratic regimes that dominated Europe until the end of the eighteenth century, the increasingly powerful commercial and industrial interests took sides with any definitions of liberty that aided them in their struggle. Liberty to speak against the state was called freedom of opinion and nicely juggled to include freedom of the press. Given the existing state of military and industrial technology, arms and hands were needed for armies and factories, and also as allies in the struggle against aristocratic privilege. Voting equality was extended to men and called part of their liberty. Thus all those who had lived in previous centuries under kings were automatically indicted as slaves, or at any rate unfree men. The artistic and cultural parts of freedom as yet were ignored. Marx, as we saw, verged on recognizing them, but then couldn't get away from the necessity of work, except in a faraway time when machines produce by themselves. The present of Marx's day of course was the nineteenth century, the time of great industrial development. The purpose of the state seems to have been to insure political liberty, considered as freedom of the press and equal voting rights. Once these were granted, then what? This was a question that did not seem to trouble political thinkers or economists. For the latter, goods got cheaper and cheaper and people could get more and more of them: this was all that mattered.

Here the *laissez-faire* economists did their share in implanting the commodity mentality. When they began their discourses, however, the idea was not so objectionable, since they were talking mainly about clothing and foodstuffs and the like, of which at the same time there was little enough. For the economist too, it seems, the question of "Then what?" never was answered. Work, it is true, got one justification from the reformed churches. One from the state, also, for once the military power of technology was recognized, work and production received credit for making the nation strong. What place had art and beauty in this scheme of things? They began to be things apart, existing by themselves, divorced from political life—if ever they had been falsely united.

Contemplation, which plays so great a part in Plato, Aristotle, Epicurus, even in Roman thought and certainly in the Middle Ages and the Renaissance, and which belongs to a life of leisure, takes on a specifically nonpolitical and nonreligious cast. Leibnitz took a first step by distinguishing one mode of apprehending that needed no reasons or grounds. It characterized knowledge obtained through the senses, and in it was the feeling of beauty. But, scientifically, only the intellect could go beyond the indistinct form of things to their true essence. So though the senses bring us beauty, they separate us from the intellect. This distinction fathered esthetics, the science of the beautiful, but a second-rate science, since intellect was foreign to it. Later Kant reasoned his way to further distinctions in which the beautiful with its *a priori* character pleases without need of a conception. But therefore doctrine in esthetics cannot exist; only a critique of taste is possible. Hence in matters of taste nothing would be gained by proofs of logic or conceptions.

Schiller even more positively relates contemplation to esthetics. With an unusual philosophic interest in art and the beautiful, of which there are intimations in his "Die Künstler," he concludes that contemplation apprehends the object without subjecting it to cognition or understanding. The enjoyment of the beautiful is independent of the practical and the theoretical reason both. Schiller went on to the educating of man through the esthetic life. Art eventually promotes morality and science. Greatly inspired as he was by Shaftesbury, he developed the ideal of the *schöne Seele*. But Schiller and then even Goethe, though they succeeded in fusing the divisions that Leibnitz and Kant had cut, left an emphasis that remains to this day, through the influence of German poets and philosophers, on "the beautiful soul," on living life as a work of art, on leisure as the way to esthetic sensibility.

Enthusiasm was what Shaftesbury had, enthusiasm for the true, the good, and the beautiful. As the Greeks would live the life of leisure, life was to be lived in science, virtue, and art. Shaftesbury glorifies the world poetically, and he sings the whole world, not one with intellect and beauty apart.

The distinction between political liberty and cultural liberty, or taste, worked out well when the issue arose of government control over any of the mass media. Since the political supposedly had nothing to do with the cultural, business interests could in effect say to the government: "Mind your own business! The vote that elected you to office was for political matters. For cultural things the people themselves decide. They use another vote to express their choice, and their candidate is whatever they spend their dollar for." Since the mass media have been defended not only as economic enterprises and therefore entitled to be let alone, but also as instruments of political liberty—freedom of opinion and the press —the government even by mandate of the people could not interfere with the cultural liberty of the mass media: upheld by businessmen and advertisers, they too were equipped with a mandate from the people.

The degradation of aristocratic authority meant that aristocratic taste had to be defamed, too. This was not an easy accomplishment. It has succeeded less well than the attempt to nullify aristocratic political competence and morality. Yet the assertion of esthetic relativism, *de gustibus non disputandum,* did make headway and prepared the ground for the succeeding dogma—majority taste, a militant doctrine asserting that what people like they have a right to, and no one can tell them they are in bad taste. Aggressive though it may be, the doctrine has never gone so far as to say that what the majority likes makes good taste. It has shied away from the word *taste.*

Leisure became apolitical. Liberty took on a restricted reference to free press and the suffrage, and later to labor association. The mass media took over entertainment, keeping the government out in the name of titles they freely appropriated—communication and a free press. Thus political theorists are confronted with the doctrine whereby the ballot box expresses political choice, and the market takes care of cultural choice.

The political and the religious spheres as well are slighted in studies of free time also for the reason given above and for another one. This latter reason, also, has a special interest: it involves two concepts that often have confused the ideal of leisure. One is time (quantitative); the other is activity (visible). After the discussion of time in the previous section, it should be evident that the importance of an activity cannot be judged by the time it consumes. In any given day, month, or year the amount of time a person devotes to religion is small compared, say, to that he spends in transportation or work or shopping. On Sundays outdoor "leisure" increases noticeably for the young and old alike. The one-hour difference is due chiefly to the mass of people who go out to church on Sunday. This, though, seems to be about the only inch of time that can wholly be assigned to religion, except for small amounts spent in church socials or receiving visits from one's pastor, Bible reading, or listening to church services on radio or television.

The same time-pettiness is true of politics. A man may not give any time whatever to the elections even in election year. Yet for his country, a political entity, he will make great sacrifices, perhaps give his life in war, something he would not do for a television program or be asked to do even for his job. Recent studies of electoral campaigns indicate that three out of every four voters voted, that one out of three tried to persuade others to his political views, and that another one out of that three did not care how the elections came out at all. Perhaps one in ten attended political rallies, only a few in every hundred donated time or money to parties or candidates, and about one in fifty belonged to a political club. This is the score once every four years. The average amount of daily time so spent would have to be measured by a stop watch.

There is something to add, though, to these figures. A citizen in a democracy is supposed to keep himself informed of what goes on in the world. The above tallies do not include the time spent on the news sections of the newspaper, radio, and television, or in reading books with political implications, or in earning the money to pay taxes. Certainly in the election heat it is almost as hard to escape the campaign as it is each year to escape taxes. Still, even if the political aspects of reading, listening, and viewing be added, the time spent is much less than that given in the evening to musical variety programs. There is no educational or news program, for example, that reaches the top ten on television.

Thus, by using the strictly quantitative assembly-line conception of time, that is time as a moving belt of equal units, one ignores the significance of much activity. A moment of awe in religion, or ecstasy in love, or orgasm in intercourse, a decisive blow to an enemy, relief in a sneeze, or death in a fall is treated as equal to a moment of riding on the bus, shoveling coal, or eating beans. As a matter of fact in most research the former kind of moments get left out altogether. In the search for the meaning of activity neither the quality of time nor the inner share of action can be ignored without damage. They go together, each lending significance to the other. The importance of activity without visible movement, as in reflecting or meditating, for example, escapes most Americans. Traditionally America is the land where action (meaning bustling activity) wns the day. For Plato and Aristotle, not horse racing, money-making, or fighting, but meditating, reflecting, speculating—these, the activities of the mind, were the ones by which men, old and young everywhere, distinguished themselves from the animals and placed themselves in relation to God. The United States in its short history among the nations of the world has gone straight ahead of everyone in rewarding bustle. This premium, I have tried to show at several points, affects not only the reporting of activity but each person's definition and description of it.

Religion is not merely going in and out of church doors. It is also a way of life, a standard for conduct, a morality, and more still. All of Sunday is a religious day, a holy day. All activity falls into its context. We saw earlier how it affects the day's character. Should the whole twenty-four hours be considered religious?

No more is politics merely going to the polls once every four years. The American as a political being has standards that regulate his conduct, or, to continue the usage here, his activities. Actually, "activities" as applied to religious and political conduct is not the right word. For activities does not connote the standard that "conduct" does. A person on free time engages in activities, but these are contained within a framework of the permissible, the moral, the framework of conduct. A strictly quantitative reckoning of time cannot take this into account. Studies and perspectives based on it will always underestimate the political and the religious action.

So, more than we have been led to believe, free time, as well as leisure, maintains close contact with politics. To the examples cited earlier— legislation affecting education and mass media, national parks, forests and museums, subsidies and taxes affecting occupations and commodities, congressional committees on recreation, passport control—we can add a most obvious one: government regulation of hours of work. At best, though, these measures reflect an underlying relationship.

What is the state for? This is the real question. In contemporary times the answer has been to provide order and a variety of liberty that gives all persons formal access to political choice (for example, universal suffrage and education). In more recent years, this liberty has been extended to provide security against certain misfortunes, like illness, old age, and unemployment—in a phrase, the welfare state. The acceptance by the government of unemployment insurance signifies that it accepts a role as the guarantor of work. Beyond this, the passing of years has seen little change in the state's part in free time; it provides a bit of space and houses a few collections of paintings or natural history. The local level, especially city governments, often offers greater variety. Since a

congressional commission administers the District of Columbia, the activities of the Federal government there resemble those of an ordinary
municipality. If there are summer band concerts in New York City, there
are United States Marine Band concerts in Washington, D.C.

Because of the conflict with private interests, of the mix-up in the mass
media of news and entertainment, and of the accepted theory that the
market is the arbiter of free-time choice, the question of the role of the
state goes begging for study and reflection. The democratic state therefore has no position to take, and, without a reasoned and strongly felt
position, no authority to act.

THE MANY PLEASURES OF THE MANY

Any real passage from free time toward leisure cannot be made, we have
seen, without leaving the confines of the present-day democratic credo,
in particular its ideas of work and equality. There thus seems little chance
of rapid change in the ways people have of spending their free time.
But one shouldn't lay the blame at the door of democracy alone. What
does Russia offer its citizens for their hard work? Free time and commodities, if not now, sometime soon. How do Russians spend their free
time now? Less in overtime, none in moonlighting, more for cultural uplifting, more in collective undertakings, less with commodities, more in
political readings, but, all told, everyone looks ahead to the goal apparently reached by Americans—much more free time.

All that need be added is consumers' goods in quantity for the pattern
to move up toward identity. Not long ago the clerical employees of a
Western oil company in North Africa went on strike, though their pay
stood among the best on the continent and their working conditions included air-conditioned offices. The reason for the strike was clearly stated
and comprehensible. The company's offer of a cost-of-living pay increase
made no provision for the inflated costs of entertainment. Being entertained was not a luxury, the union had said, but a necessity now in order
to break the monotony of employment. This little story neatly fits some
aspects of the contemporary rationalized work style. The point to be
made, though, is limited neither to democratic governments nor to industrial patterns of work.

No civilization has even seen all or even a majority of its people participate in the best standards of taste, or those highest activities of the
mind that reveal the presence of leisure. The majority typically presents
a spectacle of free-time activities resembling today's. There are important differences of time, space, and taste in these activities, but I shall
save discussion of them for a later moment. Ancient Greece, where the
ideal was brought to its pinnacle, ancient Rome with its centuries of
peace, the Republic of Venice which was called the Serenissima, Brunel-

leschi's Florence, the eye of the Renaissance—all present us with only a few capable of enjoying leisure. There is no point in saying this is bad, or that popular pleasure in free time is reprehensible. Why be a spoilsport? It is what it is. About the only thing that can be done is to rephrase things so that they sound better. The mandarin Khanh-du once improvised a moving poem on selling coal.

The contemporary American's attitude toward the theory and practice of leisure might present itself now somewhat like this: For convenience, he keeps work and leisure running on the same time schedule; he takes pleasure in moderation so that work does not suffer; freed from basic fear by the security provisions of his government, he stands ready to take the most out of life, little caring what happens afterward; an optimist, he is proud of his fellow man's progressive conquest of nature, of his country's resources, of the appliances he can buy with the work he puts in; he uses these appliances as they should be used: as means to the end of saving time and labor and of having fun; he constantly and actively seeks ways to improve his position; unimpressed by the dullness of politics and the sobriety of religion, he is not averse to raising hell every now and then; he finds social pleasure in doing what others do, being a strong believer in teamwork and team play; he is convinced that one man is as good as another, if not a damn sight better, and deserves as much as another, specially if he's a practical man; once the day's work is done he is content to relax in the humble diversions offered by the home and its accessories. Why is anything wrong with any of this? It sounds no worse than the circuses of Rome, the Parisian worker and wife's Saturday night outing at the old café-concert, the periodic fisticuffs in Venice at the Ponte dei Pugni, the cockfights of Mexico, the possession-dramas of Ghana, or the Englishman's crowded beach at Brighton.

We have seen at least two good reasons why people might not take leisure though the opportunity existed: first, there may be no strong tradition of leisure; second, in its absence, forces opposed to leisure, unless stopped, may intervene to bring not a new tradition but a follow-the-piper, day-to-day pattern for work, free time, and money-spending. There is a third reason: leisure may be beyond the capacity of most people. If history shows no people in any quantity ever enjoying its delights, perhaps we are dealing with something that only a few can enjoy in any case.

Persons democratically inclined immediately react to such a possibility with an environmental explanation: No wonder only a few can have or enjoy leisure; the rest of humanity has been brought up in such squalor as to prevent their ever arriving at leisure. Yet we can point to cases— Rome is one—where the mass of the citizenry had no need to work, being supported by the foreign tributes exacted by their government, where libraries and literacy flourished, where health and hygiene were as good as they've ever been, and still we meet the same kind of popular pursuits.

Socrates needed little to find leisure; Epicurus the same, Diogenes even less. Undoubtedly, the American's work can unfit him for leisure, but what can we say of times when it was not necessary to work? Aristotle had pointed out that the Spartans could have no leisure as long as the Helots might be expected to rise up and massacre them. The *plebs* had no such fears. Is it temperament, then, that fits only a few for leisure?

Greek thinkers had set up a different ideal, granted, in making leisure the state of being free of everyday necessity. For them this meant that a man should do nothing, or very little, in order to attend to his appetites. By and large they understood by appetites the carnal or material ones— hunger, thirst, sex. A word on the place of sex as a necessity is still in order. (I hope to be given credit here not for what I write but for what I refrain from writing.) Natural appetites should be satisfied naturally. The Greeks believed in giving the body its due. Its due should not cost much. The government, though other costs might have risen, kept the price of flute girls at two drachmas. They liked wine with grace and bodies with grace, which, however, were not spiritual things. At most they were imitations of spiritual things. Once you move from the natural appetites and the pleasures of Bacchus and Aphrodite into other lands of desire, like power or fame or riches, the ground begins to get shaky. Take away all desire from a man, he is no longer alive. Man is a desiring creature. Love for family, particularly for one's children, was recognized as natural, once the family existed. Beyond this Plato and Aristotle recognized a love for justice and for the state and, of course, for God and the gods. Epicurus put little stock in the *polis* or the gods, but admitted a desire for philosophical fame. These then were natural or at least naturally understood desires, even in a state of leisure.

For theory's sake appetites and desires had to have an acknowledged role. They defined necessity. If you were free of the necessity of food and shelter, for instance, you did not have to work, unless you were prey to false desires such as those for riches or power. If you had no desires save natural ones naturally satisfied, then whatever you did was free of obligation. You did it for its own sake.

Now in admitting natural desire and the love for virtue, the Greeks avoided trying to make a man without passions, a paper man. In letting in desire, however, they opened the door to something it was not easy to keep an eye on. They were probably right in treating corporeal desires in a natural fashion, but other desires cannot be treated so casually. Man's make-up and situation conspire to complicate all his desires. They become difficult to trace or to reduce to their origin. What appears as love of God may be a desire for riches, and a seeming drive for power may be a passion for justice. Perhaps again they were right in ignoring such subtleties. After all, given the absence of everyday necessity for toil, of sycophanting to superiors, of taking it out on inferiors, of seeking only what is needed to advance one's ends—having got rid of imperfections as gross as these, the smaller defects will not cause great harm.

The Greeks may seem to have underestimated the twists and turns personality can take, even when free of everyday necessity. Actually, they did not. They neglected such facets because they were talking about persons whose background they took for granted. What might they have said if confronted by this businessman? He was asked whether, if he had an independent income assuring him of his present standard of living, he would continue to work. He replied, "I am sole heir to four million. Does that answer you?" Some might say that the reply proves that for this man his business is his leisure; he does it for its own sake. But the Greeks would have reasoned differently. Their idea of freedom from necessity itself is foreign to most of us. Instead, "We all have to work" seems to us a self-evident law of the universe. Since we work, we have no necessity. This is the way we reason. But it is the work that creates the un-freedom. Illogically, we start from the premises of work when we try to prove our freedom from necessity, thus tying ourselves to necessity before we begin to reason.

One of the ideas the monks of the Middle Ages had was that by monotonous manual labor the mind was freed for thought and contemplation. The argument has been advanced in recent times, too, apropos of factory work. Surely a man can be spiritually free of his work, if while he is at it he can forget it. If he prefers another place for his reflections, however, and another time, and another activity—in other words, if he were doing other than what he is, and were free to choose any time and place for it—then he is unfree, and the product of his mind and hands will show it. To write poetry one man may need the clean air and solitude of wide open spaces; another may compose best in a small smoke-filled back room. This is a different matter, reflecting a choice of place only, while present-day work involves a time schedule and specified activities, too. If one is subject to a boss who says, "You work in the room filled with blue smoke over there," it will be hard not to suspect necessity. Any case where one is subject to the orders of another would raise the suspicion. It may be that some persons like to work under direction, or that some wouldn't know what to do with themselves if they didn't have to go to the office or factory in the morning, or that others would prefer a clean orderly air-conditioned office to a hot house and unkempt wife. In each instance, work, though they may like it, remains a means to particular ends. The heir to millions presents a different situation.

Perhaps these Greek thinkers did not make clear enough that a man could be unfree and not know it, that like a life-sentence prisoner suddenly pardoned, he could be too long subject to necessity ever to leave the prison once the gate was opened. In any case, their first response might be that the man was educated improperly. As we said a moment ago, the Greeks had in mind persons whose educational tradition they understood. Even in castigating Sparta, Aristotle was singling out its aristocracy. Education consisted in being brought up in an aristocratic family and being tutored privately. It formed character, developed mind and body. If a man didn't have this education there was little he could do to obtain it later in life: the impressionable years for character, mind, and body had long passed. Culture is *paideia,* something you absorb as a child.

Youth is not free in practice, law, or custom from parents, teachers, and others who tutor and watch over minors. Hence, the young can be neither free of necessity nor capable of leisure. The term *minors* expresses their inferior station. They cannot yet have formed standards for themselves; only a good upbringing will give them the proper foundation.

Bouvard et Pécuchet is the story of two men who acquire the income to do what they want but fall heir to it at too late an age for their adult studies to do them much good. As for a man brought up to like work, what chance would he have? If he didn't work, he wouldn't know what to do with himself. So Aristotle, probably, would have taken a bet that the man, if truthful, would have given the answer of one of his most famous forefathers, Abraham Lincoln. When elected to Congress, it is told, Lincoln was given a form requiring him to describe his education. He wrote one word, "Defective."

The Greek's second response might well have been that the man simply didn't have the stuff it takes to enjoy leisure. There is such a thing as intelligence. Bouvard and Pécuchet, though towering over the people around them, may have lacked some of the necessary amount of it, and perhaps also of another requisite—the leisure temperament. To any other temperament, the delights of leisure are not so delightful. Some of them can be appreciated by almost anyone, perhaps. The banqueting, the dallying, the friends chosen for their own sake, conversations about anything—love, politics, the gods—music and poetry, gambols, wining and dining, all the way through the night. "No songs can please nor yet live long," says Horace, "that are written by those who drink water."

A man of leisure cannot work in the sense of earning daily bread, but he can play, if play is what he wants to do. Generally play for him will be a distraction; the mind, after long pursuing a line of thought, may need to run playfully along a different line. In another sense, the man of leisure is always at play, since his delight is in the play of the mind. This may seem an unwarranted extension of *play,* and can only be used in the English, not the Greek, sense of the word, yet it is justified not only by long usage but also by the detachment which, we have shown, appears in leisure. This detachment and objectivity is related to the lack of seriousness in play, for the mind seems to play without disturbing a flower.

Actually the detachment is more fundamental than this. What is meant by unseriousness is that play ceases when at the player's shoulder pallid necessity appears. If starvation or death is the outcome of a contest, then it is neither game nor play. For the professional boxer, the tightrope walker, the gladiator, the contest is a matter of bread and butter or of life and death. For the spectators it may be a game. They suffer the excitement of siding with contestants in agony; they feel joy of victory or humiliation of defeat. But behind them there does not stand *chlōra anankē.*

In a true game, one without such high stakes, the players' tension does not come from fear of necessity, but from imagining that the play is serious. This is play's set of mind, acting as if the outcome counts for something vital. The idea of fair play and being a good loser belongs to the same quality of unseriousness. If absorption goes too far, it becomes a trance or ecstasy or leads to breaking the rules of the game. A justified and common complaint of players is that one or another person takes the game too seriously. But if the game loses too much of its power of illusion and absorption, it becomes uninteresting or frivolous.

In English *game* is often used metaphorically for *contest,* since both have the element of striving. Yet a contest can be to the death; a game cannot. People sometimes say that business is a game, and certainly it can be one, if not taken seriously. But for those who work at it, business is usually in earnest and counts for what it is supposed to.

Play's relation to leisure lies more on the side of pleasure. The joy of the game comes from voluntarily exciting oneself to maximum strength and skill, or acting as if the stakes are the highest, while remaining all the time aware that it really doesn't count. The duel is a contest and yet a game if both fencers stop the moment a drop of blood is drawn. The joy of the game, then, is pretending to battle or acting out a danger situation, a play of skill and risk, within a situation really without peril. The player leaves his everyday world and enters one in which for the moment he is free of necessity, namely in his free time, his time of recreation. Symbolically he does battle with necessity, knowing that he cannot lose; indeed, if he plays and acts well, he may win.

In ordinary life, of course, if a man works he is not free of necessity, and on the next day or hour returns to the workday world. But play has lifted him out of it for a moment and made him a free man, one who could choose or not to play, one who, keeping faith with all the rules, faces the bull in the arena. So, for the ordinary man, play is a taste of leisure. The festivity and the holidays are playdays, out of this world, moments when the ordinary is suspended and all rejoice in a common unconcern for everyday cares, to celebrate this and other wonders of the cosmos.

The man of leisure, we said earlier, is always at play or (as Plato would say) on the hunt, in the exercise of the mind. And in another sense also:

in his freedom from necessity. Plato, who understood play better than Aristotle, may well have meant this when as an old man he wrote in the *Laws* that the right way to live is at play, in games, in giving the gods their due, in singing and dances. The philosopher concludes this remark significantly: Then, he says, a man will be able to propitiate the gods, defend himself against enemies, and win the contest. Note that he separates play and games from contest, here. Play and games can be considered in terms of social function as preparation for work tasks in later life. But the significance here is not sociological function. With leisure comes detachment and objectivity. In play too, since the game doesn't count, there is also detachment. The player plays without the passion of a real struggle. The quality of dispassion and objectivity in play is what leads to the recommendation not infrequently heard to do a given task or job as if it were a game. Talleyrand's advice in diplomacy was *surtout, pas de zèle.* In nations where honor is a dominant virtue, the aristocrat acts as if everything others live in terror of were to him a game. Thus he is always prepared for quick and true decision. Cool and collected, he sees that all life is a game. An extreme example of this occurs in polite Japanese speech, where the speaker speaks as if his hearers did whatever they did because they wanted to, not because of necessity. On hearing that a man's father had died, one would say to him, "I hear that your father has played dying." The one who can look on life as a game, the man free of necessity, has the advantage of detachment, of the objectivity of leisure, that graces play in its brief moment. A world with leisure supports a world with play.

Whether we accept Xenophon's or Plato's description of a symposium, both of them describe pleasures that have a wide appeal. But underneath it all, moving it along and lifting it to unequaled heights, is delight in the play of the mind. These men of leisure came to the banquet well prepared in the exercise of the speculative faculty. They led a life of theory, and for them that life was the only one worth living. The businessman's job, as can be seen at once, ought to be useful for many ends— the pleasure of commanding, of a game, of outfoxing a competitor, of prestige, of carrying on a family tradition, fulfilling one's responsibilities toward employees, and so forth. The job can be a means toward any of these ends, but nowhere is it reputed to open up vistas for contemplation. One interested in the exercise of the mind gets out of a narrow field that offers no prospect of it.

The world is divided into two classes. Not three or five or twenty. Just two. One is the great majority; the other is the leisure kind, not those of wealth or position or birth, but those who love ideas and the imagination. Of the great mass of mankind there are a few persons who are blessed and tormented with this love. They may work, steal, flirt, fight, like all the others, but everything they do is touched with the play of thought. In one century they may be scientists, in other theologians, in some other bards, whatever the category may be that grants them the freedom to let their minds play. They invent the stories, they create the cosmos, they discover what truth it is given man to discover, and give him the best portion of his truth and error. It is a select, small world of thinkers, artists, and musicians, not necessarily in touch with one another, who find their happiness in what they do, who can't do anything else, their daemon won't let them. The daemon doesn't depend on environment. You have it or have not. The pleasures of this handful of persons differ sharply from those of the rest. It cannot be otherwise. The ordinary person must buy his pleasures with the time and income of his occupation, while this class is actually occupied in its pleasures. That is why no matter how much the class is underpaid, it is a luxury class and will always have its select spirits as members. As long as it has leisure. Its felicity is assured in each act and at the very moment. The others, moreover, need to rec-reate themselves from their occupation, whereas this class has, if any-thing, only a need of distraction.

The others have their mass or popular or folk cultures; the leisure kind create culture. Culture doesn't necessarily make a person happier than folk culture (it depends on the person), but it is more profound, truer, highest in skill, artistic, beautiful. Those of the non-leisure class are formed by others. The man of the leisure class may be poor or rich, noble or commoner, of the strong or the weak, but he is always powerful in that he is the only one who, by his daemon, forms himself.

Veblen thought the rich and the aristocratic made up the leisure classes. The rich, specially the newly rich, buy commodities and ape the manners and taste of the noble. The noble and the anciently rich have quite constant spare time pleasures, at best like those of Pliny. They ride and hunt and go to the theater, they make love, they converse, dance, and drink. They also work, or at least the real ones did, to keep their estate in order, to see the crops distributed, or they fight to enlarge and protect it. Some of their pleasure has its origin in the battling of land aristocracies. Thus it bears a relation to the nobleman's work, and can be called recreation. They read, too, though some may have the literary taste of the ante-bellum plantation where the fondness for Sir Walter Scott was excessive. Since that author helped feed the Southerner's idea of himself, perhaps reading in the South too was recreation. (I have been using the modern sense of work here, which, of course, does not apply to an aristocracy.) Of all these rich and aristocratic activities, be they work, play, or something else, none show a great love for the cultivation of the mind.

Class is linked to Marx, since he taught the class struggle. *Leisure class* is linked to Veblen, since he wrote *The Theory of the Leisure Class*. Both these thinkers are so far from the ideas of this book that it would be only fair to disassociate them from our use of *the leisure class. Class,* moreover, when applied to groups usually involves some communication among class members; this is not necessarily true of the class we intend. They may neither know of nor care for one another's existence. The preferable term in many cases is *the leisure kind.* The word *kind* allows more room for a temperamental element and suggests a deeper environmental imprint than class. Yet the phrase *leisure class* should not be discarded, if only because popular reaction to it is significant.

To use the phrase *the leisure class* kindly today invites hostility and envy. The phrase rubs against the grain of equality. In recent centuries the envy must date from around the time of the French Revolution. Equality was probably not the first concept to raise the war cry against the leisure class. More probably "work" antedated "equality," work in its newer factory form, with an idea of production as whatever comes out of machines.

Sometimes it is as hard to convince people that everybody does not want leisure as it is to convince them that in the days of domestics, servants pitied their masters' lot. Much of Plato's *Republic* is devoted to the simple proposition that we cannot all be philosophers. If we can't be philosophers, we'd be bored with leisure.

The practical man, in relation to thought, can take it or leave it (he thinks). Shakespeare, Bach, Cézanne, mystery stories, comic books, western films—to him it's only a question of how you want to spend your free time. But for this same practical man the question of a leisure class boils down to a privilege: there are some people around who take it easy and live in luxury. This, highly simplified, is Veblen's idea too. The non-leisure class nowadays believes that a leisure class is one that leads an enviable life. We have just agreed that we cannot all be philosophers, gentlemen, musicians, or scholars, and that most of us would not want to be.

Then what is it the non-leisured envy in their false picture of the leisured? Above all they envy the thought that the others take it easy. This element of envy brings us to another difference between the two classes. The majorities of peoples have never sought the delights of leisure. For them "delights" is a misnomer. There is another mass of evidence to be brought in. It resides in two bodies of literature, each corresponding to one of these two great classes that distinguish mankind.

Mass Society and Its Culture*

By Edward Shils

MASS SOCIETY: CONSENSUS, CIVILITY, INDIVIDUALITY

A new order of society has taken form since the end of World War I in the United States, above all, but also in Great Britain, France, Northern Italy, the Low and Northern European countries, and Japan. Some of its features have begun to appear in Eastern and Central Europe, though in a less even manner; more incipiently and prospectively so, in Asian and African countries. It is the style to refer to this new order as the "mass society."

This new order of society, despite all its internal conflicts, discloses in the individual a greater sense of attachment to the society as a whole, and of affinity with his fellows. As a result, perhaps for the first time in history, large aggregations of human beings living over an extensive territory have been able to enter into relatively free and uncoerced association.

The new society is a mass society precisely in the sense that the mass of the population has become incorporated *into* society. The center of society—the central institutions, and the central value systems which guide and legitimate these institutions—has extended its boundaries. Most of the population (the "mass") now stands in a closer relationship to the center than has been the case in either premodern societies or in the earlier phases of modern society. In previous societies, a substantial portion of the population, often the majority, were born and forever remained "outsiders."

The mass society is a new phenomenon, but it has been long in gestation. The idea of the *polis* is its seed, nurtured and developed in the Roman idea of a common citizenship extending over a wide territory. The growth of nationality in the modern era has heightened the sense of

* Reprinted by permission from *Daedalus,* Journal of the American Academy of Arts and Sciences, Boston, Mass., Vol. 89, No. 2.

affinity among the members of different classes and regions of the same country. When the proponents of the modern idea of the nation put forward the view that life on contiguous, continuous, and common territory —beyond all divisions of kinship, caste, and religious belief—united the human beings living within that territory into a single collectivity, and when they made a common language the evidence of that membership, they committed themselves, not often wittingly, to the mass society.

An important feature of that society is the diminished sacredness of authority, the reduction in the awe it evokes and in the charisma attributed to it. This diminution in the status of authority runs parallel to a loosening of the power of tradition. Naturally, tradition continues to exert influence, but it becomes more open to divergent interpretations, and these frequently lead to divergent courses of action.

The dispersion of charisma from center outward has manifested itself in a greater stress on individual dignity and individual rights. This extension does not always reach into the sphere of the political, but it is apparent in the attitudes toward women, youth, and ethnic groups which have been in a disadvantageous position.

Following from this, one of the features of mass society I should like to emphasize is its wide dispersion of "civility." The concept of civility is not a modern creation, but it is in the mass society that it has found its most complete (though still very incomplete) realization. The very idea of a *citizenry* coterminous with the adult population is one of its signs. So is the moral equalitarianism which is a trait unique to the West, with its insistence that by virtue of their sharing membership in the community and a common tongue men possess a certain irreducible dignity.

None of these characteristic tendencies of mass society has attained anything like full realization. The moral consensus of mass society is certainly far from complete; the mutual assimilation of center (i.e., the elite) and periphery (i.e., the mass) is still much less than total. Class conflict, ethnic prejudice, and disordered personal relations remain significant factors in our modern mass societies, but without preventing the tendencies I have described from finding an historically unprecedented degree of realization.

Mass society is an industrial society. Without industry, i.e., without the replacement of simple tools by complicated machines, mass society would be inconceivable. Modern industrial techniques, through the creation of an elaborate network of transportation and communication, bring the various parts of mass society into frequent contact. Modern technology has liberated man from the burden of physically exhausting labor, and has given him resources through which new experiences of sensation, conviviality, and introspection have become possible. True, modern industrial organization has also been attended by a measure of hierarchical and bureaucratic organization which often runs contrary to the vital but loose consensus of mass society. Nonetheless, the fact remains that modern mass society has reached out toward a moral consensus and a civil order congruous with the adult population. The sacredness that every man possesses by virtue of his membership in society finds a more far-reaching affirmation than ever before.

Mass society has aroused and enhanced individuality. Individuality is characterized by an openness to experience, an efflorescence of sensation and sensibility, a sensitivity to other minds and personalities. It gives rise to, and lives in, personal attachments; it grows from the expansion of the empathic capacities of the human being. Mass society has liberated the cognitive, appreciative, and moral capacities of individuals. Larger elements of the population have consciously learned to value the pleasures of eye, ear, taste, touch, and conviviality. People make choices more freely in many spheres of life, and these choices are not necessarily made for them by tradition, authority, or scarcity. The value of the experience of personal relationships is more widely appreciated.

These observations are not meant to imply that individuality as developed in mass society exists universally. A part of the population in mass society lives in a nearly vegetative torpor, reacting dully or aggressively to its environment. Nonetheless, the search for individuality and its manifestations in personal relations are distinctly present in mass society and constitute one of its essential features.

THE CULTURE OF MASS SOCIETY

The fundamental categories of cultural life are the same in all societies. In all the different strata of any given society, the effort to explore and explain the universe, to understand the meaning of events, to enter into contact with the sacred or to commit sacrilege, to affirm the principles of morality and justice and to deny them, to encounter the unknown, to exalt or denigrate authority, to stir the senses by the control of and response to words, sounds, shapes, and colors—these are the basic elements of cultural existence. There are, however, profound variations in the elaboration of these elements, for human begins show marked differences in capacity for expression and reception.

No society can ever achieve a complete cultural consensus: there are natural limitations to the spread of the standards and products of superior culture throughout society. The tradition of refinement is itself replete with antinomies, and the nature of creativity adds to them. Creativity is a modification of tradition. Furthermore, the traditional transmission of superior culture inevitably stirs some to reject and deny significant parts of it, just because it is traditional. More fundamental than the degrees of creativity and alienation is the disparity in human cognitive, appreciative, and moral capacities. This disparity produces marked differences in the apprehension of tradition, in the complexity of the response to it, and in the substance of the judgments aroused by it.

Thus a widely differentiated "dissensus" has become stabilized in the course of history. The pattern of this "dissensus" is not inevitably unchanging. The classes consuming culture may diminish in number, their taste may deteriorate, their standards become less discriminating or more debased. On the other hand, as the mass of the population comes awake when its curiosity and sensibility and its moral responsiveness are aroused, it begins to become capable of a more subtle perception, more appreciative of the more general elements in a concrete representation, and more complex in its aesthetic reception and expression.

The Levels of Culture

For present purposes, we shall employ a very rough distinction among three levels of culture, which are levels of quality measured by aesthetic, intellectual, and moral standards. These are "superior" or "refined" culture, "mediocre" culture, and "brutal" culture.*

Superior or refined culture is distinguished by the seriousness of its subject matter, i.e., the centrality of the problems with which it deals, the acute penetration and coherence of its perceptions, the subtlety and wealth of its expressed feeling. The stock of superior culture includes the great works of poetry, novels, philosophy, scientific theory and research, statues, paintings, musical compositions and their performance, the texts and performance of plays, history, economic, social, and political analyses, architecture and works of craftsmanship. It goes without saying that the category of superior culture does not refer to the social status, i.e., the quality of their attainment, or of the author or of the consumers of the works in question, but only to their truth and beauty.

The category of mediocre culture includes works which, whatever the aspiration of their creators, do not measure up to the standards employed

---

* I have reservations about the use of the term "mass culture," because it refers simultaneously to the substantive and qualitative properties of the culture, to the social status of its consumers, and to the media by which it is transmitted. Because of this at least three-fold reference, it tends to beg some important questions regarding the relations among the three variables. For example, the current conception of "mass culture" does not allow for the fact that in most countries, and not just at present, very large sections of the elite consume primarily mediocre and brutal culture. It also begs the important questions as to whether the mass media can transmit works of superior culture, or whether the genres developed by the new mass media can become the occasions of creativity and therewith a part of superior culture. Also, it does not consider the obvious fact that much of what is produced in the genres of superior culture is extremely mediocre in quality. At present, I have no satisfactory set of terms to distinguish the three levels of cultural objects. I have toyed with "high," "refined," "elaborate," "genuine," or "serious," "vulgar," "mediocre," or "middle," and "low," "brutal," "base" or "coarse." None of these words succeeds either in felicity or aptness.

in judging works of superior culture. Mediocre culture is less original than superior culture; it is more reproductive; it operates largely in the same genres as superior culture, but also in certain relatively novel genres not yet fully incorporated into superior culture, such as the musical comedy. This may be a function of the nature of the genre or of the fact that the genre has not yet attracted great talent to its practice.

At the third level is brutal culture, where symbolic elaboration is of a more elementary order. Some of the genres on this level are identical with those of mediocre and refined culture (pictorial and plastic representation, music, poems, novels, and stories) but they also include games, spectacles (such as boxing and horse racing), and more directly expressive actions with a minimal symbolic content. The depth of penetration is almost always negligible, subtlety is almost entirely lacking, and a general grossness of sensitivity and perception is a common feature.

The greatest difference among the three levels of culture, apart from intrinsic quality, is the tremendous disparity in the richness of the stock available in any society at any given time. What any given society possesses is not only what it creates in its own generation but also what it has received from antecedent generations and from earlier and contemporaneous generations of other societies. Superior culture is immeasurably richer in content because it contains not only superior contemporary production but also much of the refined production of earlier epochs. Mediocre culture tends to be poorer, not only because of the poorer quality of what it produces in its own generation, but because these cultural products have a relatively shorter life span. Nevertheless, mediocre culture contains much that has been created in the past. The boundaries between mediocre and superior culture are not so sharp, and the custodians of superior culture are not so discriminating as always to reject the mediocre. Furthermore, a considerable amount of mediocre culture retains value over long periods; and even though mediocre taste varies, as does superior taste, there are stable elements in it, too, so that some of the mediocre culture of the past continues to find an appreciative audience.

At the lowest cultural level, where the symbolic content is most impoverished and where there is very little original creation in each generation, we come again to a greater, if much less self-conscious, dependence on the past. Games, jokes, spectacles, and the like continue traditional patterns with little consciousness of their traditionality. If the traditional element in brutal culture has been large, this is due to the relatively low creative capacities of those who produce and consume it. Here, until recently, there has been little professional production, machinery for preservation and transmission is lacking, and oral transmission plays a greater part in maintaining traditions of expression and performance than in the case of superior and mediocre cultures.

The Magnitudes: Consumption

The quantity of culture consumed in mass society is certainly greater than in any other epoch, even if we make proper allowance for the larger populations of the mass societies at present. It is especially at the levels of mediocre and brutal culture that an immense expansion has occurred, but the consumption of superior culture has also increased.

The grounds for this great increase, and for the larger increase in the two lower categories, are not far to seek. The most obvious are greater availability, increased leisure time, the decreased physical demands of work, the greater affluence of the classes which once worked very hard for long hours for small income, increased literacy, enhanced individuality, and more unabashed hedonism. In all these, the middle and the lower classes have gained more than have the elites (including the intellectuals, whatever their occupational distribution).

The consumption of superior culture has increased, too, but not as much as the other two categories, because the intellectual classes were more nearly saturated before the age of mass society. Moreover, the institutions of superior culture—the collections of connoisseurs, academies, universities, libraries, publishing houses, periodicals—were more elaborately and more continuously established in the pre-mass society than were the institutions which made mediocre and brutal culture available to their consumers.

Thus in mass society the proportion of the total stock of cultural objects held by superior culture has shrunk, and correspondingly the share of mediocre and brutal culture has grown*

Note on the Value of Mediocre and Brutal Culture

Mediocre culture has many merits. It often has elements of genuine conviviality, not subtle or profound perhaps, but genuine in the sense of being spontaneous and honest. It is often very good fun. Moreover, it is often earnestly, even if simply, moral. Mediocre culture, too, has its traditions; many of the dramas and stories which regale the vulgar have a long history hidden from those who tell and enjoy them. Like anything traditional, they express something essential in human life, and expunging them would expunge the accumulated wisdom of ordinary men and women, their painfully developed art of coping with the miseries of existence, their routine pieties, and their decent pleasures.

---

* This change in the relative shares of the three levels of culture has been distorted by contrast with the preceding epochs. The cultural life of the consumers of mediocre and brutal culture was relatively silent, unseen by the intellectuals. The immense advances in audibility and visibility of the two lower levels of culture is one of the most noticeable traits of mass society. This is in turn intensified by another trait of mass society, i.e., the enhanced mutual awareness of different sectors of the society.

There is much ridicule of *kitsch,* and it is ridiculous. Yet it represents aesthetic sensibility and aesthetic aspiration, untutored, rude, and deformed. The very growth of kitsch, and of the demand which has generated the industry for the production of kitsch, is an indication of a crude aesthetic awakening in classes which previously accepted what was handed down to them or who had practically no aesthetic expression and reception.

THE REPRODUCTION AND TRANSMISSION OF CULTURE

In medieval society, the church, and, to a less effective and more limited degree, the schools (which were immediate or indirect adjuncts of the church), brought the culture of the center into the peripheral areas of a very loosely integrated society.* Protestantism and printing led to a pronounced change which showed the direction of the future. The cheapened access to the printed word and the spread of a minimal literacy (which became nearly universal within European societies only at the beginning of the present century) resulted in an expansion of each of the three strata of culture. In this expansion, the chief beneficiaries were mediocre and brutal culture.

The increased wealth, leisure, and literacy of the lower classes, and the flowering of hedonism which these permitted, would undoubtedly have produced the great expansion in mediocre and brutal, as well as superior, cultural consumption even without the further technological developments of communication in the twentieth century. This technological development did, however, supply a mighty additional impetus. The popular press of the last decades of the nineteenth century showed the way. The development of new methods of graphic reproduction in lithography and in both still and moving pictures, new methods of sound recording, and the transmission of sound and picture increased the flow of communication from the center to the periphery. Where previously the custodians of superior culture and its mediocre variants had nearly a monopoly, through their quasi-monopoly of the institutions of transmission, the new methods of mass communication have transformed the situation.

The quest for a larger audience, which would make it feasible to obtain a subsidy (in the form of advertising) to cover the difference between what the consumers pay and what it costs to produce cultural objects, has been of the greatest importance to the interrelations of the various strata of culture. The dependence of the subsidy on greatly extended consumption would in itself have required a reaching-out toward a heterogeneous audience. The increased overhead of communication

---

* A society which is far less "organic" in its structure and outlook than the critics of modern society allege and less "organic" also than the modern society which is so unsympathetically assailed by these critics.

enterprises in television, for example, as compared with book printing, has intensified the need for large and heterogeneous audiences.

Before the emergence of the most recent forms of mass communication, with their very large capital requirements, each stratum of culture had its own channels and institutions. As long as books were the chief means of impersonal cultural transmission, the cultural segregation of the classes could be easily maintained. The drive toward a maximum audience has helped change this, and the change has had momentous repercussions. The magazine is the embodiment of this new development. The form of the magazine is an eighteenth-century phenomenon; but the enlargement of its role in the reproduction and transmission of culture is the product of the latter-day need to gain the maximum audience, one in its turn impelled by the economic necessity of the subsidy. To speak to the largest possible audience, it has been necessary to make the content of what is transmitted in a single issue as heterogeneous as the audience sought.

The general principle of providing something for everyone in the family became well established in the first decades of the popular press. The principle was developed to the point where every class which could possibly increase the total audience was offered something. This principle has not succeeded in dominating the entire field. There are still specialized organs and institutions which seek to please only one particular stratum of consumers, and in Europe the tradition of a unitary public still persists—but even there not without making very substantial concessions to the new principle. Even the universities (which do not necessarily seek large numbers) in Europe, although not as much as in America, have also diversified their programs in order to meet the diversified demand. In popular periodicals like *Time, Life, Look, Picture Post, Match, Der Spiegel, Esquire,* and in distinguished daily newspapers like *The New York Times,* and recently, even in a cumbersome way, *The Times* of London, there is an intermixture of superior, mediocre, and brutal culture which is historically unique. The same can be observed in television and, of course, in the film: a single network presents a wide variety of levels, and films of genuinely high artistic and intellectual merit may be produced in the same studio which produces numerous mediocre and brutal films.

THE CONSUMPTION OF CULTURE

In modern society, the number of consumers of superior culture has never been very large; in premodern societies, it was even smaller. The chief consumers of works of superior culture are the intellectuals, i.e., those whose occupations require intellectual preparation, and in practice, the application of high intellectual skills. In the contemporary world this category includes university teachers, scientists, university students, writers, artists, secondary-school teachers, members of the learned professions (law, medicine, and the church), journalists, and higher civil servants, as well as a scattering of businessmen, engineers, and army officers.

Outside the intellectual occupations, where the largest number are found, the consumers of superior culture are spread thin and at random. This situation has probably never been different, even in periods when the princes of the church were patrons of painting and sculpture, or when in most grand-bourgeois households one could find sets of Goethe, Nietzsche, Fielding, the memoirs of Sully, or the letters of Mme. de Sévigné.

The political, technological, military, ecclesiastical, and economic elites have not usually been intellectuals, even though their members have had intellectual training and followed intellectual careers before entering their particular profession. Politician and intellectual come closest in regimes just established by revolution or by a successful nationalist movement (their quality as intellectuals, however, is usually not particularly distinguished). In established political regimes, although there may be a significant number of politicians who were once intellectuals of a respectable level, over a long period the demands of the profession of politics leave little time, strength, or sensitivity for the continued consumption of intellectual goods.

Among the leading Western countries, it is in the United States that the political elite gives a preponderant impression of indifference toward works of superior culture. The situation is probably not very different in Great Britain, France, Germany, or Italy, though there, the political elite, living amidst aristocratic and patrician traditions, possesses an external gloss of intimacy with high culture. In the United States, however, despite Woodrow Wilson, Franklin Roosevelt, the Plutarch-reading Harry Truman, and the De re metallica-editing Herbert Hoover, the political elite gives a definitely unintellectual impression.

The same is true of the American plutocracy: as a body of collectors of the works of painting and sculpture and as patrons of learning, it will take an outstanding place in the history of the great Maecenases. Yet the dominant impression is one of indifference and inhospitality to intellectual work. The great industrial system of the United States has required a large corps of engineers and applied scientists, men of great imagination and even high creativity; yet their cultural consumption (not only of superior culture but also of mediocre culture) is rather small. The vigor and pre-eminence of these sectors of the American elite, and the conventions of the media of information through which their public image is formed, fortify intellectuals with the sense that they alone in their society are concerned with superior culture.

Among the middle classes the consumption of the traditional genres of superior culture is not large. Popular periodicals, best-selling novels, political books of transient interest, inferior poetry, inspirational works of theology and moral edification, and biographies made up and still make up the bulk of their consumption. More recently, the films and radio, and most recently, television, have provided the substance of their cultural consumption. Their fare is largely philistine—mediocre culture and brutal culture. Nonetheless, because of exposure to the "mass media," e.g., periodicals like *Life* and a narrow band of the output on television, film, and radio, a larger section of these classes has come into contact with and consumed a larger quantity of extra-religious, superior culture than has been the case throughout the course of modern history.

Finally, the industrial working class and the rural population remain to be considered. Together, these classes consume almost nothing of the inheritance and current production of superior culture. Very little mediocre culture of the conventional genres reaches them except in such periodicals as *Life, Look,* and *The Reader's Digest.* Much of their culture as transmitted by mass media is brutal—crime films and television spectacles, paperbacks of violence, pornographic oral and printed literature, and the culture of the world of sports.

It would be a mistake, however, to think that the culture possessed by these classes is exhausted by what comes to them through the mass media. A large amount of traditional religious culture (and of sectarian variants of traditional religious culture) flourishes in all the nonintellectual classes. Much of regional and class culture, maintained by family, by colleagues, neighbors, and friends and by local institutions, survives and is unlikely to be supplanted by the larger culture which emanates from the center. This places limits on what is incorporated from the current flow of the mass media.*

A special stratum of the population that cuts across all classes and gives a particular tone to mass society is the younger generation, the maligned and bewildering "youth." The coming forth of youth in contemporary society rests on primordial foundations which exist in all societies. In most societies, however, the institutional structure and the niggardliness of nature have kept youth in check. In modern times, romanticism and increased wealth and (more deeply) the expanding radius of empathy and fellow-feeling have given youth opportunities never before available. The enhanced productivity of the economy of Western countries has, on the one hand, allowed young people to remain outside the hard grind of work for a longer time; it has given them opportunities

---

* Also, it should be added, this persistence of traditional and orally transmitted culture renders fruitless the effort to diagnose the dispositions and outlook of a people by analyzing what is presented to them through films, television, and wireless broadcasts, the press, etc.

to earn and spend substantial individual incomes. The resulting cultural manifestations are largely responsible for what is called "mass culture."

Before the advent of mass society, a small proportion of the youth were rigorously inculcated with superior culture; the rest were exposed to the brutal culture of their seniors. It is one of the marks of mass society, however, that youth has become a major consumer of the special variants of mediocre and brutal culture that are produced for transmission through the mass media. An extraordinary quantity of popular music, mediocre and brutal films, periodical literature, and forms of dance is produced for and consumed by youth. This is something unprecedented, and this is the heart of the revolution of mass culture.

Most of the "youthful mass" comes from strata of society which have had little connection except through religious education with high or superior culture. Not yet enmeshed in the responsibilities of family and civic life, and with much leisure time and purchasing power, youth constitutes both an eager and a profitable public which attracts the attention of the mass media. The eagerness of youth for the mediocre and brutal culture provided by the mass media, and that youth's own creative poverty are a universal phenomenon. Where the political elite does not grant this eagerness the right of direct expression, but seeks instead to divert it into ideological channels or to dam it up, it still remains powerful and indomitable. Where the political order allows this passionate and uncultivated vitality to find a free expression, the result is what we see throughout the Western world.

THE PRODUCTION OF CULTURE

The High Intelligentsia

A differentiated creative intelligentsia is the oldest stratum of Western society with a set of continuous traditions. Such a stratum still exists today, far broader than ever before, far more extended and with international ties exceeding that of any other section of our own or any other society.* There is today more internal specialization than in the past: it is impossible for any one man to be fully conversant with the inherited and currently produced stock of cultural objects. The productive intelligentsia is perhaps less intensely like-minded now than in the past, when it was smaller and the body of what it had to master was smaller. Nonetheless, despite changes in society, in the modes of financial support, and in the organization of intellectual life, this creative stratum is constantly reproducing and increasing.

---

* The internationality of the medieval church and of the European aristocracy in the eighteenth century was thin and parochial in comparison with the scope and intensity of that exhibited by present-day intellectual classes.

The Mediocre Intelligentsia

The modern age, however, has seen growing up alongside this creative intelligentsia a much larger stratum of producers of mediocre culture. In the seventeenth and eighteenth centuries, when letters and the arts began to offer the possibilities of a professional career, thanks to the advance of printing and to an enlarging public, there emerged, besides those whose creative capacities achieved the heights of greatness, a wider group of writers, artists, and scholars. From these were recruited the residents of Grub Street, who, while still trying to reach the highest levels, had to live by producing for a less discriminating public. The nineteenth century saw the stabilization of the profession of those who produced almost exclusively for the public that consumed mediocre culture. The popular press, the film, radio, and television have deepened and extended their ranks. The enlargement of university populations and the corresponding increase in the number of university teachers, the increased opportunities for careers in research, in the applied natural and social sciences, have similarly added to the producers of mediocre culture.*

The professional practitioner with a mediocre culture has developed traditions, models, and standards of his own. More frequently than in the past he engages directly in the professional production of mediocre culture without first essaying the production of works of superior culture. He can attain an excellence within his own field that often brings him satisfaction and esteem. Indeed, in certain genres of mediocre culture that are new or at least relatively new, he can reach heights of unprecedented excellence, to the point where, if the genre is admissible, his work can take on the lineaments of superior cultural achievement.

Yet despite this approximation to autonomy, the autonomy remains incomplete. The producer of mediocre culture is exposed to the standards of superior culture, and he cannot entirely escape their pressure. If he prospers and his colleagues on the level of superior culture do not, then he is guilt-ridden for having "betrayed" higher standards for the sake of the fleshpots.

This troubling juxtaposition of two consciences is rendered more acute by the physical juxtaposition of the two levels of cultural objects and the social contact of their producers in the media through which mediocre culture chiefly finds its audience, namely, the media of mass communica-

---

* The increase in numbers of persons in intellectual occupations and those that require intellectual training might well be pressing hard against the supply. The supply of high talent is limited; improved methods of selection and training can somewhat increase it, but they cannot make it limitless or coterminous with the population of any society. Hence as the numbers expand, modern societies are forced to admit many persons whose endowments are such as to permit only a mediocre performance in the creation and reproduction of cultural works.

tion. The professionals of mediocre culture cannot, even if they would, forget the standards of superior culture, because they mix with persons who often attain them, because the media from time to time present works composed according to those standards, and because critics continually refer to them. These factors provide an increasing stimulus to an awareness of and a concern for high standards, even when they are not observed.

The Brutal Intelligentsia

The producers of brutal culture confront a quite different situation. They have neither a similarly compelling historical past nor the connections with superior culture which their "colleagues" in the field of mediocre culture possess. They do not, so far as I know, justify their performance by reference to the great masters of their art. There are some exceptions among crime-story writers, boxers, jockeys, and certainly among a few of the best sports writers. But these are new professions. Their practitioners feel no continuity with their forerunners, even though the objects they produce have been produced for a long time. Brutal culture therefore has only recently developed a differentiated professional personnel.

Brutal culture has not shown great potentialities for development. Nonetheless, certain genres of brutal culture have produced works of great excellence, so that these reach through mediocre culture into the outer confines of superior culture. Some works of pornography have found a place in superior culture, some horror stories have done the same, as have the chronicles of sports. Since brutal culture is by no means restricted to the uncultivated classes for its audience, works of brutal culture, which reach a form of high refinement, also make their way upward, and with them, their producers move in the same direction. In the main, however, there is a wall which separates the producers of brutal culture from the producers of superior culture. Even where they find the same audience, the tradition of superior culture is such as to erect a barrier to a massive interpenetration.*

A few words should be said here about another kind of cultural production: the anonymous production of folk art and literature and linguistic innovation. In their highest manifestations, the production of these arts was probably never very widely spread. They grow on the edge of craftsmanship, of religious worship, and of brutal entertainment. Considerable creative talents must have impelled them into existence. Their creators must have been men of genius, working with subterranean traditions that

---

* The bohemian sector of the high intelligentsia, past and present, is an exception to this generalization. The mingling of poets and cut-purses has a long and special history which runs down to the occasional highbrow glorification of the hipster.

scarcely exist any more, and that had only a small direct connection with the great tradition of superior culture. In so far as they were inspired by craftsmanship, machine production has greatly restricted their emergence; the traditions which sustained them have atrophied.

It is sometimes asserted that the anonymous cultural production of craftsmen and peasants in the Europe of the later Middle Ages and of early modern times has been destroyed by the growth of mass culture. This is possible, but it is not the only possibility. If we assume that the production of geniuses and outstandingly gifted intelligences and sensibilities in any population remains fairly constant (not an unreasonable assumption) and that modern Western societies with their increasing cultivation of science, literature, art, enterprise, administration, and technology have been drawing more and more on their reservoirs of talent, then it appears quite plausible to assert that the talents of the type once manifested in the anonymous productions of folk culture have been recruited and diverted into other spheres and are active at different levels of culture and social life.

THE POSITION OF SUPERIOR CULTURE IN MASS SOCIETY

Has the culture created in the past forty years—the approximate age of mass society—deteriorated as much as its detractors claim? The task of assessment is most difficult.

Let us for the moment grant that contemporary refined culture may be poorer than the superior culture produced in any comparable span of years in the past. There may be any number of reasons or causes, totally unrelated to the development and impact of mass society on culture. For example, the distribution and efflorescence of genius are matters that still await full understanding. It is conceivable, if unlikely, that our neural equipment is poorer than that of our ancestors. And even if it is as good, it is also possible that our cultural traditions have passed their point of culmination, that they contain no possibilities of further development, that they offer no point of departure even for creative minds. Another important consideration is whether the alleged deterioration is being evaluated in the light of standards that are applied equally to other periods. We must be sure to comprehend in our assessment the whole range of intellectual and artistic activities. We must remember that the genius which is expressed in refined culture may be of diverse forms, and that it can flow into some domains in one age, and into other domains in other ages.

Yet these might be idle reflections. The evidence of decline is not by any means very impressive. In every field of science and scholarship into which so much of our contemporary genius flows (in physics, chemistry, and in mathematics, in biology and neurology, in logic, linguistics, and anthropology, in comparative religion, in Sinology and Indology), out-standing work is being done, not only in the older centers not yet afflicted by the culture of mass society, but in the United States as well, that most massive of all mass societies. Theology seems to be in a more vital and powerful state than it has been for several centuries. Economics proceeds on a high level, higher on the average than in past periods; sociology, barbarous, rude, and so often trivial, offers at its best something which no past age can match in the way of discovery and penetration. In political philosophy, in which our decay is said to be so patent, we have no Aristotle, Hobbes, or Bentham, but there are probably only a half dozen such masters in all human history. On the other hand, in France and America there are men and women who are at least as deep and rigorous in their analysis of central issues as John Stuart Mill or Walter Bagehot or de Tocqueville were. In the novel, we have no Tolstoy, no Stendhal or Dostoievsky or Flaubert; still, the level of achievement is high. In poetry and in painting, there may indeed have been a falling-off from the great heights; in drama there is no Aeschylus, no Shakespeare, no Racine. But these are among the highest peaks of all human history, and the absence of any such from our two-fifths of a century can scarcely constitute evi-dence of a general decline in the quality of the products of superior culture in our own time.

That there is, however, a consciousness of decline is undeniable. Intel-lectuals are beset by a malaise, by a sense of isolation, of disregard, of a lack of sympathy. They feel they have lost contact with their audiences, especially that most important of all audiences, those who rule society. This is nothing new. Romanticism is still far from dead, and it is a cardinal tenet of romanticism that the creative person is cut off from his own society and especially from its rulers. The contemporary romantic intellectual has in addition an acute sense of being cut off from the people.

The noisy, visible, tangible presence of mediocre and brutal culture has heightened his anguish. Whereas intellectuals in earlier ages of modern society could remain ignorant of the cultural preferences of those who consumed cultural objects other than their own, this is not really possible for contemporary intellectuals. By virtue of their own relations to pro-duction, the vigor with which mediocre and brutal cultures are promoted, and the evident enjoyment of their consumers, intellectuals are forced to be familiar with what takes place on these levels of culture.

But what are the specific threats to superior culture in mass society? To what extent do they differ from earlier dangers? To what extent do these dangers derive from mass society itself? For superior culture is and has always been in danger. Since it never is and never has been the culture of an entire society, it must necessarily be in a state of tension vis-à-vis the rest of society. If the producers and consumers of superior culture see further and deeper than their contemporaries, if they have a more subtle and more lively sensitivity, if they do not accept the received traditions and the acknowledged deities of their fellow countrymen, whatever they say or believe or discover is bound to create tension.

Are intellectuals more endangered in the age of mass society by the jealousy and distrust of the powerful than in other social eras? Surely, censorship, arrest, and exile are nothing new. Can the occasional anti-intellectual flurries of American politicians and businessmen be equated with the restraints imposed on intellectuals in Soviet Russia, Fascist Spain, or National Socialist Germany? None of these countries, it should be noted, are or were mass societies in the sense that the contemporary United States is, or as the United Kingdom, Western Germany, and France are becoming. Does the role played by advertising on the television screen represent a greater intrusion into the creative sphere than did the prosecutions of Flaubert and Baudelaire in nineteenth-century France, or the moral censorship which Mrs. Grundy used to exercise so coarsely in the United States and which she still does in Britain, or the political and religious censorship practiced in eighteenth-century France? Athenian society was no mass society, and there were no advertisers there, yet Socrates was executed. I do not wish to belittle the present or recent attacks on intellectual or artistic liberty in the United States, but I do wish to stress that they are not unique to mass society.

It is sometimes asserted that the culture of mass society produces its insidious effects in roundabout ways that constitute a greater danger than the crude external pressures employed by the rulers of earlier societies. It seduces, it is said, rather than constrains. It offers opportunities for large incomes to those who agree to the terms of employment offered by institutions of mediocre and brutal culture. But does this opportunity, and even its acceptance, necessarily damage superior culture? The mere existence of the opportunity will not seduce a man of strongly impelled creative capacities, once he has found his direction. And if he does accept the opportunity, are his creative talents inevitably stunted? Is there no chance at all that they will find expression in the mass medium to which he is drawn? The very fact that here and there in the mass media, on television and in the film, work of superior quality is to be seen, seems to be evidence that genuine talent is not inevitably squandered once it leaves the traditional refined media.

It is, of course, possible for men to waste their talents, to corrupt themselves for the pleasures of office, for the favor of authority, for popularity, or for income or for the simple pleasure of self-destruction. Qualitatively, the financial temptations of work in the media of mass communication are of the same order as the other temptations intellectuals encounter. Quantitatively, it is difficult to estimate the magnitude of the temptation. There are certainly more opportunities now for intellectuals to earn much money in the production of mediocre and brutal cultural objects than there were before the development of the mass media. It is clear, however, that the large majority of literary men, poets, scholars, painters, scientists, or teachers have not been tempted nor have they yielded to the temptation—even if we concede, which we do not, that their experience in the mass media prevents them from finding creative expression either in the mass media or outside them.

Popularization is sometimes cited as one of the ways in which superior culture is being eroded. Does the contact between mediocre and refined culture which occurs in popularization do damage to refined culture? Raymond Aron's thought does not deteriorate because he occasionally writes in *The New York Times Magazine* and much more frequently in *Le Figaro;* Bertrand Russell suffered no injury from an article in *Look Magazine.* There is no reason why gifted intellectuals should lose their powers because they write for audiences unable to comprehend their ordinary level of analysis and exposition. An intellectual who devotes all his efforts to popularization would soon cease to have anything of his own to popularize and would have to become a popularizer of the works of other persons. But there is no convincing evidence that persons who are capable of refined cultural production and who are strongly impelled to it are being gradually drawn away from their calling by the temptations of popularization. What has been the loss to American, British, and French science in the past forty years from the development of the new branch of journalism which is involved in scientific popularization?

The production of mediocre or brutal culture need not (so the argument goes) destroy superior culture by striking at its producers, either constrainingly or seductively. It can deprive them of their market, and especially of the discriminating appreciation they need to keep their skills at the highest pitch. The corruption of public taste, of those consumers whose natural discriminative powers are not so great that they can dispense with the cultivation which a refined cultural environment provides, is certainly a possibility. In contrast to this possibility, however, is the fact that in the United States today discrimination in a small minority (certainly no smaller than at the end of the nineteenth century or in England today) is as acutely perceptive as it ever was. The quality of literary criticism in *The Partisan Review, The Hudson Review, The Sewanee Review,* and *The New Yorker* is as informed, as penetrating, and as reflective as it was fifty years ago in the best American or British periodicals.

The demand for the products of mediocre and brutal culture certainly affects the market for the products of superior culture. If there were no inferior cultural products available and if the purchasing power were there, there certainly would be a larger body of purchasers of the products of superior culture. This was the situation in Britain during the war, and it is probably the situation in the Soviet Union today. As to whether this represents an improvement in public taste is another matter. In Britain, after the war, once inferior cultural objects became available in larger supply, the prosperity of serious booksellers markedly declined. The same would probably occur in the Soviet Union if a larger range of consumer goods, cultural and other, were to enter the market.

Therefore, when public demand is free to obtain the objects it desires, the market for superior cultural objects, given the present distribution of tastes, is restricted, and enterprisers with capital to invest will not rush in to use their resources in areas of the market where the return is relatively poor. Yet are there many manuscripts of books of outstanding merit lying unpublished today?

The relative unprofitability of the market for superior cultural objects is compensated for in part by the existence of enterprises motivated by other than profit considerations. There is no reason to assume that such uneconomically oriented investors will be fewer in the future than in the recent past. In part, the unprofitability of the market is circumvented by subsidy or patronage.

We often hear the old system of patronage praised by those who bemoan its passing. It is well to remember, however, what misery and humiliation it imposed on its beneficiaries, how capricious and irregular it was, and how few were affected by it during the period from the seventeenth to the nineteenth centuries when intellectuals were growing in numbers. Many more were supported by administrative sinecures in church and state.

The private patronage of individual intellectuals by individual patrons still exists, but it plays a scant role. The place of this older form of subsidy has been taken over by the universities, the state, and the private foundations, and they appear to be more lavish, more generous, and more just than their predecessors were in earlier centuries.

There is, however, a major deficiency in the institutional system of high culture in the United States, one that can be largely attributed to the successful competition among the best of the newer organs of mass communication. America lacks a satisfactory intellectual weekly press, and, ironically, this is in part the achievement of *Time Magazine. The Nation* and *The New Republic,* which thirty years provided something quite comparable in journalistic and intellectual quality to *The Spectator,* have declined in quality and influence.

The absence of a passable intellectual weekly* does damage to American intellectual life. The country is so large and the intellectuals so scattered that a continuous focus on intellectual concerns (including the

---

* *Commonweal* exists on a higher intellectual plane than that of our two secular weeklies, but its religious preoccupations restrict the generality of its appeal.

evaluation of political and economic affairs in a manner acceptable to a sophisticated, intellectual public) would serve invaluably to maintain standards of judgment and to provide a common universe of discourse.* There is a danger in the United States today of a centrifugal force within the intellectual classes, arising from their numbers, their spatial dispersion and their professional specialization. These factors tend to weaken the sense of community among our intellectual classes. Without this sense of community, the attachment to high standards might slacken or even collapse altogether.

PURITANISM, PROVINCIALISM, AND SPECIALIZATION

If the arguments of those who attribute to mass society the alleged misery of contemporary culture are not sound, there is no gainsaying the fact that the consumption of superior culture does not rest in a perfectly secure position in the United States. The culture of the educated classes, who in America as elsewhere should be its bearers, leaves much to be desired. One is distressed by the boorish and complacent ignorance of university graduates, by the philistine distrust of or superciliousness toward superior culture which is exhibited by university professors in the humanities and social sciences or in the medical and law schools of this country, and by journalists and broadcasters. The political, economic, military, and technological elites are no better. The near illiteracy of some of the better American newspapers, the oftentimes raucous barbarism of our weeklies and our one widely circulated fortnightly, the unletteredness of many of our civil servants, the poverty of our bookshops, the vulgarity of our publishers (or at least those who write their jacket blurbs and their advertising copy) can give little comfort.

There is undeniably much that is wrong with the quality of culture consumed by the more or less educated classes in America. Very little of what is wrong, however, can be attributed to the mass media, particularly to the films, television, radio, and popular magazines.

It is not that the cascade of mediocre and brutal culture which pours out over the mass media is admirable. Quite the contrary. The culture of the mass media is not, however, the reason that the distribution and consumption of superior culture disclose (alongside so many profoundly impressive achievements) many things that are repellent.

What is wrong, is wrong with our intellectuals and their institutions and with some of our cultural traditions, which have little to do with the culture created for and presented by the mass media.

---

* The excellent highbrow reviews are no substitute for an intellectual weekly. They are too infrequent, they are too apolitical, and even where they are not, as in the case of the *Partisan Review* or *Commentary,* they cannot maintain a continuous flow of comment and coverage.

The dour Puritanism that looked on aesthetic expression as self-indulgence does not grow out of mass society. Nor does the complacent and often arrogant provincialism that distrusts refined culture because it believes it to be urban, Anglophile, and connected with a patrician upper class. America was not a mass society in the nineteenth century, it was a differentiated society in which pronounced equalitarian sentiments often took on a populistic form. Certain tendencies which have culminated in a mass society were at work in it. However, much of its culture, although mediocre and brutal, was not produced by the institutions or by the professional personnel now producing the culture of mass society.

Refined culture in nineteenth-century America, reflecting the taste of the cultivated classes of New England and the Middle Atlantic States, did not enjoy a hospitable reception in the Middle West, as a result of the usual hostility of province against metropolis and of those who arrived later in America against those who arrived earlier and who became established sooner. American provincial culture in the nineteenth century was a variant of the British provincial dissenting culture that Matthew Arnold criticized unsparingly in *Culture and Anarchy.* Whereas this culture collapsed in England after World War I, in America it has continued powerful almost up to the present.

These are some of the special reasons for the present uncongeniality of superior culture to so many Americans. It springs from a general distrust that superior culture must always encounter in any society. In this country it expresses itself with greater strength, virulence, and freedom because the political and economic elites of American society feel little obligation to assume a veneer of refined culture, as in Great Britain and France.

Against this background of tradition and sentiment, the development of education in the United States in the past decades has created a technical intelligentsia that does not form a coherent intellectual community. While secondary education became less intellectual in its content and undergraduate education dissipated itself in courses of study of very low intensity and little discipline, a very superior and vigorous type of postgraduate education developed. In trying to make up for lost ground and in seeking to make a deep and thorough penetration into a rapidly growing body of knowledge, postgraduate training in each discipline has had to become highly specialized.

This impetus toward specialization has been heightened by the natural development of science and by the growth of the percentage of the population that pursues postgraduate studies. The development of science has greatly increased the volume of literature a student must cover in each discipline; the increasing number of students, and the necessity for each to do a piece of research no one has ever done before have tended to narrow the concentration within the discipline imposed by the internal evolution of the subject.*

The product of these educational and scientific developments has been the specialist who is uncultivated outside his own specialty. Except for those strong and expansive personalities whose curiosity and sensitivity lead them to the experience of what their education has failed to give them, even the creative American scientist, scholar, or technologist often possesses only a narrow range of mediocre culture.

The ascent of the universities to preponderance in the life of superior culture in the United States, and increasingly (though still not to the same extent) in Europe, has meant that trends within the university tend to become the trends of intellectual life as a whole to a much greater degree than in earlier periods of modern society. As the universities have become more internally differentiated and specialized, superior cultural life has also tended to become more specialized.

What we are suffering from is the dissolution of "the educated public," coherent although unorganized, with a taste for superior cultural objects with no vocational import. The "universitization" of superior culture—most advanced in America but already visible in Great Britain, too, though not at all a completely realized tendency—is part of this process of the dissolution of the body of consumers of superior culture.

At the same time, it would be disregarding the truth to overlook the extraordinary vitality of the contemporary American university. Vitality by its nature is diffuse and inflammatory. It is possible, therefore, that despite the densely specialized clutter of the postgraduate system and the prevailing pattern of research which is partly a cause and partly a result of that system, this vitality will do more than withstand the pressure; it is possible that it will ignite interest along a broader front than specialized training commands. It is also possible that the waste of undergraduate education will turn into lively cultivation through the vitality of the new generation of college teachers who are at present among the chief consumers and reproducers of superior culture.

Specialization has lessened the coherence of the intellectual community, comprising creators, reproducers and consumers; it has dispersed its focus of attention, and thus left ungratified cultural needs which the mediocre and brutal culture of the mass media and of private life have been called in to satisfy. The consumption of brutal and mediocre culture is the consequence, not the cause, of developments which are quite independent of the specific properties of mass society. As a matter of fact,

---

* The romantic idea of originality, which claimed that genius must go its own unique way, has been transposed into one that demands that the subject matter should be unique to the investigator. This has led to much specialized triviality in humanistic research.

the vitality, the individuality, which may rehabilitate our intellectual public will probably be the fruits of the liberation of powers and possibilities inherent in mass societies.

THE PROSPECTS OF SUPERIOR CULTURE IN MASS SOCIETY

The problems of superior culture in mass society are the same as in any society. These problems are the maintenance of its quality and influence on the rest of the society.

To maintain itself, superior culture must maintain its own traditions and its own internal coherence. The progress of superior culture (and its continued self-renewal and expansion) require that the traditions be sustained, however much they are revised or partially rejected at any time.

Respect for the traditions in one's own field, together with freedom in dealing with those traditions, are the necessary conditions for creative work. The balance between them is difficult to define, and it is no less difficult to discern the conditions under which that balance can be achieved and maintained. Of great importance is the morale (in its broadest sense) of the intellectuals who take on administrative and teaching responsibilities for the maintenance and advancement of high culture. Within this section of the intellectual class, there must be an incessant scrutiny of every institutional innovation, with regard to its possible impact on intellectual morale. An essential element in this internal state is a balance between respect and freedom in relation to the immanent traditions of each field of intellectual work.

Serious intellectuals have never been free from pressure on the part of sectors of society other than their own. The intellectual sector has always been relatively isolated, regardless of the role of intellectuals in economic and political life. The external world is always jealous of the devotion of the intellectuals to their own gods, and of the implicit criticism which that devotion directs against the ruling values of the other spheres. Intellectuals have always been faced with the task of continuing their own tradition, developing it, differentiating it, improving it as best they could. They have always had to contend with church, state, and party, with merchants and soldiers who have sought to enlist them in their service and to restrict and damage them in word and deed if they did not yield to temptations and threats. The present situation has much in common with the past. The responsibilities of intellectuals also remain the same: to serve the standards they discern and develop and to find a way of rendering unto Caesar what is Caesar's without renouncing what belongs to their own proper realm.

There is no doubt in my mind that the main "political" tradition by which most of our literary, artistic, and social-science intellectuals have lived in America is unsatisfactory. The fault does not lie exclusively with the intellectuals. The philistine Puritanism and provincialism of our elites share much of the blame, as does the populism of professional and lay politicians. Nonetheless, the intellectuals cannot evade the charge that they have done little to ameliorate the situation. Their own political attitudes have been alienated, they have run off into many directions of frivolity. The most recent of such episodes in the 1930s and 1940s were also the most humiliating, and temporarily the most damaging, to the position of intellectuals in American society.

One of the responsibilities implied by their obligation to maintain good relations with the nonintellectual elite is the "civilization" of political life, i.e., the infusion of the standards and concerns of a serious, intellectually disciplined contemplation of the deeper issues of political life into everyday politics. Our intellectuals have in the main lectured politicians, upbraided them, looked down their noses at them, opposed them, and even suspected those of their fellow intellectuals who have become politicians of moral corruption and intellectual betrayal.

The intellectuals who have taken on themselves the fostering of superior culture are part of the elite in any country; but in the United States they have not felt bound by any invisible affiliation with the political, economic, ecclesiastical, military, and technological elites.*

The "civilization" of political life is only one aspect of the "process of civilization," which is the expansion of the culture of the center into the peripheries of society and, in this particular context, the diffusion of superior culture into the areas of society normally consuming mediocre and brutal culture.

Within the limits mentioned earlier in this essay, the prospects for superior culture seem to be reasonably good. The overlapping at certain points on the part of the producers of superior culture and those of mediocre culture has resulted in an expansion of the elements of superior culture which reaches persons whose usual inclinations do not lead them to seek it out. Popularization brings a better content, but not all of this expansion is popularization; much of it is the presentation (and consumption) of genuinely superior cultural work. An improvement in our educational system at the elementary and secondary levels, which is assuredly practicable and likely, will also further this process of civilization. A better education of taste, which a richer, less scarcity-harassed society can afford, the opening and enrichment of sensitivity, which

---

* This is not a condition unique to the United States. Only Great Britain has managed to avoid it for most of the period since the French Revolution, yet there, too, the past few years have not provided notable examples of Britain's good fortune in avoiding this separation.

leisure and a diversified environment can make possible, and a more fruitful use of available intelligence can also push forward the "process of civilization."

Of course, men will remain men, their capacities to understand, create, and experience will vary, and very many are probably destined to find pleasure and salvation at other and lower cultural levels. For the others, the prospect of a more dignified and richer cultural life does not seem out of the question. It would certainly be an impossible one, however, if all intellectuals devoted themselves to education and popularization. In a short time the superior culture which would be transmitted through the "process of civilization" would fade and dessicate.

Thus, if the periphery is not to be polished while the center becomes dusty, the first obligation of the intellectuals is to look after intellectual things, to concentrate their powers on the creation and reproduction and consumption of particular works of philosophy, art, science, literature, or scholarship, to receive the traditions in which these works stand with a discriminating readiness to accept, elaborate, or reject. If that is done, there will be nothing to fear from the movement of culture in mass society.

A Dissent from the Consensual Society[*]

By Ernest van den Haag

Edward Shils replaces Van Wyck Brooks' high-, middle-, and lowbrow classification (lately elaborated fruitfully by Richard Chase[1]) with his own: "refined," "mediocre," and "brutal" culture. The old terminology was unsatisfactory; but the new one is much more so. The evaluative element inherent in both should be formulated independently.[2] It is stronger in the new notation. Further, this notation is misleading in its implications. "Refined" has a genteel connotation, which I find hard to apply to such highbrows as Joyce, Kafka, Dostoyevski, Céline, or Nathanael West. Nor are lowbrow and "brutal" equivalent; indeed, the belief that they are is a middlebrow cliché, a projection of ambivalent desire and fear that identifies vitality and brutality. Actually, much lowbrow culture is maudlin and sentimental rather than brutal.[3] Even the term "mediocre" culture, though less misleading than the others, is not satisfactory and provides a criterion that would be hard to apply.

In my opinion, emphasis on cultural objects misses the point. A sociologist (and to analyze mass culture is a sociological enterprise) must focus on the function of such objects in people's lives: he must study how they are used; who produces what for whom; why, and with what

---

[*] Reprinted by permission from *Daedalus,* Journal of the American Academy of Arts and Sciences, Boston, Mass., Vol. 89, No. 2.
[1] Richard Chase, *The Democratic Vista,* Doubleday, Garden City, 1958
[2] Unless it is contended that everything (and everybody) "refined" is morally and aesthetically superior to everything (and everybody) "brutal" or "mediocre," etc. Yet the possibility of excellence *sui generis* must not be excluded by definition, unless, instead of social and cultural, purely aesthetic categories are to be discussed. On this score, and in the whole taxonomic scheme, Mr. Shils is confusing.
[3] See *True Romances,* various soap operas, and lowbrow religious and familial piety. "Kitsch," which is part of low and of middle-lowbrow culture, means corny sentimentalization and, contrary to Mr. Shils, it does not "represent aesthetic sensibility and aesthetic aspiration, untutored . . ." but a synthetic, an *Ersatz* for both. Paper flowers, however real they look, will never grow.

effects. To be sure, value judgments cannot be avoided, but the qualities of the product become relevant only when related to its social functions. Middlebrow culture objects are not necessarily "mediocre." To be a middlebrow is to *relate* to objects, any objects, in a certain way, to give them a specific function in the context of one's life. A middlebrow might, for example, use a phrase, whatever its origin, as a cliché, i.e., in such a way that it loses its emotional impact and specific, concrete meaning and no longer communicates but labels or stereotypes and thus avoids perception and communication. The phrase is not middlebrow (or "mediocre"); he is. Beethoven does not become "mediocre," even though he may become a favored middlebrow composer and function as part of middlebrow culture. Mozart may "tinkle" for the middlebrow; it is not Mozart but the audience that is "mediocre." Indeed, it is characteristic of much middlebrow culture to overuse highbrow cultural objects of the past without understanding them and thus both to honor and debase them. Mr. Shils's terminology precludes the description of cultural dynamics in these terms and thus disregards one of the most important aspects of mass culture: the corruption and sterilization of the heritage of the past.

Mass culture is not the culture of a class or group throughout history. It is the culture of nearly everybody today, and of nearly nobody yesterday; and because of production, market, and social changes, it is quite a new phenomenon which cannot be reduced to quantitative changes nor identified with timeless categories. Mr. Shils dismisses the conditions under which mass culture is produced and consumed with some descriptive phrases but does not relate mass production to the qualities of the cultural objects he discusses. His categories remain ahistorical, even though garnished with familiar historical references. Thus, the problem of mass culture is defined away, instead of being analyzed.

Mr. Shils hopefully maintains that "refined" culture now has become available to more people than ever before. This is true, but it constitutes the problem, not the solution. What are people making of the cultural heritage that is becoming available to them? What impact does it have on them? What are they doing to it? Mass culture involves a change in the conditions in which objects are produced, consumed, and related to on all levels, a change in the role each level plays, and a change finally in the way people relate to each other. At times Mr. Shils seems to recognize this change; but his categories preclude analysis of it. The destruction of folk culture by mass culture is apparently denied and then explained by the hypothesis that the proportion of gifted people remains "fairly constant" in any population and that they are now "diverted into other spheres." This is, of course, what is meant by the destruction of folk culture, in addition to other effects of increased mobility and communication. It is remarkable that Shils also says that, if high culture has declined (which he denies) possibly "our neural equipment is poorer than that of our ancestors." Neither of the two inconsistent hypotheses—unchanged or changed "neural equipment"—can be proved. Does this mean that we can use both? Since we know so little about neurological change, would it not be sensible to look for social changes to explain cultural changes? Mr. Shils recognizes social changes but refuses to relate them to cultural changes, which he denies, asserts, deplores, and approves. He cannot be wrong since he has left all possibilities open.

Mr. Shils suggests that anyone critical of mass culture must be a *laudator temporis acti;* I see no basis for this, nor for his own temporal chauvinism. We have no measurements; and history is not a homogeneous stream; hence, comparisons with the past depend largely on the period selected as standard. Comparison of specific aspects and levels of culture may be instructive, or, at least, illustrative; but wholesale judgments seem futile.[4]

The crucial issue is fully comprised in the question with which Rostovtzeff concludes his *magnum opus:* "Is it possible to extend a higher civilization to the lower classes without debasing its standard and diluting its quality to the vanishing point? Is not every civilization bound to decay as soon as it begins to penetrate the masses?"

Mr. Shils describes mass society as one in which there is "more sense of attachment to society as a whole . . . more sense of affinity with one's fellows." According to him, the mass stands in a closer relationship to the center; there is a "dispersion of charisma" with "greater stress on individual dignity"; "the value of sensation has come to be widely appreciated"; individuality has been "discovered and developed," as has the value of personal relationships; the masses begin to "become capable of more subtle perception and judgment" as their "moral responsiveness and sensibility are aroused."

The society which Mr. Shils describes is not the one in which I live. I am forced to conjecture that the generosity of his wishes has relaxed the customary strictness of his methods and blunted the accuracy of his perception.[5]

---

[4] Elsewhere Mr. Shils has suggested that critics of mass culture are sour ex-Marxists. Possibly. Ex-Marxists are likely to be critical minds. That is what made them first Marxists and then ex. But though ex-Marxists may incline to be critics of mass culture (and only some, by no means all), the converse certainly does not follow. At any rate, I am tempted to paraphrase advice attributed to Lincoln: abstemious sociologists might benefit by a draught of radical ex-Marxism.

[5] John Stuart Mill (*On Liberty,* chap. 3) concludes his discussion of the power of public opinion in egalitarian societies by pointing out that as leveling proceeds, "there ceases to be any social support for nonconformity . . . any substantive power in society which . . . is interested in taking under its protection opinions and tendencies at variance with those of the public." From de Tocqueville to David Riesman, the dangers of "cultural democracy" have been considered. I do not believe that Mr. Shils comes seriously to grips with these dangers.

Progress toward the fulfillment of Mr. Shils's wishes is implied by the terms he uses. Yet there are some material doubts. Is "the value of sensation" more widely appreciated than it was in antiquity, the Renaissance, or even the nineteenth century? I find American society singularly anti-sensual: let me just mention the food served in restaurants, or preprandial cocktails intended—often charitable—to kill sensation. And the congested seating arrangements in restaurants, or the way cities, suburbs, exurbs, and resorts are built hardly support the hypothesis of increased value placed on privacy. Even sex is largely socialized and de-sensualized. Do we stand in closer relationship to the center—or are we alienated, suffering from what Wordsworth described as "perpetual emptiness, unceasing change" because in Yeats' words, "Things fall apart; the centre cannot hold"? Has there actually been a "dispersion of charisma"?[6] Or has there been a shift from real to Hollywood queens? Does our society foster "personal relationships," "individuality," and "privacy," or marketability, outer-directedness, and pseudo-personalizations parasitically devouring the genuine personalities of those who assume them? Could Jesus go into the desert today to contemplate? Wouldn't he be followed by a crew of *Life* photographers, cameramen, publishers' agents, etc.? What of the gossip columns, of people's interest in other people's *private* lives and particularly their *personal* relations; don't these phenomena suggest a breakdown of reserve, vicarious living, indeed, pseudo-life and experience?

Statistical data reveal that there is now higher income, more education and leisure, more equally distributed, increased mobility, travel, and communication. Undoubtedly there is more material opportunity for more people than ever before. But if so many people are so much better off in so many respects, is culture better than ever? The lowered barriers, the greater wealth, the increased opportunities are material achievements but only cultural promises. Mr. Shils appears to have taken all the promises of the age and confused them with fulfillments. It is as though one were to take the data of the Kinsey report and conclude that since there seems to be so much intercourse, people must love each other more than ever. I have nothing against Mr. Kinsey's entomological enterprise (though it makes me feel waspish). But we must distinguish it from sociological enterprise even though it may furnish raw data for it.

If people address each other by their first names right away do they really love and respect each other more than people who do not? Or does equally easy familiarity with all suggest a lack of differentiation, the very opposite of personal relations, which are based on discriminating

---

[6] I am not convinced even that the greater inclusiveness of our society can quite be taken for granted. The fate of the Jews in Germany cannot be that easily dismissed. Nazism was political kitsch as well as a rise of "brutal culture."

among perceived individualities? "In America," de Tocqueville wrote, "the bond of affection is extended but it is relaxed." Mr. Shils notes the extension but not the dilution. Yet extension can be bought at the price of lessened intensity, depth, and stability.

Of course we have more communication and mobility than ever before. But isn't it possible that less is communicated? We have all the opportunities in the world to see, hear, and read more than ever before. Is there any *independent* indication to show that we experience and understand more? Does the constant slick assault on our senses and minds not produce monotony and indifference and prevent experience? Does the discontinuity of most people's lives not unsettle, and sometimes undo them? We surely have more external contacts than ever before. But most people have less spontaneous and personal (internalized) relationships than they might with fewer contacts and opportunities.

We have more equality of opportunity. But the burden of relative deprivations is felt more acutely the smaller they are and the greater the opportunities.[7] People become resentful and clamor for a different kind of equality, at the end rather than the beginning, in short, invidious leveling. Does the comminution of society not alienate people from one another—as the discontinuity of their existence fragments them—and replace their sense of purpose with a sense of meaninglessness? Is the increased "conviviality" Mr. Shils hails more than the wish for "togetherness" which marks the lonely crowd?

Mr. Shils contends that we have more intellectuals, consumers, and producers of "refined" culture than before. In one sense, he is quite right. But these are intellectuals by position (university teachers, authors, et al.), and having more of them tells us nothing about the number of intellectuals by ability, interest, and cultivation. Mr. Shils almost concedes as much. But he remains on the phenomenal level, and never goes to the root:[8] the marginal role, the interstitial life, of intellectuals in a mass culture society. And I mean those who remain engaged in intellectual life and do not allow themselves to be reduced to the status of technicians or manufacturers of middlebrow entertainment.

Similarly, Mr. Shils mentions the possibility that intellectual and artistic creators may be seduced into more remunerative pseudo-creative activities only to dismiss it by pointing out that "the mere existence of opportunity will not seduce a man of strongly impelled creative capacities

---

[7] "The more complete this uniformity the more insupportable the sight of such a difference becomes," de Tocqueville notes.
[8] Even on that level, one might quarrel with Mr. Shils. England is not yet as much imbued with mass culture as we are. The class system and selective education have not been entirely overcome; nor have the traditions of elite culture. With only a quarter of our population, not to speak of wealth, England publishes more books every year than we do. And it has at least as many economists, philosophers, and novelists of the first rank as we do.

once he has found his direction." Of course, no one is impelled *only* by "creative capacities." The trouble is that the lure of mass media (and of foundation money and prestige) and the values that go with them are internalized long before the potential creator "has found his direction."

Mr. Shils declares that "the heart of the revolution of mass culture" is "the expanding radius of empathy and fellow feeling" which "have given to youth opportunities never available before." These opportunities, Mr. Shils concedes, are utilized mainly through "mediocre and brutal culture." But he does not point out (though noting the effect) that the appalling ignorance of educated youth is produced by reliance on the equally ignorant peer group which is endowed with "charisma"; by the belief, in short, that there is little to learn from the past and its representatives. The loss of respect for learning and tradition, particularly in its less tangible aspects, is not independent of the leveling dear to Mr. Shils; it is not unrelated to the widely held view that obsolescence automatically overtakes aesthetic and moral values, as it does technological invention. It should be evident that this notion is generated by the pragmatic nature of mass culture and by the high mobility that Mr. Shils extolls.[9]

To object to some of Mr. Shils's views is to agree with others. For he starts by praising and ends by deploring mass culture. This nice balance is achieved, I feel, at the expense of a coherent theory of mass culture. Let me suggest a few prolegomena to such a theory.

The most general characteristics of mass culture are deducible from premises on which there is no disagreement: they are concomitants of any industrial, mass production society. Among these are increased income, mobility, and leisure, more equally distributed; increased egalitarianism, communication, and education;[10] more specialization and less scope for individuality in work. The consequences that I deduce from these premises are consistent and fit my impressions. But there is no strict empirical proof, although I do believe it may be possible to test some of these hypotheses after appropriate reformulation. Further, other hypotheses may be consistent with these premises, and the real question turns on their relative importance and relevance. With these qualifications, I submit that this quasi-deductive method which relates the ascertainable to the less tangible is the only one that can yield a theory of mass culture deserving the name "theory."

---

[9] The phenomenon is part of mass culture everywhere, but the ignorance and rejection of the past were particularly fostered in America because of the immigrant background of many parents, the melting-pot nature of the school system, and the rapid rate of change which makes the experience of the old seem old-fashioned and diminishes their authority.

[10] Note that more has to be learned through formal instruction, partly because less culture is transmitted informally and individually. This is no advantage because our school system helps bring about the spread of a homogenized mass culture intentionally and unintentionally.

(1) There is a separation of the manufacturers of culture from the consumers, which is part of the general separation of production and consumption and of work and play. Culture becomes largely spectator sport, and life and experience become exogenous and largely vicarious. (Nothing will dissuade me from seeing a difference between a young girl walking around with her pocket radio listening to popular songs and one who sings herself; nor am I persuaded that the tales collected by the brothers Grimm remain the same when enacted on television or synthetically reproduced by Walt Disney.)

(2) Mass production aims at pleasing an average of tastes and therefore, though catering to all to some extent, it cannot satisfy any taste fully. Standardization is required and necessarily de-individualizes, as do the techniques required by mass production and marketing.

(3) Since culture, like everything else in a mass society, is mainly produced to please an average of consumer tastes, the producers become (and remain) an elite by catering to consumer tastes rather than developing or cultivating autonomous ones. Initiative, and power to bestow prestige and income, have shifted from the elite to the mass. The difference may be seen by comparing the development of ritual dogmatic beliefs and practices in the Protestant denominations and in the Roman Catholic church. The latter has minimized, the former maximized dependence on consumers. In the Protestant churches, there is, therefore, no body of religious (as distinguished from moral) beliefs left, except as an intellectual curiosity.

(4) The mass of men dislikes and always has disliked learning and art. It wishes to be distracted from life rather than to have it revealed; to be comforted by traditional (possibly happy and sentimental) tropes, rather than to be upset by new ones. It is true that it wishes to be thrilled, too. But irrational violence or vulgarity provides thrills, as well as release, just as sentimentality provides escape. What is new here is that, apart from the fact that irrelevant thrills and emotions are now prefabricated, the elite is no longer protected from the demands of the mass consumers.

(5) As a result of the high psychological and economic costs of individuality and privacy, gregariousness has become internalized. People fear solitude and unpopularity; popular approval becomes the only moral and aesthetic standard most people recognize. This tendency is reinforced by the shrinkage in the importance and size of primary groups, which have also become looser; by a corresponding increase in the size and importance of secondary groups and publics; and finally, by the shift of many of the functions of primary to secondary groups.

(6) The greatly increased lure of mass markets for both producers and consumers diverts potential talent from the creation of art. (Within the arts, the performing do better than the creative ones.) Here interesting empirical questions arise: to what extent is talent bent endogenously and exogenously? to what extent can it be?

(7) Excessive communication serves to isolate people from one another, from themselves, and from experience. It extends bonds by weakening them. People become indifferently and indiscriminately tolerant; their own life as well as everything else is trivialized, eclectic, and styleless.

(8) Mass media for inherent reasons must conform to prevailing average canons of taste.[12] They cannot foster art; indeed, they replace it. When they take up classics, they usually reshape them to meet expectations. But even when that is not the case, they cannot hope to individualize and refine taste, though they may occasionally supply an already formed taste for high culture. Half a loaf, in these matters, spoils the appetite, even with vitamins added, and is not better than none. The technical availability of good reproductions and the paperback editions of noncondensed books are unlikely to change this situation; they often add alien elements which merely decorate lives styled by mass culture.[13]

(9) The total effect of mass culture is to distract people from lives which are so boring that they generate obsession with escape. Yet because mass culture creates addiction to prefabricated experience, most people are deprived of the remaining possibilities of autonomous growth and enrichment, and their lives become ever more boring and unfulfilled.

This very brief sketch of the general features of mass culture should make it clear that I do not agree with those optimists who favor and believe possible the wide presentation of "refined" culture through the mass media. I do not think this desirable or desired. Nor, for that matter, practicable. People get what they wish and I see no way of imposing anything else on them. I have to disagree with those who appear to think that the issue is to improve the culture offered the mass of men and to try to reach the masses in greater and greater numbers. My conclusion is different: high or refined culture, in my opinion, is best preserved and developed by avoiding mass media. I should go further and give up some advantages of mass production for the sake of greater individualization. This would reverse many present policies. For instance, I should favor fairly high direct taxes on most mass media, or a tax on advertising. Perhaps we are still capable of replacing the noise that would be thus eliminated with conversation.

---

[11] For a fuller exposition of my views, see Ralph Ross and Ernest van den Haag, *The Fabric of Society* (New York, Harcourt, Brace and Company, 1957), chap 15.
[12] In Frank Stanton's words, "Any mass medium will always have to cater to the middle grounds . . . the most widely held, or cease to be."
[13] Joseph Bram has called my attention to the several distinct phases of mass culture. It often begins with a rather moving attempt of the uneducated to become seriously educated. One sees this in countries beginning their industrial development. The adulteration of, and disrespect for, education comes with full industrialization, when the mass culture market is created and supplied with goods manufactured for it.

Society and Culture[*]

By Hannah Arendt

Mass culture and mass society (the very terms were still a sign of reprobation a few years ago, implying that mass society was a depraved form of society and mass culture a contradiction in terms) are considered by almost everybody today as something with which we must come to terms, and in which we must discover some "positive" aspects—if only because mass culture is the culture of a mass society. And mass society, whether we like it or not, is going to stay with us into the forseeable future. No doubt mass society and mass culture are interrelated phenomena. Mass society comes about when "the mass of the population has become incorporated into society."[1] Since society originally comprehended those parts of the population which disposed of leisure time and the wealth which goes with it, mass society does indeed indicate a new order in which the masses have been liberated "from the burden of physically exhausting labor."[2] Historically as well as conceptually, therefore, mass society has been preceded by society, and society is no more a generic term than is mass society; it too can be dated and described historically. It is older, to be sure, than mass society, but not older than the modern age. In fact, all the traits that crowd psychology has meanwhile discovered in mass man: his loneliness (and loneliness is neither isolation nor solitude) regardless of his adaptability; his excitability and lack of standards; his capacity for consumption, accompanied by inability to judge or even to distinguish; above all, his egocentricity and that fateful alienation from the world which, since Rousseau, he mistakes for self-alienation—all these traits first appeared in "good

* Reprinted by permission from *Daedalus*, Journal of the American Academy of Arts and Sciences, Boston, Mass., Vol. 89, No. 2.
1 Edward Shils, see p. 61.
2 *Ibid.*, p. 62.

society," where there was no question of masses, numerically speaking. The first mass men, we are tempted to say, quantitatively so little constituted a mass that they could even imagine they constituted an elite, the elite of good society.

Let me therefore first say a few words on the older phenomena of society and its relation to culture: say them not primarily for historical reasons, but because they relate facts that seem to me little known in this country. It may be this lack of knowledge that leads Mr. Shils to say "individuality has flowered in mass society," whereas actually the modern individual was defined and, indeed, discovered by those who—like Rousseau in the eighteenth or John Stuart Mill in the nineteenth century—found themselves in open rebellion against society. Individualism and the "sensibility and privacy" which go with it—the discovery of intimacy as the atmosphere the individual needs for his full development—came about at a time when society was not yet a mass phenomenon but still thought of itself in terms of "good society" or (especially in Central Europe) of "educated and cultured society." And it is against this background that we must understand the modern (and no longer so modern) individual who, as we all know from nineteenth- and twentieth-century novels, can only be understood as part of the society against which he tried to assert himself and which always got the better of him.

The chances of this individual's survival lay in the simultaneous presence within the population of other nonsociety strata into which the rebellious individual could escape; one reason why rebellious individuals so frequently ended by becoming revolutionaries as well was that they discovered in those who were not admitted to society certain traits of humanity which had become extinct in society. We need only read the record of the French Revolution, and recall to what an extent the very concept of *le peuple* received its connotations from a rebellion against the corruption and hypocrisy of the salons, to realize what the true role of society was throughout the nineteenth century. A good part of the despair of individuals under the conditions of mass society is due to the fact that these avenues of escape are, of course, closed as soon as society has incorporated all the strata of the population.

Generally speaking, I think it has been the great good fortune of this country to have this intermediary stage of good and cultured society play a relatively minor role in its development; but the disadvantage of this good fortune today is that those few who will still make a stand against mass culture as an unavoidable consequence of mass society are tempted to look upon these earlier phenomena of society and culture as a kind of golden age and lost paradise, precisely because they know so little of it. America has been only too well acquainted with the barbarian philistinism of the *nouveau riche,* but it has only a nodding acquaintance with the equally annoying cultural and educated philistinism of society where culture actually has what Mr. Shils calls "snob-value," and where it is a matter of status to be educated.

This cultural philistinism is today in Europe rather a matter of the past, for the simple reason that the whole development of modern art started from and remained committed to a profound mistrust not only of cultural philistinism but also of the word culture itself. It is still an open question whether it is more difficult to discover the great authors of the past without the help of any tradition than it is to rescue them from the rubbish of educated philistinism. And this task of preserving the past without help of tradition, and often even against traditional standards and interpretations, is the same for the whole of Western civilization. Intellectually, though not socially, America and Europe are in the same situation: the thread of tradition is broken, and we must discover the past for ourselves, that is, read its authors as though nobody had ever read them before. In this task, mass society is much less in our way than good and educated society, and I suspect that this kind of reading was not uncommon in nineteenth-century America precisely because this country was still that "unstoried wilderness" from which so many American writers and artists tried to escape. That American fiction and poetry have so suddenly and richly come into their own, ever since Whitman and Melville, may have something to do with this.

It would be unfortunate indeed if out of the dilemmas and distractions of mass culture and mass society there should arise an altogether unwarranted and idle yearning for a state of affairs which is not better but only a bit more old-fashioned. And the eager and uncritical acceptance of such obviously snobbish and philistine terms as highbrow, middlebrow, and lowbrow is a rather ominous sign. For the only nonsocial and authentic criterion for works of culture is, of course, their relative permanence and even their ultimate immortality. The point of the matter is that as soon as the immortal works of the past became the object of "refinement" and acquired the status which went with it, they lost their most important and elemental quality, which is to grasp and move the reader or spectator, throughout the centuries. The very word "culture" became suspect precisely because it indicated that "pursuit of perfection" which to Matthew Arnold was identical with the "pursuit of sweetness and light." It was not Plato, but a reading of Plato, prompted by the ulterior motive of self-perfection, that became suspect; and the "pursuit of sweetness and light," with all its overtones of good society, was held in contempt because of its rather obvious effort to keep reality out of one's life by looking at everything through a veil of sweetness and light. The astounding recovery of the creative arts in the twentieth century, and a less apparent but perhaps no less real recovery of the greatness of the past, began when good society lost its monopolizing grip on culture, together with its dominant position in society as a whole.

Here we are not concerned with society, however, but with culture—or rather with what happens to culture under the different conditions of society and of mass society. In society, culture, even more than other realities, had become what only then began to be called a "value," that is, a social commodity which could be circulated and cashed in on as social coinage for the purpose of acquiring social status. Cultural objects were transformed into values when the cultural philistine seized upon them as a currency by which he bought a higher position in society—higher, that is, than in his own opinion he deserved either by nature or by birth. Cultural values, therefore, were what values have always been, exchange values; in passing from hand to hand, they were worn down like an old coin. They lost the faculty which is originally peculiar to all cultural things, the factulty of arresting our attention and moving us. This process of transformation was called the devaluation of values, and its end came with the "bargain-sale of values" *(Ausverkauf der Werte)* during the twenties and thirties, when cultural and moral values were "sold out" together.

Perhaps the chief difference between society and mass society is that society wanted culture, evaluated and devaluated cultural things into social commodities, used and abused them for its own selfish purposes, but did not "consume" them. Even in their most worn-out shapes, these things remained things, they were not "consumed" and swallowed up but retained their worldly objectivity. Mass society, on the contrary, wants not culture but entertainment, and the wares offered by the entertainment industry are indeed consumed by society just as are any other consumer goods. The products needed for entertainment serve the life process of society, even though they may not be as necessary for this life as bread and meat. They serve, as the phrase is, to while way time, and the vacant time which is whiled away is not leisure time, strictly speaking, that is, time in which we are truly liberated from all cares and activities necessitated by the life process, and therefore free for the world and its "culture"; it is rather leftover time, which still is biological in nature, leftover after labor and sleep have received their due. Vacant time which entertainment is supposed to fill is a hiatus in the biologically conditioned cycle of labor, in "the metabolism of man with nature," as Marx used to say.

Under modern conditions, this hiatus is constantly growing; there is more and more time freed that must be filled with entertainment, but this enormous increase in vacant time does not change the nature of the time. Entertainment, like labor and sleep, is irrevocably part of the biological life process. And biological life is always, whether one is laboring or at rest, engaged in consumption or in the passive reception of amusement, a metabolism feeding on things by devouring them. The commodities the entertainment industry offers are not "things"—cultural objects whose excellence is measured by their ability to withstand the life process and to become permanent appurtenances of the world—and they should not be judged according to these standards; nor are they values which exist to be used and exchanged; they are rather consumer goods destined to be used up, as are any other consumer goods.

Panis et circenses truly belong together; both are necessary for life, for its preservation and recuperation, and both vanish in the course of the life process, that is, both must constantly be produced anew and offered anew, lest this process cease entirely. The standards by which both should be judged are indeed freshness and novelty—standards by which we today (and, I think, quite mistakenly) judge cultural and artistic objects as well, things which are supposed to remain in the world even after we have left it.

As long as the entertainment industry produces its own consumer goods, all is well, and we can no more reproach it for the nondurability of its articles than we can reproach a bakery because it produces goods which, if they are not to spoil, must be consumed as soon as they are made. It has always been the mark of educated philistinism to despise entertainment and amusement because no "value" could be derived from them. In so far as we are all subject to life's great cycle, we all stand in need of entertainment and amusement in some form or other, and it is sheer hypocrisy or social snobbery to deny that we can be amused and entertained by exactly the same things which amuse and entertain the masses of our fellow men. As far as the survival of culture is concerned, it certainly is less threatened by those who fill vacant time with amusement and entertainment than by those who fill it with some haphazard educational gadget in order to improve their social standing.

If mass culture and the entertainment industry were the same, I should not worry much, even though it is true that, in Mr. Shils's words, "the immense advance in audibility and visibility" of this whole sector of life, which formerly had been "relatively silent and unseen by the intellectuals," creates a serious problem for the artist and intellectual. It is as though the futility inherent in entertainment had been permitted to permeate the whole social atmosphere, and the often described malaise of the artists and intellectuals is of course partly due to their inability to make themselves heard and seen in the tumultuous uproar of mass society, or to penetrate its noisy futility. But this protest of the artist against society is as old as society, though not older; the great revival of nearly all the arts in our century (which perhaps one day will seem one of the great artistic, and of course scientific, periods of Western civilization) began with the malaise of the artist in society, with his decision to turn his back upon it and its "values," to leave the dead to bury the dead. As far as artistic productivity is concerned, it should not be more difficult to withstand the massive temptations of mass culture, or to keep from being thrown out of gear by the noise and humbug of mass society, than it was to avoid the more sophisticated temptations and the more insidious noises of the cultural snobs in refined society.

Unhappily, the case is not that simple. The entertainment industry is confronted with gargantuan appetites, and since its wares disappear in consumption, it must constantly offer new commodities. In this predicament, those who produce for the mass media ransack the entire range of past and present culture in the hope of finding suitable material. This material, however, cannot be offered as it is; it must be prepared and altered in order to become entertaining; it cannot be consumed as it is.

Mass culture comes into being when mass society seizes upon cultural objects, and its danger is that the life process of society (which like all biological processes insatiably draws everything available into the cycle of its metabolism) will literally consume the cultural objects, eat them up and destroy them. I am not referring to the phenomenon of mass distribution. When cultural objects, books, or pictures in reproduction, are thrown on the market cheaply and attain huge sales, this does not affect the nature of the goods in question. But their nature is affected when these objects themselves are changed (rewritten, condensed, digested, reduced to Kitsch in the course of reproduction or preparation for the movies) in order to be put into usable form for a mass sale which they otherwise could not attain.

Neither the entertainment industry itself nor mass sales as such are signs of, not what we call mass culture, but what we ought more accurately to call the decay of culture in mass society. This decay sets in when liberties are taken with these cultural objects in order that they may be distributed among masses of people. Those who actively promote this decay are not the Tin Pan Alley composers but a special kind of intellectuals, often well read and well informed, whose sole function is to organize, disseminate, and change cultural objects in order to make them palatable to those who want to be entertained or—and this is worse—to be "educated," that is, to acquire as cheaply as possible some kind of cultural knowledge to improve their social status.

Richard Blackmur (in a recent article on the "Role of the Intellectual," in the *Kenyon Review*) has brilliantly shown that the present malaise of the intellectual springs from the fact that he finds himself surrounded, not by the masses, from whom, on the contrary, he is carefully shielded, but by these digesters, re-writers, and changers of culture whom we find in every publishing house in the United States, and in the editorial offices of nearly every magazine. And these "professionals" are ably assisted by those who no longer write books but fabricate them, who manufacture a "new" textbook out of four or five already on the market, and who then have, as Blackmur shows, only one worry—how to avoid plagiarism. (Meanwhile the editor does his best to substitute clichés for sheer illiteracy.) Here the criterion of novelty, quite legitimate in the entertainment industry, becomes a simple fake and, indeed, a threat: it is only too likely that the "new" textbook will crowd out the older ones, which usually are better, not because they are older, but because they were still written in response to authentic needs.

This state of affairs, which indeed is equaled nowhere else in the world, can properly be called mass culture; its promoters are neither the masses nor their entertainers, but are those who try to entertain the masses with what once was an authentic object of culture, or to persuade them that *Hamlet* can be as entertaining as *My Fair Lady,* and educational as well. The danger of mass education is precisely that it may become very entertaining indeed; there are many great authors of the past who have survived centuries of oblivion and neglect, but it is still an open question whether they will be able to survive an entertaining version of what they have to say.

The malaise of the intellectual in the atmosphere of mass culture is much more legitimate than his malaise in mass society; it is caused socially by the presence of these other intellectuals, the manufacturers of mass culture, from whom he finds it difficult to distinguish himself and who, moreover, always outnumber him, and therefore acquire that kind of power which is generated whenever people band together and act more or less in concert. The power of the many (legitimate only in the realm of politics and the field of action) has always been a threat to the strength of the few; it is a threat under the most favorable circumstances, and it has always been felt to be more dangerous when it arises from within a group's own ranks. Culturally, the malaise is caused, I think, not so much by the massive temptations and the high rewards which await those who are willing to alter their products to make them acceptable for a mass market, as by the constant irritating care each of us has to exert in order to protect his product against the demands and the ingenuity of those who think they know how to "improve" it.

Culture relates to objects and is a phenomenon of the world; entertainment relates to people and is a phenomenon of life. If life is no longer content with the pleasure which is always coexistent with the toil and labor inherent in the metabolism of man with nature, if vital energy is no longer fully used up in this cycle, then life may reach out for the things of the world, may violate and consume them. It will prepare these things of the world until they are fit for consumption; it will treat them as if they were articles of nature, articles which must also be prepared before they can enter into man's metabolism.

Consumption of the things of nature does no harm to them; they are constantly renewed because man, in so far as he lives and labors, toils and recuperates, is also a creature of nature, a part of the great cycle in which all nature wheels. But the things of the world which are made by man (in so far as he is a worldly and not merely a natural being), these things are not renewed of their own accord. When life seizes upon them and consumes them at its pleasure, for entertainment, they simply disappear. And this disappearance, which first begins in mass culture—that is, the "culture" of a society poised between the alternatives of laboring and of consuming—is something different from the wear and tear culture suffered when its things were made into exchange values, and circulated in society until their original stamp and meaning were scarcely recognizable.

If we wish to classify these two anticultural processes in historical and sociological terms, we may say that the devaluation of culture in good society through the cultural philistines was the characteristic peril of commercial society, whose primary public area was the exchange market for goods and ideas. The disappearance of culture in a mass society, on the other hand, comes about when we have a consumers' society which, in so far as it produces only for consumption, does not need a public worldly space whose existence is independent of and outside the sphere of its life process. In other words, a consumers' society does not know how to take care of the world and the things which belong to it: the society's own chief attitude toward objects, the attitude of consumption, spells ruin to everything it touches. If we understand by culture what it originally meant (the Roman *cultura*—derived from *colere,* to take care of and preserve and cultivate) then we can say without any exaggeration that a society obsessed with consumption cannot at the same time be cultured or produce a culture.

For all their differences, however, one thing is common to both these anticultural processes: they arise when all the worldly objects produced by the present or the past have become "social," are related to society, and are seen in their merely functional aspect. In the one case, society uses and exchanges, evaluates and devaluates them; in the other, it devours and consumes them. This functionalization or "societization" of the world is by no means a matter of course; the notion that every object must be functional, fulfilling some needs of society or of the individual— the church a religious need, the painting the need for self-expression in the painter and the need of self-perfection in the onlooker, and so on—is historically so new that one is tempted to speak of a modern prejudice. The cathedrals were built *ad majorem gloriam Dei;* although they as buildings certainly served the needs of the community, their elaborate beauty can never be explained by these needs, which could have been served quite as well by any nondescript building.

An object is cultural to the extent that it can endure; this durability is the very opposite of its functionality, which is the quality which makes it disappear again from the phenomenal world by being used and used up. The "thingness" of an object appears in its shape and appearance, the proper criterion of which is beauty. If we wanted to judge an object by its use value alone, and not also by its appearance (that is, by whether it is beautiful or ugly or something in between), we would first have to pluck out our eyes. Thus, the functionalization of the world which occurs in both society and mass society deprives the world of culture as well as beauty. Culture can be safe only with those who love the world for its own sake, who know that without the beauty of man-made, worldly things which we call works of art, without the radiant glory in which potential imperishability is made manifest to the world and in the world, all human life would be futile and no greatness could endure.

The Electric Aesthetic and the Short-Circuit Ethic: The Populist Generator in Our Mass Culture Machine*

By Kingsley Widmer

"Monuments, museums, permanencies, and ponderosities are all anathema," angrily commented D. H. Lawrence on the imposed order and passionless deadness of much of our traditional culture. Some such rejection of the preservative and power-protective emphasis seems to be essential in the quest for greater individual responsiveness and communal liberation. The sought for experiences are kinesthetic, an intense ritualization of bodily immediacy and relatedness, in arts open and celebratory. Responsiveness must be energetic and social rather than passive and distanced, as in the usual aesthetic appreciation. The festival rather than the monument, the exalted sensation rather than the museum object, the playfulness rather than the permanency, the quick impulses of being rather than the ponderous markers of knowing, connect the genuinely popular and protesting currents which should be recognized as part of our post-industrial mass culture.

In contrast, the power-preservative culture controls sensibility by the withdrawal of art into awesome and exclusive objects with prescribed values. These achieve fixity and scarcity, and thus authority, as masterpieces and other precious commodities and as specialist techniques and painfully learned and restricted styles. Trained mediators—we institutionalized critics and teachers—insist on a preparatory "connoisseurship" and ascetic spiritualization as the controlled way of access to aesthetic experience. We suspect the arts of the uncultivated young just as we doubt the learning of the uninstitutionalized autodidact. We can recognize

---

* This is the author's revision of two articles, "The Electric Aesthetic and the Short-Circuit Ethic," *Arts in Society*, X (Summer, 1970), and "McLuhanism," *The Village Voice* (Dec. 30, 1969), and continuous with several earlier studies, such as "The Role of the Rebellious Culture," in C. H. Anderson, ed., *Sociological Essays* (Dorsey Press, 1970). Reprinted by permission of the publishers and the author.

"popular culture" as controlled solace and exploitation aimed at the inner barbarians but not as collective innovation and vitality. What we prefer to think of as "high culture" can be defended, with some partial justice, by claims to immutable and lonely profundity. But socially, the rejection of such cultural permanency and ponderosity is also a revolt against the elitist and repressive control of sensibility. Preservative cultural processing serves social domination. The hierarchies of high culture, of values as well as of persons, fuse with those of institutional control and general social power. Culture becomes forms of power, and corrupts.

Popular and protesting culture resists controls and affirms other values less by preserving and protecting than by re-creating, by, literally, lively recreation. Given the amorphously pervasive controls and corruptions of contemporary culture, esoteric as well as popular, the dissident less assault them than attempt to outflank authority and power by furthering populist subcultures. Not surprisingly, this now gets identified—and patronizingly subsumed—as mere youthful waywardness which serves the mass culture industries. For the charged-up young seem to be threatening to blow out social control by short-circuiting the controls and corruptions of cultural processing.

The custodians of high culture, like a junta directorate denouncing guerrilla revolutionaries as "mere bandits," often refuse to acknowledge that what they war with constitutes art and meaningful culture and authentic human responses. Since they rightly see the new artistic responsiveness and variant sensibility as an implicitly powerful social movement, involving energetic and uunomesticated masses, the sycophants of power —a majority of the learned—hasten to denigrate the "weird youth culture," the "drop-out aesthetic" exploited by the media, just "another student madness," "the drug-entertainment scene," which is "largely a generational pathology" now built into a "sub-establishment" or "counter-establishment." Some small truths lurk in most such charges but we would serve the rhetoric of manipulation and domination if we were only to discuss our popular protesting culture within the petty terms of such "social problems." Our sense of the more lively currents within mass culture will be weak and contemptuous if it centers on drugs or entertainment or adolescence. That would be like discussing the delightful Medieval Goliard poets only in terms of unemployment and alcoholism (they did not have clerical sinecures and treated wine as a *sumum bonum*), or reducing the mordantly perceptive outsider view of the picaresque literary tradition to an issue of vagrancy laws (poetic wanderers and hoboes and beatniks are of course dirty and disruptive migrants), or vulgarizing the Greco-Roman Cynic philosophers and the Radical Reformation preachers into the sociology of educational surplus and delinquency. Movements of populist culture require rather more awareness than that allowed in textbook discussions of "social disorganization." Sadly, some of our pot-vague and rock-happy young dissidents seem to have been taken in by their patronizing elders and so themselves misrationalize their own freshness of artistic experience and libertarian social motives as just accusatory symptoms. It is embarrassing to hear the young smugly spouting about "the generation gap." In fact, the free-wheeling mockeries and joyous affirmations of our dissident culture go quite beyond such suburban sociology. Though we should recognize the limitations and ambiguities of the populist side of the mass culture, we must start by emphasizing the genuineness of its artistic impetus and the importance of its cultural role.

Partly for historical reasons, I prefer "populist culture" to "counter culture." For one thing, the imperatives are not "new" in the sense of unprecedented or unidentifiable. Partly a recurrence of Western populist romanticism, partly an expansion of the minority styles of several generations (American bohemian-beat-hippy rebels), and partly a cyclic recrudescence of ancient antinomian-utopian religious and social revolt, its newness comes from its curious relations to technology and its mass spread by way of the electronic media. The populist music, for example, variously combines traditional forms of the rural folk, the impassioned artistry and anguish of the ghettos, and the modes of urban-industrial entertainment, along with some of the eclecticism and exhibitionism we should expect in a late and over-done civilization. Most responsive observers agree that contemporary rock-folk-blues music results in some of the most lively and intriguing *popular* music since industrial organization effectively smashed indigenous folk arts. The populist literary imagination takes lesser ways, not least because our culture-of-the-word remains more fully controlled by the hierarchs of indoctrinating education and exploitative publishing and programming. The word arts stay within limited rhetorical forms: lyrics, titles, slogans, subjective reportage (the "personal" or "participatory" journalism of the hundreds of "underground" newspapers), broadsides, improvisational theatre, but rarely novels, contemplative essays, elaborate poetry, or intellectual dialectics. The emphasis upon transitory, parodistic, cursing, and burlesque styles assumes a great skepticism about our word culture so generally falsified for institutional rationalization and indoctrination. In contrast to the modernist aesthetic movements of the recent past, our present dissident culture no longer treats the man-of-letters as a hero. Pretty obviously, literacy has lost much of its magic. (And its transcendental egotism, as a wry contrast may suggest. In despairing moods, a noted but rather solitary literary artist I know thumbs through the inch-thick library card-catalogue of works by and about himself, or pursues the dry immortality of index references to himself. He is puzzled to the threshold of rage by some former writing students who distribute their satiric verses as anonymous broadsides and edit and write a radical and community-oriented biweekly newspaper under varied instant nicknames—collective outcast "monicker" style revived and widespread in the current underculture.)

The hundreds of "underground newspapers," with a readership of at least several millions in 1970, don't, contrary to the electronic priests of mass culture, indicate a total refusal of the written word. But they do point up some rather different styles of spreading, and parodying, the Word in their mocking variations on journalism and programming and advertising and other institutional rhetoric. Heterodox styles of sermon and prayer came back in vogue, as any observer of protest rallies and other underculture rituals can testify. While most of the populist papers seem as tiresome as seventeenth century sectarian pamphlets, with their neo-Leninist gospels and quasi-Learyist rituals, they service in rather burlesque forms of the other media a mass audience. The real news from underground is that there exists another nation, other communities, than those presented in the mass gospels of mainstream America.

The visual arts of the populist culture largely consist of costume and decoration and mixed media and transitory icons (posters, banners, graffiti) which usually "pastiche," in a surreal heightening, historical and museum motifs. The psychedelic styles, fortunately fading, were mostly *retardataire,* whether as forty-point illegible type or as arts nouveau imitation patterns. But the aesthetics of visual involvement, fracturing, and intensification continue.

We have previously experienced most of these elements of musical, verbal, and visual art but not in such peculiarly mixed, massive and electrifying ways. Part of the distinctiveness of these arts from the underculture, when they become popularized, resides in what might be summarized as their "electric increment." Traditional musical elements become one with their electronic mixture, amplification, distortion, and intensification. The otherwise historic iconology takes similar, and somewhat grotesque, visual proportions because of mergence with new techniques (day-glo paints, strobe lights, synthetic materials, etc.) and normatively gratuitous application (to automobiles, kites, human bodies). Idiomatic speech, especially that derived from minority and outcast defiance, gets heightened by unexpected enlargement (the headline obscenity), by bizarrely imaginative nomenclature (the rock group names), and by a poeticization in which quotidian technical terms transpose into ecstatic gestures (as "electrical vibrations" become spiritual "vibes"). These electric-increments characterize a post-technological popular and protesting culture which turns the media to its own imperatives, and thus carries out considerable humanization.

Much of what stands out here seems to be the *playful* use of technology. The technical gets turned into the fantastic, humorous, grotesque. Traditional aesthetic elements combine with electronics and synthetics.

The significance should be seen less in either source, the technological and the traditional, than in the fusion itself. Rebellious imperatives don't just use technology for reproduction and distribution but make something different of it. By playing with the electronic and synthetic, and not only when paradoxically mocking "plastic culture," they tend to twistingly absorb and artfully invert the more usual mass media sensibility. Our most advanced technological modes become sheer sensation and game and mystery and defiance and communion.

Perhaps here may be found some watershed points in the perplexed relations of modern technology and culture. Our prevalent theories of culture versus technology may have obscured what has been happening. For example, our allegiance to past heroic artists led us, properly enough, to see humane and imaginative culture as struggling for autonomy from the "Satanic mills." William Blake was considerably right, of course, in demanding "mental warfare" against an exploitative and dehumanizing industrial order and the science ("Newton's single-vision") on which it rested. Later cultivated allegiance to conservative craftsmen and reactive aesthetes and *symboliste* explorers of artistic autonomy furthered resistance to technocratic sensibility. They justly rejected what we now widely recognize as the lunar pieties and self-worshipping monumentalities of production for its own destructive sake. But though the scientistic and technistic certainly lack fully human dimensions, art cannot itself provide an alternative production and social order and, in the long run, countering art cannot even provide sufficient culture. In the past two centuries, artistic styles as well as media never successfully resisted for long the pressures of technological transformation. In spite of repeated attempts at archaizing and almost mystical efforts to stay with the traditional means (instruments, easels, class performances, genteel and metrical language, and all the rest), art ended up imitating technology. Even the distinctive "modernist" movements in the arts could not long defend themselves from subservient entertainment and power-preservative academicization. The break with the traditional aesthetics did not achieve a new autonomy from class or mass culture. By the middle of the twentieth century, the modernist culture of the preceding three or four generations was not only exploited by the technological media but merged with the elitist cultural depositories of museum and theater and journal and academy. Avant-gardist careerism clearly came to serve the sensibility and social order of technological society. If modernism in the arts won its battles for succession with the traditional aesthetics, succeeding in its "adversary" intellectualism, it also became merely new-traditional and lost much of its campaign for humanization. Modernism merely systematized the schizophrenia between sensitive culture and technological order. Consequently, artful protest against dehumanization today no longer pursues artistic modernism.

Now, apparently, we move within "post-modernist" responses, including the sense that the old conflicts of art and technology end Pyrrhic. But technological sensibility even more desperately needs to be humanized, transformed into the tolerable and various and responsive and communal. Culture which cannot serve tangible and social ways of living will not do it. The arts, our young make clear, must be immediate and involving, sensual and communal, to be humanly effective. They require an enlivening of the technological order, not an archaic or modernist split from the reality we inhabit.

Why is the effort to humanize the technological not recognized? Uncomfortable "liberal" members of the preservative culture plaintively qualify their attempts at sympathy for the populist art experiences: if only the music weren't so loud, the costumes so outrageous, the hair and nudity so sexually peculiar, the drugged lives so impractical, the gestures and language so gross, the gatherings so lemming-like, the parasitism on society so patent. . . . But the populist currents in the mass culture reveal an amoral strategy, a take-over rather than a fastidious withdrawal from our social realities, from our noise, affluence, polymorphous sexuality, massization, distorted language, rootlessness, and other absurdities—and our technology. The populist culture takes much of what is and makes it aesthetic experience—re-creates the dominating things-as-they-are into delightful things-in-themselves. By embracing rather than rejecting, it would transpose our social realities into realms of imagination and feeling and communion. The enlightened moralist objections, though reasonable and appealing in cast, rest on the schizophrenia between culture and technology, refined art and the mass media, and must therefore miss the connections the "new people" make.

To the degree that there is a new culture within the mass culture, it operates by what we must call an inverted "aestheticizing." In this, the official becomes pure game just as the technical becomes pure sensation. For the young especially, such misuse becomes an art. The mechanical and electrical apparatus loses its depersonalized utility and reductive control when hedonistically exploited. Our spurious commodities cease to alienate by being turned into toys. An awesome administrative center (our technological cathedral) becomes proper scene for noise, graffitti, begging, love-making, and other humanizing irreverence. The woozy public event becomes a sacred festival, the earnest political occasion a comic ritual, the pious ceremony a saturnalia—or vice versa, when inappropriate. (The famous front page pictures of the sixties, such as the bearded and denimed student smoking a stolen cigar and with his feet on a university president's desk, or the pacifist rally with pranksters dressed in guerilla-type clothes firing toy machine-guns, or the stoned, peace-medalioned and guitar-playing soldier leaning against the armoured recon car in Vietnam, or the entwined young bodies on the littered floor of a computer center—among others—illustrate the style.) To the horror of the technologically pious, the young treat machines less in terms of their function than of decoration and destruction. Science properly reverts to direct magic, or so loses its ascetic mystification and is so derided that a great technologue fearfully warns of the end of technological advance within a generation. The ideologies of patriotism and productive submission and traditional legitimacy which support the technological order get turned, literally, into grotesque and obscene comic mythologies. The decorum of "dressing up"—always an important cultural key—becomes defiantly flamboyant costuming. The "impractical" becomes normative. The pharmaceutical provides madness rather more than medicine. Our current popular but intense arts—that itself is an inversion—come within, by and through, the dominant counterfeit culture, manipulative technology, and dehumanized organization. By such reversals reality becomes art, the realm of necessity reveals itself the realm of freedom, and the mass technological culture becomes expressive, fantastic, comic, sensational, lively, communal, and subverted.

I am highlighting, of course, certain currents as the populist side of the mass culture and would readily grant that they are often only partial and ambiguous, and their future uncertain. Yet surely they have been present for some time, for those willing to hear and see and, I suppose, properly vibrate. Often cultivated responses can only lead to misapprehension. "Show me," says a long-time competent and politically conscious artist, "the key masterpieces of this populist culture, and I will predict its future." But there are no such uniquely defining works. If our populist arts produce any "masterpieces" they will be as incidental to it as those we now discover in the ceremonial artifacts of neolithic tribes. To claim otherwise usually falsifies the actual work of, say, Kesey or Dylan or Cobb or Hendrix. Or it would be to substitute a psychedelic bus for a Romanesque altar or the Grateful Dead for the London Philharmonic or *Avatan* for the New York *Times* or a California underground collective for the Pentagon —a confusion of realms and dominions.

Quite appropriate to a culture which does not seek the preservative and the masterpiece and the powerful order is the renewed emphasis on applied arts, the exceptional rise in pottery and weaving and decoration of so many kinds. This shows yet again the turn away from both the hierarchies of preservative culture and the utilities of technological organization. Accessible style, rather than rare artifact or pure function, provide the aim and end of the new craftsmen. Surely it is production for use but, as we suddenly see the contrast of much of the rest of our culture, the populist ways do not aspire to transcendental art, science, or power.

Nor will the populist culture likely produce new ideas, any more than new inventions or new masterpieces. Indeed, it implicitly questions why we should even want such things. In such culture, intellectual disinterest and aggrandizement and dialectics must be subordinated to the kinetic and communal. You can groove with, join in, the populist culture and its group art experiences, but thinking will not make it. Perhaps protectively, entree comes from a mixture of game temper—"hang loose" in an ecstatic "cool," "do your thing but don't get up-tight"—and from the electricity of touch, of communal relation. The historian can catalogue the "ideas," ranging from mystical nature doctrines to the heroization of the urban outcast and poor, but the derivations are less important than the tone, manner, and relationship, which will allow many incompatible ideas. Intellectual criticism and dialectic, those hostile arts, do not provide such connections and communions.

We intellectuals must feel irritation when faced with much of the populist culture. One of its senior mentors, for example, now bitterly mocks the results, the drastic severance and denial of authority, the ignorance and lack of high culture. Paul Goodman (in *New Reformation*) even smugly points out the aesthetic contradictions involved in playing "primitive folk music" on "electronically amplified instruments." Left-Hegelian Herbert Marcuse wants to be programmatically sympathetic to such "liberating imagination"; but, also as a good European, he really feels that culture means Bach rather than rock, and the dialectics of liberation demand tough organizational cadres, and technological mastery. Even a learned anarchist historian, George Woodcock, ended with a vociferous condemnation of the "counter-culture" for its parasitism on the technological society and its lack of "classical heroic individualism"—a strangely conservative way of negating the anarchist movement of his own time. Each of these libertarian intellectuals must miss essential imperatives of the populist culture in breaking with the preservative culture in the quest for community. Marcuse's Hegel, Homer (cited by Woodcock), and Milton (cited by Goodman) cannot possibly provide the aesthetic electricity. Also a sticking point each time is the paradoxical relation to technology, the renaturing it by play. This has some forerunners, as in dadaism, but generally contrasts with the all-too-grim attempts to fuse art and technology, as in objectivist abstraction and functionalist design, and electronic musical neoclassicism and positivistic documentary literature. In contrast, the populist culture properly subordinates the techno-order by not taking it seriously.

If enlightened liberal and libertarian critics do so poorly with the populist side of the mass culture, we can hardly expect more aesthetic awareness from the aficionados of the technological media, such as Marshall McLuhan and Buckminster Fuller. Let me consider McLuhanism a bit since that seems the most pretentious and widespread form of mass media religiosity, though difficult to take seriously because of its gross failure to make discriminations about the exploitative ways of mass culture. In such technocratic ideologies, only the media processing, the packaging not the product, is allowed to be meaningful experience. By masturbating media metaphors, one achieves a kind of electronic mysticism. Instead of seeking out the human elements in the new environment, you become the medium of your media. And instead of recognizing that people variously attempt to transform the media into culture, whether populist, preservative, or other, as I have argued, McLuhan holds that the media do the creating themselves. Such electronic mystification, like the drunk attempting to swallow the hair of the dog that bit him, would attempt to cure disorientation and dehumanization by maximizing the poison as therapy, by further blowing-up ("implosions") reality and fragmenting ("mosaic method") sensibility.

Take McLuhan's main slogan: "The Medium is the Message." This punningly became "The medium is the massage," and, later, "The Medium Is the Mess Age." Intellectually smogged-up here in old-fashioned word-play is the recognition that our mass media tend to function as self-destruct machines, properly subordinate to our socioeconomic ordering which makes production its own ostensible purpose, thus not only suppressing all content and human purpose but leaving the processing itself as the dominant experience. The mesmerized watch *something* on TV less than watch TV itself. Like Talk Show maestros compulsively joking about their inability to make jokes, or the obsessional giggling about nothing in particular which characterizes most popular comedy routines, the lack of meaning becomes the ultimate, and addicting, experience. But such processing also requires a frenzied pursuit of new programs, people, content, news, messages, to be processed and denatured. The media mess up and quickly age all, processing out all differences between the trivial and the tragic, the hardsell and the soft feeling, creation and destruction. Or more accurately—and more dialectically than any McLuhanism could allow—our media processing attempts this but comes up against the drastic resistance of "high-brow" scorn, of "drop-out" dismissal, of traditionalist demands and populist perversions, and many other common human ways of re-introducing sense, joy, defiance, community, and other unprocessed human reality. No matter how cleverly the medium absorbs, denatures, and empties experience, there is still a world outside. Contrary to McLuhanism, then, we less have a "new technological sensibility" coming from the media than the ever-human sensibilities and their varied cultures struggling with and subverting the media. The real message for the cultural dialectician is that he must seek out how the Age battles its Messes.

McLuhan, of course, quite lacks consistency and rigor, and repeatedly slips out of his own media metaphysic, as in announcing that "the citadel of individual consciousness . . . is not accessible to the mass media." That's a silly cop-out; the struggle really is, as they used to say, for men's souls. The basic McLuhanist argument is that we are undergoing a "technological transformation of our nervous system," but he has incoherently retained a ghost in the electronic machine to placate his and our fears of the destruction of human individuality. Such genial confusions, of course, are typical mass-media-processed messages and conveniently provide the style of media popularity, of "linear" aggrandizement.

By counter-playing McLuhan's puns, I do him no disservice. Summarized but not simplified, his main argument is an extended pun. In reading—up to the near-present the determining intellectual mode—we follow the "line"; ergo, "linear consciousness." Run this trope through Western cultural history: Greek thought (the syllogism's one-two-three), Monastic ordering (the rule of the bookish Word), Gutenberg's type revolution (the repetition of A-B-C), Renaissance perspective (point-of-view parallel to authorship and other condittorri egotism), the Age of Enlightenment (the alphabetical encyclopedization of knowledge), the Industrial Age (the assembly line's step-by-step production), and all the rest of what can be metaphorically reduced to a visually sequential civilization, including clock-time, the Protestant work-ethic, and modern money accountancy. Thus our civilization ended, recently, in a straight-jacket of linearity, printed words, representation, industrialism, hard-lines, rationality, and privateering individualism. Now such linearity gets blasted out by the instantaneousness, multiplicity, simultaneity, tactility, totalism, communalism—and probably pointlessness—of television and computers and the rest of our postindustrial and super-rational and beyond-literate technology and organization. That is the medium message which should solacingly massage us in our Mass Age.

Never mind that such a history of Western consciousness is like an instant beverage—a little condensed dust of learning and a lot of hot water. Also never mind that on any particular subject—literature, psychology, education, mechanics, sports—McLuhan is often either wrong or confuses puns with actualities. His is simply a mix of media metaphors, a schizoid splattering of technological terms and aesthetic tropes serving as theological entities, though quite thin in dialectics and drama. As a learned game and exorcism of mass culture this should not altogether be put down, though also not confused with reality. Others can play, too. Let me give McLuhan a case for his media catalogue. Protest movements (a subject which he dismisses, apparently in ignorance and fear) have for a decade provided a major mass culture phenomenon and a crucial (and much distorted by the processing) media experience. McLuhan style, we would have to see the protest rally as the state of its media, not its message—for example, the bull horn. That electronic megaphone, used by both cops and militants, not only makes street protest louder and more mobile but generally bullish. Note, also, of the bull horn its quickly varying directional focus, its gutteral exaggerations and sudden decibel changes, and the conditioned responses that go with such authoritative "voiceovers." In sum, the medium encourages sporadic, roaring, multifocused rioting by both protesters and cops. The handy amplifier also engenders instantaneous elitism. How else would one identify in a mob the Chief of the Tactical Squad or the Leading Revolutionary Monitor, if it weren't for their characterizing bull horns, of which they are the mere moveable stands? Small men now speak large, the old street fighter with his linear broadside and the old patrolman with his comic half-block hoarse authority now electrifyingly magnified and communally echoing because of the bull horn. And since bull horns get heavy in the right hand, this probably accounts for the increasing leftist emphasis of long protests. But if we properly look to the future and technology's new miniaturized calf horns, we may envision far more fluid street fighting on many fronts—every cop his own riot—with an increasingly pure rightist though less virile, less two-fisted, quality. Bull-shouting as well as bullshit will magically transform itself.

Although I could endlessly expound on the significance of the new street media—radical literate intellectuals, as McLuhan (the Agnew of the technological aesthetes) repeatedly warns us, remain too fixated in book-ish cud-chewing to see that revolution is about wheels and other media —any explication should be done with an amplifier, not mere print. But just think of all the metaphors connected with bull horn possibilities and you can become the latest, and probably the horniest, model McLuhan.

But you won't get at the metadynamics of street fighting if you think in a linear-logical way about the arbitrary and illegitimate institutions of our society. Such an antique concern for justice would substitute the message for the medium. Is there really a condition that somewhat relates to McLuhan's major metaphor of "linear consciousness"? Of course. That is what we mean when we say of someone that he thinks "mechanically," or when we disparage "rote learning," or when we ask for a full pattern or "gestalt" of perception, or when we insist on the "depth" of true understanding. These, of course, are usually antithetical to the mass media. A few years ago, quite autonomously of McLuhanism, John Holt (*How Children Fail*) wrote of fearfully submissive young pupils who memorized the sequence of a problem but did not probe the thinking that went into it; he described them as taking a "linear" misapproach, partly induced by directing themselves to authority rather than to the problem. People who read a poem as a series of printed words and prescribed response make a similar mistake. We all know the infuriating experience of talking with those who seem "logical" or "analytic" but exclude all the richness, extension, and life of a subject. These "linear" people make bad human mediums by reducing all to a narrow line and manipulative purpose. Although McLuhan makes such linearity the Originating Sin born of book-print culture and its abstraction "from all other senses," a more basic inattention, rote-fundamentalism, and reduction of imagination and feeling, not confined to any particular medium, seems pertinent. Main-line-media fare of all kinds depends upon just such linearity, with the electronic magnifying it instead of changing it. Bland people in institutional power not only reveal but insist upon a narrowly lined and limited sensibility. Linear consciousness is not a certain medium and kind of responding but a failure of response, a characteristic pathology encouraged for aggrandizement and control in a manipulative and counterfeit civilization.

Has such linear consciousness increased in our time? Probably. More and more in our processed schooling, for example, people "can't learn." In many areas, our expertise reduces a reality to its most controllable, exploitable, "neutral" manipulation, i.e., to linear form. Business, government, and other institutions display a straight-ahead "rationality" close to total insensitivity and insanity. The American Indo-China War can be described in terms of misplaced linear thinking, from the early "domino theory" (a linear-visual sequence) through the violent logic of applying computer tapes to strategic orders and the direct support of the Saigon dictatorship (the accepted line-of-command) to the whole pattern of Western institutional rationalization imposed on an alien and inappropriate tribal scene. (Quite late in the war, even McLuhan discovered the political analogy and finally wrote, in a characteristically dehumanized headline, "Vietnam war is extravagant pedagogical effort to Westernize the East.") No matter how sophisticated are the mass electronic methodologies applied to Vietnam, the messages come out the ultimate linear logic of miscomprehension—the technology of mass murder.

In other senses, too, our mass mediaized wars, the reporting of which as much inures as outrages, belie McLuhan's conceits such as that we now live in a "global village" with a renewed "tribal sensibility" and a more "visceral" and "organic" culture, even when he does not push his points to such comic perversity as "Bless Madison Avenue for restoring the magical art of the caveman to suburbia." We do have increasing efforts toward tribal and organic relatedness, but these arise in social fact as dissident movements that vehemently reject much of the media and Madison Avenue magic. The attempts at new community in America, the new neolithic or alternate cultures, insistently resist the McLuhanist technocracy and its lines of manipulation. This is the counter-dialectic, revulsively and yearningly arising in the mass culture, the resistance against those mesmerized by the boob tube, as linear as an IBM printout, as lively as an electronic circuitry stamping. For the media "extensions of man" do not build sensitive communalism, except by reaction to them, but institutional power networks.

Instead of the young happily "learning a living" in "new total environments," they block out responding, including that little allowed in schooling, as just more substitutes for doing and being. Even the populist enlivenings add up to brief "highs" in a long passive "downer." The technological stimuli could hardly gratify the thwarting of direct human touch and relation which they create, unless inverted and resisted back into human dimensions. The media ersatz-tactile effects end in an imposed fetishism of fantasy commodities, of projective lunacies, and of lubricities of institutional displacement of the fully and directly human.

The media hero of McLuhan (and Fuller and the other technological ideologues) is not the sexually pulsating, stoned rock-blues guitarist in Indian drag parodying electronic show-biz but the conference jetting mod-administrator pursuing "new information patterns" in expense-account elitism. As anyone should recognize who has run that dreary plastic and aluminum maze of airport-plane-airport-hotel-airport-plane-homebar TVport (you never get outside or in a different ambiance), doing it creates neither human experience nor informed awareness, only the pathetic hyped-out victims of desperate efforts to maintain pseudopersonal contact and control in a fractured ordering. The human simply serves as just another media impulse. Similarly, our "information overload" less encourages new energetic "patterns," than charges mental blocks and hot-arcs of resentment and burnt-out withdrawal. The jargonings in which such administrators, and McLuhan and the media folk, cushion crippled sensibility is not "cool" media personalizing, in place of the old "hot" and high-styled intellectual rhetoric, but the appropriate loss of humane speech. All who have endured a number of television or other mass media interviews should also recognize that response is processed (panel, interview, or excerpt style) as a means of control, censorship, and deflation of individual and passionate views. The technological medium as well as the message serves social and ideological domination. Media processing, form and content, must be understood as the restriction of experience, perfectly evident in the organization and control as well as style since the mass media order is generally corrupt, ornately bureaucratized, and usually in the command of quite contemptible people. While no simple conspiracy, our mass media pursue disorientation and reduction of the human with a teleos which finally seems to be the cosmic program of a schizophrenic deity seeking to reverse the creation.

One further necessary note on McLuhanism. He characteristically concludes his media-mad polemic against intellectuals, *Counterblast*, with, in giant type, a self-congratulatory slogan: "THE IVORY TOWER BECOMES THE CONTROL TOWER OF HUMAN NAVIGATION." Thus we return to the permanencies and ponderosities of the preservative culture. Identification with electronic mass culture serves as mere aggrandizement for the old aesthete. McLuhan calls from his imitation-ivory minaret for prayers to the one-and-all packaging. That he always sounds-off with many literary quotes (usually twisted badly out of context and meaning) from a narrow range of preservative literature of a few generations back

(Mallarmé, James, Joyce, Lewis, etc.), confirms the aestheticism. It is not at all far from the old art-for-art's sake to the new media-for-media's sake. The decadent's concern with frissons of artistic sensation easily displaces into a technological aestheticism which sanctions the power culture.

As so often, the ivory-tower critic of the mass culture not only puts himself to sea with the big fleets but insists that he is at the helm. Still practicing his narrow but now fractured linearity of intellectual culture, in books, he steers a narrow set of media metaphors into a technological port in support of the old traditional powers and hierarchies. Although I suppose that one can find in these technological ideologies some nihilistic hedonism as a homeopathic dosage for poisoned sensibility, the real crux is the same old submissive worshiping of power processing which can only result in increasing our diseases of human denigration and disorientation.

Thus I have not really diverged from my initial argument about the dialectics of the power-culture and the counter-culture. Uncritical views of either the preservative or the technological must ignore the issues of cultural controls. But how adequate against these are the rebellious responses which have risen in and around contemporary mass culture? My suggestion is that the populist arts and styles provide an important adversary which, however, cannot be an adequate and enduring culture in itself. Intellectual commentators on mass culture must therefore stay on a precarious edge between condemnation and affirmation, less interested in the techniques and essences of mass culture than in their contraries and what they existentially serve.

It seems evident, for instance, that the intellectual and individualizing cast of the poet, novelist, painter, composer and philosophical critic, in the usual senses, cannot sufficiently root themselves in the populist context, or in the rest of mass culture. Such will necessarily retain allegiance to different, alienating and elitist, cultural traditions. But from that historical necessity, we cannot derive justification for fundamentalist condemnations of, or sycophant submission to, all mass culture and populist arts. The popular protesting culture provides shortened circuits between imagination and society, between transforming impetus and mass control, though it does not and probably cannot create the forms of either. Populist culture must presuppose the exploitative technological order which it lives within and the critical and artistic culture from which it draws humanizing impetus. This makes limited and transitory any particular significant manifestation of populist culture. The rapidity of its fashions and its constant permutations and adaptabilities confirm this. Yet the counter imperatives, as well as the large need, for the populist culture remain, and retain their own truths.

What delight, vitality, and liberation our populist culture has been providing! We should sympathetically contemplate all it has been doing for

us. As the enlarged expression of rebellious views and feelings, our populist arts give public, and sometimes surprizingly pungent, expression to
art and attitudes from the dissident and outside. Minority styles and sensibilities, neither confined to "youth" nor readily "mediable" by the main-
line institutional-commercial culture, now spread with remarkable rapidity
and force because of the young populist audiences as electric inter-
mediaries. The libidinal manners and fanciful responsiveness, the "misuse" which reaffirms our *homo leudens* autonomy from our objects and
orderings, the freeing variousness in language, relationship, and work
create social transformations not only evident on campuses and in urban
purlieus of the marginal but much more widely. Of course some of this
becomes new subordination by style-conformity and market-exploitation
—sterling silver peace medallions, high-mark-up revolutionary head and
nature shops, incorporated protest figures, a counter-culture sub-establishment—but what doesn't in this society? Nonetheless, many socially
rigidified as well as cultural controls get deboned by imagination and
movement. New color, tenderness, and ecstasy flow over our bland institutional decorum. Behavior under our bureaucracies will never be quite
as structured again. Surely the ominous possibility remains that the mass
hedonism could serve, with pot as soma and various electronic fanti-
sectomies, Huxley's *Brave New World* and Zamiatin's ruthlessly benevolent *One State.* Yet now the indivisibility of freedom, to use the antique
language of our Enlightenment forbearers, means that the opening up
and varying of personal conduct and expression engenders other varieties
and imaginings of character and social structure. Historical fact: In ways
none of us predicted in the nineteen fifties, and which did not seem possible from the preservative and mass arts, the populist culture has already
generated religious and social changes.

Autocrats and authoritarians have always taken cultural change more
seriously than liberals. I'm inclined to grant their fearful insight into the
function of strict appearance, inhibiting fashions, artistic censorship, restrictive styles, and narrow sensibility. The populist culture, whatever its
conscious motives, wars with them. Some political leftists hold that the
"youth-culture syndrome" provides substitute releases for more fully
liberal or radical social changes. But yesterday's revolutionaries tend to
be peevishly doctrinaire and blind to new agents of change. The populist
culture has itself created unexpected co-optations: the peace movement
and much leftism (quite "straight" until recently), significant members
and numbers out of the preservative high-culture (on the campuses as
well as in the other mass media), and in a variety of other scenes. We can
find the arts, costuming, antimanners, multisexuality, and much else
spread by the populist culture, in surfing and skiing groups, in street
gangs and suburban parties, with Jesus freaks and right-wing political
radicals, and in all sorts of unexpected places. Part of the effectiveness
of populist culture comes from its social amorphousness.

Institutional administrators and other custodians and pundits of preservative sensibility respond with considerable perplexity and uncertainty, and thus lessened authority, to the widening manifestations of a new popular sensibility. They must because much of our mass technological transformation fractures the legitimacy of traditional orderings. Even when the power reactions are hostile and repressive, they further the de-authoritization by revealing the fears and hatreds informing the preservative culture and social domination. For obvious reasons, culture identified with youth must be naive, but the custodians of official culture and power necessarily provide an informing disenchantment, whether they try to repress or to counterfeit the populist ways.

Our old Jacobin commentators fail to see the institutional struggle under the bizarre styles, as with the liberal parent who argued about chauvinism while his daughter unargumentatively turned a nylon "Old Glory" into a mini-skirt. More social conscience gets moved by populist lyrics than by a thousand chunks of platform rhetoric. The "out-of-it" and "drop-out" responses to social and political demands (the draft, the usual corporate employment, educational discipline) may well be more effective than more overtly principled resistance. The refusal of such submissions in immediate institutions follows appropriately from the populist sensibility. When hundreds of thousands gathered for peace-sex-pot-rock-protest-soulfulness at Woodstock and Altamont, we saw the massing of the new and unemployed proletariat of the rich, technobureaucratic society creating their own consciousness between lonely resistance and the mainstream mass culture. Pretty clearly, it was, in nineteenth-century terms, a *lumpen* mass, in spite of middle-class origins, with only vaguely rebellious self-consciousness and loose allegiance to its own wider social roles. Not much directly follows from it, except the recognition that the controlled mass culture has created its own rebellious culture which will likely be a significant current, in various other shapes, for some time to come.

Will the populist current in the mass culture also short out? It constantly threatens to, but the hunger for its art and communion, and the basic human inadequacy of the mainstream technological mass culture, restore the energies. The cultural vacuum demands it, as we finally learn in practice that mass schooling and higher learning cannot successfully and satisfyingly impose much preservative culture on everyone. Granted, in protective coloration as well as in desperation for control, the manipulative institutions would and do take it over. Populist artists become rich celebrity businessmen and, in spite of a sometimes remarkable insouciance, sink into show-biz fatuousness and the usual commercial fraudulence. Our exhaustive processing of culture, like our endless bureaucratization of learning, certainly removes autonomy and difference from the populist culture and would pacify it into rococo irrelevence. Yet the populist culture has a curious elusiveness in which sleazy entertainment events become ecstatic religious festivals and in which styles start out by already ambiguously parodying themselves and those who would take them over. The weird disproportions indigenous to such minority cultures disrupt the logic of counterfeiting and control. Thus a minor indulgence such as pot becomes a politics and metaphysics. In curious defensive reversals, we have ardent youths claiming moral revelations from fatuous exoticism, e.g., from the revival of astrology and other forms of the occult, while passing off as mere youthful games revolutionary insurrections. But which of our cultures in the most mad mirror-world can be left open?

Still, an adversary culture must finally go beyond play, inversion, parody, grotesquery, and ambiguity and become something more, a full sensibility and continuing way of life. Though hardly ever in full synchronization in modern civilization, culture finally belongs to society. In the usual cultural theory, change in power allows change in institutions which then allows a change in sensibility, from political to social to cultural revolution. However, our present cultural conflicts imply that the last be first, that a change in sensibility will change the order of the world. Such is the positive force, the awesome dialectic, suggested by so many manifestations of our populist culture. And we must admit the remarkable vitality and the widespread social effects. However, direct change in institutional and other political power seems absurdly slight. Essentially the same denaturing processes, and the same types, considerably control education and entertainment. Even the populist culture's delightful revival of American utopian imagination, made tangible in some hundreds of communes and in many thousands of collectives and other tribal ways of domesticity (crucial modifications of our great anxiety machine, the competitive suburban family), often seems ambiguous. Frequently, we can suspect that marijuana substitutes for martinis, middling rock for middle-brow schmaltz, whole-earth-catalogue salesmanship for the thing of ancient hucksters, and the new messiness for the old morality. Instead of alternatives to technological organization and its passively reductive consciousness, we may find that collectives of young technologues week-end for cheap therapy and that the mass culture peddles new anesthetics.

Does the populist culture finally reveal itself as fully subordinate to the power culture? The evidence in the early seventies should leave one, I believe, rather uncertain. Surely the genuine and desirable impetus to new ways of life and more vital sensibility and communitarian order would need more rigor and fullness than they now show in order to counter the technological processing and the apathetic consciousness that demands. But at least temporarily, the populist culture has led to some significant de-powering of not only the mass culture but of some institutions, e.g., familial and educational. Still, that will hardly transform a large part of technological mass culture, much less re-create our other institutions.

Those who sardonically compare the populist currents with old fashioned rebelliousness and its minority art, alienated criticism, and moral intransigence certainly have a case. Taken in itself, our countering culture often seems a soft, vulgarized, and declining version of the culture of revolt, i.e., jazz down to rock, abstractionism and expressionism down to psychedelic decoration, bohemian literature reduced to underground journalism, philosophical radicalism reduced to ecological sentimentality, ecstatic prophecy condensed to drug "highs," and heroic nihilism to adolescent hedonism. But a popular and protesting culture must serve different purposes and roles and is therefore not comparable. For as a humane civilization we must also have an intense, kinesthetic, communal, and youthful popular culture, not just a preservative high culture (however modernist) and a piously exploitative and mind-rinsing technological mass culture. If the current populist culture gets altogether short-circuited into thin arts of passivity, surrogate experience, and institutional submission, if it is fully processed into mainstream mass culture and its technocratic ideology, then there will have to be another populist culture. Our openness to real change, to the possibilities of lively sensibility and more humane consciousness, and to communal relations are being tested by a relatively new cultural and social populism. Are we so far gone that it can have no authentic and enduring possibilities? The alternatives seem to be a violent apocalypse or a combination of a mortuary culture and a technological mass culture which will serve a fully authoritarian and debasing order. Our populist culture at least generates against this currents of a richer and freer life.

Culture and Rebellion: Dilemmas of Radical Teachers*

By Alan Trachtenberg

Student activism still looms as the foremost fact of life in schools everywhere. In the past year, demands have escalated, tactics have become more disruptive and abrasive, countermeasures more harsh and angry. Although it is too early to say what forms both protest and repression will take this year, it is apparent that the character of the student movement has already undergone a decisive change since its beginnings in the civil rights and free-speech campaign of the early 1960s. It has become more inclusive in its aims and its membership, more assured that the university is the proper battleground on which to engage a variety of enemies it sees as interconnected: imperialism, racism, corporate liberalism.

The movement seems impatient with nice distinctions: if the university behaves as a servant to militarism even in the smallest way, as a buttress to racism, as a slum landlord, then it has lost its immunity. Its practices expose its ideals of rationality as fraudulent. If the school permits the making of poison gas anywhere on its campus, in no matter how obscure a corner, then never mind what else it offers, never mind the supposed ideals of learning, the humane values allegedly enshrined there, the cherished forms of academic freedom. The presence of evil makes the other functions irrelevant for the moment, if not indeed themselves suspicious of contamination. In their rhetoric, and there is no reason to believe it is not sincere, student radicals want to represent in the halls of learning the cries of napalmed children, the anger and animosity of black and "third-world" youth, the eruptive rhythms of middle-class youth shedding the moral duplicity, the "up-tight" style of their family and their class. These are the immediate facts of the world these young people inhabit, and if the university refuses to accommodate itself to them, then the

---

* Reprinted by permission of author and publisher (copyright by *Dissent*).

university must be overhauled. They seem confident in their power to do precisely that.

In the eyes of many Americans—faculty members as well as the generally hostile public—the movement wears the aspect of a sinister contagion. We hear accusations of "left fascism," of a new barbarism at the gates. Many people see the student protests as a symptom of larger, deeper disorders, a failure of authority throughout society, a collapse of cultural values which have stood for centuries, an epidemical regression to infantilism. In regard to the university itself, a common response is that student radicals seem willing to eliminate the baby with the dirty bath water, that while they have done a service to call attention to the need of reform, they have by now gone beyond a meliorist crusade and are attacking fundamental values without which no university is possible. The resort to violence—at least what looks like violence to most people —suggests that political goals have gotten enmeshed in antipolitical intentions: it seems hard now to distinguish whatever may be sound in their moral aims from the intolerable nihilism and anarchism, so-called, of their behavior. Listen for the tune, not the words, and you hear sounds discordant with the humane goals of social transformation many academics were initially attracted to.

Does the movement take its character from the words or the tune? Has the tune, which sometimes sounds like a rock cacophony, come to prevail over the words, the principles and theories of social criticism, or is the point that tune and words are now one, that the students have achieved an authentic expressive form for their political and social vision? Some older radicals seem already to have decided: if SDS is making a revolution, they say, they might very well line up on the other side. Social justice, freedom of thought, egalitarianism seem to have better defenders, they feel, among parliamentary liberals than among New Left anarchists.

My own position is less certain, and I suspect that my mixed feelings and divided loyalties are shared by at least a small number of academics on every campus. Faced with growing pressure to line up against the students, to resist demands backed up by threat of force, to defend rational process and disinterestedness as ends in themselves, we are stuck in a dilemma. The pressure is to see the protests as discipline problems, and to define the campus issues under the heading of control and punishment. But in some moods student uprisings seem an avenging angel come to haunt us with our own little sins, compromises, and equivocations, which suddenly loom as a major guilt—the guilt of being an academic, a scholar, a teacher, while wars rage and people starve. What kind of commitment is it we have made to Truth that takes locked files and riot police to protect? Does rational process include university-supported war research, ROTC, social engineering? Do we really mean disinterestedness, or passivity, and isn't neutrality often a cover for complicity? The way most universities are run, can we honestly speak of reason and humane learning as central values?

These questions have bothered us long before the occupation of buildings. True, we may have allowed ourselves to drift into careers that have deflected our attention from such issues. For many of us, the academic campaign against the Vietnam war a few years ago represented a re-politicalization, a reactivation of older ambitions and passions. I am not sure how widespread is the feeling of a strain between demands of career and demands of politics. But that is not exactly the dilemma I refer to, for it is a personal matter, a question of priorities in use of time and energy. Whatever doubt we may feel is not over militarism, racism, or the structure of social privilege which discriminate in education against the poor and the ethnic minorities. Whatever else, we feel the university as well as society at large ought to free itself from these intolerable conditions.

But our own experiences have led us to value the university in a way apparently incomprehensible to student radicals. For most of us the university has represented access to a culture fundamentally at odds with that of the larger society, a countervailing culture that honors the development of consciousness, and reading, thinking, and writing as the faculties of consciousness. It may sound excessive to say so, but the university has been a sort of salvation for many of us, salvation from the confinements and destructive ends, the dilution of ideas and culture, in the larger society. True, the academy exacts its own price, has its own intellectual and emotional pitfalls. Yes, scholarship and criticism is often exasperatingly pretentious, overwrought, and stupid. The academic mind can be just as insulated from experiences outside its limits as any other, and just as arrogant and patronizing about its own values. But why characterize the university only by its worst features? The university is perhaps the sole institution that makes accessible to its members the grounds of self-criticism, the only formal "place" arranged for free discussion, where the inherited and the contemporary can confront each other openly, where a usable tradition can be elicited from the encounter of old and new.

This is not to say it always happens; intellectual freedom can be as empty a convention, as mindless a slogan as "up against the wall." And in the recent period, formalism and narrow professionalism did frequently place constraints on thought. But the ideal and the possibility of freedom persist, perhaps nowhere stronger than among the liberal and radical faculty who value the opportunities for critical research and discourse the university affords. It is from that ideal itself that they derive their support for many of the aims of student protest.

Only a few years ago collaboration between students and faculty in behalf of a better university seemed natural. The enemy was seen as the administration. Its extensive bureaucracy, its machinery of manipulation, its budget-minded caution seemed to represent, as Thorstein Veblen argued in *The Higher Learning in America* (1918), the invasion of business-minded habits of thought into the academy. We seemed agreed on the necessity of freeing the "higher learning" from, in Veblen's words, "the manner of life enforced on the group by the circumstances in which it is placed."

In the past year, however, the situation has tipped. Students are now more likely to find support, especially for demands of increased power over educational policy, from administrators who are coming to see their function as one of diplomacy and negotiation. And from the faculty they are more likely to meet a stubborn clinging to notions of standards and integrity and traditional prerogatives. Faculty resistance can be traced to a guild outlook, emerging tentatively from a dimly recalled past when teachers were teachers, masters of a field and carriers of a culture, and students were students, who came to learn. It is a teacher's business to decide what is to be taught. Of course in some measure his decision is made for him by his culture. But how else can you define a teacher? How can a syllabus be a negotiable issue? Moreover, teachers want to think that their subject makes a difference, that it is not merely a subject but an access to significance, an opening to a higher life.

This idea of teaching has been called elitist, and in part it is. A major sociological fact of university life in the past generation is that many teachers, particularly in the humanities (a category, by the way, that is itself part of the difficulty), bring to their work an unmistakable sense of superiority to their students. It rests not only on differences of training and expertness, but also on differences of values. It is felt to be a condition of life that to teach literature, art, and philosophy, it is necessary to wean most students from the culture of their backgrounds, a culture of provincial manners, of puritanical practices, of constricted, not to say crippling emotions. The students we have called "best" are those who display a sensibility for a "higher life," those who come to share our contempt for the mass culture of American society.

The idea of a cultural mission of the university is frequently evoked by those who worry about the anti-intellectualism of students. This worry has been transferred, it is interesting to note, from the average, sluggish student—the typical middle-class American youth—to the radical and activist student, who is often also the "best." It is worth digressing for a moment to consider the special character of this mission in American universities, and the ambiguities it contains.

Culture is one of the most difficult of our commonly used terms to define, and the difficulties themselves indicate the historical dimensions of the problem. The word is generally used in two interchangeable senses, one normative and the other neutral or "scientific." One refers to the inherited ideas and artistic monuments which express the ideal values of a society, what it collectively accepts as its best, its loftiest, its most honorific achievements in the realm of "spirit." The other refers to the "whole way of life" of a society, its manners as well as its arts, its patterns of behavior as well as its official ideas. When Matthew Arnold speaks of culture as the alternative to anarchy he means the first sense, "the best that has been thought and known in the world." This notion of culture stresses individual cultivation, refinement of sensibility, and especially the development of values, virtually religious, which lend meaning to life. Whereas the other definition of culture does not judge but describes, this version of the word implies a criticism of common life, a set of judgments of the quality of life. It values detachment and inwardness. It sees itself as Culture at odds with "culture."

Both senses of the word have had complex developments in the period of industrial society. The discriminations between "high" and "mass" culture grew out of the fear that industrialism would destroy the values attached to traditional art and thought. Although anthropologists introduced relativism into the comparative study of culture—that is, the idea that no culture had a claim to intrinsic superiority over another which arose under its own conditions—partisans of traditional culture in Europe and America felt their values threatened by bourgeois society. Intellectuals began to see themselves as critics of "mass" society, and by the beginning of the twentieth century the university was accepted as a place where traditional or "high" culture was preserved and nourished, where the student would be trained to open the mysteries of literature, art, philosophy. Academics and the public at large probably still agree that, at least in some measure, "cultivation" is an aim of higher education.

But with the new functions and services undertaken by the modern university, with the proliferating specialization of knowledge required by the economy and its technology, with the splitting apart of curriculum into quasi-feudal domains called departments each with an increasingly specialized methodology of its own, and with the rise of business and engineering schools as major political forces within the university, the operational aims of higher education became less clear. The ideal of cultivation had placed upon the university the responsibility for developing the entire apparatus of mind and feeling, for enlarging the student's sense of the world and of the self in the world. Now this ideal became the property of one branch of the university, the liberal arts, and was called upon to justify itself in terms fundamentally antithetical to its nature, terms designed to persuade the controllers of budget and curriculum of the convertability of liberal arts into concrete rewards—garlands of allusions for executives, fancier vocabularies for engineers, and for all, a "respect for values."

This picture is of course much simplified; in fact the liberal arts have been more vigorous in scholarship and criticism in the past generation than one might have expected under the circumstances. But in some crucial ways the liberal arts did acquiesce. The "Great Books" or "Leading Ideas of Western Civilization" courses, well-intentioned as they were in most cases, became a form of pandering to the belief that culture could be had through a form of purchase. Called upon to explain themselves in terms accessible to administrators, who in turn have to persuade alumni or legislators, some academic humanists tended to adopt those terms as their own and, perhaps as protective coloration, were willing to present themselves as proprietors of a particular line of goods—the "values" counter. Culture became in part identified with particular literary monuments thought of as "timeless"—a pleasant distraction for a society increasingly subject to time-study experts—and just as important, with a certain style of expression and demeanor: one is expected to be a gentleman in pursuit of Truth, Beauty, and especially Goodness.

In consequence of this defensive position the liberal arts have allowed humane culture to be pushed from the center to the periphery of education. Instead of resisting, or even recognizing the fatal loss of authority of the ideal culture, many humanists settled quite snuggly into their peripheral domain, and cultivated irony and disdain to support an inner sense of superiority to the prevailing powers. One effect of their teaching and writing was to separate their culture (call it "high" or "academic") decisively from the culture of the larger society. This gave to "high" culture a putative and precarious authority drawn not from living experience but from self-evident propositions. Humanities courses often have the tone of an initiation into a life of the mind drained of the vitality which was once its mark and is still its potentiality.

Now we are taken unawares by the fact that even—indeed, *especially* —our "best" students seem no longer interested in any version of the "higher life." This raises an extremely sensitive issue. Far from sharing our contempt, and fear, of mass culture, many students are now embracing it. A comment like Richard Goldstein's in *The Poetry of Rock,* that "America's single greatest contribution to the world has been her Pop (music, cinema, painting, even merchandising)," that "mass culture can be as vital as high art," must surely meet with wide approval among the young. But I am frankly skeptical of its truth. To be sure, notions of "high" and "low" tend to become formal conventions, genteel sanctions do frequently compete with intrinsic sanctions in "high" culture, and "official" academic values can stifle art and deny it the nourishment of new experience. The "higher life" does threaten to externalize itself, to yield to the satisfactions of an insignia, of manners and elegant speech—in short, snobbishness—instead of maintaining itself as an inner condition, a freedom and subtlety of mind and feeling.

Moreover, the badge of culture, like all badges and uniforms, can be put to antidemocratic uses. Whitman charged that the word "Culture" was an enemy of Democracy. It separated people into castes, it projected an aristocratic hierarchy of worth. A hundred years ago he wrote: "Of all the dangers to a nation, as things exist in our day, there can be no greater one than having certain portions of the people set off from the rest by a line drawn—they not privileged as others, but degraded, humiliated, made of no account." It is still a danger. The academic idea of "high" culture, which was won against the genteel tradition of earlier generations, has often, and often unwittingly, served as a fence around a special preserve of expreriences. The academy has seen itself as a means of liberation from the hold of bourgeois values—usually abstracted as "materialism," as if that exhausted the matter—and from the banalities and easy satisfactions, what Whitman called the "half sleep," of mass culture. Yes. But the alternative has tended to become a brand of its own. The exclusion of black, of immigrant, of working-class, and ethnic experiences from university culture is one instance. The insistence of "third-world" students that the university not deprive them of their historical culture (even where they have to scratch to find evidence of one), not compel them to forget their language and their customs, but instead equip them with the means to foster cultural self-consciousness among their people, is precisely to this point.

Anthropology alone should have taught us that there are many ways of conceiving a "higher life," and that cultural deprivation robs a man as ruinously as any other form of banditry. But the demand that the university redefine its cultural role in light of the multiplicity of American life (a severe undertaking under any circumstances) is one thing, and the demand, implicit in much of the protest, that it reject the life of the mind altogether, is quite another. One of the reasons for stiffening faculty resistance is an uneasy feeling that although the students may be acting out of and thereby reviving ethical imperatives, they may also be enacting a mindlessness we have always felt as an intimidating presence in American life. The quest for "pure" experience, the substitution of sensation for thought, the flight from discipline—these have been historical features of American culture. In conflict with opposite ideas identified with "Europe," ideas of tradition, authority, and complexity, they have leavened much of our literature and thought.

But detached from their opposites, celebrated as self-evident goals in their own right, these impulses toward anarchic freedom lose the very conditions which made them meaningful, and radical, in earlier periods. Yes, our young radicals have rejected, with refreshing spirit and elan, much of the musty and cramped style of middle-class life. They are loose, if they are nothing else. But their rejection takes a form that might in the end reinforce the institutions they want to overturn. The glorification of Pop, for example, suggests that as profoundly as the young feel alienated from their society, they are right at home in its culture.

Admittedly I am characterizing the movement by its most glaring outcroppings. But the times are such, the desperation for action and sensation so intense, that the most extreme can overnight become the norm. And isn't this in itself a Pop phenomenon, a condition manufactured by the machinery of mass culture, which feeds on confrontation, on theatricality on always "new" and bizarre gestures? There are times when protest has seemed a creature of the media. This is unfair of course: I do not mean to charge anyone with frivolity. But does the act of demonstrating always spring from the issues, from a considered grasp of their meaning, from a deliberative strategy regarding them? Is there no reason for concern that the political action of students might be, or become, a reflex of their culture, a compulsion to act and to prove oneself (in name of "authenticity"), rather than a participation in social change?

Insofar as the mood of rebellious students represents skepticism toward the pieties of national life, toward the evasions of intellectuals and academics, and toward the present state of knowledge—especially the split between value and fact reflected in the absurdly compartmentalized university curriculum—the mood invites faculty support and alliance. But there is cause for worry and for criticism in the degree to which student radicalism deviates from democratic and socialist thought, and veers in the direction of a "counterculture" which is capturing many Americans.

In part campus unrest conforms to a wave of changes in personal style that defy political or racial lines. It is a style that stresses the self-sufficiency of adventure, experiment, spontaneity. It is a style of repudiation, and it brooks no interference with "free" expression. We see it in the arts, in theater and film and music. Most of all we see it in fashion. It might be mistaken for a new avant-garde movement, but an avant-garde with such popular appeal should make us suspicious. It is more likely that the mass media are catching up with the earlier avant-garde movements—Data, surrealism, theater of cruelty—and detaching mannerisms and tactics from their theoretical foundations as a calculated critique of bourgeois culture and vestigial classicism and formalism. What was assault then, has by now become sheer mannerism, sheer sensation.

The mass media are playing an unprecedented role in propagating a "counterculture" with the flavor of "now!" Think of the importance of rock. Its practitioners are no longer entertainers but gurus. The music and its makers are celebrated—the proper word may be promoted—not only for the excitement of rhythm and sound, but for their message, their litany of liberation. And their message inspires a craving for what? For more of the same, as the record industry well knows. The same message, the same inducement to "do your own thing" and to "let it all hang out" can be heard in theater, in film, in the very visible "underground press," in the mushrooming "encounter groups." Writing in *Esquire* Elenore Lester has described the message as this: "Try hallucinogens: they drive you out of your wretched mind. Try nudity: it returns you to your sanity. Try multi-media baths: they stretch the sensorium. Try confrontation: it cleanses the psyche. Try revolution: it energizes the environment."

Of course radical students are not entirely responsible for how the media have popularized and cheapened the idea of cultural change. But two questions need to be considered. One, to what extent has the media version of "revolution" affected the form, particularly the inner feelings, of protest? And two, is there something about the current style of protest, including what passes for avant-garde art and theater, that lends itself to media needs, their hunger for sensation, for excitability?

In its disregard for theory generally, the New Left has pretty much ignored the media, and has failed to develop a critical point of view toward mass communications. Slogans from McLuhan and murky fragments from Marcuse have served in lieu of analysis. This is not the entire answer, but neglect of theory has helped make radicalism susceptible to media exploitation—and the exploitation is blatant; mind-blowing is a major industry. There is a belief abroad that changes in hair style, in dress, in sexual habits constitute a rejection of the social order and prepare you for revolution. The new style is supposed to be more "authentic"; the fact that it is also fashionable does not seem to occur to its defenders. Some intellectuals, whose sensibility has been formed in the modernist movement, are sometimes prone to hail any sign of the "new" as a spark of life, and to enjoy the idiosyncratic and the bizarre for their own sakes, for the "hell of it." Rather than a process of mastering social reality by will and thought, revolution has come to mean something dangerously close to sheer impulse.

Granted, the energy invested in cultural rebellion, in acid-rock insurrection against the old ethic of deferring pleasure for the sake of profit, may have a revolutionary potential. "In a culture judged as inorganic, dead, coercive, authoritarian," writes Susan Sontag, "it becomes a revolutionary gesture to be alive. . . . Bending the mind and shaking loose the body makes someone a less willing functionary of the bureaucratic machine. Rock, grass, better orgasms, grooving on nature—really grooving on anything—unfits, maladapts a person for the American way of life." But what *do* these gestures fit a person for? What social alternatives do they imply? Is the "American way" really in danger from such gestures? The fact is that the "American way" itself has cultivated these impulses, has set them up as its secretly-admired version of what it means to be "different." Are we witnessing the middle-class, in a mood of self-hate and anxiety about its "authenticity," turning against itself by turning itself inside out? The fantastic notion that if only the "up-tight" middle-class would "turn on," war and poverty would cease, the air would de-pollute itself, and capitalism self-destruct has become a pleasant fantasy, and for that reason so effective a piece of vicarious entertainment for the middle class itself. And the pugnacious idea that all authority is evil, rather than specific uses of authority, serves to obscure the causes of war and poverty within the present structure of society; it raises a straw man in place of concrete analysis.

In the student movement there is a considerable amount of discussion of theory; but theatricality, gesture, the hope for "instant revolution"— not to speak of indiscriminate terror—seem often more prominent than the effort to arrive at clear, persuasive statements of issues and mapping of strategy. The cry for "relevance" is a case in point. It is another example of an emerging pattern of impatience with analysis and contempt for history. It is also an example of the debasement of a good idea through sloganizing. Many faculty members are vulnerable to the cry because inwardly they apply a standard of relevance to their own work, but they recognize how complex, how tentative, how problematic the standard can be. The current idea of what is knowledge ought always to justify itself in light of criticism; that indeed is the function of intellectuals. Perspectives on the past always reflect, with greater or lesser degree of awareness, the influence of the present. Students make a valuable point when they attack much of what passes for "objective" knowledge as formalistic and ideological, as knowledge serving specific political and social aims under the guise of neutrality. They are right to try to penetrate to the social purposes and uses of curriculum.

But in demanding relevance students often assume that only the contemporary, which is to say the fashionable at the moment, is worth bothering about, that history, being dead, should be junked, that they themselves are the arbiters of what is relevant or not, living or dead. "Swamped with presentness," as Paul Goodman puts it, they seem unwilling to acknowledge that the "present" is a supremely difficult entity to define. Whitehead wrote that "the present contains all there is," that is, as an accumulation of the past, the present is the only possible locus of thought and action. This casts a somewhat different light on "relevance." Of course the present matters in a way the past does not; the future matters most of all. With more of a regard for history, students who cry for relevance might be better able to extrapolate from the present the best possibilities for a desirable future.

It may be that academics, even radicals, are overly fond of history, of the long and detached view. They might profit from an exchange with their students: some impatience with injustice for some historical perspective. It would be a fruitful exchange. Academics who want an organic culture in which the scholar can serve, in Emerson's words, to translate living experience into consciousness, to give meaning to life as it is being lived, have perhaps relaxed their demands on themselves by making careers in the academy. Many are now forced to admit an instability in their commitments: their political and larger cultural vision askew with the values and style of their profession. This tension is one source of the mixed feelings many have about student rebelliousness.

But it would be a hopeful sign if mixed feelings began to appear among the students as well. Recent history has raised the pitch of contradiction within society, and it would be strange if individuals did not feel the effects. Inner conflict is a sign that history still matters. Such conflicts can serve as revelations of the state of the world, within and without. The faculty might help keep alive a sense of the final uncertainty of the nature of student activism. It is senseless to exchange slogans, to hurl reproaches. It will be tragic if we allow the present agitation to settle in our minds as a discipline problem, just as it is tragic for radical students to feel no need for further education.

It is hard to say where hope for a renewed university lies. But surely it does not lie in repression of any sort. "In every era," wrote Walter Benjamin, "the attempt must be made anew to wrest tradition away from a conformism that is about to overpower it." Unexpectedly, conformism has appeared in the camp of rebellion as well as in the main body of society. But we cannot allow that fact to obscure the larger questions, of what we mean by university, by society, by culture at all. It is ironic that we are moved to punish students who have, no matter how unceremoniously, raised these questions. A better motive would be to help transform their assault into a reasoned critique and a program for change. The immediate problem is to restore the possibility of discourse.

The Journalistic Attitude*

By Joseph Bensman and Robert Lilienfeld

The journalistic attitude is related to the reporting of events by media which have, as one of their central characteristics, *periodicity of publication,* whether it be a daily newspaper, a weekly or bimonthly journal, or a radio or television program. The act of reportage is limited, not only in the sense that it conveys an image of the world defined within the framework of the reported event, but limited also by the periodicity of publication. Thus, time becomes a major dimension which determines a vast part of that subsequent reporting of events which defines and determines an image of the world.

The time feature is not the natural time of the natural man, because, given the periodicity of publication, time is an objective factor, subject to conditions and controls that are external to the events reported on, and external even to the act of reporting on the events, though they may be incorporated into it.

At the same time, the externality of time is not the preordained rhythm of a ceremony, or a ritual, in which submission to the tyranny of time (rhythm) becomes a major aesthetic end in itself. Time, for the journalist, is purely an arbitrary accident of the requirements of publication, which has no inherent rhythm other than the economics of publication and the expectations of readers that publication will occur at given times. Thus, the journalist must consciously discipline himself to the tyranny of these objective forms of time, and perhaps, having done so, enjoys the aesthetics of completing assignments within the framework of what might otherwise be purely arbitrary and capricious publication dates. Thus, regardless of the state of completeness of his research and knowledge, he must present a story which appears to be a complete entity at the time of his deadline. The element of completeness in the story, the who, when,

---

* Published for the first time in this volume.

where, and how, of journalism, creates an image of a total world as presented in a work of art,* so that in this respect the journalist is an artist, who, however, works in terms of time demands which are generally not characteristic of the artist. The requirement, however, that the story appear to be complete in and of itself forces the journalist to work for a closure which is not the closure that might have occurred had he not been subject to the time requirements.

A second characteristic of the journalistic attitude is based on the attitude of the journalist to his audience. Hemmed in by the periodicity of publication, and by the fact that he is selling some kind of media or publication, he is forced to anticipate the response of his audience in terms of what the journalist calls newsworthy, or "human interest." He must anticipate what will excite, stimulate, and titillate an audience at the time of publication. This means that the flow of his attention must be consistent with the natural flow of attention of his audience. He must drop stories and his interest in events, as the events themselves shift either in their dramatic impact on audiences, or in the journalist's estimate of the audience's rhythm of interest.[1]

Thus, the cliché that there is nothing as old as yesterday's newspaper is no less true because of its nature as a cliché.

For this reason, journalism cannot or does not necessarily have the depth and the timeless quality of art, though in other respects it resembles the image-making of art.

In a third respect, however, journalism has much in common with science and art, for one of the characteristics of outstanding journalism is that it results in a transvaluation, at least momentarily, of previous images of the world. For good journalism takes as its framework the assumptions and routines of everyday life, and the normal expectations of an audience, and discovers, through the story or event, the violation of these expectations and routines. So, the newsworthy, the dramatic, the "human interest" aspect of reporting looks either for the dramatic affirmation or the dramatic denial by events of the world of everyday life.

In dramatizing the denial of everyday life by events, the journalist ex-

---

* See Bensman and Lilienfeld, "A Phenomenological Model of the Artistic and Critical Attitudes," in *Philosophy and Phenomenological Research,* March 1968.

[1] Georg Simmel, in *Superordination and Subordination,* Section 5, *Leader and Led:* "The journalist gives content and direction to the opinions of a mute multitude. But he is nevertheless forced to listen, combine, and guess what the tendencies of this multitude are, what it desires to hear and to have confirmed, and whether it wants to be led. While apparently it is only the public which is exposed to *his* suggestions, actually he is as much under the sway of the public's suggestion. Thus, a highly complex interaction (whose two, mutually spontaneous forces, to be sure, appear under very different forms) is hidden here beneath the semblance of the pure supriority of the one element and a purely passive being-led of the other." From *The Sociology of Georg Simmel,* translated by Kurt Wolff, New York, Free Press Paperback, 1964, pp. 185–186.

poses the incongruities between image and realities, the fraud and chicanery behind many facades, and suggests the operation of structures governing the world other than those normally accepted. At times, such activities result in a renovation of values which are frequently neglected because they are taken for granted and not looked at. At other times, the effect of continuous exposures may cause the devaluation of values because these values appear to be inoperative. But in both cases, the act of good reporting is something more than reporting; it is an act of creation and re-creation. Its effects, while they may be startling at a given time, however, are likely to be temporary, because the journalist is forced continually to shift the focus of attention, as even the exposure in a given area becomes routinized, and as the response of his readership shifts.

Although the result of such activities may, from time to time, cause public scandals, the arrest of malefactors, the redesigning of automobiles, the enactment of new legislation, and changes in the sensibilities of audiences, the journalist who lives at the point of the chasm between appearances and reality is likely at a personal level to feel that all appearances are fraudulent, are managed, engineered, for reasons totally unrelated to the appearances. As a result, his personal attitude may be one of intellectual cynicism, which however is not necessarily incongruous with intellectual honesty and the maintenance of high standards of personal ethics.

In presenting these characteristics of the journalistic attitude, we have tended to neglect the simple and more obvious characteristics of technical facility in the handling, arranging, and manipulation of words and symbols, so that taken together they produce for the moment total images of a reality as adumbrated around an event or a story.

Viewed in terms of his technical virtuosity, as a craftsman and artisan, the journalist is an information-disseminator. He is able to present images of the world in apparently clear, personalistic, simple, and dramatic forms that are not abstract, academic or complicated.

This latter aspect, the technical and aesthetic virtuosity of the journalist, not only constitutes his professional and artistic methodology, but constitutes his basis for evaluation and appreciation by others, including other journalists.

THE SOCIETAL SETTINGS AND SOCIAL FUNCTIONS OF JOURNALISM

Journalism as an activity becomes meaningful only in some societal settings, and is unnecessary in others. It is appropriate to only limited kinds of social worlds. In a small-scale society, in which all available knowledge is gathered through direct and personal experience, the journalistic attitude would not develop, or would be part of the normal cognitive and perceptual equipment of every individual in this society. This also applies to the amount of differentiation within a society. For, if all individuals in the society are equipped to understand from direct experience the total range of events and activities in that society, then the normal channels of personal communication would be effective in disseminating and interpreting information within that society.

When the technical development of a society grows to the point where most of the basic issues and dynamics of a society are too complex, too abstract, too removed from the experience of the individuals in the society, there is need for the qualities of personification, dramatization, and the removal of abstraction and complexity from events and issues.[2]

The growth of large-scale civilizations, the increased differentiation within society, and the development of complex administrative, scientific, technical, and industrial processes all contribute to the development of journalism and the journalistic attitude.

The journalist, by developing professional competence in one or more of the abstract technical areas in the society, and by combining them with his "communications skills," makes distant and complex areas of the world available to audiences who are presumed to lack either the experience or the equipment to understand those events and issues directly in their own terms. As a result, he is or seems indispensable to a mass society.

The second aspect of the information function of journalism is related to the nonjournalistic uses of information in a large-scale society. Organized groups, business corporations, government agencies, universities, and other large-scale organizations are or become aware that information dissemination is related to their specialized public and private purposes. They need to employ specialists at dramatization, personalization, simplification, in order to present most effectively their specialized claims to distant publics. It is no accident, then, that the beginnings of professional propaganda began with the beginnings of professional journalism. For the information talents of the journalist develop in response to needs for substitute sources of information when genuine or direct sources of experience are not available. But this situation, in which the individual is not capable or is presumed to be not capable of evaluating issues and

---

[2] Alfred Schutz, in his essay, *The Well-Informed Citizen—An Essay on the Social Distribution of Knowledge,* formulates this problem in a somewhat different but related perspective, in which he constructs three ideal types: the expert, the man in the street, and the well-informed citizen, as three separate forms of social knowledge (see the *Collected Works,* Vol. II, p. 129 *et passim*). The present essay on the journalistic attitude focuses upon certain aspects which Schutz developed only in passing. See also W. Lippmann, *The Phantom Public* (Harcourt, Brace and Co., New York, 1925): "Modern society is not visible to anybody, nor intelligible continuously and as a whole. One section is visible to another section, one series of acts is intelligible to this group and another to that" (p. 42).

events in terms of direct experience, is precisely that situation which makes possible large-scale fraud, charlatanry, and deceit by misdirection. For the conscious manipulation of information becomes possible only when access to genuine information or direct sources of experience is obscured by the complexity of events, issues, technology, size, differentiation, etc., in a society.[3]

The development of a complex society provides the opportunity and the motivation, but the misapplication of journalism supplies the means.

PERSONIFICATION, CONCRETENESS, COMPREHENSIBILITY

The journalist, in avoiding abstraction and the cold deadness of difficult and abstract themes, seeks to find the image or the personality that embodies the idea, and deals with the image or personality in place of the idea. This enables him to communicate at levels that a large and non-professional audience is able to understand. Frequently, the characteristics of the journalistically treated personality begins to transcend that idea. Thus, the personal habits, the love stories, the leisure pursuits, the personal character or lack of it, all overpower that which would make the personality of journalistic interest originally.[4]

Thus, for Einstein, the journalistic treatment would emphasize his eccentricities: the haircut, his hatred of shaving cream, his absent-

---

[3] Leo Gurko, *Heroes, Highbrows and the Popular Mind,* Bobbs-Merrill, New York, 1953: "The enormous specialization that accompanied the spread of scientific and technical knowledge broke life up into smaller segments, and made the custodian of each segment increasingly important. In due course this custodian developed into the professional expert who, by virtue of his total knowledge of a single area (and often total ignorance of everything else), set up shop as middleman between his area and the public at large. His very concentration on a single sphere at the expense of every other kind of knowledge was a strong element in his functioning as an expert" (p. 236).

[4] Leo Lowenthal, *Biographies in Popular Magazines,* reprinted in William Petersen, *American Social Patterns,* Doubleday Anchor Books, Garden City, 1956, p. 71: "A biography seems to be the means by which an average person is able to reconcile his interest in the important trends of history and in the personal lives of other people"; also pp. 108–110: "The important role of familiarity in all phenomena of mass culture cannot be sufficiently emphasized. People derive a great deal of satisfaction from the continual repetition of familiar patterns . . . there has never been any rebellion against this fact . . . the biographies repeat what we have always known . . . (p. 110) the distance between what an average individual may do and the forces and powers that determine his life and death has become so unbridgeable that identification with normalcy, even with Philistine boredom, becomes a readily grasped empire of refuge and escape . . . By narrowing his focus of attention he can experience the gratification of being confirmed in his own pleasures and discomforts by participating in the pleasure and discomforts of the great. The large and confusing issues on the political and economic realm and the antagonisms and controversies in the social realm—all these are submerged in the experience of being at one with the lofty and great in the sphere of consumption. See also Lippmann, *op. cit.,* pp. 13–14.

mindedness, his proclivity for wearing old sweaters, etc., all at the expense of any presentation of his contribution, which is defined as so abstract that only a dozen men could understand it.[5]

The concreteness and "comprehensibility" embodied in this form of journalistic treatment results in the "hero" or the "star," who symbolizes and personifies, in terms larger than life, a field of endeavor which would otherwise not be salient. Once the attempt is made to make the "star" salient, the person who is momentarily presented as a star has a fabricated image. The dramatic aspects have to be emphasized; traits are created either in the person himself, so that he is made to resemble his journalistic image, or so that the image is made independent of his genuine characteristics or qualities.[6]

In this sense, journalism not only reports on the operation of appearances, and on realities underlying appearances, but also creates appearances or the appearance of realities.

JOURNALISM IN PUBLIC RELATIONS

The manipulator of public opinion, the propagandist, the public relations man, seeks from whatever source is available, those individuals whose technical skills, knowledge, and artistry will implement his purposes. The journalist possesses some of these skills, though in modern society he is not too different from the artist, the intellectual, the researcher, or the academician, who can become, if he desires, available for the same purposes. Each becomes, if he works for the government, an information specialist.

The information specialist translates the often complex, scientific, abstract procedural documents of quasi-literate technicians into the

---

[5] Orrin E. Klapp, *Symbolic Leaders—Public Dramas and Public Men,* Aldine Publishing Company, Chicago, 1964, especially Chap. 8: "Hero Stuff," p. 217, for other props of famous characters: sweaters, spectacles, mustaches, stovepipe hats, etc.

[6] Edgar Morin, *The Star—An Account of the Star System in Motion Pictures,* Grove Press, New York, 1960: "The actor does not engulf his role. The role does not engulf the actor. Once the film is over, the actor becomes an actor again, the character remains a character, *but from their union is born a composite creature who participates in both, envelops them both: the star.* G. Gentilhomme gives an excellent primary definition of the star (in *Comment devenir vedette de cinema*): 'A star appears when the interpreter takes precedence over the character he is playing while profiting by that character's qualities on the mythic level.' Which we might complete: 'and when the character profits by the star's qualities on this same mythic level'" (p. 39). "Possessed by her own myth, the star imposes it on the film universe of which she is the product. Stars demand or refuse roles in the name of their own image. P. Richard Wilm wanted to make only films in which he would be victorious in love; Gabin, before 1939, demanded his death in every film he made" (p. 67). "The star is in effect subjectively determined by her double on the screen. She is nothing since her image is everything. She is everything since she is this image too" (p. 66).

dramatic, the personal, the concrete imagery characteristic of pure journalism.

But, in addition to this, as an employee of a specialized agency which has vested interests of its own, the job of the information specialist entails the repression of information which is not consistent with those specialized interests, the concealment of weaknesses, of original documents, and their restatement so that the positive interests of the agency are enhanced.

In the private sphere, the same function is called public relations, and includes all of the same activities.

In addition, the essential devices of dramatization and personification enable both the public and the private agency to attain visibility or salience in a world where the overabundance of information tends to clog all avenues of information.

Thus, the journalist must work out dramatic devices; thus, the public-relations man, by means of hokum, teasers, and fraudulent stories, gains access to media which allow the favorable story to become visible.

To the extent that journalism makes itself available for such uses, it destroys one of its original basic attributes: that of revealing conflicts between appearances and underlying structures. Instead, it reverses this relationship, in that it contributes to the manufacture of pseudo-appearances, and contributes to a fraudulent public climate.

When this is conducted for a vast number of institutions and organizations, the public life of a society becomes so congested with manufactured appearances that it is difficult to recognize any underlying realities. Fraud itself becomes the basic reality.

As a result, individuals begin to distrust all public facades and retreat into apathy, cynicism, disaffiliation, "privacy," and to forms of psychological sabotage and rebellion. At this point the journalist *qua* journalist can expose the workings of the journalist *qua* public-relations man or *qua* information specialist, if he operates within the framework of a genuine journalistic attitude.

Unfortunately, in a complex society where the sources of information are so varied and numerous, the journalist and his enterprises in their basic news reporting function are frequently forced to accept pseudo-journalism in the form of the press release, the handout, as a substitute for the genuine legwork that results in journalism as a peculiar art form.[7]

---

[7] Daniel J. Boorstin, *The Image, or What Happened to the American Dream,* Atheneum Books, New York, 1962: ". . . our whole system of public information produces always more 'packaged' news, more pseudo-events . . . The common 'news releases' which every day issue by the ream from Congressmen's offices, from the President's press secretary, from the press relations offices of businesses, charitable organizations, and universities are a kind of *Congressional Record* covering all American life. To secure 'news coverage' for an event, . . . one must issue, in proper form a 'release' . . . The release is news pre-cooked, and sup-

The journalistic attitude, when separated from the act of writing itself can become independent of a specific occupation, and can become applied to spheres other than that of juornalism itself, or of bureaucratic information-control and information-manipulation. This is especially true since the social conditions which evoke the journalistic attitude are independent of journalism itself. The complexity and differentiation of modern society force everyone who wishes to communicate with outsiders to do so in manners and styles that flow from the journalistic attitude.

These manners and styles, we have indicated, are: use of drama, personification, concreteness, simplification, imagery, etc.[8]

JOURNALISTIC TREATMENT

The use of the objective techniques of journalism can become independent of professional journalism in its primary and original sense. Once this occurs, it is followed by what we call journalistic treatment, in which the methods of journalism are used in nonjournalistic enterprises.

Journalistic treatment, then, results in a reduction or transvaluation of materials that have been written or developed for nonjournalistic purposes, into new forms which are given journalistic treatment.

Thus, whenever a new idea, institution, technological development, or art work or form appears, in a society imbued with highly developed journalistic tradition, these new forms are almost immediately redeveloped, reported, and publicized, within the framework of journalistic treatment.

Modern art, or a new development in modern art, will become within a relatively short period of time, in journalistic form, invested with the

---

posed to keep till needed . . . The account is written in past tense but usually describes an event that has not yet happened when the release is given out . . . The National Press Club in its Washington clubrooms has a large rack which is filled daily with the latest releases, so the reporter does not even have to visit the offices which give them out. In 1947 there were about twice as many government press agents engaged in preparing news releases as there were newsmen gathering them in . . ." (pp. 17–19).

[8] Israel Gerver and Joseph Bensman, "Towards a Sociology of Expertness," in *Social Forces,* Vol. 32, No. 3, March 1954: . . . "symbolic experts may personify complexities not only for the distant public, but also for insiders under conditions which are sufficiently complex so that these complexities cannot be understood exclusively and immediately in terms of direct participant experience. . . . In many fields of endeavour the symbolic expert is not actually a substantive expert but appears to be one. The symbolic expert is not necessarily a particular living person but may be a complex of traditional evaluations and definitions which become personified . . . such as Rembrandt, Beethoven, Bach, Van Gogh . . . Copernicus and Galileo . . ." (pp. 227–228); also "The interpretive expert who is attached to the organization publicizes the results and creates and maintains the symbolic expert. Both emphasize the magic of scientific technique to the public at large. Both are likely to pressure the substantive experts for publicly demonstrative results, and both are more likely to announce these results before the substantive expert would do so . . ." (p. 229).

glamour, the exoticism, and the "chic-ness" inherent in a "hero" or "star" system.

Given the appeal of the journalistic treatment to audiences whose interests have been aroused and jaded by past journalistic treatment, there is a high probability that the new development will have almost instantaneous currency, via both the form of its treatment, and the media of mass dissemination for such material.

As a result, within the last 100 years, it can be argued that the time interval between the development of a style, a form, an innovation, and its acceptance at a popular level, has been shortened and shortened, so that by now, instant acceptance of innovation is often guaranteed, even before the idea can be properly understood and developed by its protagonists. The individual as worker or innovator is pulled into the world of the stars and of public characters, before he has time to assess, criticize, and develop the innovation.[9] There is a probability that basically good ideas are exhausted, vulgarized, or bowdlerized before their immanent meaning emerges. Or, in the absence of general ideas, effects may be forced by a willful experimentalism and sensationalism. As a further result, changes, innovations, and restructuring develop autonomous virtues regardless of their content.

If this is true of innovators, it is even more true of audiences, who must be prepared, if they wish to be *au courant,* to leap from one journalistically created vogue to another, preferably before the high point of each succeeding vogue has been reached. The artist or innovator must risk the danger of becoming outmoded before he has done his work. And if he values his recently acquired stardom, he must learn to leave that work which becomes passé as new styles replace it. In this sense, the dangers of journalistically induced success are greater than the dangers of obscurity.[10]

---

[9] Bernard Rosenberg and Norris Fliegel, *The Vanguard Artist—Portrait and Self-Portrait,* Quadrangle Books, Chicago, 1965: "by becoming celebrities too soon, many of the young are deprived of experience. The quiet novitiate, an extended period of steady work without public celebration, toughens and inures a man to success. With adequate pre-conditioning and time to grow he can take it in stride. Young men in a hurry, overambitious to start with, who "click" on the marketplace find it difficult to resist the ballyhoo which envelops them" (pp. 57–58).
[10] Rosenberg and Fliegel, *ibid.,* "To get their work before a sizable audience, artists feel they are forced into alien procedures; they must also accept the fact that much of their work will be acquired by aesthetically unappreciative buyers. They are elated when things go otherwise, but there is rarely any expectation that they will. Few can hold out for the "perfect buyer." The size of the purchasing audience often makes it difficult for the painter to know who his "customer" is. The pervasive feeling is that the patron of yesteryear and the collector of yesterday have been replaced by a new and difficult-to-define breed of art consumers—a group whose motivations are at best suspect. Painters seem to accommodate themselves to these realities without excessive rancor. Understandably, they deplore the fact that the buying group . . . is often guided by extraneous considerations . . ." (pp. 194–195).

Other forms of journalistic treatment abound. The most frequent form occurs when journalistic treatment combines with academic treatment, in which the journalistic explicator must explain in journalistic terms how work that is independently valuable was really done, or how it can be understood in more simplified and "basic" terms. This results in the industry of commentaries. But it is not enough for the journalist (or non-journalist who provides journalistic treatment) to simplify, and explain the original work. He must add elements to the original work and to previous commentaries, to justify his present commentary. This results in journalistic "improvements" of the original work by individuals who are not equipped to do that work, but who know how to write about it after the fact.

Thus, as one example, in the field of music, one of the largest critical industries is that of writing annotations—explanations of the systems of interpretation of such works as the Beethoven piano sonatas, and other works. Thus, for many original compositions, there are a host of editions, each annotated by an inferior musical mind, each introducing his own personal idiosyncrasies, preferences, and personality into his revision of Beethoven's works. In the process, the original annotations by Beethoven are frequently lost or obscured, so that at a later date, a more advanced critical industry is forced to emerge, that of the discovery of the musical work in its original form. It is a tribute to recent musicological scholarship that it has discovered the necessity for removing the barnacles of journalistic and critical growths.

THE JOURNALISTIC ATTITUDE OUTSIDE OF JOURNALISM

Perhaps the simplest form of application of the journalistic attitude outside of journalism is the use of this device by a scholar or expert toward his peers who presumably have the experience, the background, and the technique, at levels which do not require the simplifications of the journalistic attitude. Why this should occur so pervasively is not directly perceivable. Perhaps the habits of mind developed from dealing with outgroups become so pervasive that the trained professional presents his own materials to other trained professionals in ways that previously would have been considered inappropriate.

But other factors might be relevant as well. Among these is the technicization of society to the extent that professional, technical, and occupational peers are so distant from each other that one treats them as strangers, as laymen, or as a general public. In addition, even within relatively narrow technical areas, the amount of information to be transmitted is so great that to gain the attention of one's peers requires the development of dramatic devices, which in specialized technical areas necessarily falsifies the data so presented. And, thirdly, the amount of specialization even within a narrow technical area is so great that the specialist does not feel confident that another specialist in a closely related field will be able to understand specialized information in its own terms.

Regardless of the cause, then, the specialist as receiver of information must guard himself against the forms of information which might mislead him, even though he himself, in his dissemination of information, might use the very same forms.

Related to these activities is the journalistic institution of the book review, as a means of coping with the immense flow of information to be found in technical and specialized journals. This flow is so great that the academician is often forced to subscribe to reviewing journals, and to engage clipping services and graduate students to provide abstracts, digests, and quotations from unread books, monographs, and articles.

Beyond this, the specialist in all areas must deal with audiences that do not and cannot have the technical equipment to comprehend his communication in the sense that he himself (hopefully) understands. He must thus become his own journalist.

The physician, for example, has a choice between developing or presenting descriptions of disease which are beyond the comprehension of the layman, or of vulgarizing the description. He may, in vulgarizing it, seek to maintain the essential accuracy of the description, or he may slant the information in order thereby to dramatize himself and the quality of his practice.

If, on the other hand, he presents the data in its original technical complexity, he can do so in order to be accurate but incommunicable, or he can do it in order to evoke the aura of science, of complexity, and of professional esotericism, and thus to magnify and enhance his professional image. In this latter case, the use of the professional mysteries of science in its original complexity can become a public-relations device in all the implications of the term. The example of the M.D. in dealing with the layman is the prototypical case, in which the complexity of a given field promises opportunity for material and psychological profitmaking through either the simplification or the complexity of the specialized worlds of the expert. Given the size of the various lay audiences for the products and by-products of specialization, the opportunities for such simplification or manipulation are boundless. Thus, the textbook industry, swollen in size by the number of subcollege and college students, provides vast opportunities for the specialist to simplify his materials so that they can be packaged and sold to neophytes in the field. A successful textbook can provide more material rewards than an entire career of undramatic but serious technical work. The problem involved in such work is: what level of simplification, dramatization, and personification, etc., is necessary to present the neophyte with a working knowledge of a field?

At the present time, some publishers employ professional writers to write textbooks in fields with which they are not familiar, and engage prominent academicians to sign their names to them. The journalistic attitude treats the audience as a consumer; i.e., knowledge disseminated should excite, stimulate, titillate, entertain, surprise, and evoke temporary interest, but no effort, on the part of the consumer.[11] But a genuine educational attitude must treat the neophyte as a producer, must teach him to handle the complexity, the difficulty, the abstractness, etc., of the data of his field, in its own terms. When the journalistic attitude becomes part and parcel of the process of education, then the would-be producer is treated as a consumer, and his perception of the field is distorted by the importation of dramatic elements into what might be serious, undramatic, persistent, long-term technical work. Disillusion must follow an orientation to work based on the expectation of the drama of work. In addition, the student develops the expectation that scholarship should be easy, dramatic, or exciting, and that his major function is to be entertained.

But more important, the use of the dramatization inherent in the journalistic attitude delays the entry of the neophyte into the work itself, so that it is difficult for him to learn what work is. Again, to repeat a cliché, he learns *about* the work, instead of learning the work.[12]

Ordinarily, genuine learning takes place as part of and during the process of working on real problems in real settings. Knowledge is acquired if and when it becomes useful to the worker in the solution of specific problems. The salience of a technique or a method, or of information, is immediately perceptible in the light of the ongoing activity. Knowledge is never "theoretical," distant, or "abstract," because it is never removed from the problem.

However, with the substitution of the consumer's point of view for the producers point of view, via the journalistic presentation of non-journalistic material, the pseudo-glamour and drama of the activity puts distance between the image of the work and the work itself, and creates a gap which cannot be closed until problems are confronted in the attempt to solve them.

---

[11] See Bensman and Lilienfeld, *op. cit.*

[12] William James, *The Principles of Psychology*, Henry Holt & Co., New York, 1896: "There are two kinds of knowledge broadly and practically distinguishable: we may call them respectively *knowledge of acquaintance* and *knowledge-about* . . . In minds able to speak at all there is, it is true, some knowledge about everything. Things can at least be classed, and the times of their appearance told. But in general, the less we analyze a thing, and the fewer of its relations we perceive, the less we know about it and the more our familiarity with it is of the acquaintance-type. The two kinds of knowledge are, therefore, as the human mind practically exerts them, relative terms. That is, the same thought of a thing may be called knowledge-about it in comparison with a simpler thought or acquaintance with it in comparison with a thought of it that is more articulate and explicit still" (pp. 221–222).

JOURNALISM IN INTELLECTUAL WORK

We can distinguish between two ideal types: "self-generated" material, and "externally generated" material. "Externally generated" material is that material which is developed simply to meet a deadline, and to fill up space in a journal, or to fill time, as at a broadcast or popular lecture. "Self-generated" material includes all those books, art works, scientific reports, etc., which are developed out of concern for immanent empirical or theoretical problems, out of perceptions or improvisations on the part of a writer or artist which are seen by him as promising and requiring further development or investigation, but which do not inherently take their genesis from any immediate external pressures. Preoccupation with the material alone generates the work to be done.

A major component of journalistic activity and of the journalistic attitude is, however, the pressure to have something written in time for a deadline, and of sufficient volume to fill the space or the time allotted to it. Thus, to paraphrase Karl Kraus, the journalist must write though he has nothing to say, and the journalist has something to say, because he must write.[13] If, under this pressure, it happens that the journalist finds something to say, all is well, but if not, he must then have recourse to various devices.

One such device is to have recourse to that body of material which is, as described above, "self-generated," and to "popularize" it; to explain it, "clarify" it, make it amusing, dramatic, etc.; or, one may go further, and in the process may "improve" the material by removing from it what one takes to be offensive to an audience, or merely boring, or threatening to one or another interest group. Here, the journalistic attitude actually acts as mediator between two groups; toward the public, it decides what that public is fit or able to understand; toward the producers of work, it will dictate what may or may not be appropriate for an audience presumed to be rather lightly educated and having a short attention span. If this journalistic attitude becomes internalized by a producer of self-generated material, he may become induced to shape this material in ways different from those he would have chosen had he not anticipated public responses. Thus, the extent to which the journalistic attitude becomes internalized may serve to distinguish various classes of intellectual work from one another, ranging from speculative philosophical works, works of high art, original theoretical treatises, on one hand, to works of popularization, "introductions to" one or another subject matter field, "how to" books, anthologies, readers, etc.

---

[13] Karl Kraus, *Beim Wort Genommen*, p. 212. This and many other features of the journalistic attitude were first developed in the polemic and satirical writings of Kraus, e.g., "A historian is often just a journalist facing backwards," *ibid*, p. 215, Kösel Verlag, Munich, 1955.

The distinction made here between "self-generated" and "externally generated" material actually describes the opposite poles of a continuum; at one end stands, in Schutzian terms, the expert, at the other end the journalist or the propagandist; somewhere in between stands the ideal of the well-informed citizen.[14]

JOURNALISM AND PROPAGANDA

Part of journalistic treatment is to present arguments for or against a given issue or idea in such a way that the arguments of the advocate can be understood and accepted without access to the complexities, the abstractness, or the legality of the issue in its original form. Most points of contention in a complex society are necessarily dealt with in terms of their legalistic, technical, administrative, procedural, and economic complexities. Their substantive merits are not always immediately visible, especially as major substantive points will frequently turn on relatively innocuous but abstract legal or technical issues.

The technical aspects of these arguments are often difficult to present, especially to lay publics, are difficult to understand, and have difficulty in evoking loyalties and passions, even though these arguments may involve the life and growth of major groups and institutions within a society. The journalistic treatment of these issues provides a solution to this problem. Journalistic treatment can, at its highest technical development, provide a description of a story concerning the issue, in which no argument is ever made. The selection of words and the emotional loading of words, the slanting of the treatment of events, the sympathetic or unsympathetic treatment of personalities, all constitute the application of journalistic treatment to complex issues. The argument is contained in the form of the treatment of the story, rather than in the argument itself. Argumentativeness, that is, the ideologized form of argument, is frowned upon from this point of view, for the ideological or logical form of the argument might alert the individual to the idea that an argument is about to be presented. This would signal him to adopt a critical stance in which the argument is to be subjected to logical or empirical criticism, or simply to emotional resistance. The argumentative form in its essential nature implies that the "other" should be prepared to resist the argument, and invites him to develop counter-arguments. In using these subtler forms of journalistic treatment, the individual is not alerted to the polemic situation, is not warned, alarmed, and invited to use his critical faculties. The argument is presented in such a way that the individual does not know that an argument has been made. If the presentation is successful, he accepts the argument as a series of facts, emotional tones, or as a reality. He has

---

[14] See Schutz, *op. cit.*, pp. 122–123 and 132–133.

been manipulated. This form of journalistic treatment finds its most concentrated expression in "mood advertising," in magazines like *Time,* and in indirect public-relations campaigns. It is for this reason that ideology as a form of disputation has become unfashionable in a world where journalistic treatment replaces ideological or polemic treatment of controversial issues.[15]

JOURNALISM AND PUBLIC RELATIONS

The public-relations attitude requires a state of continuing innovation, i.e., one needs to have a story re something new and exciting occurring within an institution at relatively frequent intervals, so that press releases, handouts, etc., can be made. Since the routine operation of an able and efficient institution is not by itself newsworthy, items that are newsworthy have to be manufactured. This means that new programs, new ideas, new personnel, the employment and application of new technology, machinery, and inventions, all evoke the possibility of newsworthy public relations. When public prominence becomes a primary need for an institution, then the rate of innovation must be increased, even though on technical or intrinsic grounds there is no need for innovations. Thus, perfectly good ideas, programs, or techniques can be instituted even when unnecessary or misapplied, because their use is not intrinsic to the operation itself but only to the publicity. This is very important when related to considerations of the rate of innovation or change within a society. In a public-relations world paralleling the development of innovation in the arts the use of public-relations techniques accentuates the rate of innovation and application beyond what one might expect from the need for such inventions or their usefulness.

At this point, for such reasons, the journalists as cynics or as insiders in large-scale institutions who are aware of both the public image and the internal image of the operations of institutions tend to be skeptical regarding the applicability of publicly valued technology to the institutions, such as high-powered computers, team teaching, teaching machines, operations research and linear programing, PERT systems, systems development, and many other similar ideas. As indicated, the concepts of

---

[15] A by-product of this process is the development of a special journalistic language which conveys meaning by indirection, and by surrounding familiar words with new emotional connotations to convey meanings opposite to their traditional sense. In addition, new language, spelling, and coinages, elisions, acronyms, etc., are invented. These debase the traditional usages of language, and introduce new forms of barbarisms. They do however, facilitate the above-described journalistic treatment of events. See, for example Dwight MacDonald, *Against the American Grain,* Vintage Books, New York, 1962, pp. 12–13, and the essays, "The String Untuned," pp. 289*ff,* and "The Decline and Fall of English," pp. 317*ff.* See also Karl Kraus, *Untergang der Welt durch Schwarze Magie.*

change, innovation, and restructuring, all develop positive connotations regardless of their substantive content.

Under this heading come such developments as the establishment of university chairs at very high salaries, for which an outstanding scholar is hired, primarily to enhance the "image" of the institution, the establishment of special curricular and educational programs and degrees, new construction of various types, and the establishment of various research institutions.

JOURNALISM AND BOOK PUBLISHING

The "migration" of the journalistic attitude out of journalism and into various fields has been discussed above. Its effects in the publishing of books may be briefly indicated. There are three principal loci of the journalistic attitude in book publishing. A firm may wish to fill out its catalogue in various subject-matter fields, for reasons of competition, and so may commission or generate books (often in the trade called "non-books") which would otherwise not have existed. Textbooks for schools, and "Introductions to etc." for the general trade, come under this heading; thus, externally generated material. The second principal locus of the journalistic attitude in publishing is frequently located among editors. An editor who receives a manuscript from a subject-matter expert may find that its obscurity and disorganization of style require reordering clarification. In so acting, the editor operates with the model of the well-informed citizen. But a book editor may follow another model, as described above (pp. 144–145), namely that of anticipating audience responses to original, controversial, difficult, or otherwise disturbing material, and may in the process truncate, disfigure, or suppress a book entirely. This may be operative especially in the area of translating a major work into English, either from a foreign language or from technical jargon, in the process of which the editor frequently announces his deletion of considerable amounts of material which he has considered as not suitable for the English reading audience. Here, the editor has clearly adopted the journalistic attitude.

A third locus of the journalistic attitude in the field of book publishing lies in the area of reference books. The development of a complex technological world has led to a need for information about areas and fields which an individual cannot be expected to know at first hand. For "the well-informed citizen" reference books may serve a legitimate purpose, but they of course may serve journalistic purposes as well, enabling a popularizer, rewrite man, commentator, etc., to assume the mantle of a depth of scholarship he does not possess. The influence of journalism may be shown not only in the proliferation of encyclopedias, textbooks, and reference books, but in the regularity with which they are revised and updated to include the latest developments, to the point that they come to resemble periodicals in being constantly updated, even though the developments may be peripheral or of ephemeral interest in a subject-matter field. This has been called "instant knowledge."

It remains to consider one more function of the journalistic attitude as it is applied not only by journalists, but also by scholars in the presentation of their fields.

At any given point in time in any field of study, the sum total of working knowledge in that field is fragmentary, unorganized, and quite frequently disorganized. A vast number of individuals are working on a series of frequently unrelated problems, while others are working in terms of intellectual traditions which are often competing, antagonistic, or anomalous. An accurate summation of knowledge in any field, for those who expect a unified, organized, progressive march of science and knowledge, might prove discrediting to that field. When public-relations purposes are first in mind, the presentation of the state of the art or science requires that the field be presented in an orderly, systematic, unified, and dramatic front, such that all professionals have two orders of data about their own field: *(1)* one, of inside knowledge which determines the operative data for the professional in his intramural work; *(2)* the other, which is a pseudo-integration of his field, which is presented to laymen, neophytes, the general public, and to outside administrators whose work impinges on the field.

This may appear at times to be necessary; however, the attempt to treat the pseudo-order as genuine often results in a falsification of the entire field. Further, when a field is full of the conflicts and divergences of approach which is necessarily characteristic of a search for knowledge based upon free inquiry by independent minds, then the problem of orientation to the various approaches within a field is important not only to the public and to the neophyte, but also to the professional. Here, the scholar as intramural journalist operates by defining "lines" along which an individual can find avenues for the expression of loyalties and commitments. At the same time, the lines define the "enemies," and, with it, those schools of thought and approaches that are to be ignored, disdained, or accorded low prestige.

One conceptual device which has become a major part of the critical industry, and which can be traced back to journalistic usages, is that of the establishment, within a subject-matter field, of a pantheon of the major historical figures of that field. Many a survey of a field for the beginner or for the layman has the model of a guided tour of the pantheon, in which the leading figures are brought forth, their lives and works briefly sketched using the techniques of personification, simplification, etc., and then their relative merits are established. Thus, one figure will be established in the main section, others in the lesser wings of the pantheon, according to their stature, as established by the critic describing the field. Thus, we will be given ratings of the figures in the field: the greatest and most important, the second after him, the next, and so on. This device of establishing, as though once and for all, the relative merits of the figures in a field, is journalistic in nature, borrowed primarily from the sports pages of the newspapers, in which individual athletes and teams are rated either according to their standings in the season's competition, or on the basis of long-term statistical measures, or according to public-opinion polls.

In scholarly work, this results in the use of the biography or the anthology of biographical essays in which the life, the glamour, the travails and tragedies, and the agonies and ecstasies of creative geniuses are presented as a substitute for the great work or thought itself.

This industry of commentaries also serves the political organization of an intellectual field in the problem of according recognition for original or valuable work which originates in an opposing or rival school of thought. If the concepts or findings developed are really indispensable, they can be gradually and anonymously appropriated, and sources for the appropriation can be eventually cited only among scholars of an allied, rather than an opposing, school of thought.

In the above cases, we have presented the development of a phenomenological model of an attitude as related to a specialized kind of treatment of information appropriate to given types of social and societal structures. The journalistic attitude is evoked by the needs for the periodistic presentation of images of the world to distant publics who are not able to comprehend necessary parts of their world in terms of their direct experience. At its best, journalism performs an extremely important function in the creation, re-creation, and re-emphasis of world images. It transvalues the world even in the process of trying to present it.

But the very development of the skills and techniques for manifesting such images demonstrates the possibility of use and abuse by those who would use the journalistic attitude for nonjournalistic purposes, and in a society in which the need for information is so great that, when fulfilled, the fulfillment cancels the need by drowning the public in information.

But in addition to the overabundance of information presented to the society at large, one finds that public-relations treatment has been imported into most other areas of life, even by those who are not professionally aware of using the journalistic attitude. Thus, when journalistic treatment begins to pervade a great part of the major institutions and the thinking processes of a society, the creation of images and appearances becomes an autonomous process in which the institutions, techniques, and methodologies of the society become the product of the attempt to manufacture images.

Thus, the image is no longer a by-product of the generic and necessary operation of an institution, but becomes a major *raison d'être* for the institution. When this occurs, the activities and operations of the institutions are depleted of their intrinsic meanings, and extrinsic meanings become the only meanings available. If and when this occurs, self consciousness concerning image-building, that is, the journalistic attitude and journalistic treatment, results in the devaluation of all intrinsic meanings. The articulation of meaning thus becomes a device by which meaning is depleted of its content.

THE OVERVIEW: FURTHER READINGS

Books

Boorstin, Daniel, *The Image,* Harper and Row, New York, 1964.

Heckscher, August, *The Public Happiness,* Atheneum, New York, 1962.

Hoggart, Richard, *The Uses of Literacy,* Beacon, Boston, 1961.

Lowenthal, Leo, *Literature, Popular Culture, and Society,* Pacific Books, Englewood Cliffs, 1961.

Read, Herbert, *To Hell with Culture,* Schocken, New York, 1963.

Rivers, William L., and Schramm, Wilbur, *Responsibility in Mass Communication,* rev. ed., New York, 1963.

Toffler, Alvin, *The Culture Consumers: A Study of Art* and *Affluence in America,* St. Martins Press, New York, 1964.

Articles

Fontaine, A., "Mass Media: A Need for Greatness," *Annals of the American Academy,* May 1967.

Kronenberger, L., "Staggered Culture," *Nation,* Sept. 20, 1965.

Mannes, M., "They're Cultural, but Are They Cultured" *New York Times Magazine,* July 9, 1961.

Mott, F. L., "Twentieth Century Monster: the Mass Audience," *Saturday Review,* Oct. 8, 1960.

Read, H., "Art and Alienation," *Saturday Review,* Dec. 2, 1967.

Resnick, H. S., "What Culture? What Boom?" *Atlantic Monthly,* Feb. 1967.

Steinem, G., "What Culture?" *Look,* Nov. 26, 1968.

Toffler, A., "Quantity of Culture," *Fortune,* Nov. 1961.

Television

There is no more sensitive barometer of mass culture than television. As frightening as it may seem to elitist critics, television is the mass medium *par excellence.* There is at least one television set in 95% of American homes, and approximately one in three of these sets is a color receiver. Unqustionably, the American public has invested billions of dollars in the hardware of television, an investment made primarily to be entertained. Clearly, anyone of television's millions of viewers who witnessed the events of President Kennedy's assassination realizes that the medium touches and affects him in diverse ways far beyond the pleasure principles of entertainment. Whether as viewers we deprecate or extoll television, it is difficult to imagine our lives without it.

Granted that any medium that feeds its public seventeen or eighteen hours a day of programs rarely reaches and sustains creative heights. Still, television's uniqueness as a mass communications medium (as McLuhan continually reminds us) goes beyond the ephemeral banalities of a Red Skelton or *Hee Haw.* It alone has the technological capacity to unite hundreds of millions of viewers all over the world, as it did in the Apollo 11 moon landing, in a simultaneously shared experience.

Do the "shared experiences" provided by television foster the global solidarity of men, or does television unwittingly promote only an illusion of human participation without the substance of real interaction? Gerhart Wiebe discusses this problem in his essay in this section. He suggests

151

that given the psychological setting of television viewing it is difficult for this medium to exercise more than an entertainment function. Thus the use of television for didacticism is at best tenuous no matter how well-intentioned the program may be.

Nicholas Johnson, a member of the Federal Communications Commission, is one of the most outspoken critics of commercial television. A prolific writer, his commentaries on the state of electronic communication evoke a response from the National Association of Broadcasters not unlike General Motors' impression of Ralph Nader. In his essay for this section, Mr. Johnson accuses the television industry of negligence in coming to grips with the social problems that foster violence. He earnestly proposes some wedges that would force the broadcasting industry to "improve its contribution to our society." These encompass such things as an alternative system of public broadcasting, more citizen participation in evaluating a station's performance prior to renewal of its license by the F.C.C., and more accessibility to television for people of varying viewpoints.

Although his orientation in television is almost opposite to Commissioner Johnson's, Fred W. Friendly examines another facet of the way the mass media deal with violence, in this case the war in Indo-China. How did television cover what Michael Arlen aptly termed "The Living Room War"?

Since Mr. Friendly himself was president of CBS News during the escalating days of the Tonkin Gulf resolution and thereafter, the critical thrust of his "poor performance" assessment applies to *all* who were in key editorial positions at the time. Rather than an "I told you so" attitude, Friendly candidly admits his own mistakes. He cites specific cases, (U. Thant's peace appeal in 1965, for example), and sadly concludes, "There has been such obfuscation, distortion, and mishandling of interpretation concerning Vietnam—such a climate of distrust between the Government and the news media—that the end result may be a deadly sense of cynicism."

Finally, in this section, Richard J. Stonesifer, although sharing both

Messrs. Johnson's and Friendly's caveats about the medium, is not without hope that television can be a "great technological force working for good in our world." He agrees with André Malraux that cinema and television constitute the two most powerful modern influences on men's mind but that these media regrettably are allowed to cater to what is least civilized and most elemental in man's nature.

The implacable cynic will say that these appeals cannot be satiated and that the mass media, particularly television, exist to exploit these tastes. Dr. Stonesifer demurs to this line of reasoning by urging educators, opinion-makers of all persuasions, and individual citizens of taste to become today's action-critics of television.

The Social Effects of Broadcasting*

By Gerhart D. Wiebe

THE PROBLEM

The central problem to be explored may be introduced by reference to two familiar observations. The first is that the broadcast media in the United States generate huge audiences. The second is that the content of very popular programs is generally regarded by members of the intellectual community as being light, superficial, trivial, and in some cases, as vulgar and even harmful. That is, it is regarded as of little use, or even as being negative in its effects on the quality of people's lives.

The remarkable size of audiences is regularly documented by the rating services, and the calibre of program content is deplored by critics and scholars with comparable regularity. The situation is documented and deplored, but it is not explained. The implications for broadcasters devoted to education, the arts, and religion are serious and perplexing. The media seem to open the way to intellectual, cultural, and spirited refinement for the millions, but the millions elude the proffered enlightenment, preferring the light, the superficial, the trivial.

The problem is familiar. So also are several prescriptions for improvement. It is frequently argued that tastes would improve if people were exposed to programs of high calibre. But the record is discouraging. Consider for example, the twenty-year history of Sunday afternoon concerts by the New York Philharmonic Orchestra, broadcast by the Columbia Broadcasting System. Despite vigorous promotion, a good and unchanged position in the schedule, and excellent production, the audience for these concerts did not grow nor did it ever achieve a size considered minimal

---

* Reprinted by permission of the author. This paper was prepared for World Assembly of the World Association for Christian Broadcasting in Oslo, Norway, in June 1968. A version of this speech appeared in the *Public Opinion Quarterly,* Vol. 33, Winter 1969–1970.

for successful commercial programs. Similar examples can be cited in other content areas. Opportunity is apparently not enough.

A second proposal for improving public taste would restrict program offerings to those of high intellectual, moral, and artistic quality for a period of time long enough so that discriminating taste would become habitual and normative among the public. Given twenty years of consistently high quality programming, it is suggested, people would not tolerate programs of comparatively low quality. This proposal, like the earlier one, finds rough going in the light of experience. After some twenty years of programming in England, controlled exclusively by the BBC, commercial television came to England. With it came some commercial entertainment series from the United States which, according to the present hypothesis, should have found a very chilly reception. But that isn't what happened.

The appetite in the United States for light diversion on television is perhaps most thoroughly and authoritatively documented in the late Dr. Steiner's book, *The People Look At Television* (Knopf, 1963, especially Chap. 6).

Steiner studied both attitudes toward television and actual viewing behavior by the same respondents. He found that people verbalized more interest in fine programming than their viewing behavior demonstrated. And further, that although the college educated respondents differed in their program preferences from the less well educated in expected ways, the degree of difference was remarkably small. For example, during periods when cultural entertainment, public information programming, and light entertainment were available simultaneously, a random distribution of the audience would allocate 33% to each type. Since light entertainment predominates most of the time, the simultaneous availability of the three types constitutes an unusual opportunity for those with discriminating tastes to tune in quality programming. Still, even during these periods, 40% of those with college education chose the light entertainment (Steiner, p. 201).

The impact of broadcasting ranges from slight to sweeping appeal and we have no explanation for this phenomenon beyond the descriptive observation that in general there is a tendency toward an inverse relationship between audience size and the cultural merit of the program.

This observation is not peculiar to our time nor is it observed exclusively with reference to the broadcast media. With the introduction of printing in the fifteenth century the treasures of learning, which had been severely restricted, were henceforth as widely available as was literacy. But instead of grasping the unprecedented opportunities for enlightenment, the public appetite, from the first decades of printing, was for the light, the superficial, the trivial, and it may be added for the scandalous, the seditious, and the vulgar. H. A. Innis, in his book, *Empire and Communication,* quotes a seventeenth century observation that "The slightest pamphlet is nowadays more vendable than the works of learnedest men." This pattern even appears to pre-date the press. A pre-Gutenberg example appears in the relation of the wandering minstrel to the public appetite for messages that offend refined taste.

I share the concern expressed by musicians, scientists, poets, dramatists, educators, critics, and others of comparable intellectual accomplishment regarding the apparent waste, the loss of opportunity in the general preference for the trivial while the mass media make it practical for the peoples of the earth to advance their education, to refine the quality of their experience, and to share in the finest achievements of human intellect. But I no longer believe that what has been called "the taste for trash" can be remedied by scholarly exhortation or by attempting to teach good taste or by increasing budgets for cultural offerings. The best hope of understanding this problem, and then perhaps improving the situation in some degree, seems to lie in posing the hypothesis that the observed behavior has positive psychological utility. If this utility can be identified, then perhaps, as we learn to understand it, we may be able to apply this knowledge to the general welfare. In pursuing this path I have set aside observations on the media themselves, turning instead to patterns of psychological and sociological behavior that are independent of the media.

Two such patterns will be discussed. Both appear to contribute to a theoretical understanding of media audience behavior. The first is the apparent difficulty with which we humans aquire *the concept of the other.* By "the other," I mean simply a person other than oneself.

RELUCTANCE TO COPE WITH THE OTHER

We begin with findings relating to infant egocentrism. The term egocentrism is used here, not in the pejorative sense of selfishness or conceit, but simply in nonvalued reference to preoccupation with self. The psychologist Piaget has contributed much to our understanding of infant egocentrism. His ingenious experiments indicate that when an object at which an infant had been looking is screened from his view, it is not just hidden. For the infant, it apparently ceases to exist. (Jean Piaget, *The Construction of Reality in the Child,* Basic Books, New York, 1954, pp. 20–40.) There is a learning process that precedes the child's recognition that objects and persons actually occupy space and exist as permanent and substantial entities.

The child's early preoccupation is in the discovery and maintenance of self. His success in this early learning obviously depends on the solicitude of the mother or her substitute, but the relationship is not reciprocal. The human infant levies demands on the outside, and apparently perceives the objects and persons that make up the outside as ephemera among which he seeks satisfaction—primarily nourishment and comfort.

Unlike some animals, human young do not mature without elaborate care. Studies of the so-called feral children and others raised in near isolation demonstrate the dependence of the maturation process on association with others. I believe, however, that developmental psychologists have tended, until recently, to underemphasize the unilateral, taking orientation of the young child's interaction with the outside.

The traditional concept of the mother-child relationship during the first year as one of reciprocal love must be re-examined. Findings suggest that in the normal process of maturation during the first year, a child cannot be said to perceive another person as an individual, autonomous, other. The psychoanalyst Rene Spitz has recently reported experiments showing that the treasured smiling response, observed at about six months, is elicited equally well by mother or stranger, male or female, old or young, even by a person in a mask, so long as the face presented to the baby is animated, and is presented head on. (Rene Spitz, *The First Year of Life,* International Universities Press, Inc., New York, 1965, p. 86.)

The crucial period of the infant's dependence on solicitous care by a specific individual during the last part of the first year appears to be largely a need for stimulation and nourishment in accustomed ways as the child practices his early and precarious attempts to cope with the insubstantial outside.

Mothers know that a two-year-old, left in reach of an age mate treats him as if he were a thing rather than as another person. The concept of *the other* has not yet emerged.

Margaret Greene, in her charming and informative book, entitled *Learning to Talk* (Harper and Brothers, New York, 1960) reports this incident: "Heather," she writes, "when three, enjoyed building a snowman, and when he was complete, ... begged him to talk to her. ... But he didn't and her eyes filled with tears of disappointment. Quickly I made some kind of remark in a gruff snowman-sort-of voice. Immediately, she laughed and in a moment was impersonating him herself."

The point here is that the bright child of three who probably had a vocabulary of some 600 or 800 words was still so vague in her perception of other people *as people* that she thought the snowman she had just helped to make would be able to talk. And then after momentary disappointment, she didn't mind that he couldn't.

Moving along in time, we come to a series of findings on six-year-olds reported by Piaget. He observed and then studied what he called egocentric language among six-year-olds. He divides egocentric speech into three subgroups—repetition, monologue, and collective monologue. The point in common among these three categories is that the speech is not addressed to anyone. Although the presence of others sometimes seems to serve as a general sort of stimulus, the child during egocentric speech apparently does not actually address other persons. He seems rather to "talk past them."

Piaget found that something over a third of the speech of the six-year-olds he studied fell into this category of egocentric language. (Jean Piaget, *The Language and Thought of the Child,* The Humanities Press Inc., London, 1952, Chap. 1.) Thus, even in groups of six-year-olds where language would seem so obviously to be a tool of interaction, much of their behavior contradicts this expectation, and consciousness of the other is only inconsistently observed.

More recently the work of Dr. Melvin H. Fiffer (*Journal of Personality,* 1960, **28,** 383–396) proceeding from that of Piaget indicates that the ability to assume different social perspectives is only gradually developed, that it is correlated with chronological age, and that its measurement, still far from precise, may well turn out to be an important index to psychological maturation.

These findings from developmental psychology document the relatively slow emergence of the concept of *the other* in contrast with the precocious development observed in what might be called the unilateral achievement of self-expression and need gratification.

Such concepts as sharing, mutuality, reciprocal relationships, empathy, service, interaction, all of these positively valued concepts, endlessly stressed in the process of socialization, turn out, on examination, to refer to rather sophisticated, psychologically demanding processes which call for a well-developed sense of *the other.* They are essentially *social* processes which require the surrender or at least the inhibiting of the early deep-seated pattern of egocentrism.

How does this late developing sense of *the other* relate to media behavior? The relationship seems quite direct when it is recalled that the media, by definition, remove *the other.* The media present printed symbols or sounds or images, but never persons. The media reinstate the opportunity to enjoy the early pattern of taking, without deference to the reciprocal needs of the giver. The media offer immediate need gratification without "paying the piper." They provide the sense of experience without the accommodation required in true participation. One may weep or laugh or hate or fear and escape the necessity of acknowledging the physical existence and the reciprocal demands of those others who arouse the emotion. The media allow the audience member to resume the infantile posture observed by Piaget in which, when the stimulus is removed, it ceases to exist. Reality, on the other hand is beset with people and things that resist, react, counterthrust, encroach, demand. Small wonder then, if when people are weary, frustrated, and crowded, they embrace the media where people and things are ephemera—as they once were for each of us. It is characteristic of popular media content that it maximizes immediate need gratification, minimizes intellectual effort, and excuses the audience member from acknowledging a substantial *other.*

But the point appears to have reference to broadcasters as well as to audiences. Broadcasters tend to consider their mission accomplished when their message is released. The sequel is seldom investigated except by commercial broadcasters who are disciplined by the buying responses of those others out there. Perhaps this deep-seated reluctance to cope with *the other* influences behavior on both the sending and the receiving sides of the media.

It is often said that the media bring people into contact with each other. We must be more literal. The media only transport symbols. They do not bring people together. On the contrary, the media stand between people. The media may *invite* subsequent interaction, but they do not and cannot provide it.

This is the first idea that seems to merit careful study. Facility in personal interaction comes late in the developmental sequence. The phenomenon of talking past people rather than with them is familiar. Interpersonal frictions plague adult life. The fact that media messages provide the illusion of interaction together with immunity from *the other* seems to relate a basic psychological factor to media audience behavior.

THREE ASPECTS OF SOCIALIZATION

The second point relates to the process of socialization, and particularly to the individual's resistance to this process.

Socialization has been defined by the Hartleys as "the process by which an individual becomes a member of a given social group." (Eugene L. and Ruth E. Hartley, *Fundamentals of Social Psychology,* Alfred A. Knopf, New York, 1952, p. 202.) The identity of the "actor" and the "acted-upon" in this process is clear. The group requires. The individual adjusts. Ruth Benedict says "culture exists in the habituated bodies and minds of the people who belong to the culture." Margaret Mead reminds us of the extent and pervasiveness of this habituating process in observing "that the growing child is systematically patterned in every detail, in posture as well as in gesture, in tempo as well as in speech, in his way of think-ing as well as in the content of his thinking, in his capacity to feel as well as in the forms which his feelings take." (Hartley and Hartley, pp. 202, 203.) Professor George Herbert Mead built an entire school of thought around the concept of the individual as a cumulative composite of the environmental feedback he himself experiences.

The Hartleys add to this "nature-nurture" discussion what they call a psychological truism, namely "that all development depends on both the innate qualities of the organism and the external environment in which the organism exists" (p. 203). This recognition that both the innate nature of the individual and the demands of a structured environment are involved in the process of socialization may indeed be self-evident, but its importance has perhaps been underestimated. Each human being has inherent tendencies, innate patterns, which would direct growth in ways different from those that actually occur if this growth were uninfluenced by the requirements of the group.

It follows that the socializing process does not simply mold inert stuff. It is rather the modifying and changing of a dynamic system, deflecting it from the course it would otherwise follow. Socialization is alteration of forces in motion, and when one alters the direction of forces in motion, he encounters resistance. This resistance to socialization is familiar, but it has received rather little attention from social psychologists except as an inconvenience that must be handled in order to proceed with the essential business of qualifying the individual for group membership.

The typical example of socialization is the parent training the child. The child's changing toward normative behavior is seen as the essential content of socialization. Seen from the child's point of view, however, the process of socialization is a series of defeats and compromises in which what he wants to do must bow to what he is required to do. In a good parent-child relationship, the child's sacrifice is in some degree compensated by praise and other rewards. Even so, however, viewed as the child sees it, the process is coercive. Impulse is inhibited. Spontaneity is modified. The individual must adapt to the group prescription.

It would be remarkable indeed if all of this compromising, substituting, bending, changing, and giving up to which the growing human is subjected during socialization did not generate a deep and persistent pattern of counteraction. Behavior that fits this expectation is, of course, familiar. In addition to their outright opposition against prescribed behavior, the young retreat and restore themselves somewhat through secret retaliation against authority figures. In solitude and with peers, in both manifest and symbolic behavior, in their play and their fantasy, children assuage the discomforts of the socializing process and find some degree of psychic face-saving that makes the losing battle tolerable.

From the child's point of view, socialization can be seen as consisting of three sorts of behavior. The first includes learning, refinement, or improvement in the direction of prescribed behavior. The second includes the relatively stable and acceptable everyday behavior at one's achieved level of socialization. The third includes the retaliatory, assuaging, and indemnifying counterstrokes just discussed. These three phases of socialization may be referred to as *directive, maintenance,* and *restorative.* For convenience these labels will be used as if they referred to discrete categories. Actually I see them as zones in a continuum.

The process of socialization is inconceivable without communication. Professor Merton calls communication the instrument of social process. If we view socialization in terms of the messages involved, we find the *directive, maintenance,* and *restorative* aspects of socialization clearly identifiable in corresponding categories of messages.

Directive messages come from authority figures. They command, exhort, instruct, persuade, and urge in the direction of learning and new understanding that represent progress in the estimation of authority figures. Directive messages call for substantial and conscious intellectual effort on the part of the learner.

Maintenance messages include all the every-day messages sent and received in the customary business of living. They call for relatively little conscious intellectual effort.

Restorative messages, including individual fantasies, are those with which the individual refreshes himself from the strain of adapting, the weariness of conforming. They provide an interim for the reasserting of impulse. The child, seemingly with perverse precociousness, articulates his restorative messages as he screams, complains, jeers, taunts, defies, says forbidden words, and gleefully plays out cruel and destructive fantasies.

The socializing process is concentrated in childhood and youth, but it continues in adult society. Many elements of media audience behavior seem to fit into a coherent pattern if they are viewed as responsive to *directive, maintenance,* and *restorative* messages in the context of adult socialization.

In beginning this exploration we must differentiate between the purpose a message is meant to perform by the sender, and the purpose it actually performs for the receiver. Communicators tend to speak primarily in terms of the sender's intention. But much of the following discussion is couched in terms of the receiver's reaction. Certainly the two points of view cannot be assumed to be identical. We will frequently refer to a message that is intended as *directive,* but received as *maintenance,* or one that is intended as *maintenance* but is received as *restorative.*

DIRECTIVE MEDIA MESSAGES

Directive messages call for learning, for changed behavior, new differentiations, refined perceptions. Such responses require the expenditure of intellectual effort on the part of the neophyte. In childhood, these changes customarily take place, whether in home, church, or school, in a disciplined face-to-face relationship. This pattern appears to extend beyond childhood. If a person can read and has access to a good library, the prerequisites for a college education would appear to be present. But professors who command the respect of their students continue to be required. The printed Bible has not made the church obsolete nor has it reduced the role of the clergy. Granting the existence of the exceptional few with unusually high motivation, it seems to be true that the large majority of people do not move to higher spiritual, artistic, or intellectual levels except within the disciplined context of face-to-face pupil-teacher relationship.

The media do not provide this relationship. Certainly they can supplement and enrich the learning process. But I find no evidence that by themselves they will bring about substantial learning among the rank and file of a society—presumably because most people will not expend the required intellectual effort in the absence of an authority figure. This generalization finds strong support in Dr. Wilbur Schramm's book *The New Media,* published in 1967. (UNESCO, International Institute for Educational Planning, 1967). In this survey of education by radio and television in many nations, Dr. Schramm reviews twenty-three projects. He reports many reasons for failure or success. But in no instance does he report success in the absence of a face-to-face relationship between the learner and a teacher, monitor, parent, or comparable authority figure.

Once an individual has achieved a unit of learning within such a structured situation, he may voluntarily enter the audience for broadcasts featuring these recently acquired concepts and insights, but he then experiences such programs as *maintenance* messages rather than as *directive.*

MAINTENANCE MEDIA MESSAGES

Who then among the general public, tunes in media messages intended to educate, to elevate, to present substantial new insights, to refine? Even though such programs do not command very large audiences, people do tune them in. The answer, in substantial degree, seems to lie in the familiar observation that the large majority of those who tune in religious programs are already religious. Most of those who tune in a science series already understand science at about the level presented in the series. I believe Dr. Paul Lazarsfeld first documented this pattern of media audience behavior years ago when he found that the audience for a radio series entitled "Americans All, Immigrants All," changed significantly from program to program, each nationality group tending to tune in the program about itself, but being less faithful in listening to the programs about other nationality groups where more learning would have been achieved. *Thus, given a range of choice, media audiences, through a self-selecting process, tend to turn messages intended to be directive into maintenance messages.*

Stated differently, given a permissive situation with available alternatives, people avoid the intellectual effort required in a true learning situation, preferring messages that review or embellish or elaborate what they already know. This, in essence, is what *maintenance* messages do. News programs will serve as the prototype of media *maintenance* messages. They are intended to extend or up-date the audience member's information about the world he already knows, and they seem, in general, to perform that function. They do not call for disciplined intellectual effort.

There is a second way in which messages intended as *directive* are transformed into a *maintenance* function. Child psychologists have long known that children, exposed to programs intended for adults, perceive what they are ready to perceive, but miss many points that seem quite obvious to adults. I hypothesize that this same pattern persists in adult audiences so that in listening to a news program, a political speech, or a sermon, people hear what they can comfortably accommodate in the context of their present knowledge, and very little more.

When do media messages move audience members to subsequent action? The answer, in terms of the present hypothesis, must be sought in a combination of at least three factors. First, in the existing readiness, the present predisposition among audience members to react. Secondly, in the social provisions for facilitating such action, and third, in the appeal of the message. Media messages themselves are only one of at least three factors. Seen in this way, the limitations as well as the power of media messages become less obscure. By way of illustration, consider the general experience in the United States regarding advertising on the one hand and sermons about brotherhood on the other. Successful advertising, if my observations are correct, succeeds not by the power of the medium and the message alone. Its success depends on these elements in combination with at least two other factors, namely a favorable predisposition among the audience and a retail establishment that facilitates the completion of the requested behavior. Sermons on brotherhood, on the other hand, though they have been numerous, and often eloquent, as in the case of the late Dr. King, bring very little positive change in behavior. Why? Our hypothesis suggests that audience members are not favorably disposed toward changing accustomed ways, and further, that social and institutional arrangements tend to impede rather than to facilitate changed behavior in this area.

Perhaps an interim summary is appropriate here.

1. Broadcasts seldom move audience members to substantially new and higher levels of intellectual, artistic, or spiritual experience except when such messages are received in the context of a face-to-face teacher-pupil relationship.
2. Given a permissive situation with available alternatives, media audiences avoid *directive* messages which require disciplined intellectual effort.
3. Those who choose programs intended to be *directive* are in many

cases those who already know all or most of what is presented so that the program is *perceived,* not as *directive,* but as *maintenance.*

4. Others with less understanding who attend to *directive* messages tend to hear only what can easily be accommodated in the context of present knowledge, and so, again, experience the *directive* message as *maintenance.*

5. Programs *intended* as *maintenance* messages, for example news shows, and in religious broadcasting, programs of familiar hymns and sermons that stay on ground familiar to the general public—such programs are received as *maintenance,* and are preferred over *directive* messages.

6. *Maintenance* media messages are the counterpart of everyday conversation. They review, elaborate, extend the audience member's experience at approximately his achieved level of sophistication and accordingly do not demand the disciplined intellectual effort characteristic of substantial learning experiences.

7. Maintenance media messages like conversations with acquaintances lead to responsive behavior provided the suggested behavior is a feasible and convenient extension of an existing predisposition.

RESTORATIVE MEDIA MESSAGES

What of the *restorative* category? The adult counterpart of youthful protest and retaliation against authority figures appears spontaneously and apparently inevitably as an antidote for the strictures of organized living. Mimicry, caricature, pantomine, satire, gossip, ribald ballads, malicious rhymes, broad humor, and scandalous drama were popular before the days of Gutenberg. They have appeared persistently through history and have withstood the most harsh attempts at suppression. Their counterparts in media content fit our expectations for *restorative* messages and lend strong support to the hypothesis that the *restorative* aspect of socialization is served copiously, though of course not exclusively, by the kinds of media content that seem so deplorable to those with discriminating taste.

Restorative media messages feature crime, violence, disrespect for authority, sudden and unearned wealth, sexual indiscretion, and freedom from social restraints. The themes of these most popular media messages seem to make up a composite reciprocal of the values stressed in adult socialization.

Because the very essence of restorative messages is their token retaliation against the establishment, the likely effect of well-intentioned attempts by proponents of high standards to "improve" popular *restorative* content is clear. Let's take out the violence, we say, and substitute a theme of cooperative problem solving. The *restorative* essence is removed and *directive* content is substituted. The psychological utility of the message is altered and its popularity is correspondingly reduced.

It was observed earlier that messages intended as *directive* are often received as *maintenance*. There is a similar mechanism that appears regarding the *maintenance* and *restorative* categories. News messages, for example, are supposed to inform the audience about happenings of significance so that audience members will be better able to maintain a clear view of the world in which they live. But if we examine the contents of news programs or of newspapers, it is hard to escape the conclusion that other criteria have also gotten into the picture. Crime, scandal, sports, accidents, fires, and comics receive more attention than would seem to be justified by their true importance in shaping our concept of the reality in which we live. I believe their prominence can be better understood by seeing them as *restorative* messages in a *maintenance* format.

The *restorative* mechanism hypothesized here, has as perhaps its chief merit the characteristic of releasing hostility in small amounts. Seen in quantitative terms, it follows that if an individual or members of a subgroup or indeed of a whole society perceive themselves as oppressed or frustrated in nearly intolerable ways, the *restorative* mechanism may not suffice to accommodate the required relief. In such cases, messages intended as *restorative* may trigger overt retaliatory behavior in grossly antisocial forms. The pattern suggested here is familiar in its childhood version where, among inhibited children, fun often escalates into fighting.

Throughout history, authority figures, and particularly those in autocratic hierarchies have kept anxious watch on popular satire, comedy, songs, rhymes, stories, dramas, and festivals. There is always the question of whether retaliation against the establishment will remain token, and so, restorative, or whether it will override social restraints. The answer is appropriately sought, less in analysis of message content than in the psychological condition of audience members. Perhaps one measure of a society's health is the degree to which it can tolerate the *restorative* mechanism without risking escalation into action that threatens some segment of the social structure.

Should a society regulate the amount of restorative content to which adults have access? In childhood the amount of make-believe, petty sadism, and noisy play is limited by authority figures. But in adulthood, given a permissive situation and available alternatives among media offerings, no comparable institutionalized regulation exists. Whether such regulation should exist is a matter of momentous significance, but it is beyond the scope of the present discussion.

The two mechanisms discussed here interact with each other and, no doubt, with many other factors too. In concluding, I will attempt to relate *reluctance to cope with the other,* successively with *directive, maintenance,* and *restorative messages,* and to do this with reference to the current and crucial problem of race relations in the United States.

RELUCTANCE TO COPE WITH THE OTHER
AND DIRECTIVE MESSAGES

We have observed that *directive* media messages, that is messages intended to bring about substantial learning, do not generally succeed unless they tie in to a structured, face-to-face teacher-pupil relationship. This observation even applies to the teaching of content that does not call for changes in interpersonal behavior, such as mathematics, or the understanding of serious music. If in addition to the intellectual work required, the lesson also requires greater refinement and discipline in interpersonal relationships, reluctance to cope with the other intervenes to further reduce the chances of success.

If Dr. Martin Luther King had expected whites who heard his broadcast messages to substantially increase their understanding of Christianity and also to reflect this understanding in their behavior toward blacks, he would have been unrealistic according to the present hypotheses. But apparently he had no such expectations. He did not stay in the broadcasting studio. Even though he had no special liking for the hurly-burly of the pavements, he carried his mission into face-to-face interaction and it is there that changed behavior was accomplished.

The present formulation appears to accommodate the remarkable and tragic fact that in a nation where Christianity has been the dominant religion for three centuries, and where few living adults have not heard Dr. King and others of like mind via the media, behavior patterns toward blacks have not changed substantially except as such behavior has been compelled by law or in physical confrontations.

RELUCTANCE TO COPE WITH THE OTHER
AND MAINTENANCE MESSAGES

We have mentioned two ways in which messages intended as *directive* are transformed into *maintenance* messages at the receiving end. Although I do not have specific data to prove it, it seems highly likely that both mechanisms have transpired with regard to media messages on civil rights. First, the media audiences for civil rights leaders, I speculate, have included a much larger proportion of those already favorable to the civil rights campaign than of those who oppose it. Secondly, among those who favor the civil rights campaign, such exhortations as those of Dr. King have been selectively perceived so that, for example, northern audience members could sincerely agree that blacks should be served in southern restaurants while still feeling no need to take specific steps in breaking through established patterns of discriminatory housing in their own northern neighborhoods.

Maintenance messages provide additional information that extends, updates, and elaborates one's view of reality at approximately his achieved level of socialization. The media perform this function in the United States with remarkable success. By doing so, audience members with a predisposition or readiness to behave in a given manner may be notified of a new or improved social situation in which such behavior is facilitated. Thus the announcement of a civil rights protest demonstration, according to our hypothesis, will activate that small proportion of audience members who have reached the conviction that they must participate in such an activity, and the probably somewhat larger number of those who like to go as spectators to see what happens while avoiding the personal commitment of actual participation. The very large majority, however, receive the news, perceive it in a manner consonant with their existing view of things, and then continue behaving very much as they ordinarily do.

RELUCTANCE TO COPE WITH THE OTHER AND RESTORATIVE MESSAGES

The function of the *restorative* mechanism is to provide token retaliation against authority figures. It reverses deference lines so that the acted upon becomes the actor. In order to insure victory in these forays of the weak against the strong, *restorative* messages typically involve symbolism, metaphor, or fantasy. Institutionalized ceremonies, often featuring costumes and masks, provide occasions in many societies where the weak are guaranteed immunity in acts that would bring stern punishment in everyday life. Either by social or by individual devices, the *restorative* mechanism evades the danger of a forthright test of power with established authority figures. The *restorative* mechanism thus accommodates reluctance to cope with the other.

We have hypothesized a tendency on the part of media audience members to transform messages intended as *directive* or *maintenance* into *restorative* messages if content lends itself to such transformation. This opportunity is certainly present in the case of speeches, documentaries, and televised news reports on the civil rights campaign. In one way or another, these messages say "we are oppressed and we appeal for justice." But the white audience member, preoccupied with his own frustrations, can easily perceive such a message as symbolic reference to his own problems, and so, treat such reports of social reality as if they were drama. Black audience members, on the other hand, many of whom carry nearly explosive accumulations of resentment, are more likely to experience such messages in a personal and literal rather than metaphorical sense, and in some cases are stimulated to gross antisocial behavior.

The hypothesis that civil rights media messages are intuitively transformed for purposes of individual psychological utility seems to contribute toward an understanding of several perplexing and tragic reactions to the assassination of Dr. King; for example:

1. The fact that a significant number of blacks reacted to the death of this disciple of nonviolence with violence.

2. The fact that a significant number of whites reacted to this tragic event by asking, "What can *I* do?"—a question sincerely asked by many whites, but heard as the ultimate in hypocrisy by blacks.

3. The fact that capable and resourceful leaders in the white community preach the efficacy of orderly and peaceful appeals for change, but seem to respond only to the destruction of property or the dislocation of commerce.

The media offer the illusion of participation together with immunity from interaction with the other. The media make it easy to look and pass on, a pattern that has been familiar since ancient times:

"A certain man went down from Jerusalem to Jericho, and fell among thieves, which stripped him of his raiment, and wounded him, and departed, leaving him half dead. And by chance there came down a certain priest that way: and when he saw him, he passed by on the other side. And likewise a Levite, when he was at the place, came and looked on him, and passed by on the other side. But a certain Samaritan, as he journeyed, came where he was: and when he saw him, he had compassion on him, and went to him, and bound up his wounds . . ." St. Luke: 10.

The media make it easy to pass by on the other side.

Television and Violence: Perspectives and Proposals*

By Nicholas Johnson

John Gardner has characterized as perceptively as anyone the process of which this Commission on Violence is a part.

> The Paul Revere story is a very inadequate guide to action in a complex modern society. It was all too wonderfully simple. He saw danger, he sounded the alarm, and people really did wake up. In a big, busy society the modern Paul Revere is not even heard in the hubbub of voices. When he sounds the alarm no one answers. If he persists, people put him down as a controversial character. Then someday an incident occurs that confirms his warnings. The citizen who had refused to listen to the warnings now rushes to the window, puts his head out, nightcap and all, and cries, "Why doesn't somebody tell me these things?" At that point the citizen is ready to support some new solutions, and wise innovators will take advantage of that fact. A man working on a new air-traffic control technique said recently, "I haven't perfected it yet, but it wouldn't be accepted today anyway because people aren't worried enough. Within the next two years there will be another spectacular air disaster that will focus the public mind on this problem. That will be my deadline and my opportunity."

The same thing can be said, of course, for the "air disaster" represented by the chemicals and soot that fill the air, and our lungs. It also applies to the air pollution problem which is ours today: radio and television.

The academicians, research scientists, and critics have been telling us for years of television's impact upon the attitudes and behavior of those who watch it. They cite very persuasive statistics to indicate that television's influence has affected, in one way or another, virtually every phenomenon in our present day society.

There are sixty million homes in the United States and over 95% of

---

* Reprinted from the *Television Quarterly,* Vol. 8, No. 1, by permission of the author and publisher. Copyright 1969 by the National Academy of Television Arts and Sciences. This article is based on Mr. Johnson's testimony before the Commission on Violence in the United States.

them are equipped with a television set. (More than 25% have two or more sets.) In the average home that set is turned on some five hours and forty-five minutes a day. The average male viewer, between his second and sixty-fifth year, will watch television for over 3000 entire days—roughly nine full years of his life. During the average weekday winter evening nearly half of the American people are to be found silently seated with fixed gaze upon a phosphorescent screen, experiencing the sensation of its radiation upon the retina of the eye.

Americans receive decidedly more of their "education" from television than from the 19th century institutions we call elementary and high schools. By the time the average child enters kindergarten he has already spent more hours learning about his world from television than the hours he would spend in a college classroom earning a B.A. degree.

So the problem is not that the modern-day Paul Reveres have not warned us, or even that they have not told us what to do. The problem is similar to that described by John Gardner's air-traffic controller: "Today even the most potent innovator is unlikely to be effective unless his work coincides with a crisis or a series to crises which puts people in a mood to accept innovation."

We have by now experienced television's own form of "air disaster" in a series of crises.

During 1966 and 1967 there was a dramatic upsurge in the amount of rioting and demonstrations in our cities. As Pat Moynihan reminded us all in the NBC Special, *Summer 1967: What We Learned,* "We have no business acting surprised at all this. The signs that it was coming were unmistakable." The signs had been reported by those who had been observing, studying, and writing about the plight of black Americans. But these modern-day Paul Reveres were either not heard or were put down as "controversial characters." So the crises came, captured our attention, and put us in a mood to listen. The Kerner Commission was established, conducted a thorough-going investigation, and wrote a thoughtful and persuasive report. In this report the Commissioners found it necessary to devote an entire chapter to the mass media. They found themselves at every turn with evidence of the implications of the mass media in a nation wracked with civil disorders. There was not only the matter of the relationship between the reporting of incidents and subsequent action. They also discovered a shocking lack of communication and understanding between blacks and whites in this country. As they put it, "the communications media, ironically, have failed to communicate." But Dr. Martin Luther King had told us very much the same thing: "Lacking sufficient access to television, publications and broad forums, Negroes have had to write their most persuasive essays with the blunt pen of marching ranks."

The Kerner Commission report had no more than found its way to the coffee tables of white suburbia before this nation was torn apart once again—this time with the agonizing, heartwrenching sorrow accompanying the assassinations of two beloved and controversial leaders, Dr. Martin Luther King and Senator Robert F. Kennedy. Once again a crisis, once again national attention, once again a commission—this time yours. And as you have searched about for the causes of violence in our land you, too, have inevitably had to confront the evidence of the implications of the mass media. And you have discovered in the literature, as Dr. Albert Bandura, Professor of Psychology at Stanford University, has recently said, that

> It has been shown that if people are exposed to televised aggression they not only learn aggressive patterns of behavior, but they also retain them over a long period of time. There is no longer any need to equivocate about whether televised stimulation produces learning effects. It can serve as an effective tutor.

But it has taken another crisis to make us listen.

A National Commission was not even permitted to conclude its deliberations and issue a report before the third in this recent series of crises hit the American people. It was, of course, the confrontation at Chicago and the Democratic National Convention. This has been the subject of the report submitted to you by Daniel Walker, *Rights in Conflict.* In this instance the mass media were not only implicated in the confrontation, they were an active party. (In the words of the Walker Report, "What 'the whole world was watching,' after all, was not a confrontation but the picture of a confrontation, to some extent directed by a generation that has grown up with television and learned how to use it.") Subsequently television was the target for an outpouring of public criticism. But once again we find that we have not been without forewarnings of the impact of corporate television upon the process of politics and the subject matter and method of news reporting—to cite but two books from this year, Harry Skornia's *Television and the News,* and Robert MacNeil's *The People Machine* (a study that gives special attention to the involvement of television in the American political process).

How many more crises must we undergo before we begin to understand the impact of television upon *all* the attitudes and events in our society? How many more such crises can America withstand and survive as a nation united? Are we going to have to wait for dramatic upturns in the number and rates of high school dropouts, broken families, disintegrating universities, illegitimate children, mental illness, crime, alienated blacks and young people, alcoholism, suicide rates, and drug consumption? Must we blindly go on establishing national commissions to study each new crisis of social behavior as if it were a unique symptom unrelated to the cause of the last? I hope not.

Of course, no one would suggest that television is the *only* influence in our society. But I hope that this Commission will possess both the perception and the courage to say what is by now so obvious to many of the best students of American society in the 1960s. There is a common ingredient in a great many of the social ills that are troubling Americans so deeply today, that is the impact of television upon our attitudes and behavior as a people, and we ought to know much more about it than we do. One cannot understand violence in America without understanding the impact of television programming upon that violence. But one cannot understand the impact of television programming upon violence without coming to grips with the ways in which television influences virtually all of our attitudes and behavior.

When we speak of television's influence we may be referring to any one of four factors. *(1)* The impact of television watching (without regard to program content) upon the way we spend our time, and so forth. *(2)* The impact of television programming upon our attitudes and behavior. *(3)* The ways in which television is "used" by groups seeking "news" coverage; its creation of and effect upon events actually or potentially portrayed on television. *(4)* The results of abuses by television: serving economic self-interests, self-censorship, staging of events, and so forth. With these directions in mind let's examine the industry's arguments.

TELEVISION'S IMPACT AND THE INDUSTRY'S BIG MYTH TECHNIQUE

Whenever the question arises of the impact of television programming upon the attitudes and behavior of the audience, industry spokesmen are likely to respond with variants of three big myths. *(1)* We just give the people what they want. The "public interest" is what interests the public. The viewer must be selective, just as he would be in selecting magazines. He gets to choose from the great variety of television programming we offer. He can always turn off the set. *(2)* Entertainment programming doesn't have "any impact" upon people. It's just entertainment. We can't be educational all the time. *(3)* We report the news. If it's news we put it on; if it's not we don't. It's as simple as that. We can't be deciding what to put on the news or not based upon its impact upon public opinion or national values. We can't be held responsible if someone sees something on television and goes out and does the same thing.

The Myth of Serving Public Taste

Regulation of broadcasting was begun at the Federal level under two basic premises. One was that without regulation users could not allocate frequencies among themselves. The other premise was that the spectrum was a limited resource, owned by the public, and that its use was to be permitted under license to private users. These private users, given the right to use a public resource that was valuable, were expected to return public benefit; their use of the resource was to be in the "public interest." When faced with competing applicants for use of the spectrum the FCC, an arm of the Congress, was to choose the one who would best serve the public interest.

We have come a long way since those days. It is useful to remember the hopes and ideals expressed at the beginnings of this industry. But it should be clear that the performance of the broadcasting industry is quite different from what the drafters of the Communications Act might have expected.

By and large broadcasting today is run by corporations which have a virtual lease in perpetuity on the right to broadcast. These corporations are like all other businesses, they are interested in maximizing their profits. The value of their business, including the right to broadcast, is directly related to the profits the business returns. And this value is realizable in a virtually free market for the sale of established stations. This is not to be viewed as a hostile judgment of these men and corporations. America has been served well by the profit motive in a competitive system. It does suggest, however, that the system today is different from that envisioned by those who molded the present regulatory framework.

But we must examine the economic incentives as well. Broadcasters act to gain as large an audience as possible, and the audience is attracted by the broadcasters' programming. Programming is chosen for the number of people it can command. Its selection need not reflect the intensity of the audience's approval, or what the audience would be willing to pay for the programming. In fact, the incentive to get the largest audience regardless of good taste has on occasion driven the networks to arrogant indifference to "what the public wants." The Dodd Committee Report refers to an incident in which an independent testing organization conducted an advance audience reaction test of an episode of a series show for a network. Of the men, women, and children tested, 97% believed there was too much emphasis on sex, and 75% felt the show was unsuitable for children. The network ignored the findings, and televised the episode.

The concentrated ownership of the national television market and its effect on programming is clear. The dominant impact of the three networks on programming is apparent for first-run programming and syndication alike, since much of syndication is network reruns. Roughly 85% of the prime-time audience watches the networks. Each network is trying for its slice of that 85%, and for most purposes that audience is viewed as homogeneous, that is, one person counts the same as another in the ratings. Thus no programming will be shown by the networks unless aimed at the whole audience, and each network strives to gain no less than one-third of the audience.

This is not to suggest that stations and networks engage exclusively in profit-maximizing behavior, but rather that this is the predominant component of their business motivation. And, I repeat, I am not now passing moral judgment on this behavior. I am simply pointing out that this is the system we have created, and that it is significantly different from the one that was envisioned thirty years ago.

Stations and networks sometimes do engage in programming that is not the most profitable available to them. Thus, Justice Hugo L. Black was permitted to speak to some ten million Americans in December 1968 on CBS. The concern of CBS was not only whether its relatively low programming costs were covered by the commercial revenue from that program (there were eight products or services advertised), but the "opportunity cost" in the form of *additional* return CBS might have obtained from regular programming aimed at a larger audience. (It is also concerned about losing audience on the shows to follow, since there is some viewer carry-over from program to program. This is another force that has precluded advertisers from sponsoring public service shows of their own choosing, even when they are willing to pay handsomely for the opportunity.) Of course, there are many responsible individuals, associated with stations and networks alike, who realize the great power of this medium for good and who try to use it. The point is simply that each of them is limited by the functioning of the system—a system that doesn't allow significant deviation from the goal of profit maximizing. Some have left commercial broadcasting because of that constraint.

It should be clear why attempts to affect the quality of programming have often focused on changing the rules of the system. Shouting exhortations at an edifice is a poor substitute for some structural changes. Proposals have been designed to open up the program procurement process, to restructure the affiliate-network relationship, to increase the number of TV stations, and to make rules concerning the types of programming to be presented. Educational broadcasting, as well as the potential of subscription television and cable television, are fundamental responses to the functioning of the present commercial system.

The Myth of Lack of Impact

Dean George Gerbner of the Annenberg School of Communications has stated:

> In only two decades of massive national existence television has transformed the political life of the nation, has changed the daily habits of our people, has moulded the style of the generation, made overnight global phenomena out of local happenings, redirected the flow of information and values from traditional channels into centralized networks reaching into every home. In other words it has profoundly affected what we call the process of socialization, the process by which members of our species become human.

He continued:

The analysis of mass media is the study of the curriculum of new schooling. As with any curriculum study, it will not necessarily tell you what people do with what they learn, but it will tell you what assumptions, what issues, what items of information, what aspects of life, what values, goals, and means occupy their time and animate their imagination.

I share Dean Gerbner's sense of television's impact upon our society. Many spokesmen for the broadcasting establishment, however, do not. And so I would like to anticipate their rebuttal with a little more discussion of the matter.

The argument that television entertainment programming has no impact upon the audience is one of the most difficult for the broadcasting industry to advance. In the first place, it is internally self-contradictory. Television is sustained by advertising. It is able to attract something like $2.5 billion annually from advertisers on the assertion that it is the advertising medium with the greatest impact. And it has, in large measure, delivered on this assertion. At least there are merchandisers, like the president of Alberto Culver—who has relied almost exclusively on television advertising and has seen his sales climb from $1.5 million in 1956 to $80 million in 1964—who are willing to say that "the investment will virtually always return a disproportionately large profit." The manufacturer of the bottled liquid cleaner, "Lestoil," undertook a $9 million television advertising program and watched his sales go from 150,000 bottles annually to 100 million in three years, in competition with Procter and Gamble, Lever Brothers, Colgate, and others. The Dreyfus Fund went from assets of $95 million in 1959 to $1.1 billion in 1965 and concluded, "TV works for us." American industry generally has supported such a philosophy with investments in television advertising increasing from $300 million in 1952 to $900 million in 1956 to $1.8 billion in 1964 to on the order of $2.5 billion this year. Professor John Kenneth Galbraith, in the course of creating and surveying *The New Industrial State,* observes that, "The industrial system is profoundly dependent upon commercial television and could not exist in its present form without it. . . . [Radio and television are] the prime instruments for the management of consumer demand."

The point of all this was well made by the sociologist Dr. Peter P. Lejins. He describes four studies of the impact upon adult buying of advertising directed at children. Most showed that on the order of 90% of the adults surveyed were asked by children to buy products, and that the child influenced the buying decision in 60 to 75% of those instances. He observes, If the advertising content has prompted the children to this much action, could it be that the crime and violence content, directly interspersed with this advertising material, did not influence their motivation at all?" There is, of course, much stronger evidence than this of the influence of violence in television programming upon the aggressive behavior of children which I will discuss later. My point for now, however, is that television's salesmen cannot have it both ways. They cannot point with pride to the power of their medium to affect the attitudes and behavior associated with product selection and consumption, and then take the position that everything else on television has no impact whatsoever upon attitudes and behavior.

The evidence of the impact of television advertising upon human attitudes and behavior tends to be confirmed by the growing reliance upon visual materials in education and propaganda. Films and television material are being ever more widely used throughout our schools and colleges, and in industrial and military training. Studies tend to support assertions of their effectiveness. We appropriate on the order of $200 million annually for the United States Information Agency on the theory that its activities do have an impact upon the attitudes of the people of the world about the United States. Presumably those who go to the expense and effort to "jam" the programming of the Voice of America and Radio Free Europe share this view.

Nor is our evidence of commercial television's influence limited to the advertising. Whatever one may understand Marshall McLuhan to be saying by the expression "the medium is the message," it is clear that television has affected our lives in ways unrelated to its program content. Brooklyn College sociologist Dr. Clara T. Appell reports that of the families she has studied 60% have changed their sleep patterns because of television, 55% have changed their eating schedules, and 78% report they use television as an "electronic babysitter." Water system engineers must build city water supply systems to accommodate the drop in water pressure occasioned by the toilet flushing during television commercials. Medical doctors are encountering what they call "TV spine" and "TV eyes." Psychiatrist Dr. Eugene D. Glynn expresses concern about television's ". . . schizoid-fostering aspects," and the fact that "it smothers contact, really inhibiting inter-personal exchange." General semanticist and San Francisco State President, Dr. S. I. Hayakawa asks, "Is there any connection between this fact [television's snatching children from their parents for 22,000 hours before they are 18, giving them little 'experience in influencing behavior and being influenced in return'] and the sudden appearance . . . of an enormous number of young people . . . who find it difficult or impossible to relate to anybody—and therefore drop out?"

A casual mention on television can affect viewers' attitudes and behavior. After *Rowan and Martin's Laugh-In* used the expression, "Look that up in your Funk and Wagnalls," the dictionary had to go into extra printings to satisfy a 20% rise in sales. When television's *Daniel Boone,* Fess Parker, started wearing coonskin caps, so did millions of American boys. The sales of Batman capes and accessories are another example. Television establishes national speech patterns and eliminates dialects, not only in this country but around the world; for example, "Tokyo Japanese" is now becoming the standard throughout Japan. New words and expressions are firmly implanted in our national vocabulary from television programs, among them Rowan and Martin's "Sock it to me," or Don Adams' "Sorry about that, Chief." Television can also be used to encourage reading. The morning after Alexander King appeared on the late-night Jack Paar show his new book, *Mine Enemy Grows Older,* was sold out all over the country. When the overtly "educational" Continental Classroom atomic age physics course began on network television 13,000 textbooks were sold the first week.

Politicians evidently think television is influential. Most spend over half of their campaign budgets on radio and television time, and some advertising agencies advise that virtually all expenditures should go into television time. When Sig Mickelson was President of CBS News he commented on "television's ability to create national figures almost overnight . . ."—a phenomenon which by now we have all witnessed.

The soap operas have been found to be especially influential. Harry F. Waters recently did a piece in *Newsweek* on the soap operas. He estimates they have a loyal following of about 18 million viewers, and contribute much of the networks' $325 million daytime revenue.

> Judging from the mail, the intensity of the audience's involvement with the soap folk easily equals anything recorded in radio days. . . . It may even provide an educational experience. Agnes Nixon, a refreshingly thoughtful writer who has been manufacturing soaps for fourteen years, likes to point out that episodes concerning alcoholism, adoption and breast cancer have drawn many grateful letters from those with similar problems.

Seizing upon this fact, educators in Denver and Los Angeles have used the soap opera format to beam hard, factual information about jobs, education, health care, and so forth, into the ghetto areas of their cities. The Denver educators' soap received one of the highest daytime ratings in the market. There is, of course, no reason to believe the prime-time evening series shows have any less impact.

Indeed, as Bradley S. Greenberg of Michigan State reported, "40 percent of the poor black children and 30 percent of the poor white children (compared with 15 percent of the middle-class white youngsters) were ardent believers of the true-to-life nature of the television content." And he went on to underline further the "educational" impact of all television.

> Eleven of the reasons for watching television dealt with the ways in which TV was used to learn things—about one's self and about the outside world. This was easy learning. This is the school-of-life notion—watching TV to learn a lot without working hard, to get to know all about people in all walks of life, because the programs give lessons for life, because TV shows what life is really like, to learn from the mistakes of others, etc. The lower-class children are more dependent on television than any other mass medium to teach these things. They have

fewer alternative sources of information about middle-class society, for example, and therefore no competing or contradictory information. My only caveat here is that we do not know what information is obtained through informal sources. Research is practically non-existent on the question of interpersonal communication systems of the poor. Thus, the young people learn about the society that they do not regularly observe or come in direct contact with through television programs—and they believe that this is what life is all about.

Knowing these things, as by now all television executives must, society is going to hold them to extremely high standards of responsibility.

What do we learn about life from television? Watch it for yourself, and draw your own conclusions. Here are some of my own. We learn from commercials that gainful employment is not necessary to high income. How rare it is to see a character in a commercial who appears to be employed. We learn that the single measure of happiness and personal satisfaction is consumption, conspicuous when possible. Few characters in televisionland seem to derive much pleasure from the use of finely developed skills in the pursuit of excellence, or from service to others. "Success" comes from the purchase of a product—a mouthwash or deodorant, say—not from years of rigorous study and training. How do you resolve conflicts? By force, by violence, by destroying "the enemy." Not by being a good listener, by understanding or cooperation and compromise, by attempting to evolve a community consensus. Who are television's leaders, its heroes, its stars? Not educators, representatives of minority groups, the physically handicapped, the humble and the modest, or those who give their lives to the service of others. They are the physically attractive, glib, and wealthy. What is to be derived from a relationship between man and woman? The self-gratification of sexual intercourse and little else—whatever the marital bonds may or may not be. What do you do when life throws other than roses in your hedonistic path? You get "fast, fast, fast" relief from a pill—a headache remedy, a stomach settler, a tranquilizer, a pep pill, or "the pill." You smoke a cigarette, have a drink, or get high on grass or more potent drugs. You get a divorce or run away from home. Or you "chew your little troubles away." But try to "work at" a solution, assume part of the fault lies with yourself, or attempt to improve your capacity to deal with life's problems? Never.

The Myth of "News"

News and public affairs is, by common agreement, American television's finest contribution. The men who run it are generally professional, able, honorable, and hard-working. To the extent the American people know what's going on in the world much of the credit must go to the networks' news teams. It's a tough and often thankless job. Eric Sevareid has said of trying to do network news that the ultimate sensation is that of being eaten to death by ducks. These men have fought a good many battles for all of us—with network management, advertisers, government officials, and news sources generally. We are thankful. And, by and large, I think we ought to stay out of their business, with the exception, perhaps, of providing them protection from physical assault. I would not for a moment suggest that either your Commission, or mine, ought to be providing standards for what is reported as "news." At the same time, I think that neither of us need feel under compulsion to avoid any comment whatsoever on the subject. And the point of my particular observation is simple, and its explanation brief.

Whenever one begins discussing the violence quotient in televised news, the broadcasting establishment (far more often than the thoughtful newsmen themselves) is apt to come out with something about the First Amendment and journalistic integrity. The suggestion is made that there is a socially desirable, professionally agreed-upon definition of "news"— known only to those who manage television stations and networks— which is automatically applied, and that any efforts to be reflective about it might contribute to the collapse of the Republic.

My view is simply that this is nonsense, and that the slightest investigation of the product of journalism will demonstrate it to be such. As Robert Kintner once wrote, "But every reporter knows that when you write the first word you make an editorial judgment." "Education" does not become news until the *New York Times* sets up a special Sunday section on it. Whether and how "television" is reported as news in *Newsweek* depends in part upon what they call the sections of the magazine—and those headings change. The same is true of "science" or "medicine." We do not get much meaningful reporting about the federal budget, the choices it represents and the processes by which they were made. We could get more simply because an editor or a newsman took an interest in the matter.

I would agree with Reuven Frank's statement in the Dec. 16, 1968, *TV Guide* that we benefit from living in a nation with "free journalism," which he defines as "the system under which the reporter demands access to facts and events for no other reason than that he is who he is, and his argument is always accepted." I want the check of the news media upon government officials, including myself. But I do not believe, and he does not suggest, that free journalism need function as irresponsible journalism, completely free of check, comment, or criticism from professional critics, a concerned public, and responsible officials. Journalists can alter what subjects they report and how they report them, and they do. They can do this in response to a sense of professional responsibility. They often have. I ask no more; we should expect no less.

THE IMPACT OF TELEVISION PROGRAMMING ON VIOLENCE

The principal thrust of my position is that television programming—commercials, entertainment, and public affairs—is one of the most important influences on all attitudes and behavior throughout our society. To the extent that television "reflects" society, it is but a reflection of an image that has earlier appeared upon its screen. This is a perspective that I believe necessary to an understanding of the impact of television upon violence. It is an understanding that prompts one to reevaluate the most appropriate mission and focus of this Commission, and those that inevitably will follow.

There is not much point in my simply repeating the evidence that has accumulated in the literature and been brought to your attention. It is, after all, the findings and assertions of the scientific community on this point—not mine—that are most relevant to your inquiry.

The Interim Report of the Dodd Committee in 1965 concluded:

> [I]t is clear that television, whose impact on the public mind is equal to or greater than that of any other medium, is a factor in molding the character, attitudes, and behavior patterns of America's young people. Further, it is the subcommittee's view that the excessive amount of televised crime, violence, and brutality can and does contribute to the development of attitudes and actions in many young people which pave the way for delinquent behavior.

This was back in the days when we investigated "juvenile delinquency." And the subcommittee bearing that name had been brought to the need to study the amount of violence in television programming as early as 1954. Subsequently, it concluded, "If the 1954 findings suggested the need for . . . a closer look at television programming as it relates to delinquency, the 1961 monitoring reports were shocking by comparison." By 1964 it concluded, "the extent to which violence and related activities are depicted on television today has not changed substantially from what it was in 1961. . . ."

Nor have things changed much today. *The Christian Science Monitor* reported in October 1968:

> Staff members of this newspaper watched 74½ hours of evening programs during the first week of the new season, and during that time recorded 254 incidents of violence including threats, and 71 murders, killings, and suicides.
> The results were almost unchanged from a survey conducted by this newspaper last July which counted 210 incidents and 81 killings in 78½ hours of television.

Throughout the years network officials have been quick to promise reform, but slow to deliver. After the 1954 hearings they acknowledged the programming ought to be improved, and promised it would be. Ten years later the Dodd Committee found it was worse. A study was promised in 1954 by the NAB. It was referred to again in 1961 by CBS. It was finally produced, nine years late, in 1963, but contained little or nothing about the impact of violent programming on children. In spite of renewed promises, nothing more has been heard from the industry. Violence continues.

In spite of the industry's protestations that they do not use violence for its own sake, the Dodd investigation turned up some rather revealing memoranda to the contrary. An independent producer was asked to "inject an 'adequate' diet of violence into scripts" (overriding a sponsor's objections to excessive violence). Another network official wrote, "I like the idea of sadism." Still another was advised by memorandum: "In accordance with your request, spectacular accidents and violence scenes of the 1930–36 years have been requested from all known sources of stock footages. You will be advised as material arrives." "Give me sex and action," demanded one executive. Several shows were criticized as being "a far cry" from top management's order to deliver "broads, bosoms, and fun." A producer testified, "I was told to put sex and violence in my show." No wonder the Committee concluded that the networks "clearly pursued a deliberate policy of emphasizing sex, violence and brutality on [their] dramatic shows."

Dr. Wilbur Schramm of Stanford University has written:

[W]e are taking a needless chance with our children's welfare by permitting them to see such a parade of violence across our picture tubes. It is a chance we need not take. It is a danger to which we need not expose our children any more than we need expose them to tetanus, or bacteria from unpasteurized milk.

CENSORSHIP

We have heard a great deal from the broadcasting establishment about "censorship." Because the issue is an important one, however, I should like to attempt a restatement.

The First Amendment expressly provides that "Congress shall make no law . . . abridging the freedom of speech. . . ." And Congress provided in 1934 in Section 326 of the Communications Act (the Act establishing the Federal Communications Commission) that "Nothing . . . shall be understood or construed to give the Commission the power of censorship. . . ." (Although the same section went on to give the Commission authority to prohibit any "obscene, indecent, or profane language.") The commitment to freedom of speech runs deep in our history and our law. It is a commitment I personally hold with a fervor molded by years of study and a year as law clerk to Justice Hugo L. Black. As a public official, I welcome the mass media as a check upon government. And should the occasion arise when I felt the FCC was granting or withholding access to broadcasting licenses based upon the political, economic, or social ideology of the licensee (or the content of his programming) I would help lead the broadcasters' parade of protest.

But I do not believe it is "censorship" for Congress to provide that a broadcast licensee must accord "equal opportunities" to all competing candidates for public office once one is allowed the use of his station (the "equal time" rule), or to require that "broadcasters . . . afford reasonable opportunity for the discussion of conflicting views on issues of public importance" (the "fairness doctrine"). Nor is it censorship for the Commission to conclude that the Congressional mandate that licensees operate in the "public interest" (Section 307) requires that they "take the necessary steps to inform themselves of the real needs and interests of the areas they serve and to provide programming which in fact constitutes a diligent effort, in good faith, to provide for those needs and interests" (as it did in its Programming Policy Statement of July 29, 1960). Nor do I believe Congress violated the constitutional prohibitions against censorship when it authorized the FCC to require stations to keep "records of programs" (Section 303(j)), or that the FCC did so when it required all broadcasters to announce publicly the source of payment for paid messages and programming.

The examples could be multiplied, almost without end—regulation of lotteries, false and misleading advertising, and so forth. But the point has been made. There are many court decisions, statutes and government regulations that affect speech in ways designed to serve other desirable social ends that are, appropriately, not held to violate the letter or the spirit of the First Amendment. Like the young boy who cried "Wolf!" the broadcasting establishment has shouted so loudly and so often that any statutes or regulations relating to their industry violate the First Amendment that they are not likely to be believed if, someday, a real threat does come along.

I think my own position is fairly clear. Suppose the FCC was about to order a national network to produce news film that was taken by its cameramen but not used over the air—what are called "out takes" in the trade. I would urge my colleagues that we not do so as a matter of propriety. A small point perhaps, but I am pleased the Commission has not voted to pursue such a request. In an opinion involving the indifference to a newsman's conflict of interest by the management of another national network, I wrote, "I enthusiastically join the statements [of my colleagues of the majority] insofar as they urge that this Commission should constantly be on guard against actions of government—especially this agency—that might impede 'robust, wide-open debate' or 'aggressive news coverage and commentary.'"

I share Arthur Schlesinger, Jr.'s, judgment that the people retain "a certain right of self defense" from the mass media. And if corporate arrogance and intransigence become intolerable I am prepared to reassess the issue. But in general, and for now, I would prefer occasional abuses by a responsible broadcasting industry, capable of reform, to license revocations for irresponsibility.

I think investigation and public disclosure quite useful and appropriate. But I do not believe that the FCC should revoke the license of a television station because of its coverage of a political convention, a war, a riot, or a government official. With all the admiration I have for Secretary Orville Freeman, I do not believe he—or I—should be able to prevent CBS' showing of "Hunger in America." I do believe that some independent expert entity should be making program evaluations, and that they should be expert, candid, hard hitting, and generally available to the American people. I do not believe the FCC should deny license renewals to network-owned stations because those networks used excessive violence in action dramas, children's cartoons and other programming in an effort to secure greater audiences. Nor do I believe the FCC should take action against stations which show movies that large segments of the populace find objectionable—movies that have been cleared by the courts for showing in theaters. But I believe some independent entity should investigate and report the impact of radio and television entertainment programming, should criticize what the broadcasting establishment is doing, and should make its views known to the American people.

I am prepared to reevaluate my present position. But I now believe that networks do not tighten fraud procedures on game shows out of fear of the FCC; it is from the fear of adverse public opinion and the economic impact of that opinion. The same is probably true when networks attempt to control the conflicts of interest of their commentators. Broadcasters made reforms after the quiz show scandals, and the revelations concerning payola and plugola, not out of fear of Congress or the FCC but from the realization that the economic health of their industry depends upon public trust. If the public receives believable information that news is deliberately slanted, or programming has deleterious effects, I hope and believe that broadcasters will necessarily move to correct it.

This is not to say the FCC is without power to act in the area of broadcaster conduct and program content. We require stations to announce if they have received money or other consideration for the presentation of programming. A station must make available equal facilities and opportunities to opposing candidates. We have taken action against stations for sponsoring fraudulent contests over the air. The Federal Trade Commission acts against false and misleading advertising. The Communications Act prohibits obscenity, although this is a matter I believe we might be hard pressed to defend in court. We have held that licensees must make known any corporate conflicts of interest in their handling of programming matters. It is less clear whether we could take positive punitive action against a station for fraud in the presentation of news. That does not mean we should not investigate such a matter—and in public hearings. I would see nothing wrong with the FCC using its powers of compelling disclosure to insure that the public learns about fraud, corporate censorship, or falsehood in media practices that are protected by the First Amendment. The penalty would be the same as when any private figure criticizes the media: the effect of public opinion. No institution in our society should be immune from that kind of criticism.

But governmental power is not the only, or even the most important, threat to the freedom of speech of the broadcasting industry. Economic, corporate power over free speech is today, in my opinion, an even greater limitation than those feared by the drafters of the Bill of Rights. All Americans have felt the oppression of corporate censorship.

There are many forms of actual and potential censorship in broadcasting. A good many of them are self-imposed. I deplore them all. The problem is serious. But I do believe that any fair, impartial evaluation would have to conclude that your Commission and mine are not the principal threats to free speech in America today.

PROPOSALS

There have been efforts to "investigate" and "study" television and radio since their beginnings. There have been uncounted words written in books, articles and speeches about broadcasting's ills. The question, as always, is "What do we *do* about it?"

What we propose depends in great part upon what we think will alter men's behavior. My own view is that a meaningful reform must be premised upon its capacity to be carried out by self-serving men of average intelligence. To dream schemes of institutions that will only function when men are angels is futile. This is not to say that the world is not populated with a significant number of very decent guys who are willing to risk future and fortune to do "the right thing"; only that you cannot count on one of them being in all the right places at all the necessary times. Indeed, there are even some who question whether one can pass moral judgment on a man who simply finds himself carried along by the system of incentives—rewards and punishments—of his institutional environment. To some extent, that's what Fred Friendly's book, *Due to Circumstances Beyond Our Control,* is all about. It is not enough to wish that networks were being run by men who would televise Senate hearings instead of a rerun of *I Love Lucy.* For such a wish requires them to refund pocketed profits to advertisers and giveaways for free time already sold—in an institutional environment in which their performance, their "success," is measured almost exclusively in terms of how much they can increase profits.

The history of industrial safety is illustrative. There were efforts at moral suasion throughout the 19th and early 20th centuries, all to little effect. The real turning point in industrial safety came when plaintiffs' awards in lawsuits, workmen's compensation schemes, and insurance premiums rose to a level that made it more profitable to protect human arms, legs, and eyes than to continue to pay for the quantity consumed in the manufacturing process.

It is in this sense that I concluded, early in my term as an FCC Commissioner, that speeches by me about the "vast wasteland" would not have much lasting effect upon the contribution of radio and television to the quality of American life. What is needed are institutional realignments.

Let me make abundantly clear that the kind of realignments I am talking about are evolutionary rather than revolutionary. Indeed, the process of adaptation and self-renewal is, in my view, the essence of conservatism. There are forces of revolution and alienation abroad in our land. There are those who preach that our system cannot work, that it cannot adapt fast enough, and that our institutions, government, universities, corporations, and so forth, must be destroyed.

I am not among them. I want to conserve our institutions. But I believe they can only be conserved by evolution and adaptation to changed conditions and needs. Those who practice corporate arrogance and preach the haughty disdain of legitimate demands for popular participation are the real handmaidens of revolution in this country today.

In my view, government regulation of business seeks to make the free private enterprise system work better, not to stifle it. It seeks a relationship between government and business such that legitimate public demands and needs and interests will be met by institutional adaptation within the private sector, not by nationalization. As McGeorge Bundy has said, "more effective government, at every level, is the friend and not the enemy of the strength and freedom of our economic system as a whole." The American industrial system was strengthened, not stifled, when corporations began paying a fair market price for the human beings consumed in the manufacturing process. The very purpose of the antitrust laws is to encourage competition, and establish some ground rules for its perpetuation. The food and drug industry is made more profitable, and popularly acceptable, by laws that prohibit profiting from products that produce disease and death. Laws requiring fair employment opportunities for Americans of all races do not hamper big business; they produce more potential customers and reduce the corporate tax burden to sustain the unemployed. We can argue about the details of such proposals in this country, and we do, but I think we can all agree that what we are trying to do is make the American system work better. In the process, we also make it competitively possible for basically decent men to do the right thing. Shareholders may expect corporate officials to maximize profits, but they do not expect them to violate the law.

Let us, in this light, examine some of the proposals that have been made to alter slightly the system of institutional pressures within the broadcasting industry in ways designed to improve its total contribution to our society.

Public Broadcasting

There are a number of sources of public broadcasting today: National Educational Television's programming and occasional networking service, National Educational Radio, the Public Broadcasting Laboratory's Sunday evening show, the Eastern Educational Network, the programming of now some 150 stations throughout the country, and so forth. The Public Broadcasting Corporation is just beginning. The National Foundations on the Arts and Humanities have provided some financial support already. The Ford Foundation has, of course, been by all odds the most significant source of support for public broadcasting over the years. This programming is significant in a number of ways. It is, first of all, an available alternative when and where it is available. A few people listen, and watch, and are enriched. In view of the relatively small audiences, however, public broadcasting's principal value must be measured today in terms of its impact upon commercial television. This has been significant. It is a professional training ground for all of the various jobs in commercial broadcasting. It is a source of programming ideas, public affairs issues, and technical innovations. It is commercial broadcasting's graduate school, its farm club, its underground press, its research and development laboratory.

It is a $90 million tail (or, perhaps I should say, head) on the $3 billion dog of commercial broadcasting that, when it can move the animal, can have a tremendous impact upon our nation with very little investment. As McGeorge Bundy has said, "Twenty years of experience have made it very plain indeed that commercial TV alone cannot do for the American public what mixed systems, public and private, are offering to other countries, notably Great Britain and Japan." The Japanese people have chosen to fund their equivalent of our Public Broadcasting Corporation (NHK) at a proportion of their gross national product that would be equivalent to $2 billion a year in this country. They are richer for it. The United States is now on the threshold of finding out whether it can muster the national will to do as well. I think that it is crucial that the Public Broadcasting Corporation be adequately funded, and, in line with the Carnegie study, in such a manner as to be independent of the government. Such an effort would be a classic example of an institutional change that could benefit everyone affected by broadcasting far more than its costs suggest —and harm no one.

Citizen Participation

A statesman has been defined as a man who stands upright, due to equal pressure on all sides. It is, in this sense, that the Federal Communications Commission is made up of statesmen. Mr. Bundy has said of the FCC that "its weakness is a national scandal. . . ." But it is not true that the Commission just responds to pressure from the broadcasting industry. It responds to pressure from anybody. Increasingly, citizens all around the country are learning that the FCC's adversary process will only work if they will make it work. For you can only make an adversary process work if you have adversaries.

The typical station's license renewal proceeding goes like this. The FCC gathers at ringside and offers to referee. At the sound of the bell the licensee jumps in the ring and begins shadow boxing. At the end of three minutes he is proclaimed the winner by the FCC majority, found to have been serving the public interest in his community, and given a three-year license renewal.

Members of the public are learning how to make this a more meaningful contest. In Seattle, a voluntary citizens-media council has brought interested parties together to improve coverage of the black community. (The general concept of local broadcasting councils has worked in other countries and might well be tried here.) Negroes in Jackson, Mississippi, along with the United Church of Christ, are challenging in court the FCC's renewal of the license of station WLBT. John Banzhaf, who established the "fairness doctrine" requirement that broadcasters inform their audiences about the harmful effects of cigarette smoking, is contesting the license renewals of stations which have not complied. Labor unions are contesting the license renewals of stations which do not fairly present labor's story. Citizens in Chicago, Seattle and Atlanta are, independently, protesting changes in the programming format of their favorite local stations from classical music to something more popular—and profitable. A number of organizations are fighting the renewal of license for a station that broadcasts a surfeit of what they consider right-wing hate programming. Other groups are protesting children's programming, violence on television, and the absence of meaningful local service programming. (As one group of young blacks' picket signs put it, "Soul Music is Not Enough.") Needless to say, I am not expressing a view on the merits of these cases. But I believe this trend is going to continue. And I think that it is, in most cases, basically healthy for listeners and viewers to be able to participate in the Commission's proceedings. It creates the reality, as well as the illusion, that it is possible to "do something" to make our seemingly intractable institutions respond to popular will, that you *can* fight city hall. It removes the pressure for revolutionary action that otherwise heats up without escape like infection in a boil. Finally, it should be welcomed by the vast majority of American broadcasters who are responsible, involved with their community, and who are already making efforts to obtain more audience interest in their stations' programming.

Public Service Time

Businessmen who would like to perform a public service that does not maximize immediate profits often have difficulty convincing their shareholders they should do so unless their competition undertakes a similar burden. Take the safety record of commercial aviation, for example. It would be competitively difficult for a single airline to establish and follow the kind of maintenance and safety standards imposed by the FAA and CAB. There would always be a competitor who, by taking a few more risks, could cut costs, reduce rates and attract customers.

By having industry-wide standards enforced by a government agency, however, everyone is competitively equal—and everyone benefits from an industry-wide reputation that builds confidence in airline transportation. Because of the almost total absence of programming standards from the FCC, the broadcasting industry is at a substantial disadvantage. It becomes competitively difficult for a single network to put very much news and public affairs in prime time, to increase its financial commitment to public service, or to broadcast programming without commercial sponsorship so long as the other two can continue to maximize profits. Competitive position as well as profits are involved. The FCC owes the industry, and the public, the assist that only government, with its antitrust immunity, can provide: the establishment of standards that will create for the industry the opportunity to more often do its best.

Such standards could take a number of forms. We could require that a given proportion to gross income be invested in programming. We could require that each network provide a given proportion of its prime time, each evening or each week, to public service programming; stations could have similar standards, especially for local programming. (For example, each of the three networks could be required to provide a single hour of such programming Monday through Saturday between 7:00 and 10:00 p.m. on a staggered basis. Thus, at any moment of this segment of prime time, viewers would have a choice of something other than advertiser-supported, lowest-common-denominator programming.) We could require that, for some programs, there be no commercial interruption. We could set standards for the size of the news staff, or news budget, as a proportion of gross income. Such standards could, of course, be worked out with the networks and station owners, for—as with the commercial airlines' safety record—it is the responsible, professional elements in the industry that ultimately have the most to gain from such proposals.

Program Diversity and Ownership Standards

Many of the FCC's policies in the broadcasting field are premised upon the assumption that the more independently owned broadcasting outlets the better. That is, minority tastes will be better served, and programming quality improved, by increasing the number of sources of broadcast programming. There has never been a thorough-going effort to find out if this theory has worked out in fact, and thus each of us must judge for himself. But today's 7350 operating radio and television stations do represent about a tenfold increase over the number of broadcast outlets in the 1920s and 1930s. This has come about through the addition of relatively lower-power, day-time-only, local AM radio stations, the wholly new FM radio service, and television, first VHF and then UHF. Cable television, which now serves some two million homes, has the potential of bringing twenty or more television signals into the home (compared with the four or five signals in most major markets today). Additional individual choice is provided by services that do not involve broadcasting. Music can be obtained from phonograph records and audio tapes. The sale of tape recorders is up markedly, including stereo tape players for automobiles, and there is widespread taping of music from radio stations for subsequent personal use. Films have always been available, but have been expensive and difficult to operate; now the prospect of video cameras, tape recorders, and video disc and tape recordings opens up a whole new consumer market.

Diversity in broadcast programming is also affected by FCC rules regarding programming practices. In the largest 100 markets the FCC requires that jointly owned AM–FM stations not duplicate programming more than 50% of the time. The Commission has under consideration a proposal that would limit a network's ownership interest to a maximum of 50% of the networked programming. We have put out for comments the Westinghouse proposal to limit the amount of prime time programming that any station affiliate can take from one network. Of course, the mere joint ownership of broadcast properties in the same market decreases the likelihood of diversity in programming. And the FCC has also proposed a rule that no single owner can hold a license to more than one full-time facility in a single market—which the Justice Department believes should be expanded to take account of newspaper ownership. (The limits now are five VHF, two UHF, seven AM, and seven FM stations for a single owner. No commonly owned TV signals may overlap, nor

AM nor FM, but a TV plus AM plus FM may be commonly owned in a single community.) To the extent that diversity of signals, programming, and ownership has led to greater audience choice, service to minority tastes, and improved quality, such efforts are to be encouraged.

Professionalism

Members of the radio and television industry like to think of themselves as members of a profession. No one would question that there are, within the industry, individuals with impressive records of academic training, and participation in programming that represents a high sense of responsibility, creativity, and technical standards. The fact remains, however, that most of the ingredients one associates with a profession are not to be found in broadcasting. There are no academic standards. There are no professional qualifying examinations. There are no moral or character standards. There are no professional associations. There is no procedure for processing public grievances addressed to one of the members. A lawyer, by contrast, must hold college and law degrees from accredited institutions. He also must be found to be academically qualified by examiners from the legal profession. He must meet character qualifications. The courts before which he appears must first "admit" him to practice, after satisfying themselves as to his qualifications. He belongs to a "bar association" which may be a requirement to practice. Grievances filed against him are evaluated by a "grievance committee" against the standards of professional "canons of ethics" and prior decisions interpreting those canons. Similar qualities are associated with doctors, dentists, engineers, architects, accountants, and so forth.

Or consider for a moment the rigors of qualifying as a third grade teacher. The applicant must have a college degree from a school of education. She must be qualified under standards established by the state for a teachers' certificate. She must meet the standards of the local school board. She must have spent some time as a practice teacher. She may continue to take in-service training. She must meet these standards because she is going to spend time with a group of perhaps twenty-five children for a few hours a day for a few months out of the year. She will be giving them ideas, information, opinions, attitudes, and behavior patterns that must hold them in good stead throughout life. We don't want to trust their minds to any but the most skillful and responsible of hands. Contrast these concerns and standards, if you will, with those we associate with broadcasters, with their access to *millions* of young minds for far more hours every week. As Harry Skornia has said, "Although broadcasting is one of the most powerful forces shaping social values and behavior, broadcast staffs and management in the United States generally have no specific professional standards to meet. . . ." There are exceptions. But of the NAB Code Skornia says, "A document so vaguely worded, so defensive, and so flagrantly violated, can hardly be seriously considered a real code of either ethics or practices." He believes that the mass media "should be entrusted only to professionals, who study their effects as carefully as new drug manufacturers are expected to test new drugs before putting them on the market." News is, of course, a special concern: "It must be recognized that news, like medicine or education, is too important to be entrusted to people without proper qualifications." Let me hasten to make clear that I do not urge that the FCC is the most appropriate agency to establish such professional standards, or to engage in licensing. But I do urge that the American people have the right to expect professional standards from those who instruct millions of young people Saturday morning that are at least as high as those it imposes upon the teachers who instruct a classroom of twenty-five students on Monday morning.

Programming Liability

Legal liability for a monetary damage award has often proven to be an effective spur to reform. Manufacturers' concern for the safety and suitability of their products has undoubtedly been enhanced by the "product liability" standards that have been laid down by the courts. It is simply too expensive to try to run a manufacturing business with the threat of suits from injured customers. The same principle has applied to industrial safety practices. Safety procedures and equipment that once seemed "too expensive" appear much more reasonable when balanced against adequate plaintiffs' awards for injuries and death. Perhaps the networks' concern about the quality and impact of their programming could be intensified in this way, either by principles of liability found in the common law or from new legislation. I appreciate that this is a provocative suggestion, that it could sometimes raise First Amendment problems, and that proof of causation would be difficult.

Public's Access to Television

We are living in an age in which television has become confused in a crazy way with reality. If it's not on the tube it hasn't happened. And if you, or those with whom you can identify, are not on the tube, you don't exist. A poll by Louis Harris found that a sense of alienation is growing among many Americans, principally, it seems to me, among those who are excluded from participation in television. The right to petition one's government, guaranteed in the First Amendment of the Bill of Rights, has become the need to petition one's media, usually television. That's how you change things. That's how you communicate with your fellow citizens. We've discovered that a riot is a form of communication.

We might as well face up to the fact that television *is* responsible for violence to the extent it insists upon action from those with legitimate grievances to share with their fellow citizens. People with something they must say will do whatever is necessary to be heard. What is necessary is what the gatekeepers of our television channels define as necessary.

Another conclusion is that we probably ought to be giving more thought to principles of public right of access to television. The FCC's "fairness doctrine" is, of course, designed and administered in ways which seek to serve this need in part. But it is inadequate. Professor Barron has argued in the Harvard Law Review that in order to breathe life into First Amedment freedoms today they must mean something more than the right to establish one's own multi-million-dollar TV station, network, or newspaper, there must be a public "right" of access to the mass media. Television networks and stations today retain a very tight control over who uses their facilities—even to the point of causing a company such as Xerox to set up its own "network" to show some of its more creative documentaries. The only public access comes during news programs and interview shows when, of course, the outsiders are carefully screened.

It is in part this control which has required the necessity of establishing the rather expensive duplicate facilities represented by 150 educational television stations. Corporations have made contributions to help sustain educational broadcasting. But some have also used commercial television to bring the same kind of programming to the American people—Xerox, Hallmark, AT&T, Union Carbide, to name but a few. It is the means chosen by the National Geographic Society. If we are to limit the surfeit of advertiser-supported, network entertainment programming during prime-time, perhaps we should consider a rule making a proportion of this time available for non-commercial programming of an educational, scientific, or cultural nature paid for by foundations or similar institutions. Such time would then be available to them as a matter of right, rather than as a matter of sufferance from the networks. The FCC has recently proposed a similar principle with regard to cable television systems, namely that extra channels be made available on a common-carrier basis for lease to those who wish to distribute programming, the costs for which may be relatively low.

Citizens' Commission on Broadcasting

Twenty-two years ago, with the leadership of Robert M. Hutchins and the funding of Henry R. Luce, the "Commission on the Freedom of the Press" took a look at our mass media at that time and recommended "the establishment of a new and independent agency to appraise and report annually upon the performance of the press."

The National Advisory Commission on Civil Disorders (the Kerner Commission) recommended, among other things, the establishment of an "Institute of Urban Communication on a private, nonprofit basis" with the responsibility to "review press and television coverage of riot and racial news and publicly award praise and blame."

In between, similar suggestions have come from such distinguished citizens and students of the mass media as Professor Harold Lasswell, former Senator William Benton (who proposed a National Citizens Advisory Board for Radio and Television to the Senate, along with Senators John W. Bricker, Leverett Saltonstall, and Lester C. Hunt in 1951), Jack Gould of *The New York Times,* Harry S. Ashmore (now of the Center for the Study of Democratic Institutions), and Professor William Rivers of the Institute of Communication Research at Stanford. Representative Oren Harris, when Chairman of the House Committee on Interstate and Foreign Commerce, proposed a similar idea, as did CBS President Frank Stanton (although his proposal was for industry funding). Dr. Otto Larson called for an "institute" to conduct "continuing, systematic, objective comparative surveillance of mass media contents. . . ." The National Citizens Committee for Broadcasting could develop in this direction. (Even former FCC Commissioner (Lee) Loevinger has recently urged the industry to establish its own "American Broadcasting Council on Fairness and Accuracy in Reporting.")

What form should such a citizens' commission or institute take? Others have spoken on the details and I will not attempt to repeat all of the proposals here. A few general characteristics, however, seem to run throughout.

Although there may be some appropriate ways to funnel some federal or industry funds to such an institute, I believe that most proponents would agree that the organization ought to be completely free from any suggestion of government or industry influence. It may already be impossible, in this day and age, to isolate any institution from the overpowering political pressures of Big Television. But the institute should, at least, not draw its membership or employees from either government or broadcasting.

Funding should come from foundation and other private sources and would probably have to be in the range of $1 to $10 million a year. There is a certain "critical mass" of individuals necessary to undertake an effort of this kind in terms of the quality and range of professionals, and sheer quantity of work involved. This is somewhere between fifty and 200 professional people. To the extent projects are contracted out to others; or training programs are undertaken, that would, of course, require additional funding. Federal funding might be possible through the National Science

Foundation, the National Institutes of Health and of Mental Health, the National Foundations on the Arts and Humanities, the Public Broadcasting Corporation, or the Department of Health, Education and Welfare. But I would assume that government and industry funding combined should not exceed, say, 30% of the annual operating budget and that it would be far more desirable, if possible, to do without it altogether.

What would such a citizens' commission or institute do? There would be, of course, a wide range of potential activities that would evolve with the interests of the participants. But the following may be illustrative:

1. The analysis and evaluation of broadcasting standards.
2. The creation and evaluation of programming standards.
3. The monitoring and evaluation of broadcasting.
4. The evaluation of media grievance machinery.
5. Analysis of the economic structure of the media.
6. Analysis of media employment practices.
7. The evaluation of the effectiveness of government agencies charged with media-related responsibilities.
8. Development of standards and programs for improving community-broadcaster relations.
9. The provision of training in areas of critical social significance.
10. Research contracts, and the stimulation of public-interest programming through grants and awards.

Now, what powers should an Institute have to carry out such a formidable array of functions? Certain minimal powers seem apparent.

1. Authority to publicize its findings and conclusions.

The Institute would be expected to seek the widest possible dissemination of its statements and reports. While the Institute should be authorized, if the occasion necessitates, to purchase media time or space for the publication of its findings, the media would normally be expected to provide adequate coverage for Institute releases.

2. Authority to request data and reports through Government agencies.

The Institute should be able to obtain, through FCC processes, broadcast information which it deems relevant to its tasks, but which it cannot obtain voluntarily. Similarly, the Institute should have access to relevant economic data. The Institute could cooperate with the Equal Employment Opportunities Commission in obtaining information on hiring and task assignment practices.

3. Authority to appear as advocate for the public interest.

While the Institute would have no regulatory authority, it is essential that its findings be widely circulated—not only through publicity, but also through advocacy in all appropriate forums.

4. Annual report.

Finally, to provide a check on its own activities, as well as a formalized occasion for evaluation of the overall performance and trends within broadcasting, the Institute should annually prepare and present to the public—and to the President and the Congress—a comprehensive report detailing its activities and rendering its judgment.

The American people are calling for some meaningful response to the corporate arrogance that posts a high wood fence around the television business with "Keep Out!" written on one side and "First Amendment" on the other. As Arthur Schlesinger, Jr., has observed in his book on *Violence:*

> No rational person wants to reestablish a reign of censorship or mobilize new Legions of Decency. . . . Yet society retains a certain right of self-defense.

We do retain a right of self-defense. The people are looking to you to exercise it. One useful way in which you could do so would be to recommend the creation of a non-governmental, non-industry Citizens' Commission on Broadcasting.

TV at the Turning Point[*]

By Fred W. Friendly

As a wise old physician, an eminent teacher of clinical surgery, awaited a desperate effort to repair his ruptured aorta, he whispered to me, "I just don't want them to save the organ and kill the man." The analogy is relevant to the Vietnam operation, particularly in the summers of 1964 and 1965 when, based on faulty x rays and a naïve diagnosis, the United States attempted to save an organ—a government—by radical surgery which destroyed the patient. It is imprecise to say that the patient perished on the operating table, but the reality is that for all the transfusions and desperate transplants Vietnam as a sociological community never really regained consciousness. In South Vietnam, the trauma of war has so ruptured the human fabric that what is left may hardly be worth saving.

The failure to understand this tragic reality and the battery of brutal facts that exploded the State Department's simplistic theories about Vietnam cannot be blamed on the U.S. Government alone. The news media, and particularly broadcast journalism, which owned "first rights" on this violent little war, must share that responsibility. It was not our war to win or lose, but it was our war to understand and to explain. I refer specifically to 1964 and 1965 when, as an Undersecretary of State later testified, escalation at the time of the Tonkin Gulf resolution amounted to the functional equivalent of a declaration of war, and when Danang and Cam Ne signaled the intensification and brutalization of the American effort. It was a time when the military's failure to understand the complexities of the Asian mainland and mind—"We don't know beans about what Hanoi is thinking," one Pentagon official said—caused an entire administration to flirt with deception. All of Walter Lippmann's Seven Deadly Sins of Public Opinion—hatred, intolerance, suspicion, bigotry, secrecy, fear, and

---

[*] Reprinted from *Columbia Journalism Review,* Winter 1970–71, by permission of the author and publisher.

lying—were marshalled to obscure a series of decisions which could be justified only by further drastic acts of war.

Those of us who were in key editorial posts at the time can blame it all on the President, or his advisers—Robert McNamara, Dean Rusk, McGeorge Bundy, Maxwell Taylor—but we cannot forever paint over the stain left by our own ineffectiveness. With few exceptions, "the world outside and the pictures in our heads," as far as Vietnam was concerned, were not appreciably different from those of the Administration. The broadcast journalist went into Vietnam the same way he went into World War II and Korea—"as a member of the team." (The extent of cooperation was such that the U.S. Navy's official film on Tonkin was narrated by NBC's Chet Huntley.) Because the Tonkin Gulf resolution was not by the letter of the law a declaration of war, and for other complicated reasons, we operated without censorship in Vietnam. It was a unique responsibility to avoid bringing aid and comfort to the enemy without doing commercials for the Pentagon. The delicate balance between those two objectives and the complications of the times in which we lived were conditions for which we were unprepared.

In 1965 Dan Schorr, returning from his highly successful assignment in Europe, was so impressed with CBS News' intensity of Vietnam coverage that he wryly accused me of attempting to make it television's war. I do think we succeeded in capturing the battles, the skirmishes, the human interest, and the inhuman strategies. But we never captured the whole war. Again I am describing 1964 and 1965, when the reporting in the field far outran the editing and much of the reporting at home. "The Living Room War," as Michael Arlen called it, transported millions of Americans to Pleiku, Quinhon, and Cam Ne. As we watched, 2500 years of historical humbug about the glory of battle was dissolved into a montage of miserable little firefights in which GI Joe was often cast in the role of the heavy. It was Morley Safer who first focused the TV eye so dramatically. For his work, the Johnson Administration not only tried to bring about Safer's recall but to my certain knowledge trafficked in phony charges about the Royal Canadian Mounted Police having questions about this Canadian national's loyalty.

With his colleagues, Peter Kalischer—"the brass wants us to get on the team, but my job is to find out what the score is"—and young Jack Laurence, Safer helped to invent a new kind of battle coverage that combined threads of Murrow's shortwave reports from the London Blitz with David Duncan's battle photos from Korea. The combat cameramen, many of whom were Asians, pioneered new ground, usually at the risk of their own lives. (Assistant Secretary of Defense Arthur Sylvester asked me by phone one night after viewing a damaging piece of film on the Cronkite broadcast, "What do you mean by hiring Vietnamese nationals as cameramen?" Several weeks after I left CBS in 1966, I met Mr. Sylvester at a Gridiron Club dinner. His after-dinner greeting to me was, "Well, we got rid of you, now we have to get rid of Morley Safer." Sylvester's tour of duty ended long before Safer's whose record in Vietnam endures.)

The Pentagon's and the President's admonitions that the news media were giving and the public was getting a distorted picture "because they couldn't know all the facts" had a hollow ring when nightly broadcasts seemed to indicate that the Commander-in-Chief and his generals, for all their orchestrated briefings and charts, themselves did not know what was happening in the elephant grass and rice paddies. What seemed to come across on the tube and between the lines of every newspaper report was the frightening reality that the hunted in this search-and-destroy scenario was a foe whom no one really hated. Pleiku was no Alamo, even if the President on a visit to Camranh Bay urged the troops to "nail the coonskin to the wall."

The Commander-in-Chief, watching those three Sony TV sets of his, would, I am told, swear at the sets, denounce the NBC or CBS report, order his staff to warn the network and then call the Pentagon to find out if it was true—about the Marines burning a village with cigaret lighters, or what the patrol said after that unsuccessful walk-in-the-sun mission. In the end, the film would be shipped to Washington and often back to Saigon, where it would be denounced all the way to the line outfit, where the commander would merely shake his head.

If the combat reporting was so effective in 1965, why all the second guessing at this late date? Although the performance naturally varies with the three networks, the record looks impressive on paper and in the film library. There were some excellent reports on refugees, on nationbuilding, on air evacuation, on Saigon's black market, on the Chinese colony of Cholon; and, always from Washington, those polarizing hawk and dove debates. Charles Collingwood, who commuted to Vietnam, teamed up with Les Midgely to do several penetrating documentaries; and Frank McGee and Walter Cronkite did some very tough news analyses in 1967. But that was already 1967 and we had more than 300,000 troops in Vietnam.

There were really four Vietnam stories: the military, diplomatic, political, and economic. We may have been providing most of the parts of that mosaic but in my view we lacked the will and imagination to relate them to one another. The three-minute snippets between the Marlboro man and the Dodge girl, together with an occasional documentary or debate, just didn't add up to interpretive journalism. The coefficient of loss between what the correspondent corps in Washington—Elie Abel, Marvin Kalb, Ed Morgan—knew and what those in Saigon—Peter Kalischer, Bernard Kalb, and Welles Hangen—could see was a lag of enormous proportions. It was not just a shortage of air time, although the continuous coverage that could be cleared for Space, Presidential junkets, and football, compared to air time for Vietnam, is a commentary of its own. Nor can we blame it all on the profit demands of the networks and the unwillingness of some local stations to carry serious Vietnam coverage. The equally disturbing problem was our inability to understand the complexities of the Vietnam puzzle and to assemble a comprehensive profile early enough to make a difference. The most succinct definition of news analysis I know comes from Alexander Kendrick, who calls it the "Yes, but . . ." school of journalism. To have used that formula in 1965 when President Johnson proclaimed, "I'm not going to be the President who saw Asia go the way China went," might have made a difference.

Various correspondents understood segments of it. A few editors, like Russ Bensley of the Cronkite News and Herb Mitgang, for three years CBS News' Executive Editor, had a solid overview of the war. But all this energy and talent produced only a fraction of the maximum effort required by this decisive moment in history. Perhaps what was needed was a primer on how to watch a war—for both journalists and viewers. If the military experts didn't understand that nasty little war where there were no fronts, no reliable body counts, and no aerial reconnaissance worthy of the name, how could working journalists get a fix on so fluid and inscrutable a situation?

Part of the answer lay in more editorial coordination, more imagination in stitching together what we did know, and more accurate identification of those clouded areas where we had no experience. Arthur Schlesinger wrote: "The United States salvation of Asia represents an extravagance in national policy. The fact is our government just doesn't know a lot of things it pretends to know." The same criticism was true of experts in the news media.

The mistakes we journalists made in 1964 and 1965 almost outran those of the statesmen. One useful example is the sad case of U Thant's abortive peace effort in the summer of 1965. The story begins with what was in many ways the most distinguished single piece of journalism done outside Vietnam in 1965 by a broadcast journalist—Eric Sevareid's essay about his last meeting with Adlai Stevenson in London just before the Ambassador's tragic death. Although Sevareid broadcast some of the insights from London in abbreviated form, the heart of the interview—evidence of the Stevenson desire to resign—burst with explosive force in *Look* Nov. 30.

It was a rough week for CBS News. Top management was upset because the White House was challenging the accuracy and delicacy of the Sevareid report—"He [Stevenson] simply had to get out of the UN job." My colleagues' and my own embarrassment was compounded by the fact that we had to quote *Look* to report what our own chief correspondent had written. Eric was surprised at the impact of the story. He pointed out that he had aired parts of it on CBS radio and/or TV that summer and wrote it for *Look* because an article provided more space and a more suitable forum for what was intended as a eulogy. David Schoenbrun, then of Metromedia Broadcasting, buttressed the story by reporting a similar interview with Stevenson, who expressed the same discouraged tone. But Adlai Stevenson III countered with an unmailed, unsigned letter that his late father had drafted, indicating to some of his Stateside friends that he had no intention of resigning. Elie Abel, then NBC bureau chief in London, had his private interview the day after Sevareid's meeting and came away with the impression that Stevenson was not going to resign. Abel is convinced, as I am, that the contradiction is probably more a reflection of the Hamlet-like approach to decision making that was the Stevenson style than a reflection on the accuracy of the journalism. What Abel and Sevareid each heard loud and clear was Ambassador Stevenson's disappointment over his mission and his ineffectiveness in the Johnson Administration during the Dominican intervention and in Vietnam. He was particularly depressed over his failure to get through to the White House the seriousess and promise of Secretary General U Thant's peace negotiations with the Hanoi government.

U Thant, then under growing pressure in the UN, was convinced he could bring Ho Chi Minh's representatives to the peace table in Rangoon, that a truce line could be drawn across not only Vietnam but adjacent Laos, and that the U.S. Government "could write the terms of the cease-fire offer exactly as they saw fit" and that he (U Thant) would announce it in exactly those words. Stevenson had told interviewers that Secretary of Defense McNamara was not interested and that he could not even get Secretary of State Rusk to respond.

Sevareid reported much of the U Thant peace effort on CBS radio without attribution to source. Several weeks later, the Paris edition of the *Herald Tribune* and other European newspapers reported the U Thant peace expedition, but the Government in Washington discounted the seriousness and even credibility of the overture. Stevenson did not.

The Sevareid-Stevenson episode taken alone is perhaps just a fascinating footnote to history. But viewed against the concurrent developments of that fateful summer, it could have meant far more than a footnote. So frustrated and disturbed was U Thant that in a news conference held in February, 1965, he tried to use Asian shorthand to telegraph a message to the American people: "I am sure the great American people, if only they know the true facts and the background to the developments in South Vietnam, will agree with me that further bloodshed is unnecessary. And also that the political and diplomatic method of discussions and negotiations alone can create conditions which will enable the United States to withdraw gracefully from that part of the world. As you know, in times of war and of hostilities the first casualty is truth."

Other events, more or less known by broadcast reporters and editors at the time, add substance to U Thant's sense of foreboding. The battle situation in Vietnam was deteriorating. Premier Khan's government was swiftly decaying. Corruption in Saigon and desertion from the Army were putting heavier demands on the 50,000 men on the ground there. Pleiku had been a disaster, but as one high government official put it, "If there hadn't been a Pleiku, it would have had to be invented." General Maxwell Taylor, commuting between Saigon and Washington, was telling the President that escalation by as much as 115,000 additional troops would be necessary to prevent a total rout. Within the Government there was disagreement on strategy between Rusk and his Undersecretary George Ball, and some between Taylor and McNamara. Although there were important backgrounders by the Administration about the desire to strengthen the role of the United Nations, the truth was that high officials of the Johnson Administration were constantly sabotaging the effectiveness of the world organization and even the credibility of its Asian Secretary General.

The fact is that on the night of the Sevareid-Stevenson interview, when U Thant was still desperately trying to get both sides to that Rangoon table, the White House was making the decision to send 115,000 troops to Vietnam. Soon afterward the decision was enlarged to bring U.S. troop strength in Vietnam to a total of 380,000 by 1966.

Recently I asked former White House press chief Bill Moyers, who in 1965 had the assignment of downgrading the Sevareid story, what he believed now about the reliability of the Stevenson message. Moyers said he believed Stevenson went to his grave convinced that Hanoi was prepared to negotiate on U Thant's terms. But Moyers also believed that Johnson was in July of 1965 unaware of such peace possibilities. The State Department's role in this massive misunderstanding was largely unreported then, as it is now. What is clear is that our Ambassador to the United Nations had no direct access to the President of the United States and that Rusk and/or his bureaucracy applied a pocket veto to a peace plan whose validity they rejected.

U Thant's peace plan was not the only casualty that July. Interpretive journalism suffered a wound from which we are still bleeding. It is not just hindsight which enables us to see this now with 20/20 vision. Most of the information was known to a variety of able broadcasters, each capable of incisive interpretation of the pattern that the various parts reflected. Kalischer and Safer knew about the deterioration after Pleiku. Richard Hottelet at the UN was aware of the frigid attitudes between the Secretary General and the President. Marvin Kalb and John Scali were at the State Department every day and understood the hardening Rusk position. Sevareid, Abel, and Schoenbrun had been present when Stevenson bared his soul and frustrations. The tragedy was that what emerged on the home screen was at best a series of sharply edited, professionally honed episodes. As a news executive often accused of being more involved with production and content than with administration, I was certainly aware of each of these stories. Yet the failure to assemble all these elements into the kind of interpretive journalism that would have enabled the American people to understand the magnitude of the decision their leadership was about to make was a serious lapse.

For those not familiar with a broadcast news operation, let me state that there were editors. The Vietnam content of the evening and morning news is carefully structured by dedicated, serious newsmen. But too often the problem turns into a question of logistics. The foreign editor, although that is not his title, must be more concerned with the plane schedule from Saigon, the transfer time in Hong Kong or Tokyo, and the cost of the satellite than with the content of the story. Within each program the pressure is on getting the film in and out of the lab, evaluating it, reconciling it with the reporter's script—often recorded on the run in the field—and getting it down to time. Because broadcast correspondents must fight daily with the clock and because producers are traditionally averse to too many talking heads, we often produced one-dimensional stories which accentuated the urgent rather than the important.

The time, the skill, and, if you like, the sophistication to put it all together were, at least in 1964 and 1965, absent. Of course there were documentaries and specials; the titles and scope make an imposing list: Fred Freed's three-and-a-half-hour study of U.S. foreign policy and Ted Yates' *Secret War in Laos,* both of which NBC broadcast in 1965; CBS's *Vietnam Perspectives,* our half-hour interview with Senator Fulbright that so upset the White House; and of course the 1966 Foreign Relations Committee hearings, which NBC and CBS covered in considerable but not equal depth.

But the lost opportunity that must haunt print as well as broadcast journalists was the Tonkin Gulf incident in August of 1964. We in journalism have to share the guilt with the commanders of the *Maddox, Turner Joy,* and the admiral who commanded the task force, with the officials who drafted the resolution, with the President who brought it to the Congress, and with the Senator from Arkansas who steered it through in record time. The fact that CBS News chose to do some five minutes of wrapup rather than the kind of comprehensive analysis our Washington bureau was capable of is something that will always haunt me. President Johnson went on the air at 11:36 and spoke for less than eight minutes. Our entire broadcast lasted eleven minutes, and I didn't even fight for more time.

The only phone call I got that night came from Ed Murrow, then desperately ill in Pawling but still caring enough to castigate me for insufficient interpretation. Of course we had no way of knowing how dangerous a swamp that resolution and accompanying action would lead to.

Certainly we had the warnings of Lippmann, and that painfully prophetic prediction of Wayne Morse:

> We're at war in violation of the Constitution of the U.S. Article I, Section 8 of the Constitution specifically provides that only Congress has the power to declare war. No President has the right to send American boys to their death on a battlefield in the absence of a declaration of war. But one thing I do know and that is we're going to be bogged down in Southeast Asia for years to come if we follow this course of action and we're going to kill thousands of American boys until, finally let me say, the American people are going to say what the French people finally said: they've had enough.

Senator Morse spoke those words on Aug. 2, even before the actual Tonkin Gulf resolution. The coverage in print and broadcast was that accorded a "reckless and querulous dissenter."

Morse and Gruening of Alaska were the only two Senators who voted against the resolution. Most newspapers and broadcast organizations supported it as an act of great restraint under provocation. We reported that Senator Goldwater, then running for President on a GOP ticket with a hawkish plank, saluted the Johnson action and its subsequent escalation. We never emphasized that in order to nullify one of Goldwater's chief campaign issues, Johnson had repudiated a promise as old as his Presidency, a promise "not to send American boys nine to ten thousand miles from home . . . [to be] tied down in a land war in Asia." Walter Lippmann's criticism of the quality of editing at this time, although directed at Washington's leading newspaper, was also an indictment of me and every other broadcast editor: "If I had been editor of the Washington *Post* when Johnson was planning to move to a full-scale war in Vietnam, I'd have raised a great stink and told the people what was happening."

Without raising that "great stink," which might have required broadcasters to cross that fine line from news analysis to editorializing, we certainly should have raised and explored in depth a series of obvious questions which might have illuminated those dark shoals and jagged reefs which came to be known as the credibility gulf:

1. How does a major power declare war? What was the legal difference between the Tonkin Gulf resolution and a declaration of war? Senator Fulbright and Undersecretary of State Katzenbach clashed over this in 1967, and even today the printed text reads like a confrontation in a Hochhuth drama. We could have brought about a debate on these questions when it mattered.

2. What were the 1954 Geneva Accords and how did we interpret them? How did we interpret the Manila agreement that was so often used as the basis for our intervention? What were the commitments President Eisenhower made? How could the Senate majority leader (LBJ) who helped

persuade President Eisenhower not to involve the United States in the French Indochina war in 1954 reverse his field in 1964 in the name of a SEATO treaty?

3. What was the *Maddox* evidence? If the Tonkin Gulf situation was understandably confused during that frantic first week in August, 1964, what about some investigative reporting between Aug. 4 and the following July, when the major escalation decisions were made?

4. What was the cost of the war in 1964? What was it likely to cost after we first sent in ground troops to protect the air units and then when we sent more to fight a jungle war together with sufficient service troops to supply the combat units? Even in 1965 and 1966 war costs were approaching $2.5 billion a month, and Congressman Melvin Laird of Wisconsin was asking why there was such a gap between what the Pentagon said the war was costing and the facts.

5. What about the Vietnam extravagance when measured against the unfulfilled commitments to our urban obligations, when riots in Watts, Harlem, and Rochester were already sending out early-warning signals every bit as challenging as those from the *Maddox* and from the *Turner Joy?*

6. Why did the President tell journalists and Senators that he knew the war had to be won and could be won on the nonmilitary side when the plan to escalate had become a virtual certainty? Did the President purposefully avoid calling up the reserves and forego making obvious budgetary plans in order to obscure what was to be a maximum effort to teach Ho Chi Minh a lesson?

In a recent forum in Atlanta on credibility, Agnew, and the news media, I was asked the recurring question: Why do broadcasters feel they must do instant analysis after every Presidential speech? The answer was that it is seldom on an instant basis, that White House briefings and advance texts often give newsmen a lead time of two to five hours. I then went on to explain, as I have before, my own sense of guilt over CBS's failure in 1964 to provide serious news analysis after the Tonkin Gulf resolution. Another panelist, Sidney Gruson of the *New York Times,* gently chided me for my hair shirt, insisting that nothing CBS News could have done the night of Aug. 4 and in the days following could have changed history. Gruson may be right, but that does not excuse us for not trying. Perhaps if we had all done more to convince the President that his plans would be carefully scrutinized by a series of well informed broadcasts and searching analyses in the nation's press, there might have been a chance for some sober second thoughts. Perhaps the contagion of such "Yes, but . . ." interpretive journalism might have encouraged others to dig deeper. William Shirer at the time of Hitler, and Murrow and Elmer Davis during the McCarthy ordeal affected the entire level of reporting. Perhaps some of the self-deception might have been minimized. Perhaps some of the false assumptions from which our leadership suffered might have been challenged.

I have always believed that the news media's improved performance during the Dominican intervention may have prevented that Caribbean caper from escalating. It may be an overstatement to say that the presence of news cameras at Mylai might have prevented that massacre. But I doubt it. Certainly more news analysis on the kind of war it was could have made a difference. The present criticism of broadcast journalism—Mr. Agnew notwithstanding—is that there is too little interpretation, not too much.

What of the future?

As the State Department has suffered from a lack of Asian scholars, so, too, American journalism suffers from a shortage of expertise on Southeast Asia. Broadcasting will need specialists in the field, whether it be on Asia, Hough, Wall Street, or for Santa Barbara oil slicks. Perhaps what is needed is the equivalent of the Election Unit and the Space task forces which have provided the networks with highly specialized teams for major developing stories. A new kind of editor will be required, one who perceives the national predicament early enough to turn on the kind of searching light that permits a choice of options while there is still time.

Broadcast newsrooms, like newspapers, suffer from lack of seasoned, dedicated men on the desk; there seems to be more reward in reporting or in being an anchorman. The notable exception is the documentary producer, who is really an editor. But the future of the serious documentary is now in doubt except on public television, where there is at least air time.

Brilliant combat reporting has not been enough, or Vietnam would not continue to be the best reported and least understood war in history. Even today too many Americans remain oblivious to the confusions at the time of Tonkin Gulf. An extended documentary such as NBC's *Decision to Drop the Atomic Bomb* might be a relevant place to begin. A history of the Vietnam struggle may not be as glorious as Solomon's *Victory at Sea* or Wolff's *Air Power,* but the lessons to be learned might be as valuable as those of Pearl Harbor and Dresden. CBS News once did a documentary called *1944.* What about 1964 and 1965? What about a study of the effect of jungle bombing from Nam-dinh through Sontay in December of 1970? A dialogue between all three defense Secretaries—McNamara, Clifford, and Laird—on what the generals were always telling them was certain and what events have taught them was not might be a useful primer.

Finally, as we continue to challenge assumptions, let the news media face up to their own. There has been such obfuscation, distortion, and mishandling of interpretation concerning Vietnam—such a climate of distrust between the Government and the news media—that the end result may be a deadly sense of cynicism. Just as Munich and Czechoslovakia have become shorthand pejoratives for appeasement and apathy, Vietnam may create a new generation of knee-jerk isolationists unwilling to involve America in any cause, regardless of its merit. The tragedy of Vietnam would indeed be compounded if, like the characters in Plato's Cave, we saw only shadows and became the prisoners of the preconceived "pictures in our heads"—pictures placed there by journalistic failures we have only begun to see and remedy.

A New Style
for TV Criticism*

By Richard J. Stonesifer

Leslie Fiedler once wisecracked that the analysis of mass culture is in fact assuming proportions which threaten to make it a branch of mass culture itself. Hence anyone who produces anything about the media—and particularly something centered on the newest and the most spectacular of the media, television—ought to provide a reasonable defense for doing so.

In 1962 Gilbert Seldes, then Dean of the Annenberg School of Communications of the University of Pennsylvania, invited me to establish a graduate seminar studying "the educational, instructional, and cultural aspects of American television." I met his invitation with laughter and a remark about not knowing much on a subject so vast. And he, smiling benignly, remarked that no one really did, so I should not feel intimidated.

I was, however, essentially a teacher and a critic of literature. In order to accept his invitation, I had to convince myself not only that my qualifications were passable but also that I could justify putting aside my more strictly literary interests to do so. For the first time, I had to sit back and straighten out in my own mind precisely how I felt about all of television, whether or not it was worth worrying about.

I recall an incident at a dinner party which occurred at about this time. My hostess was introducing me to one of the guests and, paving the way for conversation, informed the lady that I might be getting ready to do some writing on television. "For or against?" she asked automatically. It was a significant rejoinder which she probably would not have made had she been informed that I was thinking of surveying the world of books, or some aspect of art, or music, or the theater. Television, it seems, is some-

* Reprinted with permission of the author and publishers from *Television Quarterly*, Vol. 6, No. 2 (copyright 1967 by National Academy of Television Arts and Sciences).

thing about which one takes sides, perhaps violently—a symptom of an attitude about the medium that its management might view with some qualms when contemplating its future.

In a little more than two decades, the Television Revolution has produced a giant that not only threatens to but already does bestride our culture like a colossus, for good or bad. English teachers occasionally hear disquieting rumbles abouts the demise of "the Print Culture" or barbs hurled at "those who are merely print-oriented." The name of Marshall McLuhan looms large, and the populace manages at least to understand from what he says that something monumental is happening in our world. It is evident that electronic journalism might slowly relegate the newspaper to a secondary position in the scheme of things and change the major concerns of print journalism at the same time. It seems equally likely that a new electronic literature is destined to emerge, in fact is emerging even as the networks in the 1966–67 season began to commission artistic works for television. Its emergence might change the nature and scope of printed literature from our time onward, detestable as the bulk of the present electronic output might be.

I decided that I have little sympathy for those of my critical colleagues who think that probing studies of such things as broadside ballads or the "realism" of Daniel Defoe constitute proper concerns for the literary analyst, but who are inclined to snort in derision at the idea that television merits any critical concern. I have read too many bad Elizabethan and Jacobean plays to denounce categorically everything of television's attempt at drama as a decline from some past, and largely imagined, theatrical majesty. I have some logical difficulty in separating the antics of a country booby in an 18th-century play and the farce of *The Beverly Hillbillies,* in elevating the one as an object worthy of students' attention (perhaps largely because of its antiquity) and in condemning the other wholly as prefabricated trash cooked up for something called the tasteless Mass Man of our own time, and so beneath notice.

I have even more difficulty accepting without qualification the sort of sharp pigeon-holing statements about true art and popularity that many of my professional colleagues accept as having the rigidity of Scripture to a fundamentalist—"literature embraces two powerful cultural complexes: art on the one hand, and a market-oriented commodity on the other."[1] I have seen too many cultural continuities in evidence as the

---

[1] Lowenthal, Leo, *Literature, Popular Culture,* and *Society,* Prentice-Hall, Inc., Englewood Cliffs, N.J., 1961, p. vii. Lowenthal then goes on to dogmatize even more rigidly: "At least since the separation of literature into the two distinct fields of art and commodity in the course of the 18th-century, the popular literary products *can make no claim in insight and truth.* Yet, since they have become a powerful force in the life of modern man, their symbols cannot be over-estimated as diagnostic tools for studying man in contemporary society." (italics mine) Isn't this just a shade too cavalier a categorization?

Television Revolution has swirled around me to ignore it. And I have long since rejected the thesis that there are, and ought to be, two rigidly defined cultures, one for an elite and one for the masses, with a high fence hopefully erected between them; and that it is virtually hopeless to attempt to lift mass tastes to higher levels. The fencing off process can't be worked in the first place. And the evidence simply cannot be shrugged aside that, speaking broadly, popular culture since 1900 has been a slowly maturing culture. Or that the best of what appears in the mass media constitutes something of a new art form, falling between what is usually called "folk" and "high" culture and thus helping to form a desirable continuum between them.

Moreover, I had to reject the high-fence thesis, pragmatically at least, because I am a teacher, and no teacher can accept it and continue to work effectively with anyone outside the supposed elite. Accepting it is to embrace a kind of sterility, comfortable as that may be, in which one deals only with younger versions of oneself. My ego, for one thing, is not that large. Moreover, such an intentional cultural dichotomy creates a rift in society which seems to me untenable if we hope that our tomorrows will be much of an improvement over our todays. A teacher has to accept Matthew Arnold's "The Last Word" as his credo ("Let the victors, when they come,/When the forts of folly fall,/Find thy body by the wall") even if he knows assuredly that the forts of folly will not fall within many generations, if ever—and even if he feels privately that Arnold was a mite sententious in phrasing it all that way!

I know that British intellectuals, battling against the introduction of commercial television in the early 1950s, took to calling television "the idiot's lantern," fashioning the scornful epithet to sum up a number of things: the shock of cultured sensitivities exposed (as if for the first time) to the inanities and barbarities of vulgar, unformed tastes; the fear of the responsible and socially concerned that the populace would be lulled into mindless apathy; the distate for an expected deluge of American-style programming—"it's pretty dreary living in the American Age . . ." says Osborne's Jimmy Porter in *Look Back in Anger*. The modern Diogenes, British or not, hardly sees himself carrying an image orthicon tube around as *his* lantern. Indeed, what he fears most is that in his search for men possessing the proper human virtues, he is more likely to find most of them huddled in front of their flickering screens, intent on the gibberings of a Zsa Zsa Gabor: a prospect which is, let us admit quickly, far from pleasing. Even the tycoons currently presiding over television in America cannot be happy facing the horrible allegation that mankind has slowly climbed from the primeval muck to the present to end up enthralled by a world of antic shadows—no matter how much toothpaste is sold.

But the epithet was really unmerited. That too I know. If television can be "the little mind rotter" that Eugene Paul called it in his *The Hungry*

Eye in 1962, too often just a distractor, a convenient baby-sitter, a pacifier for children and the childish, the "boob tube" or the "idiot box," it can be, and frequently is, a great deal more. Gilbert Seldes himself put it in a phrase when he wrote in *The Great Audience* that television can be "a sort of Platonic ideal of communication." Or Charles Siepmann when he called it "a kind of language."

It is of staggering importance that in the average daytime minute millions of American homes supposedly have television sets turned on in them, rising to many millions more per prime-time minute in the evening hours. Or that the parts of the average American family watch television for more than a total of five hours each day. Or that television's programming is readily available to 94% of the population, a percentage which is calculated to rise to 98% by the decade's end. These are important if only to assess the size of the giant that has developed since June 17, 1941, when commercial television operation was first authorized.

But they are "facts" which are important chiefly when viewed against the observations cited from Seldes and Siepmann—that here in television is the ideal communications set-up; that here is a medium which involves virtually a new language in the sense that its way of communicating is new and different and all-encompassing; above all, that here is a fact of our technological civilization that simply must concern all of us, for it may be vital if we would preserve ourselves as a race and lift ourselves as men.

Anyone who has watched television with any consistency has had more than enough moments for despair. But he can, if he is fair, produce his own list of unforgettable moments too, moments when its being "a sort of Platonic ideal of communication" came through strongly, moments which reached a *massed* audience (which is different from but includes the *mass* audience) with a force impossible in any other way. Many might cite, and have, that evening—March 7, 1955—when one out of every two Americans watched Mary Martin flying around as Peter Pan, a marvel that enhanced the fairy-tale magic of Tinkerbell and her crew. Others would cite Edward R. Murrow's *See It Now* exposure of McCarthyism, which some have called the single most important program ever done on television. But I would submit five key moments, all of them from the public affairs sector of telecasting, which seem to me to stand as essential symbols, proof positive that television can be, as Bob Hope once said, a "21-inch looking glass that shows you the world full-length." And that too has a Platonic ring to it. All of them were times when, almost literally, everyone was watching.

The first was that moment when the TV camera focused on the fumbling hands of the gangster Costello during the March, 1951, Kefauver hearings. Denied the opportunity of photographing his face, cameramen focused instead on his hands, hands which twisted and turned and rubbed each other, quickly convicting Costello in the eyes of the citizenry and demonstrating, thus early in television's history, the incomparable value of the close-up; and demonstrating too the validity of another of Seldes' contentions in *The Great Audience:* that television can be "incomparably the conveyor of truth."

The second was in the Army-McCarthy hearings in April of 1954, when Attorney Joseph Welch turned on the demagogic Senator and rebuked him for besmirching the good name of Frederick Fisher, one of Welch's young colleagues in his New England law firm. There has not been a better confrontation of good versus evil seen in the mass media, not even on that deserted street in front of the saloon in *High Noon.*

The third was when Robert Frost, blinded by the sun, had to discard his manuscript and to work from memory in reciting a poem at President Kennedy's Inaugural on January 20, 1961. In the process, he humanized and ennobled the merely formal ceremonies. Everyone, at such a moment, is in the position "of seeing Shelley plain."

The fourth and fifth come, as certainly they would have to come on any list, from the Four Days (November 22–25) in 1963 when television reached its greatest glory so far in covering the events of the Kennedy assassination and funeral. The shooting of Oswald by Ruby, an event which television *should not have been present to record,* must inevitably be included, sordid and degrading as it is, but included because television was there and so everyone could witness what history will call something of a tragicomic sequence.

Finally, and with equal inevitability, that almost too poignant moment when three-year-old John John Kennedy, responding to his mother's whispered instructions, straightened and saluted the passing coffin bearing his father's body.

I watched this last standing amidst a crowd of college professors in a lounge in the Faculty Club at the University of Pennsylvania. Archibald MacLeish, then a writer-in-residence there for a few weeks, was standing with me. I looked at his face and thought of the words he had written in his *Poetry and Experience:*

> To feel emotion is at least to feel. The crime against life, the worst of all crimes, is *not* to feel. And there was never, perhaps, a civilization in which that crime, the crime of torpor, of lethargy, of apathy, the snakelike sin of coldness-at-the-heart, was commoner than in our technological civilization in which the emotionless emotions of adolescent boys are mass produced on television screens to do our feeling for us, and a woman's longing for her life is twisted, by singing commercials, into a longing for a new detergent, family size, which will keep her hands as innocent as though she had never lived. It is the modern painless death, this commercialized atrophy of the heart. None of us is safe from it.

Even television's severest critics will agree to the medium's utility in making such moments as I have mentioned available to the massed public. But they also will echo MacLeish's concern, or go beyond it to condemn all of television because of its commercial excesses and the scarcity of valuable moments. Moreover, it is intellectually fashionable, very much the "in" thing, to be anti-TV. The serious critics of television, who are few in number, give way quickly to the Television Snob, a specimen met, I regret to say, frequently within the Groves of Academe.

A leading university, contemplating awarding an honorary degree to TV-host Dr. Frank Baxter, found that it had to give up the idea when a faculty committee rebelled in distaste. Baxter had, someone pointed out, jocularly referred to himself as "the intellectuals' Liberace," a bit of whimsy that effectively cut him off from being considered as a serious scholar, at least by this high-minded group. I recall vividly a day in 1957 when I had introduced John Mason Brown at a meeting. A television newsman stopped us as we left the auditorium, thrust a microphone under Brown's nose and asked, "Mr. Brown, what do you think of people who refuse to own television sets?" Brown thought for a moment, and then out it came, a little gem of icy criticism which he later put into print: "I feel this—and I feel it passionately—people who deny themselves television deny themselves participation in life today. They are horse and buggy; they are atrophied; they are self-exiled from the world. They suffer from the most painful illiteracy, which is that of the literate!"

I, like Brown, have little sympathy for the Television Snob. But I have great respect for the thoughtful critic—like MacLeish—who condemns much, even most, of television in its present state. When Walter Kerr referred to television on one occasion as "an unfortunate medium," he was, I hope, referring to its present programming practices, not to its ultimate possibilities.

President Eisenhower's 1960 Commission on National Goals reported simply that "thus far, television has failed to use its facilities adequately for educational and cultural purposes, and reform in its performance is urgent." But we must be fair and reasonable in our demands for its reform. We have already seen enough of television to know that the early cries of anguish about its probable effects were probably too shrill and hysterical. When television appeared in the late 1940s, the critical argued that it might fatally disrupt and corrupt American family life. Or that it could irreparably damage the morals and taste of youth and lead to a catastrophic passivity among the citizenry. It might even open the future to domination by the Russians or Chinese—presumably to the one of those two resisting its electronic blandishments longest! These were the more fearful prognostications. But it was also alleged that television might create over the next few generations a race incapable of locomotion, broad in the hams and weak in the eyes, drugged into meek acceptance of whatever TV conveys, manipulated into consent by whatever Mustapha Mond benevolent or despotic, ruled at the moment.

It is still too early in television's history to say categorically that some or all of these things might not ultimately happen. But the possibility seems unlikely. Commercial television has now worked through its obsession with wrestling, with cowboys-in-the-saddle, and with quiz shows. It has recently passed from its preoccupation with nurses-in-the-corridors and medical syringes to an emphasis on filmed comedy series, a phase which is also destined to pass. It would be hard to build a case for a swing upward toward sustained quality in any of this. Some critical watchers-of-the-screen have professed to see nothing in it but massive evidence of television's gradual deterioration from its own Golden Age, which centered loosely on *Robert Montgomery Presents, Kraft Theatre,* or *Garroway at Large,* depending on what one wishes to denigrate in the 1960s. Meanwhile, the middle-class American family has gone through a similar progression—going out to see TV, then bringing the instrument into the home and enthroning it in a central position in the living room, then relegating it to the den or bedroom or even to a playroom in the basement.

It seems profitless to pursue the matter further by considering the descent of the television set into the cellar as a new middle-class symbol, though some have tried. Gunther Anders, for example, waxed eloquent in a similar vein:

> Decades ago it was possible to observe that the social hallmark of the family—the massive table in the center of the living room, which served as the gathering point of the family—had begun to lose its force of attraction, had become obsolete. Eventually the living room table was eliminated from the modern home. Now it has found its authentic successor, the television set, a piece of furniture whose social symbolism and persuasive power can measure against those of the former table. This does not mean, however, that the television set has become the family center; on the contrary, what the set embodies is rather the decentralization of the family, its eccentricity: it is, so to speak, the negative family table. It does not provide a common center, but rather a common avenue of escape . . .[2]

Anders seems not to realize that the main reason for the disappearance of the bulky central table as the center of family activity was the development of the electric light, allowing the efficient and economical brightening up of the corners to which the family members were delighted to disperse, perhaps to get away from each other!

The whole game is simply too confusing to be worthwhile, especially when one can't believe in it. And I can't, anymore than I can believe that television alone ought to be charged with a number of deleterious effects

---

2 Anders, Gunther, "The Phantom World of TV," *Dissent,* **3,** 14–24 (1956).

on American family life. The American family (working-class, middle-class, or aristocratic) has now survived the greatest possible impact of television. No really conclusive evidence exists to show that the revolution in domestic morality of the 1950s and 1960s can be attributed any more to television than to other significant forces on the social scene since World War II, *even though television may be related to those forces and may accentuate their impact on the populace.*

In March of 1954, a prominent Philadelphia clergyman, groping for the ultimate in earthly privations for his flock, suggested that they give up television for Lent, meeting with no success. His success would be no better in the 1960s. The poor padre, of course, should have been able to foretell his failure, and probably did. For no matter how one feels about television's impact, one thing stands clear: the people seem to be hooked by the thing, though they may not stay that way. It took the motion picture decades to reach the peak of its power to draw audiences—82,000,000 persons in the U.S. in 1946. Radio took far less time. But television, within six years of its widespread entrance on the American scene, gained audiences that surpassed all of the other media.

A statistical parade to make this point has become a standard feature of books on television. Instead of setting down again the all-too-familiar but staggering figures, let me utilize an already existing tabulation and show what is wrong with it. Here is a paragraph from Stan Opotowsky's *TV: The Big Picture:*

> The eagerness with which the American public grabbed at the opportunity to become hollow-eyed zombies is graphically demonstrated by television's growth. It took 62 years for electric wiring to reach 34,000,000 homes. It took 80 years for the telephone to reach the same number of homes. It took the automobile 49 years and the electric washer 47 years. But it took television only 10 years.

Very interesting. And very graphic. But logically misleading and in need of a great deal of qualification. When TV arrived, electricity was already available; one merely had to buy a set, install an antenna, plug the set in, and sit back to attempt to develop an interest in Milton Berle. A lot of time was spent in getting the telephone distributed because an entire system had to be built; the automobile needed an expanding network of hard-surfaced roads. These networks were infinitely more difficult to build than the coaxial cable uniting the continent for television. In short, radio had built television's essential "system" before television's arrival. And television arrived in the United States in the aftermath of World War II, when personal incomes were high. Money saved during the war could be spent on sets, and the national urge to be amused was strong. Not the least of Milton Berle's attainments was that he did his best to make some Gold Star Mothers forget!

In sum, my credentials for the task with which Gilbert Seldes asked me to cope were not impeccable, though I at least had the considerable virtue of knowing my own limitations.

But I worried nevertheless, chiefly because I am not a formally trained social scientist. And because I knew that as a student of literature I am not much interested in distilling seemingly cosmic symbolizations and significances from the trivia that is inevitably a sizable part of any popular culture ("From Dagmar to Mary Tyler Moore: A Commentary on Changing Female Types on Television," accompanied by statistical tables resulting from a survey done in Sheboygan, Wisconsin, on the relative impact of low-cut dresses and stretch pants in stimulating the id). I would not, *I will not,* take that path!

I soon came to see these supposed deficiencies in my academic orientation as decided virtues. This conviction grew stronger as I delved into the intricacies of the research that the Television Revolution has produced and as I pondered the musings of the analysts of mass culture. In their pages, however, I discovered twin texts on which to hang my new endeavor, texts which might be carved in some enduring stone and placed over the entrances of the schools of communication now springing up on the nation's campuses.

Leon Arons and Mark A. May provided the first: ". . . the proper study of mass communications is Man."[3] This says what I want said, though I am certain that its authors may interpret it to include things which I don't. Which is why I am anxious to couple it with a few sentences from Leo Lowenthal in which he lashes out at the restricted and essentially barren nature of much of the research so far directed to television. But listen to Lowenthal directly:

> A study of television . . . will go to great heights in analyzing data on the influence of television on family life, but it will leave to poets and dreamers the question of the actual human values of this new institution. Social research takes the phenomena of modern life, including the mass media, at face value. It rejects the idea of placing them in a historical and moral context.[4]

If the reader has detected that I can control my unmitigated enthusiasm for much that has been done in the field thus far, he has gotten my point. One can't help thinking of Albert D. Lasker's famed definition of market research: "something that tells you that a jackass has two ears." I stand ready to be both corrected and educated. But I try to be objective, to avoid excesses of enthusiasm or distaste, and to remember always that

---

[3] Arons, Leon, and May, Mark A., eds., *Television and Human Behavior—Tomorrow's Research in Mass Communications,* Appleton-Century-Crofts, New York, 1963.
[4] Lowenthal, Leo, "Historical Perspectives in Popular Culture," *American Journal of Sociology,* **55,** 323–332 (1950). In his *Literature, Popular Culture, and Society* (p. 7), Lowenthal reworkd this article into the opening section, and he significantly changes one sentence to read, "Social research takes too much of modern life, including the mass media, at face value."

television in our time involves something like an evolving art form; which means that one ought occasionally to apply to it the regular artistic and aesthetic yardsticks rather than only the measurements of the opinion pollsters or the social-theory makers.

Obviously, as an educator my primary interests are in the educational and cultural possibilities which television opens to us. But there is, I submit, little point in discussing the strictly educational uses of television and their impact on our cultural health without considering the much greater impact that current commercial television has on the nation's populace.

My primary concern is the one voiced by André Malraux to the French Chamber of Deputies on November 11, 1963, when he pointed out that motion pictures and television constitute the two most powerful modern influences on men's minds and that these media today are allowed to appeal in the large to what is least civilized and most elemental in man's nature. Malraux warned that these influences must be counteracted.

I would add, I think, that simple counteraction is likely to be strikingly ineffective. A far more challenging and nobler task faces us: making the visual mass media what they can truly be, great technological forces working for good in our world. We can, if we will, follow the sage advice of Dr. Samuel Gould and make television, for instance, "one of the major tools in sharpening and deepening our aesthetic appreciations." Or we can allow it merely to help the hucksters sell soap. The choice is ours as free men.

And the choice may now well be upon us. Burton Paulu, writing in *British Broadcasting in Transition,* remarked that "thinking Americans are questioning their broadcasting system as never before."

It is well that they should. For the gravest threat to television's future is simply this: that those who ought to be most concerned about its health and welfare have either largely deserted it or have never been brought to feel that it mattered—the educators, the critics, the clergy, the opinion-makers, the individual citizens of taste.

What is needed, obviously, are some strident voices resounding across the American landscape. And they have started to sound, most significantly from within television itself.

It seems, in short, a good idea to join the voices.

TELEVISION: FURTHER READINGS

Books

Arlen, Michael J., *Living-Room War,* New York, 1969.

Bluem, A. William, *Documentary in American Television: Form, Function, Method,* Hastings, New York, 1965.

Lyle, Jack, and Parker, Edwin B., *Television in the Lives of Our Children,* Sanford, 1961.

Minow, Newton N., *Equal Time: the Private Broadcaster and the Public Interest,* Atheneum, New York, 1964.

Opotowsky, Stan, *TV the Big Picture: a Close Hard Look at the World of Television,* Collier, New York, 1961.

Skornia, Harry J., *Television and Society: an Inquest and Agenda for Improvement,* McGraw-Hill Book Co., New York, 1965.

———, *Television and the News: a Critical Appraisal,* Palo Alto, 1968.

Steiner, Gary, *The People Look at Television: a Study of Audience Attitudes,* Alfred A. Knopf, New York, 1963.

Toffler, Alvin, *The Culture Consumers: a Study of Art and Affluence in America,* St. Martins Press, New York, 1964.

Whale, John, *The Half-Shut Eye: Television and Politics in Britain and America,* New York, 1969.

White, David Manning, and Averson, Richard, eds., *Sight, Sound and Society: Motion Pictures and Television in America,* Boston, 1968.

Articles

Arthur, R. A., "TV: the 21-inch Bore," *Nation,* Sept. 20, 1965.

Dempsey, D., "Social Comment and TV Censorship," *Saturday Review,* July 12, 1969.

Goden, H. H., "American Media Baronies: a Modest Atlantic Atlas," *Atlantic Monthly,* July 1969.

Hentoff, N., "Irrigating the TV Wasteland," *Commonwealth,* Aug. 11, 1961.

Packard, V., "New Kinds of Television: Where Do We Go from Here?" *Atlantic Monthly,* Oct. 1963.

Film

Perhaps nothing is more symbolic of the changes in American films since the mid-fifties than an ad in *The New York Times* in April 1970 which announced the public auction of MGM's complete inventory of set-pieces, costumes, and properties. For those mass-media critics who equate pop culture with the assembly lines of the Hollywood dream factories, the announcement was no doubt joyous; Leo the Lion's rapacious roar had been reduced to a whimper. But there are probably millions of movie-goers who nostalgically clipped the advertisement to tuck it away with other memorabilia of the silver screen—with souvenir programs of *Ziegfeld Follies* and *Mrs. Miniver,* autographed photos of Clark Gable and Judy Garland, and back numbers of *Photoplay.*

Mutatis mutandis . . . Just as today's over-thirty fan might treasure a wheel from Charlton Heston's chariot in *Ben-Hur,* in 1984 a film-buff of the "now" generation may bid for the handlebars of Peter Fonda's motorcycle in *Easy Rider.*

If the movies have changed, it is because audiences have changed. Fifteen years ago, when the first edition of *Mass Culture* appeared, the tremors of upheaval were only beginning to be felt in the celluloid Establishment. Despite declining box-office receipts due to television's competitive entertainment, the content of American films was still aimed at a broad audience. In 1957 a *Midnight Cowboy* was unthinkable; no member-company of the Motion Picture Association would even submit such a script to the Code office, let alone taken an option on the property. One can only speculate about Louis B. Mayer's reaction had he been present at the awarding of an Oscar to *Midnight Cowboy* as the best picture of 1969: incredulity mixed with a few censorable thoughts. Perhaps with grudging fanfare, the award to *Midnight Cowboy* was Hollywood's way of acknowledging where it's at.

In his essay, Robert Steele examines the films which, if box-office is any indication, make strong rapport with the young filmgoers of the Age of Aquarius. Mr. Steele underscores in films what has been happening in theater, music, and literature—less concern for "tradition" and *art pour l'art* and far more concern for what the under-thirty generation considers relevant. Relevance to the young audiences who now make up the bulk of the moviegoing public may often seem contradictory: on the one hand a film like *Medium Cool* stressed the need for political and social involvement on the part of young people; whereas a film like *Easy Rider* or *Alice's Restaurant* glorifies the values of the social drop-out (with or without pot).

Whatever their ambiguity, today's films, Mr. Steele posits, speak the language of the young and reflect the contemporary life style. Steele has serious doubts whether the film-makers of classical cinema, such as F. W. Murnau, Jean Renoir, and Sergei Eisenstein, would understand, let alone enjoy, the movies that enrapture today's youth. Perhaps we are today experiencing an outburst of film experimentation, a neo-Romanticism if you will, in which old cinema forms are disappearing.

Are we witnessing the demise of the traditional *story* film and the expansion of the *personal* cinema? The increasing critical emphasis on the film director as "author," the fragmenting of the once-mass movie audience, and the availability of inexpensive photographic and sound-recording equipment seem to be clues to a new use of cinema for individual expression. This is not to suggest that the films of George Stevens and Alfred Hitchcock are necessarily going to be replaced by the experimental and lyric films of a Robert Downey, a Jonas Mekas, or a Stan Vanderbeek, at least not on tomorrow's marquees. The "old pros" are not beyond adapting to the tastes and audiences of the times. William Wyler, for example, followed a very successful, conventional Hollywood musical, *Funny Girl,* with a contemporary, social-message film dealing with racial problems, *The Liberation of L.B. Jones.*

Yet, whether a film be narrative or experimental, realistic or surrealistic, "traditional" in style or contemporary, it offers clues to the particular culture and social structure which yielded it. Diana Trilling, in her incisive examination of *Easy Rider* and the milieu in which this film became so popular, raises some provocative questions about the role of film in today's mass culture. Should critics be concerned with morality? In her affirmative answer to this question, Mrs. Trilling urges us not to forget that codes for the guidance of our moral lives are constantly being offered by popular culture institutions such as cinema. If the artists of mass culture— whether Peter Fonda and Dennis Hopper, John Lennon, or Jimmy Hendrix —play a primary role in the fashioning of these codes, what is the proper role of popular culture critics? To warn us not to be too seduced by art; to ask questions about the reliability and feasibility and worth of the codes now being offered us.

Art, Youth Culture, and the Movies*

By Robert Steele

Looking over a panorama of films of the late sixties makes one wonder how we will get through the seventies. Whether accurate or not, they show America failing in every direction.

The signs that are repeated in these films offer numerous interpretations. It's easy to guess how a prophet would read them. A Satan would read them as evidence of his triumph. A god would read them as a depiction of the absurdity of his creation and the signal of the demise of his influence; he might take comfort in his decision to have silently withdrawn and accept the accusation of his being a *deus abscondi*.

A Shiva would interpret the movies of our times as the crack of a pistol giving him the starting time for his eighth dance around the world to terminate the conflagration which he initiated and represents. A Brahma would regard them as a harbinger proclaiming to him that his time of retirement and rest is over. Shiva's destruction, which is a cleaning of putrescence, will soon subside. The hills and valleys, the rivers and sears, the ghettos and cities will soon be decontaminated, and Brahma's creative work can begin anew. (A cyclic view of history, found in Hinduism, can bolster us when contrasted with our Judeo-Christian philosophy of human events.)

Or an unknown god that has stayed close to the scene may be waiting in the wings for a cue to make his stage entrance.

The reaction of the artist to the movies of the late sixties would be a curious mixture of admonition and regret. He may find comfort walking in the shoes of a Jeremiah, but in 1970 he wears rubber boots so that his tears do not soak his feet and cause him to die of pneumonia.

The difficulty is that today's films defy traditional ideas of art. The cinema is in more flux than ever. Today's films are both unconventional

---

* Published for the first time in this volume.

222

and successful, especially in their appeal to young people. Meaningful hypotheses are not easy.

The word "art" has become dated and almost mawkish. Pronouncing a film or a play a "work of art" is no longer a sought-after critical endorsement. In an era of pop culture such a sobriquet can give a deathly sting to an expressive object. While art has been a yardstick measuring the heights reached by past cultures, it is now considered a measure verging toward the antediluvian. Faulkner's eloquent description of art as that which endures no longer seems pertinent:

> The aim of every artist is to arrest motion, which is life, by artificial means and hold it fixed, so that a hundred years later, when a stranger looks at it, it moves again, since it is life. This is the artist's way of scribbling "Kilroy was here" on the wall of the final and irrevocable oblivion through which he must someday pass.

Until recently, we made much use of the words "nonart," "antiart," and "nouveau art" to describe contemporary phenomena. But much that passes for art today cannot be explained by its being dadaistic. Rather than mocking the art of the past, artistic practitioners today don't give a damn about it. The art of the past has no more to do with them than past medicine, past theology, and past plumbing. They are not concerned with merely bringing down the past to gain freedom to create new forms. Formlessness itself, or antiform for its own sake, gets closer to *au courant* intentions. The art of the past no longer stands over and above artisans, it no longer commands respect. Becoming an artist by being apprenticed to a master, or copying art objects in the Prado, makes today's practitioner the part of the totem pole that is buried six feet underground. A copyist of past art is considered only a dreg. Technique which made him a valuable link in the perpetuation of art styles is held in low esteem.

A revolution in what used to be called the art world has taken place. More radical changes have occurred between World War II and the present time than took place in previous centuries. It is a misnomer exhibiting the remoteness of a "square" to even discuss created objects of today as art objects. Only children, old folk, and nonmakers of today's artistic commodities go to conventional museums, theaters, and concert halls. The practitioner does not go very much, and when he does go, it is not to enjoy and learn but to satisfy curiosity. In the midst of this revolution, we move fast and destroy indiscriminately. The fabricators of plays, graphic arts, sculpture, and especially films today are unmoved by an art heritage. Contemporary work in the domain that used to be called art is being taken over by a new breed of creators. These new creators are a generation of the species who give us a revision of our old world as well as a vision of their new world.

The Oscar Wilde aesthetic, "art for art's sake," is no longer being discussed. Life for art's sake also seems Victorian. Art for life's sake puts the "squares" on speaking terms with the "cool people," but the square was born too late or has a hangup with his professor, art school, or mentor. Life for life's sake, or more life for more life's sake, is an aesthetic summation of current artistic expression. Although raw material may be the stuff that is handled with an ambiguous feeling that its use may contribute to more life, it may remain in its virginal state. In many instances, the less done to the raw material, when it is supposedly transformed into an arbitrary creation, the better.

What a tizzy the state of today's "art world" puts our art critics in! All some critics can do is rant against what's happening. (What can you say about a happening? What can be said about something that is so bizarre that there is no standard from the past that has any relevancy when confronted with an outlandish exhibition?) Some critics of the past feel that they have little or nothing to work with today. Art objects for them are nonexistent. But it is only they, the critics, who seem to notice or care. The creators whom they might analyze after failing to analyze new works couldn't care less. Daily and weekly, in a chorus, some critics come close to divulging their furor and exploding about the degradation of art by the Johnny-come-latelies. These *parvenus* may have moved into the galleries and theaters, but to the critic they are still outsiders.

In the gamesmanship of get-the-critic, the new artistic nonartist takes a don't-give-a-damn pose when he encounters the critic. He has no expectation of his work's making sense to the critic. Perhaps he truly doesn't care a hoot about what the critic thinks if he is strong enough or secure enough to be impervious to the good that the patronization of a critic might be to him.

We need television around for a bit longer, so that we can have the rich comedy shows of the critic interviewing the artist. The "artist" wished he had never agreed to be on the show in the first place, but he was conned into it because he needed the money. He sits back invisibly smiling at the interviewer and the television audience, and listens while the critic-interviewer explains to the audience the nature of his work.

A shattering experience for many a middle-aged critic today is to run into a twenty-two year old punk kid who has not spent an hour studying art history or aesthetics, but who speaks and writes brilliantly. (See the new journal *Interview*.) The kid dances around the august critic with his insights into what is going on in the new scene. He makes sense to his peers while the name-critic is good only for a laugh. An encounter of this sort makes the established critic resolve to learn more, to try harder to perceive beneath surfaces, to take a second look at the film or the play that may have eluded him. He has the disturbing hunch that he has overlooked something, else how could this youngster make such good sense.

Yet the followers and devotees of this young and forceful expositor may be bores. Their enthusiasm and commitment to the latest film of a Godard or a Lester can be explained by their having been stunted emotionally and intellectually by all of the television upon which they have feasted for their whole lives. The older person believes that when he was their age he knew more, and had superior aesthetic judgment and taste, than today's hordes of young people. The films that are so popular with the masses of the young seem puerile to him. He has seen the same thing before countless times, and many times he has seen it expressed with much more meaning and finesse. The young oftentimes seem to him sickly solemn and debauched; the veteran of the arts bolsters his ego and feels less archaic because he sees *kitsch* where the young see the *bona fide*.

Joseph Wood Krutch argues that today the arts are being corrupted. They are responsible for swinging us back into primitiveness or else our increasing primitievness is transforming our arts into the artistic expressions of the aboriginal. Their closeness to the values and nonvalues of our hip communities results in an "infatuation with the primitive." "Primitive had at one time," Krutch says, "connotations entirely derogatory; whereas today it implies, as often as not, admiration and praise. Primitive, say we, and therefore beautiful. Has anyone ever suggested that this preference today for what used to be called barbarism may have chilling implications."

Krutch hopes that his fears are unfounded, but he says, "Developments in the arts have often been paralleled in other fields, and as I contemplate political, social and military events rather than those merely artistic or cultural, I find them suggesting the gloomier alternative . . . The anthropologists' pet theory that customs are the only basis of a moral code is very up to date, but it is also a return to the concept of the tribal god whose rules and regulations are valid only for his chosen people."

This erudite man and distinguished critic feels the pulse of contemporary arts, and the count that he gets could make us feel that Spengler and Schopenhauer foresaw the changes in society which we now perceive on motion-picture screens at the neighborhood cinema. Television moves the images of our decline and societal demise into our living rooms. Other arts that many young people are refurbishing to make them their own are undergoing similar transformations, but it is the movies that seem to be the most pervasive burning bushes to give us cause for somber thought.

Despite the upheavals in the motion-picture industry, movies are economically stronger than ever; some are making more money for the lucky investors than ever before in movie history; films and music, rock, and country music, of course, have left theater, graphic arts, and literature scrounging for survival. The electric guitar and percussion instruments are such an inseparable part of the movies that are most successful at the box office, that hip movies and hip music have become as necessary to each other as shoes and socks. Even Antonioni landed on the Grateful

Dead for *Zabriskie Point*. Jerry Garcia, "Pink Floyd," and "Kaleidoscope" have become hot-selling albums for M.G.M.'s record division.

Some recent films that have forced themselves into the rapping, thinking, and behavior of young audiences are worth analysis. They are in the contemporary life style; they appeal to that half of the population which is under twenty-five. Some of these films are idolized like gods and studied like scripture; seeing them a half dozen times is not unusual. They have something that satisfies the appetites of audiences who want to belong to rebellion. Some contain seeds of revolution. Many of them bamboozle the no-longer-young who wish they knew why the movies become religious or cult objects for a hip congregation.

What do these movies say about the state of American society, and how do young audiences read their signs and messages?

Capitalism and its "good" ways of life in America are put down in *The Graduate*. The upper-middle class, with its swimming pools and electric toasters, is pillaged. The persons who have "made it" are presented as immoral, stupid, corrupted, and beyond repair. But young persons who went into spasms over this film (which enabled Joe Levine, its financier, to become the wealthiest film mogul around today) are vague when questioned about the appeal of the film. Dustin Hoffman's sounding and looking as if he has spent most of his life at Nebraska Wesleyan University doesn't bother his acolytes. Supposedly, he has come from an Eastern Ivy League college. An older person feels certain he would not have been admitted, let alone been graduated, from an urbane university. He is a dope but is loved all the more for his doltish ways. Unlike more recent films, *The Graduate* is pink-lemonade romance. Sex without love is not so interesting as an "intellectual" conversation with Mrs. Robinson at the very moment she is panting for him.

Love is foiled for the latter part of the film, but the young man gets into his convertible, seduces his beloved, who has just spoken her marriage vows to another young man, and whisks her off to that somewhere promising to be paradise for them both. Love amounts to her face, hair, and attractiveness. Benjamin doesn't know her well, and they never say anything to each other that gets beneath their skins. But at the end of the film his future happiness is nailed down by his striking those in the church who would stop him. The cross functions as his weapon and then as a door bolt. The boy gets the girl, and we have a happy ending. A plastic economy is exchanged for a plastic romance.

But *The Graduate*, even though it is one of the films of the late sixties, already seems old-fashioned. Happy endings are no longer the patent for "now" films, and boys don't always get their girls.

Easy Rider feeds the love-hate affair young people have with America. They emphathize with Fonda and Hopper: "they could be me!" The cyclists went in search of American life, and look what happened to them.

This country will do the same to me, read the young moviegoers. Freedom, doing your thing, and individualism make you the enemy of the people, especially Southerners. If you don't cut your hair and shape up, you've had it from your employer, university authorities, and, of course, your parents and the military. The use of an all-American maneuver as the springboard of *Easy Rider* (buying and selling drugs to finance the odyssey) is neither considered nor objected to by the film's young ticket-buying supporters. It is excused because the cyclists are free souls *wanting* to do the right thing, and that's the way it is. One way or another, we all blow it.

Shoppers passing Tiffany's in *Midnight Cowboy* do not see a man who is prostrate on the sidewalk. This is an inkling of how much those who have arrived care about me, reflects the young moviegoer. Money talks and only money talks and money is evil. But not having it makes for misery and violence to get it. Joe learns to be somebody only when his money runs out; only then does he cease to be a braggart and gum-chewing fake cowboy. He grows enough to have a loyal and loving relationship to Ratzo, and this relationship helps him to face reality. He puts his cowboy identity in the trash can. Rather than compromising with the city, the doorway to fame and fortune, Joe and Ratzo withdraw. Ratzo keeps some of his delusions about how he will climb to the top of a pinnacle and gorge on the good life, but he dies. His dream of success was ridiculous. Joe, by the end of the film, has no appetite for the climb and will be content to sell used cars. Later on he may find someone who loves him, like the girl he left in Texas, whom he can love.

Last Summer is about one deceitful parent and a sycophant prospective parent. Sporting behavior results in the rape of a good girl as a comeuppance. Nobody really relates to anybody. All there is is a beautiful sunset to conclude a day, and a hope that next summer might be different—but how different? Nobody knows.

In *The Sterile Cuckoo* Warren is a square. He looses his elan for Pookie; because he's failing in college, in order to hit the books, he cancels his vacation plans to be with her. But his determination not to fail is not the real reason for his dropping Pookie. He likes her a lot, really cares about her, but he is not going to get tied down. He is so dense, even though she is a kook; he can't see how great she really is. He is a sorry sight. She is unappreciated, unrewarded goodness; she is all free spirit. Every Saturday morning may be just like last Saturday morning for her. Love? Pookie has heard about it, but it is a phantom.

Arlo Guthrie in *Alice's Restaurant* is as sweet and innocent as a baby, and it is not in him to hurt anybody. He couldn't even say anything unkind. But look what does or can happen to him: the draft, and the idiotic police arresting and fining him. An overdose can kill, and loving care does not heal. The bulwarks, Alice and Ray, evaporate. The girl who is nothing but a warm body is the one he beds down with. Even love is slight and tenuous; romance gives way to convenience and mutuality. Love is sex. Violence is not the way, but action isn't either. Withdraw and retire from the fray seems to be the answer. Conflict with authority is amusing for a while, but even it becomes pointless. The dispossessed have no recourse. They can't even count on their friends.

Loving is an exacerbation on suburbanite *angst*. George Segal becomes Faust when, instead of being a painter, he becomes a commercial illustrator. Probably his cataclysmic misstep was moving out of his loft in the Village to take on a house, wife, kids, and neighbors in Westport, Connecticut. He is trapped in the business world. He is trapped in monogamy with a respectable, conventional wife. He pays for her dresses even though she doesn't select the one he likes. He looks at a new house to please her when he doesn't have the next payment for the old and smaller one. His soul, which ought to belong to Vermeer, goes to the marketplace every time he takes the commuter's train to Manhattan. He has two onerous daughters who are kids rather than cherubs. He is an artist—or was an artist—whose mistress makes more demands for "respectability" and security from him. His lot is one of daily agony. Getting smashed no longer helps. His life is measured out in trips to see his agent in the city, redoing drawings to placate clients, working nights, getting up tired, and shopping with the family on Saturdays. There is no way out. He is damned.

Jane Fonda has had it before *They Shoot Horses, Don't They?* gets its marathon dancing under way. She is a thirty-minute hard-boiled egg. Until the end of the film she doesn't speak a line that is not spewed-out venom. Agents have had her; producers have had her; everyone that has arrived in Hollywood, male and female, has had her. She has moved out of her body in order to climb to the top. Life is a mad merry-go-round interspersed with a physical-endurance derby that goes nowhere. If that is all that life is, and if there is no exit from the insane marathon, voluntary death is preferable. Nothing, even if there is a hell, could be worse than the battle to be admitted to heavenly Hollywood. Her withdrawal is the ultimate withdrawal. Alternates are nonexistent. Horses are treated better; they are shot.

In *Putney Swope* a black becomes chairman of the board of a Madison Avenue ad agency; he renames it "Truth and Soul." The previous chairman had a heart seizure and lies dead on the conference table. The board members voted for the black musical director of the agency, Putney, the least likely candidate, so that they would be throwing away their votes to cut down the competition for their becoming the new chairman.

After he assumes power Putney announces that he is not planning to rock the old boat—he will sink it. Blacks replace whites. The agency refuses to make television commercials promoting cigarettes, booze, and war. Guilts are romped through by the manic chairman and his henchmen, all blacks—guilts about sex, money, success, and race relations.

Life in an army camp can be unforgetable fun experience if one manages to have olives for his martinis, says M*A*S*H; black humor, that is, humor at the expense of the fundamentalist surgeon who is hauled off in a straitjacket, and Hot Lips, the up-tight nurse who becomes a pig-tailed cheerleader, throws light on the idiocy of the Korean War and MacArthur. No one from the top to the bottom of the hierarchy in the military establishment of the Mobile Army Surgical Hospital can resist being bought.

U.S.A. doctors give a draftable Korean the high-blood-pressure treatment to try to pull the wool over the eyes of Korean physical examiners to save the Korean draftee from the Korean army. Marriage and kids that are back home in Illinois are far, far away. Maybe they no longer exist. A stoned American football team become killers going out to the football field to separate American heads from American bodies while the war carries on. Mansonlike surgery is performed on the casualties brought in on stretchers from the front three miles away. The surgery looks like a game of charades when sausages and egg-beaters are pulled out of an open stomach behind a sheet. When we are drafted for psychotic war and pressed into an insane situation, the sane man maintains his sanity by splitting a gut laughing. People are all right as long as they are left alone, but when they are interfered with, why shouldn't all hell break loose?

Daria glances through the back window of her car and thinks she sees an explosion. She gets out of the car and sees explosion after explosion that is no mirage: the whole hilltop house is blowing up. It's the blowing up of contemporary architecture, modern Scandinavian furniture, candle-light dinners, executives' wives lolling around swimming pools, servility, Muzak, telephones, and all the material accoutrements of a capitalistic society. The apocalyptic vision at the end of *Zabriskie Point* is the only justifiable recourse. One terrific explosion that sets off more and more explosions. Why shouldn't the mess be blown up? Fire is clean. If you don't murder the pig, he will murder you. That's all one can expect now. Fun, play, running away, and love are impossible in our crevice of the cosmos.

The foreign films which young moviegoers enthusiastically endorse offer similar interpretations. In the quest for the world film market, the content breech between Hollywood and the "imports" has narrowed.

The heroine of the Swedish *I Am Curious (Yellow)* thinks her droopy breasts and fat stomach will turn men off. She has ideals for a better world, but her disconnected experiences teach her that she is alone in her idealism. Nothing comes out right for her, and everyone conspires to use her as an object. Maximum respect for an emancipated and demo-cratic way of life, as verbalized in her new ten commandments, are put down, along with the whipped cream she consumes when she breaks her fast. There's plenty in this film about what's wrong with the world, as well as Sweden, but there's even more. The evil of the prison system and what mothers do to destroy their daughters is taken on in *I Am Curious (Blue)*. These films tell us again what we already know: cities and the self-centeredness they nurture destroy us; they cause poverty and slavery. The economic and political systems of a nation offer us no hope. Non-violence has lost its appeal. Only a revolution will bail out Lena and us. And you can't trust anybody, really you can't, except for the moment.

That man who radiates goodness, Yves Montand, casts his presence over the totality of *Z* despite his being beaten on the head, run over by a car, and killed early in the film. The message of the film is obvious: individual resistance can do only so much. You can give your life resist-ing, and for an interim you may think you have won, but evil forces cannot be beaten. They are always there. They take only a brief holiday after they have been momentarily trounced for fracturing skulls and shedding the blood of the martyrs. Political and military systems are more durably woven together than the warp and woof of the Aubusson tapestry. The man with a long view knows that in the end he will be the victim of the state's ruthlessness. The courageous man who pits himself against the world of the generals and politicians wins love from his followers, but their love does not save him or them from the inevitable final demolition.

The protagonist of Truffaut's *Stolen Kisses* is a lovable bumbler. He has little ambition—except to get a dishonorable discharge from the Army —and clearly he will never get ahead. It's his nature to do the wrong thing at the wrong time; he never fails in this. But he gets the girl, and she and her family will see to it that he always gets another job or, at least, doesn't starve. Why worry about the future?

If . . . is somewhat atypical because the English-schoolboy rebels do break through a morass of stupidity and cruelty. They rubberstamp the violence and hatred of their oppressors, but their ends justify their means. They will take what they want and get away with it. In contrast to the cop-out, which characterizes many American films about young people, the boys in *If* . . . fight back. Unlike the rebellious schoolboys in Jean Vigo's *Zero de Conduite,* made in 1933, who pelt their school authorities from the school rooftop with trash, the rebels in *If* . . . have a machine gun on the roof and throw bombs. They wear uniforms like revolution-aries. They will take no more of the nonsense of the Establishment. They become blood brothers and are ready to die for their self-styled revolu-tion.

In all of these films pessimism and negation abound. Our film pop culture is rife with disintegration, decay, disillusionment, destruction, and decay. Doomsday is due next week, and there's no doubt about it.

Films such as these are speaking in the language of many young people who find it difficult to articulate their confusion and anger. Movies become the language that speaks to their unformed and ill-formed thoughts. "Movies make me feel the way I know I think . . . Movies help me to realize that the U.S.A. is not my scene." Not unexpectedly, those movie moguls who manufacture movies they hope to sell, cater to the confusion of young people, and cast and wish to shape their products to fit into the hip ap-perceptive mass.

If we would listen carefully to young people—as carefully as the movie moguls and savants do—their soliloquy would go something like this:

"Authority equals conflict today. Homes are places that we go to if there is absolutely no place to go; even if you did screw them, the home folks have to take you in.

Marriage? Monogamy? That's for the hix in the stix. Being wild in the streets with Christopher Jones and his houseful of stoned cats is a lot better. In *The Graduate* they got married in a church, but that marriage was put asunder by Dustin. The real marriage happened at the end of the bus ride after Dustin kidnapped Katherine from the church.

Happy endings don't exist in life. Love? Let's get together and think about love later. Maybe we won't even need to think about it.

No political solution exists. Jefferson was a good man but Nixon would take him for a Communist and get Mitchell to track him down and put him in the poky. The American dream? What was that? There's not enough freedom in the American political system to let me patch my pants with a piece of the flag. Also, I can't take my clothes off with Uncle Sam looking on. I want to take my clothes off! Why do you say I can't? Who are you to tell me I can't? I want to take my clothes off. I am what I am. Look all of me over. If you pinch me, I say, "Ouch!"

I'd go to the country, to some open land somewhere, but I can't farm and I don't want to farm. But if a farmer I must be, then I'll do it the Indian peasant way. I'll use a stick in the ground pulled by my chick. Ploughs and tractors? Why man, they're *machines!* Technology, for me? Steel, plastic, chrome? Bikes and cars are all right. But I go for the ways and tools of the aboriginals. Show me a tribe I can join.

Anguish is on exhibit in our films today for anyone to see who can empathize. One reason we like movies more than other entertainments is because they are cheaper, but that's not the real reason. Movies show us as we are because they have gotten closer and closer to life as we know it.

We have no definition of art that comes from God or anybody else who makes it *ex cathedra.* Art is what I like. Or if you prefer, don't call it art at all. What's in a name? A rose is a rose. You do your thing, and I'll do mine, but if we do it together too much, the pig will come along and yell, 'Keep moving.' We don't know why. We were just standing there until we sat on a bench which we thought was there for sitting."

*   *   *

The youth movies have put art, as we have known it, on the shelf.

Perhaps in some ways art can be dangerous and even an evil. To the extent we live only for art, it can become a pernicious surrogate for living. We have usually considered art as a vision of a better life and a world made tangible in a perfected object. True, a vision of perfection can be therapeutic by helping us to endure disorderly times and circumstances, but such therapy is always temporal; it can't make life bearable over the long haul.

The contemporary revolt against art, and the addiction to certain movies that are the pop culture of the hip, can hopefully help to bring about a resurrection of the aesthetically half-dead, unless it is already too late for salvaging to be possible. Paul Tillich understood a great deal that is pertinent to the psyche of the young and the movies they idolize:

> Man cannot begin to think less of art without, at the same time, begin-ning to think more of religion, of love, of equality, of possessions, of power, of all else by which his mind and spirit are engaged. The values are interdependent, and it is the duty of criticism, which is something more than the impression of one book, one picture or one play to be alive to this interdependence.

Hail, Hero was the worst movie of the sixties despite its attempt to present a free-spirited young man who loved music, all kinds of people, and who took life in his stride in an untamed way. That film gives us, however, an apt greeting to those young people and the youth films which reveal the interdependence of values and their contemporary expression: Hail to the young and the films of youth culture if they can conquer more good life for more people!

If we can manage to survive our bad times, who knows, we might have spent these years whetting appetites for art.

Easy Rider
and Its Critics[*]

By Diana Trilling

Bernard Shaw's *Quintessence of Ibsenism* was first presented in 1892 as a lecture to the Fabian Society in London. Shaw's justification for bringing the theater into discussion with people chiefly engaged in government, politics, economics, and the law was his belief that the drama has a significant influence upon the individual life and the life of society. "Art," Shaw wrote, but he was speaking primarily of the theater, "should refine our sense of character and conduct, of justice and sympathy, greatly heightening our self-knowledge, self-control, precision of action, and considerateness, and making us intolerant of baseness, cruelty, injustice, and intellectual superficiality and vulgarity." A formulation like this was possible eighty years ago as it of course no longer is; today, its language must seem to verge on quaintness. We nevertheless recognize that Shaw is voicing a conviction which in transmuted form is still very much alive for us. Certainly it is some such appreciation of the high moral function of the theater that warrants our appeals for government support of the stage and makes the basis of our contempt for the philistine and commercial theater.

And his statement of the high purpose of the dramatic art makes plain why Shaw found it appropriate to talk about Ibsen to a group of people whose first commitment was to political and social improvement. For if it is the purpose of the theater to instruct us in character and conscience, then clearly all men of character and conscience, all persons devoted to the public good, should be informed of the way in which the theater is discharging, or might discharge, this important duty.

There can be no question that were Shaw addressing himself to present-day affairs he would put the film under quite as strict scrutiny as the stage, or even stricter, and not merely because the movies reach so

---

[*] Reprinted from *The Atlantic Monthly* by permission of the author and publisher, Atlantic Monthly Company.

much wider an audience than stage plays but also because he would be bound to respond to the special force of the visual as compared to the predominantly verbal medium. Indeed, I have only a most formal hesitation in borrowing his authority for the opinion that no art now exerts more moral influence than the films, and that for the present generation, and particularly among our best-educated young people, more than personal character is being formed by our film-makers: a culture, a society, even a polity.

It is as an exemplification of this power of moral and social instruction that I wish to discuss *Easy Rider*. But perhaps I should first say what I mean by instruction in this context. I do not mean overt pedagogy, and I do not even mean what the famous director Jean-Luc Godard presumably had in mind when he was speaking at Harvard recently about his film *See You at Mao,* and said, "The movie is like a blackboard. A revolutionary movie can show how the arms struggle may be done." *Easy Rider* is not at all a film of this order. Although it is highly tendentious, it wears the mask of disengagement; its atmosphere, in fact, is that of a pastoral. Its method is that of implication and suggestion rather than that of assertion. Its notable achievement lies in its ability to communicate states of feeling: it is through its skill in the creation of emotion and mood that it does its work of persuasion.

An air of purposive mystification, a sense of the existence of tensions which are perhaps made the more significant by never being named, is established from the start of the film. *Easy Rider* opens with its two main characters, Wyatt, played by Peter Fonda, and Billy, played by Dennis Hopper, having crossed the border from California into Mexico to do business with a Mexican peasant. Both the young men are long-haired, one of them bearded, and both wear clothes which, like their style of hair, at once authenticate their dedication to freedom. Both are riding simple motorbikes. It is of some importance, I think, that Fonda and Hopper are the leading actors in a film which they wrote together, with some unspecified assistance from Terry Southern, and which Hopper directed. *Easy Rider* represents an unusually direct statement on the part of its authors: there are no paid "stars" to intervene between them and us, no interposition of an alien personality or will.

The business on which Wyatt and Billy have crossed to Mexico is the purchase of heroin. At least, we conclude it is heroin although it could of course be cocaine—it is a white powder and the two men sniff it. Apparently the purchase is satisfactory, because they then go on to their next rendezvous: a chauffeur-driven Rolls-Royce meets them at what seems to be the edge of an airfield, and a sallow and sleazy man of about forty—we notice that he is close-shaven and wears city clothes—gets out and takes their supply of drugs, in exchange for which he gives Wyatt and Billy a wad of money which they will later stash away in their bikes. Before this unalluring character drives off and out of the film, he takes his own revitalizing snort of the powder he has purchased. Although he is doing precisely what the two young men had done just a moment before, his use of the heroin is made to seem ugly and furtive whereas theirs has been presented as an exercise in connoiseurship—apparently with dope as with sex it is the style of the agent which makes for the moral meaning of the act.

As a first gain from the sale of the heroin, the simple motorbikes on which Wyatt and Billy were riding at the start of the picture are replaced by a pair of the biggest, flashiest, most expensive motorcycles ever to fill the male American heart with envy. It is on these splendid vehicles—Fonda-Wyatt's is decorated with a splash of American flag—that the two men now begin their beautiful journey from California to near New Orleans, where their trip will be suddenly and violently cut off. It is a handsome travelogue, this West to East tour of the Southwestern United States. And we are no doubt the more moved by the loveliness and variety of the country because it is offered to us as the stage on which two people already certified as heroes of dissidence are about to act out their fate. Too, this is an America whose purity has not been polluted. The landscape of *Easy Rider* would seem to have known no human desecration other than the building of the highways which Wyatt and Billy ride—they pass no cars, no buses, no billboards or roadside stands or motels. When there is any form of human encounter, which is rare, it is played for its symbolic meaning.

Thus, the two young riders stop at a lone ranch for repairs on one of the motorcycles. The rancher is shoeing a horse, and in his barn the wheel on which the camera fixes its editorializing gaze is that of a wagon. But even the farm itself is something of an anomaly in Fonda and Hopper's vision of the American West: we have been shown no other such instances of human enterprise. And indeed, the rancher inhabits a boundless universe; the land is his as far as the eye can see—what the film appears to be asking us is why, in an America this big and empty, we crowd as we do in our cities. He receives the two strangers at his table and within his family in the kind of openness and trust which consorts with the freedom and openness of the life he lives. His wife serves him in sweet docility, surrounds him with the happy-faced children she breeds for him. In a brief colloquy over their meal—in the idyllic imagination of *Easy Rider* farmers eat their meals at picnic tables set outdoors—Wyatt inquires whether all this vast spread belongs to the farmer, and he receives his host's assurance that it does. It is a good life to live, is Fonda-Wyatt's comment, and it is of course our response as well.

A counterpoint to this scene is provided very little later in the film when Wyatt and Billy, once again on the road, pick up a traveler—his style is not unlike their own—who takes them to his rural commune. Until now, *Easy Rider* has engaged in considerable conscious evasion: it has not told us where its two main characters come from or where they are going, what drug they have trafficked in or what use they plan to make of the money they earned by its sale, or, for that matter, what in their previous personal or social experience has brought them to their present condition. But now the film becomes not so much mystifying as surrealist. The commune contains some thirty or more young people and a few small children who all live together in what is no doubt meant to represent an entire goodness and harmony, each pursuing his concern. Playacting appears to be one of the group occupations: we see bits of miming in the manner of the guerrilla theater and even a rude outdoor stage. There is also a prayer scene similar to the Thanksgiving devotions in *Alice's Restaurant;* I took it, perhaps wrongly, to be an appeal for rain to water the crops—for it is a gentle point of this commune sequence that these young people would wish to grow their food but do not know how, their unnatural modern upbringings having cut them off from the vital springs of life: dazed but intent, they stamp barefoot upon the unharrowed, even unplowed, ground on which they have dropped the seed. Drugs are not mentioned; for one viewer, they were nevertheless omnipresent in the appearance and behavior of the members of the commune. There is a moment when the camera circles the group, moving slowly from one vacant-eyed face to the next: they are the faces of madness, of a perhaps irremediable break with reality, or so they looked to me, but I am afraid that what I saw was not necessarily what the makers of the film intended. Before Wyatt and Billy again take to the road, they have an innocent naked romp in a nearby stream with two of the commune girls.

The beautiful journey resumes. At the end of each day's run Wyatt and Billy camp at the roadside. We do not discover them buying or preparing their food, washing themselves or their clothes, or even actually building the fires over which they sit at night, quietly smoking their pot, quietly getting stoned. The inessentials of life have been eliminated to reveal life's essential joyous simplicity—obviously the two men supply each other with the kind of companionship in which marijuana is said to make its happiest effect: at any rate, they laugh together for no apparent reason. And if there is any doubt in the viewer's mind as to what it is that provides this nightly relaxation, it is nicely dispelled when the two men offer a cigarette to a drunk they have picked up who refuses it in terror—hasn't he, he asks, enough trouble already with the booze? Wyatt can reassure him: this anodyne has no devil in it as whiskey does.

The new member of what now becomes a trio of riders had joined them in the jail of his Southern town where he was sleeping off a binge. Riding into the town, Wyatt and Billy had playfully got entangled in a parade and been arrested. After a night in jail, the third young man, an ACLU lawyer, arranges for their release. Gentle, liberal, idealistic, he is the defeated son of the big man of the town, whose power is to be withstood only by drinking—the symbol of the son's remembrance of joy is a football helmet cherished since boyhood. Wearing his helmet, he hops a ride with his new friends: he is bound for a brothel in New Orleans. At a modest restaurant the trio attracts the attention of the sheriff and some cronies of his who mobilize a quick brutal hatred of the hippie outsiders; that night, as the three men sleep at the roadside, the sheriff and his people sneak up on them—they manage to kill only the local lawyer. Just as the sheriff stands for American xenophobia and violence, the lawyer represents, we must suppose, the soft liberal underbelly of American establishment. Well-meaning but misguided, he is first to succumb to a repressive social authority with which he had attempted to live and even deal, blind to its implacable enmity.

The pop music which functions as a kind of Greek chorus to the mounting doom of *Easy Rider* carries much of the emotion with which Wyatt and Billy receive the death of their new friend. They now undertake to complete his journey for him, and they go to the brothel in New Orleans, where they join up with two young prostitutes—but not sexually, only in comradeship. The four go together to the Mardi Gras, then continue the day in a cemetery where they get high on pot and liquor. By the time Wyatt distributes the LSD he has in his pocket, the girls are too intoxicated to care what they are taking. The inhabitable world vanishes from the screen: as in one of Dr. Leary's psychedelic celebrations, the film now is given over to describing the psychic states induced in Wyatt, Billy, and the two girls by the acid. We watch them writhe among the gravestones, suffering the apparently joyous agony of their self-willed release from the limitations of our reality-bound consciousness. When one of the girls takes off her clothes, no one has use for her naked body: with the help of drugs Wyatt and Billy have transcended more than our society, more even than their minds: their bodies. *Easy Rider* celebrates not only a pretechnological but also a presexual, or at least a pregenital, world.

But they have not transcended death. The acid trip over, the other journey across an America which once was, and presumably might still be, must once more begin. The two men get but a short distance beyond New Orleans, however, when they are overtaken on the deserted road and shot down, in coldest blood. Whether it is the same sheriff of their previous encounter or a counterpart who commits the murder, I am uncertain. But it cannot matter. What matters is that we have been shown vigilante America at work, out to destroy whatever loves freedom and is different from itself. The film ends in a bloody dawn, with Wyatt's and Billy's smashed bodies lying in the road. We understand that their murderers will go unapprehended.

This is, I think, a fair synopsis of *Easy Rider,* though not uncharged with my adverse feelings about the film. But it is necessary for me to make plain that although, while I was in the theater, I was aware of weighty reservations on the score of its moral content—they were provoked from the very start of the picture, by the sale of the heroin—I was also considerably seduced by it. It is not difficult for me to identify my seducer—ironically, it was America. I say ironically because, even apart from the fact that the point of the film is its attack upon America for failure to fulfill its promise to us, the America of *Easy Rider* is largely a pictorial illusion. The landscape it spreads out for us is mythic—I had almost said epic—in its lack of industrialization, of technology, even of population: I daresay there are still sections of the Southwest where one can travel big distances without seeing a billboard or a hamburger stand and where such farms as there are exist in isolation, but I doubt that one can travel from California almost all the way to New Orleans on main highways that are this totally bare of other humans and vehicles. And yet no other film that I can recall has so poignantly reminded me of the beautiful heritage we have in this country. It was the American land which seduced me in *Easy Rider*—and this would seem to suggest that I too, like the makers of the film, am caught in the dream of a country unscathed by modernity.

But the longing for an unravished land is obviously not a new emotion for Americans. It appears in our literature even before the existence of what can properly be described as a technological society, in the work of Cooper, Thoreau, Whitman, and of course Mark Twain—when Huck Finn lit out for the territory he too, even in his time, was trying to escape the restrictions of civilized modern life; and in our more recent literature it has played a decisive part in the imagination of Hemingway. For all of these men the unspoiled forests, prairies, mountains, and rivers of America make not only the setting for their quest of freedom but also the actual condition by means of which they discover their wholeness and worth as human beings. *Easy Rider* leans heavily upon the charm and authority of this literary tradition. But the unravished countryside which makes the landscape of its dream of the free life has, in fact, no integral relation to the film's representation of freedom—it is nothing *but* landscape. Its beauty is used, or misused, to validate the only freedom of which Fonda and Hopper have any genuine conception, that which is imputed to the drug experience. It is a first and basic dishonesty of *Easy Rider,* that is, that it proposes more than a kinship, actually an equivalence, or at least an interdependence, between the fulfillment which may be sought by moving beyond the frontiers of civilization and the gratifications which are sought in extending the frontiers of consciousness by the use of drugs.

But a dishonesty of this dimension requires other deceptions to sustain it. The search for a new frontier beyond which life will have retained its old innocence is, to be sure, recurrent in American literature, but we know it is not our sole American dream, nor ever has been: there has always gone along with our nostalgia for the fair and innocent land another dream, that of F. Scott Fitzgerald's Gatsby—the American dream of happiness through power and wealth. This was the conqueror's dream, and today we direct our sternest disapproval to those who submit themselves to it. Wyatt and Billy are so clearly presented to us as the very antithesis and negation of the predator's America that when at the end of *Easy Rider* they are destroyed by the forces of darkness, we are meant to feel that more than individual lives have been wiped out: virtue itself has been defeated.

Gatsby, we recall, tried to buy his transcendence over limiting social circumstance by bootlegging: Fitzgerald conceals from us no part of Gatsby's moral implication in this way of getting rich. Wyatt and Billy try to buy their transcendence over limiting social circumstance by trafficking in drugs, but they are made to bear no moral responsibility for *their* way of getting rich—unless we were perhaps to argue that their death at the end of the film is a punishment for wrong-doing, in which case *Easy Rider* would have to be accused of having vested its moral authority in cold-blooded murderers. The transaction in heroin is indeed embedded in moral obfuscation. We see the expensive white powder being given to the man in the Rolls-Royce, we never see to whom he gives it other than himself: we are never shown, say, the schoolchildren in Los Angeles who will become our newest statistics in heroin addiction and death. Certainly nothing in the film suggests that the money with which Wyatt and Billy undertake to escape this tainted world of ours is itself tainted—the sale of the heroin behind them, Wyatt and Billy represent the film's appeal on behalf of America's lost purity.

And just as the filthy business in which the heroes of *Easy Rider* make their wad is somehow disinfected by the presumed decency of their intentions in life, just so their recourse to heroin and LSD is somehow obscured by the innocent pleasure they have from marijuana. In general, the enlightened public now makes a distinction between marijuana and the other drugs which have come into wide use. In fact, the argument, not that all drugs should be legalized in order to take them out of the sphere of criminality, but that marijuana should be legal because it is harmless, rests on the belief that the use of marijuana is a quite separate activity from the use of "real" drugs. The evidence of *Easy Rider,* however, is against such a distinction. For Wyatt and Billy pot seems to be the basic daily fare which makes life supportable for them between their adventures with more potent medicines. We see the two men sniff heroin only once, at the start of the film; their practiced performance with it nevertheless makes us fairly sure that this is not an initial experience. Similarly, their composure after their bad acid trip suggests that this is not their first excursion in LSD. It is difficult to see how the young filmgoers who chiefly make up the audiences of *Easy Rider* can fail to conclude from the example of Wyatt and Billy that the sniffing of heroin and the taking of LSD are simply alternative to smoking pot, or, at least, that the taking of these more drastic drugs can be slipped in and out of at will, between joints, dreary medical injunction to the contrary notwithstanding.

Nor can we place more confidence in the social-economic import of *Easy Rider* than in its moral instruction. The film implies that spiritual freedom depends upon an escape from technology, and it gives us the happy rancher in example. In his barn a horse is being shod, and we are shown the wheel of a wagon—there is no farm machinery, there are no farmhands, and the rancher's sons are too young to help him. Apparently we are to believe that it requires only one man plus a horse and wagon to put a great tract of land under cultivation. We could perhaps accept a simplification of this sort as merely an aesthetic concentration, were it not for the extreme social and political disingenuousness of the film as a whole, including, as a prime instance, its assumption that one has only, like Wyatt or Billy, to be the target of evil forces within our corrupt society to be oneself wiped clean of all corruption. This curious assumption of course established itself in American liberal thought in the McCarthy period, when one had only to be the object of McCarthy's malignity to be warranted as forever blameless.

As in a traditional Western, *Easy Rider* divides the world into the good and the bad guys. But what gives *Easy Rider* its chic is its definition of good guys and bad in the sentimental terms which are at present being sanctified by left-wing thought: good guys want to be left in peace to live out their lives of natural freedom, bad guys want to impose their way of being upon others. In the revolution of the seventies the contending social forces are, of course, no longer labor and capital. They are the passively virtuous and the actively wicked. In *Easy Rider* the proletariat, with its auspicious place in history and its decisive role in determining the fate of mankind, is transformed into a pair of mindless cop-outs (not to say criminals) for whom there is neither past nor future, imagination, curiosity, desire. Symbols of what we are to suppose is the idealism and aspiration of this revolutionary day, Wyatt and Billy lack the energy to create anything, comment on anything, feel anything except the mute pleasure of each other's company.

But the muteness of *Easy Rider* not only accurately represents the anti-intellectualism of the contemporary revolution, it is also essential to the myth-making impulse of the film. By this I mean, simply, that were *Easy Rider* more verbal, more given to the exposition of its ideas, it would be more accessible to the skeptical intellect. For example, the pivotal point of the film, or at any rate what many viewers have taken to be its moral climax, depends upon our interpretation of a sudden statement by Wyatt—the statement consists of three words. Wyatt and Billy are once again about to hit the road after their acid trip, and Billy murmurs something about their having made it. To this Wyatt replies, "We blew it." This utterance might perhaps indicate that Wyatt thinks their journey has failed in its spiritual intention, or it might even suggest—which is not too different—that Wyatt has come to recognize his moral responsibility for the drug transaction. But nothing in the film supports such interpretations, and I am myself inclined to believe that the ambiguousness of the statement is a deviousness, and that it was formulated to allow the viewer to draw from it whatever moral conclusion would make him most comfortable. By staying with so few words and refusing to explicate Wyatt's summary assessment of his and Billy's quest, the authors of *Easy Rider* concur in an adverse moral judgment of the central characters of the film, if that is how we prefer it. But at the same time they protect the central figures of the film against adverse judgment so that they can be retained as examples of innocent victimization. And it is as examples of innocent victimization that Wyatt and Billy of course enter the pantheon of contemporary heroic dissent.

Here, then, are some of the lessons taught in this popular film, and an enticing brew of the fashionable, the false, and the pernicious they are. How are we to respond to such an offering? Surely not by legal censorship, which in America doesn't even raise questions of the control of moral and social ideas, only of what may be thought pornographic or obscene, and which in countries where it does treat such questions necessarily operates to suppress anything which challenges the assumptions of the official culture. But the rejection of censorship implies that we put our faith in moral and social intelligence either as exercised by the artists themselves or by those who receive their work.

It is a piety of our art-loving culture that between moral and social intelligence and artistic intelligence there is an inevitable congruence. *Easy Rider* is demonstration that this is not so. As an instance of the art of film-making, it is much to be praised: it is well played and well directed, imaginative, adroit, visually pleasing, and undoubtedly fulfills the intentions of its authors. But these positive qualities not only coexist with grave deficiencies of moral and social intelligence; they give authority to the film's false view of the moral and social life. If *Easy Rider* were less attractive as a piece of film-making, we would not need to be concerned about its influence. It therefore rests with us who receive the film to exercise the moral and social discrimination which the authors show themselves unable to exercise. In particular, this responsibility devolves, I think, upon those whose work it is to tell us how well the theater is fulfilling its high mission of instructing us in character and conscience: the critics.

It is my sense that more than any other group within the critical profession the film critics have the public's attention—for instance, less than a week after the warm critical welcome that was given the film *Z*, it was impossible to get a seat in the theater at eleven o'clock in the morning. I was out of the country when *Easy Rider* opened; but from the reviews I have since retrieved I have the impression, certainly not of general unqualified approval—only Penelope Gilliat of the *New Yorker* would seem to have given it that—but of a response in which any critical unease engendered by the film was always eventually, and effectually, buried in the reviewer's need to concur in what was taken to be its invaluable social message: it was as if Fonda's and Hopper's observation of Middle America's hatred of anything different from itself and of the American capacity for mindless violence constituted an insight of such freshness and magnitude as to render paltry or carping any adverse judgment the critic might be moved to make on the film's validity as a document of American life. Except for Paul Schrader in the Los Angeles *Free Press,* who boldly ridiculed *Easy Rider* for its indulgence in stale left-wing ritualisms—and it is worth noting that with the publication of this review Mr. Schrader's connection with the paper was terminated—even critics who, like Richard Schickel in *Life,* spoke of the air of self-congratulation in which Wyatt and Billy have their being, or, like Joseph Morgenstern in *Newsweek,* mocked the sententiousness of the film, raised these objections in a context of appreciation.

And even Mr. Schrader went but half the course. Although he did indeed firmly denounce the nondimensional politics of *Easy Rider,* he mentioned not at all the means by which Wyatt and Billy financed their journey. The oversight, however, little distinguishes his reception of the film from that of the other reviewers. To be sure, Vincent Canby of the *New York Times* wrote: "After all, Wyatt and Billy, the heroin pushers, may be the same kind of casual murderers as the southern red necks." Stanley Kauffmann of the *New Republic* wrote: "In cold factual terms, Fonda and Hopper are pretty low types—experienced drug-peddlers, criminal vagabonds. . . ." And Joseph Morgenstern, again in *Newsweek,* wrote: "Neither of these two riders . . . is conspicuously innocent. They've gotten the money for their odyssey by pushing dope." But these comments, which at least announce disapprobation of drug-trading, are curiously brief, unreverberant—they scarcely describe a rousing opposition to the film's own bland acceptance of drug-dealing—while the other reviews I have read fail to make even this small obeisance to the moral occasion. For Dan Wakefield, writing in this magazine, the drug in which Wyatt and Billy traffic is cocaine—he is positive in the identification. And extensively and eloquently outraged as Mr. Wakefield is by the bad treatment hippies receive at the hands of their fellow-citizens, he finds it possible to concentrate the whole of his judgment of Wyatt and Billy's drug transaction into a single sentence of narration: "The two hippies . . . make a highly profitable sale of some cocaine they score in Mexico to a sinister-looking connection in Los Angeles, and with the money stashed in the red-white-and-blue Stars-and-Stripes painted fuel tank of Wyatt's motorcycle, they take off east for New Orleans. . . ." In fact, later in his piece Mr. Wakefield makes explicit his faith in the two central characters of *Easy Rider* as figures of virtue: "Why," he inquires, "the needless death and destruction of these fairly innocuous, generally pleasant, and harmless young men?" But it is left to Miss Gilliat of the *New Yorker* to bring the moral and social-political concerns of the film into most reassuring accord with each other. Of Wyatt and Billy she writes: "By smuggling dope across the frontier and selling it to a gum-chewing young capitalist disguised as a fellow-hippie, they make enough money to live life their own way." With a stroke of the pen, that is, Miss Gilliat certifies the heroes of *Easy Rider* as proper symbols of the lost freedom and decency of American life: they are genuine hippies rather than capitalists disguised as hippies, and they do not chew gum.

We are accustomed, of course, to the reluctance of our critics to submit to rigorous examination any political or social idea which offers itself as enlightened dissidence. It is indeed by its accessibility to whatever is opposed to established values or whatever may be regarded as innovative thought that criticism defends itself against the imputation of academicism and brings itself into the full current of strenuous contemporary life. Are we to conclude, then, from Mr. Wakefield's or Miss Gilliat's unperturbed acceptance of drug-dealing and from the self-effacing comments upon this enterprise on the part even of the critics who oppose it that drug use has made good its claim to radical-ideological status?

I do not think so. I think, rather, that what we are seeing in the less than satisfactory response of the critics to *Easy Rider* is their obedience to the modern injunction against moralizing about art. Quoting from Shaw, I said that the language in which Shaw described the function of the theater could only sound quaint to our contemporary ears. I meant that such outright moralizing puts us in mind of a culture in which there could be good firm working formulations of right and wrong and in which there were wise men, teachers, whose job it was to guide us through the few possible areas of doubt. Obviously, our sense of our own times is just the opposite of this. So extreme, in fact, is our awareness of the absence of such rules and of the lack of such persons, and of the consequent need for each one of us to improvise his own morality, that we have all but lost sight of the dynamics of culture. We forget that codes for the guidance of our moral lives are constantly being proposed for us by the culture.

In the fashioning of these codes the artists—especially, nowadays, artists in the popular media—have a primary role. But the role of the critics is far from negligible. It is the critics who are supposed to warn us not to be seduced by art and who are delegated to ask questions about the reliability and feasibility and worth of the codes which are being offered us. Theirs is always, if you will, a moralizing function. It is today, when they seem to be most moved to forget this responsibility, that they are perhaps most to be recalled to it.

FILM: FURTHER READINGS

Books

Houston, Penelope, *The Contemporary Cinema,* Baltimore, 1968 (c1963).
Jacobs, Lewis, ed., *The Emergence of Film Art,* New York, 1968.
Kael, Pauline, *I Lost It at the Movies,* Little, Brown and Company, Boston, 1965.
————, *Kiss Kiss, Bang Bang,* Little, Brown and Company, Boston, 1968.
Kracauer, Siegfried, *Theory of Film: the Redemption of Physical Reality,* Oxford University Press, New York, 1960.
Macdonald, Dwight, *Against the American Grain,* Random House, New York, 1962.
Sarris, Andrew, *The American Cinema: Directors and Directions,* 1929–1968, New York, 1968.
Tyler, Parker, *Classics of the Foreign Film: a Pictorial Treasury,* Citadel, New York, 1964.
————, *Every Artist His Own Scandal: a Study of Real and Fictive Heroes,* Horizon, New York, 1964.
————, *Sex, Psyche, Etcetera in the Film,* New York, 1969.

Articles

Alpert, H. "Retrospective: Fifteen Years of Movie-going," *Saturday Review,* Nov. 27, 1965.
Alpert, H., Knight, A., and Fuller, J. G., "Do the Movies Have a Future?" *Saturday Review,* Aug. 29, 1964.
Kael, P., "Are Movies Going to Pieces?" *Atlantic Monthly, Dec. 1964.*
Macdonald, D., "After Forty Years of Writing About Movies, I Know Something about Cinema," *Esquire,* July 1969.
Reed, R., "And Now Some Sacred Cows to the Kill," *Holiday,* May 1969.
Sarris, A., "Hollywood Haters: Illusions and Independents," *Saturday Review,* Dec. 24, 1966.
Schillaci, A., "Film as Environment," *Saturday Review,* Dec. 28, 1968.

Magazines and Newspapers

Despite stringent competition from television (which now usurps more than thirty hours a week of the average American's leisure hours) the magazine is still a hearty vegetable in the mass culture garden. There are no less than 8000 magazines (according to Ayer's Directory) if we count trade publications and weekly magazines in newspapers. Whether the *Reader's Digest* with fifteen million readers has as much influence as *The New Yorker,* whose circulation is less than 500,000 or the *Saturday Review's* 390,000, depends on one's definition of influence. Do the nearly eight and one-half million women who read *McCall's* seek anything more than entertainment? In the early 1900s magazines in the United States were synonymous with the word "muckraker." But as John Hohenberg so aptly puts it, "today's mass circulation magazines for the most part merchandise sex, sympathy and dreams." *Playboy,* which soared to the top of the field in men's magazines during the last fifteen years doesn't even bother to merchandise sympathy or dreams—sexual fantasy, spiced with intellectual promiscuity and culture chic has apparently held Hugh Hefner's audience of more than three million clients each month.

The world of magazine fiction has often been accused of promulgating stereotypes about various American minorities. In our first edition of *Mass Culture* we included Berelson and Salter's noted 1946 study which analyzed some 200 short stories from eight leading magazines of that period. That study showed that native, WASP Americans were the ideal characters, achieved their goals because they were clean, honest, rich, desirable, etc.

For this volume we asked Alan B. Kotok, a young sociologist, to replicate the Berelson-Salter study to see if there were any changes in the quarter-century span. Kotok's study indicates there have been considerable changes in the presentation and treatment of foreign and minority characters in current magazine fiction. Even though "Americans" still tend to rule the roost, minority characters are more numerous and today play more important roles. The reasons for these changes are presented cogently by Mr. Kotok.

A factor to be reckoned with in any assessment of mass culture in the sixties would be the growth of the so-called "underground" press. The values of the hippie movement are mirrored in these publications, which led two sociologists, Jack Levin and James L. Spates, to undertake a content analysis of Underground Press Syndicate periodicals. In contrasting the *expressive* values found in the hippie publications to the *instrumental* values found in that bulwark of middle-class magazines, *The Reader's Digest,* the authors note certain changes which are occurring in our social structure. They see the hippie emphasis on expressive values as illustrative of a process of "balancing" in American society as a whole —a counterbalance, as it were, to the extreme *instrumentalism* of our social system.

In the final essay in this section, Nathan B. Blumberg sharply criticizes the "orthodox" (as opposed to the "underground") press for its coverage of news of dissent. His thesis is that the press is almost invariably an ally of those in political and/or economic power who have a stake in the *status quo.* The particular relevance of his article lies in his documentation of the manner in which the Chicago press covered the national Democratic Convention of 1968. Newsmen, stung by police assaults on their own personnel, enjoyed a few "days of glory" and then lapsed into their habitual apologetic torpor.

Foreign Nationals and Minority Americans in Magazine Fiction, 1946-1968[*]

By Alan B. Kotok

The presentation and portrayal of ethnic minorities and foreigners in the mass media has become a major concern of behavioral scientists today. This stems from concern over the media's responsibility to the general public, as well as the recognition of the media's powerful effect on the formation of attitudes toward and images of different groups in our society. The mass media have been accused, at times, of perpetuating the characteristic stereotypes of many American minorities: the lazy Black, the cheap Jew, the emotional Italian, the ignorant Pole. They have also been accused of setting up the native, white, Protestant Americans as the ideal characters: rich, responsible, honest, clean, and desirable.

Bernard Berelson and Patricia Salter, in a 1946 study of magazine fiction, were among the first to point out these discrepancies.[1] They content-analyzed 198 short stories from eight leading magazines of the time (Saturday Evening Post, Collier's, American, Cosmopolitan, Woman's Home Companion, Ladies' Home Journal, True Story, and True Confessions) and found the native, white, Protestant Americans to be the most numerous, richest, and most highly approved characters at the expense of the foreigners and American minorities.

Berelson and Salter employed several criteria in their analysis. Besides being the most numerous group, they found the "Americans" (the white, native, Protestant majority) to be totally out of proportion when compared to the ethnic distribution of the United States population at the time. The "Americans" were found in the most major roles in the stories, as well as being given the most approved treatment.

The "Americans" lived the most luxurious lives and had the most pres-

* Published for the first time in this volume. The author gratefully acknowledges the guidance of Dr. F. Earle Barcus during the preparation of this study.

tigious occupations. Their high social and occupational status was rarely explained, justified, or qualified.

The "Americans" were found to pursue the most altruistic goals while the foreign and minority characters were left to pursue the most pragmatic and mundane goals. "Americans" were likewise found in most of the superordinate interactional positions. Love and marriage in these stories was found to take place within rather than between ethnic groups.

Few stories in the 1946 sample were found to deal with ethnic-group problems. In fact, only four of the 198 stories even remotely dealt with these issues.

Since 1946, great changes have taken place in the mass media and the society in general. Bogart noted that fiction in mass-circulated magazines had dropped off sharply due to the influence of television. He also found that men's magazines had grown extensively since the rise of television and had begun to offer more fiction to their readers.[2] Colle, in his discussion of the Negro in the mass media, saw new marketing patterns and social pressures on the communications industries prompting more presentation and more favorable portrayal of Negroes.[3]

A recent study of magazine fiction disputes this contention by Colle. Jack Levin found the majority characters in majority-oriented magazines to follow the same pattern found in the Berelson and Salter study, in relation to Negro characters. Only in Black-oriented magazines did Negro characters have more equitable presentation and treatment.[4]

American society, needless to say, has undergone great change since the 1940s. Americans are more urbanized, more mobile, better educated, and in general, better off financially. People in our society tend to be more aware and concerned about minority-group problems in this country. Larger involvement in world affairs and the advent of world-wide telecommunications has made the American people take a larger interest in problems and issues outside the North American continent. Most importantly, however, is the social and economic power gained by most ethnic minorities since the 1940s.

With these changes in the society and the mass media, one may also expect changes in the presentation and portrayal of foreign and minority groups since the 1940s. More specifically, one may expect to see more stories dealing with racial or ethnic-group problems, and the ethnic distribution of characters should better approximate the ethnic distribution in the American population. Foreign and minority characters should occupy more major and submajor roles in their stories, higher socioeconomic statuses, and more prestigious occupations. There should be less justification or explanation of foreign and minority characters in high-status positions. Foreign and minority characters should occupy less subordinate interactional positions and seek more altruistic goals. There should also be more intergroup love and marriage relationships.

In order to better understand the position of foreign and minority characters in magazine fiction, two more indicators will be added to the Berelson and Salter model. They include means and barriers to goal achievement. Since no prior findings are available for comparison, one can expect the majority characters under study to employ more approved means of goal achievement and overcome more disapproved barriers than the foreign and minority characters.

Berelson and Salter looked at the presentation and treatment of foreign and minority characters *in toto.* No attempt was made to compare the results of different types of magazines. In this study, the magazines aimed for upper-middle and upper class readers (the "slicks") will be compared to those aimed for lower-middle and lower class readers (the "pulps"). Albrecht, in a study of values in magazine fiction, found the pulps to be the least tolerant of deviation from established norms whereas the slicks were the most tolerant of deviation.[5]

From this model, one can expect the slicks to give more equitable presentation and treatment to foreign and minority characters. More specifically, one can expect to see more stories dealing with race and ethnic-group problems in the slicks, a larger proportion of foreign and minority characters, more foreign and minority characters in major and submajor roles, and less foreign and minority characters given neutral and disapproved treatment.

In their study, Berelson and Salter selected eight publications from the years 1937 and 1943. Their sample consisted of 198 stories generating nearly 900 characters. From each magazine, in each year, four magazines were selected at regular intervals to avoid possible bias of seasons or events. The first, third, and fifth stories in each of these issues was then analyzed.

Since the 1940s, three of the original eight publications dropped out of the market and men's magazines have grown in circulation and become major vehicles for fiction. In order to approximate the Berelson and Salter sample, but still reflect these changes, three leading men's magazines, *Esquire, Playboy,* and *Argosy,* replaced *American, Collier's,* and *Woman's Home Companion* which were no longer in circulation..They were added to *Saturday Evening Post, True Story, True Confessions, Cosmopolitan,* and *Ladies' Home Journal* to complete the sample.*

The calendar year 1968 represented the time period from which the issues were selected. One story from each issue of each magazine was randomly selected. The resulting sample consisted of eighty stories and 511 characters. Serials, condensed novels, and "short-short" stories were omitted.

Each story was individually coded and the following data were col-

---

* After the study had begun, *Saturday Evening Post* also ceased publication.

lected for each:

> Story name
> Magazine name
> List of characters
> Summary of story line or plot
> Time period in which the story takes place
> Geographic setting of the story
> Primary subject matter
> Secondary subject matter

Characters were selected for analysis only if they individually appeared in the story. In other words, the character must be presented "in the flesh" by the author. Those characters only mentioned by other characters or presented in groups were not included. The characters were coded for the following data:

> Character's name
> Summary of the character's role in the story
> Citizenship, race, or ethnic group
> Character's role in the story (major, submajor, or minor)
> Approval or disapproval of the character
> Socioeconomic status (as depicted from the character's life style)
> Occupational prestige or status
> Explanation of character's high prestige or status
> Love and marriage relationships (between or within ethnic groups)
> Interactional position (superordinate, subordinate, neutral)
> Character's goals in the story
> Means employed in achieving these goals
> Barriers faced in achieving these goals

The data on the characters were then punched and stored on IBM cards.

The stories and characters were coded by the author. A second coder was also trained by the author who independently coded seven stories and forty characters. A measure of intercoder agreement, "Scott's pi" was used to check reliability.‡ The mean reliability score for all criteria was 0.8590.

---

‡ Computation for "Scott's pi":

$$pi = \frac{P - PE}{1 - PE} \quad \text{where}$$

$$P = \frac{\text{the number of intercoder agreements}}{\text{the number of intercoder agreements and disagreements}}$$

PE = the proportion of agreement expected by chance

See W. A. Scott, "Reliability of Content Analysis: The Case of Nominal Data," *Public Opinion Quarterly*, **19**, 321–325 (1955). See also Dennis J. Arp, "The Problem of Reliability in the Human Coding of Textual Data," paper presented at the Annual Meeting of the American Educational Research Association, Los Angeles, 1969, pp. 4–5.

THE STORIES

Berelson and Salter found the stories in their sample to follow a virtually standard pattern. They were designed mainly for entertainment and were largely concerned with love, marriage, or domestic relations. Their stories were usually set in the United States. Of those set in the United States, most of them took place in New York City or the Eastern Seaboard.

In the present sample, the geographical settings of the stories changed noticeably. A larger share of the stories were set outside the territorial limits of the United States. Of those set in the United States, there was a marked shift towards the West, especially California. This is not surprising when one considers the rapid development of the American West since the 1940s.

The subject matter of the stories also changed. Although most of the stories dealt with love, romance, or domestic relations, as was the case with Berelson and Salter, there seemed to be more serious subjects discussed. Many stories dealt with crime, war, and mystery, as well as race and ethnic-group relations. One of the focuses of this study was the change in the number of stories dealing with race and ethnic-group relations (Table 1). While neither study had a large proportion of stories dealing with these topics, the present sample's was considerably larger, thus supporting the contention that there would be more stories of this type since the 1940s.

TABLE 1. Stories Dealing with Ethnic-Group Relationship in the Two Studies

| | Year of Study | |
Story Theme	1946	1968
Ethnic-group relationships	2.0%	16.3%
Others	98.0	83.7
Total	100.0%	100.0%
n	198	80
p		< 0.001

THE CHARACTERS: ETHNIC DISTRIBUTION AND STORY ROLE

The characters in magazine fiction stories come from a wide range of nationalities and backgrounds. Berelson and Salter combined these various groups into three main categories: "Americans," Anglo-Saxon and Nordic (AS&N)—immigrants and nationals from Britain, Canada, Australia, and New Zealand, as well as immigrants, descendants and nationals from Ireland, Scotland, and Western Europe—and "Others," all other racial, ethnic, and national groups. The same categorization was used in the present study.

TABLE 2.   Ethnic and National Group Distribution of Characters by Year of Study

Ethnic or National Group	Year of Study	
	1946	1968
"Americans"	84.0%	47.5%
American Minorities		
Anglo-Saxon/Nordic	3.0	7.2
Other hyphenates	2.5	8.5
Blacks	2.0	5.3
Jews	1.0	2.9
Foreign Nationals		
Anglo-Saxon/Nordic	4.0	12.8
Other nationals	3.5	15.7
Sub-total: "Americans"	84.0	47.5
Sub-total: Anglo-Saxon/Nordic	7.0	20.0
Sub-total: "Others"	9.0	32.5
Grand total	100.0%	100.0%
n	889	375

The ethnic and national distribution of the characters has changed considerably since 1946. The proportion of "Americans" has dropped off, while all foreign and minority groups have increased to various degrees (Table 2).

How the ethnic distribution of American characters reflects the ethnic distribution of the United States population is of interest here. It can be expected that the distribution of characters in 1968 would be more representative of the population than was the distribution of characters in 1946. This was found to be the case, although the Anglo-Saxon/Nordic characters seem somewhat overrepresented while the "Others" seem underrepresented in the 1968 sample (Table 3).

TABLE 3.   Ethnic Distribution of American Characters and Population by Year of Study

Ethnic Group	1946		1968	
	Population	Characters	Population[a]	Characters
"Americans"	60.2%	90.8%	62.8%	66.4%
AS&N	8.8	3.3	5.8	10.1
Others	17.6	2.8	17.6	11.9
Blacks	9.8	1.9	10.9	7.5
Jews	3.6	1.2	2.8	4.1
Total	100.0%	100.0%	100.0%	100.0%
n		822		268
p		0.001		0.01

[a] United States Bureau of the Census, *Statistical Abstract of the United States: 1967*, 88th ed., Washington, D.C., 1967.

TABLE 4.   Story Role by Ethnic Category and Year of Study

Story Role	1946			1968		
	Americans	AS&N	Others	Americans	AS&N	Others
Major	52%	38%	30%	47%	39%	34%
Submajor	16	18	14	25	28	31
Minor	32	44	56	28	33	35
Total	100%	100%	100%	100%	100%	100%
n	745	61	77	176	75	122

Characters in magazine fiction can range in importance from the hero or heroine to supporting or submajor status, to minor or "bit" parts. Berelson and Salter found the "Americans" to be cast mainly in the major and submajor roles whereas the foreign and minority characters were most often relegated to the minor parts. In the 1968 sample, the foreign and minority characters were found to occupy many more submajor and slightly more major roles. The "Americans" decreased in their proportion of major roles, but increased their share of submajor roles slightly (Table 4).

An important means of determining a character's portrayal in magazine fiction is by his approval or disapproval by the author. The approved characters are presented as clean, honest, respectable, and desirable. Disapproved characters are the opposite. Berelson and Salter found most of their characters, regardless of ethnic or national group to be cast in approved roles, although there was a greater likelihood of the foreign and minority characters to be cast in neutral or disapproved status (Table 5).

It can be expected that in the present study, foreign and minority characters would occupy less neutral and disapproved roles. The figures, however, show just the opposite. The foreign and minority characters were found to occupy more neutral and disapproved roles than before. The "Americans" were also found in more neutral and disapproved roles than in 1946, however.

TABLE 5.   Approval/Disapproval of Characters by Ethnic Group and Year of Study

Treatment	1946			1968		
	Americans	AS&N	Other	Americans	AS&N	Others
Approval	80%	78%	62%	72%	67%	45%
Neutral	4	14	14	18	17	33
Disapproval	16	8	24	10	16	22
Total	100%	100%	100%	100%	100%	100%
n	726	60	77	172	75	120

In sum, the foreign and minority characters are being presented more often and more importantly than in the 1940s. The lack of approved status for all characters, be they "American," foreign, or minority, is characteristic of a different type of fiction story. With more stories dealing with such topics as war, crime, race, or ethnic-group relations, one would probably find less lovable characters. One example is a story dealing with the Arab-Israeli Six-Day War of 1967 where two Israeli officers brutalized and tortured a Jordanian prisoner to gain some secret information. This is a far cry from the standard boy-meets-girl format found in the Berelson and Salter study.

SOCIAL CLASS CHARACTERISTICS

The character's social class provides another indicator of his portrayal. Approved characters will make the most money, live the best lives, and work at the best jobs, in general. Rarely will you find a common laborer as the hero of the story.

Berelson and Salter found the "Americans" to be cast mainly in the higher-income groups, whereas the foreign and minority characters were most often found in the middle- and lower-income groups. It was expected that more foreign and minority characters would be found in the higher brackets in the 1968 study, and this was indeed the case.

Gains were made by all foreign and minority groups towards the higher classes, but the Anglo-Saxon/Nordic characters made the largest jump. "Americans" made some small advances (Table 6).

Berelson and Salter found the "Americans" to be in most of the prestigious occupations like the professions and business. Foreign and minority characters were most likely found in jobs of lesser distinction. Also, the "Others" had a sizable proportion in illegal or suspect positions like embezzler, gambler, or hoodlum.

The foreign and minority characters in this study were expected to carry better jobs and this was found to be the case. As before, both of

TABLE 6. Socioeconomic Status by Ethnic Group and Year of Study

SES[a]	1946			1968		
	Americans	AS&N	Others	Americans	AS&N	Others
A	39%	24%	16%	39%	57%	17%
B	33	18	28	41	39	31
C	23	49	37	19	4	31
D	5	9	19	1	0	21
Total	100%	100%	100%	100%	100%	100%
n	722	55	76	119	44	65

[a] Socioeconomic status: the scale runs from high (A) to low (D).

TABLE 7. Occupational Status by Ethnic Group and Year of Study

Occupational Status	1946			1968		
	Americans	AS&N	Other	Americans	AS&N	Other
High	59%	29%	20%	39%	59%	23%
Middle	19	23	20	35	28	31
Low	11	27	36	8	8	18
Illegal	1	2	15	3	0	9
Armed Forces	10	19	9	15	5	19
Total	100%	100%	100%	100%	100%	100%
n	602	52	66	129	49	103

the foreign and minority categories moved upward on the scale and most of the progress was made by the Anglo-Saxon/Nordic characters (Table 7). Interestingly, the "Others" had a sizable number in the armed forces. Considering the high prestige generally offered to military personnel in this country, this can also be interpreted as a movement up the social ladder.

Closely related to these traditional indicators of social class is the explanation or justification of high social or occupational status (Table 8). Whether or not this high status is explained or justified to the reader is one means of discerning favorable or unfavorable portrayal. When a character's high status is justified or explained, it is assumed that the character is somewhat undeserving of this high status. Berelson and Salter found that the foreign and minority characters in their study, more often than not, needed such justification or explanation. In the present study, it was expected that fewer foreign and minority characters would be treated in this way, and this turned out to be the case.

With economic success a highly valued goal in our society, it can be assumed the high social, economic, or occupational status is indicative of positive portrayal or presentation. One can conclude, therefore, that foreign and minority-group characters have made substantial gains up the social ladder.

TABLE 8. High Status Explanation by Ethnic Category and Year of Study

Status Explanation	1946		1968	
	Americans	Foreign/ Minorities	Americans	Foreign/ Minorities
No	78%	43%	89%	60%
Yes	22	57	11	40
Total	100%	100%	100%	100%
n	93	14	63	40

Upon closer scrutiny, however, it becomes apparent that this was not completely true for all the foreign and minority characters. In both socioeconomic and occupational status, the gains made by the Anglo-Saxon/Nordic characters outran those by the "Others." In the 1968 sample, there were stories about British noblemen and lawyers, Irish priests, and Scandinavian businessmen. There were still a sizable number of "Others" cast in stereotypical situations like the Jewish tailor, the Black maid, or the large Italian family stuffed in a small house. On the other hand, there were a large number of "Others" in the armed forces, both as officers and enlisted men. It must be remembered that due to the number of foreign characters, these servicemen were not confined to American forces. Still, some Blacks, as well as others in this category, were found as American officers.

SOCIAL RELATIONSHIPS

The way in which a character interacts with other characters will offer some clues to his portrayal. One way is through the love and marriage relationship. Berelson and Salter called this the "acid test" of personal relationships. These are the most intimate relationships in which two characters can indulge and the degree of intergroup activity in this area would serve as an indication of inter-ethnic group tolerance.

In 1946, love and marriage relationships involving only the "Americans" took up the great bulk of all the relationships of this type. In 1968, "all-American" relationships were still the most numerous, but not nearly as prevalent as they were in 1946 (Table 9). In the present study, the "Americans" were found to have relations with the "Others" to a much larger extent. Intergroup romance was found in many cases as "Americans" linked up with Blacks and Polynesians, as well as white minorities like

TABLE 9.   Love and Marriage Relationship by Ethnic Group and Year of Study

Ethnic Groups	1946	1968
American-American	85%	85%
American-AS&N	5	8
American-Other	4	15
AS&N-AS&N	3	13
AS&N-Other	2	0
Other-Other	1	16
Sub-total: intergroup	11	24
Sub-total: intragroup	89	76
Total	100%	100%
n	153	71

TABLE 10. Interactional Position by Ethnic Group (1968)

Position	Americans	AS&N	Others
Superordinate	53%	50%	38%
Subordinate	33	31	45
Equal	14	19	17
Total	100%	100%	100%
n	168	72	110

Jews, Italians, and Greeks. Intergroup love and marriage had indeed in-creased substantially, as was expected. The Anglo-Saxon/Nordic char-acters, however, had little romantic contact outside their own group.

The interactional position a character assumes offers another indication of favorable or unfavorable portrayal (Table 10). Approved characters, heroes, or "good guys" will be in superordinate positions, giving com-mands, orders, advice, or counsel. Neutral or disapproved characters will be in subordinate positions.

Berelson and Salter, although giving no quantitative data, found the "Americans" to be mainly in these superordinate positions, whereas the foreign and minority characters were found in subordinate positions. It was expected that foreign and minority characters in the present sample would occupy more superordinate positions. All the foreign and minority characters were well represented in the superordinate group, although the Anglo-Saxon/Nordic characters were the more prevalent.

Interactional position is closely related to occupational status. The occupations of higher prestige will more likely have more command re-sponsibilities than those of lower prestige. Since the "Americans" and the Anglo-Saxon/Nordic characters were cast in occupations of higher prestige more often than the "Others," it is not surprising that they should also be in more superordinate positions.

GOAL ACHIEVEMENT

Of the many means used to evaluate character portrayal in this study, one of the most useful is the analysis of goals. What the character seeks or wishes in a story is indicative of his presentation to the reader. Approved characters will seek altruistic, expressive, or honorable goals like justice, love, domestic harmony, pride, patriotism, loyalty, honor, and adventure. Disapproved characters will seek the more rational, pragmatic, or mundane goals like self-preservation, material success, power, ambi-tion, or knowledge.

Berelson and Salter found the "Americans" to seek the altruistic (or "heart") goals, while the foreign and minority characters sought the prag-

TABLE 11. Characters' Goals by Ethnic Group and Year of Study

Goals	1946			1968		
	Americans	AS&N	Other	Americans	AS&N	Other
Altruistic	69%	61%	49%	82%	66%	71%
Pragmatic	31	39	51	18	34	29
Total	100%	100%	100%	100%	100%	100%
n	793	57	53	152	67	104

matic (or "head") goals, in general. It was expected that more foreign and minority characters in the present sample would seek more altruistic goals than in the earlier study. This was found to be the case (Table 11). The "Others" made the largest gains of the two foreign and minority categories, although "Americans" also increased.

In order to expand the analysis in this important area of goal achievement, the means and barriers to goals were also studied. Approved characters can be expected to achieve their goals through approved means like legal authority, personality, charm, good fortune, industry, or intelligence. Disapproved characters can likewise be expected to seek their goals through disapproved means like violence, threats, deceit, trickery, or sponging off others.

On the other hand, approved characters can be expected to face more disapproved barriers like violence, trickery, deceit, or their own personal deficiencies, while disapproved characters would face approved barriers like constituted authority, industry, and intelligence of other characters.

It was expected that the "Americans" would use more approved means and face more disapproved barriers than the foreign and minority char-

TABLE 12. Means and Barriers to Goal Achievement by Ethnic Category

	Americans	Foreign/Minorities
Means		
Approved	69%	64%
Disapproved	31	36
Total	100%	100%
n	150	171
p	n.s.	
Barriers		
Approved	35%	36%
Disapproved	65	64
Total	100%	100%
n	114	110
p	n.s.	

acters. This was not found to be the case. The figures show little difference between the groups, if any (Table 12).

The relationships between goal achievement and the other criteria are interesting. The others, as mentioned above, have a large proportion of characters in the armed forces. This, of course, would make them seek more goals like patriotism and military duty, which are placed in the "altruistic" category. They would also be more likely to employ violence, a disapproved mean, and face violence, a disapproved barrier, in their goal achievement. The greater numbers of "Americans" and Anglo-Saxon/Nordic characters in high status occupations and superordinate interactional positions would make them more likely to seek more altruistic goals, and employ more approved means.

"PULPS" VS "SLICKS"

Another extension of the Berelson and Salter model is the investigation of the treatment and presentation of foreign and minority characters in different types of magazines. Albrecht found the "pulps" (those magazines aimed for lower-middle- and lower-class readers) to be the least tolerant of deviation from established norms, while the "slicks" (those aimed for upper-middle- and upper-class readers) to be the most tolerant of deviation, as far as fiction stories are concerned. It can therefore be expected that the "slicks" would give more equitable treatment to foreign and minority characters than would the "pulps."

The "pulps" in this study were *Argosy, True Confessions,* and *True Story.* These publications elicited thirty-one stories and 221 characters. The "slicks" were *Saturday Evening Post, Cosmopolitan, Ladies' Home Journal, Playboy,* and *Esquire,* in which were found forty-nine stories and 290 characters. One measure of foreign and minority group treatment is the number of stories dealing with race and ethnic-group relations. It can be expected that the slicks would have the greater share of stories dealing with this matter, but just the opposite was the case (Table 13).

Another measure is the proportion of foreign and minority characters. It can be expected that the slicks would have a larger percentage of

TABLE 13.   Race and Ethnic-Group Stories by Magazine Type

Story Theme	Magazine Type	
	Pulp	Slick
Ethnic-group relations	29.0%	8.2%
Others	71.0	91.8
Total	100.0%	100.0%
n	31	49

TABLE 14. Ethnic Group by Magazine Type

Ethnic Group	Pulp	Slick
"Americans"	45.4%	49.1%
American Minorities		
Anglo-Saxon/Nordic	12.3	3.3
Other hyphenates	5.5	10.8
Blacks	11.0	0.9
Jews	1.9	3.8
Foreign Nationals		
Anglo-Saxon/Nordic	4.9	18.9
Others	19.0	13.2
Total	100.0%	100.0%
n	163	212

these characters. The ratio of foreign and minority characters to "Americans" was roughly equal, although the pulps stressed the American minorities, and slicks emphasized the foreign characters (Table 14).

The slicks can be expected to portray more foreign and minority characters in major and submajor roles than the pulps. This turned out to be the case, although the slicks had more "Americans" in major and submajor roles as well (Table 15).

Finally, it can be expected that the slicks would give more foreign and minority characters approved status in their stories than would the pulps. Just the opposite was the case (Table 16). The pulps gave foreign and minority characters more approved treatment than the slicks, although more "Americans" appeared in approved roles as well in these magazines.

What does all this have to say about the difference between pulps and slicks as far as foreign and minority characters are concerned? First, it appears that the pulps are more interested in racial and ethnic-group problems than the slicks. This is evident from the greater proportion of stories dealing with these matters and the larger share of American minority characters. This is understandable when one considers the

TABLE 15. Story Role by Ethnic Category and Magazine Type

Story Role	Americans		Foreign/Minorities	
	Pulps	Slicks	Pulps	Slicks
Major and submajor	74.3%	83.7%	61.8%	68.5%
Minor	25.7	16.3	38.2	31.5
Total	100.0%	100.0%	100.0%	100.0%
n	74	86	89	108

TABLE 16. Approval/Disapproval by Ethnic Category and Magazine Type

Treatment	Americans		Foreign/Minorities	
	Pulps	Slicks	Pulps	Slicks
Approval	78.4%	68.0%	57.3%	49.5%
Neutral and				
disapproval	21.6	32.0	42.7	50.1
Total	100.0%	100.0%	100.0%	100.0%
n	74	100	89	107

market they try to reach. Their readers are the ones most affected by social change in these areas. Either they belong to the deprived ethnic group like Blacks, or Spanish-speaking minorities, or they feel the most threatened by their advancements.

The slicks, however, give more play to stories and characters of a foreign nature. This is pointed out by the greater proportion of foreign characters. Their readers tend to be better educated and more aware of international events.

The difference in the foreign and minority characters being given approved treatment is also explainable, in part, by the difference in stories and audience. The stories in the pulps tend to parallel the stories in the Berelson and Salter sample. They tend to be simple in structure with highly idealized heroes and villains. The slicks, however, are aimed for readers with a greater education and their stories tend to be more complex with heroes and villains which tend to be less differentiated. Stories of this type would be more difficult for the average reader of pulp magazines to understand. It can also be contended that fiction in the two types of magazines play different functions to the readers. Fiction in pulps may very well play a socializing role, "teaching" their readers about the middle-class values they tend to seek. In the slicks, fiction could play more of an entertainment function, although catering to more sophisticated tastes.

CONCLUSION

Changes in the presentation and treatment of foreign and minority characters in magazine fiction have been considerable. Although the "Americans" still tend to predominate, foreign and minority characters are more numerous, play more important roles, live better lives, and seek more honorable goals. This has been the case for all the groups, although the Anglo-Saxon/Nordic characters have made the most progress.

These changes can be explained, in part, by the changes in the sample and the audience. The market for magazine fiction has changed considerably, with men's magazines becoming a major vehicle for fiction. Men's magazines, in general, tend to be less concerned with love, marriage, or domestic relations, and more with war, action, and adventure stories. This would mean more foreign locales and foreign characters.

Another explanation lies in the competition from television. Light, simple, humorous stories, which characterized the Berelson and Salter sample, are now a major commodity on prime-time TV. Although these stories still turn up in the 1968 sample, the stories, in general, tend to be more varied, and offer the reader material which TV does not carry, at present.

Finally, one must consider the great social changes which have occurred since the 1940s. It is inconceivable that these changes would affect the major institutions in our society without affecting magazine fiction. The writers, editors, and publishers must take into account the awareness of racial and ethnic-group problems as well as the greater involvement of the United States in world affairs.

The effects which these stories have upon the formation of images and attitudes relating to foreign and minority groups is only a matter for conjecture at this point. Because of their ability to involve the reader's fantasy, however, they can be of some consequence over a period of time. Those readers with rigid stereotypes of certain foreign and minority groups would probably not be affected by a favorable portrayal of these groups in magazine fiction. For those people in changing social situations, however, old ideas and stereotypes may be questioned. Here, magazine fiction may be one factor which affects attitudes towards people of different foreign, racial, and ethnic backgrounds.

REFERENCES

1. Berelson, Bernard, and Salter, Patricia, "Majority and Minority Americans: An Analysis of Magazine Fiction," *Public Opinion Quarterly,* **10,** 168–197 (1946).
2. Bogart, Leo, "Magazines Since the Rise of Television," *Journalism Quarterly,* **33,** 157–158, 162, (1956).
3. Colle, Royal, "Negro Image in the Mass Media: A Case Study in Social Change," *Journalism Quarterly,* **45,** 55–60 (1968).
4. Levin, Jack, "The Ethnic Groups in Majority and Negro Fiction: Their Social Positions and Social Relations," (Unpublished M. S. thesis, Boston University. 1965), pp. 31, 47–49, 77–79.
5. Albrecht, M. C., "Does Literature Reflect Common Values?" *American Sociological Review,* **21,** 722–729.

ADDITIONAL REFERENCES

Albrecht, M. C., "Does Literature Reflect Common Values?" *American Sociological Review,* **21,** 722–729 (1956).

Arp, Dennis J., "The Problem of Reliability in the Human Coding of Textual Data," paper presented at the Annual Meeting of the American Educational Research Association, Los Angeles, California, 1969.

Berelson, Bernard, and Salter, Patricia, "Majority and Minority Americans: An Analysis of Magazine Fiction." *Public Opinion Quarterly,* **10,** 168–197 (1946).

Bogart, Leo, "Magazines Since the Rise of Television," *Journalism Quarterly,* **33,** 168–197 (1956).

Colle, Royal, "Negro Image in the Mass Media: A Case Study in Social Change," *Journalism Quarterly,* **45,** 55–60 (1968).

DeFleur, Melvin L., *Theories of Mass Communication,* David McKay, Inc., New York, 1966.

Johns-Heine, Patricke, and Gerth, Hans, "Values in Mass Periodical Fiction, 1921–1940," *Public Opinion Quarterly,* **13,** 105–113 (1949).

Levin, Jack, "The Ethnic Groups in Majority and Negro Fiction: Their Social Positions and Social Relations," Unpublished M.S. thesis, Boston University, 1965.

Lipset, Seymour M., *Political Man: The Social Bases of Politics,* Doubleday, New York, 1960.

Shuey, A. M., "Stereotyping of Negroes and Whites: An Analysis of Magazine Pictures," *Public Opinion Quarterly,* **17,** 281–287 (1953).

Siegel, Sidney, *Nonparametric Statistics for the Behavioral Sciences,* McGraw-Hill Book Co., New York, 1956.

Steele, Henry, "Majority and Minority Americans in Magazine Fiction During 1967," Unpublished term paper, Boston University, 1968.

United States Bureau of the Census, *Statistical Abstract of the United States: 1967,* 88th ed., Washington, D.C., 1967.

Hippie Values: An Analysis of the Underground Press*

By Jack Levin and James L. Spates

There is little doubt by this time that the hippie phenomenon of the late 1960s is a social movement of some consequence for American society.[1] Whatever its greater significance, the movement has already contributed to a "revolution" in modern dress, hairstyles, music, art, and youth culture.

Since 1966, the mass media have analyzed, scrutinized, supported, and condemned the movement, so that almost all Americans, whether or not they have had direct experience with the hippies, presently hold some opinion regarding the "merits" of this group of young people.

Why have the hippies attracted so much attention? It is doubtful that the answer lies solely in the number of hippies: percentage-wise, they are a very small proportion of the American population, numbering, at highest estimate, only 200,000 full-time participants.[2] Nor does it seem likely that the concern is a direct product of the much publicized "generation gap." Despite ample evidence that most hippies are young (under 30) and that most of their critics are "old" (over 30), support for the movement ranges far beyond age lines: many of the hippies' most ardent admirers, if not participants, are over 30 and many of their detractors under 30.

After this widespread popularization, social scientists have recently attempted to account for the American reaction to the hippie phenomenon.[3] Some have specifically focused upon the value gap between the hippies and the middle class, a gap which has been characterized as an attempt by the hippie movement to substitute a viable alternative in place of the traditional American value pattern.[4] From this standpoint, the hippie problem becomes distinctly ideological, being directly related to those values or ideals which serve as the most general guidelines for action within society (e.g., the general American ideal that everyone, in

* Published by permission of the authors. A version of this essay appeared in *Youth and Society* II (1), 59–73 (Sept. 1970).

order to be an American in good standing, must achieve individual success through his own occupational efforts).

The value argument raises an important aspect of the problem—that of conflict between different values as an expression of the basic gap between the hippie and middle-class views of life. Values being the most general directives for action in society means that they are the most generally *shared* ideas about the correct way to behave. A challenge to the values of a social system is therefore regarded by the members of that system as a basic threat to the very *raison d'etre* of their social structure. Hence, one might expect the expansion of strong concerns regarding the challenging elements of the hippie phenomenon.

THE MIDDLE-CLASS PATTERN

The hippie mode of existence cannot be understood apart from the value structure of American society as a whole. More specifically, hippie culture has arisen directly out of the middle-class value system within which the majority of hippies were initially socialized. It has been estimated that over 70% of all hippies come from this middle- (or upper-) class orientation.[5]

Characteristically, middle-class values tend to specify acts which are oriented to the future and normally require the individual to inhibit emotional expression in order for his resources to be fully directed toward the cognitive or rational solution to life-tasks.[6]

In the American case, the middle-class pattern typically manifests itself in the pursuit of economic concerns, i.e., in rationally constructed efforts to increase economic production, profits, and occupational status by means of extended formal education and hard work. The achievement dimension of this pattern cannot be overemphasized: the middle-class value structure places major demands upon each individual to achieve occupational success, not merely in terms of personal wealth, power, or status, but as a moral obligation to contribute to the building of the "good society."[7] In other words, middle class achievement cannot be purely utilitarian: a person cannot use *any* means to a particular end, but must use instead socially legitimized (normatively sanctioned) means to ends. Basic success, then, is defined in *social* as well as personal terms; and rewards are commensurate. Thus, from the middle-class perspective, the hard-working businessman who makes $10,000 a year is much more *respectable* than the gangster who makes ten times that amount; and, all things being equal, it is the businessman who will be given the "upstanding" positions in the society.

These essential features of the middle class pattern, i.e., its economic, cognitive, and achievement dimensions, all of which denote the goal-oriented nature of activity within the system, can be summarized for convenience under the term "instrumentalism."[8]

THE HIPPIE PATTERN

The hippies contend that their subculture offers a radical departure from the dominant American value structure which they see as thoroughly materialistic, dehumanizing, inauthentic, and alienating.[9] This point of view is reflected in the hippies' "almost total rejection of economic individualism and the 'dog eat dog' or 'do unto others before they do unto you' attitude that is seen by them as the driving force behind contemporary American society."[10] The following responses are illustrative of the hippies' rejection of middle class values:

> (A hippie drop-out since 1960) To me, dropping-out means to reject the dominant moral, economic, and social values of one's society. I dropped out because the values in our society have become obsolete . . . Our society is simply full of internal contradictions between its values and the reality of what people actually think and do. Forty percent of America is terribly poor and yet we have tried to hide this from ourselves and the world because the dominant American middle-class has interests in perpetuating the myth.

> (A hippie) In order to act with freedom, one must not be constrained by the oppressive systems of orientation and the selfish, meaningless goals that were learned while a member of the uptight, plastic society.

> (A twenty-three-year-old hippie) We (America) have reached a high level of material development, many people have become hypnotized and obsessed with a desire for material good. There is a strong feeling of "us" and "them" . . . This is a negative part of contemporary American life and is blocking people from seeing the essence of one another.[11]

In sum, then, it would appear that the hippie views the instrumental values of American society, whatever their original purpose, as presently generating dehumanized life-styles, even to the point where human beings themselves, in the active quest for "success," have become objects of manipulation to one another.

Such a negative reaction to his own society's dominant values (and to his own original values) has led the hippie to form a life-style that is quite at odds with the typical American ideal of the hard-working, self-denying, rational businessman or professional. Yablonsky has set forth what he sees as the basic elements of the ideal hippie: he is a philosopher who claims to be "tuned-in to the cosmic affinity of man"; he thus loves all men (the love ethic); "he has achieved this insight, at least in part, from the use of drugs (marijuana, LSD) as a sacrament"; he is a role model for new hippies to look up to; he is creative; he does not work in the traditional sense of American culture, rather preferring to "do his own thing," whatever that may be; he is, in a word, "totally dropped out of the larger society," which he regards as "plastic," and is actively engaged in "fostering another mode of existence."[12]

This other "mode of existence" is for the hippie an alternative which completely de-emphasizes the economic and achievement criteria of American society, and focuses instead upon all objects and actions as *ends-in-themselves,* as valuable and necessary foci of immediate gratification and present (rather than future) time orientation. More specifically, rather than attempting to deal with their affairs on a cognitive-rational level, or in terms of economic value, the hippie's ideals stress nonmaterial or spiritual concerns (e.g., participation in cosmology, mysticism, and the occult)[13] as well as the search for love and intimacy in human relationships.[14] In addition, the achievement aspects of the middle-class pattern are replaced by the quest for self-expression as experienced in the immediate on-going situation (i.e., by "grooving on" or "getting into" music, art, and psychedelic drugs, etc.). Whereas the middle class individual is rewarded for following socially legitimized paths to achievement, the hippie is expected to follow his own personal path to wherever it leads him. That is, whatever his "thing" is, he does it.

The essential components of the hippie value pattern—as indicated by self-expression, affiliation, concern for others, and religious philosophical interests—can be conveniently characterized under the term "expressivism."[15]

The value gap between the hippies and the middle-class, though often suggested by previous investigations of the hippie phenomenon, has, for the most part, lacked systematic, quantitative substantiation.[16] For this reason, it was the central purpose of the present study to test the hypothesis that *contrary to the middle-class pattern, hippie values stress expressive concerns and de-emphasize instrumental concerns.*

METHOD

To delineate the value structure of the hippie movement, a sample was taken from Underground Press Syndicate (UPS) periodicals published in 1967 and 1968—a recent period during which hippie literature was available. The UPS has an estimated, combined circulation of one million and, as self-described, consists of an "informal association of publications of the 'alternative press' . . . produced in storefronts and basements by feelthy hippies, distributed by unorthodox channels and free-thinking bookstores and from curbs."[17] Ron Thelin, the editor of a representative underground newspaper has expressed the purpose of his publication in the following manner:

> (To) provide an organ for the hip community, an evolution of communications consciousness and group consciousness to reflect the universal spirit and the miracles of light in this community (Haight-Ashbury) . . . To show that LSD provides a profound experience . . . To provide communication of the historical and ancient discoveries that are coming out of the hip culture, to spread the word, to get everyone to turn on, tune in, and drop out.[18]

Most hippie underground papers appeared in the mid-sixties, many of them after the publicity of 1967, and many of them short-lived. But their common components were an emphasis on hippie argot, psychedelic lettering and art, the glorification of folk rock, flower power, and love-ins—all, as Thelin says, in an attempt to describe the hip experience to its readers.

To obtain a representative sample of underground newspapers, the following most widely circulated periodicals were selected from major centers of recent hippie activities, including both eastern and western regions; *Avatar* (Boston), *Distant Drummer* (Philadelphia), *East Village Other* (New York), *Los Angeles Free Press, San Francisco Oracle,* and *Washington Free Press*.[19] A single issue of each UPS periodical from every second month in the period from September 1967 to August 1968 was selected.[20] Every second nonfictional article appearing in this sample of issues, excluding poetry and letters to the editor, was subjected to analysis ($N = 316$).

To provide a comparable sample of articles representative of middle-class values, an analysis was also conducted of concurrently published issues of the *Reader's Digest*.[21] Excluding fiction and poetry, each article appearing in every other issue of the Reader's Digest was studied ($N = 162$).

The major value-theme of articles in both samples was coded by means of a modified version of Ralph K. White's Value Catalogue.[22] All materials were coded using a detailed set of definitions of the value-themes and appropriate coding sheets.[23]

The central hypothesis regarding expressive and instrumental values was tested in the following manner. On the basis of the theoretical discussion above, the categories of self-expression, concern for others, affiliation, and religious-philosophical were treated as aspects of expressivism, while the categories of achievement, cognitive, and economic became the basis for instrumentalism. Categories of the value analysis are listed below:

Instrumental
A. *Achievement:* Values which produce achievement motivation for the individual in terms of hard work, practicality, or economic value are often expressed by means of contributions to society through occupation and high regard for ownership.
B. *Cognitive:* These represent the drive for learning as an end in itself as well as the means for achieving success, welfare, or happiness.
C. *Economic:* Economic values are at the collective level (e.g., national, state, industrial), thus differing from individual goals such as achievement.

Expressive
D. *Self-expressive:* This area includes all the self-expressive values and goals. The main ones are humor, play, and fun in general, relaxation, or exciting new discoveries, and travel. Art and beauty are included as well as other creative-expressive activities.
E. *Affiliative:* These may be the product of social conditioning, or a result of the need to belong to a group, to affiliate with another per-

son. This category focuses upon the gregariousness of individuals and the friendships which they develop. These affiliative aims may be expressed as conformity, loyalty to the group, friendship, or other-directedness.

F. *Concern for others:* Concern for others does not depend upon a drive to interact. Unlike the affiliative values, this category focuses upon attitudes and feelings toward particular groups or toward humanity in general. Therefore, this category tends to include more abstract objectives than those associated with affiliation.

G. *Religious-philosophical:* This category includes goals dealing with ultimate meaning in life, the role of deity, concerns with after-life, etc.

Other

H. *Individualistic:* This category is concerned with values which stress the importance of the individual, the development of his unique personality, individual independence, and the achievement of individualized personal fulfillment including rebellion.

I. *Physiological:* These are goals created by simple physiological drives such as hunger, sex, physical health, and physical safety.

J. *Political:* This category includes collective goals (e.g., state, community, national, international objectives), in their central reference to group decision-making processes.

K. *Miscellaneous:* Any other goals not covered above (e.g., hope, honesty, purity, modesty, and manners).

The reliability of the value analysis was tested by having three coders independently code thirty articles from both the UPS and the *Digest* samples. Using a two-out-of-three criterion (i.e., where two of three coders agreed), agreement reached 90%. Total agreement (e.g., three of three coders agreed) was 78%.

RESULTS AND DISCUSSION

Results obtained in an analysis of UPS and *Reader's Digest* value-themes suggest that expressivism occupies a central position in the hippie value structure, whereas instrumentalism occurs only peripherally. As shown in Table 1, expressive concerns accounted for 46% of the value-themes in the underground press, whereas instrumental concerns were the major focus of only 10% of these articles. In sharp contrast, instrumental concerns represented the major value-theme in the *Reader's Digest* sample (42%), whereas expressive concerns were substantially less important (23%).

Within the expressivism of the hippie sample, the dominant emphasis appeared to be Self-Expression (28%). For example, typical articles in the underground press dealt with the "mind-blowing" psychedelic properties of drugs; the relationship of early rock-and-roll music to contemporary rock groups (e.g., the Beatles and Rolling Stones); the influence of such figures as Ken Kesey, Timothy Leary, and Lenny Bruce on the hippie movement.

In the *Reader's Digest* sample, Achievement was the dominant component of instrumentalism, representing 28% of all value-themes. Typically, *Reader's Digest* articles emphasized methods for occupational

TABLE 1. Value-Themes in the Underground Press and Reader's Digest[a]

Value-Theme	Underground Press		Reader's Digest	
Expressive	46%		23%	
Self-expressive		28%		9%
Concern for others		8		6
Affiliative		4		3
Religious-philosophical		6		5
Instrumental	10		42	
Achievement		3		28
Cognitive		5		7
Economic		2		7
Other	44		35	
Individual		20		10
Political[b]		19		12
Physiological[c]		4		12
Miscellaneous		1		1
Total		100%		100%
(N=)		(316)		(162)

[a] A chi-square analysis was conducted by comparing the Underground Press and *Reader's Digest* on the two major value-themes, expressive and instrumental ($\chi^2 = 61.17$, $df = 1$, $p < 0.001$).
[b] The distribution of Political values reveals an important aspect of the nature of the underground press: a secondary appeal of these newspapers is often to politically "radical" or "New Left" types, though most of the material is designed for hippie consumption (see, Wolfe, op. cit., pp. 135–144)—a group known for its apolitical stance (see, Yablonsky, op. cit.).
[c] In the *Reader's Digest,* this category consisted primarily of health-related topics such as methods of weight reduction, physical diseases (e.g., cancer), and aging. In the Underground Press, it contained references to physiological sex.

achievement, including business enterprises created by college students; advice concerning financial investments and taxes; the careers of well-known persons who had achieved occupational success, etc.

An independent analysis of a random sample of underground press advertisements appearing in our sample yielded the following supportive data: almost 90% of the hippie advertisements focused on expressive-related products, i.e., on products which are designed either for expressive behavior or expressive consumption, such as music (rock, folk, blues, soul, etc.), movies, plays, psychedelic shops, clothing (mod), and coffee and tea houses. The most important of these expressive categories contained music-related products such as concerts, records, recording artists, and stereophonic equipment; these products accounted for 25% of all hippie advertisements. These results lend support to the suggestion that expressive concerns are a staple of great magnitude for the readers of the underground press, and, more generally, for the hippie movement as a whole.

An examination of the relationship of individualism to the expressive-instrumental dichotomy may shed additional light on the above findings. As is well known, social scientists have long been concerned with the position of individualism in the American value structure. In the middle-class case, individualism has the major task of locating responsibility for contributions to the building of the "good society." Thus, each individual must actively strive to accomplish those objectives which society has defined as legitimate concerns.

Similarly, the hippies show a characteristic American concern for the individual. As shown in the present study, 20% of the articles appearing in the underground press contained an individualistic value-orientation. However, the hippie version may indicate an individualism of a different order: an individualism closely tied to the expressive value-orientation. It is here that the hippie phrase, "Do your own thing!" has particular relevance, in that it essentially directs attention to the immediate gratification of needs by means of creative self-expression—an "expressive individualism" which stands in sharp contrast to the dominant middle-class pattern.[24]

The hippies form a unique phenomenon in contemporary America—a large-scale movement which has arisen out of the mainstream of American life to form a contra-culture within its societal boundaries. Results obtained in the present study support the contention that the hippies are attempting to stress values of an expressive nature, values which they feel have been neglected by the highly instrumental middle-class.

From the sociological point of view, this is where the concern of Americans over the hippies comes home to roost: a way of life is being criticized and sides are being taken. The ideology of the hip movement attempts to cut to the core of the instrumental view of things. The middle-class ideology, the hippies are saying, neglects the personal needs of the individual to be a *human* being; it neglects his need to be affective, loving, and trustful of other people; it neglects his need for self-realization by following his own individual needs; in a word; it neglects his need to be expressive.

Yet, how "expressive" can a social system be? There is increasing evidence that the strongly reactive nature of the hippie value system may in large part account for the general failure of the movement to form viable communities or other social structures.[25] The perceived overemphasis of the middle-class on instrumentalism seems to have been matched by a similar overemphasis by the hippies on pure expressivism. In structural terms, extreme expressivism poses a significant problem for long-term, stable patterns of interaction, i.e., the basic tasks of maintaining the system are not performed on a regular basis, which, in the extreme, can result in social disorganization and decay. Indeed, the literature on the hippies is replete with examples of community and group termination because food was not taken in, rent was not paid, etc. Clearly, for a stable society, everyone "doing his own thing" has its limitations.

It is just this aspect of "system dissolution" that the middle-class American intuitively, and, we think, rightly, feels may be a consequence of a purely expressive mode of existence. Knowing this, he, like the hippie, takes a stance of defense of his life-style. Though the ideological "stance" of each group often becomes a battle of "ego defenses" (i.e., "My way of life is right because it is *my* way of life"), there seems to be objective merit in both positions; extreme instrumentalism does appear to neglect the necessities of personality and organismic expression, whereas extreme expressivism appears to neglect the requirements of stable social systems. For this reason, it may well be that neither the "expressive" or "instrumental" value structures may come to be dominant in this ideational conflict. Rather, the solution may be in the form of systems which combine elements of both these systems; systems which are already in the process of formulation.

It already appears that the hippie's purely expressive solution to life is considered too radical as a viable solution for the society as a whole. Very few people completely "drop out" (which the totally expressive solution necessitates). But, there is evidence that fewer and fewer people are taking the "straight life" in its extreme sense as their life-style either. Rather, some sort of balance apparently is being worked out on both sides of the fence.

From a more general perspective, the hippie emphasis on expressive values could be regarded as partially illustrative of a process of widespread "balancing" in American society as a whole, whereby the social system, being pushed more and more to an instrumental extreme, is re-introducing various modes of expressivism at all levels of its structure. If this is the case, then the society-wide trend toward expressivism, exemplified in its most extreme form by the hip movement, could be seen as part-and-parcel of other strong trends in contemporary America—civil rights, freedom of speech, representation, life-style, etc. Though the end result will most likely not be the extreme expressivism found dominant in many hip sub-cultures, it may very well be, over time, that an expressivism suitable to all age levels and classes of American society will become part of the American ideology. It is in this sense that the hippie movement may have its most profound influence on the character of the American value system.

Acknowledgment: We wish to especially thank Herbert J. Greenwald for his many helpful suggestions. We are also grateful to Stephen R. Marks, Kingsley H. Birge, and William F. Macauley for their critical review of earlier versions of this paper.

REFERENCES

1. For a discussion of the hippies as a social movement, see Lewis Yablonsky, *The Hippie Trip,* Pegasus, New York, 1968, p. 290ff.
2. *Ibid.,* p. 36.
3. See, for example, *Trans-Action,* **5**(2) (Dec. 1967): Bennett M. Berger, "Hippie Morality—More Old Than New," pp. 19–27; Fred Davis, "Why All of Us May Be Hippies Someday," pp. 10–18; Geoffrey Simon and Grafton Trout, "Hippies in College—From Teeney-boppers to Drug-Freaks," pp. 27–32. Michael E.

Brown, "The Persecution and Condemnation of Hippies," *Trans-Action,* **6**(10) 33–46 (Sept. 1969); Stephen R. Marks, "The Hippies and the Organism: A Problem for the General Theory of Action," an unpublished manuscript, Department of Sociology, Boston University, 1969. Yablonsky, *op. cit.*

4. Marks, *op. cit.* In this paper, the relationship of the hippies to the instrumental-expressive continuum was originally delineated.

5. Yablonsky, *op. cit.,* p. 26.

6. Talcott Parsons, *The Social System,* The Free Press, New York, 1951, p. 48. See also Talcott Parsons and Winston White, "The Link Between Character and Society," in Talcott Parsons, ed., *Social Structure and Personality.* The Free Press, New York, 1964, pp. 196ff.

7. Parsons and White, *op. cit.,* p. 196.

8. *Ibid.,* pp. 196ff. See also Morris Zelditch, Jr., "Role Differentiation in the Nuclear Family: A Comparative Study" in Talcott Parsons and Robert F. Bales, et al., eds., *Family: Socialization and Interaction Process,* The Free Press, New York, 1955, pp. 309–312.

9. Yablonsky, *op. cit.,* pp. 361–366.

10. *Ibid.,* p. 358.

11. *Ibid.,* pp. 350–351, 358, 365.

12. *Ibid.,* pp. 29–31.

13. Andrew M. Greeley, "There's a New Time Religion on Campus," *New York Times Magazine* (June 1, 1969), pp. 14–28.

14. Yablonsky, *op. cit.,* pp. 366, 358.

15. See Zelditch, *op. cit.,* p. 311.

16. See those cited in footnote 2. One major exception is Yablonsky, whose methods include lengthy participant observation and a questionnaire approach *(N*=600). However, the study has been severely criticized on methodological grounds, particularly in its participant observation aspect: see, for example, Bennett M. Berger, "Sociologist on a Bad Trip," *Trans-Action,* **6**(4), 54–56 (Feb. 1969).

17. *Underground Press Syndicate* Directory, Orpheus, Phoenix, 1969, pp. 17–18.

18. Ron Thelin, editor of the *San Francisco Oracle,* as quoted in Burton H. Wolfe, *The Hippies,* Signet, New York, 1968, pp. 143–144.

19. The UPS periodicals in the sample have a combined circulation of more than 200,000 (UPS Directory, *op. cit.*)

20. Monthly issues of weeklies and biweeklies were sampled on a random basis.

21. *Reader's Digest* was selected for its variety of middle-class articles taken from diverse sources. See Genevieve Ginglinger, "Basic Values in 'Reader's Digest,' 'Selection,' and 'Constellation,'" *Journalism Quarterly,* **32**(1), 56–61 (Winter 1955).

22. Ralph K. White, *Value-Analysis: The Nature and Use of the Method,* Society for the Psychological Study of Social Issues, New York, 1951.

23. We gratefully acknowledge the coding assistance of Ann MacConnell, Kenneth Sweezey, and Marilyn Thomas.

24. Marks, *op. cit.,* also notes this particular individualistic pattern in the hippie phenomenon.

25. Because of harassment by various agencies of the dominant culture, a significant number of hippies have literally taken to the woods to form communes. While some of these social systems have existed for a number of years, their long-term stability has not yet been confirmed. In addition, even if successful, the price of their success may be more instrumentally oriented behavior. Such groups are in the minority if one takes the hippie population as a whole: most hippies still reside in major urban centers and exist in extremely loose confederations. See Brown, *op. cit.,* esp. p. 37.

The 'Orthodox' Media Under Fire: Chicago and the Press[*]

By Nathan B. Blumberg

We have been somewhat sympathetic to the problems of policemen and police authorities who have been charged with unwarranted brutality in critical mob situations when much if not all of it has been a result of provocation. However, we have no sympathy for them when they appear to be deliberately assaulting news reporters and cameramen in what appears to be an effort to prevent coverage of their mob-controlling tactics whatever they might be.

—*Editor & Publisher,* Aug. 31, 1968

The news media of the United States were subjected to an attack unprecedented in modern times for their coverage of events during the Democratic National Convention in Chicago. The reason is that the news media did their jobs in Chicago in a way unprecedented in modern times.

Mayor Richard Daley made several dreadful miscalculations in his handling of the Democratic National Convention, but the decisive mistake was a frontal attack on the men sent to cover the events in the convention hall and on the streets. Two things happened that didn't have to happen and that made all the difference. Unfortunately, it took some assaults on newsmen by police to push the print media into telling a story that otherwise, we must assume from the record, would have remained essentially untold, and it took some ham-handed attempts at censorship by Chicago's political boss, accustomed to having his way, to infuriate the television networks to the point that they showed the way things were and are in Chicago.

Only ten months earlier, when 100,000 persons assembled at the Lincoln Memorial to protest the war in Vietnam and more than 30,000 demonstrators later pressed against the Pentagon, the confrontation was reported by the news media in ways that only could have delighted the authorities—governmental, military, police, and industrial. Following an

* Reprinted from the *Montana Journalism Review*, No. 12, 1969, by permission of the author and publisher.

analysis of the reporting of that event and the coverage of other activities of dissent, I hopefully had concluded:

> Perhaps it is too much to expect, as the hostile critics of the press have contended through the years, that a press with an undeniable stake in the economic and political system would report fairly on those who are fundamentally dissatisfied with the status quo. But the history of journalism is not without instances in which "orthodox" publications went "underground," and some examples cited herein demonstrate that sometimes some organs of information report facts that tend to disrupt the hegemony of the industrial-military-governmental complex.*

What happened in Chicago was that incidents of repression that in the past almost always had been kept hidden from the public were reported in detail. Naturally, those persons committed to perpetuating present policies and conditions were infuriated by this unexpected and unusual turn of events and they struck back with all the considerable power in their hands. They were joined by those millions of Americans who for varying reasons favor authoritarian repression of minority groups and minority opinions.

Conversely, events in Chicago were shocking to millions of other Americans because just as the orthodox press covered up what happened in the demonstration leading to the doors of the Pentagon, it has covered up illegal police behavior in countless cities where police officers daily harass and intimidate large numbers of our citizens. Chicago was a catalyst. It brought out in one agonizing ordeal all the frustrations that overwhelm our people—on the one hand the young, the disenchanted, the revolutionary, the pacifistic and idealistic, the draft resisting, the McCarthy-supporting, and those concerned with the desperate plight of the blacks and of a nation in a horrendous war; on the other hand the complacent and the content, the Nixonites and Humphreyites, the ones who have it made in government or in business or in the military, the people who don't want niggers next door or niggers taking their jobs. Agonizing, that is, to everyone except, in one of those poignant and delicious ironies of history, the blacks and the other aggrieved men and women of color who could stand back and watch in amusement whitey's battle in which The Man took after The Kids.

[Chicago's brooding ghettos remained calm during the entire week of the convention because their black inhabitants knew very well why the troops were there. The reported 7,500 regular army troops—flown from Fort Hood, Fort Sill and Fort Carson and bivouacked in armories, at air stations, in Washington Park in the heart of Chicago's south side—were

---

* For the full account see "A Study of the 'Orthodox' Press: The Reporting of Dissent" in the Montana Journalism Review, No. 11, 1968, reprinted in The American Oxonian, October, 1968, or a condensed version, "The Defaulting Press and Vietnam," in Commonweal, July 12, 1968.

ready along with an announced 6,000 Illinois National Guardsmen, an estimated 1,000 Secret Service and FBI agents and about 12,000 Chicago police. In addition, three full regular army armored divisions, totaling more than 40,000 men, were earmarked for Chicago, if needed. The 26,000 men on hand were not there for the scruffy legions of pacifism and hipdom or the McCarthy kids or even the hard-eyed revolutionaries—in all the "weapons" displayed by police as captured from demonstrators, not one gun had been picked off a protester. The soldiers were there for the blacks, who are armed. Mayor Daley had the sign up in blazing capitals: "YOU BETTER NOT MOVE." And if the blacks on the west and south sides did move, Daley and the police wanted troops ready for the battle in the streets, the sniping and the guerrilla warfare they fully expect, nervously await and patently escalate toward fulfillment. As a result, many black militant leaders moved out of Chicago before the delegates moved in and the others cooled it or watched in carnival spirit as the cops busted heads of the self-proclaimed new niggers in Lincoln and Grant parks, in front of the Hilton or the Palmer House, in Old Town or at 18th and Michigan.

Some publications of the orthodox press scantily reported that 43 black soldiers at Fort Hood were arrested after they refused to board planes to go from Texas to Chicago. But the orthodox press quickly dropped the matter and certainly did not try to explain why black soldiers preferred the stockade to duty in Chicago where they might be ordered to patrol ghetto streets. The black Chicago Daily Defender *named one of these soldiers from Chicago and quoted him: "I don't want to knife any one of my brothers or sisters. We fought for one whitey in Vietnam, and we don't want to go home and destroy the freedom that we fought in Vietnam for."]*

No doubt about it: The people of the United States split, if not down the middle somewhere close to it, over what happened in those four days that seemed like forty to anyone who was there. Those thoroughly angry with American policies in Vietnam, with a fixed convention programmed to nominate a man who hadn't won a primary, with the lack of understanding of the plight of the minorities were arrayed against those other millions thoroughly fed up with noisy demonstrators, with bearded and often dirty youths, with uppity people, with those who mocked their desperate longing for a return to a time when, in retrospect, life was so ordered and pleasant.

An equally indisputable fact is that the closer reporters and cameramen were to the action in Chicago, the more they were infuriated by what they saw and experienced. The violence was far worse than what television showed; the savagery was too widespread to be picked up by a few cameras. No person of decent instincts could witness that hell on the streets and in the parks without revulsion, and that revulsion was communicated effectively. Whether the story would have been told so completely had not Mayor Daley's police clubbed and beaten and threatened scores of newsmen can of course be argued, but the overwhelming evidence is that it was the thumpings suffered by journalists that was decisive.

A MYOPIC APPROACH TO PROBLEMS

Look, for example, at the quotation above from an editorial in *Editor & Publisher,* once justifiably called the "Bible of the Newspaper Industry" and now a flaccid weekly propagandist and apologist for the fattest cats of newspaper publishing. It is an unabashed confession that the trade magazine of the American press had seen little wrong with police handling of "critical mob situations" until some newsmen and photographers got theirs in Chicago. Translated from the code words employed these days by most editorial writers of the orthodox press, the two sentences in the editorial mean simply that it was okay, cops, to bang the heads of those dirty hippies and lousy yippies, those pacifists and peaceniks, those draft-card burners and bearded students, those coons and spics and all the others who have been beaten up through the years by policemen for daring to protest matters of inequity or of conscience. But lay off, ya hear, our reporters and cameramen. As if to delineate the limits of its concern, *Editor & Publisher* in the following weeks editorially repeated its fervent concern for the safety of newsmen in future demonstrations without appending a word of apprehension for the safety of nonjournalists who also might be beaten. "We're not interested in who was responsible for the demonstrations, who provoked the police or how they did it, or how the police reacted to the onslaught of the mob," the publisher and editor of *Editor & Publisher* emphasized in his personal column. "But we want to know only why easily identifiable newsmen got it in the neck and what can be done to prevent similar incidents in other cities in the future." This is typical of the myopic approach of the newspaper industry's spokesmen to the problems of the press and the society in which the press operates. A subsequent by-lined, "news story" reporting Mayor Daley's side of the story went far out of its way to quote seven moronic paragraphs from a column by Betty Beale, a cocktail party chatterer who covers social gatherings of bureaucrats and politicians for the *Washington Star,* and three equally ludicrous paragraphs from a syndicated column by James J. Kilpatrick, a practicing racist. It was a sad but unfortunately typical performance by a publication supposedly dedicated to the legitimate concerns of the profession of journalism.

[*The decline and fall of* Editor & Publisher *from its splendid critical stance in the 1930s to its present state of serving as a flack for the newspaper industry is another story. But one more example: The article following the one out of Chicago was a long account of how the press covers the annual Miss America Pageant, which included, among the details usually reserved for fan magazines published for teenagers, the informa-*

tion that "there are a number of those in the communications media who serve as judges and select the new Miss America . . . and here effort is always made to get one or more people who can give the Pageant and the resort a good break in publicity." It works, too, the article proudly announced. "Payoffs in other years were invitations which brought columnists Earl Wilson and Norton Mockridge here. Both featured the resort and the Pageant in their columns during the week and even after, a publicity break which could not have been secured by any other means." Obviously Editor & Publisher *remains, in its way, an indispensable medium for an understanding of the American press.*]

When the billy clubs began busting open the skins of journalists, it was too much to bear for four publishers—Arthur Ochs Sulzberger of the *New York Times,* Mrs. Katharine Graham of the *Washington Post,* Otis Chandler of the *Los Angeles Times,* and Bailey Howard of the *Chicago Daily News* and *Sun-Times.* They joined with the three top network television executives and the editor-in-chief of *Time* magazine, Hedley Donovan, to dispatch to Mayor Daley a telegram stating that newsmen "were repeatedly singled out by policemen and deliberately beaten and harassed. . . . The obvious purpose was to discourage or prevent reporting of an important confrontation between police and demonstrators which the American public has a right to know about."

Suddenly the American public's right-to-know became pressingly important to these publishers, simply because they had been backed into a corner and had little choice but to rush to the defense of their front-line troops. If they had failed to support their employes in that charged situation, the whole delicate arrangement by which reporters serve the wishes of publishers would have been threatened. We thereby witnessed the token protest, quickly forgotten as things were patched up with Mayor Daley once the four days had passed. But surely it must have occurred to more than one person that policemen who did not hesitate to beat up newsmen (and even sought out victims) would have less restraint when it came to popping demonstrators who have very little going for their defense in the power structure. And the same concern for victims of beatings had not been expressed by publishers when police or United States marshals had illegally and unjustifiably beaten other protesters at other times in recent months—for example, at the Pentagon, in Oakland and earlier in Chicago.

[*Many of the 6,500 participants in the April 27 Peace Parade in Chicago suspected that police actions in clashes with marchers were a "dress rehearsal for August" and "a warning to potential dissenters that demonstrations will not be tolerated" in that city. The quoted words are from a prophetic document, "Dissent and Disorder," issued by an independent investigating committee on Aug. 1—more than three weeks before the opening of the Democratic National Convention. The report, financed by the Roger Baldwin Foundation of the American Civil Liberties Union of*

Illinois, reviewed the disturbances of April—an eerie preview of the events of August—and concluded: "The police were doing what the Mayor and Superintendent had clearly indicated was expected of them. If we are to erase the causes of the peace parade disorder, we must look to the responsible officials, and the dilatory and obstructive way in which they handled preparations for April 27."]

Other publications clearly demonstrated their furious reaction to the beatings of newsmen. *Newsweek* made a special point in its "Top of the Week" column of what had happened to six of its nine men assigned to the streets, "all wearing prominent press credentials," who were "chopped down in the free-swinging police charges." A photograph of the six and what had happened to them ("Clubbed on back," "Beaten on back and leg," etc.) was the first item in its Sept. 9 issue. And the two-page "Press" section of that issue was devoted to stories entitled "Beat the Press" and "Sizing Up Chicago" that struck hard at the police for their treatment of newsmen.

Even the *Wall Street Journal* was twice as upset about what had happened to newsmen as it was about anyone else. Referring to the "on-the-scene reports" of its writers and others, it editorially concluded: "Throughout the week security forces had displayed an undercurrent of ugliness. When middle-aged women are pushed through plate-glass windows, when newsmen covering demonstrations are repeatedly attacked, when a television reporter is slugged by a policeman with the rank of commander obviously the police are out of hand."

Significantly, the conservative *National Review,* although editorially attacking the "myth" that Mayor Daley and the police had acted badly, had no trouble getting at the cause of all the trouble. The "news media distorted the hell out of all this," it pointed out, probably "because they were mad as hell—the police did, after all, club or otherwise injure 32 reporters and photographers, and hell hath no fury like a journalist when his comrades are kicked around."

Perhaps the best example is closest to home, where a close examination of late editions of the Chicago dailies shows that the news columns of three of Chicago's four major newspapers, which with rare exceptions have purred like pussycats for Major Daley, literally overnight became snarling tigers clawing at the mayor and his cops. The fourth paper remained unmoved by the carnage, none of its reporters having been injured and none of its reporters showing evidence of having been near the action, but the *Chicago Tribune* merits special diagnosis later in this examination.

II

A suburban Democrat accused Mayor Daley of undermining liberals at a closed session of the Cook County Democratic Central Committee last week, it was disclosed Tuesday. . . .
Daley responded by listing his own liberal credentials as a legislator

and party leader, and denied any intention of driving liberals out of the party.

"After all," Daley said, "I am a liberal myself."
—News item, *Chicago Sun-Times,* Oct. 23, 1968

In the maelstrom that is Chicago politics, almost nothing can be regarded as unusual. The editorial unanimity of the Chicago daily press in support of a fourth term for Mayor Richard Dailey in 1967 was not especially strange, although in the case of the *Tribune* and the mayor it meant the queerest sort of bedfellows: The bitchiest of Republicans sleeping with the kingmaker of Democrats. Nor was this curious consensus unexpected, since Chicago business executives, in the words of a preconvention story in *U.S. News & World Report,* "keep organizing to help Mr. Daley win re-election," and the Chicago daily press throughout the thirteen years of Daley's rule had treated him as some sort of sacred cow meriting no more than an occasional slap on the rump when some particularly scandalous caper among the herd was uncovered. This political-journalistic alliance was rudely severed when Chicago police began clubbing reporters and photographers. Suddenly—and it was so sudden that customary policies and procedures could not be put into effect—three of Chicago's four major dailies, in varying but nonetheless significant degrees, began reporting news about their police and their mayor as they never had before. It did not last long—from three to five days, depending on the newspaper involved—but they certainly were among the most glorious days in the history of Chicago journalism.

The first signs of the transition were only barely visible in the Monday morning *Sun-Times,* which buried the events of Sunday night in Lincoln Park and the Old Town area on page five—behind at least six other convention stories—but nonetheless showed a deep concern for journalists who had been clubbed. The newspaper was especially disturbed about the beating administered to one of its photographers who "identified himself, but the police kept swinging." It had difficulty, however, adjusting to the demonstrators, whom it generally called "hippies" in headlines and "youths" in stories and photographs (where they often looked like young people anywhere), and on Monday it even described the protesters as "a mixed band of hippies, yippies, motorcyclists and flower children."

ALLITERATION WITH A SNEER

Chicago's American, once a Hearst newspaper and now a satellite launched daily from the Tribune Tower, appeals to an earthy group of readers, nearly 90% of whom, according to an *American* poll reported on the eve of the convention, "indicated they would order police to 'shoot to kill' if they were attacked by militant civil rights agitators." On the Friday before the convention the paper had thought it hilarious to run on its front page a three-column photograph of a human being, a "fuzzy-haired delegate to the Pigasus 'nomination,'" under a line: "Yippies' Pig Goes to Pokey." Its coverage on Monday afternoon featured a banner over a page of photos, "Police Halt Hippie Invasion at the Bridge," which is, admittedly, one way of looking at the march that had developed after the demonstrators had been flushed from Lincoln Park.

The *Chicago Daily News* coverage of the Sunday night events included an evenhanded, enlightening front-page story concerning the views of some of the demonstrators. Another story served especially to tell how the situation was shaping up in Chicago. It began:

> Beneath the hoopla there was a grimness and—unlike other years—the cops had no time for jokes.
> And it wasn't only the hippies and the Yippies and the peace kids they were up tight about.
> It applied to ordinary, shirt-and-tie folks, too.

By Tuesday, however, following a night of indiscriminate beatings of newsmen, the three newspapers were almost equally incensed. The front page of the *Sun-Times* featured a photograph and caption: "Police knock down a fleeing demonstrator near Wells and Division early Tuesday morning after hundreds of young demonstrators were routed from Lincoln Park by police using clubs and tear gas. . . ." The headline was "Police Gas Yippies In Lincoln Pk." but the overline was the giveaway: "BEAT NEWSMEN AT SCENE." The headline on the lead story on page 5 was "Police Continue To Beat Newsmen; More Attacked Despite Probe," and the twenty-five inch story was devoted to the difficulties of newsmen with the exception of a single paragraph—fourth from the end—which announced that a *Sun-Times* staff member "also reported numerous unprovoked attacks by police on young people, including girls." An accompanying photograph carried this caption: "As *Sun-Times* photographer Bob Black photographed this policeman skirmishing with a demonstrator at Division and Wells Monday night, two other policemen attacked Black with their clubs." Pages six and seven were devoted to the story of Lincoln Park and included six photographs, one of which was captioned: "Beaten up in his back yard, a resident shouts his protest."

Chicago's American, obviously angry, ran two photographs across the top of the front page with the streamer: "Photographer Gets the Picture, Then Gets It." The first photo showed a photographer taking a picture of two young men fleeing several policemen, and the second showed the battered photographer on the sidewalk as the police walked away. Also on page one was a story about what was happening to journalists in Chicago and including the intelligence that editors of three of Chicago's four major daily newspapers had asked Police Supt. James B. Conlisk "to investigate the beatings of their newsmen assigned to cover hippie and yippie demonstrations." On page three another photo showed "one of many newsmen beaten by police."

The *Chicago Daily News* similarly concentrated on brutal treatment of journalists by Chicago's police, but it also published a photograph captioned: "In wake of sweep, a clubbing victim lies bloodied and gasping from tear gas." A long story on the police action contained a revealing paragraph: "Bystanders and couples strolling home after dates were swept up in the melee and pummeled by the police." Among many similar items:

> [*Chicago Daily News* Reporter John] Linstead was assaulted by policemen who broke away from 200 policemen sweeping across the intersection of LaSalle and Clark. Police chanted "Kill, kill, kill," as they rushed across the street.
>
> Linstead said the police turned on him after he protested their clubbing three or four young girls in a red foreign convertible that was caught in the traffic jam at the intersection.
>
> "The girls hadn't been doing anything. I yelled at the policemen to stop and they started to come at me," said Linstead.
>
> "I said I was a reporter. I was told to move and then was shoved. That's when they started beating me."
>
> Linstead was taken to the hospital by bystanders. . . .
>
> [Delos] Hall, the CBS cameraman, said a policeman clubbed him from behind as he filmed police dispersing some youths near N. Wells and W. Division.
>
> "No one stopped me and asked who I was. He (the policeman) came by and took a running shot at me just for standing there."
>
> Hall said he fell to the pavement and several more police beat him. . . .
>
> U.S. Atty. Thomas A. Foran said Tuesday he believed the police detail that clashed with newsmen and hippies acted with "wonderful discipline" and that he could not understand the allegations of police brutality.

The last paragraph above caught the eye of Mike Royko, the *Daily News* columnist who on Tuesday had unlimbered a heavily ironic attack on police behavior ("The following people can be assumed to be non-press: young couples holding hands; long-haired youths of either sex; people playing guitars or bongos; clergymen; people distributing antiwar literature. They can be beaten on sight. And so far, they have been."). He pulled even fewer punches in his Wednesday column, entitled "Cops threaten law and order."

> Thomas A. Foran, the U.S. attorney for northern Illinois, says Chicago police have shown "wonderful discipline" in their handling of Lincoln Park demonstrators.
>
> Foran is either stupid or a liar. . . .
>
> Chicago's police, for his information, have been beating innocent people with, to coin a phrase, reckless abandon. . . .
>
> In general, the biggest threat to law and order in the last week has been the Chicago Police Department.
>
> When Foran talks about "wonderful discipline," he sounds like a boob. He's not. It's just that he, like anyone else on the public payroll in Chicago, is a flunky for the mayor. . . .

But our mayor, the architect of the grand plan for head-bashing, is wandering around loose and making predictable statements. . . .
He's been conning people so easily, I'm sorry to say about my fellow Chicagoans, that he thought he could keep it up this week.

What Royko didn't add, and couldn't add, is that the mayor had been conning people so easily all those years with the full support and blessings of the proprietors of Chicago's daily newspapers.

The *Daily News* also turned its attention more effectively to non-journalists being bloodied by Chicago's police. As an example, a cutline on a four-column photograph Wednesday:

A youth, about 20, and his bike head for the Lincoln Park lagoon after two policemen had grabbed him and rushed him toward the water, according to witnesses. The witnesses said the police then just stood back and laughed. The youth reportedly had just been riding through the park; he had not even been part of the Yippie gathering in the park, for which the police were on duty there.

The story of the alternative convention took up almost the entire front page of the Wednesday *Sun-Times,* topped by a three-line head ending with an exclamation point: "NATIONAL GUARD VS. HIPPIES AT THE HILTON!" The account was rich in details of police action against non-journalists. Page five was allotted completely to the police problem; the lead story had a two-line banner: "News Media Assured by Conlisk Of Their Right To Cover Protests." Below it was a four-column photograph of a just-punched Dan Rather and a headline, "CBS Reporter Is Knocked Down By Punch On Convention Floor." Two other stories described rough police treatment of important visitors to the city. On another page a story about the Illinois convention delegation—"Until Daley Moves, Not A Figure Stirs"—detailed the iron grip of the "will of one man" on the "perfectly disciplined delegation." Other stories told of oppressive convention security, "pushy ushers" and the "President Johnson anti-birthday party" held by protesters.

EXTRAORDINARY COVERAGE PROVIDED

The next day the *Sun-Times* greatly expanded its news role to provide its readers with extraordinary coverage, demonstrating what can be done when a newspaper provides the necessary space for reporters and editors who know what they are doing. "Big Hilton Battle!" was the front-page headline; below it, "Speakers At Convention Blast Daley And Police." Seven photographs, including a magnificent shot covering the entire back page, showed what had happened. Among the many outstanding articles that caught the mood and significance of the preceding day and night were "Bandages And Stitches Tell The Grant Park Story" and "Street Sweeper Confronts Debris Of An Insane Day."

By Thursday even *Chicago's American* had had quite enough of the behavior of its local police. Across the top of page one it ran verbatim conversations of its reporters over the newspaper's radio communications network. Some samples (ellipses are the *American's*):

Jackson: I'm at 14th and State streets. . . . There's about 200 demonstrators headed towards me. And here come the boys in blue. Man . . . look at those hippies run!
Sullivan: People are screaming . . . running! The cops are clubbing everything in sight. God . . . they don't care who they slug. Girls, kids . . . anything that moves.
Murray: Man, these convention delegates are mad. They don't like that gas. Neither do I.
Rezwin: I thought it was going to calm down. Then that damn gas.

Its coverage opened up, too. A news story: "Dozens of innocent bystanders on Michigan Avenue and on Loop streets were caught up in the melee and injured." A photo caption. "Once-idyllic Grant Park becomes horror scene as police chase demonstrators." Another photo caption: "A policeman's club is raised over head of falling protester after a group had left the park and charged police. In background one Yippie [a young man in a white shirt] aids injured comrade."

The Thursday afternoon *Chicago Daily News* also poured it on. A streamer across the top of the front page proclaimed: "Mayor Daley convention's big 'casualty' " and the gist of the splendidly detailed story was that "club-swinging cops outside the Hilton Hotel" had served to "smash Daley's exalted political reputation into small pieces." Another front-page story was headlined "New protest tactic: Cops help it work," and a third story announced: "Dissident delegates plan march." Page 8 was given over entirely to seven photographs and text describing what the headline called *"Daily News* cameraman's ordeal," whose travail included a right hand broken by a police club. The caption on one photograph:

Soldier who appeared to be in Chicago on furlough—and not part of the military forces detailed to keep peace here during the Democratic convention—beats a peace demonstrator at S. Michigan and E. 7th St. The beating was without apparent provocation. Police formed a ring, and did not try to stop the beating. When photographer [Paul] Sequeira snapped this picture, five policemen went at him, knocking him down, knocking off a protective helmet he was wearing and hitting him repeatedly with nightsticks. Shortly afterward, in response to charges of police brutality during Wednesday's peace demonstrations, Police Supt. James Conlisk Jr. issued a statement saying that his men used only as much force as was necessary to handle the situation.

On another page, under an eight-column photograph, two captions read:

The police sweep through the bandshell area of Grant Park like a cyclone, clubbed peace demonstrators in their wake.

The day that terror struck the band concert area, normally a place of serenity.

Columnist Virginia Kay had free rein:

> I wonder how long it will be before Chicago's name stands for anything but horror in the minds of the world.

The *Daily News* carried the official versions, as of course it should, but they were on page 18 ("Daley puts blame on 'terrorists' ") and on page 28 ("Police deny excess, vow to uphold law"). Surrounded by factual coverage, the authorized versions looked ludicrous, just as authorized versions would much of the time if surrounded by factual coverage.

The Friday *Daily News* did not let up. Front-page stories reported the mayor's press conference ("Candidates Periled: Daley") and, just below it, the latest example of policemen beating up unresisting civilians ("Cops raid McCarthy HQ"). Mike Royko struck again: "Down below, the mayor looked so happy, and all his Illinois flunkies looked happy. When he is happy, they are happy. . . . His big moment came when Alabama's Bull Connor, the legendary wooly-head-breaker of yesteryear, gave the mayor a vote for vice president. The guys in the gallery let out a mad scream. It might have been a scream of terror because if he ever went to Washington, they'd have to go to work." And the *Daily News* television critic, Dean Gysel, who before the convention opened had written that "Mayor Daley does not like television, nor does he like any media he cannot control," contended "TV showed Chicago like it is." Excerpts:

> Television did not disgrace the city; it merely showed it the way it was. Mayor Daley used force because it was the natural and easy thing for him to do. . . . The mayor is two generations away from the young people in age, but epochs away in understanding.

The *Daily News* published a full page of photographs of the confrontation of marchers and guardsmen at 18th and Michigan and some other revealing stories: "A black eye for Chicago" (overline: "Police Assailed"); "Newsman tells how gassing kayoed him," and "Military seeking GI involved in beating" (concerning the soldier who had beaten a demonstrator).

By Friday, however, *Chicago's* very own *American* was solidly and safely back behind the Chamber of Commerce line. Two last feeble gasps were expelled—one by columnist Dorothy Storck protesting the mockery of Mayor Daley's stacked galleries at the Amphitheater and pleading for understanding what the demonstrators were protesting against; the other a wire-service story headlined "London Papers Rip Daley as 'City Boss Disgrace'; Police Called Hooligans." Otherwise the *American* was back in camp. Its banner: "Daley Bares Assassin Plot," with an overline: "Story Behind Tight Security." A front-page photograph carried the caption: "Battered and cracked helmet worn by an injured Chicago policeman is displayed at police headquarters as proof of demonstrators' violence during disorders." And a large part of the front page was given over to a broadside by the paper's television columnist, "Blast Networks for Coverage of Convention," which explained "how television can distort and manage its coverage."

Inside stories also were carefully stacked. One, locally written, proclaimed "World Criticizes but Chicago Backs Cops." Another story and a two-column photo were devoted to a policeman hit by a brick in Grant Park. Another long local story, based on an interview with Henry J. Taylor, "whose column appears in *Chicago's American,*" was headlined: "How Agitators Stirred Revolt."

On Saturday the reins of *Chicago's American* were tightly held. On page three were two stories: "Block U.S. Probe of Attacks on Newsmen, FBI Studies Yippies," and "How Chicago Cop Got Yippie Plans." On page five an Illinois National Guard commander interviewed by an *American* reporter concluded that his troops "in many ways, had a tougher time dealing with 'peace' demonstrators this week than they did with angry Negro mobs last April." The only story on the front page concerning the convention in Chicago was an item at the bottom: "Chicagoans, Police Redeem Reputations," which told of a man who had been robbed and subsequently had been helped by witnesses and police and who was quoted as saying: "I've heard screams all week about police brutality and it's simply not true. People holler about tough cops and tough mayor, but they are only doing their job—protecting Chicagoans and visitors like me."

The Saturday *Daily News* carried a short front-page story, "Guardsmen wind up city patrol," and featured on page two "Our Great Debate":

The protesters: Cops created revolt in the streets
The police: Radicals vowed to destroy city

Below those two stories, a third: "Stiff mental tests for cops urged," the view of a Chicago psychologist who contended the screening process for the Chicago Police Department allows emotionally ill candidates to slip through.

Other stories were similarly informative: "Delegates sing our praises— or condemn us," and "City cops backed in national poll" with an overline "61% praise Daley." Two columnists, however, got in their licks. Charles Nicodemus described the "raw brutality" of "the shouting, cursing police charge that swept past me down Balbo Drive," and added:

Mayor Daley and Police Supt. James Conlisk belatedly contend that this abdication of civic sanity occurred because the demonstrators charged police lines.
But the unblinking electronic eye, the resulting TV tapes, and the experience of several hundred bystanders scattered within 30 yards of that clash indicate otherwise.

Another columnist, Richard Christiansen, asked "Just how stupid could they be?" and castigated police who "intimidated delegates, terrorized women, clubbed reporters and whacked the hell out of young people who were not even resisting." He added:

When criticism against this display was voiced on television, the public information officer of the Chicago Police Department stood up at a press conference and petulantly blamed the trouble on the "intellectual" (spoken with disdain) commentators from the East. . . .
The rest of the nation, however, can shudder at this city, turn away and return home. We are stuck with it. And we are left to hate it all the more, because we love it so much.

The *Daily News* is not published on Sunday and by Monday it, too, had been pulled back to where it had been before the battle of Chicago. On the following Monday, Sept. 9, it not only published the text of Mayor Daley's "Official White Paper" without comment, but designed it as a special section "to be folded in thirds, stapled or taped closed, and mailed merely by affixing postage and filling in address area on back page."

DECLINE AND FALL OF THE SUN-TIMES

Now witness the decline and fall of the *Chicago Sun-Times.*

The day following its magnificent Thursday issue it gave front-page display to the official version, "Police Action Defended By Daley," but stories on inside pages nonetheless effectively told what had happened. Especially noteworthy were four stomach-turning photographs captioned "How One Cop Used His Nightstick," in which a policeman, identified by name and number, was shown delivering an unmerciful beating to a black youth in Old Town. The accompanying metallic text added that "an eyewitness said the attack of the youth was for no apparent reason." The Saturday *Sun-Times* also reported the official accounts ("Daley Reports Assassination Plot" and "Conlisk Gets Daley's Praise") but balanced them with a statement by several medical groups challenging the mayor's claim that "terrorists" had brought "their own brigade of medics" to Chicago. A reporter also interviewed the black young man whose beating had been reported the preceding day and added some details concerning what is an almost daily but generally unreported occurrence. That, however, was to be the last issue of the finest week in the history of the newspaper Marshall Field III had established twenty-seven years earlier.

The results of feverish high-level wits-gathering were strikingly evident in the Sunday *Sun-Times.* The message was spelled out for all to read in four clustered items on page three:

Item—A four-column photo showing three girls presenting a cake to a police captain. The girls reportedly had been arrested during the Tuesday disturbances and the gift was "in gratitude for considerate treatment they received when they were arrested."

Item—"HHH Says He Was Marked For Chicago Assassination." Humphrey: "We ought to quit pretending that Mayor Daley did something that was wrong."

Item—Story and photo with the following caption: "From his bed at

Mercy Hospital, [a patrolman] describes being hit by a brick during last Wednesday night's demonstration at the Conrad Hilton."

The most significant item of all—"Bailey K. Howard, president of Field Enterprises Newspaper Division, publishers of *The Sun-Times* and *The Daily News,* Saturday issued a statement calling for prompt prosecution and appropriate penalties for those individuals among the rioters responsible for physical attacks upon the police."

Yet there are those who deny the existence of an "establishment" and an "orthodox" press that serves its purposes.

[*The* Sun-Times *subsequently emitted one more shout of unorthodox protest, muffled on page 14 of the Sept. 15 issue. A splendid investigative story by Basil Talbott Jr. revealed that "a majority of objects listed as weapons used against police during convention-week disorders were collected from the streets after clashes." He also pointed out that the list included a dozen items (bull horn, protest signs, marijuana, "Senator McCarthy press pass") that could not be considered weapons and documented the fact that many of the other items were not related to demonstrators or the demonstrations. The most interesting revelation concerned the famous black widow spider weapon, about which much had been made in the Chicago newspapers and by the wire services. According to Talbott, the spider was inventoried after police picked it up from a railroad employe in his auto Sept. 1, after the convention had adjourned. Talbott wrote: "The railroad worker told police a man had tossed a jar containing the spider in his car, shouted 'I've threw 25 of these in squad cars last week,' and then fled." The orthodox press then threw the black widow at its readers, but don't bother ducking; although poisonous, it was just another police-journalistic hoax. Ask yourself: If you knew about the black widow spider incident, did you know how it really happened?*]

No examination of local coverage during the fateful week would be complete without witnessing the edifying transformation of Jack Mabley, assistant managing editor of *Chicago's American,* from chief cheerleader of Chicago's police to rabid civil liberatarian—and then back again.

Before the convention, Mabley's personal columns about the protesters had been filled with incomprehension ("I'm so square that I missed the message") and he had served as a vehicle for the most nonsensical kinds of official pap ("This is what has been threatened: . . . Yippies said they would paint cars as independent taxicabs and take delegates away from the city. Yippies' girls would work as hookers and try to attract delegates, and put LSD in their drinks").

Then his journalistic co-workers began getting the kinds of lumps other citizens had been receiving. In his Wednesday column he suffered only from a slow burn as he related how one of the *American* reporters was on Wells Street, "well away from the park, when a policeman clubbed him to the ground as he shouted his identity and waved his press card. [He] was not interfering with police work. He had been standing on the side-walk talking with a plain clothes man he knew." Mabley summed up what he had seen:

> Trying to be as objective as possible, I'd say some [reporters and photographers] perhaps were asking for it, pushing into the way of the police. Some were just caught in the skirmishing, and some were singled out and deliberately chased down because they had cameras.

Not a word of sympathy, however for those whose travail the camera-men were trying to film when they were "singled out and deliberately chased down." That had to wait until the next day, after he had seen more than he could tolerate. His Thursday column included a photograph with the following cutline: "Pedestrians caught up in sweep near Conrad Hilton Hotel got taste of police state and found explanations futile in a world where reason suddenly stopped." [Please note this caption. We shall return to it later.] The headline on the column was "A Horrifying View of the Police State." He was appalled "when policemen started beating pedestrians on State Street." He was more than appalled at other scenes:

> Scores of people under the Palmer House canopy watched in horror as a policeman went animal when a crippled man couldn't get away fast enough. The man hopped with his stick as fast as he could, but the policeman shoved him in the back, then hit him with the nightstick, hit him again, and finally crashed him into a lamppost.
> Clergymen, medics, and this cripple were the special pigeons last night. At State and Adams a nightstick cracked open the head of a clergyman who didn't move fast enough. He was lying in a store doorway, bleeding heavily, when I left. Across the street a policeman cracked a clergyman across the back because he walked instead of ran.

[This is one of the rare references in print or on the air to the fact that the police attacked not only newsmen and photographers but became even more frenzied when confronted by clergymen. Part of the reason may have been that Protestant and Catholic clergymen had formed a "North Side Co-Operative Ministry" to provide lodgings for hundreds of protesters who had been banned from sleeping in Lincoln Park. An incredible episode of unrestrained police behavior occurred Tuesday night in Lincoln Park when about 70 persons, wearing white collars and arm bands to identify them as clergymen, seated themselves around a circle of young men and women who sang songs and spoke quietly under a 12-foot wooden cross that appeared to be made of railroad ties. A few in the group were coun-terfeit clerics who had obtained the religious garb with the idea it would restrain the police from beating them, an idea they shortly were compelled to abandon. The leaders of the group professed the hope of holding an all-night religious meeting and of serving as a buffer between the police and those who had gathered to protest the war in Vietnam and the con-duct of the convention. Any hope they had held that they somehow would be able to prevent the police from acting violently while making arrests vanished as the first clubs smashed against them with what appeared to

be particular viciousness. In the days following at Grant Park, many of the most disillusioned and bitter protesters were seminarians.]

In Mabley's torment, a confession:

It sickens me to write this because I am on the police's side, and I went out at 1 o'clock yesterday to write exactly what I saw and I was sure it would bring credit to the police.

Finally, he is driven to concern for the constitutional and legal rights of a citizen he despises, followed by a ringing peroration:

No blood flowed in one of the most ominous happenings. Jerry Rubin, a leader of the radicals, was walking west on Washington, turning onto Dearborn at 10:20. A girl was with him. They were alone. I'd seen Rubin shortly before on State Street, just walking with the girl.
An unmarked car with four policemen skidded to a stop beside Rubin. Three men jumped out. "Come on, Jerry, we want you," one called as they grabbed Rubin. The girl screamed "We haven't done anything! We were just walking."
An officer grabbed the girl and twirled her around. "You want to come, too?" he shouted.
Rubin now was doubled over beneath two officers. They carried him to the squad car and sped toward State Street. The girl stood screaming on the corner.
I have heard Rubin speak, and he was obscene and revolting. In America a man may be arrested for obscenity or revolution. But Rubin was grabbed off the street and rushed to jail because of what he thinks.
This is the way it is done in Prague. This is what happens to candidates who finish second in Viet Nam. This is not the beginning of the police state, it IS the police state.

[*What happened to Rubin in the 26 hours after he was picked off the street was reported in the Sept. 6* Los Angeles Free Press: *"The three cops came out of the car and pulled me by my hair and pushed me into an unmarked police car and drove away. One cop said, 'Now that we've got you, all the trouble will stop on the streets.' The other cop said, 'We're gonna take you in an alley and take care of you.' And another cop said, 'We're gonna dump you in the river and nobody will ever know the difference.' They took me to the eighth floor of 11th and State Street, the police department, and prevented me from making a phone call by saying that I was not under arrest but that I was under investigation. These members of the intelligence department of the police said that we had no right coming to Chicago to demonstrate and that they were going to try to put all the leaders in jail for a long, long time. After three hours of interrogation I was charged with disorderly conduct, resisting arrest and 'solicitation to commit mob action.' Bail was then set at the astronomical figure of $25,000." One of the major contributions of the underground press has been its relentless reporting of illegal police behavior, a subject the orthodox press almost never explores and almost always covers up.*]

On Friday, however, Mabley was jerked sharply back into line. His column: "Here's Police Side of Story in City Rioting." The final humiliation on Saturday was complete. His employers again published the photograph that had appeared in his column on Thursday [see above], along with a news story:

> Here is a correction *Chicago's American* is very happy to make. The caption appearing under the above picture in Thursday's editions was in error.
> The caption said that the people involved were victims of the police. This was caused by a transposition of caption material and was inadvertent.

There followed the "corrected" caption:

> Police assist brother and sister who were caught in confrontation between Yippies and police Wednesday near Conrad Hilton Hotel. Originally, it was believed they were police "victims," but their father has explained that the security men were courteous and trying to protect the pair.

Any way you look at it, whether the first caption was a "mistake" or not, *Chicago's American,* the shoddy remnant of what was once Hearst's Chicago empire, has no shame.

Chicago's fifth newspaper, the black *Daily Defender,* gave little coverage to whitey's battle in the streets. Its reporting of the Democratic convention similarly was limited almost exclusively to developments involving black delegates. It rose editorially only once during the convention week, but that was a front-page editorial on Wednesday entitled "Police Brutality." It deplored attacks on newsmen and photographers by Chicago police—"Their reputation for brutality has been established long ago beyond peradventure of a doubt"—but said nothing about the clashes between demonstrators and police. "The charge by various investigating commissions," it concluded, "that police brutality is at the bottom of most urban riots can scarcely be dubbed an irresponsible conclusion when one examines the outlandish conduct of Chicago policemen in recent days."

By Saturday, however, it was back in line with its white journalistic brothers under the skin with a banner headline: "REDS TO BLAME: COP CHIEF," which gave the views of the police director of public information that Communists were responsible for the riots.

EDITORIAL SCREWS ALSO TIGHTENED

Just as the proprietorial screws were tightened on the news columns, which for a few brief shining moments had known glory, the editorials of the newspapers were returned to normal as the week ended. The *Chicago Daily News* on Tuesday had pointedly noted in an editorial entitled "The law is for cops, too" that reporters "have seen incidents develop from the sheer numbers and visibility of 'the law,' when a lesser number of officers, equally firm, might well have kept the peace and spared broken heads." It also was critical of "a rising number of cases of deliberate savagery by police clubbing down photographers, reporters and television cameramen," and concluded that "all citizens should be law-abiding, including the cops." The following day a local editorial cartoon elaborated the theme, depicting a figure labeled "Chicago Police," with "BRUTAL UNPROVOKED ASSAULTS" lettered across his chest, clubbing a newsman from behind. The caption was "The Daley Clout." The next day a caustically labeled editorial, " 'Democracy' in Chicago," closed with these words:

> But there is more here than a few dozen cracked heads, painful and inexcusable as they may be. Mayor Daley's house is badly awry, and needs to be put in order. Just now the paramount danger is not from hippies, yippies, or other demonstrators; it is from an establishment that has lost sight, temporarily at least, of the right of all the people to their fundamental freedoms.

Whatever the establishment may have lost sight of, temporarily at least, it had not taken its eyes off what it expected from the *Chicago Daily News* editorial page. Chastised, the page appeared Saturday and meekly proclaimed: "There's another side." The editorial writer, stripped to the buff, was allowed to keep his fig leaf—for two paragraphs. "We have said before, and say again," he said, "that much of what went on here was inexcusable, that the police overreacted to provocation, and that the hard-line attitude of the city administration, beginning with Mayor Daley, bears a large burden of blame." Enough; off with the fig leaf . . .:

> That being said, is there another side to the story? We believe there is. And it is important to the life of the city—as well as its reputation—that it be noted. . . .

Five paragraphs whitewashing Mayor Daley and the police followed, leading to the conclusion that "many of the critics have overreacted in their way just as some policemen overreacted in theirs." In this fashion was the record set straight, and one should be forgiven the fleeting thought that writing editorials for the *Chicago Daily News* obviously is not one of the blessed journalistic vocations.

Editorially, *Chicago's American* went through a similar pattern. On Wednesday it angrily asked "Who Controls the Cops?" and warned the police with no ifs, ands or buts that "we have had it right up to here with the King Kong tactics used by a few of them against newsmen. These attacks are going to stop or there is going to be court action." It noted that it "is also clear that, in most cases, the club-swingers zeroed in on photographers who had taken pictures that might prove embarrassing to the police," although no word of concern was expressed for those particular victims. Then it bravely concluded with a note to those in authority that the newsmen "are not there to make you look either good or bad;

they are reporting what happens, whether it makes the Chicago police look like heroes or bums."

The bravura was diminished considerably by the following day when another editorial, "Controversy on the Cops," expressed sympathy for the police who "have been the targets of everything imaginable in the last four days," and concluded: "We have no interest in insulting the Chicago police." Two days of editorial silence followed and then came the Sunday editorial summary, "Police and the Public," calling for "some sober consideration on all sides." The editorial admitted that there were "instances of brutality that cannot be disguised or ignored—repeated, unnecessary clubbing, knee-in-the-groin assaults, three or four policemen battering a single person," but then went on with seven paragraphs "on the other side." Finally, a pathetic last-paragraph confession:

> It may well be that the press has paid too little attention in the past to reports of police brutality, and has let a few uniformed thugs get the idea that they're free to knock people around. If so, that's over too. Police brutality is now a very live issue in Chicago. How long it stays that way is up to the police.

Consider the threat of court action if attacks on newsmen did not stop —an action that was not undertaken when the attacks on newsmen did not stop—and do not hold your breath while *Chicago's American* keeps police brutality a very live issue in Chicago.

MASSIVE POLICE POWER SUPPORTED

Nor, sadly, was the situation improved in the *Chicago Sun-Times,* a newspaper that largely succeeds in achieving lively, well-edited news columns and then produces one of the flabbiest editorial pages of any metropolitan newspaper in the United States. Not without justice has it been observed that Mayor Daley could not exist in a city with a *St. Louis Post-Dispatch;* it is the *Sun-Times* that should fulfill this duty but it has abdicated. Its editorial on the morning of the opening of the convention, for example, included side-by-side photographs of the barbed wire outside the Amphitheater and a wire fence in Miami Beach· and contended that the security measures in Chicago "are the same as those that were taken at Miami Beach for the Republican convention." That asinine observation drew what charitably can be described as snorts from reporters who had been to both places. And although Chicago indisputably had the atmosphere of an armed camp, the *Sun Times* berated "the TV networks and others, who because of anger at the mayor over not being able to have their own way, have misrepresented Chicago as having the atmosphere of an armed camp."

After the clubbing of newsmen, the *Sun-Times* in an editorial, "The Police And The Press," reaffirmed its support of "the plans of Mayor Daley and Police Supt. Conlisk to use massive police power to preserve order on the city streets" but warned that the "force, however, must not be indiscriminate, used against every person on the scene of disorder." It then went on with a stirring protest of the beatings suffered by two *Sun-Times* men and other representatives of the press, without even a suggestion that the police ought to stop clubbing other law-abiding citizens. On Friday it reconsidered the omission and lashed at the authorities in an editorial, "The Rule Of Law For All." The rule of law, now, "applies to those who are authorized to enforce the law." Convention officials who in the *Sun-Times'* previously held opinion had been doing no more than what was done at Miami Beach are told, now, that "oppressive and excessive security checks that have no place in an open convention share responsibility for the ugly mood that permeated the hall." Comparisons of Chicago with Prague, which had been called "extreme" and "far-fetched" in two editorials earlier in the week, come quickly to mind, now, as "pictures of police fighting the mob of invading peace protesters were like a newsreel from a police state such as Prague." Good Friend Police Supt. Conlisk, who had received the strong support of the *Sun-Times* editorial page "to use massive police power to preserve order on the city streets," is informed, now, that the *Sun-Times* editorial page did not mean "to turn the police ranks themselves into a melee of club-swinging individuals subject to no discipline." Good Friend Mayor Daley, applauded earlier for his wonderful convention arrangements and for taking "proper precautions by making a visible display of police and military manpower," is told in no uncertain terms, now, that he "must share the blame for what has happened to his city's reputation."

After that performance, the *Sun-Times* could not be expected to sink again soon to such depths, but on Sunday its sole editorial comment on the extraordinary times through which Chicago had just passed was as follows:

> We Pause
> For A Message . . .
> Now that the Democratic Convention is over . . .
> Good Night, Chet.
> Good Night, David.
> AND
> *Good-by*
> Walter Cronkite.

[*Little wonder that a group of about 65 Chicago daily newspapermen organized to publish the* Chicago Journalism Review *(5000 S. Dorchester Ave., Chicago 60615, $5 a year) soon after the battle of Chicago. The first issue in October set the publication's formal purpose, to provide "an uncompromisingly professional analysis of the press and its problems," but the appeal for editorial contributions was more earthy: "Newsmen, we need your help. If you're sulking in frustration over a killed story—if you have a gripe about an editor's—or reporter's—news judgment or about the general treatment of a news event—you now have an outlet. Don't*

*cry over a beer or grumble to your peers—write it down and call us up."
It especially protested that "all too often, the media act in complicity with
the news manipulators—not through back-room deals and explicit conspiracies, but through the conspiracies of silence, Chicago-style cynicism,
and formula journalism which doesn't rock the boat (Example: 'Mayor
Daley Monday unveiled bold new plans for a new ———')." If the working
press of other major cities had a similar review, or if a national publication
of this kind could be published, as some of us have been urging for years,
many of the problems of press performance could be aired. The foundations, especially those with publishers on their boards, essentially are
interested in preserving or only insignificantly altering the status quo
and have been resolutely cold to such proposals. The* Columbia Journalism Review, *which in early issues showed promise of at least partially
fulfilling this function, has become a tame organ indeed, and* Nieman Reports, *published at Harvard, has abandoned the role it served as a critical
appraiser of the press. No coincidence, despite public pronouncements
that the* Columbia Journalism Review *was free from institutional censorship, is the fact that the man responsible for the birth of the publication,
Edward W. Barrett, has resigned as dean of the Graduate School of
Journalism after fundamental disagreements with the Columbia trustees
and administration.*]

III

The precautions were taken because the city received many warnings
from radical leftists, student groups, and black power zealots. They
threatened to have a million or more demonstrators here for the purpose of disrupting the convention and the life of the city.
—Editorial in *Chicago Tribune*, August 29, 1968.

In the fantasy world of Chicago's incredible *Tribune,* every act of God
or man is made to conform to an elaborately constructed journalistic
masquerade. The warped, distorted view of the world that Robert R. Mc-
Cormick pressed daily on his staff and readers until his death in 1955 is
memorialized by his carefully selected successors. The *Tribune,* one
national magazine observed after the recent events in Chicago, "imposes
its Little Orphan Annie value judgments on the whole realm." Its news
coverage was characterized in another national publication two years ago
as "eccentric." It more accurately can be classified as psychopathic
(Webster's Second: "Psychopathy—1. Mental disorder in general. 2. More
commonly, mental disorder not amounting to insanity or taking the specific
form of a psychoneurosis, but characterized by defect of character or
personality, eccentricity, emotional instability, inadequacy or perversity
of conduct, undue conceit and suspiciousness, or lack of common sense,
social feeling, self-control, truthfulness, energy, or persistence. Different
psychopathic individuals show different combinations of these traits").
The *Chicago Tribune* manifests all of the symptoms. Furthermore, it is

impossible to separate the *Tribune's* news coverage and its opinions, and the same disorder afflicts the newspaper's editorial page.

AN EFFORT TO SUPPRESS DISSENTERS

For example, although the *Tribune* is a classic dissenter, disapproving of much that has happened during this century and in a minority on almost every political, economic and social issue, it regularly seeks to suppress other dissenters. Furthermore, as it made clear in the "Whose Riot?" editorial of Dec. 3, 1968, it approves only certain methods of dissent: "The vote is one. Written petitions and protest are others. Dissenters can always hire a hall and let off steam. The authorities will even agree to the marches which have become nuisances all over the country." The limits of dissent, therefore, are to be set not by the Constitution and the courts but by the *Chicago Tribune;* in fact, it let one of its mangiest cats out of its editorial bag in an editorial Dec. 23 when, in the process of denouncing an individual whose views it despises, it tellingly added: ". . . nor is he going to be very sympathetic to attempts to maintain law and the existing order." Witness: Not to maintain order (Webster's Second: "Order—conformity to law or decorum; freedom from disturbance; general tranquillity; public quiet; rule of law or proper authority; as to preserve *order* in a community"), but the entirely different matter of maintaining the *existing* order. Rarely has the *Tribune* doctrine on dissent been so clearly enunciated.

For another example, the *Tribune* constantly tries to make believe Chicago suffers no unusual crime problem—"First of all," it contended in the "Whose Riot?" editorial, "Chicago is normally a peaceful and orderly city, disturbed at times by professional crime which is the bane of all urban centers." Nonetheless, the Chicago Crime Commission, after examining the real world, insisted on concluding that crime is one of the most flourishing trades in town, a fact easily accepted by anyone who knows anything about Chicago. The *Tribune* also likes to pretend it was easy for dissenters to "hire a hall and let off steam" or to demonstrate peacefully preceding and during the convention, when the facts are that Mayor Daley, assisted by the courts, saw to it that theaters, stadiums and other assembly points were not available. For instance, the pro-McCarthy Coalition for an Open Convention, after seeking permission for several weeks to hold a peaceful rally at Soldier Field on the Sunday night before the convention, was turned down in its petition to Federal District Judge William J. Lynch. He also ruled that when the city agreed to an afternoon rally in Grant Park and "offered alternate routes for a march" it had "acted in a reasonable and nondiscriminatory manner so as to preserve public safety and convenience without deprivation of any first amendment guarantees of free speech and public assembly." The *Tribune* applauded those rulings.

[Lynch is Mayor Daley's former law partner. He also figured in another interesting case. The Youth International Party had filed suit to force the city to allow visitors to sleep in Lincoln Park during the "Festival of Life," but withdrew it before the convention opened. Standing before Lynch, Yippie Abbie Hoffman explained that the suit was being dropped because "we have as little faith in the judicial system of this city as in the political system."]

The pre-convention Sunday *Tribune* announced in a headline on page three that "Tribune News Staff Is Tops" and proclaimed that "one of the largest and most experienced news teams of any newspaper in the country" would "bring to Chicago readers the vivid details of every exciting moment." By *Tribune* standards the qualification "one of" was an extraordinary concession to modesty on the part of the "World's Greatest Newspaper." It listed the thirteen persons who would cover the convention but neglected to include the name of anyone assigned to cover possible disorders, although the front-page story that same day had suggested strongly that disorders by what it called "peaceniks" were likely. As it turned out, readers had no difficulty discovering that security and disorder stories clearly were the province of one Ronald Koziol, a writer steeped in the *Tribune's* tradition of unremitting irrelevance and calculated viciousness.

On Monday the *Tribune* slightly stepped up its coverage. A front-page headline stated that "Police Repel Jeering Mob of Peaceniks," and in the story the protesters were called "peaceniks" (three times), "radicals" (twice), and "radical detachment," "anti-war demonstrators," "demonstrators," "hippies, yippies and other radical groups," and "hippie-clad people." No mention of police clubbing demonstrators was made in the story or in the cutlines accompanying four demure photographs. Mention was made of a *Tribune* automobile that was stoned and a *Tribune* reporter who was "pelted" but not seriously hurt, both by demonstrators. The one-column headline and story appeared next to a three-column color photograph of Mayor and Mrs. Richard J. Daley, "Host and Hostess," holding hands. On page nine was the headline, "Mayor Finds Time to Be a Host, Father; His Honor Seems to Be Everywhere," which accurately reflected the tone, quality and content of the long story. The daily index of the news failed to include the events in Lincoln Park and environs as one of the eight important local stories of the preceding day, although they had been reported on the front page.

The Tuesday *Tribune* continued to play down the fact of convention week disorders, burying a short story under a one-column headline on the fifth page. Throughout the fanciful account, which differed extensively from what non-*Tribune* reporters saw, five separate references were made to injuries reportedly suffered by policemen while no mention was made of injuries to "hippies," which is what the demonstrators were called throughout. A second story, also under a one-column headline, briefly reported that "more newsmen were injured in the battles between hippies and police early today than either demonstrators or lawmen," and dismissed in one paragraph the "vigorous protests" filed by officials of the three television networks, the *Sun-Times* and the *Daily News. (Chicago's American* also had protested, according to itself, the *Sun-Times* and the *Daily News,* but it is owned by the *Tribune* and therefore could be omitted in the *Tribune's* fantasy-world reporting.)

While the three other major Chicago daily newspapers were furiously reporting what had happened Tuesday in Chicago, the Wednesday *Tribune* kept its cool. It ran a weird tale of the flushing of Lincoln Park which included the information that the protesters were "hippies, yippies, and other nondescripts." It referred to "50 Negroes wearing patches identifying them as Black Panthers, the California black nationalist group," a scoop of monumental proportions since no other reporter in Chicago mentioned their presence. Its readers also were treated to the following wildly simplified account of the Lyndon Johnson "un-birthday party":

> Before the largest group of hippies left the Coliseum, at 1513 Wabash Ave., [Note the splendid example of significant detail] they were whipped up by provocative speeches made by Dick Gregory, comedian and civil rights worker; Allen Ginsberg, hippie poet; William Burroughs, author; and Jean Genet, French writer.
> The theme of the speeches was vigorously against the Chicago police [!], comparing them with Russian troops occupying Prague. At one point folk singer Phil Ochs sang an anti-war song called "We Won't Go Marching Anymore" [*sic*] and his performance was greeted with a 10-minute ovation and the burning of what were said to be draft cards by about a dozen persons in the audience.

Other stories contained other goodies: "While the yippies, hippies, dippies, and others were massing in the south end of Lincoln Park . . . ," and "Dick Gregory, who insists that he is a candidate for president. . . ." Six photographs purportedly covered the action in and near Lincoln Park, but none showed police hitting demonstrators and one was captioned "Hippie Attacks Policeman." And in what surely was sufficient to set the authors of "The Front Page" whirring in their graves, a paragraph in another story pathetically revealed how one newsman coped with his problem:

> A Tribune reporter who was at the melee in Lincoln Park early yesterday reported that police told him that he would get his "head busted" if he continued to stay near the demonstration. At one point, he said, he had to ask a police lieutenant for protection against policemen with nightsticks.

Whether that stark incident was the spark that ignited the *Tribune's* sudden concern about police behavior must remain moot to anyone outside the Tribune Tower. Nonetheless, the *Tribune* listed the names of newsmen reportedly beaten by the police and ran a story and photograph of Dan Rather being punched in an exercise of security precautions at the convention. Yet another story said editors of the three other daily newspapers in Chicago had sent telegrams to the superintendent of police protesting the beatings of their reporters. Apparently the *Tribune,* although unwilling to join in the protest, joined in the subsequent meeting with the superintendent since it reported that "representatives of four Chicago newspapers" were present. (The *Trib* hardly could be expected to include the *Daily Defender* in any listing of Chicago's daily press.) Furthermore, its participation in the meetings would not be out of character, for part of the *Tribune's* psychopathy is an overweening pride in its role as a defender of freedom of the press, by which it means freedom for itself and most other segments of the orthodox press but no freedom whatsoever for those persons and organs whose views it finds obnoxious.

THE ART OF UNDERSTATEMENT

Thus driven, the *Tribune* editorially denounced "Bad Judgment by the Police," which turned out to be a denunciation of "the rowdy demonstrations conducted by the hippies, yippies, and other young punks who have gathered in Chicago by the thousands." Again demonstrating its mastery of the art of understatement, it suggested: "Their presence is unnecessary for the work of the Democratic national convention, which they apparently are trying to influence." It expressed concern for the safety of newsmen, announced its solidarity with the editors who had requested an investigation by the police superintendent and concluded with the following paragraph, presented in its entirety and without comment:

> The press is not the enemy of the police force; it is the policeman's friend. Policemen so lacking in judgment that they needlessly beat up a representative of the press don't belong on the police force.

On Thursday, Aug. 29, 1968, that remarkable day in the history of Chicago journalism, even the *Chicago Tribune* told its readers—briefly, in three paragraphs buried deep in a news story—what its police had been up to. Under a six-column front-page headline, "Cops, Hippies War in Street," played second only to the Humphrey nomination, a hint of something unusual in *Tribune* coverage came in the last sentence of the eighth paragraph: "The police waded into the crowd." Then came the stunning ninth and eleventh paragraphs:

> Many convention visitors and others watched the battle from upper windows of the hotel. Many were appalled at what they considered unnatural enthusiasms of the police for the job of arresting demonstrators. There were cries of "Cut it out . . . don't hurt him . . . how can you do this?" from hotel windows. . . .
> Some observers said the demonstrators were caught between two groups of police which, instead of pushing them back into Grant Park,

were squeezing the demonstrators between police lines. Neither of the police groups was aware of what the other was doing.

Elsewhere the *Tribune* carried eight photographs of street and park action, but none showed the police doing anything to which any reasonable person might take exception. In other stories the names of 29 policemen reported injured during the preceding day were announced, and "Police Injure 6 More Newsmen" told, among other harassments of journalists, about a *Tribune* photographer arrested after he took a picture of a magazine photographer being arrested. Although the *Trib* man reportedly was released soon after being taken to central police headquarters and no mention was made of his film being confiscated, the photograph he took was not published. If it was in focus it unquestionably would have been more revealing than any of the eight selected for inclusion in the Thursday *Tribune.*

Another story, "Hilton Hotel Has Wartime Appearance," included a sentence that simply was a lie: "A group of demonstrators smashed a window of the Haymarket bar facing Michigan avenue and 15 to 20 were able to clamber thru into the Hilton before police stopped them." As anyone knows who was there, and all media except the *Tribune* reported, the window was broken by pressure of bystanders who were charged and clubbed by police.

In another curious example of *Tribune* reporting, a photograph of Dick Gregory and Mark Lane captioned "Write-In Candidates" and a story of a press conference held by them were carried on page twenty-two. Somehow the *Tribune* reporter got the idea that Gregory was announcing his candidacy for the presidency, which he had in fact done 16 months earlier. Nonetheless, in the story the only title granted to Gregory was "comedian." Since the gist of the story was that Gregory predicted a Republican victory in November, it fit neatly into the *Tribune's* fantasy world.

The lead editorial of the day, " 'Fortress Chicago,' " complained that "television commentators and some newspaper writers are making a great fuss about the security measures taken for the Democratic national convention." (News item eight days earlier in *Chicago Tribune,* Aug. 21: "When asked if he anticipated trouble, Daley replied: 'No, we don't anticipate or expect it unless certain commentators and columnists cause trouble.' ") The editorial then repeated the literally endless litany that "it was necessary to mobilize the national guard, federal troops, and many federal agents to keep order" because "radical leftists, student groups, and black power zealots . . . had plans to ignite widespread rioting." Again it ignored the issue, which was not primarily the security measures but the illegal excesses to which the police had resorted. The *Tribune* long ago mastered the technique of evading the point and focusing attention on another point; a long row of straw men parades constantly through the fantasy world.

On Friday the *Tribune* unleashed itself as only the *Tribune* can. It took to the front page for an editorial, "Chicago: A Great City," addressed to "delegates and visitors who have been in Chicago during the week of the Democratic national convention." They were promptly informed that Chicago is a beautiful city with a lakefront setting and lovely parks, fine hotels, superior restaurants, among the best universities, museums and cultural life, an enterprising and energetic business community and working population, and good, responsible and decent Americans. In the last paragraph the delegates were urged to "come back again" so that they could "appreciate our city and its people as they really are." Sandwiched between those two slices was the baloney: "This orderly city" has been beset by a "bearded, dirty, lawless rabble" and has responded with "such force as was necessary to repel them." In a monstrous understatement it maintained that "Chicago did not invite these street fighters to come here in the hope of disgracing the city." In a typical *Tribune* distortion of statistics it quoted police records that "disclosed that 136 of the 309 persons arrested did not live in Chicago or any suburb"; a page nine news story in the same issue, giving later figures, did not resort to this sleight-of-hand and revealed that only 170 persons of the 568 who had been arrested were not citizens of Illinois. The *Tribune* also continued to evade the only pertinent matter worth discussion: Whether the police had reacted violently and illegally both in situations of provocation and non-provocation.

Another editorial, in its customary position on the editorial page, was entitled "No Right to Assemble in Michigan av." After a brief introduction, the *Tribune* approvingly quoted, without a trace of irony, some views on the limitations of constitutional rights of assembly expressed by Justices Black and Fortas and former Justice Goldberg, three Supreme Court members whose views on almost every other subject had been anathematized editorially in that newspaper for years.

The lead paragraph of the principal news story on the demonstrations, headlined "2,000 Flee to Park in Tear Gas Attacks," dripped with sarcasm: "Anti-war demonstrators, Hippies, Yippies, and numerous disgruntled Democratic convention delegates appeared to have finally calmed down early today in the Grant park trouble area across from the Conrad Hilton hotel." But buried in the long story was a startlingly revealing—for the *Tribune*—item of information concerning the confrontation at 18th and Michigan, where a march led by Dick Gregory had been halted:

> Guardsmen kept demonstrators confined to the east sidewalk of Michigan avenue.
> "Use your rifle butts. Use your rifle butts. Move them back," came the order to guardsmen over a loudspeaker. The guardsmen followed instructions.

That was what had happened. Two days later the *Tribune* decided that its reporter had not seen what had happened. The fantasy world of Sunday will be examined shortly.

In another of its inexplicable eccentricities, the *Tribune* decided in this story to identify Dick Gregory for probably the first time in its news columns as "Negro candidate for president," after consistently contending that he was nothing more than a "comic," a "comedian," a "civil rights activist" or, at best, a man "who insists that he is a candidate for president."

[*The* Chicago Tribune *was not alone. One of the better-kept secrets of the orthodox press in the 1968 presidential campaign was the candidacy of Dick Gregory, who was nothing more than a "Negro activist" to* Life, *a "night club entertainer" to David Brinkley, and a "Negro comic" to the wire services. The announcement of his candidacy was news in many overseas newspapers, but the white press of the United States ignored it or laughed it off. The London* Observer, *for example, in its Sept. 8, 1968, issue identified Gregory as an active candidate and concluded of his write-in campaign for the presidency: "Anyone who thinks this must be some kind of irrelevant gimmick is very much mistaken." Among the many peculiarities of domestic press coverage of Gregory is the fact that soon after the Chicago convention when Mike Wallace interviewed Attorney General Ramsey Clark on the first program of the CBS television series "60 Minutes," his first question was: "Dick Gregory said the cop is the new nigger. Do you understand that?" It's nice that Mike Wallace knew this and used it, but one can look in vain in the orthodox media for coverage of Gregory's Chicago speech in which he made the observation. Nor were any other speeches at the "Alternative Convention" in Grant Park reported in the daily press or on radio or television. Many newspapers of the underground press, of course, covered them in detail. Furthermore, Gregory had been openly and actively a candidate since April, 1967. He had the buttons to prove it; he had a platform which had a Preamble and Pledge and planks on Moral Pollution, Vietnam, Welfare and Poverty, Unemployment, Starvation in America, Voting Age, Indians, Foreign Aid, Youth, Education, Civil Rights, Gun Law and Veterans; he had a considerable volunteer campaign staff; he had the mandatory paperback, "Write me in!"; he was on the ballot in several states and a write-in candidate in the others, yet the white press persisted in calling him a comedian and entertainer. Lester Maddox ran a restaurant and got himself elected governor and when he declared himself a candidate for the presidency he was given national television coverage and the front pages of almost every newspaper in the country. He subsequently withdrew, of course, but in the meantime he was briefed by the President of the United States and had a Secret Service detail to usher him around. Gregory asked the President for briefings and some protection—which he genuinely needs —and he got a brushoff. Who's funny? Joseph Heller said it all: Dick Gregory, meet Yossarian.*]

Two other front-page stories parroted the official line: "Daley Backs Cops' Action; Planned Disruption Is Cited," and "Demonstrator's Seized

Diary Details Plan to Disrupt City." Pages four and five were devoted almost entirely to the disorders. "Cops Pressed Beyond Limit, They Assert; Charge News Reports Favor Demonstrators" was a by-lined piece seventeen inches long, followed by a wire story from Fort Lauderdale, Fla., in which a policeman there said Chicago officers "let down the many honest policemen thruout the nation." It was two inches long. "Actor Asserts He Did Not See Cop Brutality" was Ralph Bellamy's view that the disorders were "started by dissenters" and directed "from outside." Then there was "Girl Arrested for Peddling Pot to Hippies," which was a story out of Grant Park, and "Lady Bird's Aid Jabs Needle Into TV News," which was the apologia of the press secretary to Mrs. Lyndon Johnson ("Frankly," said Mrs. Elizabeth Carpenter at a Democratic women's luncheon, "I like the politics of happiness a heck of a lot better than the politics of hippiness, yippiness, or whatever it is over in Grant Park trying to take over this convention"). "Violence, Not HHH, Big News in Britain" was a *Tribune* correspondent's contribution from London accurately reporting the hostile reaction of the British press to events in Chicago, followed by stories of reactions in Moscow and Saigon. "Police Do Excellent Job, Dirksen Says" was nine inches of local interview enterprise, and "Court Curbs Cop Squeeze on Press Here" was fourteen inches of concern for newsmen. "Negro Leader Blames Whites for Chicago 'Police Brutality'" was the first of seven items on the police action (five against, two for).

The remainder of the coverage, extensive by *Tribune* standards since it had played down disorders until they no longer could be ignored, was a journalistic smorgasbord emphasizing support for Daley and the police: "HHH Defends Tight Convention Security"; "Most Callers Praise Daley for Tough Stand on Rioters"; "Daley Now Symbolizes Dems' Rift," (giving more of the mayor's views on events outside the convention); George C. Wallace praises Chicago police for their "restraint" in coping with demonstrators; Governor Agnew condemns both the "provocations" of demonstrators and "to some extent, an overreaction on the part of the Chicago police"; and a list of arrested persons ("Large Minority From Out of Town" said the deck, which means at least that a majority was from in town).

The Saturday *Tribune* concentrated on a long "dramatic account of operations of the Youth International Party" by an undercover policeman, a television interview in which "Mayor Daley supported *Tribune* reports on the plots on the lives of Vice President Humphrey and Senators George McGovern and Eugene McCarthy," and a *Tribune* reporter's story announcing that "Riot Diary Names 38 Hard-Core Reds."

In the weeks following the convention hardly a day passed without the news pages being used for a running defense of Mayor Daley and the police. Worthy of special note is the issue of Sunday, Sept. 1, a collector's item. On the first and second pages appeared a summary and analysis of the convention by the *Tribune's* political writer, Willard Edwards, who must be read regularly to be fully savored. "Daley," he concluded, "emerged as a central figure at the convention, saving it from utter chaos on at least two occasions. He was often the target of booing but on the final night when he showed up on the podium with Humphrey, he was given a thunderous acclamation." No mention, of course, of the galleries packed with the mayor's City of Chicago employes who did much of the thunderous acclaiming, a fact that did not escape the attention of other newsmen who covered the story. He quoted Senator Abraham Ribicoff as saying: "With McGovern, we wouldn't have a national guard," which is about as close as a *Tribune* analyst is expected to come. (What Ribicoff said was: "With George McGovern as president, we wouldn't have Gestapo tactics in the streets of Chicago.") The uncanny recital also would have us believe that at the end of the Tuesday session "the Wisconsin delegation which, with New York and California, seemed intent upon provoking chaos, sought to adjourn the proceedings until the following afternoon." The delegations got their way, he pointed out, when the permanent chairman "saw Daley drawing his finger across his throat in a signal to adjourn." Then follows one of the startling insights of our times, proving that in the fantasy world no dream can be too wild: "If Albert had permitted it to continue, his apparent intention, until a pre-dawn vote, the consequences might have been fatal. The peace advocates, moved by a zeal of fanatic proportions, might have prevailed because of absentees among administration supporters." It was, of course, the peace-plank advocates who furiously sought adjournment until the next day, and it was Mayor Daley who finally was reluctantly forced to give the necessary signal. The fabrication, incredible as it may be, becomes even more ludicrous in the light of Edwards' own by-lined account in the preceding Wednesday *Tribune,* which stated bluntly and accurately that "a leader of the insurgent minority against the Viet Nam plank in the platform sought to move for adjournment." To a *Chicago Tribune* political analyst in retrospect Daley must never be wrong; thus it became, in a final soaring flight into the *Tribune's* private Elysium, Mayor Richard J. Daley's brilliant tactical maneuver that made it possible for "administration strategists to mobilize their forces" and defeat the peace plank the following day.

The remainder of page two, with the exception of one story, was devoted to post-convention coverage from a dedicated point of view. The headlines:

Hippies Frolic on a Serene Du Page Farm; Cops Protect Leaders of Riot Hordes
Court Action Asked Against Leftist Chiefs
Leftists Plan College Riots, Hoover Warns
Viet Vet Hails Suppression of Mob Here
Daley's Wife Is His No. 1 Fan
Call Guard 'Cool' Under Attack

It was in the story about the "coolness" of the National Guard that the *Tribune* went out of its way to rewrite the record. In its Friday issue two days earlier, as pointed out above, it had correctly reported that guardsmen had used rifle butts to disperse a protest march south of Grant Park. By Sunday, however, the lie is set with an appalling deliberateness:

> When a mob of demonstrators assaulted the troops when trying to pass thru their line across Michigan avenue at 18th street Thursday, the troops drove them back with minimum force, newsmen observed, using tear gas effectively to break up the mob without resorting to outright clubbing with their rifles.

Tribune employes require no special antennae to pick up the managerial signal that everyone is expected to follow the official line. Writers stray no farther from the proclaimed dogma than do writers on *Pravda* or *Izvestia,* to which the *Tribune* bears several resemblances. On the beam, for example, was its television columnist who was never far behind the editorial writers in bemoaning television's violent intrusion into the fantasy world; on one occasion he deplored the fact that "television screens were cluttered night after night with scenes of long-haired, wild-eyed, foul-mouthed young people, many of them alien to this city, rioting in the streets of Chicago. . . ." Similarly, throughout the week and subsequently, *Tribune* readers were treated daily to the views of Robert Wiedrich, ordinarily a night club gossip columnist on the order of Walter Winchell ("Curvy Betty Grable drew rave reviews from the girl watchers on duty at the Sheraton-O'Hare"), but for the occasion a political commentator on the order of Winchell ("We hear that Songstress Jane Morgan is miffed at Mayor Daley's failure to endorse Hubert Humphrey early in the convention"). His "Tower Ticker" column is a gossamer part of the fantasy world, banality following closely on banality, separated only by Winchellian dots. Typical of his contributions were the following:

> We have in our hands [a phrase familiar to all who lived through the 1950s] a copy of a hippie battle plan intended to block the deployment of national guardsmen from the Chicago avenue armory and its immediate neighborhood. It demonstrates the hand of a professional agitator.
> The plan involves using wooden horses to divert traffic from Lake Shore drive into the armory area to create confusion. It involves flattening tires and stalling cars at the armory vehicle exits to destroy the guard's mobility. It involves opening fire hydrants to furnish water for first aid in case of tear gas attacks. And it describes escape routes thru alleys and passageways. . . .
> And on Sunday, a hippie pamphlet announced, "There will be a demonstration of police brutality at 11 p.m. tonight." Was somebody thinking about provoking the police? Are these the plans of "peaceful" demonstrators?

When someone is that far out of it, there is no hope that he can be brought back.

[This account must necessarily include reference to the conduct of the Chicago Tribune in the days following the issuance of the Walker Report, "Rights in Conflict," which termed the events of the convention week a "police riot." The Tribune practice of using its news columns to puff up persons it likes and punish (and preferably, destroy) persons it doesn't like can be documented in almost any issue. It set out to discredit Daniel Walker and the Walker Report with a single-minded vengeance rarely equaled in American journalistic history. Following are the front-page headlines of the one-star editions between Dec. 3 and Dec. 10:

Ad Sought Testimony for Report; Berkeley Students Solicited for Facts on Disorders Here

Mayor Supports Police; Quiz Aid Admits Ad Role

RIOT REPORT HIT BY JUDGE (Banner)
Suggest Probe of Motives and Timing of Quiz

Walker Report Cost Disclosed as $86,000

RIOT REPORT FIGHT GROWS (Banner)
Clark Denies Editing Summary; Document Mine, Walker Vows

Ignored, Says Riot Expert; Tells How Testimony Was Brushed Off

Study's Role in Democrats Split Is Told; Called Weapon for Daley Foes

Walker Broke Word: Judge

It reached a journalistic nadir, even for the Tribune, in the Dec. 10 six-column headline—"Walker Broke Word: Judge"—and the accompanying by-lined story. Federal District Judge William J. Campbell was quoted as saying Walker "went back on his word to me." Nowhere in the 22-paragraph story was Walker allowed to reply to or comment on the charge. But buried in the eighth paragraph is a quotation from Judge Campbell: "When I reminded him of the agreement, he said he had made no agreement."]

IV

Mrs. Humphrey said the Chicago protesters had received entirely too much attention, presumably from the press, radio and television. She said that they were "noisy and rude." And she said she, her husband and their children certainly wanted to hear young America's views, but that they already were aware of them.

"Our youngsters are all over talking with young executives and young Jaycees," she explained.

—Charlotte Curtis in the *New York Times*, Aug. 31, 1968.

The primary journalistic—and ultimately, perhaps, historical—lesson of Chicago is that the news media of general circulation have been guilty of a massive failure, especially during the past decade, to describe and interpret what has been happening in the United States and in the world.* The "orthodox" press, essentially satisfied with the prevailing conditions of life, has resisted or ignored the inequities of our society and has attempted to perpetuate governmental, economic and social abuses. It is not enough to open the columns and the electronic channels for a few hours or days to report what is really happening as they were opened during the battle of Chicago; the reports Americans saw and heard and read in much of the orthodox media should be their steady diet. Significantly, the "underground" newspapers had little to add to what happened in what it termed "Czechago" except for accounts of speeches delivered in Lincoln and Grant parks. In effect, by doing its job, the orthodox media briefly made the underground press irrelevant.

No valid purpose is served by attempting to analyze the political situation in the United States as most editorial writers, columnists and commentators employed by the orthodox press persist in viewing it. It is an acute form of journalistic self-deception (which, especially in recent years, has been the gravest single sin of commission by our press) to write and speak of Democrats and Republicans, Wallaceites and McCarthyites, or the maneuverings and machinations of politicians and bureaucrats as if these are the significant and ultimately crucial divisions in our society. It emphatically is not simplistic to suggest that the central political fact of our times is that there are only two sides: Those who do not want to see any fundamental change in the status quo are pitted violently against those who find the status quo intolerable. Of course there are degrees and nuances on both sides, but it is useless to deny that when large numbers of our citizens are frustrated and angry with the established system, those who are not on their side are against them. Thus: "You are either part of the problem or part of the solution."

[*And there, on the last page of* Newsweek, *is poor Stewart Alsop's column which begins: "There is no more dismaying experience for a political writer than being confronted with an important political phenomenon he really doesn't understand. I had this experience on a Wednesday afternoon during Chicago's hell week." Intended to be a disarming admission, it is in fact a damning indictment. All he had done was cross the street from the Hilton Hotel to Grant Park, there to stage his personal confrontation with the political realities of contemporary America. And how does he view the scene? He sees with the same old eyes he has used*

---

* This section incorporates most of the address of the author at the opening session of the Association for Education in Journalism convention at the University of Kansas last summer. It was delivered approximately two hours before the Chicago police made their first sweep of Lincoln Park on Sunday evening, August 25.

for years, in which everything is adjusted to the context of traditional (and essentially trivial) political maneuvering. He suggests that we always have had a "generational conflict" and right now we have one because a kid, if he's 18, has "passively watched a television screen for some 22,000 hours" (if you think this is all made up, see for yourself on page 108 of Newsweek, Sept. 16, 1968), and we suffer from affluence, to which other empires have succumbed, "vide the Roman Empire." Then the peroration: Something bad is happening—"some political poison, some Virus X" that "is beyond the capacity of the middle-aged to understand, or the young to explain." Finally, he is staggered by the possibilities: "In Chicago, for the first time in my life, it began to seem to me possible that some form of American Fascism may really happen here." (He stopped there, choosing not to roast the one remaining chestnut: Huey Long's observation that if Fascism ever came to the United States it would come in the name of Americanism.) It should be added, however, that Alsop is no more irrelevant than many other political columnists and commentators who have demonstrated in their premises and their conclusions that they live in a world of political phenomena they really don't understand, a world that has swept past them, a world to which they respond ritualistically, burdened by experience that no longer applies and accrued wisdom that provides no answers to current questions. To point out that Eric Sevareid, for example, to the very moment of this writing has never had a beginning understanding of what the dissent movement is all about is to state the obvious. If one accepts the frame of reference and the pattern of logic of the politician in the traditional posture of "making it," one cannot understand and thereby interpret even a Eugene McCarthy, much less an Abbie Hoffman. And it matters not whether the columnist is "liberal" or "conservative." Examine the following:

—After the dust had settled in Chicago, Newsweek columnist Kenneth Crawford saw the whole thing as a television plot in which the networks were out to get his boys. In what must rank among the most paranoiac pronouncements on the entire Chicago affair, Crawford pondered what would have happened "had Daley acted on the notion he once entertained of supporting Kennedy instead of Humphrey." Wondrous things would have happened, Crawford concluded. Television reporters would have made no references to mysterious security men following them around; excuses would have been found for police excesses and the news would have been spread that "Ribicoff's innocents were responding to agitators bent upon raiding the convention's hall or at least its biggest hotel." Of such stuff is nonsense fabricated. But there was in Crawford's column a single startlingly suggestive sentence, which revealed far more than he probably had intended; finally, he wrote, if Daley had appeased the networks by rejecting Humphrey and adopting Edward Kennedy, "parallels would have been found between the Chicago riots and earlier bloodlettings decreed and brought off by some of the same leaders at the Pentagon and at Columbia." He obviously ached for the good old days when dissenters got what was coming to them with the full approval of the networks and the print media, including the news magazine that publishes his column.

—Max Lerner, smarting over criticism of coverage of the week in Chicago, was driven in his fashion to examine the deficiencies of the American press and came up with an extraneous assortment of failures. "Mostly," he wrote, "our sins are lack of analysis in depth, lack of venturesomeness in the realm of ideas, lack of historical background, a tendency to treat every isolated event as equal to every other event in a kind of democracy of news, a fear of hurting fat cats, a chasing-off after every new fad and a vulgarization of sensitivity and taste." Note that in every case with the possible exception of one—"a fear of hurting fat cats"—he averted his eyes from the major flaws of the news media. This frustrated and frustrating analysis was so palpably meretricious that it was, of course, picked up and run in Time magazine. And the way it was run tells all that anyone needs to know about that particular publication. It not only altered Lerner's words within quotation marks, but without showing ellipsis put a period after "democracy of news" and then went on to quote other parts of the column. Thus Time readers were not informed of Lerner's other listed sins of the press—"a fear of hurting fat cats, a chasing-off after every new fad and a vulgarization of sensitivity and taste." The editors of Time know when someone is hitting too close to home.

—James J. Kilpatrick, one of the leading exponents of the right-wing viewpoint: "If the police and troops had not done their job, these pug-ugly scavengers would have torn the Hilton to the ground," a sentence that leaves even more unanswered questions than usual for our friend from the South. "Almost no one," he concluded incredibly, "has said thanks to the mayor and thanks to the cops. I do." If he meant that almost no one who had witnessed the horror in Chicago had afterwards dropped by to thank the police, he certainly was correct; but if he meant that approving letters, telegrams and telephone calls had not flooded Mayor Daley's office and police headquarters, he was badly misinformed.

(When it was all over, only two signs of property damage were visible along Michigan avenue. One was the plate glass window of the Haymarket Lounge of the Conrad Hilton, which had been shattered by terrified bystanders backing away from a group of club-swinging police. The other was the glass front of an office which had been pelted with stones. Some student demonstrators obviously had been selective; the damaged establishment was that of IBM.)

—James Reston's incredible column on the day following the climactic battles in the streets and parks: "The Democratic party was deeply hurt politically by the vicious clashes between demonstrators and police on the streets of Chicago. Though the party itself had no direct responsibility for the incidents, it held its convention here knowing of the dangers of violence and counted on Mayor Daley and his police to handle the situation without embarrassment to the party. This gamble failed. . . ." And so forth. One can look into the future and visualize 100,000 white students streaming into Chicago to aid West Side ghetto residents who had barricaded the streets and declared war on half a million troops flown into the city the previous day, and then Reston's column in the New York Times and other daily newspapers: "Sen. Edward Kennedy's drive for the Democratic presidential nomination suffered what may be a serious setback yesterday as events transpired in Chicago. President Nixon still holds one of the two keys to this puzzle. . . ."

Some columnists and commentators of the orthodox media, on the other hand, went out on the streets to see what was happening and reported the story. Notable among these was John S. Knight, editorial chairman of the Knight newspapers, who probably has been more accurate down through the years about the war in Vietnam than any other American journalist and who has demonstrated a remarkable understanding of young people and what is happening in this country. He is, unfortunately, a rarity among publishers ("I know from personal observation," he later wrote, "that some of the editors who defended Daley to the hilt never left their safe shelters in the Hilton Hotel"). In his interpretive coverage of Chicago, he emphasized that most of the demonstrators were "of good presence and surprisingly well dressed . . . in no way resembled the hippies and yippies of the cartoons . . . displayed no hostility and were eager to talk when not chanting anti-war songs and slogans." He wrote that for his part he "could not see that their assembling in the park constituted any threat to anyone. The police took another view. . . . Abuse of police power only raised tensions when a firm but fair police could have controlled any real or threatened mob action. . . . If these kids came to their rally skeptical of government and duly constituted authority, they must have left it completely disillusioned on all counts." The hostile response to Mr. Knight's views predictably was heavy, but the following Sunday in his weekly "Notebook" he held firm, continuing to deplore "the overkill used by Chicago police in clubbing innocent people." Another exception to the columnar pap poured daily into the editorial pages of the orthodox press was Tom Wicker, whose lucid and accurate analyses from Chicago under deadline pressures emphasized both the specific and general significance of unleashed and unrestricted police power. A few excerpts: "The marchers were political dissidents, some radical, most idealistic, determined to exercise the right of free speech and free assembly and —as Edmund Muskie recognized in his acceptance speech—to have something to say about the kind of future they will inherit. . . . Contrary to Humphrey's banalities, the lesson is that raw, unchecked police power *is not the answer to anything. It is not the answer to the race problem, which is real, nor the answer to the crisis of American youth, which also is real. It is the last resort, instead, of angry and fearful old men who see 'order' as a rigid freezing of the America they have made, and who think 'law' has no higher function than to preserve that order. . . ." Still another columnist (now lost to the profession) who on the night of the nomination of the Democratic candidate for president chose the streets instead of the convention hall was Jimmy Breslin. He looked back on 20 years of "having policemen in the family, riding with policemen in cars, drinking with them, watching them work in demonstrations and crowds in cities all over the world," and concluded that "the performance of the police of Chicago on Michigan Avenue last night was the worst one I ever have seen." He documented his case fully.]*

A RARELY SPOKEN TRUTH

And it is time, too, for recognition of the stark, naked but almost never spoken truth that hundreds—perhaps thousands—of reporters and copy editors and even editors who draw their pay from the owners of the orthodox press are disgusted with the policies of their employers, but the economic necessities of their situation force them to vent their frustrations in the bars, in letters to friends, in their homes or wherever they gather with fellow professionals. What, finally, can they do? Where, finally, can they go? With the orthodox press dominated by the Hearsts, the Scripps-Howards, the Pulliams, the Ridders, the Copleys, the Mc-Cormick heirs, they stick grimly and unhappily with their jobs. And even if they could go to the *New York Times,* the *Washington Post,* the *St. Louis Post-Dispatch,* the Cowles or the Knight or the Field papers—to name a few of the newspapers that display at least some significant measure of decency, fairness and respectability—they have discovered they still are up against editors and publishers who order stories killed, or buried, or covered up when the pressures of the business community or the country club are applied. The men and women of the working press know better than anyone the truth of A. J. Liebling's essentially accurate aphorism that without a school for publishers no school of journalism can have meaning.

All of us need desperately to look with fresh eyes at some of the ways in which the news media have helped to stifle reforms and perpetuate injustices. Until illegal and brutal conduct by some members of police forces is reported regularly in our press, the residents of our ghettos and those who seek legitimate redress of grievances will continue to suffer at the hands of their tormentors. What Americans saw and read during those four days in Chicago is a twenty-four hour reality every day, perhaps in lesser quantity but in undiminished quality, in hundreds of local-ities. The police reporters know it, the city editors know it, the editors and the publishers know it. It is known to many of those who control the content of magazines, radio and television. Many persons have died or suffered terribly from mistreatment, but only the underground press reports it regularly. It has been the unwritten code of the orthodox press that stories of police beating up people or otherwise violating the law don't get into the paper—unless, of course, the scandal becomes so obvious, as the not-so-funny joke has it, that people are afraid to call the police.

One of the few blessings emerging from the events in Chicago was the massive breakthrough made in police reporting not only by newspapers and wire services but by magazines. Especially noteworthy among the news magazines was Newsweek, *which in contrast to its limited and orthodox coverage of the march on the Pentagon the preceding October reported and interpreted at length what had occurred in Chicago. "Miraculously,"* Newskeek *stated, "no one was killed by Chicago Mayor Richard Daley's beefy cops, who went on a sustained rampage unprecedented outside the unreconstructed boondocks of Dixie. 'Kill 'em! Kill 'em!' they shouted as they charged the harum-scarum mobs of hippies, yippies, peace demonstrators and innocent onlookers in the parks and on the streets outside the convention headquarters hotel, the vast Conrad Hilton. Time and again, the police singled out reporters and photographers for clubbing—attacking more than a score. . . . In the midst of all the bloodletting, a middle-aged man in a dark business suit pleaded with an onrushing cop, 'I'm only watching,' he cried. 'You don't belong here, you bastard,' retorted the cop—and clubbed him across the shoulder. . . . Pushed up against a wall by a phalanx of cops, a pretty blonde begged for mercy. No one listened. Instead, a group of police prodded her in the stomach with their clubs, sending her to her knees, her face in her hands, screaming: 'Please God, help me. Please help me.' When a neatly dressed young man tried to help, the police beat him over the head—leaving boy and girl, blood-drenched and whimpering, wrapped in each other's arms. 'You're murderers,' screamed a youth—until a cop silenced him with a rap across the face." The same kind of reporting marked other accounts in the post-convention issue, capped by extraordinary pictorial coverage of events on the streets (27 photographs, seven of them in gory color). Time also reflected its stunned reaction to Chicago by forgoing its customary flippant style for a serious attempt at significant interpretation. Nothing changed, however, at U.S. News & World Report, which weighed its article heavily in favor of Mayor Daley and what it termed "the city's tough policy on law enforcement" and concluded with an approving quotation of a sentence in a* Chicago Tribune *editorial. Nothing more should be expected from a magazine which, in discussing possible Supreme*

Court appointments in the same issue, could assert: " 'Liberals' seem to show more concern for rights of suspected criminals; 'conservatives' tend to show most concern for rights of law-abiding people."

General interest magazines and opinion magazines, almost without exception, expressed shock at the behavior of the Chicago administration and police. Four of the magazines merit special notice:

—Life in its post-convention issue published what is unquestionably the outstanding example of group coverage and interpretation in its history. It ran four articles, two editorials and several revealing photographs devoted to the confrontation in Chicago and left no doubt where it believed the blame rested for the ugly events. Especially dramatic was its editorial departure from bland acceptance of the status quo, including a bristling indictment of Mayor Daley and a memorable last sentence: "But has Chicago now learned that he is an anachronism and an embarrassment?"

—The New Yorker, not noted for timeliness or concern with current affairs of social or political importance, rushed into print in its Sept. 7 issue two articles on Chicago and a highly sympathetic account in "Talk of the Town" of a protest demonstration outside Humphrey's New York headquarters. In one article Michael J. Arlen described a police action he had witnessed ("You can have only a partial idea of how rotten it was") and in the second article Richard H. Rovere, although not as successful as when he examines the innards of the political establishment, lacerated Chicago's mayor and police force ("This is a peculiarly violent city; there may be no higher ratio of brutes among the police here than among the police anywhere, though it certainly seemed as if there were to those who watched them in action the last two nights").

—Business Week, considerably sobered in its coverage and opinion by the actions of Chicago's authorities, placed the blame for the disaster on "Daley's extreme security precautions and the heavy-handedness of his police." Editorially, it moved even farther away from its established position. Examining in the wake of events in Chicago why the nation has seen "things turn sour," it noted that "something of a consensus has developed on the key issue of Vietnam. The U.S. wants to get out."

—The National Review confirmed the suspicion that something mighty peculiar is going on at William Buckley's place when it featured an article by Garry Wills sympathetic to the dissenters. Wills, who in an earlier article on the Republican convention patently mocked the sacred cows of the conservative pasture, deplored "Mayor Daley's untenable first-line toughness" and chastised him for giving the protesters "no place to stay and demonstrate peacefully." The article was illustrated, furthermore, with drawings clearly anti-police and just as clearly not anti-demonstrators. The "New Politics," Wills concluded, "is unworkable in the long run; but Daley made it work, beautifully, in Chicago." He even made the *ultimate admission for a* National Review *writer when he ruefully observed that "the convention in the streets may have been of more lasting importance than that held in the Amphitheater."*]

Similarly documented is the fact that the news media have been guilty of a generally uncritical acceptance and often advocacy of the established policy in foreign affairs (i.e., the policy of the President and his State Department) through successive administrations during the past twenty years. That is the primary reason why it took so many months and years for millions of Americans and, at long last, for many American publications to be upset about the war in Vietnam. That calamitous conflict stands as confirmation of the fact that a major portion of the orthodox press was hesitant to question or provoke the government-industrial-military complex of which President Eisenhower gave the first warning signals. Our foreign policy has been controlled and militarized by the huge bureaucracies in the State Department and the Pentagon, which have effectively promoted the need for an arms race which has no visible end. Part of the revolution that is taking place concerns not only the necessity for a fresh look at the American commitment in Vietnam but the need for a comprehensive revision of the entire American foreign policy. It is not enough that we escape from the current quagmire; there simply must be no more Vietnams. Bismarck observed that every nation eventually must pay for the windows broken by its press, and we are paying a dear price at this time. Despite the massive reversal of position in the editorial pages and columns of orthodox publications on the issue of the war in Vietnam, it is a rare sight indeed to read or hear of any questioning of State Department and/or Pentagon policies in other areas of Southeast Asia, in the Middle East, in Latin America, in Africa, or in Western Europe, to name a few places where we are likely to be fighting new battles with the blood of young Americans.

Furthermore, if the white majority does not sleep well these nights, in too many cases the reason is that the news media have warned of agitators and militants, rioters and looters, but have not pointed out sufficiently the genuine grievances of our black brothers. If—or, more accurately, when—the United States becomes an apartheid society, the blame will rest in large part on a blind and selfish and unconscionable white power establishment and its almost unfailing and subservient ally, the orthodox media. There has been, and there remains, a curious curtain of silence dropped by the white press to keep white people from knowing about events and conditions concerning black people. The record of reporting black attitudes and activities during the fifties and sixties is so dismal that it is openly admitted by many executives in high places of the media. Attempts to remedy that situation, no matter how worthy and how noble, cannot erase the record. We should refuse, for example, to join in the applause for *Newsweek* magazine for its analysis of "The Negro in America" and its advocacy of a program for action—"That in order to deal with the racial crisis effectively, there must be a mobilization of the nation's moral, spiritual and physical resources and a commitment on the part of all segments of U.S. society, public and private, to meet the challenging job." That twenty-three page report, which subsequently was awarded a journalistic prize, had one major flaw: The date on the cover. It was November 20, 1967, when it was probably too late, rather than November, 1957, when there was still time. The orthodox press too often squarely faces up to societal pressures and issues only to prevent the greater of evils. And we should not fall victim to the hypocrisy of many organs of the news media which finally have begun their examinations of black history, black heritage, black culture and the centuries of repression of black people. Even the *Chicago Tribune* now attempts to paint over a history of unremitting indifference to the sufferings of black people in its city by publishing, in May 1968, a special section on the history of the Negro in America. Beyond and beneath comment is the pious pronouncement of the American Newspaper Publishers Association Foundation that grants-in-aid totaling a miserable $14,340 had been awarded to twenty-six Negro college journalism majors. The fund was established by a $100,000 contribution announced by the publisher of the *Chicago Tribune* last April and the grants were announced in August by Eugene S. Pulliam, thus keeping the record clear: Penance, such as it is, by the publishers of papers which rank among the most racist in the United States.

The orthodox press has failed, consciously or otherwise, to report and inform effectively in many other areas where we now face or soon will face critical problems. In large measure the failures resulted from a lack of gutsy local and state reporting, the glossing over of underlying conditions, the reporting of social abuses only when they no longer can be kept hidden. And even if publishers do not seek to slide over the sordid details of our society, the incontrovertible fact (ask almost any reporter or any former reporter now in public relations) is that newspapers in this country, with rare exceptions, simply have been unwilling to commit a reasonable portion of their profits to the production of effective, probing, well-researched investigative reporting. Thus, for example, the comfortable and unafflicted probably would be astonished to learn of the blazing hatred with which our judicial system is regarded by the poor and aspiring as a powerful weapon of the establishment to maintain order by using law as a bludgeon. The corruption and brutality of our courts, especially the lower courts, is not a subject of discussion in the ghettos of our land; it is accepted by the imprisoned inhabitants as a part of their hopelessness. Yet this corruption, witnessed daily not only by the victims but by the reporters for the media, is rarely reported. Well within the restrictions and penalties of "contempt of court," it is possible for the media in their day-by-day reporting to report newsworthy, but unpleasant, items reflecting on the integrity of our judicial system and the right of every person to equal treatment and equal penalty under the law.

THREATS HIDDEN OR PLAYED DOWN

Still another revealing and damning indictment of the orthodox press is the steadily deteriorating quality of the American environment under a man-made miasma. It is not surprising that the orthodox press has splendidly lifted the mask of science and technology to reveal the horrible face of nuclear war; the catastrophic consequences of an atomic holocaust would be about as severe for the establishment as for the rest of us. But in other areas where science has revealed the depth of the crises we are in, the news media have not been nearly so eager to report facts that threaten to shake the existing economic order. Well reported are the technological triumphs that make it possible for us to enjoy the magnificent material base of our society, but kept hidden or played down or explained away until very recently have been the threats to human health and survival, because to solve the problems would necessitate grave economic, political and social disruptions opposed by those who derive economic profit from contaminating our environment. It was bad enough in the nineteenth century when the predator industries, especially mining and lumbering, plundered our natural resources to make possible a new industrial society. The results of their rape of the land are visible from one end of the country to the other. But that was child's play compared with what is happening in this century as industries dare to destroy not only our land but the basic necessities of life: Our air and our water.

One can dwell on air pollution, on water pollution by urban and industrial wastes, on the barbaric desecration of land called strip mining, the noise levels of our cities to which can be added the barely explored dangers of sonic booms, the radiation hazards from nuclear fallout, lead poisoning, the several ways we can get cancer of the lung, the shockingly unrestricted use of insecticides, herbicides and fungicides, military experiments with gas and chemical warfare (of which the Utah story stands as a monumental example of the complaisance of the news media), not to mention the possible synergistic efforts of various man-made poisons, chemicals and pollutants. Bluntly, the coverage of the California grape strike is a continuing national journalistic disgrace, and the superficial handling of campus dissent and demonstrations has alienated large numbers of university and college students who understand what is happening. As for young students, it was George Beebe, senior managing editor of the *Miami Herald,* writing in *APME News* last July, who said he had studied what interests young minds and concluded: "It is pretty obvious that only the sheltered child could enjoy the teen-age sections I have seen." Most segments of the orthodox media not only lag behind the Supreme Court in their definitions of "obscenity" but are wildly out of touch with millions of young people who see the genuine obscenities of the world about them and are not upset by some words regarded as taboo by their elders.

[*Among the curious arguments used against the demonstrators by Humphrey, Daley and others was that they were "obscene." Nonetheless, as anyone who was there can categorically confirm and as quotations in the Walker Report to the National Commission on the Causes and Prevention of Violence make abundantly clear, a majority of the audible "obscenities" were uttered by police, most of whom appeared unable to address even each other without employing scatological or sexual allusions. Let it be noted, too, that several general-circulation magazines— including* Life— *published some of these "obscenities" and William Buckley's* National Review *in its Chicago coverage exposed that magazine's readers for the first time to two words that previously had been withheld from them. It was Buckley himself who, in full view of millions of television viewers on ABC, lashed out at Gore Vidal with the following words: "Shut up, you queer. Don't call me a crypto-Nazi again or I'll sock you in your goddamn face. Go back to your pornography writing." Vidal, author of a novel that features a hero or heroine who is a hermaphrodite, simply responded the next day: "I've always tried to treat Buckley like the great lady that he is." Then there was Mayor Daley, paragon of virtue, who publicly deplored alleged excremental excesses: "When I ask you as a law-abiding citizen not to proceed any further, and you linked arms and someone in your outfit kicks them in the groin or spits at him in the face or hits them with a bag of urine or a bag that begins with 's' and ends with 't,' what would you do? I just wonder what you would do?" Esquire magazine gave the answer the question deserved: "Duck."*]

Fortunately, some hopeful signs can be noted. We know what the industrial establishment and the orthodox press did to Rachel Carson when in *Silent Spring* she exposed the surface of this putrescent problem. But just as it now is becoming fashionable to explore the urban crises and the conditions of the black people, so it is now permissible to report on our noxious air and our filthy water—even *Life* magazine has come to that. Again too little, too late. The acquiescence and even the cooperation and approbation of the orthodox press in the pollution of our environment constitute one of the darker chapters in the history of the American press.

The many other examples that could be cited would only serve to emphasize that pragmatic modifications of the structure, operation, function, and purposes of the press no longer are enough. If Xerox can demonstrate that it has received the message from McLuhan when it announces that it is not in the business of selling copiers but is "in the business of making it easier for people to understand one another," then it is time for the orthodox press to recognize that it is not in the business of selling papers and perpetuating the status quo but is in the business of telling what is really happening in our society. Journalism by paroxysm has been a way of muddling through, but we are paying a terribly high price for covering up and explaining away our problems. There may still be time for the United States if the press fulfills the mission assigned it two centuries ago as the estate that stands above and often against the three other estates.

But not much time remains. Let no one minimize the fact that only small incalculables and coincidences—acts of God, if you will—kept Chicago from becoming the scene of an imponderable catastrophe. During the beautifully cool days and nights of convention week the temperature peaks ranged from 69 to 78 degrees. Temperatures during the week preceding the convention hit highs of 89 to 94, but the heat wave broke on the Sunday eve of the gathering and did not return until four days after the delegates departed. In that kind of heat and humidity, how many would have been killed? What we now debate would be as nothing compared to what might have been.

Spy Fiction

The entertainment moguls of mass culture might well have boasted of the three B's during the 1960s—the Beatles, *Bonanza,* and James Bond. Few heroes, folk, real, or literary, have ever achieved the renown of Ian Fleming's 007, the adventurer nonpareil. By the end of the decade, perhaps, the James Bond balloon was somewhat deflated, probably because the unrelenting mills of the publicity gods had ground even this demigod into apathy, and the fickle mass public needed a new divinity to adulate and emulate. But in his hey-day of the mid-1960s the handsome, rugged Sean Connery's face seemed to appear from every other page of our mass magazines, nearly fifty million copies of Fleming's novels (in twenty-six different languages) had been sold, and spydom had been given a status and mystique that its routine, day-by-day activities of agents would belie.

Any revisit to mass culture, then, during the period of the 1960s would be incomplete without an analysis of why James Bond was so enormously popular. The Canadian novelist, Mordecai Richler, in his essay in this section, finds this adulation of Bond hard to conceive, since *(1)* Fleming was an inept, wooden writer, *(2)* the plots in virtually every Bond novel followed the same formula, and *(3)* Fleming exhibited a xenophobia of genuine dimensions. Richler doesn't like Fleming or his brain-hero, Bond, and his essay minces no words in telling us why.

The relationship between fictional spies and their counterparts in the real world is examined with great insight by British sociologist, Joan Rockwell. What has happened, she queried, to the gentleman spy of British fiction or his real-life models? Kipling's gentlemanly Kim has now become a coarse practitioner of the art of espionage in the person of Le Carré's Leamas. If Somerset Maugham and his Ashenden were gentlemen par excellence, playing The Game, what can be said of the redoubtable James Bond? Like Richler, Miss Rockwell finds Bond less than acceptable, either as a spy or a fellow Briton.

Normative Attitudes of Spies in Fiction*

By Joan Rockwell

The spy in British fiction, like the real-life British spy, used to be a gentleman; or, at the very least, he was governed by a gentlemanly ideal. Now he is rather seedy, tough, and lower-middle-class (Le Carré's Leamas in *The Spy Who Came in from the Cold* is the prototype, and it covers most of Le Carré's and Deighton's characters) or even working-class (Turner, in *A Small Town in Germany,* or *Callan,* in an excellent and popular British TV series). Le Carré's gentle scholarly middle-class spy, George Smiley, quit the service in disgust.

Kipling's *Kim,* the prince of all British fictional spies, whose influence on life and literature is noticeable to this day, was certainly not a gentleman. Orphaned (but legitimate) son of an Irish color-sergeant ("but his mother had been nursemaid in a Colonel's family"), his origins were low enough; he was raised by a "bazaar-woman," which puts him right outside the lowest area of the caste-system of the British Army in India. Nevertheless, he is shown to be sincerely admiring the "gentlemanly ideal"—rank, power, and arrogance when dealing with the Indians. This comes to him as a revelation when he overhears the C.-in-C. planning reprisals against some dissident princes:

> . . . . "Warn the Pindi and Peshawur brigades. It will disorganise all the summer reliefs but we can't help that. This comes of not smashing them thoroughly the first time. Eight thousand should be enough."
> "What about artillery, sir?"
> "I must consult Macklin"
> "Then it means war?"
> "No. Punishment.

---

* Published for the first time in this volume.

> . . . . Send off those telegrams at once—. . . I don't think we need keep the ladies waiting any longer. We can settle the rest over the cigars. I thought it was coming. It's punishment—not war."

and Kim, lost in admiration, reflects

> "Every time before that I have borne a message it concerned a woman. Now it is men. Better."

His ambition thenceforth is tied to the maintenance of the machinery of power, and he is chosen as having a special talent to be "one of those who hunts out men who have done a foolishness against the State." There is nothing he wants more than to have a number in the files and a price on his head—to be one of those who play "The Great Game which never stops night or day."

It is significant that Kipling/Kim calls espionage The Great Game. Gentlemen play games, especially elegant, dangerous, and exciting games, but they don't do dirty work for pay. Writers of contemporary spy fiction emphasize that this is what their spies are doing all the time. In Kipling's time, all on the English side engaged in spying are animated by both patriotism and gentlemanly, sporting instincts: this even includes natives like Mahbub Ali and Hurree Babu. The enemy, however, are beastly outsiders with no gentlemanly instincts at all. They are despised by their very coolies. Pretending to be on a shooting trip, they buy the heads they are supposed to have shot, they have no retinue of servants, and are even stingy enough to cook their own food. They are also over-familiar with natives—Kipling is very specific in observing that no British officer would offer a native a drink, but then neither would he strike him. Gentlemen do not lose their heads or their tempers.

Kipling, of course, was a major apologist for Imperialism when *Kim* was published (1901). Just then the British Empire was reaching its greatest extension of territory, power, and prestige. Kipling favors anything which will consolidate this position. Somerset Maugham, in *Ashenden, or The British Agent* (1928), a book based on his own experiences in World War I, takes to the job of spy quite naturally, regarding it as a patriotic duty, perfectly compatible with being a literary figure and an educated man from an upper-class milieu. One of the particularly fascinating aspects about the spy in British fiction is the exceptionally close connection between fact and fiction.

> The administrative reality has been overlaid by thick fictional and semi-fictional accretions. The vogue for books about espionage is today at such a point that the spy ranks as one of the most potent images of mid-twentieth-century life; but the stream of works in English about espionage, intrigue and secret service goes back at least to the latter part of the nineteenth century, and there is a curious inter-relationship between secret service work and literature. . . . The list of writers of fiction who have worked in one way or another for British secret organ-

izations includes some of the most widely read of our time, like John Buchan, Compton Mackenzie, Somerset Maugham, Grahame Greene, Dennis Wheatley, Ian Fleming and John Le Carré (and even, perhaps, Rudyard Kipling). . . . .

Philby, pp. 134–135

That there is "a stream of works in English" about spying is perfectly true; but it is also true that the gentleman-as-spy is peculiarly English, never American. Americans read spy stories with avidity, but they read Le Carré, Fleming, and Deighton, not an American equivalent of these. A new mass-produced American spy story has appeared, which will be discussed below, but it has little claim to literary or psychological interest.

The lack of the gentleman-spy as a serious protagonist in the American thriller is due to two things: the populist tradition in classic American literature, and the actual position with respect to real espionage in American society, and the consequent low tolerance of the image of the spy-as-hero.

Unlike British fiction, American literature has never taken its heroes from the gentry or even the middle-class until very recently. Who are the heroes of Cooper, Melville, Mark Twain, and Dreiser? The commonest of common men. Hawthorne and Poe, to be sure, avoided these protagonists, but the ones they chose were psychotics. Faulkner divides his attention between the cabin and the mansion-house, but the chief thing he says about the latter is that it is falling down. Hemingway's heroes are serious middle-class professional people, who find themselves among the rich and their hangers-on, with a sprinkling of upper-class Bohemia and exceptionally skilled lower-class "friends"—but he was an expatriate, like the only two American writers who reverence the rich, Henry James and Scott Fitzgerald.* The middle-class and upper-class protagonist has only recently become a legitimate character in American fiction, and this development is in marked contrast to the English literary tradition, which has consistently projected gentlemanly or middle-class heroes; if they are poor (Tom Jones, Oliver Twist, Tess d'Urberville), some kind of social displacement is at work—they are really lost heirs, belonging rightfully to the upper classes after all.

The different social situation has probably at least as much influence on types of protagonists as differing literary traditions. England had an Empire, and an upper-class consciously devoted to maintaining it by all means. As Le Carré says in the Introduction to *Philby*, membership in the upper-class was identified with loyalty. The loyalty is understood to be not only to the country, but also and specifically to the Empire as such: Chapter 2 of *Philby*, entitled "The Boyhood of Three Spies," is

---

* And a case for extreme ambivalence could be argued for both: in *The Golden Bowl* and *Gatsby*, for instance.

headed by a sentence taken from the dossier on Donald MacLean. It reads as follows:

"Why shouldn't the Indians win? After all, it's their country."
—Donald Maclean, aged 17

America has never had an Empire in this sense, one not only acknowledged but acclaimed, and viewed as a just cause rightly demanding loyalty manifested in any and every service. With the fading of the Kennedy-Johnson dream it seems unlikely that we ever will. Americans go abroad to make money, to acquire culture, to promote a cause, to avoid the draft, but not by any means to sit for thirty years in some awful swamp or jungle to serve the Queen, God bless her!

America has certainly national money-making interests abroad, but has only lately developed a spy network which gentlemanly writers could join and use as a literary source, even if the ideal did prevail. American espionage never enjoyed anything like the scope and public acceptability of the spy network in Great Britain or of Continental European countries. Alexander Orlov, a Russian defector who was formerly a General in the NKVD, mentions in his *Handbook of Intelligence and Guerrilla Warfare,* the deficiencies of American Intelligence which lagged

> . . . . far behind those of other countries. General George C. Marshall frankly admitted at the Senate Committee on Military Affairs (Oct. 18, 1945) that until World War II the American intelligence abroad was "little more than what a military attaché could learn at dinner, more or less, over the coffee cups"* When in 1941 President Roosevelt asked Col. Wm. J. Donovan to organize an intelligence service (the O.S.S.) he told Donovan: "You will have to begin with nothing. We have no intelligence service."** Dwight D. Eisenhower also deplored the "shocking deficiency" of American intelligence at the outset of the war, and General Omar Bradley*** stated that "the British easily outstripped their American colleagues in military intelligence." The state of the so-called diplomatic intelligence was no less deplorable. . . .
>
> —*Handbook,* pp. 2–3

Orlov attributes this state of affairs to what he calls *"The American doctrine of intelligence"* (p. 8). The basic error, in his opinion, is dependence on the massive collection of data from

> . . . legitimately accessible sources, such as library research, foreign newspapers, military and scientific journals, foreign parliamentary debates, encyclopedias and statistics. According to a reliable source, the American intelligence agencies monitor as many as five million words

---

* William Donovan, "Intelligence; Key to Defense," *Life,* Oct. 30, 1945.
** *Crusade in Europe,* 1948, p. 32.
*** *A Soldier's Story,* 1951, p. 33.

daily from foreign radio broadcasts alone (which equals fifty books of average size) and condense them into a few short pages . . . the intelligence officers and trained analysts derive, process, and distill much information about foreign countries, their economies and finances, industries, agriculture and trade, populations and social trends, education, political systems, structure of governments, and biographical data on political and military leaders . . .

Admiral Ellis, who was deputy chief of Naval Intelligence in World War II, wrote that in the Navy 95% of peacetime intelligence was derived from legitimately accessible sources, four per cent from semiopen sources, and only one per cent was procured through secret agents.*

—*Handbook,* p. 7

Orlov estimates that in fact between 10–20% of U.S. intelligence comes from secret sources, but he amply demonstrates, by his use of public statements by high-ranking officials, that this is played down: no acceptably devious image of the spy in constant danger, playing the Great Game with a lone hand, emerges. He seems rather to be a bureaucratic personality, buried beneath a mountain of paper work. The five years since Orlov's *Handbook* was published (1963) have not changed the official image. The *New York Times* of June 22, 1969, gives substantially the same picture:

The bulk of the agency's (CIA) work consists of gathering intelligence from radio broadcasts, from agents and other sources all over the world and then evaluating it for the President. . . . . The CIA and the Atomic Energy Commission between them, he added, probably lead the government in the use of computers and data retrieval procedures. By contrast, other sources say, the clandestine work or "dirty tricks" side as it is called inside the agency, plays far less a role than is popularly supposed.

"Every covert action must first be authorized by a top-level White House committee. . . .

"Moreover," he added, "James Bond to the contrary,—absolutely no one is authorized, licensed, permitted or encouraged to kill anyone."

—Benjamin Welles, Special to the
New York Times, June 2, 1969

This soothing image of the bureaucratic spy is evidently desired by the public and actively promoted by those in a position to judge the true nature of espionage. Orlov, a Continental, is strongly in favour of the secret-agent type of spy; he quotes with contempt MacArthur's explanation of the lack of intelligence at the start of the Korean War: *"There is nothing, no means or methods, except spy methods . . . that can get such information as that."* Orlov's point is that spy methods are what ought to be used.

Important state secrets, and especially clues to the intentions and plans

---

* Captain Ellis M. Zacharias, USN, *Secret Missions: the Story of an Intelligence Officer,* pp. 117–18.

of potential enemies *cannot be found in libraries and encyclopedias,* but only where they are being kept under lock and key. The task of intelligence services is to acquire the keys and lay the secrets before their governments and thus provide them with *foreknowledge.*

—Handbook, p. 12

Whether Orlov was aware of electronic spying devices such as U-2 and *Peublo,* not to mention the activities of Michigan State University, located eighty miles from the University of Michigan, which published his book, not to mention the spying activities of U.S. academics abroad, is immaterial. He was trying to popularize and legitimize the image of the non-bureaucratic spy, engaged as often as not in "dirty tricks," to a public opinion which rejected that image. Without the image there was no possibility of developing a literature of espionage in America comparable to that in Britain where the spy was acknowledged, admired, and identified with the exemplary upper class.

One interesting question about the spy in British fiction is, how and why has his social status slipped downhill so disastrously that now (1969), far from being a gentleman, he expresses a great deal of conscious and subconscious aggression toward the upper class? The TV series, *Callan,* mentioned above, ended abruptly when Callan (working-class) is brainwashed into shooting his (upper-class) Control, and is shot down himself.

It used to be different. Maugham and his *Ashenden,* who took so naturally to the job of agent, were gentlemen par excellence. Ashenden was much higher on the stratification scale of the outside world than M., his superior in the service. M. lacks social grace; he is far from well-bred and finds himself ill at ease in the smart restaurants to which Ashenden spitefully takes him, mostly to gloat over M.'s discomfort: his incompetent way of appearing "a little too much at ease," and his naive pleasure in sharing the same room with so many celebrities, pointed out by Ashenden. Ashenden's insistence on his social superiority would make most modern readers uneasy, but he is quite complacent about it. He has another source of superiority: as a professional man of sensibility, a writer, it is more or less his duty to note the human qualities of the people he is tracking down. Caypor, the English spy, is devoted to his wife and dog and charming to elderly people in the hotel, but he is not only betraying his country for £40 a month, he has "lived his furtive life in shabby side-streets." In one of the stories there is an interesting beginning of a conflict between sensibility and loyalty. M. sets Ashenden on to trap Chandra Lal, a man "who has done a foolishness against the State" —an Indian Nationalist who is stirring up a good deal of trouble for the British in India during the War. Ashenden conceives quite a romantic admiration for this man, for which he is rebuked by M., who tells him not to get sentimental because he's only a common criminal and must be put down. Nevertheless, Ashenden is struck by this little, fat, middle-aged man, who besides tackling the total might of the Empire more or less single-handed, has a genuine and passionate love affair with an equally ridiculous actress/prostitute, the *Giulia Lazzari* of the title. It should be said that real and reciprocal love is one of the few human situations that Maugham (in fiction) truly admires; he gives it the respect appropriate to a miracle. Ashenden however, on instructions, traps the Indian by bullying his lover into betraying him. How he avoids the self-disgust which would immediately overwhelm a Le Carré or Deighton character is most revealing. Chandra Lal has committed suicide to avoid arrest, and Maugham has Giulia come to Ashenden and ask for the return of his wristwatch, which she had given him for Christmas: "It cost £12." This of course lets Ashenden off the moral hook—these low-class wogs are hardly human.

Perhaps the most interesting story for our purpose, however, is the last one in the book. On this occasion Ashenden is sent to Moscow (1917) to prevent the Revolution. He remarks that the reader will be aware that in this he did not succeed, but he can't help feeling that if he had been sent a little earlier. . . .

This is an expression of the prime myth of the British upper-class, the delusion that it is a genuine elite, distinguished by an "effortless superiority." It does everything better, with no trouble, than the lower orders do with great effort. This belief, which might be called the Pimpernel Syndrome, is persistently displayed in British thriller fiction. It includes the maintenance of ritual frivolity, which proves that the superiority is really effortless. A typical example is the correspondence of Lord Peter Wimsey, the model aristocratic detective of the thirties, with a friend in the foreign office, about a possible foreign agent:

Dear Clumps,—Here's a cipher message. Probably Playfair but old Bungo will know. Can you push it off to him and say I'd be grateful for a construe? Said to hail from Central Europe but ten to one it's in English. How goes?

Yours,
Wimbles

The answer is as follows:

Dear Wimbles,
   Got your screed. Old Bungo is in China, dealing with the mess-up there, so have posted enclosure off as per instructions. He may be up-country, but he'll probably get it in a few weeks. How's things? Saw Trotters last week at the Carlton. He has got himself into a bit of a mess with his old man, but seems to bear up. You remember the Newton-Carberry business? Well, it's settled, and Flops has departed for the Continent. What-ho!

Yours ever,
Clumps
—*Have his Carcass* (1932)
by Dorothy Sayers

This baby-talk, which infuriated Orwell, is part of the upper-class image of "the inspired amateur." Lord Peter, of course, sets to and solves the cipher in about twenty minutes. Whatever the modern reader may think, and here, as with Ashenden, standards of admiration have certainly changed, the intention is to present Lord Peter as totally admirable for his superiority in every single human activity and emotion, throughout the series of books in which he figures. And this is typical of thriller fiction as well as spy fiction right through the thirties and up to 1945. The "mess-up in China" to which Clumps refers, was the Shanghai Massacre of Communists by Chiang-Kai-Chek, the Battle of Nanking, and the beginning of the long March to Yenan by the Chinese Red Army under Mao-Tse-Tung. Perhaps if old Bungo had been sent a little earlier. . . . ?

Doubtless the belief in upper-class ability led to staffing high posts, including the secret services, with upper-class people. It was accompanied by another assumption, and one much more rationally founded, in the total identification of class with loyalty. Le Carré points out, in his introduction to *Philby,* that this assumption made the service continue to employ Philby long after it had more than enough evidence to get rid of him. The assumption of loyalty is not only based on the obvious material interest which members of the upper-class have in maintaining the status quo—plenty of people are capable of putting larger interests above their own—but on the fact that the British ruling class runs its affairs as if it were a primary group. There is great emphasis on personal acquaintance with family and social background. Anthony Samson, in *Anatomy of Britain,* has sufficiently demonstrated the interlocking web of alliances by birth, education, and marriage, which constitute a "clan" of rulers having almost a relationship of blood kinship. Whatever their surface characteristics they can be assumed to be basically loyal. There is necessarily a great tolerance of eccentricity of various kinds. Thus it didn't count against MacLean that he was a drunkard, or against Burgess that he was demonstratively homosexual and Bohemian (although the Consul at Cairo is reported to have said, when he saw Burgess' fingernails (filthy): "Can he really be one of us?"); or against Philby that he was, as his dossier records, "a bit of a bastard with the girls." Neither did youthful left-wing tendencies count against anyone: they were presumed to be outgrown, and were in any case a normal stage in the development of young gentlemen of the brighter sort. Malcolm Muggeridge assumes that blindness to this partial trait was due to a breakdown in the instinctual detection apparatus of the "clan":

A ruling class on the run, as ours is, is capable of every fatuity. It makes the wrong decisions, chooses the wrong people, and is unable to recognise its enemies—if it does not actually prefer them to its friends.

—reprinted in *Tread Softly,*
You Tread on My Jokes, 1968

and there may be something in this, since the recognition of friends was based on two false premises: ability and loyalty as inevitable class characteristics. But the reason there was such an outburst of fury in Britain over the defection of Burgess, MacLean, and especially Philby, was that they had shown themselves to be true deviants, not merely eccentrics, by challenging the existence of their own clan: a crime tantamount, in clan society, to shedding kindred blood. This explains the prominence given, by the authors of *Philby,* to the remark of the seventeen-year-old Mac-Lean, cited above: it shows that he was rotten to the core, a criminal deviant, and not merely a generous-hearted boy, as anyone outside the Empire-ideology might suppose.

The secret service is part of the ruling-clan most exactly like a primary group—the inner core of the family. The method of recruitment supports this hypothesis. Graham Greene, for instance, was asked on the BBC "How was it you went into intelligence work?" Answer: "I was recruited by a relation. They wanted somebody who had a little knowledge of Africa" (*The Listener,* Nov. 21, 1968). *Ashenden* had a long chat with a high-ranking officer at a party, and was asked to go to a seedy house in Kensington, where he was recruited. This seedy house in Kensington still haunts spy-fiction: see, for instance, the opening of Len Deighton's *Funeral in Berlin.*

Given the social assumptions set out above, it is not surprising that in the late thirties and during the war, Intelligence was recruited on the basis of class membership. Page, Leitch, and Knightley give extensive and very funny documentation of this. Leitch, for instance, reports the following conversation with

> . . . an amiable gentleman who passed the war excitingly in a series of very clandestine operations.
> They were discussing the quality of the intake in those hectic days of the early forties, and the exchange was as follows:
> Leitch: "An amazing amount of crooks seem to have got into SOE, SIS and all those outfits during the war, don't you think?"
> Veteran: "Well, have to take what you can get in wartime, don't you?"
> Leitch: "They seem to have got most of these chaps out of the bar at White's, so far as one can see."
> Veteran: "Yes, well you wouldn't find anything except crooks there, would you?"
> Leitch: "Where were you recruited?"
> Veteran: "Boodle's"

White's, we are informed on p. 146, "is usually bracketed with the Turf at the apex of the subtle hierarchy of London clubland." Boodle's is lower down, but not by much.

> During the war, an etiquette grew up among members of White's that one was not to bother Menzies and Koch de Gooreynd when they were together at the bar, because it was understood that they were 'running the secret service, or something.' It would hardly have struck anyone

at White's as odd that the club should occasionally be a sort of partial, alternative headquarters of the secret service; rather the reverse, in that the major clubs of the West End are, quite unselfconsciously, citadels of the British ruling orders.

—Philby, p. 146

By 1945, then, the upper-class, in real life as in fiction, had moved in and taken over the executive posts in the secret services; they were no longer gentlemanly outsiders, patriotically offering their services as a duty, which might entail the laughable requirement that they take orders from their social inferiors. Now the gentlemen are running the Game, including the "dirty tricks"—"I can see them working it out, they're so damned academic"; says Leamas in a burst of bitterness, "I can see them sitting round a fire in one of their smart bloody clubs. . . ."

From admiration of the gentlemanly Imperial ideal to the bitterness and sometimes hatred toward gentleman-superiors which is shown again and again by the best British spy-writers—Le Carré, Deighton, Adam Hall *(The Quiller Memorandom)*—is a considerable distance. I think the watershed in that change of attitude is the postwar ambience most accurately presented in Michael Innes' masterpiece, *The Journeying Boy.*

This delightful book, first published in 1949, is extraordinarily cheerful. Besides being a tour-de-force of Donnish writing, it is full of the post-war optimism which was general in England at the time, before everything began to go wrong (for this, see *Age of Austerity,* Sissons and French, eds., Penguin). Mr. Thewless, the tutor, muses not about social superiority but about "the building of a better England. For the achieving of that, after all, how many people more talented and powerful than he must passionately care!" This hope and attitude implies a down-grading of mere wealth as a moral value. Thewless* outside the door of Sir Bernard Paxton, who is "beyond doubt the greatest of living physicists," is visited by sharp misgivings, and this despite being, "as he sometimes told himself, a sober and self-respecting snob, just as by vocation he was a hanger-on of people themselves no more than desperately hanging-on."

Often enough before he had been in this sort of house, but never with comfort for very long. Positive opulence was something which he found uncomfortably to jar with the spirit of the time; the poet whose social occasions obliged him to spend a day at Timon's villa was not rendered more uneasy by its splendours than was Mr. Thewless by anything

---

* Innes amuses himself by using characters to define their roles, in the manner of a medieval Morality and in the literary tradition of Dickens and Henry James. Not only is the tutor named Thewless, but Paxton's researches are presumably to be used for peace; the lady secret agent is called Miss Liberty; the two men from Homicide are called Cadover and Morton; a psychiatrist named Lord Polder is mentioned (polder: "a piece of low-lying ground reclaimed from the sea. (Du.)"; even the village where the crime takes place is called Killyboffin, and Boffin = Scientist in England, since Dickens created the first Boffin in Bleak House.

resembling their latter-day counterpart. And why—the question suggested itself even as he raised his hand to the doorbell—yes, why in the world should a really great man take the trouble to surround himself with so emphatic a material magnificence?

—p. 6 (Penguin ed.)

The social assumption in this context is that society is really changing. The "idle rich" are disappearing—"no more than desperately hanging-on" —there is to be a true aristocracy of merit and moral worth. It counts against Sir Bernard that he indulges himself in a display of wealth; nevertheless it is Mr. Thewless' duty to help him because of his scientific genius, which is used for the public good. The values are not to be gross material gain and the brutal exercise of power, as with Kipling and Ian Fleming, or the arrogance of hereditary superiority, as in the whole snob school of thrillers from Maugham through John Buchan and the snob murder-queens: Dorothy Sayers, Agatha Christie, Margery Allingham, and Ngaio Marsh (their American counterparts are Elizabeth Daly and Mary Roberts Rhinehart). On the contrary, in *The Journeying Boy* the admired values are: intelligence, social responsibility, and honorable behavior directed at promoting the good of the whole society. In this situation idealism is consonant with patriotism, which may account for the optimistic tone. The privileges of the upper stratum are noted, but allowable because of superiority due to great effort, not by right of birth. They have constantly to make hard moral decisions, and their consciousness of kind is based on virtue not class. The villains, unlike those of Kipling, Maugham, and Fleming, are neither foreign nor low-class, but cousins of Sir Bernard's late wife, in hot pursuit of unenlightened self-interest.

We encounter frequent jabs at the gentlemanly snob ideal—phrases like "our faded institutions of privilege"—and this attitude is not exclusive to this particular book and author, but general in the tone of thriller literature of the time. Thus in a contemporary work of Allingham, an eccentric countess who has used the prerogatives of rank to move the body and generally interfere, is castigated, the other character noting that "ninety-nine percent of the world's population were in agreement" as to the illegitimacy of this Old Girl arrogance.

But the optimal social situation reflected in *The Journeying Boy* came quickly to an end. The resumption of Parliamentary power by the Conservatives in 1951 made it clear that, some social gains notwithstanding, the New Jerusalem had not been built in England. So far as the Secret World was concerned, its upper-class administrators had remained uninterruptedly in command since the War, and beginning with Graham Greene's *Our Man in Havana* (1958), a new type of mocking, disillusioned spy literature appeared; in this first instance, the attack was on the delusion of the effortless superiority of the "inspired amateurs" in command, whose gullibility and incompetence are the target. There is also an implied attack on the whole wrong-headed mystique of spying, which ignores the real miseries of the island (Cuba), but is infatuated with fake photos of a vacuum cleaner.

With the appearance of Le Carré's *Call for the Dead* (1961; later reprinted as *The Deadly Affair*) and *A Murder of Quality* (1962), and Len Deighton's *Ipcress File* (1962) a really jeering attack on the upper-class comes to be mounted, and the new type of spy fiction is established. The distinguishing features are: detestation of the middle- or lower-class spy in the field for his upper-class administrative superiors; emotional attachment, sometimes only consciousness of kind but sometimes real affection, of the spy for his enemy opposite number; revulsion at the dirty work of spying in general, and in particular at having to kill his enemy/friend; and finally, a basic loyalty after all to his own country and service, not because it is superior but because he happens to have been born in it.

The alienation of operatives in the field from superiors in safe spots is not unknown in real life. Vilhelm Aubert, the Norwegian sociologist, discusses this in "Secrecy: the Underground as a Social System" *(The Hidden Society,* 1965), with respect to the members of the Norwegian resistance who remained in Norway during the Occupation, running the risks and doing the work, while the Norwegian exile Government attempted to direct them from London. By the end of the war their distrust and dislike had turned to real hatred: most of them contemptuously refused the decorations they were offered by the exile government. There may also have been an element of age and class antagonism in all this: field commanders were necessarily unknown and young, and Norwegians of high rank and influence in ordinary life could not be used for resistance work as they were watched. If they were present, they took orders from the young commanders; but they were naturally in command if they were in London, and if they were in the Government they were upper-class or professional people. Aubert gives no indication that the Resistance fighters felt any attraction toward the Germans; on the contrary, their emotional involvement was all with each other. People were recruited if deemed to be trustworthy by their friends, and it was necessary for their confidence to be well-founded, as the penalty for mistaken judgment was extreme; namely to be taken by the Gestapo. Friendship among themselves alone was the single available reward and solace, and Aubert reports that it was sometimes impossible to resist the temptation of telling one's real name, as a mark of trust, although this was of course contrary to security and good sense. It marked the total cut-off in intimate life, not only from the Germans but also from the general population.

The invaluable Orlov, however, reports a different attitude among Soviet intelligence officers, an attraction for their professional opponents which is similar to that described in the new spy fiction. He says:

The fifth line of Soviet intelligence is *Infiltration of Security Agencies and Intelligence Services of Foreign Countries.** This activity contains a special challenge to Soviet intelligence officers and holds for them a peculiar kind of fascination. Although they regard foreign intelligence officers as professional spies (they think of themselves as revolutionaries carrying out dangerous assignments of the party) *they do have a feeling of kinship with them* (my emphasis-JR) and react to a suddenly encountered foreign intelligence agent with the same thrill and curiosity with which two enemy pilots sight each other over the wide spaces of the sky. The general attitude of the Soviet intelligence officer towards his foreign counterpart is hostile, but *it is sincerely friendly from the moment the foreign intelligence man becomes an informant for Russia.* (my emphasis, JR)

—Handbook, p. 23

Kinship, sympathy, attraction, fascination, admiration: these sentiments of a spy toward his opponent are heavily emphasized in contemporary spy fiction. Ashenden's romantic admiration for Chandra Lal, the Indian Nationalist, is a prefiguration of this change. George Smiley in *The Deadly Affair,* quits the service in self-disgust at having killed his enemy/friend (a former student, to be sure):

Dieter was dead, and he had killed him . . . And Dieter had let him do it, had not fired the gun, had remembered their friendship when Smiley had not. . . . They had come from different hemispheres of the night, from different worlds of thought and conduct. Dieter, mercurial, absolute, had fought to build a civilization. Smiley, rationalistic, protective, had fought to prevent him. "Oh God," said Smiley aloud, "Who was then the gentleman? . . ."

Leamas and Fiedler, in *The Spy Who Came in from the Cold,* are similarly bound in sympathy—"We're all the same, you know, that's the joke," says Fiedler. There is doubtless an element of the "sincerely friendly" attitude mentioned by Orlov, in Fiedler's attitude to Leamas, a supposed defector; but we are given to understand that Leamas likes Fiedler, Liz says he is good and is horrified at Leamas' betrayal of him, as he is himself:

"It gives him a chance to secure his position," Leamas replied curtly. "By killing more innocent people? It doesn't seem to worry you much." "Of course it worries me. It makes me sick with shame and anger and . . . But I've been brought up differently, Liz; I can't see it in black and white. People who play this game take risks. Fiedler lost and Mundt won. London won—that's the point. It was a foul, foul, operation. But it's paid off, and that's the only rule."

Leamas, in spite of accepting the necessity of this rule, in effect com-

* "Those familiar with CIA operations assert that the agency has never been penetrated, unlike its principal rival, the Soviet Union's KGB, several of whose officers have defected to the West." Benjamin Wells, *The New York Times,* June 2, 1969.

mits suicide. Len Deighton's "I," in *Funeral in Berlin,* shudders to hear his superior hint at liquidating Johnny Vulkan (finally killed by "I"), a double agent; and a systematic search of the literature would yield many more examples, even excluding the old-fashioned commonplace of sexual involvement. Attraction to the literally mortal enemy seems to be a characteristic trait of modern spies, based not just on occupational identification but also on a genuine emotional involvement.

As Orlov shows, the phenomenon is not confined to fiction, and it is not confined to Russia either. We are told in *Philby* of:

> William Skardon, the crack MI5 investigator, who with his usual deceptive gentleness, had extracted an enormous amount of information from Klaus Fuchs (to whom he always referred as "dear old Klaus") . . . .
> —*Philby*, p. 259

The ability to lead a convincing double life is of course the basic operational necessity of an agent, and although this must give an area of tolerance to the fascination with real enemies recorded by Orlov (and made much of in the brilliant American film *The President's Analyst,* which features a very nice Russian spy named Kropotkin), it must also lead to the operational incovenience of agents becoming double-agents. I suppose that every spy is at least potentially a double-agent, just as every portrait is a self-portrait.

The agent attracted to the enemy, and the double-agent serving two Powers at the same time, whether or not with equal enthusiasm, is not the opposite but of a different kind from the old-fashioned spy as seen in Kipling, or the Norwegian resistance fighter. There the commitment to one's own side is absolute. It is unthinkable for Kim to give the despised and detested enemy a few secrets, for money or any other consideration. Their employment was a devotion to what they knew to be right. The bright nostalgic quality of *The Journeying Boy* derives from a more sophisticated version of the same allegiance: one's own side is, in fact, virtuous, and the Others are villains of the deepest dye; no confusion of moral issues here. *Ashenden* speciously preserves this façade by an unfair moral degradation of the enemy. The unspeakable James Bond reverts to the social morality of Kipling's Empire, the personal morality of the toughest American private-eye and gangster literature, and the most vulgar possible one-up-manship in material possessions and their conspicuous consumption. The fact that books and films about him break all records shows that the sensitive and introspective agent, doing his distasteful duty despite moral revulsion, does not by any means dominate the field, even today. There is a demand for hard-headed recognition that much espionage is morally repulsive, but necessary out of tribal loyalty. But there is a larger demand, measured in the standard mass-culture measure of sales, for approval of any kind of brutality whatsoever, provided it is associated with expensive consumer goods and machinery, and directed against political enemies, national or ethnic aliens, or women.

An interesting mass-culture phenomenon is the spy-fiction factory recently reported in the *New York Times* book review section. As indicated above, American culture has no immediate Imperial or literary connection with espionage such as that which involved British writers of respectable talents and serious intentions. But the market has been created, and an entrepreneur named L. Kenyon Engel employs sixty-four writers to fill in the outlines of plots and characters as directed by him. Like James Bond, the values revert to an earlier type: the principal figure is Nick Carter, a railroad detective created in the 1870s, tales about whom were manufactured for years by Street and Smith. It is safe to bet that no moral issues arise in these productions, no self-doubt, no detestation of superiors.

Whether real or fictional spies are right in distrusting their administrators, and vice versa, may perhaps be partially illuminated by the following jocular exchange between a couple of their ultimate employers:

> Allen W. Dulles (then director CIA): "You, Mr. Chairman, may have seen some of my intelligence reports."
> Mr. Khrushchev: "I believe we get the same reports—and probably from the same people."
> Mr. Dulles: "Maybe we should pool our efforts."
> Mr. Khrushchev: "Yes. We should buy our intelligence data together and save money. We'd have to pay the people only once."
> —News Item, Sept. 1959

Quoted by Len Deighton, at beginning of *Funeral in Berlin.*

REFERENCES

Aubert, V., *"Secrecy: the underground as a social system,"* in *The Hidden Society*, Bedminster Press, 1965.

Orlov, Alexander, *Handbook of Intelligence and Guerilla Warfare*, First U.S. publication, 1963, The Univ. of Michigan Press, Ann Arbor. Preface to this edition:

"Before World War II, when I was one of the chiefs of the Soviet intelligence, I lectured at the Central Military School in Moscow on the tactics and strategy of intelligence and counterintelligence. In 1936 I wrote down the basic rules and principles of Soviet intelligence in the form of a manual which was approved as the only textbook for the newly created NKVD schools for undercover intelligence officers and for the Central Military School in Moscow.

Because intelligence has gained considerable importance in world affairs and has become a regular subject in the curricula of American and other Western military colleges, the University of Michigan Press has commissioned me with the reconstruction of the intelligence manual. I did it in a way that I thought would be suitable for the specialist and the layman alike.
> —Alexander Orlov,
> New York

Page, Bruce, Leitch, David, and Knightley, Phillip, *Philby, The Spy Who Betrayed a Generation,* Intro. by John Le Carré, Andre Deutsch Ltd, 1968; rev. ed., Penguin, 1969.

Bruce Page is Executive Editor of the *Sunday Times;* David Leitch is a Special Correspondent of the *Sunday Times,* based in Paris; Phillip Knightley is also a special correspondent of the *Sunday Times.*

Sissons, Michael, and French, Philip, eds., *Age of Austerity, 1945–1951,* Hodder and Stoughton, 1963; Penguin, 1964.

Fiction and Semifiction

Deighton, Len, *The Ipcress File,* 1962; *Horse Under Water,* 1963; *Funeral in Berlin,* 1964; *Billion Dollar Brain,* 1966; *An Expensive Place to Die,* 1967; *Only When I Larf,* 1968.
Greene, Graham, *Our Man in Havana,* first pub. 1958.
Innes, Michael, *The Journeying Boy,* Gollancz, first pub. 1949.
Kipling, Rudyard, *Kim,* first pub. 1901.
Le Carré, John, *Deadly Affair,* first pub. as *Call for the Dead,* 1961; *A Murder of Quality,* 1962; *The Spy Who Came in from the Cold,* 1963; *The Looking-Glass War,* 1965; *A Small Town in Germnay,* 1968.
Maugham, Somerset, *Ashenden, the British Agent,* Doubleday Doran, first pub. 1928.
Sayers, Dorothy L., *Have his Carcass,* Gollancz, first pub. 1932.

James Bond Unmasked*

By Mordecai Richler

In our time, no books, no films, have enjoyed such a dazzling international success as the James Bond stories. But the impact was not instantaneous. When *Casino Royale* appeared in 1953 the reviews were good, but three American publishers rejected the book and sales were mediocre, which was a sore disappointment to Bond's unabashedly self-promoting author, Ian Fleming, then forty-three years old.

By the spring of 1966 the thirteen Bond novels had been translated into twenty-six different languages and had sold more than forty-five million copies. The movie versions of *Doctor No; From Russia With Love; Goldfinger;* and *Thunderball* had been seen by some one hundred million people and were in fact among the most profitable ever produced. Bond has spawned a flock of imitators, including Matt Helm, Quiller, and Boysie Oakes. More than two hundred commercial products, ranging from men's toiletries to bubble gum, have been authorized to carry the official Bond trademark. Only recently, after a fantastic run, has the boom in Bond begun to slump. Or has it? Kingsley Amis, an honest devotee, has been commissioned to continue the adventures of Fleming's hero. A new Bond, *Colonel Sun,* has been published recently, and is already a best-seller in England.

The success of Bond is all the more intriguing because Ian Fleming was such an appalling writer. He had no sense of place that scratched deeper than Sunday-supplement travel articles or route maps, a much-favored device. His celebrated use of insider's facts and O.K. brand names, especially about gunmanship and the international high life, has been faulted again and again. Eric Ambler and Graham Greene (in his entertainments) have written vastly superior spy stories, and when Fleming

---

ventured into the American underworld, he begged comparison with Mickey Spillane, not with such original stylists as Dashiell Hammett and Raymond Chandler. He had a resoundingly tin ear, as witness a Harlem Negro talking, vintage 1954 *(Live and Let Die):*

> Yuh done look okay yoself, honeychile . . . an' dat's da troof. But Ah mus' spressify dat yuh stays close up tuh me an keeps you eyes offn dat low-down trash'n his hot pants. 'N Ah may say . . . dat ef Ah ketches yuh makin' up tah dat dope Ah'll jist nacherlly whup do hide off'n yo sweet ass.

Or, as an example of the recurring American gangster, Sol "Horror" Horowitz *(The Spy Who Loved Me):*

> The lady's right. You didn't ought to of spilled that java, Sluggsy. But ya see, lady, that's why they call him Sluggsy, on account he's smart with the hardware.

As Fleming was almost totally without the ability to create character through distinctive action or dialogue, he generally fell back on villains who are physically grotesque. So Mr. Big has "a great football of a head, twice the normal size and very nearly round," hairless, with no eyebrows and no eyelashes, the eyes bulging slightly and the irises golden round black pupils. Doctor No's head "was elongated and tapered from a round, completely bald skull down to a sharp chin so that the impression was of a reversed rain drop—or rather oildrop, for the skin was of a deep almost translucent yellow."

Each Bond novel, except for *The Spy Who Loved Me,* follows an unswerving formula, though the sequence of steps is sometimes shuffled through the introduction of flashbacks:

1. Bond, bored by inactivity, is summoned by M for a mission.
2. Bond and villain confront each other tentatively.
3. A sexy woman is introduced and seduced by Bond. If she is in cahoots with villain, she will find Bond irresistible and come over to his side.
4. Villain captures Bond and punishes him (torture, usually), then reveals his diabolical scheme. "As you will never get out of this alive . . ." or, "It is rare that I have the opportunity to talk to a man of your intelligence. . . ."
5. Bond escapes, triumphs over villain, destroying his vile plot.
6. Bond and sexy woman are now allowed their long-delayed tryst.

This basic formula is usually tarted-up by two devices:

1. We, the unwashed, are granted a seemingly knowledgeable, insider's peek at a glamorous industry or institution—say, diamond or gold smuggling; the Royal College of Arms, Blades, and other elegant clubs. This makes for long chapters of all but unbroken exposition, rather like fawning magazine articles.

2. We are taken on a Fleming guided tour of an exotic locale: Las Vegas, Japan, the West Indies. This also makes for lengthy, insufferably knowing expository exchanges, rather thinly disguised travel notes, as, for example, when Tiger Tanaka educates Bond to Japanese mores *(You Only Live Twice).*

Not surprisingly, considering Fleming's boyish frame of mind, competitive games figure prominently in the Bond mythology, as do chases in snob cars or along model railways. The deadly card game, Bond against the villain, is another repeated set piece *(Casino Royale, Moonraker, Goldfinger).*

A recurring character in the Bond adventures is the American Felix Leiter, once with the CIA, later with Pinkerton's. Leiter, an impossibly stupid and hearty fellow, is cut from the same cloth as the cold-war comic strip heroes Buzz Sawyer and Steve Canyon. A born gee-whiz, gung-ho type.

If Fleming's sense of character is feeble and his powers of invention limited, the sadism and heated sex I was led to expect turned out to be tepid. A roll-call of Bond's girls yields Vesper Lynd, Solitaire, Gala Brand, Tiffany Case, Honeychile Rider, Pussy Galore, Domino Vitali, Kissy Suzuki, Mary Goodnight. As the perfume-brand labels indicate, the girls are clockwork objects rather than people. The composite Bond girl, as Kingsley Amis has already noted, can be distinguished by her beautiful firm breasts, each, I might add, with its pointed stigma of desire. The Bond girls are healthy, outdoor types, but they are not all perfectly made. Take Honeychile Rider, for instance: café au lait skin, ash blonde hair, naked on first meeting except for a wide leather belt round her waist with a hunting knife in a leather sheath, she suffers from a badly broken nose, smashed crooked like a boxer's. Then there's the question of Honeychile's behind, which was "almost as firm and rounded as a boy's"—a description which brought Fleming a letter from Noel Coward. "I was slightly shocked," Coward wrote, "by the lascivious announcement that Honeychile's bottom was like a boy's. I know that we are all becoming progressively more broad-minded nowadays but really, old chap, what *could* you have been thinking of?"

Descriptions of clad Bond girls tend to focus on undergarments. Jill Masterson, on first encounter in *Goldfinger,* is naked except for a black bra and briefs. Tatiana, in *From Russia, With Love,* is discovered "wearing nothing but the black ribbon round her neck and black silk stockings rolled above her knees." Not that I object to a word of it. After all, sexy, unfailingly available girls are a legitimate and most enjoyable convention of thrillers and spy stories. If I find Fleming's politics distasteful (more about this, later), his occasional flirtation with ideas embarrassing, I am happy to say that I am in accord with him in admiring firm, thrusting, beautiful breasts.

Unlike Harold Robbins, Ian Fleming does not actually linger overlong on sexual description. Or perversion. He is seldom as brutalized as Mickey Spillane is page after page. If anything, he's something of a prude. The closest he comes to obscenity is "- - - - you" in *Dr. No.* Mind you, this fastidiousness is followed hard by a detailed description of a Negro punishing a girl by squeezing her Mound of Venus between his thumb and forefinger, until his knuckles go white with the pressure. "She's Love Moun' be sore long after ma face done get healed." Other, more exquisite tortures of women follow in further adventures, usually enforced when the girls are deliciously nude, but James Bond's language never degenerates beyond an uncharacteristic imprecation in *You Only Live Twice.* "Freddie Uncle Charlie Katie," he says, meaning fuck, I take it.

The Bond novels are not so much sexy as they are boyishly smutty. James Bond's aunt, for instance, lives "in the quaintly named hamlet of Pett Bottom." There's a girl called Kissy and another named Pussy. Not one of the Bond girls, however, lubricates as sexily as does Tracy's Lancia Flaminia Zagato Spyder, "a low white two-seater . . . [with] . . . a sexy boom from its twin exhausts."

Ian Fleming was frightened of women. "Some," he wrote, "respond to the whip, some to the kiss. . . ." A woman, he felt, should be an illusion; and he was deeply upset by their bodily functions. Once, in Capri, according to his biographer, John Pearson, Fleming disowned a girl he had liked the looks of after she retired for a few moments behind a rock. "He had," a former girl friend told Pearson, "a remarkable phobia about bodily things. . . . I'm certain he would never have tied a cut finger for me. I feel he would also have preferred me not to eat and drink as well." Fleming once told Barbara Grigg of the London *Evening Standard* that "women simply are not clean—absolutely filthy, the whole lot of them. Englishwomen simply do not wash and scrub enough." So, added to the image of James Bond, never traveling without an armory of electronic devices, the latest in computerized death-dealing gadgetry, one now suspects that his fastidious creator also lugged an old-fashioned douche bag with him everywhere.

James Bond is well worth looking at in juxtaposition to his inventor, Ian Fleming.

In *Casino Royale,* Bond, staked by British Intelligence, plays a deadly game of baccarat at Royale-les-Eaux with Le Chiffre of SMERSH, and wins a phenomenal sum, thereby depriving the USSR of its budget for subversion in France. This adventure, Fleming was fond of saying, was based on a wartime trip to Lisbon with Admiral Godfrey of Naval Intelligence. At the casino, Fleming said, he engaged in a baccarat battle with a group of Nazis, hoping to strike a blow at the German economy. Alas, he lost.

Actually, John Pearson writes, "It was a decidedly dismal evening at the casino—only a handful of Portuguese were present, the stakes were low, the croupiers were bored." Fleming whispered to the unimpressed Admiral, "Just suppose those fellows were German agents—what a coup it would be if we cleaned them out entirely."

Fleming had other imaginative notions while serving the British Naval Intelligence during the war, among them the idea of sinking a great block of concrete with men inside it in the English Channel, just before the Dieppe raid, to keep watch on the harbor with periscopes. Or of freezing clouds, mooring them along the coast of southern England, and using them as platforms for anti-aircraft guns.

Fleming's trip with Admiral Godfrey did not terminate in Lisbon, but carried on to New York. Armed for the occasion with a small commando fighting knife and a fountain pen with a cyanide cartridge, as well as his Old Etonian tie, Fleming (with the Admiral) was supposed to slip into New York anonymously. "But as they went ashore from the flying boat," Pearson writes, "press photographers began to crowd around them. Although they soon realized that it was the elegant, sweet-smelling figure of Madame Schiaparelli that was attracting the cameras, the damage was done. That evening the chief of British Naval Intelligence was to be seen in the background of all the press photographs of the famous French couturiere arriving in New York."

Fleming said he wrote his first novel, *Casino Royale,* at Goldeneye, his Jamaica home, in 1952, to "take his mind off the shock of getting married at the age of forty-three." It seems possible that the inspiration for his villain, Le Chiffre, was The Great Beast 666, necromancer Aleister Crowley, who, like Mussolini, had the whites of his eyes completely visible around the iris. Crowley, incidentally, was also the model for the first novel by Fleming's literary hero, Somerset Maugham.

M, also initially introduced in *Casino Royale,* was arguably a composite figure based on Admiral Godfrey and Sir Robert Menzies, Eton and the Life Guards. M remains an obstinately unsympathetic figure even to Bond admirers. ". . . . It may be obvious," Kingsley Amis has written, "why M's frosty, damnably clear eyes are damnably clear. No thought is taking place behind them." John Pearson writes of Bond's relationship with M, "never has such cool ingratitude produced such utter loyalty." When Bond's father-figure of a villain, Le Chiffre, threatens him with castration in his first adventure, then Bond, last time out *(The Man With The Golden Gun)*, is discovered brainwashed in the opening pages and attempts to assassinate M, the unpermissive M. "In particular," Amis writes, "M dis-approves of Bond's 'womanizing,' though he never says so directly, and would evidently prefer him not to form a permanent attachment either. He barely conceals his glee at the news that Bond is after all not going to marry Tiffany Case. This is perhaps more the attitude of a doting mother than a father."

A really perceptive observation, for Fleming, as a boy, was frightened of his stern and demanding mother and did in fact call her M.

Pearson writes in *The Life of Ian Fleming:*

Apart from Le Chiffre, M, and Vesper Lynd, the minor characters in *Casino Royale* are the merest shadows with names attached. The only other character who matters is Ian Fleming himself. For James Bond is not really a character in this book. He is a mouthpiece for the man who inhabits him, a dummy for him to hang his clothes on, a zombie to perform the dreams of violence and daring which fascinate his creator. It is only because Fleming holds so little of himself back, because he talks and dreams so freely through the device of James Bond, that the book has such readability. *Casino Royale* is really an experiment in the autobiography of dreams.

Without a doubt Fleming's dream conception of himself was James Bond, gay adventurer, two-fisted soldier of fortune, and ever the complete gentleman.

Bond renounces his occasionally vast gambling gains, donating his winnings to a service widows' fund; he is self-mocking about his heroics, avoids publicity, and once offered a knighthood, in *The Man With The Golden Gun*, he turns it down bashfully because, "He has never been a public figure and did not wish to become one . . . there was one thing above all he treasured. His privacy. His anonymity." In this Bond parts company sharply with his creator. Ian Fleming was a chap with his eye always resolutely on the main chance.

"Most authors, particularly when they begin," Pearson writes dryly, "leave details of publication to their agents or to the goodwill of the publisher." Not so Fleming, who instantly submitted a plan for "Advertising and Promotion" to his publisher, Jonathan Cape. Copies of *Casino Royale* were ready by March 1953. Without delay, Fleming wrote a letter to the editors of all Lord Kemsley's provincial newspapers, sending it off with an autographed copy of his book. "Dr. Jekyll has written this blatant thriller in his spare time, and it may amuse you. If you don't think it too puerile for Sheffield or Stockport, Macclesfield, Middlesborough, Blackburn, etc., it would be wonderful if you would hand a copy with a pair of tongs to your reviewer."

This jokey little note, properly read, was an order from the bridge to the chaps on the lower-deck, for Fleming was a known intimate of Lord Kemsley as well as foreign news manager of the *Sunday Times,* then the Kemsley flagship, so to speak.

Fleming also astutely sent a copy of his novel to Somerset Maugham, who replied, "It goes with a swing from the first page to the last and is really thrilling all through. . . . You really managed to get the tension to the highest possible pitch." If James Bond would have cherished such a private tribute from an old man, Ian Fleming immediately grasped its commercial potential, and wrote back, "Dear Willie, I have just got your letter. When I am seventy-nine shall I waste my time reading such a book and taking the trouble to write to the author in my own hand? I pray so, but I doubt it. I am even more flattered and impressed after catching a glimpse of the empestered life you lead at Cap Ferrat, deluged with fan mail, besieged by the press, inundated with bumpf of one sort or another. . . . Is it bad literary manners to ask if my publishers may quote from your letter? Please advise me—as a 'parain,' not as a favor to me and my publishers."

Maugham replied, "Please don't use what I said about your book to advertise it."

As the sales of *Casino Royale* were disappointing, Fleming turned to writing the influential Atticus gossip column in the *Sunday Times,* which provided him with a convenient platform to flatter those whose favors he sought. After Lord Kemsley refused to run a *Sunday Times* Portrait Gallery puff of Lord Beaverbrook on his seventy-sixth birthday, he did allow Fleming, following some special pleading, to celebrate Beaverbrook in his column. "History will have to decide whether he or Northcliffe was the greatest newspaperman of this half century. In the sense that he combines rare journalistic flair, the rare quality of wonder . . . with courage and vitality . . . the verdict may quite possibly go to Lord Beaverbrook. . . ."

Beaverbrook, who had an insatiable appetite for flattery, bought the serial rights to the next Bond novel and later ran a Bond comic strip in the *Daily Express,* with the upshot that James Bond, once only a *Times* reader, began to take the *Express* as well.

Once Macmillan undertook to publish *Casino Royale* in America, Fleming's self-advertisement campaign accelerated. He wrote to a friend asking him to influence Walter Winchell into plugging the book. He wrote to Iva Patcevitch, saying, "If you can possibly give it a shove in *Vogue* or elsewhere, Anna and I will allow you to play canasta against us, which should be ample reward." He also wrote to Fleur Cowles and Margaret Case. "You will soon be fed up with this book as I have sent copies around to all our friends asking them to give it a hand in America, which is a very barefaced way to go on. . . . I know Harry Luce won't be bothered with it, or Clare, but if you could somehow prevail upon *Time* to give it a review you would be an angel."

In 1955, the sales of his books still dragging, Fleming met Raymond Chandler at a dinner party. At the time, Chandler was an old and broken man, incoherent with drink. "He was very nice to me," Fleming wrote, "and said he liked my first book, *Casino Royale,* but he didn't really want to talk about anything except the loss of his wife, about which he expressed himself with a nakedness that embarrassed me while endearing him to me."

If the battered old writer, whom Fleming professed to admire, was tragically self-absorbed, he was, all the same, instantly sent a copy of Fleming's forthcoming *Live and Let Die.* "A few days later," Pearson writes, "Chandler telephoned Fleming to say how much he had enjoyed it, and went on to ask the author—vaguely, perhaps—if he would care for him to endorse the book for the benefit of his publishers—the kind of thing he was always refusing to do in the United States and a subject on which, in his published letters, he displays such ferocious cynicism. 'Rather unattractively,' Fleming wrote later, 'I took him up on his suggestion.' "

Chandler was as good as his word, Pearson goes on to say, "although it sounds as if it was rather a struggle. On May 25 he wrote pathetically to Fleming apologizing for taking so long—'in fact, lately I have had a very difficult time reading at all.' " But a week later he came through for Fleming, his blurb beginning, "Ian Fleming is probably the most *forceful* and *driving* writer of what I suppose still must be called thrillers in England . . . ." (Emphasis mine.) Chandler's letter of praise ended, somewhat ambiguously, "If this is any good to you, would you like me to have it engraved on a slab of gold?"

Fleming was also able to find uses for a burnt-out prime minister. In November 1956, twelve days after the Suez cease-fire, it was announced that Prime Minister Anthony Eden was ill from the effects of severe overstrain. It became necessary to find a secluded spot where Eden could recuperate, and so Alan Lennox-Boyd, then Secretary of State for Colonial Affairs and a friend of the Flemings, approached Ian Fleming about Goldeneye, his home in Jamaica. Fleming, flattered by the choice, neglected to say there were only iron bedsteads at Goldeneye, there was no hot water in the shower, and there was no bathroom, but there were bush rats in the roof. He did not advise Lennox-Boyd that Noel Coward's home nearby, or Sir William Stephenson's, would have been far more commodious for an ailing man. He did not even say that the Prime Minister would be without a telephone at Goldeneye. "The myth of Goldeneye was about to enter history," John Pearson writes, "it was too much to expect its creator to upset it."

Sir Anthony and Lady Eden set off for Goldeneye and Fleming sat back in Kent to write to Macmillan. "I hope that the Eden's visit to Goldeneye has done something to my American sales. Here there have been full-page spreads of the property, including Violet emptying ashtrays and heaven knows what-all. It has really been a splendid week and greatly increased the value of the property until Anne started talking to reporters about barracuda, the hardness of the beds, and curried goat. Now some papers treat the place as if it was a hovel and others as if it was the millionaire home of some particularly disgusting millionaire tax dodger . . . ." Two weeks later the bush rats caught up with Fleming. The London *Evening Standard* reported that Sir Anthony, troubled by rats during the night, had organized a hunt. Fleming, distressed, wrote to a friend, "The greatly increased rental value was brought down sharply by a completely dreamed-up report to the effect that Goldeneye was overrun by rats and that the Edens and the detectives had spent the whole night chasing them . . . ."

The Prime Minister's stay at Goldeneye brought Fleming to the attention of a public far wider than his books had so far managed for him. It was now, Pearson writes, that Fleming's public began to change. "Up to then he had been 'the Peter Cheyney of the carriage trade'. . . . After Eden's visit . . . many people were interested . . . (and) . . . began to read him. After five long years the 'best-seller stakes' had begun in earnest . . . if Fleming with his flair for self-promotion had planned the whole thing himself it could hardly have been better done."

*   *   *

Commander James Bond, CMG, RNVR, springs from a long line of secret service agents and club-land heroes, including William Le Queux's incomparable Duckworth Drew:

> Before I could utter aught save a muffled curse, I was flung head first into an empty piano case, the heavy lid of which was instantly closed on me . . . I had been tricked!

Sapper's Bulldog Drummond; and John Buchan's Richard Hannay:

> He began to snort now and his breath came heavily. "You infernal cad," I said in good round English. "I'm going to knock the stuffing out of you," but he didn't understand what I was saying.

Bond, whose double-O prefix in the Secret Service gives him a license to kill, sees himself as a "gay soldier of fortune," without personal animosity against England's enemies:

> This was merely his job—as it was the job of a pest control officer to kill rats. He was the public executioner appointed by M to represent the community. . . .

But he is distressed by an England where carrots have become all the fashion, and the government, at home and abroad,. "doesn't show teeth any more—only gums." The trouble is that while he risks his neck abroad, ungrateful England continues to deteriorate. Typical is a "foxy, pimpled" young taxi driver whom Bond encounters on a visit home. The young man slowly runs a comb through both sides of his duck-tail haircut before starting his car:

> The play with the comb, Bond guessed, was to assert to Bond that the driver was really only taking him and his money as a favor. It was typical of the cheap self-assertiveness of young labor since the war. This youth, thought Bond, makes about twenty pounds a week, despises his

parents and would like to be Tommy Steele. It's not his fault. He was born into the buyer's market of the Welfare State. . . .

Duckworth Drew, Drummond, Hannay, carried with them on their adventures abroad an innate conviction of the British gentleman's superiority in all matters, a mystique acknowledged by wogs everywhere. Not so James Bond, who in his penultimate adventure, *You Only Live Twice,* must sit through the humiliating criticism of Tiger Tanaka, Head of the Japanese secret service, who tells Bond that the British have not only lost a great empire, they have seemed almost anxious to throw it away, stage-managing, at Suez, one of the most pitiful bungles in the history of the world:

> . . . Furthermore, your governments have shown themselves successively incapable of ruling and have handed over effective control of the country to the trade unions, who appear dedicated to the principle of doing less and less work for more money . . . sapping at ever-increasing speed the moral fiber of the British, a quality the world once so much admired. In its place we now see a vacuous, aimless horde of seekers-after-pleasure, gambling at the pools and bingo, whining at the weather and the declining fortunes of the country . . . .

Richard Hannay, to be sure, would have knocked the stuffing out of just such a jabbering Jap. Hannay, in his thumping, roseate time, could boast that in peace and war, by God, there was nothing to beat the British Secret Service, but poor James Bond could not make the same claim without appearing ludicrous even to himself.

If once British commanders sallied forth jauntily to plant the flag here, there, and everywhere, or to put down infernally caddish natives, today they come with order books for Schweppes. Duckworth Drew, Drummond, and Hannay, were all Great Britons: Bond's a Little Englander.

England, England.

James Bond is a meaningless fantasy cutout unless he is tacked to the canvas of diminishing England. After the war, Sir Harold Nicolson wrote in his diary, he feared his way of life was coming to an end; he and his wife, Victoria Sackville-West, would have to walk and live a "Woolworth life." Already, in 1941, it was difficult to find a sufficient number of gardeners to tend to Sissinghurst, and the Travellers' Club had become a battered caravanserai inhabited only by "the scum of the lower London clubs."

In 1945, Labor swept into office with the cry, "We are the masters now." Ten years later in Fleming/Bond's time, the last and possibly the most docile of the British colonies, the indigenous lower-middle and working-class, rebelled again, this time demanding not free medical care and pension schemes, already torn from the state by their elders, but a commanding voice in the arts and letters. Briefly, a new style in architecture. So we had Osborne, Amis, Braine, Sillitoe, and Wesker, among others.

The gentlemen's England, where everyone knew his place in the natural order, the England which Sir Harold Nicolson, Bobbety [the 5th Marquess of Salisbury], Chips [Sir Henry Channon], and Boofy [the Earl of Arran], had been educated to govern, was indeed a war victim. Come Ian Fleming we are no longer dealing with gentlemen, but with a parody-gentleman. Look at it this way: Sir Harold Nicolson collected books because he cherished them; Ian Fleming amassed first editions because, with Britain's place unsure and the pound declining, he grasped their market value. Similarly, if the cry of God, King, and Empire, was now laughable, it was also, providing the packaging was sufficiently shrewd, very, very salable.

Little England's increasingly humiliating status has spawned a blinkered romanticism on the Left and on the Right. On the Left, it has given us CND (the touching assumption that it matters morally to the world whether or not England gives up the Bomb unilaterally) and anti-Americanism. On the Right, there is the decidedly more expensive fantasy that this off-shore island can still confront the world as Great Britain. If the brutal facts, the familiar facts, are that England has been unable to adjust to its shriveled island status, largely because of antiquated industry, economic mismanagement, a fusty civil service, and reactionary trade unions, then the comforting right-wing pot-dream is that virtuous Albion is beset by disruptive Communists within and foreign devils and conspirators without.

Largely, this is what James Bond is about.

Bond's most pernicious enemies head, or work for, hidden international conspiracies, usually SMERSH or SPECTRE. SMERSH, first described in *Casino Royale,* is the conjunction of two Russian words: *"Smyert Shpionam,"* meaning roughly: "Death to Spies." It was, in 1953, under the personal direction of Beria, with headquarters in Leningrad and a sub-station in Moscow, and ranked above MVD (formerly NKVD).

SPECTRE is The Special Executive Counterintelligence, Terrorism, Revenge, and Extortion, a private enterprise for private profit, and its founder and chairman is Ernst Stavro Blofeld. SPECTRE's headquarters are in Paris, on the Boulevard Haussmann. Not the Avenue d'Iena, the richest street in Paris, Fleming writes, because "too many of the landlords and tenants in the Avenue d'Iena have names ending in 'esou,' 'ovitch,' 'ski,' and 'stein,' and these are sometimes not the ending of respectable names." If you stopped at SPECTRE's headquarters, at 136 *bis* Boulevard Haussmann, you would find a discreetly glittering brass plate, that says FIRCO and, underneath, *Fraternité Internationale de la Résistance Contre l'Oppression.* FIRCO's stated aim is to keep alive the ideals that flourished during the last war among members of all resistance groups. It was most active during International Refugee Year.

SMERSH and SPECTRE are both inclined to secret congresses, usually called to plot the political or financial ruin or even the physical destruction of the freedom-loving West. As secret organizations go, SMERSH is growth stuff. As described in *Casino Royale,* in 1953, it was "believed to consist of only a few hundred operatives of very high quality," but only two years later, as set out in *From Russia, With Love,* SMERSH employed a total of forty thousand men and women. Its headquarters had also moved from Leningrad to a rather posh setup in Moscow, which I take to be a sign of favor. In *Goldfinger,* there is a SMERSH-inspired secret congress of America's leading mobsters brought together with the object of sacking Fort Knox. The initial covert meeting of SPECTRE, elaborately described in *Thunderball,* reveals a conspiracy to steal two atomic weapons from a NATO airplane and then threaten the British Prime Minister with the nuclear destruction of a major city unless a ransom of 100 million pounds sterling is forthcoming. SPECTRE next conspires against England in *On Her Majesty's Secret Service.* Blofeld, the organization's evil genius, has retired to a Swiss plateau and hypnotized some lovely British girls, infecting them with deadly crop and livestock diseases which they are to carry back to England, spreading pestilence.

Foreign conspiracy. In an earlier time, John Buchan, 1st Lord Tweedsmuir of Elsfield, Governor-General of Canada, and author of *The Thirty-Nine Steps* and four other Richard Hannay novels, was also obsessed with vile plots against Albion, but felt no need to equivocate. We are barely into the *Thirty-Nine Steps,* when we are introduced to Scudder, the brave and good spy, whom Hannay takes to be "a sharp, restless fellow, who always wanted to get down to the roots of things." Scudder tells Hannay that behind all the governments and the armies there was a big subterranean movement going on, engineered by a very dangerous people. Most of them were the sort of educated anarchists that make revolutions, but beside them there were financiers who were playing for money. It suited the books of both classes of conspirators to set Europe by the ears:

> When I asked Why, he said that the anarchist lot thought it would give them their chance . . . they looked to see a new world emerge. The capitalists would . . . make fortunes by buying up the wreckage. Capital, he said, had no conscience and no fatherland. Besides, the Jew was behind it, and the Jew hated Russia worse than hell.
> "Do you wonder?" he cried. "For three hundred years they have been persecuted, and this is the return match for the *pogroms.* The Jew is everywhere, but you have to go far down the backstairs to find him. Take any big Teutonic business concern. If you have dealings with it the first man you meet is Prince *von und* zu Something, an elegant young man who talks Eton-and-Harrow English. But he cuts no ice. If your business is big, you get behind him and find a prognathous Westphalian with a retreating brow and the manners of a hog. . . . But if you're on the biggest kind of job and are bound to get to the real

boss, ten to one you are brought up against a little white-faced Jew in a bathchair with an eye like a rattlesnake. Yes, sir, he is the man who is ruling the world just now, and he has his knife in the Empire of the Tzar, because his aunt was outraged and his father flogged in some one-horse location on the Volga."

The clear progenitor of these conspiracies against England is the notorious anti-Semitic forgery, *The Protocols of the Elders of Zion,* which first appeared in Western Europe in 1920 and had, by 1930, been circulated through the world in millions of copies. The *Protocols* had been used to incite massacres of Jews during the Russian civil war, being especially helpful in fomenting the pogrom at Kishinev in Bessarabia in 1903. From Russia, the *Protocols* traveled to Nazi Germany. Recently, they were serialized in a Cairo newspaper.

The history of the *Protocols,* and just how they were tortuously evolved from another forgery, *Dialogue aux Enfers entre Montesquieu et Machival,* by a French lawyer called Maurice Joly, in 1864, has already been definitively traced by Norman Cohn in his *Warrant For Genocide;* and so I will limit myself to brief comments here.

Editions of the *Protocols* are often preceded by an earlier invention, *The Rabbi's Speech,* that could easily serve as a model for later dissertations, on the glories of power and evil as revealed to James Bond by Auric Goldfinger, Sir Hugo Drax *(Moonraker),* and Blofeld. Like Auric Goldfinger, the Rabbi believes gold is the strength, the recompense, the sum of everything man fears and craves. "The day," he says, "when we shall have made ourselves the sole possessors of all the gold in the world, the real power will be in our hands." Like Sir Hugo Drax, the Rabbi understands the need for market manipulation. "The surest means of attaining [power] is to have supreme control over all industrial, financial, and commercial operations. . . ." SMERSH would envy the Rabbi's political acumen. "So far as possible we must talk to the proletariat. . . . We will drive them to upheavals, to revolutions; and each of these catastrophes marks a big step forward for our . . . sole aim—world domination."

The twenty-four protocols purport to be made up of lectures delivered to the Jewish secret government, the Elders of Zion, on how to achieve world-domination. Tangled and contradictory, the main idea is that the Jews, spreading confusion and terror, will eventually take over the globe. Like SPECTRE, they will use liberalism as a front. Like Mr. Big *(Live and Let Die),* they will foster discontent and unrest. The common people will be directed to overthrow their rulers and then a despot will be put in power. As there are more evil than good men in the world, force—the Elders have concluded—is the only sure means of government. Underground railways—a big feature in all versions of the *Protocols*—will be constucted in major cities, so that the Elders could counter any organized rebellion by blowing capital cities to smithereens—a recurring threat in the Bond novels.

In fact the more one scrutinizes the serpentine plots in Ian Fleming's novels, the more it would seem that the Elders *are* in conspiracy against England. Not only are they threatening to blow up London, but they would seize the largest store of the world's gold, back disruptive labor disputes, run dope into the country, and infect British crops and livestock with deadly pests.

Which brings me to two final points. It is possible to explain the initial success of the Bond novels in that if they came at a time when vicious anti-Semitism and neo-Fascist xenophobia were no longer acceptable in England, then a real need as well as a large audience for such reading matter still existed. It was Fleming's most brilliant stroke to present himself not as an old-fashioned, frothing wog-hater, but as an ostensibly civilized voice who offered sanitized racialism instead. The Bond novels not only satisfy Little Englanders who believe they have been undone by dastardly foreign plotters, but pander to their continuing notion of self-importance. So when the Head of SMERSH, Colonel General Gruboza-boyshikov, known as "G," summons a high level conference to announce that it has become necessary to inflict an act of terrorism aimed at the heart of the Intelligence apparat of the West, it is (on the advice of General Vozdvishensky) the British Secret Service that he chooses:

". . . . I think we all have respect for [England's] Intelligence Service," General Vozdvishensky looked around the table. There were grudging nods from everyone present, including General G. ". . . Their Secret Service . . . agents are good. They pay them little money. . . . They are rarely awarded a decoration until they retire. And yet these men and women continue to do this dangerous work. It is curious. It is perhaps the Public School and University tradition. The love of adventure. But it is odd they play this game so well, for they are not natural conspirators."

Kingsley Amis writes that "To use foreigners as villains is a convention older than our literature. It's not in itself a symptom of intolerance about foreigners. . . ."

Amis's approach is so good-natured, so ostensibly reasonable, that to protest no, no, is to seem an entirely humorless left-wing nag, a Hampstead harpie. I am not, God help me, suing for that boring office. I do not object to the use of foreigners per se as villains. I am even willing to waive moral objections to a writer in whose fictions no Englishman ever does wrong and only Jews or black or yellow men fill the villain's role. However, even in novels whose primary purpose is to entertain, I am entitled to ask for a modicum of plausibility. And so, while I would grudgingly agree with Amis that there is nothing wrong in choosing foreigners for villains, I must add that it is—in the context of contemporary England—an inaccuracy. A most outrageous inaccuracy. After all, even on the narrow squalid level of Intelligence, the most sensational betrayals have come from men who, to quote General G of SMERSH, were so admirably suited to their work by dint of their Public School and University traditions: Guy Burgess, Donald Maclean, and Kim Philby. It should be added, hastily added, that none of these three men, contrary to the Fleming style, was an ogre or sold out for gold. Rightly or wrongly, they acted on political principle. And their real value to the KBG (a final insult) was not their British information, but the American secrets they were a party to.

Kingsley Amis and I, the people he drinks with, the people I drink with, are neither anti-Semitic nor color prejudiced, however divergent their politics. We circulate in a sheltered society. Not so my children, which brings me to my primary motive for writing this essay.

The minority man, as Norman Mailer has astutely pointed out, grows up with a double-image of himself, his own and society's. My boys are crazy about the James Bond movies, they identify with 007, as yet unaware that they have been cast as the villains of the dramas. As a boy I was brought up to revere John Buchan, then Lord Tweedsmuir, Governor-General of Canada. Before he came to speak at Junior Red Cross Prize Day, we were told that he stood for the ultimate British virtues. Fair play, clean living, gentlemanly conduct. We were not forewarned that he was also an ignorant, nasty-minded anti-Semite. I discovered this for myself, reading *The Thirty-Nine Steps.* As badly as I wanted to identify with Richard Hannay, two-fisted soldier of fortune, I couldn't without betraying myself. My grandfather, *pace* Buchan, went in fear of being flogged in some one-horse location on the Volga, which was why we were in Canada. However, I owe to Buchan the image of my grandfather as a little white-faced Jew with an eye like a rattlesnake. It is an image I briefly responded to, alas, if only because Hannay, so obviously on the side of the good, accepted it without question. This, possibly, is why I've grown up to loathe Buchan, Fleming, and their sort.

Advertising

Aldous Huxley, in a parody of Winston Churchill's famous epithet aptly described the phenomenon of modern advertising, "Never have so many been manipulated so much by so few." We are constantly being reminded by the Madison Avenue savants that without their skills and guiles, their empirical know-how and symbol-transforming magic, the wheels of industry would slow down, God forbid, to a grinding, corrosive halt. Without their selfless labors on behalf of Mr. Average American, the cost of a tube of toothpaste or some underarm deodorant would be so expensive that only the economic elite could afford these items. These doctors of words proudly claim to have saved America from athlete's foot, halitosis, and hemorrhoids, and thus preserved the American way of life. Always abreast of the times, modern advertising technology does not shy away from even the most delicate areas of the consumer's privacy, successfully marketing in recent years gynecological products flavored with raspberry, lemon, and lime fragrances.

Perhaps the majority of Americans thrive on being persuaded several times each day that a blue toothpaste with red and white stripes is better for their love life than a red dentrifice with green flecks. After all, it gives us a chance to "vote" for one product over another, to be sought after by giant industries, and to keep the American Dream an economically viable entity.

But these benefits are not without a price, for whether the consumer realizes it or not, the $20 billion spent for advertising each year in the United States becomes part of the cost of a bar of Ivory soap, Westinghouse dishwasher, or General Motors automobile. There is another kind of price: to have your sensibility constantly bombarded with innocuous jingles, mind-insulting television commercials, and the constant gnawing innuendo that unless you have the latest model of everything you are some kind of unpatriotic, almost subversive, alien who is out of tune with American values.

Samm Sinclair Baker, an émigré from Madison Avenue, describes advertising as "the permissible lie." His essay, in this section, not only considers the "flatulent puffery" of many ads, but the outright absurdity as well. He cites a two page spread in *Life* magazine for which Quaker Oats spent about $85,000, which stated "Mama, make them (the kids) laugh, tell them Quaker Oats is a kind of love-pat for tummies." Absurd? Maybe, but in the world of marginal differentiation who cares?

It was inevitable that the techniques and casuistic logic of the advertising world would become an integral part of the electoral process. Television was the ultimate tool for selling a president, for here at last was the instrument that enabled the candidate to come into your home, to be seen by fifty million voters at a time. Now the only reason for campaign whistle-stops (with a few thousand partisans in the crowd) was to snag a minute or two on Walter Cronkite's news show, or to draw a comment from David Brinkley or Howard K. Smith.

No doubt about it, by 1968 television had become *the* medium. In *The Selling of the President, 1968,* Joe McGinnis produced a circumstantial account of that TV campaign, the contempt which its manipulators felt for the political goods they were merchandizing and the consummate skill with which they did it. The document, a part of which we excerpt in this section, is clearly tendentious—and utterly revealing. Written with much malice aforethought, this little narrative nevertheless thrusts us squarely into the dark side of a new decade through which mass culture will loom larger than ever.

Advertising: The Permissible Lie[*]

By Samm Sinclair Baker

"Only truth smells sweet forever," wrote a philosopher, "and illusions are deadly as a cankerworm." Admen frequently use tricks of illusion and distortion, knowing that the eye is quicker than the ear, as in TV commercials like the following:

In a Bayer Aspirin commercial exposed repeatedly to millions, the announcer said: "Yes, aspirin is what doctors recommend. . . ." He simultaneously held up a package of Bayer Aspirin. He didn't *say* that doctors recommend Bayer, but this is the impression the viewers I questioned received from his gesture. Such "innocent" misleading stratagems are a specific part of many TV commercials.

The ad-lib radio commercial contributes to this problem. Here is a sequence by the popular team of Klavan and Finch on a leading New York station, WNEW:

"I wouldn't be here if it weren't for Bayer Aspirin."

"Oh, you felt terrible and Bayer made you well enough?"

"No. It takes a certain number of commercials to pay our salaries, and Bayer is one of the best-paying sponsors. So if it wasn't for them I wouldn't be here."

"Hmmm. Well, anyhow, you were smart to take it because doctors say take Bayer Aspirin for a cold because it's the best," etc., etc.

Undoubtedly the copy prepared by Bayer's agency was: "Doctors say take aspirin for a cold." However the ad-lib boys said that doctors recommend Bayer specifically.

Admen generally know that ad-lib deejays (disc jockeys, record spinners) can get away with statements that would bring disapproval from

---

* This article is an excerpt from the author's book *The Permissible Lie, the Inside Truth About Advertising,* published by Beacon Press in a paperbook edition, and is reproduced by permission of the author.

government agencies. The ad-lib boys encourage this practice in order to get more advertising. There's very little chance of FTC inspectors listening and catching such infractions. If caught, the adman shows the original "safe" copy and says, "Sorry, the ad-lib boys went overboard in their enthusiasm. We'll caution them to make sure it never happens again."

Meanwhile, back at the station, an agencyman is telling the deejays, "Look, fellows, if you want to slant the commercial a little, exaggerate some, the sponsor won't mind at all." Although some agencymen frown on this trickery, it's practically standard procedure, as agencies strive to please the sponsor.

I met a disc jockey at a party a few days after I'd heard him tell on the radio how much his family loves "Popsies." I said, "We tried them at home and sent the remainder off to the advertiser and got our money back. We thought they tasted like shredded cardboard seasoned with glue."

"So did we," he said, "but 'sincere' personal endorsement is my stock in trade."

A tricky approach often used is the line, "There's nothing just like—" as in *"There's nothing just like Sego,"* Pet Milk's reducing product. A dozen other items are very much like Sego, which followed Metrecal's success. True, none is "just like" Sego. The intent is to make you think it's much different and has a special magic which cannot be duplicated by others.

Other examples of this gambit: *"This is color television as only Sylvania makes it."* It may not be the best, as the statement implies, but it's truly "as only Sylvania makes it." Another: *"No other shortening has Crisco's formula."* A different brand of shortening may have a better formula, but it's not Crisco's. And: *"No other vermouth can endow your cocktails with the unique taste and flavor of Tribuno."* The "unique taste and flavor" may not be palatable, but it's difinitely Tribuno's.

Note the word "stay" in all kinds of hackneyed copy—"stay slim," "stay healthy," "stay young." The inference is that the product will *make* you slim, healthy, or young. Analyzed, the promise is only that if you're now slim, healthy and young, the item will help you *stay* that way.

Have you noticed the tricky comparative "er"? The advertiser has been warned that he can't promise that his product will "make you healthy." But he is permitted to say it will "keep you health*ier*." Healthier than what? Healthier than a product that contains cyanide?

"Scott [ScotTissue] *makes it better for you."* The "better" can mean most anything—better ingredients, better manufacture, better everything. Scott or any other manufacturer can't know this because they don't know all the competitors' ingredients, methods, and other vital information that establish superiority in fact as well as in words.

An advertiser may counter: " 'Better' means many things—that our products are better than they used to be, better than any other brand; if a toilet paper, better than sandpaper or carbon paper. We're not saying that our product is better than all others." But without question that's his purpose—otherwise the advertiser wouldn't spend millions on the claim.

Watch out for that treacherous word "helps." Government regulations have stopped advertisers from saying that a product *"cures* your *cold."* So copywriters switched to the glib *"helps* relieve your cold," *"helps* you stay slim." The announcer says loudly, "BRAND X WORKS FIFTEEN WAYS TO *(low)* help *(loud)* RELIEVE YOUR COLD!"

Constant subterfuge is employed by advertisers in comparisons with "other leading products." Lavoris mouthwash, a division of Vick Chemical Company, headlined: *"Tests confirm one mouthwash best against mouth odor."* They know, just as surely as any adman does, that many people won't read any copy beyond the headline and the name Lavoris. Few note that only "the four leading mouthwashes" were compared, although any one of dozens on the market might be more effective than "best" Lavoris.

I sent for "a new scientific research report" offered in the ad, and a scientist friend questioned three points instantly: First, only sixty persons were tested and form too small a sample. Second, the technique requiring "no food or drink taken during three-hour test period" after using the mouthwash isn't normal living. Third, the testing method—"direct mouth-to-nose technique" (one person blows his breath into another's nose through a concealing curtain)—is highly unscientific.

Naturally you're never told of test projects that cost millions of dollars and are thrown out because they prove advertisers' products to be inferior to others. A cartoon showed a conference with one adman saying: "Seventeen hospitals tested our product and found it completely ineffectual—but we can still advertise it as 'hospital-tested.' "

A scientist told me that he had been offered three times his present university salary to become head of the "scientific research division" to be newly established by one of the largest advertising agencies. His conscience forced him to reject the offer—"I found that they didn't want to invest in comparative projects of scientific value. Their only aim was to prove some tiny edge of superiority for the product they handled. They didn't care if it was 90% inferior in most aspects and only 10% better in one; the latter is all they would disclose. That would be 'truthful' but only as far as it went, and *untruthful* in total. I call this 'iceberg research,' where only a small part of the entire finding is revealed to the onlooker. I couldn't buy that—my family isn't that hungry."

What is deliberately left out of an ad can result in grave deception. In October 1966 the FDA took action to force revisions in medical journal ads of Upjohn Company's Lincocin, a fast-selling new prescription drug. The FDA stated that although the ads emphasized that the product would not cause kidney or nervous disorders, they did not stress equally that use sometimes resulted in severe diarrhea and blood poisoning; and that the ads did not advise doctors that sensitivity tests are recommended. Other drug firms were accused of similar omissions in their ads. An observer labeled such advertising as *"renditions of the truth."*

Listerine, Micrin, and other mouthwashes make patently exaggerated promises that use of their product spells the difference between success and failure. A typical TV commercial shows a salesman who's a flop until his daughter tells him to rinse with Listerine—then he lands the big order. In another, an executive who is slipping tries Micrin, whereupon his boss embraces him and invites him to lunch. Is there any factual basis for these preposterous claims which insult the intelligence of the viewer? I saw none in over three decades in advertising.

It's offensive at any time, and especially at the dinner hour, when commercials for Procter and Gamble's Scope and Johnson and Johnson's Micrin scream the same foul words: *"You have bad breath!"* To top them, along came a multimillion-dollar campaign: *"Listerine fights bad breath BEST!"* To compound such unproved claims, two different advertisers had their leering announcers follow up unbelievable statements with the ultimate insult: "You know it's true because you can't lie on television."

As the stench of bad-breath advertising fouled the airwaves, Wizard Deodorizer spread the miasma beyond humans with the pronouncement: *"Your HOUSE has bad breath—House-i-tosis!"* The bad-breath hurly-burly proved again that there are no limits to bad taste on Madison Avenue.

The shocker headline is a favorite decoy. An ad for St. Joseph Vitamins for Children slammed in letters half an inch high: *"Stop vitamin shortage in Children."* Then in type an eighth inch high: "A 'balanced' diet can supply all the vitamins your child *normally* needs." The headline's aim is to frighten mothers into feeling that their children have a vitamin shortage —and that St. Joseph Vitamins are a must to combat it.

An inch-high headline: *"Is baldness necessary?"* The long copy rambles on without a single direct promise or conclusion that baldness is not necessary and can be cured. Does the advertiser figure that the headline will make men feel that hair *can* be grown on bald heads?

Some ads are amazingly naïve in their deceptions, such as a sign in a store window: "Our adding machines will last a lifetime. Guaranteed for one year."

Significant oversights in advertising copy, intentional or not, are commonplace. A Volkswagen ad showed a car with a crumpled fender. The copy stated that the repair would cost only $24.95 for a new fender plus labor. A VW owner pointed out that the repair of the headlight assembly, also smashed in the photo, would add about another $18.

Much advertising aims to convince by confusing. Ads for Condition by Clairol stated: "Actually makes your hair feel stronger. . . . Revitalizes your hair's inner strength, outer beauty." A dermatologist commented, "This is advertising nonsense. No one could explain 'hair feeling stronger' sensibly because scientifically it's baseless. As for 'revitalizing inner strength,' I don't know what it means, do you?"

Another type of advertising flummery: An ad for Wolfschmidt Vodka, made in the United States, stated: "Odd . . . but true! There is a vodka labeled *genuine* that actually costs less! Its name is Wolfschmidt . . . and it costs only $3.89 a fifth." Asked what is meant by "genuine" vodka, a liquor dealer said, "Well, if it's labeled vodka, I figure it's genuine vodka. Of course if it's gin, it ain't genuine vodka, is it?"

Regarding the ad claim "actually costs less," he reacted dazedly: "At $3.89 a fifth it doesn't cost less than this 'genuine' vodka here at $3.59, or that brand at $3.49. Less than what? Do you figure that ad writer has ever been in a liquor store? One look at the shelves would show him that $3.89 vodka doesn't 'cost less' than $3.49 vodka. Who do those jerks think they're kidding?"

It's illuminating to consider further what an ad does *not* say. A number of makers of different autos and various brands of gasoline all claim to have won first prize in racing and mileage tests; an auto buff explained, "You want to know how they could all win? Easy. The cars and gasolines may be entered in many races. But they only tell in the ads about the ones they won, not those that came out the wrong way for them. A brand may win in one race and lose in six or seven others, but the ads only mention the win."

Weyenberg Shoes ran ads competing with Portage Shoes, and Portage hit at Weyenberg in their ads. For example: "The Weyenberg Shoe Company wishes the Portage Shoe Company lots of luck . . . without going into a whole treatise on the economics of competition, the Portage people have really kept us on our toes. We've had to come to grips with the fact that they make a fine shoe, and that makes us make ours a little finer." What readers were not told is that *both brands are owned by the same corporation.*

Some bank advertising was criticized as "deceptive and misleading" by New York State Superintendent of Banks, Frank Wille. "Banking institutions occupy a special position of trust," he noted. Then he pointed to deceptive ads that emphasize the high interest rate paid on a savings certificate but fail to indicate that the penalty for withdrawing the money before maturity is a loss of much of the interest. Whenever ferocious competition arises, which has happened with banks in an interest war, the penalties for withdrawal are always in small print.

With the exception of savings-bank advertising, it has been noted that any ad headlined *"Save!"* usually has one aim—to make you *spend.*

A common kind of advertising fraud is the use of foreign names on labels of merchandise made in the United States, such as Paris Sportswear made in Hoboken, New Jersey. The FTC had to order one of the biggest manufacturers of men's and women's clothing to stop printing "London" wear large on labels with "Made in U.S.A." in tiny type.

Are testimonials to be believed? A magazine ad for a product that promises a miraculous slimming effect: "Users have made enthusiastic statements like 'Lost thirteen pounds.' . . . 'Lost eighteen pounds." . . . 'Lost nine pounds.' " Admen know by experience that there are always a few people who are enthusiastic about any product. The big point that testimonials *don't* reveal is how many users were helped, whether most were happy over results, or whether three out of 300,000 were satisfied and 299,997 were disappointed.

Testimonials in general are suspect. Athletes, only one category, have recommended cereals, cigarettes, candy bars, and dozens of other products that they rarely or never use. If an advertiser wants a celebrity testimonal, several services will supply a star who will proclaim publicly, "I love Brand X," or Y, or Z—whichever pays the highest. The more the advertiser is willing to shell out, the bigger a celebrity he'll get; there's a $500 list, a $1,000 list, etc. It's that simple and commercial.

Liggett and Myers announced an expenditure of a million dollars to launch a new pipe tobacco, Masterpiece. A color magazine ad featured a photo of Eva Gabor with her dress neckline plunging. It showed her bending toward a can of tobacco and asking: *"Darling, have you discovered Masterpiece? The most exciting men I know are smoking it!"* Do you think that the most exciting men Eva Gabor knows really smoke Masterpiece?

"Joan Fontaine throws a shot-in-the-dark party and her friends learn a thing or two." That's one headline in a celebrity campaign for Fleischmann's Whiskey. The ad pictured "Joan and her friends" sampling shots of whiskey in a room with all lights out, and guessing the brand name, the proof, and the price. Does any adman in his right mind (there are some) think that people reading the ads will throw shot-in-the-dark parties as Fleischmann suggests? No. Then why spend perhaps a million dollars on such a campaign? Only Mad. Ave. could provide a mad-enough answer.

Do most testimonials constitute "fraudulent advertising?" Well, when a movie star poses with a bottle of whiskey and a glass from which he's about to sip with clear delight (I was present), and then says privately, "I'd never touch this cheap poison!"—is that deceitful?

An example of another type of "candid" testimonial: An acquaintance was stopped in a railroad station by a woman who offered him a cup of steaming coffee. She held a microphone and asked, "How did you like it? That's new X-brand instant coffee." The man answered, "I hate every kind of instant coffee. I refuse it at home. Every morning my wife brews a fresh pot of regular coffee and *I love it.*"

The interviewer offered to pay him a sizable sum of money if he signed permission to let them use the tape recording of his remarks in "edited" form. For the money he agreed. Soon his voice was on the air as one of the "candid interviews." In the edited tape he was asked how he liked new X-brand instant coffee. His own voice came through with only the last three words of his original reply: *"I love it."*

*   *   *

The following ad filled one third of a *Good Housekeeping* magazine page: "Time to consult your bun-eez horoscope for news of size-pruf holeproof and truly whymsy hy-test quality panties. If you are feminine sissy britches or imps sport-eez at heart your best bet in sportswear, twinklette playwear, strutwear is found in the fashion names of nolde and golden nolde." The ad bore a large *Good Housekeeping* seal.

Since "many of my best friends are admen," I've become involved in bitter arguments when attacking some advertising approaches as deceptive. A frequent reaction: "Advertising fraudulent? No! Just plain silly? Well, maybe. . . ." The latter always referred to the competitor's efforts.

"Silly" advertising is well defined by David Ogilvy as "flatulent puffery." According to Webster, "flatulent" means: *"(1)* Of or having gas in the stomach or intestines. *(2)* Producing gas in the stomach or intestines, as certain foods [for thought?]. *(3)* Windy or empty in speech; vain; pompous; pretentious." It all fits the asinine in advertising.

Here are a few examples from the overwhelming mass of ads exuding the offensive odor of "flatulent puffery." It's almost impossible to believe that otherwise level-headed businessmen spend millions of dollars on so many nonsensical ads.

Advertising spokesmen proclaim in speeches that it's an outmoded concept to consider that the general public has an average twelve-year-old mentality. Countless ads still confirm the "outmoded concept." A twelve-year-old friend of mine asserts that most ads, especially TV commercials, are created to appeal to those far below his mental level.

You would think that admen and advertisers, rereading the fantastic (using this much-abused word advisedly) copy quoted here would feel embarrassment, possibly even shame. You might even hope they would think twice before releasing similar nonsense in future ads. I wouldn't bet on it. Admen are too much in love with their own words and ideas to amend their approach. Furthermore, it's almost impossible for an adman to confess, "I goofed." That's especially true of agencymen within client's ear range.

Admen frequently talk to themselves in ads, in a language comprehensible only to themselves: "Evan-Piconery! Is to wonderful in. Whimsy in. Very appeal to him in. These sweater wonderfuls. . . ." Another: "Is to poor little boy sweater in. More of a great big girl in. . . . These pure wool poors. . . ."

Another candidate for Silliest Ad of the Decade: *"Likable beautiful Buick. Affordable and reachable. Smack in wallet range."* The car was shown at an angle that you could see in a showroom if you got down on the floor on your hands and knees and looked up. Our local Buick salesman commented, "Those ad guys are nuts. They sure don't know anything about cars or people."

Quaker Oats spent about $85,000 for a two-page spread in *Life* magazine and hundreds of thousands of dollars elsewhere to state: *"Mama, make them* [the kids] *laugh. Tell them Quaker Oats is kind of a love-pat for tummies."* Even an adman would be nauseated to hear his wife tell his youngsters at breakfast, "Eat your Quaker Oats, it's a love-pat for tummies."

A Green Giant Corn ad conveyed this homily: "The world liked this corn very much—even Uncle Augbert liked it. And now the Green Giant has a well-worn path to his door. Which is nice because he does like people." Feeling a little green? Leo Burnett, head of the agency which prepared the ad, once said, "I am one who believes that one of the greatest dangers of advertising is not that of misleading people, but that of boring them to death."

A Celanese ad showed a pretty pop singer surrounded by chefs: *"Singer Leslie Uggams makes great lasagne."* The ad has her tell at length how she makes lasagne, how it helps her "unwind." "She laughed. 'I go to small Italian restaurants [when too busy to cook lasagne] and eat other people's lasagne.' " Is the ad selling Leslie's Celanese Lasagne? No. "For this [eating lasagne] we have the perfect dress. . . ." Surprise—it's made out of a Celanese fabric, not lasagne.

A Philadelphia Carpet Company ad featured carpeting in "Tintinnabulating bell tones . . . twelve colors that stir, soothe, set the spirits soaring and chime as melodically as a carillon . . . inspired by Edgar Allan Poe's noble poem, 'The Bells.' " People I queried said they prefer a carpet that just lays there quietly without pealing. The rattling sound you hear now is Edgar Allan Poe turning over in his grave.

An Armstrong Vinyl ad showed a woman fencing fiercely on a vinyl floor: *"Any man (swish!) who reneges (swish! swish!) on his promise (swish!) to buy his wife (swish! swish! swish!) a Montina vinyl Corlon floor (swish!) is in for big trouble (touché)."* The headline combined eight "swishes!" and one "touché"—a new record.

Does No-Cal tell you right out that its quinine water is the one with no calories and helps you control your weight? No. Their ad pictured a shivering man saying, "This is the t-t-tonic with the colder t-t-touch. There's no sugar, no c-c-calories to heat you up! Strictly a chilling jolt of authentic tonic f-f-flavor! Even the price keeps you cooler under the c-ccollar!" Why all this c-c-confusion? To impress the c-c-client with the agency's c-c-cleverness.

Are such examples of "silly copy" in print or on the air the exception? Are they effective? Stockton Helffrich of the National Association of Broadcasters commented in a speech to admen: "Experience in my office reveals a steady flow of copy which borders on the ridiculous and which common sense viewers cannot identify with or believe in. They shrug it off as being typical nonsense fed their way in return for the program. But purchase and use of products should result in consumer confirmation of the advertising message. Anything less results in built-up, long-range resentment from the public, damaging to advertisers and media alike."

Women are continuously assaulted with cosmetic copy such as: "Revlon Ultima II non-makeup makeup . . . transparesscent . . . souffléd texture . . . spins out a complexion like a sweep of silk . . . sweeps across your cheeks like an unexpected compliment . . . the perfect fraud . . . as though this were not makeup at all but something fed to you on a silver spoon."

A woman reading this winced and said, "I think I get it. This 'transparesscent, souffléd' goo looks like makeup but you don't smear it on, you eat it."

Another cosmetic excrescence: "With Avon Rapture [fragrance] you feel happily free but captivating—for Rapture is sensitive to you. . . . Rapture has beautiful hopes for you." Avon sells through home representatives. One of them looked disgusted upon reading this ad and remarked, "Imagine me sitting in any living room and telling a woman, 'Rapture has beautiful hopes for you.' Isn't an ad supposed to speak person-to-person? If I talked that way to my customers they'd think I just escaped from a mental hospital."

The slogan of Riker's Counter Luncheonettes in New York City: "No finer food at any price." The same ownership runs The Four Seasons, The Forum of the Twelve Caesars, and other restaurants where dinner checks can easily run to $25 or more per person. Is the slogan then based on the conviction that people will believe anything—or is it just plain foolishness? Or is the $25 dinner check at The Four Seasons a gyp since they can't serve finer food than Riker's at a dollar or two—according to their own slogan?

A Madison Avenue stereotype is the preposterous Big Brag ad: "Open up the White Rock and live! White Rock creates a light-hearted atmosphere that makes everyone feel in-tune, ready for a good time. Your party is off to a lively start and lively is the way it will stay until the last goodnight is said. . . . Stamp out dull parties . . . pour fun-filled White Rock!"

A wine advertiser warned: *"It can't be gay without Chauvenet Red Cap."* If such advertiser's own parties depend for success on the brand of soda or wine they serve, heaven help their guests. Another advertiser took advantage of the current advertising silliness with the headline: *"Will this club soda make you the perfect host? Canada Dry says No."*

A slogan has been defined as "a good old American substitute for the facts." The value of a slogan is generally overrated. One problem is that the repeated slogan may not fit the rest of the ad copy as conditions change. Kelly's Print Shop in Columbia, Missouri, found this out with their slogan, "Kelly Did It." They imprinted it in small type somewhere on every piece of their output. Objections developed when they printed the slogan on birth announcements.

An ex-adwoman, founder of Switzerland's English-language newspaper, the *Weekly Tribune,* Mrs. Casey I. Herrick, attacked "Sloppy Copy" in an article in *Printers' Ink* magazine:

> In a single half hour of browsing through magazines I found more than a dozen ads claiming that their products were smoother; longer-lasting; cheaper; better; washed whiter; stayed fresh longer. Admiral TV lasts longer and works better. Mani Magic removes cuticles three times faster (than that pair of scissors my son used to cut his hair with, no doubt).
>
> Are we really such suckers that we swallow those pointless hooks? I doubt it—and I think the public is being cheated by the manufacturers if there is nothing more to be said about their products, or the manufacturers are being taken by their agencies if this is the best copy they can turn out.

Magazines spill over with examples of "sloppy copy": "Durene is the miracle cotton yarn that makes clothes wash cleaner, look brighter, feel more comfortable, and wear far longer." Than *what?* The finish: ". . . nothing stays as new as Durene." Said a puzzled woman, "I guess it means I should buy 'nothing' because it 'stays as new as Durene.' "

Another embarrassing blast: "Among all the wonderful Italian things America has discovered, nothing is more so than Fiat's 1100D Sedan! That includes the wine, the women, the music, the art—even great, historic Roma." A traveler to Italy and an admirer of Sophia Loren commented, "After that absurd claim, how can I believe anything said in favor of Fiat?"

An ad for Contadina Tomato Paste, a division of the giant Carnation Company, showed a tintype-style photo of an old-fashioned Italian lady: "Mama cried when we took the Bay of Naples off the Contadina can. Mama was born in Naples. Nobody can explain to her why the picture of the Bay had to go off the Contadina can when we began to make our Tomato Paste in California."

A neighbor envisioned dear old Mama bending over a hot kitchen stove and cooking and crying (all the way to the bank) into millions of cans of tomato paste while she paid about $50,000 for this page in *Life* magazine. She said, "It enrages me that the advertiser considers me so stupid. It's a sure way to keep Contadina out of *my* kitchen."

An ad for Rolex watches featured a photo of A & P multi-millionaire Huntington Hartford and Edouard Cournand with this copy: "Where did you get your Rolex?' Mr. Cournand asked Mr. Hartford. You might think that's a pretty silly way to start a conversation." "Yes," a noted engineer friend remarked, "and a pretty silly way to try to sell thousand-dollar watches to adults who can afford that price."

This full-page ad for *Look,* a publication noted for clear illuminating editorial matter, appeared in *The New Yorker* and other magazines:

> "Views make news
> News makes views.
> *Look* views news.
> Views views.
> Makes news.
> Makes LOOK."

How does the asininity come about? Such nonsense ads commonly grow from constant, desperate pressure on agencymen from advertising clients to be different, original, and creative. Often dozens of writers and artists are put to work in an agency in a frenzied rush to produce "genius ideas." This habitually occurs when product sales are dipping or if the client is dissatisfied with the current advertising.

"Press the panic button!" is the cry at the agency. Meetings are called and disbanded. Harried writers and artists work night after night. Everything is tabbed "Rush! Rush! Rush!" The craziest ideas are created, rejected, revised, accepted, twisted, bulled through in a kind of mass hysteria. Ads erupts in a chaotic fury in which neither the agencymen nor the client group can finally see straight or think clearly. When the dust clears and the blood has been mopped up, the campaign has been approved at last for better or worse—invariably worse.

Later the client is likely to scream after watching the resultant commercials on his TV set at home, "My God, how the hell did that ever get by—who approved that? Get that ridiculous stuff off the air—as of now!" More often, no one at either the agency or advertiser's office sees the commercials objectively—ever. TV viewers suffer accordingly, and so do product sales.

Researcher Eric Marder has stated that based on the results of a series of studies, "Occasionally we've had to tell a client, 'It would have paid you to pay someone *not* to run this ad.' "

*   *   *

"The advertising business is made up of 1% innovation and 99% imitation," said an executive.

Madison Avenue imitated radio and borrowed a stereotyped lineup of artificial voices, unlike any used in natural, straightforward conversation among people. The voices include the overpowering, unctuous, superior, wheedling, pseudo-jolly, intimate, the peep-show whisper, baby-talk, hokey-jokey, unschooled housewife, twangy hick, and many other aberrations. An observer said that the confidential voice, for instance, sounds like someone peddling hot hub-caps.

A few admen have tried to use pleasant voices that would address the audience naturally. Almost impossible to find among professional announcers, the natural sound could be achieved by some able actors. When innovators played their audition records for other agencymen and advertisers, the reaction was invariably negative: "But he doesn't sound like a professional announcer. Why can't we get a pro?"

Furthermore, the insistence was on using only the most-heard announcers. Those with a familiar voice and the accustomed "advertising sound" were most acceptable on Madison Avenue. The fact that such voices adhere to a pattern of sound which makes most ears tune them out automatically as "Ugh, more advertising!" makes little difference to admen. Their safest way to acceptance among their cohorts is to repeat the familiar—the unnatural.

The same is true of the types of people used in TV commercials. The housewife must be either a glamor girl who has never bent over a dishwasher except in front of the TV camera, or a harsh-voiced, supposedly comical drab whom you'd shudder to have for a neighbor, and fortunately never encounter in real life. People like the boss and the mother-in-law, who are the targets of "odor" attacks, are stereotype caricatures unlike anybody you know.

Why do commercials picture such a phony never-never land? The artificial standards for radio voices spawned a similar abnormality in TV toward exaggeration. What matters if a shrieking, pop-eyed housewife in a commercial disgusts women who are potential product purchasers? What counts is that adman can nudge adman and burble, "Isn't she the most gruesome ever?"

A man from Mars could hardly find anything more ridiculous in our modes and mores than laundry product advertising, especially on TV commercials. Their inanity is compounded by the fact that the bad examples are inevitably followed by worse imitators. An advertising trade magazine reported a housewife as saying, "I have yet to see a television commercial for a household soap that wasn't an insult to a woman's intelligence." An irate gentleman damned TV's emphasis on "the dull, the mediocre, the meaningless.

A typical "people-talk" commercial for Final Touch Fabric Softener showed two young couples on a suburban terrace. The jovial white-toothed slick-haired husbands—unlike any you ever saw outside of a model agency—are about to take off for a tennis game. But there's trouble a-brewing. . . .

Wife A looks worried. Wife B asks what's bothering her. Wife A wails something like, "I feel awful that my Fred's tennis shorts aren't as white and don't hang as well as your Tom's tennis shorts." Wife B tells her about Final Touch, which makes her Tom's tennis shorts look so whitest white and hang so well. With this cleared up, presumably they all live happily ever after.

Is that what "young marrieds" are talking about these days? Those I asked retorted: "It's an insult to our intelligence."

Perhaps not quite so demeaning to women is the epidemic of "action" gimmicks that hit the boob tube. In an Ajax Powder Cleanser commercial, as a housewife is being shot out of her kitchen as though from a cannon, she clenches the product that "gets you out of the kitchen fast." Comedienne Selma Diamond on Johnny Carson's "Tonight" show said that the government could save a lot of money by sprinkling the cleansing powder on astronauts and "off they would go into space to the moon."

A teacher asked his class to write a composition on "What I Think About Advertising." One future housewife wrote: "If you want my opinion of advertising, well, it's there so I have to accept it, but I despise it. For instance: There's a new 'miracle' product that cleans so fast you fly out of the kitchen. My mother naturally bought it and washed the supper dishes with it. She flew out of the kitchen all right, after eleven P.M. Do you know where she flew? Right into bed to collapse." Another student wrote, "On TV most advertising is fake."

Ajax Laundry Detergent featured a white knight who was "stronger than dirt." He raced around on a white charger, touching various persons, such as a street cleaner, and turning their clothes dazzling white. One woman said she was going to hang her dirty clothes on the line and, "Let that creep on the white horse come along and turn them clean—or I'll sue the advertiser."

I would nominate as worst-of-the-worst the Fab commercial "for a wash that is wedding white . . . you look like a bride every time you use Fab." In this epic, a swarm of women of all ages walked into a laundry room and their clothes were transformed from house clothes into bridal costumes by using Fab. When this was described to a visiting European at a dinner party, he refused to believe it. The hostess told him, "I'm with you. Even watching the commercial I couldn't believe that anything so imbecilic would be thrown at people anywhere!"

"The giant in the washer" sent up out of the tumbling water, his hairy fist gripping a box of Action Chlorine Bleach. This aimed to prove that Action is "a giant of a bleach." A commuter grumbled that he hated leaving his pretty wife at home with that giant in the washer. "How do I know," he complained, "that he *stays* in the washer?"

How do such wild advertising devices come about, all in the same field of products, in a festering rash? Primarily it's a matter of one agency and advertiser trying to be more clever, dramatic, and impressive than the competitors. An adman admitted, "It's just another case of follow the leader." One launches a wacky idea and all the others panic to top it with a greater exaggeration.

Rosser Reeves, Bates agency chairman, called such gimmicks "vampire video" which "suck strength away from your main story . . . [making] commercials often dazzling in their art, but miserable as salesmen." Yet Mr. Reeves' agency created some dillies, such as scenes of fashionable ladies in white gloves eating M & M's candies without getting any messy chocolate on their pristine gauntlets.

George Wolf, vice president and TV executive at Lennen and Newell (Number 19), stated, "We're fascinated with anything that tells a story in a new and different way. The 'gimmick' commercials are interesting. Anything that makes the point is valid." Whether it makes the sale is a secondary point.

To check on the effect of the gimmicks I donned a sweatshirt, gathered some wash, and stopped at a couple of laundromats. I started a conversation with several women about the TV fantasy commercials and asked them which ad applied to which product.

After deliberation, one ventured, "Well, the white knight is Fab's—no, that's the green giant, no, I mean the giant fist. . . ."

"It is not. The ten-foot-tall washer is Dash—or is it Ajax?"

"You're wrong, it's Tide. No—Salvo—or is Salvo the bulldozer in the kitchen—or is it the lady plumber?"

Others tried to link each product with its matching TV commercial gimmick. The result was utter confusion and bewildered laughter. Then a large lady asked, "Does it really matter? None of us pays any attention to those commercials anyhow. They go in one eye and out the other. It's like they're put together by a bunch of kids playing with their toys. The advertising people can't be stupid enough to think we believe that stuff or are impressed by it."

Another summed up, "Who's got the patience or time to pay attention to all that nonsense? And then to remember who's advertising what? And who cares?"

"Then how do you choose your brand?"

One said instantly, "I usually go for the special offer—cents off, a coupon deal, two-for-one, like that y'know? I grab whatever seems to be the best buy in the supermarket. Of course if I find a product is terrible, I won't buy it again at any price. If I like one very much I stick with it, or maybe go for another only when there's a specially big bargain. They're all pretty much the same anyhow." The other women nodded agreement.

Hundreds of millions of dollars are spent annually on advertising and promotion of laundry products, using such idiotic approaches. You can be sure of one thing in regard to the commercials described here—they will change and be replaced by worse.

Even gorillas won't take it. In an experiment in the Bronx Zoo, four gorillas calmed down from their bickering and brawling when a TV set was placed just past the bars outside their cage. As with benumbed children, the pictures on the screen acted as a tranquilizer. However, one of the biggest gorillas started tearing up badly at times. "My theory," said Joseph A. Davis, the zoo's curator of mammals, "is that he behaved this way during commercials."

A medical journal reported on a West German study that poodles who watched TV for several hours daily suffered from loss of appetite, became snappish and very nervous; parakeets came down with fever. TV and its commercials can now be indicted for cruelty to animals as well as humans.

Each year brings new outbursts which are quickly imitated. At this writing the follow-the-leader troops of Madavenuers are on the trail of *tigers*. Like the other trends, it's easier to follow than to lead or innovate, especially when the client says, "Hey, that's a clever tiger campaign those people are running—I want one just like it."

Esso tells you to *"Put a tiger in your tank."* In France it's *"Mettez un tigre dans votre moteur."* In Germany, *"Pack den tiger in den tank."* In a popular joke a mama tiger asks her mate, "Where have you been? You smell like gasoline."

Soon Pontiac LeMans and GTO became *"Quick Wide-track tigers."* Another car became the Sunbeam Tiger. The modest Ghia was termed "a pussycat." There appeared U.S. Royal Tiger Paw tires, Tiger Coats, Tiger-tail Drink by Julius Wile, Tiger Tails bubble gum, Tigress Perfume, Tiger Sandwiches by Seeman Brothers, and Tiger Beast bracelets by Abraham and Straus.

If you "feel like a tiger is in your throat," reach for Guardets lozenges. Bovril "turns your cub into a tiger." You "make like a tiger" with Chenango Deodorant for Men, reminder of a cartoon caption in an advertising magazine: "The client says that the deodorant ad smells." A new men's cosmetics line was named "Tom Cat," with the slogan: "A Tom Cat is a Tiger State of Mind."

Ideal Toy Corporation offered a new game, Tiger Island. A hamburger stand sign advertised *"Put a tiger in your tummy."* Painted on the back of a lumbering truck: *"I got a turtle in my tank!"* Tiger Beer in the Japanese *Times* sloganeered: *"Put a tiger in your tankard."* Standard Rochester Beer countered: *"Put a tankard in your tiger."* Purina Cat Food meowed: *"Put some tuna in your tiger."* Goldblatt Brothers in Chicago advertised *"A tiger of a sale . . . savagely slashed prices."* An add for Arthur Murray Dance Studios asked: *"Are YOU ready to r-r-roar? . . . be a tiger, starting right now!"*

Why the chase for tigers on Madison Avenue? President Truman's remark probably sums it up: "Within the first few months [after being in office] I discovered that being a President is like riding a tiger. A man has to keep riding or be swallowed." The frantic adman chasing ad trends fears that he has to keep running or be swallowed by the competition.

English essayist Walter Pater suggested that happiness is "the attainment of a true philosophy." Peanuts of cartoon fame gently defined happiness as a warm puppy. Admen hopped the happiness band wagon, of course, and offered far easier solutions. Esso ads stated that *"Happiness is a quick-starting car!"* Thus, turning on happiness became as simple as turning an ignition key. Or: *"Happiness is being elected team captain— and getting a Bulova watch!"* Brancusi furniture claimed: *"Happiness is a $49 table."* Cone Sporterry: *"Happiness is giving Dad a terry shave coat for Christmas."* A Las Vegas hotel: *"Happiness is the Sands."* A decorator: *"Happiness is a bathroom by Marion Wieder."* Miss Clairol: *"Happiness can be the color of her hair."* Lest there be any mistake about degree: "REAL *happiness is being at the Puerto Rico Sheraton."*

An ad boasted: *"Happiness is reading* [and advertising] *in Holiday."* This inanity is in contrast to the thoughts of a nineteen-year-old Peace Corps volunteer from Iowa in a *Holiday* article: "Happiness is the realization that one's efforts and one's work have been worthwhile." Another teen-ager wrote: "My two strongest convictions are that man can attain happiness only through selflessness, and that every man has a profound responsibility to his fellow man." Statements like these by the "juvenile delinquent generation" spotlight Madison Avenue's pursuit of the happiness theme as sick-sick-sick. A psychiatrist said, "Such callous debasement of what constitutes happiness must weaken the traditional American concepts of high ideals, especially with the very young."

Turning to liquor advertising, the same approaches are used so often that they've lost meaning for anybody, including agencies and advertisers. Agencymen alibi that liquor advertising restrictions are so strict that they prevent any creativity, although Madison Avenue boasts of a bottomless well of ideas.

Practically every liquor has been promoted for years as "light." The beers too are "light." Piel's, like others, promoted it both ways: *"The light beer made for men—have a BELT of Piel's"*—thus trying to tab it as the light beer with a wallop.

An adman explained, 'We must describe a whiskey as 'light' or it's hard to get the campaign okayed by the client. Research and sales trends show that drinkers want their whiskey 'light,' not heavy. So whether the brand is actually 'light' or not, we say so. What can we lose?"

A Chivas Regal ad showed scraps of copy torn from many ads for Scotch. All claimed "lightness." Included were "world's lightest Scotch" and "first light Scotch." The headline scolded: *"Come, come, gentlemen. one of us has to be kidding."* (Or lying?) Then the baffling follow-up: "What we mean by 'lightness' is smoothness"—the meaningless compounded by the trite.

I stopped after counting over two dozen ads that called each different brand "smooth," including Martini and Rossi Vermouth, which claimed to be not only "smooth" but also "serene." A Johnnie Walker Red ad asked the obvious question: "With over 208 to choose from . . . how can you select the Scotch that's smoothest?" Of course you can't. So Johnnie Walker Red says, "just smooth"—then, lest this appear too modest, adds, "very smooth." Nevertheless, the same advertiser didn't hesitate to acclaim Johnnie Walker Black as "world's finest Scotch." With over 208 brands to choose from, how can anyone truthfully name the one Scotch that's "finest"?

"Gentleness" became a popular descriptive. Old Angus Scotch is "gentle as a lamb." House of Stuart Scotch is "gentled." Bellows Partners Choice Whiskey boasted that its "gentle taste is even gentler" and now "pours from a gentle-shaped bottle." Man, that's gentle!

As softening of the adman's brain progressed, a new campaign appeared for Calvert's Soft Whiskey—it "does anything any other whiskey can do. It just does it softer." What was "soft" to one brand was bound to become "softest" for another. Maker's Mark bragged that it's "the softest spoken of the bourbons." Michter's Whiskey "sips softly." Inver House Scotch advertised: "Soft as a kiss."

When greater safety in cars became a national issue, auto manufacturers voiced pious approval—and yet they increased the emphasis on model names suggesting wildness, ferocity, and speed: Barracuda, Wildcat, Mustang, Cutlass, Le Sabre, Rocket, Impala. Ford marketing consultant Stanley Arnold planned the image of the Cougar as "a car with some bite in it." Satirist Russell Baker then suggested specialized names, for example, to appeal to the gourmet: Dodge Soufflé, Oldsmobile Ossobucco, Pontiac Eggs Benedict; and for timid drivers, Chevrolet Chicken.

The sex-silly ads are always popular on the Madison Avenue sheep run. Revlon aimed to lure women with *"colors on the naked side."* Fabergé showed a sultry striped exultantly female female: *"Wild! is the word for the uninhibited jungle beat of tigress Parfum Extraordinaire."* Ondine Perfume cautioned: *"Save it [Ondine] for the real men in your life. Men who want you all to themselves . . . and keep you out too late . . .* DON'T WEAR ONDINE UNLESS YOU MEAN IT."

"That gleam is back in George's eye . . . again." The photo showed a leering George in bed, tousling his wife's red hair. Why the imminent attack? He switched to a Serta Perfect Sleeper mattress, offered as the modern man's aphrodisiac, Sealy mattress chipped in with the headline: *"After the pill: Posturpedic."*

Admen disavow blatant sex in ads, but they get as close to the borderline as possible to try to make sales. National Oil Fuel Institute devoted over three quarters of its ad to the question: *"Is your wife cold?"* Others: *"Kayser is marvelous in bed." "What makes a shy girl get intimate?"*

"When a chic woman undresses, what do you see?" "Tiffany Eubank won't without her Green Stripe [Scotch]."

Howard Clothes headlined: *"Howard makes clothes for men who make love." "Howard makes clothes for men who make babies."* Mort Wimpie of Howard's agency explained that the basic idea is to get across that Howard makes clothes for men who do all the normal things of life: "The headline is an empathy pitch—an unsubtle phrase, but it hits an empathy button." Not long after, Howard changed the theme, the advertising manager, and the agency.

Photos of sultry come-hither women highlighted ads with headlines: *"Perhaps we could, Paul, if . . . you owned a Chrysler." "Move up to Chrysler, Marty. We'll make it easy."* An agency spokesman asserted that the ads were not meant to be sexy. The adman's defense is generally, "Only a dirty mind will read something dirty in it." Every insider knows that such ads are planned specifically to appeal to the "dirty minds" which admen believe are in the majority. Otherwise they wouldn't stake millions of dollars on the ads. A lady asserted, "It takes a dirty mind to try to reach another."

In a speech, Fairfax M. Cone, chairman of the executive committee of Foote, Cone and Belding (Number 6), said: "We are now engaged in making a great deal of advertising a joke. And the question I think we must ask ourselves is whom are we kidding? When someone asks me whom I think we are talking to, whether we think the public is mentally defective after all, or what, I can only blush a deep dark red." Later he said, "The best test of any advertisement is this: could you say it to a friend without feeling like an idiot?" He's the adman who dreamed up the line: *"Aren't you glad* YOU *use Dial Soap! Don't you wish* EVERYBODY *did?"* One wonders whether Mr. Cone tries that on his friends.

Words composing offensive or silly statements and empty promises are used repeatedly, mindlessly, imitatively, as admen tramp on each other's heels in the chase for your dollar. James Bryant Conant of Harvard said about the dangers of such misuse: "Some of mankind's most terrible misdeeds have been committed under the spell of certain magic words or phrases."

The Selling of the President: 1968*

By Joe McGinniss

He was afraid of television. He knew his soul was hard to find. Beyond that, he considered it a gimmick; its use in politics offended him. It had not been part of the game when he had learned to play, he could see no reason to bring it in now. He half-suspected it was an Eastern liberal trick; one more way to make him look silly. It offended his sense of dignity, one of the truest senses he had.

So his decision to use it to become President in 1968 was not easy. So much of him argued against it. But in his Wall Street years, Richard Nixon had traveled to the darkest places inside himself and come back numbed. He was, as in the Graham Greene title, a burnt-out case. All feeling was behind him; the machine inside had proved his hardiest part. He would run for President again and if he would have to learn television to run well, then he would learn it.

Nixon gathered about himself a group of young men attuned to the political uses of television. They arrived at his side by different routes. One, William Gavin, was a thirty-one-year-old English teacher in a suburban high school outside Philadelphia in 1967 when he wrote Richard Nixon a letter urging him to run for President and base his campaign on TV. Gavin wrote the letter on stationery borrowed from the University of Pennsylvania because he thought Nixon would pay more attention if the letter seemed to be from a college professor.

Dear Mr. Nixon:

May I offer two suggestions concerning your plans for 1968?

1. Run. You can win. Nothing can happen to you, politically speaking, that is worse than what has happened to you. Ortega y Gasset in his The Revolt of the Masses *says: "These ideas are the only genuine ideas; the*

---

ideas of the shipwrecked. All the rest is rhetoric, posturing, farce. He who does not really feel himself lost, is lost without remission. . . ." You, in effect, are "lost"; that is why you are the only political figure with the vision to see things the way they are and not as Leftist or Rightist kooks would have them be. Run. You will win.

2. A tip for television: instead of those wooden performances beloved by politicians, instead of a glamor boy technique, instead of safety, be bold. Why not have live press conferences as your campaign on television? People will see you daring all, asking and answering questions from reporters, and not simply answering phony "questions" made up by your staff. This would be dynamic; it would be daring. Instead of the medium using you, you would be using the medium. . . . Television hurt you because you were not yourself; it didn't hurt the "real" Nixon. The real Nixon can revolutionize the use of television by dynamically going "live" and answering everything, the loaded and the unloaded question. Invite your opponents to this kind of debate.

Good luck, and I know you can win if you see yourself for what you are; a man who has been beaten, humiliated, hated, but who can still see the truth.

A Nixon staff member had lunch with Gavin a couple of times after the letter was received and hired him. Gavin began churning out long, stream-of-consciousness memos which dealt mostly with the importance of image, and ways in which Richard Nixon, through television, could acquire a good one: "Voters are basically lazy, basically uninterested in making an *effort* to understand what we're talking about," Gavin wrote. "Reason requires a high degree of discipline, of concentration; impression is easier. Reason pushes the viewer back, it assaults him. . . . The emotions are more easily roused, closer to the surface, more malleable. . . ."

So, for the New Hampshire primary, Gavin recommended "saturation with a film, in which the candidate can be shown better than he can be shown in person because it can be edited, so only the best moments are shown. . . . [Nixon] has to come across as a person larger than life, the stuff of legend. People are stirred by legend, including the living legend, not by the man himself. It's the aura that surrounds the charismatic figure more than it is the figure itself that draws the followers. Our task is to build that aura. . . ."

William Gavin was brought to the White House as a speechwriter in January of 1969.

Harry Treleaven, hired as creative director of advertising in the fall of 1967, immediately went to work on the more serious of Nixon's personality problems. One was his lack of humor: "Can be corrected to a degree," Treleaven wrote, "but let's not be too obvious about it. Romney's cornball attempts have hurt him. If we're going to be witty, let a pro write the words."

Treleaven also worried about Nixon's lack of warmth, but decided: "He can be helped greatly in this respect by how he is handled. . . . Give him words to say that will show his *emotional* involvement in the issues. . . . He should be presented in some kind of 'situation' rather than cold in a studio. The situation should look unstaged even if it's not."

Some of the most effective ideas belonged to Raymond K. Price, a former editorial writer for the New York *Herald Tribune,* who became Nixon's best and most prominent speechwriter in the campaign. Price later composed much of the Inaugural Address. In 1967, he concluded that rational arguments would "only be effective if we can get the people to make the *emotional* leap, or what theologians call 'leap of faith.' "

To do this, Price suggested attacking the "personal factors" rather than the "historical factors" which were the basis of the low opinion so many people had of Richard Nixon. "These tend to be more a gut reaction," he wrote, "unarticulated, nonanalytical, a product of the particular chemistry between the voter and the *image* of the candidate. *We have to be very clear on this point: that the response is to the image, not to the man. . . ."*

So there would not have to be a "new Nixon." Simply a new approach to television.

This was how they went into it. Trying, with one hand, to build the illusion that Richard Nixon, in addition to his attributes of mind and heart, considered "communicating with the people . . . one of the great joys of seeking the Presidency," while with the other they shielded him, controlled him, and controlled the atmosphere around him. It was as if they were building not a President but an Astrodome, where the wind would never blow, the temperature never rise or fall, and the ball never bounce erratically on the artificial grass.

And it worked. As he moved serenely through his primary campaign, there was new cadence to Richard Nixon's speech and motion; new confidence in his heart. And, a new image of him on the television screen, on live, but controlled, TV.

I first met Harry Treleaven on a rainy morning in June of 1968 in his New York office at Fuller and Smith and Ross, the advertising agency. Treleaven was small and thin. He had gray hair and the tight frowning mouth that you see on the assistant principal of a high school. He seemed to be in his middle forties. He looked like William Scranton. Treleaven, it turned out, did not work for Fuller and Smith and Ross. He worked for Richard Nixon. Fuller and Smith and Ross was only incidental to the campaign. An agency was needed to do the mechanics—buying the television time and the newspaper space—and this looked like a nice, quiet one that would not complain about not being permitted to do creative work.

Treleaven had been born in Chicago and had gone to Duke University, where he was Phi Beta Kappa. After that, he moved to Los Angeles and worked on the Los Angeles *Times* and then wrote radio scripts. One night he and his wife were having dinner in a restaurant in Los Angeles with a couple he did not like. Halfway through the meal he turned to his wife.

"Do you like it here?"

"You mean the restaurant?"

"I mean Los Angeles."

"No, not especially."

"Then let's go."

And Harry Treleaven threw a $20 bill on the table and he and his wife walked out. He took a plane to New York that night and found a job with the J. Walter Thompson advertising agency. He stayed with Thompson eighteen years. When he left it was as a vice president. He did commercials for Pan American, RCA, Ford, and Lark cigarettes, among others.

Harry Treleaven was sitting on the beach at Amagansett one day in September of 1967, drinking a can of beer. A summer neighbor named Len Garment, who was a partner in the law firm where Richard Nixon worked, approached him. Harry Treleaven knew Garment from a meeting they had had earlier in the summer. Garment had vaguely mentioned something about Treleaven and the advertising needs of the Richard Nixon campaign. Now he was more specific. He offered Treleaven a job. Creative director of advertising. Treleaven would devise a theme for the campaign, create commercials to fit the theme, and see that they were produced with a maximum of skill.

Len Garment's office was on the third floor of Nixon headquarters, at Park Avenue and 57th Street. A man named Jim Howard, a public-relations man from Cleveland, was with him the day I came in. Jim Howard was talking to Wilt Chamberlain on the phone.

"Wilt, I *understand* your position but they just don't pay that kind of money."

Garment was a short, pudgy man, also in his middle forties, who once had played saxophone in a Woody Herman band. He had voted for John Kennedy in 1960. Then he met Nixon at the law firm. He was chief of litigation and he was making money but he hated the job. He found that Nixon was not so bad a guy and very smart. When Nixon asked him to work in the Presidential campaign, he said yes. He had been practically the first person to be hired and now he was chief recruiter.

Jim Howard had been trying to get Wilt Chamberlain to appear on the Mike Douglas show for free. The idea was for Chamberlain to explain why Richard Nixon should be President. Chamberlain was the only Negro celebrity they had and they were trying to get him around. The problem was, the Douglas show did not pay. And Chamberlain wanted money.

Len Garment started to explain the Nixon approach to advertising. Or the Garment-Treleaven approach to advertising Nixon. "The big thing is to stay away from gimmicks," he said.

"Right," Jim Howard said. "Never let the candidate wear a hat he does not feel comfortable wearing. You can't sell the candidate like a product," he said. "A product, all you want to do is get attention. You only need 2% additional buyers to make the campaign worthwhile. In politics you need a flat 51% of the market and you can't get that through gimmicks."

Two weeks later, I met Frank Shakespeare. Treleaven, Garment (who this June became special consultant to the President in the area of civil rights), and Shakespeare made up what was to be called the media and advertising group. But of the three equals, Shakespeare was quickly becoming more equal than others. He had come from CBS. He, too, was in his forties, with blond hair and a soft, boyish face. When he was named director of the United States Information Agency, after Nixon's election, a *New York Times* profile reported that, although he had spent eighteen years at CBS, no one he worked with there could recall a single anecdote about him. He was working for free because his progress at CBS had been stalled when Jim Aubrey got fired. He had been one of Aubrey's boys. Now, it was said, he was trying to give his career some outside impetus. An association with the President of the U.S. could hardly hurt.

On the morning after the Russians invaded Czechoslovakia, Harry Treleaven got to his office early. He was in an exceptionally good mood. The invasion had proved Nixon was right all along. The Russians had not changed.

"Makes it kind of hard to be a dove, doesn't it?" he said, smiling.

Treleaven was leaving for Teletape, the film-editing studio, right away. The day before, he had cut Nixon's forty-five-minute acceptance speech to thirty minutes, and he wanted to see it.

Len Garment was at the studio when Treleaven got there. "What about this Czech thing?" he said. He looked really worried. Treleaven smiled. "Oh, I don't know, Len. Look at the positive side."

"Well, yes," Garment said. "I think it will bring a restoration of realism to American political discussion."

But Treleaven had been thinking of something else. "Unless we make some really colossal mistake," he said, "I don't see how we can lose."

Then Shakespeare came in. He was exuberant. "What a break!" he said. "This Czech thing is just perfect. It puts the soft-liners in a hell of a box!"

Harry Treleaven had used the CBS tape of the acceptance speech to make the commercial. "Better camera angles," he explained. "And besides, NBC has a peculiar form of editorializing. For instance, they'll cut to some young colored guy who's not applauding while Nixon talks of bridges to human dignity."

In the beginning of the acceptance speech, Richard Nixon had made a sweeping motion with his arm and shouted, "Let's win this one for Ike!" and all the Republicans cheered. Harry Treleaven had cut this line from the speech.

"Good," Shakespeare said, "very good, Harry. That's the one line Rose Mary Woods wanted out of there." Rose Mary Woods was Richard Nixon's secretary. Because she had stuck with him through all the bad years, she emerged in 1968 as an adviser, too.

Another thing he had cut was a reference to "the era of negotiation" with the Russians. Shakespeare was very happy this had gone. It would have been awful, he thought—they all thought—to have a reference to negotiations now that this invasion had occurred. This was the Cold War again, and adrenalin was flowing.

A big meeting was scheduled at Fuller and Smith and Ross for lunchtime. The agency had ordered ham sandwiches with a lot of lettuce and big pots of coffee. Everyone sat down and took little bites out of their sandwiches while Frank Shakespeare stood up and talked.

Already, there was bad feeling between the agency people and the Nixon group. In the beginning, the agency had believed it actually was going to create commercials. Then Harry Treleaven walked in. Without even saying good morning. Now the agency was making money but it was embarrassed. Treleaven would not tell them what he was doing. "No need to," he said. He said he had been thinking it over, and rather than rush something new into production he would prefer to continue the sixty-second excerpts from the acceptance speech that had been running as radio commercials.

Art Duram, the president of the agency, immediately lit his pipe. "But your exposure on that speech—" he said. "You're going to be horrendously overexposed."

"I'm not sure that's bad, Art," Treleaven said. "He's saying some awfully good things."

"But psychologically—"

"Well, the problem is we have nothing else to use and there's nothing else we could have ready that quickly unless it were a real emergency and I just don't think it is."

Duram shrugged.

Then a red-haired lady named Ruth Jones spoke up from the other side of the table. She had been hired by Shakespeare to supervise the buying of television and radio time for the commercials. "Nixon should go on the air tonight with a special broadcast about Czechoslovakia," she said.

Shakespeare shook his head. "He'd have to be too good. He couldn't get ready. He's better off not saying anything. He's been Mr. Cool and Mr. Calm through this whole thing."

Ruth Jones shrugged. "I still think he should do it," she said. "But let's move on to something else—we're going to get bold listings in the *Times* starting immediately."

"Bold listings?" Shakespeare asked.

"Yes, in the TV section. Listing our commercials in bold type in the schedule. They had been doing it for McCarthy and not for us. But I tossed a couple of hand grenades. At the networks and the *Times*. And I got immediate results."

Then a man walked into the room with a big colored poster under his arm. The poster was a closeup of Richard Nixon smiling. Beneath it were the words: *This time vote like your whole world depended on it.*

"This is the new slogan," he said. "And together with the picture, this will run in the center spread of *Life* Magazine and on our billboards."

Frank Shakespeare was staring at the picture. "Do you like the photograph?" he said, turning toward Len Garment.

"I have a little bit of a problem with that tremendous smile, tied in with the serious line," Garment said.

The man with the poster was nodding. "We're still looking for the right picture," he said, "and it's difficult. But this expression is not a laugh to me. It's a youthful expression. It has vitality. To look at it inspires confidence. The picture has sensitivity, and one of the reasons we ran the line behind him—in back of his head—is so he wouldn't appear to be speaking it. See, it's there, but just as part of the image. The connection is not direct."

"Yes," Frank Shakespeare said. "All right."

"It will make a tremendous billboard," Treleaven said.

"There's character in the face," Shakespeare said.

"We've got the best-looking candidate, no doubt about it," Treleaven said.

"So it's a cheerful, grim, serious, and optimistic picture," Len Garment said, smiling.

"And youthful," Shakespeare added.

"Ah," said Ruth Jones, who still wanted him to speak on Czechoslovakia, "a man for all seasons."

Then they talked about fund-raising. "The first McCarthy telecast raised a hundred and twenty-five thousand dollars," Ruth Jones said.

"Who gave the pitch?" Shakespeare asked.

"Paul Newman."

"Oh, well, that made a difference."

"It was a personal involvement pitch. Dick Goodwin wrote it for him."

"We'll use the same pitch," Shakespeare said, "but we don't have as strong a man."

"Who do we have?"

"Bud Wilkinson."

At four o'clock, Treleaven walked to a West Side theater to look at a film that had been made with Spiro Agnew at Mission Bay, California, the week after the Republican convention.

"It could be a great help, particularly with Agnew, if it's any good," Treleaven said. Shakespeare and Garment already were at the theater. So was the man who had made the films—a TV documentary man whom Shakespeare had hired especially for this job. He was wearing sneakers and shifting nervously from foot to foot. There were two separate films, each containing an interview with one of the candidates. The Agnew film was shown first. It had been shot in color, with sailboats in the blue bay as a backdrop. Spiro Agnew was squinting in the sun.

"All life," he said, "is essentially the contributions that come from compromise." His voice was sleepy, his face without expression. The questions fit right in.

"It must have really been a thrill to have been picked for Vice President, Were you happy?"

"The ability to be happy is directly proportional to the ability to suffer," Agnew said. His tone indicated he might doze before finishing the sentence, "and as you grow older you feel everything less."

He stopped. There was silence on the film. Then the voice of the interviewer: "I see."

"Jesus Christ," someone said out loud in the dark little theater. Spiro Agnew's face kept moving in and out of focus.

"Is that the projector or the film?" Garment asked. The man who had made the film disappeared into the projection booth. The technical quality of the film did not improve.

"Loyalty is the most important principle," Agnew was saying, "when coupled with honesty, that is. And I think that such values are in danger when you hear people advocate violence to change situations which are intolerable . . . and most of the people who are cutting the United States up are doing so without offering a single concrete proposal to improve it."

"How did you become a Republican?"

"I became a Republican out of hero worship." Then Spiro Agnew went on to tell a long story about an old man in the law office where he had first worked as a clerk, and how the old man had been a Republican and how he had admired the old man so much that he had become a Republican too. There was more silence on the film. The focus was very bad.

"And . . . and . . . you just sort of went on becoming more and more Republican?"

"That's right," Spiro Agnew said. More silence. The sailboats moved slowly in the background. The water was very blue. Then the focus made everything a blur.

"What a heartbreak," the man who had made the films said, standing in the back of the theater.

"It looks like you're looking through a Coke bottle," Garment said.

"And he comes across as such an utter bore," Treleaven said. "I don't think the man has had an original observation in his life."

"He is rather non-dynamic," Garment said.

Frank Shakespeare was up now and pacing the back of the theater. "We can't use any of this," he said. "That picture quality is awful. Just awful. And Agnew himself, my God. He says all the wrong things."

"What we need is a shade less truth and a little more pragmatism," Treleaven said.

"I think Dexedrine is the answer," Garment said.

"I am not going to barricade myself into a television studio and make this an antiseptic campaign," Richard Nixon said at a press conference a few days after his nomination. Then he went to Chicago to open his fall campaign. The whole day was built around a television show. Even when ten thousand people stood in front of his hotel and screamed for him to greet them he stayed locked up in his room, resting for the show.

Chicago was the site for the first of ten programs that Nixon would do in states ranging from Massachusetts to Texas. The idea was to have him in the middle of a group of people, answering questions live. Shakespeare and Treleaven had developed the idea through the primaries and now had it sharpened to a point. Each show would run for one hour. It would be live to provide suspense; there would be a studio audience to cheer Nixon's answers and make it seem to home viewers that enthusiasm for his candidacy was all but uncontrollable; and there would be an effort to achieve a conversational tone that would penetrate Nixon's stuffiness and drive out the displeasure he often seemed to feel when surrounded by other human beings instead of Bureau of the Budget reports.

One of the valuable things about this idea, from a political standpoint, was that each show would be seen only by the people who lived in that particular state or region. This meant it made no difference if Nixon's statements—for they were not really answers—were exactly the same, phrase for phrase, gesture for gesture, from state to state. Only the press would be bored and the press had been written off already. So Nixon could get through the campaign with a dozen or so carefully worded responses that would cover all the problems of America in 1968.

Roger Ailes, the executive producer of the Mike Douglas show, was hired to produce the one-hour programs. Ailes was twenty-eight years old. He had started as a prop boy on the Douglas show in 1965 and was running it within three years. He was good. When he left, Douglas' ratings declined. But not everyone he passed on his way up remained his friend. Not even Douglas. Richard Nixon had been a guest on the show in the fall of 1967. While waiting to go on, he fell into conversation with Roger Ailes.

"It's a shame a man has to use gimmicks like this to get elected," Nixon said.

"Television is not a gimmick," Ailes said.

Richard Nixon liked that kind of thinking. He told Len Garment to hire the man. Ailes had been sent to Chicago three days before Nixon opened the fall campaign. His instructions were to select a panel of questioners and design a set. But now, on the day of the program, only six hours, in fact, before it was to begin, Ailes was having problems.

"Those stupid bastards on the set-designing crew put turquoise curtains in the background. Nixon wouldn't look right unless he was carrying a pocketbook." Ailes ordered the curtains removed and three plain, almost stark wooden boards to replace them. "The wood has clean, solid, masculine lines," he said.

His biggest problem was with the panel of questioners. Shakespeare, Treleaven, and Garment had felt it essential to have a "balanced" group. First, this meant a Negro. One Negro. Not two. Two would be offensive to whites, perhaps to Negroes as well. Two would be trying too hard. One was necessary and safe. Fourteen percent of the population applied to a six- or seven-member panel equaled one. Texas would be tricky, though. Do you have a Negro *and* a Mexican-American, or if not, then which?

Besides the Negro, the panel for the first show included a Jewish attorney, the president of a Polish-Hungarian group, a suburban housewife, a businessman, a representative of the white lower middle class, and, for authenticity, two newsmen: one from Chicago, one from Moline.

That was all right, Roger Ailes said. But then someone had called from New York and insisted that he add a farmer. Roger Ailes had been born in Ohio, but even so he knew you did not want a farmer on a television show. All they did was ask complicated questions about things like parities, which nobody else understood or cared about. Including Richard Nixon. Besides, the farmer brought the panel size to eight, which Ailes said was too big. It would be impossible for Nixon to establish interpersonal relationships with eight different people in one hour. And interpersonal relationships were the key to success.

"This is the trouble with all these political people horning in," Ailes said. "Fine, they all get their lousy little groups represented but we wind up with a horseshit show."

There was to be a studio audience—three hundred people—recruited by the local Republican organization. Just enough Negroes so the press could not write "all-white" stories but not enough so it would look like a ball park. The audience, of course, would applaud every answer Richard Nixon gave, boosting his confidence and giving the impression to a viewer that Nixon certainly did have charisma, and whatever other qualities they wanted their President to have.

Treleaven and his assistant, Al Scott, came to the studio late in the afternoon. They were getting nervous. "Nixon's throat is scratchy," Treleaven said, "and that's making him upset." Al Scott did not like the lighting in the studio. "The lights are too high," he said. "They'll show the bags under RN's eyes."

Then there was a crisis about whether the press should be allowed in the studio during the show. Shakespeare had given an order that they be kept out. Now they were complaining to Herb Klein, the press-relations man, that if three hundred shills could be bussed in to cheer, a pool of two or three reporters could be allowed to sit in the stands.

Shakespeare still said no. No *newspapermen* were going to interfere with his TV show. Klein kept arguing, saying that if this was how it was going to start, on the very first day of the campaign, it was going to be 1960 again within a week. Treleaven and Ailes went upstairs, to the WBBM cafeteria, and drank vending-machine coffee from paper cups. "I agree with Frank," Ailes said. "It's not a press conference."

"But if you let the audience in . . ."

"Doesn't matter. The audience is part of the show. And that's the whole point. It's a television show. Our television show. And the press has no business on the set."

"Goddam it, Harry, the problem is that this is an electronic election. The first there's ever been. TV has the power now. Some of the guys get arrogant and rub the reporters' faces in it and then the reporters get pissed and go out of their way to rap anything they consider staged for TV. And you know damn well that's what they'd do if they saw this from the studio. You let them in with the regular audience and they see the warm-up. They see Jack Rourke out there telling the audience to applaud and to mob Nixon at the end, and that's all they'd write about. You know damn well it is." Jack Rourke was Roper Ailes's assistant.

"I'm still afraid we'll create a big incident if we lock them out entirely," Treleaven said. "I'm going to call Frank and suggest he reconsider."

But Shakespeare would not. He arranged for monitors in an adjacent studio and said the press could watch from there, seeing no more, no less, than what they would see from any living room in Illinois.

It was five o'clock now; the show was to start at nine. Ray Vojey, the makeup man borrowed from the Johnny Carson show, had arrived. "Oh, Ray," Roger Ailes said, "with Wilkinson, watch that perspiration problem on the top of his forehead."

"Yes, he went a little red in Portland," Ray Vojey said.

"And when he's off camera, I'd give him a treated towel, just like Mr. Nixon uses."

"Right."

Ailes turned to Jack Rourke, the assistant. "Also, I'd like to have Wilkinson in the room with Nixon before the show to kibitz around, get Nixon loose."

"Okay, I'll bring him in."

The set, now that it was finished, was impressive. There was a round blue-carpeted platform, six feet in diameter and eight inches high. Richard Nixon would stand on this and face the panel, which would be seated in a semicircle around him. Bleachers for the audience ranged out behind the panel chairs. Later, Roger Ailes would think to call the whole effect "the arena concept" and bill Nixon as "the man in the arena." He got this from a Theodore Roosevelt quote which hung, framed, from a wall of his office in Philadelphia. It said something about how one man in the arena was worth ten, or a hundred, or a thousand carping critics.

At nine o'clock, Central Daylight Time, Richard Nixon, freshly powdered, left his dressing room, walked down a corridor deserted save for Secret Service, and went through a carefully guarded doorway that opened on the rear of the set.

Harry Treleaven had selected tape from WBBM's coverage of the noon-time motorcade for the opening of the show. Tape that showed Richard Nixon riding, arms outstretched, beaming, atop an open car. Hundreds of thousands of citizens, some who had come on their own, some who had been recruited by Republican organizations, cheered, waved balloons, and tossed confetti in the air. One week before, at the Democratic convention, it had been Humphrey, blood, and tear gas. Today it was Nixon, the unifying hero, the man to heal all wounds. Chicago Republicans showed a warm, assured, united front. And Harry Treleaven picked only the most magical of moments for the opening of his television show.

Then the director hit a button and Bud Wilkinson appeared on the screen, a placid, composed, substantial, reassuring figure introducing his close personal friend, a man whose intelligence and judgment had won the respect of the world's leaders and the admiration of millions of his countrymen, this very same man who had been seen entering Jerusalem moments ago on tape: Richard Nixon. And the carefully cued audience (for Jack Rourke had done his job well) stood to render an ovation. Richard Nixon, grinning, waving, *thrusting,* walked to the blue riser to receive the tribute.

It was warmly given. Genuine. He looked toward his wife; the two daughters; Senator Ed Brooke, the most useful Negro he had found; Charles Percy, the organization man; and Senator Thurston Morton, resigned if not enthusiastic. They sat in the first row together.

He was alone, with not even a chair on the platform for company, ready to face, if not the nation, at least Illinois. To communicate, man to man, eye to eye, with that mass of the ordinary whose concerns he so deeply shared, whose values were so totally his own. All the subliminal effects sank in. Nixon stood alone, ringed by forces which, if not hostile, were at least—to the viewer—unpredictable.

There was a rush of sympathy; a desire—a need, even—to root. Richard Nixon was suddenly human: facing a new and dangerous situation, alone, armed with only his wits. In image terms, he had won before he began. All the old concepts had been destroyed. He had achieved a new level of communication. The stronger his statement, the stronger the surge of warmth inside the viewer.

Morris Liebman, the Jewish attorney, asked the first question: "Would you comment on the accusation which was made from time to time that your views have shifted and that they are based on expediencies?"

Richard Nixon squinted and smiled. "I suppose what you are referring to is: Is there a new Nixon or is there an old Nixon? I suppose I could counter by saying: Which Humphrey shall we listen to today?"

There was great applause for this. When it faded, Richard Nixon said, "I do want to say this: There certainly is a new Nixon. I realize, too, that as a man gets older he learns something. If I haven't learned something I am not worth anything in public life. . . . I think my principles are consistent. I believe very deeply in the American system. I believe very deeply in what is needed to defend that system at home and abroad. I think I have some ideas as to how we can promote peace, ideas that are different from what they were eight years ago, not because I have changed but because the problems have changed.

"My answer is 'yes,'" there is a new Nixon, if you are talking in terms of new ideas for the new world and the America we live in. In terms of what I believe in, the American view and the American dream, I think I am just what I was eight years ago."

Applause swept the studio. Bud Wilkinson joined in.

The farmer asked a question about farming. The Polish-Hungarian delivered an address concerning the problems of the people of Eastern Europe. His remarks led to no question at all, but no matter: Richard Nixon expressed concern for the plight of Eastern Europeans everywhere, including Northern Illinois.

Then Warner Saunders, the Negro, and a very acceptable, very polite one he seemed to be, asked, "What does law and order mean to you?"

"I am quite aware," Richard Nixon said, "of the fact that the black community, when they hear it, think of power being used in a way that is destructive to them, and yet I think we have to also remember that the black community as well as the white community has an interest in order and in law, providing that law is with justice. . . ."

John McCarter, the businessman, asked about Spiro Agnew. Nixon said, "Of all the men who I considered, Spiro Agnew had the intelligence, the courage, and the principle to take on the great responsibilities of a campaigner and responsibilities of Vice President."

McCarter came back later wanting to know if Nixon thought the Chicago police had been too harsh on demonstrators in the streets.

"It would be easy," Nixon said, "to criticize Mayor Daley and by implication Vice President Humphrey. But it wouldn't be right for me to lob in criticism. I am not going to get into it. It is best for political figures not to be making partisan comments from the sidelines."

The show went on like that. At the end the audience charged from the bleachers, as instructed. They swarmed around Richard Nixon so that the last thing the viewer at home saw was Nixon in the middle of this big crowd of people, who all thought he was great.

Treleaven plunged into the crowd. He was excited; he thought the show had been brilliant. He got to Nixon just as Nixon was bending down to autograph a cast that a girl had on her leg.

"Well, you've got a leg up," Treleaven said.

Nixon stood up and grinned and moved away.

"Gee, that was sure a funny look he gave me," Treleaven said. "I wonder if he heard me. I wonder if he knew who I was."

Originally, Treleaven had wanted David Douglas Duncan, the photographer, to make commercials. Duncan was a friend of Richard Nixon's but when Treleaven took him out to lunch he said no, he would be too busy. Then Duncan mentioned Eugene Jones. Treleaven wanted Duncan because he had decided to make still photography the basis of Richard Nixon's sixty-second television commercial campaign. He had learned a little about stills at J. Walter Thompson when he had used them for some Pan American spots. Now he thought they were the perfect thing for Nixon because Nixon himself would not have to appear. The words would be the same ones Nixon always used—the words of the acceptance speech. But they would all seem fresh and lively because a series of still pictures would flash on the screen while Nixon spoke. If it were done right, it would permit Treleaven to create a Nixon image that was entirely independent of words. Obviously, some technical skill would be required. David Douglas Duncan said Gene Jones was the man.

Treleaven met Jones and was impressed. "He's low-key," Treleaven said. "He doesn't come at you as a know-it-all."

Gene Jones, who was in his early forties, had been taking movies of wars half his life. He did it perhaps as well as any man ever has. Besides that, he had produced the *Today* show on NBC for two years and had done a documentary series on famous people called *The World of*—Billy Graham, Sophia Loren, anyone who had been famous and was willing to be surrounded by Jones's cameras for a month.

Jones understood perfectly what Treleaven was after. A technique through which Richard Nixon would seem to be contemporary, imaginative, involved—without having to say anything of substance. Jones had never done commercial work before but for $110,000, from which he would pay salaries to a nine-man staff, he said he would do it for Nixon.

A day or two later Jones came down to Treleaven's office to discuss details such as where he should set up a studio and what areas the first set of spots should cover. "This will not be a commercial sell," Jones said. "It will not have the feel of something a—pardon the expression—an agency would turn out. I see it as sort of a miniature *Project 20.* And I can't see anyone turning it off a television set, quite frankly."

That same day Jones rented two floors of the building at 303 East 53rd Street in Manhattan, one flight up from a night club called Chuck's Composite. Within three days, he had his staff at work. Buying pictures, taking pictures, taking motion pictures of still pictures that Jones himself had cropped and arranged in a sequence. I'm pretty excited about this," Jones said. "I think we can give it an artistic dimension."

Harry Treleaven did not get excited about anything but he was at least intrigued by this. "It will be interesting to see how he translates his approach into political usefulness," Treleaven said.

"Yes," Frank Shakespeare said, "if he can."

Gene Jones would start work at five o'clock in the morning. Laying coffee and doughnuts on his desk, he would spread a hundred or so pictures on the floor, taken from boxes into which his staff already had filed them. The boxes had labels like *Vietnam . . . Democratic Convention . . . Poverty: Harlem, city slums, ghettos . . . faces: Happy American people at work. . . .*

He would select a category to fit the first line of whatever script he happened to be working with that day. He would select the most appropriate of the pictures, and then arrange and rearrange, as in a game of solitaire. When he had the effect he thought he wanted he would work with a stopwatch and red pencil, marking each picture on the back to indicate what sort of angle and distance the movie camera should shoot from and how long it should linger on each still.

"The secret is in juxtaposition," Jones said. "The relationships, the arrangement. After twenty-five years, the other things—the framing and the panning—are easy."

Everyone was excited about the technique and the way it could be used to make people feel that Richard Nixon belonged in the White House. The only person who was not impressed was Nixon. He was in a hotel room in San Francisco one day recording the words for one of the early commercials. The machine was turned on before Nixon realized it and the end of his conversation was picked up.

"I'm not sure I like this kind of a . . . . format, incidentally," Nixon said. "Ah . . . I've seen these kind of things and I don't think they're very . . . very effective."

Still, Nixon read the words he had been told to read.

In the afternoons, Treleaven, Garment, and Shakespeare would go to Gene Jones's studio to look at the spots on a little machine called a Movieola. If they were approved, Jones would take them to a sound studio down the street to blend in music, but they never were approved right away. There was not one film that Garment or Shakespeare did not order changed for a "political" reason. Anything that might offend Strom Thurmond, that might annoy the Wallace voter whom Nixon was trying so hard for; any ethnic nuance that Jones, in his preoccupation with artistic viewpoint, might have missed: these came out.

"Gene is good," Treleaven explained, "but he needs a lot of political guidance. He doesn't always seem to be aware of the point we're trying to make."

Jones didn't like the changes. "I'm not an apprentice," he said. "I'm an experienced pro and never before in my career have I had anyone stand over my shoulder telling me to change this and change that. When you pull out a shot or two it destroys the dynamism, the whole flow."

The first spot was called simply VIETNAM. Gene Jones had been there for ninety days, under fire, watching men kill and die and he had been wounded in the neck himself. Out of the experience had come *A Face of War*. And out of it now came E.S.J. [for Eugene S. Jones] #1, designed to help Richard Nixon become President.

Harry Treleaven and Len Garment and Frank Shakespeare thought this commercial splendid.

"Wow, that's powerful," Treleaven said.

The fourth of the ten scheduled panel shows was done in Philadelphia. It was televised across Pennsylvania and into Delaware and New Jersey. Roger Ailes arrived in Philadelphia on Wednesday, September 18, two days before the show was to go on the air. "We're doing all right," he said. "If we could only get someone to play Hide the Greek." He did not like Spiro Agnew either.

The production meeting for the Philadelphia show was held at ten o'clock Thursday morning in the office of Al Hollender, program director of WCAU. The purpose was to acquaint the local staff with what Roger Ailes wanted to do and to acquaint Roger Ailes with the limitations of the local staff. Ailes came in ten minutes late, dressed in sweat shirt and sneakers, coffee cup in hand. He had a room at the Marriott Motor Hotel across the street.

"One problem you're going to have here, Roger," a local man said, "is the size of the studio. You've been working with an audience of three hundred, I understand, but we can only fit 240."

"That's all right. I can get as much applause out of 240 as three hundred, if it's done right, and that's all they are—an applause machine." He paused. "That and a couple of reaction shots."

"I'm more concerned." Ailes said, "about where camera one is. I've talked to Nixon twice about playing to it and I can't seem to get through to him. So I think this time we're going to play it to him."

"You ought to talk to him about saying, 'Let me make one thing very clear,' ten times every show," someone said. "It's driving people nuts."

"I have, and Shakespeare told me not to mention it again. It bugs Nixon. Apparently everybody has been telling him about it but he can't stop."

After half an hour, Roger Ailes left the meeting. "Those things bore me," he said. "I'll leave Rourke to walk around and kick the tires." He went across the street to the motel. The morning was clear and hot.

"The problem with the panels is that we need variety," Ailes said. "Nixon gets bored with the same kind of people. We've got to screw around with this one a little bit."

"You still want seven?" an assistant, supplied by the local Republicans, asked.

"Yes, and on this one we definitely need a Negro. I don't think it's necessary to have one in every group of six people, no matter what our ethnic experts say, but in Philadelphia it is. *U.S. News and World Report* this week says that one of every three votes cast in Philadelphia will be Negro."

"I know one in Philadelphia," the local man, whose name was Dan Boozer, said. "He's a dynamic type, the head of a self-help organization, that kind of thing. And he is black."

"What do you mean he's black?"

"I mean he's dark. It will be obvious on television that he's not white."

"You mean we won't have to put a sign around him that says, 'This is our Negro'?"

"Absolutely not."

"Fine. Call him. Let's get this thing going."

"Nixon is better if the panel is offbeat," Ailes was saying. "It's tough to get an articulate ditchdigger, but I'd like to."

"I have one name here," Boozer said. "Might be offbeat. A Pennsylvania Dutch farmer."

"No! No more farmers. They all ask the same dull questions."

The morning produced an Italian lawyer from Pittsburgh, a liberal housewife from the Main Line, and a Young Republican from the Wharton School of Finance and Commerce.

"Now we need a newsman," Roger Ailes said.

I suggested the name of an articulate reporter from the *Evening Bulletin* in Philadelphia.

"Fine. Why don't you call him?"

"He's a Negro."

"Oh shit, we can't have two. Even in Philadelphia. Wait a minute—call him, and if he'll do it we can drop the self-help guy."

But the reporter was unavailable. Then I suggested Jack McKinney, a radio talk-show host from WCAU. Ailes called him and after half an hour on the phone, McKinney, who found it hard to believe the show would not be rigged, agreed to go on. Then I suggested a psychiatrist I knew: the head of a group that brought Vienamese children wounded in the war to the United States for treatment and artificial limbs.

"What his name?"

"Herb Needleman."

Roger Ailes called him. Herb Needleman agreed to do the show. Roger Ailes was pleased. "The guy sounded tough but not hysterical. This is shaping up as a very interesting show."

A newsman from Camden, New Jersey, was added, and, at four o'clock, Ailes called Len Garment in New York to tell him the panel was complete.

". . . That's six," he was saying, "and then we've got a Jewish doctor from Philadelphia, a psychiatrist, who—wait a minute, Len, relax . . . I— yes, he's already accepted, he . . . Well, why not? . . . Are you serious? . . . Honest to God, Len? . . . Oh, no, I can get out of it, it'll just be a little embarrassing . . . No, you're right, if he feels that strongly about it. . . ." Roger Ailes hung up.

"Jesus Christ," he said. "You're not going to believe this but Nixon hates psychiatrists."

"What?"

"Nixon hates psychiatrists. He's got this thing, apparently. They make him very nervous. You should have heard Len on the phone when I told him I had one on the panel. Did you hear him? If I ever heard a guy's voice turn white, that was it."

"Why?"

"He said he didn't want to go into it. But apparently Nixon won't even let one in the same room. Jesus Christ, could you picture him on a live TV show finding out he's being questioned by a shrink?"

There was another reason, too, why Herb Needleman was unacceptable. "Len says they want to go easy on Jews for a while. I guess Nixon's tired of saying 'balance of power' about the goddam Middle East."

So, at 4:15 P.M., Roger Ailes made another call to Dr. Needleman, to tell him that this terribly embarrassing thing had happened, that the show had been overbooked. Something about having to add a panelist from New Jersey because the show would be televised into the southern part of the state.

"You know what I'd like?" Ailes said later. "As long as we've got this extra spot open. A good, mean, Wallaceite cab driver. Wouldn't that be great? Some guy to sit there and say, 'Awright Mac, what about these niggers?' "

It was five o'clock in the afternoon. The day still was hot but Roger Ailes had not been outside since morning. Air conditioning, iced tea, and the telephone.

"Come on," Roger Ailes said. "Let's go find a cab driver." He stepped out to the motel parking lot and walked through the sun to the main entrance. The Marriott was the best place they had in Philadelphia. Eight cabs were lined up in the driveway. The third driver Roger Ailes talked to said that he was not really for Wallace, but that he wasn't really against him either.

"What's your name?" Roger Ailes said.

"Frank Kornsey."

"You want to go on television tomorrow night? Right across the street there, and ask Mr. Nixon some questions. Any questions you want."

"I've got to work tomorrow night."

"Take it off. Tell them why. We'll pay you for the hours you miss, plus your expenses to and from the studio."

"My wife will think I'm nuts."

"Your wife will love you. When did she ever think she'd be married to a guy who conversed with the next President of the United States?"

"I'll let you know in the morning," Frank Kornsey said.

Back in the motel room, the talk drifted to some of the curious associations into which Nixon seemed to fall. People he sought to align himself with, whose endorsement he was so pleased to accept, when even in political terms they probably did him more harm than good.

"That Wilkinson, for Christ's sake, he's like a marionette with the strings broken," Ailes's director said. The director had come over from the studio in midafternoon, after working on final placement of the cameras.

"Oh, Wilkinson's a sweet guy," Ailes said, "but he's got absolutely no sense of humor."

"If you're going to keep using him as a moderator, you should tell him to stop applauding all the answers."

"He's been told," Ailes said, "he's been told. He just can't help it."

Ailes got up from the table. "Let's face it, a lot of people think Nixon is dull. Think he's a bore, a pain in the ass. They look at him as the kind of kid who always carried a book bag. Who was forty-two years old the day he was born. They figure other kids got footballs for Christmas, Nixon got briefcases and he loved it. He'd always have his homework done and he'd never let you copy. Now you put him on television, you've got a problem right away. He's a funny-looking guy. He looks like somebody hung him in a closet overnight and he jumps out in the morning with his suit all bunched up and starts running around saying, 'I want to be President.' I mean this is how he strikes some people. That's why these shows are important. To make them forget all that."

Richard Nixon came to Philadelphia the next day: Friday. There was the standard downtown motorcade at noon. Frank Kornsey took the whole day off to stay home and write questions. "I got some beauties," he told Roger Ailes on the phone.

Ailes went to the studio at two o'clock in the afternoon. "I'm going to fire this director," he said. "I'm going to fire the son of a bitch right after the show. Look at this. Look at the positioning of these cameras. I've told him fifty times I want closeups. Closeups! This is a closeup medium. It's dull to shoot chest shots. I want to see pores. That's what people are. That's what television is."

He walked through the studio, shaking his head. "We won't get a shot better than waist-high from these cameras all night. That's 1948 direction. When you had four people in every shot and figured you were lucky you had any shot at all."

The audience filled the studio at seven o'clock. The panel was brought in at 7:15. Frank Kornsey was nervous. Roger Ailes offered him a shot of bourbon. "No thanks," he said. "I'll be all right." He tried to grin.

At 7:22 Jack Rourke stepped onto the riser. He was a heavy Irishman with a red face and gray hair. "Hello," he said to the audience. "I'm Frank Sinatra."

The Nixon family, David Eisenhower, and the Governor of Pennsylvania came in. The audience applauded. This audience, like the others, had been carefully recruited by the local Republican organization. "That's the glee club," Jack Rourke said, pointing to the Nixons.

The director walked into the control booth at 7:24. "He's crazy," the director said, meaning Roger Ailes. "He has no conception of the mechanical limitations involved in a show like this. He says he wants closeups, it's like saying he wants to go to the moon." The director took his seat at the control panel and spoke to a cameraman on the floor. "Make sure you know where Mrs. Nixon is and what she looks like."

A member of the Nixon staff ran into the booth. "Cut the sound in that studio next door. We've got the press in there and we don't want them to hear the warm-up."

"Now when Mr. Nixon comes in," Jack Rourke was saying, "I want you to tear the place apart. Sound like ten thousand people. I'm sure, of course, that you'll also want to stand up at that point. So what do you say we try it now. Come on, stand up. And let me hear it."

"One forty-five to air," the director said in the control booth.

"Tell Rourke to check the sound level on the panel."

Jack Rourke turned to Frank Kornsey: "Ask a question, please. We'd like to check your microphone."

Frank Kornsey leaned forward and spoke, barely above a whisper. His list of "beauties" lay on a desk before him. He was still pale, even through his makeup.

"I was just wondering how Mr. and Mrs. Nixon are enjoying our wonderful city of Philadelphia," he said.

Pat Nixon, in a first row seat, gave her tight, closemouthed smile.

"No, they don't care for it," Jack Rourke said.

"Thirty seconds," came a voice from the control room. "Clear the decks, please, thirty seconds."

Then, at exactly 7:30, while a tape of Richard Nixon's motorcade was being played for the viewers at home, the director said, "Okay, cue the applause, move back camera one, move back one," and Richard Nixon stepped through a crack in a curtain, hunched his shoulders, raised his arms, wiggled his wrists, made V-signs with his fingers and switched on his grin.

Jack McKinney, the talk-show host, was wearing his hairpiece for the occasion. Nixon turned to him first, still with the grin, hands clasped before him, into his fourth show now and over the jitters. Maybe, in fact, ready to show off just a bit. A few new combinations, if the proper moment came, to please the crowd.

"Yes, Mr. McKinney," he said.

Jack McKinney did not lead with his right but he threw a much stiffer jab than Nixon had been expecting: "Why are you so reluctant to comment on Vietnam this year when in 1952, faced with a similar issue in Korea, you were so free with your partisan remarks?"

Not a crippling question but there was an undertone of unfriendliness to it. Worse, it had been put to him in professional form. Nixon stepped back, a bit off balance. This sort of thing threatened the stability of the whole format; the basis being the hypothesis that Nixon could appear to risk all by going live while in fact risking nothing by facing the loose syntax and predictable, sloppy thrusts of amateurs. He threw up an evasive flurry. But the grin was gone from his face. Not only did he know now that he would have to be careful of McKinney, he was forced to wonder, for the first time, what he might encounter from the others.

The Negro was next. Warily: "Yes, Mr. Burress." And Burress laid Black Capitalism right down the middle, straight and soft. Nixon had it memorized. He took a long time on the answer, though, savoring its clichés, making sure his wind had come back all the way.

Then Frank Kornsey, who studied his list and asked, "What are you going to do about the *Pueblo?*" Beautiful. Nixon was honing this one to perfection. He had taken 1:22 with it in California, according to Roger Ailes's chart, but had brought it down to 1:05 in Ohio. Now he delivered it in less than a minute. He was smooth again, and grinning, as he turned to the liberal housewife, Mrs. Mather.

Was civil disobedience *ever* justified, she wondered. Nixon took a quick step backwards on the riser. His face fell into the solemnity mask. There were philosophic implications there he did not like. He could understand the impatience of those less fortunate than ourselves, he assured her, and their demand for immediate improvement was, indeed, healthy for our society in many ways. But—as long as change could be brought about within the system—and no, he was not like some who claimed it could not—then there was no cause, repeat, *no* cause that justified the breaking of a law.

But he knew he would have to watch her, too. The first line of sweat broke out across his upper lip.

The young Republican from Wharton wanted to know how to bring the McCarthy supporters back into the mainstream, which was fine, but then the newsman from Camden asked if Nixon agreed with Spiro Agnew's charge that Hubert Humphrey was "soft on Communism."

He knew how to handle that one, but while sidestepping, he noted that this fellow, too, seemed unawed. That made three out of seven who were ready, it appeared, to mix it up. And one of them a good-looking articulate woman. And another, McKinney, who seemed truly mean.

It was McKinney's turn again: Why was Nixon refusing to appear on any of the news confrontation shows such as *Meet the Press?* Why would he face the public only in staged settings such as this, where the questions were almost certain to be worded generally enough to allow him any vague sort of answer he wanted to give? Where the presence of the cheering studio audience was sure to intimidate any questioner who contemplated true engagement? Where Nixon moved so quickly from one questioner to the next that he eliminated any possibility of follow-up, any chance for true discussion . . . ?

"The guy's making a speech!" Frank Shakespeare shouted in the control booth. Roger Ailes jumped for the phone to Wilkinson on stage. But McKinney was finished, for the moment. The question was, had he finished Nixon, too?

"I've done those quiz shows, Mr. McKinney. I've done them until they were running out of my ears." There was no question on one point: Richard Nixon was upset. Staring hard at McKinney he grumbled something about why there ought to be more fuss about Hubert Humphrey not having press conferences and less about him and *Meet the Press.*

It did not seem much of a recovery but in the control room Frank Shakespeare punched the palm of one hand with the fist of the other and said, "That socks it to him, Dickie Baby!" The audience cheered. Suddenly, Nixon, perhaps sensing a weakness in McKinney where he had feared that none existed, perhaps realizing he had no choice, surely buoyed by the cheers, decided to slug it out.

"Go ahead," he said, gesturing. "I want you to follow up."

McKinney came back creditably, using the word "amorphous" and complaining that viewers were being asked to support Nixon for President on the basis of "nothing but a wink and a smile" particularly in regard to Vietnam.

"Now, Mr. McKinney, maybe I haven't been as specific . . ." and Nixon was off on a thorough rephrasing of his Vietnam non-position, which, while it contained no substance—hence, could not accommodate anything new—sounded, to uninitiates, like a public step forward. The audience was ecstatic. Outnumbered, two hundred forty-one to one, McKinney could do nothing but smile and shake his head.

"Be very careful with McKinney," Shakespeare said, bending over Roger Ailes. "I want to give him a chance but I don't want him to hog the show."

"Yeah, if he starts making another speech I'll call Bud and—"

But Shakespeare was no longer listening. He was grappling with a cameraman who had come into the control booth and began to take pictures of the production staff at work.

"No press," Shakespeare said, and when the man continued shooting his film, Shakespeare began to push. The cameraman pushed back as well as he could, but Shakespeare, leaning hard, edged him toward the door.

Meanwhile, Frank Kornsey, consulting his written list again, had asked, "What do you intend to do about the gun-control law?" Then, quickly, the others: Are you writing off the black vote? What about federal tax credits . . . water and air pollution? And then the Camden newsman, whose name was Flynn, asking about Nixon's action in 1965 when he had called for the removal of a Rutgers history professor who had spoken kindly of the Vietcong—on campus.

Nixon assured Mr. Flynn that academic freedom remained high on his personal list of privileges which all Americans should enjoy, but added, "There is one place where I would draw the line. And that is, I do not believe that anyone who is paid by the government and who is using government facilities—and Rutgers, as I'm sure you are aware, Mr. Flynn, is a state institution—has the right to call for the victory of the enemy over American boys—while he is on the campus."

But now McKinney gathered himself for a final try: "You said that the Rutgers professor 'called for' the victory of the Vietcong, but as I recall he didn't say that at all. This is what I mean about your being able, on this kind of show, to slide off the questions. Now the facts were—"

"Oh, I know the facts, Mr. McKinney. I know the facts."

Nixon was grinning. The audience poured forth its loudest applause of the night. But Wilkinson joined in, full of righteous fervor. Of course Mr. Nixon knew the facts.

McKinney was beaten but would not quit: "The facts were that the professor did not 'call for' the victory—"

"No, what he said, Mr. McKinney, and I believe I am quoting him *exactly,* was that he would 'welcome the impending victory of the Vietcong.' "

"Which is not the same thing."

"Well, Mr. McKinney, you can make that distinction if you wish, but what I'll do is I'll turn it over to the television audience right now and let them decide for themselves about the semantics. About the difference between 'calling for' and 'welcoming' a victory of the Vietcong.''

He was angry but he had it under control and he talked fast and hard and when he was finished he swung immediately to the next questioner. The show was almost over. McKinney was through for the night.

"Boy, is he going to be pissed," Roger Ailes said as he hurried down from the control room. "He'll think we really tried to screw him. But critically it was the best show he's done."

Roger Ailes went looking for Nixon. He wound up in an elevator with Nixon's wife. She was wearing a green dress and she did not smile. One thought of the remark a member of the Nixon staff had made: "Next to her, RN looks like Mary Poppins."

"Hello, Mrs. Nixon," Roger Ailes said. She nodded. She had known him for months. "How did you like the show?" She nodded very slowly, her mouth was drawn in a thin, straight line.

"Everyone seems to think it was by far the best," Ailes said. "Especially the way he took care of that McKinney."

Pat Nixon stared at the elevator door. The car stopped. She got off and moved down a hallway with the Secret Service men around her.

After the long-awaited *Meet the Press* show in Southern California, Ailes drove an hour and a half to an airfield, where a friend had arranged for him to make his first parachute jump. He missed the landing zone on his first try and decided to jump again. The second time, he hit the landing zone but ripped ligaments in his ankle. He had to take pills for pain that evening.

The NBC studio in Burbank, location of the grand finale telethon the next day, was very big. One hundred and twenty-five telephones had been installed for the operators who would take calls during the show. The operators had been recruited by the local Republican organization. There also were seats for several hundred spectators, to be recruited by the organization, too. Richard Nixon had grown accustomed to hearing his answers applauded. It seemed foolish to deprive him on the final night of the campaign.

Roger Ailes hobbled to the front row of the audience section. Immy Fiorentino, the lighting man, who had been used for the later panel shows and the Madison Square Garden rally, was there.

"It's going to be a dull two hours," Roger Ailes said. "That's for openers."

Immy Fiorentino shrugged. Dull, sparkling, he did not much care. As long as it was properly lit. "How are these questions going to work?" he asked.

"Well, what's going to happen," Roger Ailes said, "is all of the questions are going to come through the operators over there and then runners will bring them down to the producer's table, which will be set up here, and from there they'll go to a screening room where the Nixon staff will tear them up and write their own. Then they'll go to Bud Wilkinson who will cleverly read them and Nixon will read the answers off a card."

Later, Jack Rourke was asked how it really would work.

"I understand Paul Keyes has been sitting up for two days writing questions," Roger Ailes said. Keyes was a friend of Nixon's who supervised the writing of the *Laugh-In* show.

"Well, not quite," Jack Rourke said. He seemed a little embarrassed.

"What's going to happen?"

"Oh . . ."

"It's sort of semi-forgery, isn't it?" Ailes said. "Keyes has a bunch of questions Nixon wants to answer. He's written them in advance to make sure they're properly worded. When someone calls with something similar, they'll use Keyes' question and attribute it to the person who called. Isn't that it?"

"More or less," Jack Rourke said.

At first, they were going to have Richard Nixon sit on the edge of a desk. The first desk that the NBC set designer had provided was on wheels.

"Jesus Christ, he'll lean against that and go sliding off the set." Roger Ailes said. "It will be the highlight of the campaign."

Then Frank Shakespeare called. Since there were going to be two separate telethons (one for the East, one for the West), lasting two hours each, it was felt that the edge of the desk would tend to be uncomfortable. Nixon preferred a "comfortable black swivel chair." Roger Ailes told the set designer to produce one. Then Ailes hobbled through the studio again, trying to develop a feel for it. Some sense that would enable him to infuse the program, somehow, with imagination. To give originality and élan to what seemed doomed to tedium.

"If we put Tricia and Julie over there, answering phones, we have to be careful who we put around them." He turned to an assistant. "Dolores, make a note of that. Make sure we get good-looking girls around Julie and Tricia."

He talked to the cameramen: "Sixty, sixty-five, seventy percent of the show will be RN on camera talking. You've got to watch him—I like to shoot him close but two hours on stage and he's going to perspire. So get away from him every once in a while and let him mop."

"Do you want Kleenex on stage?" a floor man asked.

"No, he'll have a handkerchief in his inside breast pocket."

In the control room, most attention centered around the splicing of a Jackie Gleason endorsement which was going into the beginning of the tape. Gleason had made the tape in Miami and it had been used first at the start of the Madison Square Garden rally: *"My name is Jackie Glea-*

son and I love this country. I've never made a public choice like this before—but I think this country needs Dick Nixon and we need him now."

Roger Ailes had his right ankle in a bucket of ice. "Jesus Christ, this hurts," he said. "Dolores, give me another of those pills, will you? I wish there were some way to pipe the Humphrey thing in here tonight. It will be a hell of a lot more interesting." He was in bad pain. And tired. And facing four hours of live direction in the evening. And—as the only member of Richard Nixon's staff who would have thought to jump from an airplane the day before the biggest TV production of the campaign—feeling quite alone. He sat with his foot in an ice bucket in the control room through the afternoon, wishing he were done and in Grenada, where he was going on vacation later in the week.

Frank Shakespeare and Paul Keyes got to the studio at three o'clock. Shakespeare was in his standard dark suit, Keyes in a sky-blue turtleneck. Ailes struggled out to meet them.

"Watch," he said. "Now they'll rip the whole thing up and start again."

The first change Shakespeare made was moving Julie and Tricia up from the second row to the first. Ailes had wanted them in the second row to make them seem simply part of the crowd, but Shakespeare said Nixon wanted to greet them as he entered and it would be awkward to have him leaning over other girls. "And he'll walk over," Shakespeare was saying, "and when he greets them I think he should kiss them."

"Well, I think kissing is a bit much," Paul Keyes said.

"But if he comes over, he's got to kiss them."

"No, it looks stagy," Keyes said. "We'll have him go right to his chair."

"Have him kiss one of the other broads," Ailes said.

Paul Keyes continued to check the set. "Roger, can you put that camera one in closer so RN will be physically conscious of it?"

Ailes explained why moving the camera would be a problem. "I know that," Keyes said, "But this was the one specific thing he asked for this morning. That we give him a camera close enough so he would be physically conscious of it. He wants this to be a very intimate show between him and the American people. And the only way he can do it is if that camera is right on top of him."

Ailes explained more of the technical problems.

"But RN wants to *converse* tonight. Low-key, easy, informal. He doesn't want to make a speech. And he needs the camera there to push him into the low key."

Ailes rearranged the cameras.

"Okay," Paul Keyes said. "Now can two come in a little closer?"

"Yeah, but if I bring two in—"

"He needs it close, Roger."

"Okay. You position two where you want it and I'll restage . . . Wait a minute, is four any good or is that too far away?"

"Four is perfect," Keyes said. "The important thing is the relationship between him and the camera. He needs that nearness."

"Okay," Ailes said, and he told the floor manager to mark with tape how far forward and to the left camera four should go without moving into the range of any of the other cameras. "Just tell RN he'll have that one camera he can play to and we'll screw around with the others," he said, and the problem was solved.

Paul Keyes sat in the chair that had been brought out for Richard Nixon. "It's too loose. It's got to have a solid back to it."

"Okay, I'll take care of that," Roger Ailes said, and he went slowly back to the control room and called the set designer and told him they needed another chair. The designer protested.

"Do you want him to tip over?" Ailes said. "The back is loose. Do you want him to lean back and go over on his ass?"

The designer suggested using an orange chair he had brought out earlier.

"Goddam it, no, we're not going to use an orange chair. We've been through that . . . I said we're not going to use an orange chair. Forget it. I'll get the goddam chair." He put down the phone and turned to Dolores Hardie, the assistant.

"Get the designer to get a goddam chair. I told that creepy bastard as soon as he brought it out that we weren't going to use an orange chair." It was four o'clock in the afternoon. Frank Shakespeare was worried about the studio getting too hot. "Make sure you've got that handkerchief soaked in witch hazel," Roger Ailes told someone. "I can't do that sincerity bit with the camera if he's sweating." Shakespeare got more worried about the temperature. "He's going to be out there four hours tonight."

It was decided to cancel the five o'clock rehearsal of the opening so the lights could be shut off, the studio sealed, and cold air piped in. Roger Ailes went across the hall to a dressing room and lay down on a couch.

"This is the beginning of a whole new concept," Ailes said. "This is it. This is the way they'll be elected forevermore. The next guys up will have to be performers. The interesting question is, how sincere is a TV set? If you take a cold guy and stage him warm, can you get away with it? I don't know. But I felt a lot better about jumping out of that plane yesterday than I do about this thing tonight."

The announcer who was to do the opening called to ask if his tone was too shrill.

"Yeah, we don't want it like a quiz show," Roger Ailes said. "He's going to be Presidential tonight so announce Presidentially."

The studio was opened and the hundred and twenty-five girls who had volunteered to answer the phones were led in. Frank Shakespeare watched them take their places and an expression of horror came over his face.

"Oh my God!" he said. "This is terrible! Where are the black faces? Where are the black faces?" He turned and went running off to find the woman who was in charge of the volunteers. She was a heavy woman with gray hair.

"We're going live across the country on Election Eve in an hour and a half and there's not one black face up there. We can't do that. It looks terrible."

"I know," the woman said. "I know. We tried. In fact we had twenty who agreed to come. But none of them showed up."

"This is terrible," Shakespeare said.

The woman gave a shrug that said, "What do you expect me to do? After all, you know they're undependable."

There was one Negro girl, sitting near the end of the next to last row. Someone pointed her out to Shakespeare. "Oh, yeah," he said. Staring.

"I could ask her to come down front so you'd be sure to get her in the picture."

Shakespeare never faltered. "Would you? Gee, that would be terrific. Terrific."

The Hubert Humphrey telethon, which started half an hour before Nixon's, was being shown in the press room. Humphrey was on with Paul Newman, Buddy Hackett, Danny Thomas, and others. He was obsequious to them all. Cue cards, other cameras, and a morass of wires and unused folding chairs were visible all over the stage. The Humphrey producers, apparently, had left their shirttails out on purpose, to point up the contrast with what they considered to be the contrived slickness of Nixon.

More startling, Humphrey was answering questions live. Actually talking to the people who called him on the phone. There was no Paul Keyes, no Bud Wilkinson to protect him.

"That's crazy," Al Scott said, appalled at what he saw. "They've got no control."

Richard Nixon was in a good mood. He sat in his comfortable black swivel chair with the back that had been tightened, his legs crossed, his smile seeming less forced than usual, his voice and rhetoric pleasantly subdued. If camera four had been any closer it would have put out his eye. He leaned into it as Bud Wilkinson read each question and responded in his most conversational tone. The substance was no different from what it had been all along, but the style was at its peak. The Social Security question was repeated at the beginning of each hour—on both shows—so that anyone who had just tuned in would be sure to hear that Richard Nixon did not intend to have senior citizens forming bread lines in the streets.

Paul Keyes had added a few twists to break the monotony of the answers. At one point, Bud Wilkinson walked across the room to where

Julie and Tricia were answering phones and asked them what seemed to be on most callers' minds. Then David Eisenhower read a letter from his grandfather. Earnestly. Then there was the chat with Mrs. Nixon. She answered a couple of Wilkinson/Paul Keyes questions of less than monumental importance, and then, as the audience—on cue—applauded, she grinned and . . . began to applaud herself.

It was simply a reflex. There had been so much applause in her life. And all through this campaign. She had sat, half-listening, then with her mind drifting more and more as the weeks and speeches passed so slowly into one another. Bringing her finally to this television studio on this final night where all that was left of her was reflex: you hear applause —applaud.

Then, in a cruel instant, she realized what she had done and that no doubt her error had been communicated to the nation by those evil black cameras she had learned to dread. Here, on the last night, with everything fitting neatly into place as it had from the start, she had spoiled it. She jerked up her hands to cover her face. Roger Ailes switched quickly to another shot.

Other than that, the two hours went smoothly, though after the immense effort of preparation it was inconceivable that they could have gone any other way. All along, whatever else the campaign was not, it was smooth.

Between shows, Richard Nixon disappeared into a dressing room for a ham and cheese sandwich, a cup of coffee, a shower, a rubdown, and a clean shirt.

David Eisenhower, looking tall and bewildered, wandered down from his seat. He was carrying two colored photographs of Richard Nixon. He approched Jack Rourke. "Do you suppose I could get these autographed?" he said.

"You know him as well as I do," Jack said.

"Yeah," David Eisenhower said. He walked away slowly. Then he saw Dwight Chapin, Nixon's personal aide. He repeated his request.

Now?" Chapin asked, straining to believe what he was hearing. "You want those autographed now?"

David Eisenhower managed a tentative nod.

"Oh, no," Dwight Chapin said. "Not now."

Richard Nixon tired a bit during the second show and started talking about those hundreds of confessed murderers who had been set free by the Supreme Court, but it was not noticeable enough to prevent Frank Shakespeare from patting people on the shoulder in the control booth and saying, "He's strong. He's strong."

Toward the end, Bud Wilkinson began a question by saying, "This one is from a carpenter named Bob Will in Orlando, Florida . . ."

And Richard Nixon started his answer with, "Well, you see, Mr. Carpenter . . ."

But the campaign was over.

"I'm not a showman," Richard Nixon was telling America. "I'm not a television personality."

Afterwards, Paul Keyes strode down the building's main corridor. "Perfect! Perfect! He did it just like he said he was going to. He said it was Nice Guy time tonight. He said he wasn't going to go for punch lines. He wasn't going to go for applause. Just come in low and thoughtful. And he did it!"

Roger Ailes was helped down the stairway and out to the car.

"Tonight," he said, "this was the Nixon I met on the Douglas show. This was the Nixon I wanted to work for."

Alternatives

Art and sub-art are everywhere in crisis. The ferment which always accompanies their many manifestations is more pronounced than ever. One finds it harder and harder to make sweeping *ex cathedra* judgments. Emergent forces keep startling us: a decadent form suddenly turns green, promise remains unfulfilled, beauty goes sour. Turn and turn about. The message of these concluding essays is perhaps that however hopeful or gloomy the situation may appear to be, it is subject to complete reversal at any given moment.

John Lahr decries the role of mass culture in standardizing contemporary language. To him, the *Time* style, the CBS style, and their innumerable offspring have "a smooth, efficient banality, a corporate ring which is unequivocal." In contrast to earlier ages when, he maintains, language re-created and stimulated the imagination, words today are the victims of ethnic anxiety and political abuse. The golden days of stage laughter, the humor of America's great clowns (like his own father, Bert Lahr) have been lost to technology. In all this Lahr's scorn is unsparing. And yet, he says, there may be hope for our scientifically sterilized language after all; *Hair* and *Muzeeka* and similar shows, the monologs of Lenny Bruce, the unique if oft-imitated Jules Feiffer—here are straws in the wind that encourage Lahr to believe that "laughter on stage will return not only to the broadness of acrobatic gesture but the flair and variety of language of the madcaps from an earlier, more intimate type of American entertainment.

That a moribund pop-art form is capable of taking on new life, that it can also express important aspects of the grim and surreal *zeitgeist* which envelops us, is the news that Bob Abel has to report. He refers us to the proliferation of Comix, strange but "refreshingly irreverent" and portentous offspring of Lil' Orphan Annie out of The Yellow Kid. Up from the underground *Hippie Sex Comix* and other more bizarre types come clawing their way up to challenge the institutionalization of funnies. It remains to be seen whether they and their creators will not themselves undergo institutionalization and conventionalization.

In Greil Marcus we have an articulate and enthusiastic chronicler of Rock 'n' Roll. Marcus traces the origins of that global cult. He finds them on the East Coast and the West Coast of America, in the Negro rhythm and blues, incarnate in Elvis and Dylan, dormant for a while and resurgent in the Beatles, the Rolling Stones, in a host of lesser lights and their avatars whether here or abroad. A barbaric yawp, preeminently a symptom of youth culture in the fifties and sixties, Marcus as an insider sees Rock in terms of the adolescent frustrations that it sets forth and relieves. To his ear, it is sound and soul, a non-verbal celebration of the senses, a matter of feeling over meaning, a mystique conveying metaphors of consciousness and unconsciousness. He is a young man, and be it noted that most of his analysis is cast in the past tense—with a ho-ho for the lyric that goes "Rock 'n' Roll forever will stand." His self-image is already that of a person who huddles together with other aficionados of his age for the warmth they need in their isolation.

The transitory nature of what looks so permanent to myopic participants is given historic perspective by a detached but involved sociologist, Irving Louis Horowitz, who himself refers ironically to a line sung not long ago by a rock group called Danny and the Juniors, to wit: "I don't care what people say/ Rock 'n' Roll is here to stay." Here today and gone tomorrow! Horowitz spots a powerful trend back to sweet dance music called *Bubblegum* and away from the current increasingly esoteric stress on instrumentation which itself originated in a terpsichorean impulse. Round and round we go.

Symbols like Woodstock and Altamont will continue to reverberate for those who lived through those tribal Be-Ins. Richard Todd confers immortality on an equally significant happening: the Alternative Media Project, an assemblage of anti-establishment communicators, communicants, and communards which took place in the hills of Maine at opulent Goddard College. Rock, propelled by LSD, had passed through Raga Rock to Acid Rock. Media freaks tripped to Goddard in defiance of the straights who, however, were also present, especially to represent the record companies. Workshops proceeded while couples engaged in casual and far from "outasight" copulation. Drugged, crazed, turned on and off, swathed in videotape, the Media Project people pant for Cable TV wherewith to spread their "radical software." Sadly, Todd watches them package cultural commodities in a manner little different from that of the establishmentarians they profess to abhor. The antagonistic forces are perceived to be in a symmetrical and symbiotic relationship: mirror images, two sides of one coin, each in its own way—one from below, the other from above—bent upon obliterating the distinction between public and private behavior. Are we in Weimar? In Rome just before the Fall? Is *this* our Alternative?

The Language of Laughter[*]

By John Lahr

Stage laughter, once the gaudy barometer of America's feverish leap into the twentieth century, now limps in search of a new voice. The society on which it comments is still shackled with injustice; the grotesque has not been ironed out by prosperity. Yet, if comedy has the targets, it lacks the language to encompass contemporary experience. The humor of America's great clowns owed its untamed brashness and variety to the street; today, the metropolis has been partially tamed by technology, and it is from the impulses of science that speech takes its pattern. Where immigrant tongues brought liveliness and variety to the stage action, the sense of immediacy with the contemporary moment has been lost to today's laughter since the real language of science must be mathematics, not words.

Language bears the scars of history. It was inevitable that the dialect humor of the early twentieth-century stage would vanish. World War II would put an end to the Baron von Münchausens of the American imagination, the civil rights struggle would banish its Amos 'n' Andys. A sophisticated society would be more self-conscious in its use of words, and even the ghetto-born comedians would speak in the uninflected tones of modern, democratic America. The buffoon, who had responded to the language of his new land with wonder and laughter at its eccentricities would give to the American stage an energy and an openness comparable to the Elizabethan merry-andrews. The rough language, like the violent broad gestures, bowed to the decorum of the times. Society now frowns upon pratfalls—man brought low—and winces at vernacular. The mass media which replaced theatrical satire as "popular" entertainment brought with them a special censorship and a uniformity which would castrate

---

* Reprinted by permission of the author and publisher, Grove Press, Inc. from *Up Against The Fourth Wall*. Copyright 1968, 1969, and 1970 by John Lahr. This article originally appeared in *Evergreen Review*.

the eccentric instincts of comedy. The innundation of the public by television has not moved language to life but away from it. Comedy has been seriously hurt.

The hollowness of contemporary vernacular—its smooth, efficient banality has a corporate ring which is unequivocal. There is a *Times* style, a *Time* style, and a CBS style. Americans listen and read, assuming the inflections without realizing their effect on the way they see the world. Language no longer vividly recreates life or stimulates the imagination as fully as in earlier eras. Too much rhetoric has been passed off as truth, too many inequities have been foisted on the public with the language of logic. Words which added richness and ambiguity to our language are lost because of ethnic nervousness or political misuse. The politics of exploitation undermine the country's speech. Can Americans use such simple words as "black," "justice," "dream," "liberal," "baby," "burn," "cool," without demeaning their argument? In the same way, as George Steiner has pointed out in *Language and Silence,* Hitler reduced the coinage of the German tongue by the atrocities carried out in its words. Terms like "roll back," "clean up," "break through," "peace," "victory," "nation" lost their poetic, evocative power. The tension felt by the German writers from Mann to Brecht is being felt by satirists in America today.

The early twentieth-century argot—with its malapropisms and ebullient idiocy—laughed at the world, but with a kindness which acknowledged a faith in it. The language of the streets, like the terms uttered to the groundlings at the Globe, had a primitive responsiveness to the world which spoke with the voice of the moment—one of longing, of failure, of carnival indifference. The effect could be both poignant and surprising.

Teacher: Gladys, vot is de opposite of misery?
Gladys: Happiness.
Teacher: Dot's right. Now Abbey, tell me vot is de opposite of woe?
Abbey: Giddyap!

(School Act, 1910)

Death filters into the language and its misuse, the grit of experience is captured in the playfulness of the funmakers, who would refer to the various types of routines as the "wop act," "the straight and the Jew," "double Dutch act," "blackface"—violent terms accepted for a brutal moment in history. The puns, the free-association of terms were part of the amusement and the curious wonder at the spoken word. "The Double Wop Act" epitomizes the intention:

Straight: I gotta good job for you.
Comic: What doin?
Straight: Manicurin boulevards.
Comic: How mucha you pay?

Straight: Twenty-two dollars a week.
Comic: Twenty-two dollars a week?
Straight: Yeh—two twos.
Comic: Datsa nice. Whatsa the hours?
Straight: You start at eight in the morning and stop at six ata night.
Comic: Datsa too much work.
Straight: Okay. I makea it easier for you. You start at six anda finish at eight.
Comic: Datsa nice man. I go now and tella my friend at the city hole.
Straight: Whatsa your friendsa name?
Comic: He lives at the city hole, I nunga remember hisa name. Hisa gotta name somethin like a horse.
Straight: You don't mean the mayor?
Comic: Sure, datsa him, the mare . . .

The American public still appreciates the outlandish wordplay of the Marx Brothers or Bert Lahr's inarticulate bellowing—"Gnong, gnong, gnong." Like the ad-lib wit, the noise was simply the random conjunction of guttural sounds which Lahr never understood. ("One day I did it; the audience laughed. So, I kept it in.") The comedians' response to language, their instinct for going beyond the bounds of the spoken word to express an emotional idea, was a special moment for American culture, and, indeed, an often impressive cultural phenomenon in other societies. As Otto Jespersen has pointed out in *Language: Its Nature, Development and Origin:*

> When we say that speech originated in song, what we mean is merely that our comparatively monotonous spoken language and our highly developed vocal music are differentiations of primitive utterances. These utterances were, at first, like the singing of birds and crooning of babies, exclamative, not communicative—that is, they came forth from an inner craving of the individual without any thought of any fellow-creatures . . .

The urgency of the early American laughter was precisely this exclamatory function, conscious of its audience, but sounding at the boundaries of experience with honest and individual statement. The effectiveness of the malapropism was its vivid image and surprise. These word pictures, a relatively primitive form of language, would evolve to a more analytic, cerebral discourse in which experience was broken down into more elaborate speech units. The freezing of verbal experiment accompanies the penchant for clinical analysis that accompanies a maturing culture. As Jespersen points out:

> Just as here the advance is due to a further analysis of language, smaller and smaller units of speech being progressively represented by single signs, in an exactly similar way, though not quite so unmistak-

ably, the history of language shows us a progressive tendency toward analyzing into smaller and smaller units that which in the earlier stages was taken as an inseparable whole.

The linguistic ossification of America by its mass media has other historical parallels. The metaphysical wit that gave language a bold inventiveness and comedy a raucous flexibility in Elizabethan England (Shakespeare had a writing vocabulary of 21,000 words), gave way to the banal, passive tone of a more scientific concept of wit. Ultimately, this instinct would lead to the buffooneries of Grub Street which Alexander Pope skewers in *The Dunciad* where "light dies before her uncreating word." It was not merely a fascination with print technology which made language uncreative, it was the instinct to reduce it to a streamlined equation. As early as 1667, the impulse of science to remodel language was being discussed. Thomas Sprat in his *History of the Royal Society* chronicled the discussion of reform, stripping English of its "vulgar" eccentricities and metaphoric potential for something efficient and dry. Criticising "those specious *Tropes* and *Figures* of imaginative writing which result in only mists and uncertainties," the Society felt that it was necessary to be "arm'd against all enchantments of *Enthusiasm.*" The plan was straightforward:

> [The members of the Society] have therefore been most rigorous in putting into execution the only Remedy that can be found for this extravagance: and that has been, a constant Resolution, to reject all the amplifications, digressions, and swellings of style: to return back to the primitive purity, and shortness, when men delivered so many *things,* almost in an equal number of *words*. They have exacted from all their members, a close, naked, natural way of speaking; positive expressions; clearness; a native easiness; bringing all things as near the *Mathematical plainness* as they can.

Restoration and eighteenth-century stage comedy would reach a linguistic and emotional dead end precisely because the language (and the plays) never confronted the reality of their environment and never offered the stage the one asset it must exploit—immediacy. Jonathan Swift satirized the folly in a language which opted for the general and eschewed the particular and colloquial. In *Gulliver's Travels*, a book which Dr. Johnson maintained was "written in open defiance of truth and regularity," Swift pricks the bubble of contemporary disenchantment:

> We next went to the school of languages, where three professors sat in consultation upon improving that of their own country.
> The first project was to shorten discourse by cutting polysyllables into one, and leaving out verbs and participles because in reality all things imaginable are but nouns.

If this sounds suspiciously like the famous *Times* pyramid style, Gulliver would meet others reminiscent of present-day avant-gardery:

The other project was a scheme for abolishing all words whatsoever; and this was urged with a great advantage in point of health as well as brevity. . . . An expedient was therefore offered, that since words are only the names of *things,* it would be more convenient for all men to carry about them such things as were necessary to express the particular business they are to discuss on . . .

Swfit understood the bondage of a language stripped of variety and a tactile fascination with the world. Today, man is coaxed into believing he has free and liberal speech, that American arts still represent a freedom and honesty in the mass media, which is everywhere denied. Kenneth Tynan back from his most recent New York scouting party reported in the March 17, 1968, *Observer:* "Say what you like about America, it can't be denied that you can say what you like . . ."

Tynan misses the point. Language and life are not honored. He is chanting the party line of mobility which is simply not true. Television not only bleeps out the vulgarities and jagged edges of life, but commissions plays in which the playwright *by contract* is not allowed to use certain political and commercial terms which might impede advertising as well as offend the audience. Worse still is the language that is allowed: a consensus argot of market research where banalities generally blanket experience, sell products as well as coat emotions. Although theater, even in its prolific Elizabethan days, had its censors, the paradox in a society "free" of censorship is a language and theater without variety, where the uniformity of output matches the uniformity of taste.

Vaclav Havel's *The Memorandum,* which recently made its American debut, was interpreted by the majority of critics as a statement about bureaucracy in Communist countries. Although Mr. Havel is a Czech, he has fashioned a tale of brilliant and acerbic universality in which the encroaching bifurcation of man's function is matched by a similar change in his language. What Americans fail to realize is that bureaucratic efficiency is even more pervasive in America than in Russia or its satellites. If the price of technocracy is an increasing limitation of human potential, language too becomes an extension of this dehumanized, split personality. In *The Memorandum,* a new language is introduced into the office— Ptydepe. The members of the office must adopt the terminology or be eliminated. While Havel explores the dynamics of conformity, his inventiveness uncovers a language which exhibits the lack of wholeness, the loss of man's responsiveness to his total environment.

In the Ptydepe classroom, the teacher expounds the principles of the new vocabulary:

Ptydepe, as you know, is a synthetic language, built on a strictly scientific basis. Its grammar is constructed with maximum rationality, its vocabulary is unusually broad. It is a thoroughly exact language, capable of expressing with far more percision than any current natural tongue all the minutest nuances in the formulation of important office documents. . . .

The language itself, intended to eliminate redundancy and ambiguity, is almost totally unmanageable. If there is no hint of the street or of the flesh in Ptydepe, the absurdity of matching scientific complexity with words is ballooned into hilarity. Ptydepe becomes a scientific malapropism, a twenty-first-century burlesque. The exclamation, that primordial response to nature, becomes lost in convoluted syntax:

> And now I shall name, just for the sake of preliminary orientation, some of the most common Ptydepe interjections. Well, then, our "ah!" becomes "zukybaj," our "ouch!" becomes "bykur," our "oh!" becomes "hayf dy doretob," English "pish!" becomes "bolypak juz," the interjection of surprise "well!" becomes "zyk," however, our "well, well!" is not "zykzyk!" as some students erroneously say, but "zykzym."

In the end, the attempt to make Ptydepe the organizational language is squashed when the managing director finally gets his memorandum in Ptydepe translated. It announces that Ptydepe is a bastard tongue. There is a purge, an apology, and a new language, Chorukor, is hatched. The final irony of Havel's tale rests with language. The girl who translates the memorandum loses her job; the managing director now back in power will not repay her kindness by reinstating her. In a final speech, he analyzes his condition with clinical accuracy:

> . . . Manipulated, automatized, made into a fetish, Man loses the experience of his own totality; horrified, he stares as a stranger at himself, unable to be what he is not, nor to be what he is . . .

He speaks clearly, but separated from life, he cannot act. His words set him apart from his own experience. The girl, overwhelmed by the weight and import of his language, accepts his gross inhumanity with wonder. ("Nobody ever *talked* to me so nicely before.") This dumb acquiescence to the contemporary vocabulary underscores passivity and overlooks the cruel indifference of its proponents locked into a system which manufactures its own staleness.

Havel's tale has great implications to American life and the silent violence of its clichéd language. Lenny Bruce's scurrilities were not merely low-blows to hypocrisy, but a clearly defined search to make American humor break through the synthetic language and responses which isolated an audience and kept it from confronting reality. In his own combination of gutter slang, Yiddish, and literacy, Bruce melted stereotypes with language larger than the word, images which vaulted the tepid balance of contemporary speech.

The first sentence of his autobiography *How to Talk Dirty and Influence People* raises the erotic folklore of the streets to consciousness and cuts into contemporary America with a jolt that brings the mind's eye back to life (and the streets).

Filipinos come quick; colored men are built abnormally large ("Their wangs look like a baby's arm with an apple in its fist"); ladies with short hair are Lesbians; if you want to keep your man, rub alum on your pussy.

Wild, unpredictable, using the vernacular of every aspect of the culture to strafe society, Bruce's intention was to explode the present, to make his audience immediately and incontrovertibly aware of the moment in American life. The instinct is much the same as the early twentieth-century American clowns; it is perhaps more literate and more cynical about the dream to which they aspired. There is a confidence in its mission and a willingness to stand alone, where the impulse for humor in earlier eras had been social acceptance and mobility. Bruce's autobiography resounds with a simple existential idea. "There is only what *is*. The what-*should*-be never did exist, but people kept trying to live *up* to it. There is only what *is*." His comedy glories in the particulars of life —the dialects, the outrageousness, the inequities. The language is at once thrilling and difficult, obsessed and oppressive—but it is the syntax of modern life with all its polyglot confusions. There is no way to escape the voice or the world—unless you kill it.

Bruce begins with reality and moves into the surreal world of his imagination where only brittle honesty can test experience in safety. His satire of the absurd repressiveness of language, divesting itself of possibility and pertinence because of self-conscious decorum, is reflected in his monologue on the evil aura of the term "hotel":

It's a real hang-up, being divorced when you're on the road. Suppose it's three o'clock in the morning, I've just done the last show, I meet a girl, and I like her, and suppose I have a record I'd like her to hear, or I just want to talk to her—there's no lust, no carnal image—but because where I live is a dirty word, I can't say to her, "Would you come to my hotel?"
And every healthy comedian has given "motel" such a dirty connotation that I couldn't ask my *grandmother* to go to a motel, say I want to give her a Gutenberg Bible at three in the morning.
The next day at two in the afternoon, when the Kiwanis Club meets there, then "hotel" is clean. But at three o'clock in the morning, Jim . . . Christ, where the hell can you live that's clean? You can't say hotel to a chick, so you try to think, what won't offend? What is a clean word to society? What is a clean word that won't offend any chick? . . .
Trailer. That's it, *trailer.*
"Will you come to my trailer?"
"All right, there's nothing dirty about trailers. Trailers are hunting and fishing and Salem cigarettes. Yes, of course, I come to your trailer. Where is it?
"Inside my hotel room."
Why can't you just say, "I want to be with you, and hug and kiss you."
No, it's, "Come up while I change my shirt." Or coffee. "Let's have a cup of coffee."
In fifty years, coffee will be another dirty word.

Bruce's language weaves in and out of experience; the pratfalls are no longer physical but psychic. "What won't offend" becomes a commercial call-word which strips away honesty and enforces a humorless sterility. Without risks of language as well as spirit nothing can be learned, no new terrain charted.

The attempts at recent stage satire have been struggling with the onus of the spoken word. Barbara Garson's *MacBird* looked to Elizabethan rhythms for a fresh voice for humor; S. J. Perelman's masterful *The Beauty Part* (1963) brought the satirist's eye for hypocrisy and his ear for the dead phrase to the stage. With characters like Monroe Sweetmeat, Harry Hubris, and Vernon Equinox, Perelman's gallimaufry of gargoyles spoke in stylized tones which were funny but indisputably *dead.* A typical exchange between the rich Weatherwax parents and their Ivy League Candide has the airy lightness of a thirties filip for the jazz age:

Octavia: Why, our twenty-year-old son, which he's home from Yale on his midyears and don't suspicion his folks are rifting.
Milo: Of course, of course. Reached man's estate already, has he? Where is our cub at the present writing?
Octavia: In the tack room, furbishing up the accoutrements of his polo ponies.
Milo (acidly): Far better to be furbishing up on his Euclid, lest he drag the name of Weatherwax through the scholastic mire.
Lance: Dads! Mums!
Octavia: Shush! Here he comes now. You had best handle this. I'm laying down on my chaise lounge with a vinegar compress *(Exists).*

The alabaster inflections are original, the butchery of diction amusing; but the effectiveness of Perelman's satire for the American stage is minimized because his vernacular humor is a glance backward at a society already slightly passé. There are greater evils than movie moguls, more outrages than philistinism. The language never stalks those culprits in contemporary life, but in Perelman's special man-made waxworks of social gorgons.

Part of the immediate appeal of *Boys in the Band,* a current Off-Broadway study of homosexuality, is the complete emotional and linguistic reversal of conventional response. In arguing (or demanding) for social understanding, a patter of movements and vocabulary stretch the audience's concept of the "real." The shock brings laughter. Commonplace words take on a new weight. One gay lover flounces around a cocktail party with a lap-dog coyness, asking, "Who do you have to fuck to get a drink around here?" The effect on an audience is visceral and surprising. The drama has a superficial glitter of language momentarily turned back on life. "There's one thing about masturbation. You don't have to look your best." The sadness and hilarity, the admission of man's bondage to his own flesh has its moments of insight. However, the ultimate effect of this flashy style, like the homosexual fascination with clothes and a carefully preened existence, is to skirt experience, painting over anxiety with quick sleights of hand.

> Give me Librium
>
> Or give me Meth

The words amuse, but also foreshadow the ultimate limitation of homosexual theater and its laughter. Everything returns to their single, sexual obsession. What begins as wit moves into the weird boredom of paranoia where life is tortured into nightmare or a flossy camp—both of which lose sight of the world.

Homosexual laughter gathers its peculiar force from the fact that it is comparatively rare to the stage. Playwrights dealing with more familiar terrain must resort to different tactics in confronting the new dimensions of contemporary life. Jean-Claude van Itallie's *Motel* changes man's proportions, creating papier-mâché brutes in a ritual of mindless destruction. The figures act in the larger-than-human gestures of the clown, matching a mammoth and technically streamlined society. As the figures sport themselves in a world which is supra-human, tape-recorded voices mouth the commercial banalities of contemporary speech:

> There now . . . There's a button push here for TV. The toilet flushes on its own accord. All you've got to do is get off. Pardon my mentioning it, but you'll have to go far before you see a thing like this one on the route.

Van Itallie's image of vulgarity is beyond words. The rape of the room, like so much of the grotesque in American life, cannot be conveyed adequately by contemporary language.

The growing vapidity of the American vernacular, the hollowness of language to encompass the truth of experience, has been one of the key brickbats of satirists from Swift to Jules Feiffer. Swift's *A Modest Proposal* uses the syntax and vocabulary of the moment to expose the hypocrisy of the uncreating word. Feiffer's brilliant *Little Murders* (1967), which lasted three performances, is one of the few thorough attempts to inch language into a more careful understanding of its own limitations. Feiffer's play, mounted on Broadway for the very audience it wanted to chastise, went unappreciated because of their numbness to the subtle changes in the vocabulary of the life and society he was challenging. Feiffer's language is wily, building to surreal proportions while keeping the ring of everyday naturalness. When a police inspector comes on the scene after the love interest has been picked off by a sniper, he speaks in the rhythm and vagueness of the public cliché we have come to accept.

> We are involved here in a far-reaching conspiracy to undermine respect for our basic beliefs. Who is behind this conspiracy? Once again ask the question: Who has the most to gain? People in high places. Their names would astound you. People in low places. Concealing their activities beneath a cloak of poverty. People in all walks of life. Left

wing and right wing. Black and white. Students and scholars. A conspiracy of such ominous proportions that we may not know the whole truth in our lifetime and we will never be able to reveal all the facts. We are readying mass arrests . . .

The violence and ignorance which appeals to reason is deceptive, and Feiffer's effectiveness is in showing up both the language and the process which inculcates its special stupefication to moral and social problems.

The betrayal of language and its misuse is now finally being met by playwrights in hand-to-hand combat with the mass media. The fact that in *Hair* one of the performers runs around a Broadway stage yelling "Fucky, fuck fuck, fuck fuck," may be self-indulgent but also a necessary means of letting the grit of life, its wonder and ugliness, back into the dingy pleasure domes, a way of acknowledging that man is neither deodorized nor fitted out with chandeliers between his legs.

The misuse of the word creates false heroes and false terms for analyzing them. In John Guare's *Muzeeka*, a recent Obie-award-winning fantasy about a dreamer who goes to work for a Muzak corporation and hopes to change the world with his special music only to find himself fighting for CBS in Vietnam, a death chorus makes the point about language. In a cruelly acerbic take-off on the Martha Raye mentality, a girl leaps out of her Marine jump suit, decked in a skirt made of torn copies of *The New York Times*. She pulls at her skirt, singing the print as she reads each transient name:

> Bonnie & Clyde and Jesus Christ
> Governor Wallace and Jesus Christ
> Ronald Reagan and Jesus Christ
> Hubert Humphrey and Jesus Christ
> LBJ was Jesus Christ.

Heroes are born anew with each headline; and after each betrayal, the words that praised them lose a part of their coinage. The instinct for satire is not, as it has so often been, a conservative argument for return to the past. The theater laughter, when it is effective, has been arguing for a progressive future and a new language to meet it. The emphasis, finally, is on freedom—a poetry composed of the artifacts of experience where object and idea counterpoint one another in glistening amusement and insight. The hero of *Muzeeka* states his vision of how to revitalize the world. It is a satirist's aesthetic—a plan for change. He will pipe in his music and count on the cocoon of the media to dull the mind:

> I'll wait till all humans are inured to the everpresent inescapable background ocean blandness of my music . . . then on a sudden day that is not especially Spring, not especially Summer, a day when the most exciting thing around is the new issue of the *Reader's Digest* and you read with interest an ad that says Campbell is putting out a new flavor soup. That kind of day. I'll strike. I'll pipe in my own secret music that I keep hidden here under my cartigal overlay and I'll free all the

Etruscans in all our brains . . . and the country will remember its
Etruscan forebearers and begin dancing . . .

The impulse is to return to the individual the gift of response, to free
him from repression and free the words with which he conveys his understanding of the world. American theater is in the process of rediscovering
playfulness on stage and with it, new possibilities for words. For the first
time since the clowns made mayhem on stage with their own individual
patois, the theater is returning to an intimate relation between experience
as lived and experience as played. What is needed in stage laughter is
what is needed in the society—honesty, responsiveness, flexibility. As
American society changes drastically in the next few years, it will demand
new terms to convey its dynamism and skewer its myopia. As the mass
media increase in popularity, the theater may become the last outpost
for the eccentric and individual voice and a life of the active mind. There
is reason to be hopeful that laughter on stage will return not only to the
broadness of acrobatic gesture, but the flair and variety of language of
the madcaps from an earlier, more intimate type of American entertainment.

Up from Underground: Notes on the New Comix*

By Bob Abel

"Allow a diffident foreigner to tell you that among the curious and characteristic native products of America, the trivialities such as compose the real originality and flavor of countries, the comic strip is one of the most to be appreciated. Nations are almost always slightly ashamed of their truly admirable idiosyncrasies; they all want to be distinguished only for massive virtues, which, even if they possess them in a remarkable degree, they only share with the mass of humanity.

"So without any critical insolence whatsoever, I confess the comic strip is a more interesting institution than, say, the mid-western novel, or the mystical voyages of O'Neill, et al., in search of God, or sophistication in all its branches."

—William Bolitho in *Camera Obscura*

"Comics in the 1930s dealt with things that were important to everyone —getting a job, marriage, children—and if we'd been around then, we'd have been doing that kind of comic strip. But today our comix are dealing with drugs and sex—there's a big concern with taboo breaking —and with paranoia and police brutality and like that."

—Art Spiegelman, underground comix artist

For the great majority of Americans, probably the first news of underground comics—or comix, to speak a properly underground English— came with the arrival of a late 1970 issue of *Playboy* which signalled the advent of "The International Comix Conspiracy." The blurb for the article, which was by Jacob Brackman, was no less sweeping: "obscene, anarchistic, sophomoric, subversive, apocalyptic, the underground cartoonists and their creations attack all that middle america holds dear." Moreover, since *Playboy* is a liberal magazine—pubic hair was being liberated from the tyranny of the air brush around this same time—its readers could feel secure from the hostile scrutiny of the underground artists.

---

* Copyright 1971 by Bob Abel. Substantial portions of this article originally appeared in *Cavalier* Magazine.

Now the *Playboy* audience, large though it may be, is dwarfed by the prime-time evening television audience, and so a great many Americans doubtless first learned of underground comix while watching CBS-TV's *Sixty Minutes* program on the underground press movement in January 1971. Although the program did not dwell on the strips for any length, it did mention them as a regular feature of many of the underground papers.

However, lest future cultural anthropologists be ill-advised on the matter, be it here noted that it was on the 15th of December 1968—roughly two years earlier—that underground comix officially came of age. On that date, *The National Insider*, whose editorial attributes include being "informative," "provocative," and "fearless," not to speak of "entertaining," exposed—the favorite headline verb of this scandal sheet par excellence—the "Latest 'Art' Trend—Hippie Sex Comics.." Inside the *Insider,* along with stories on Barbra Streisand ("Color Barbra Sexless") and the civilized world's latest sexual hangup ("Big Breasts Scare Men Stiff!"), the tabloid's puritanical readers were apprised that most of the comic strips found in underground newspapers will "make you sick." A highly indignant article predicting that "If the sick, sick comics continue in Underground newspapers, we will soon see the end of the movement" was surrounded on three sides by specimens of the offending strips, and it is interesting to note that the *Insider* had no compunction about reproducing strips with nasty words in them, nor did it bother about the niceties of running copyright notices or even crediting the material. Oh, well, one editor's sense of legality is another editor's freedom of choice, and the significant thing is that, given this scolding by *The National Insider,* which clearly enough leans toward (and on) a moral imperative, underground comix had surely arrived.

The National Insider notwithstanding, no one has ever accused American culture of being too generously predictable. Thus, while the journey of comix from the easily smudged pages of the *Insider* to the smart walls of the Whitney Museum in Manhattan and other prestigious strongholds of Real Art would seem to be a highly unlikely one—even along those routes so recently charted by the counter-culture—it is nonetheless a fact that by mid-1970 underground comix had already proved intriguing enough to the straight culture for museums to be including them in major shows and for major publishing houses to be readying collections of the work of several artists. Robert Crumb, the best-known artist in the field has had his drawings exhibited, among other places, as part of the Whitney's powerful "Human Concern/Personal Torment" show during the fall of 1969 and both the Viking Press and Ballantine Books have published his work in oversized paperbound editions. (Ballantine now publishes both *R. Crumb's Fritz the Cat* and *R. Crumb's Head Comix,* which Viking originally issued.) In addition, Bantam Books and Dell Books, two of the nation's paperback giants, had by early 1971 committed themselves to underground comix collections, and so the Great American Reading Public was about to be tested on whether it would accept in the home these new subversives out to crease its middle brow. On the other hand, these soft-cover volumes, written by young people with young people in mind, could be sales triumphs simply if enough young people bought them—which if nothing else would keep the whole movement nicely incestuous.

Of course what this may also prove is that whatever American culture does not reject outright, it somehow manages to assimilate. Prior to their modest integration into the straight culture, the creators of underground comix—whatever their degree of professionalism as artists and writers—were characterized chiefly by their unwillingness even to *try* and produce work that might be acceptable either to newspaper syndicates or the publishers of comic books. So, logically enough, underground comix got that way because the first medium in which they appeared for the edification and entertainment—not to speak of titillation—of large numbers of readers was the underground newspaper. Later on, there was a small population explosion of comix magazines, usually sold in paperback galleries—*Zap, Feds 'n Heads, Yellow Dog,* and *Bijou Funnies* were the important pioneering titles, followed in profusion by (are you ready, Middle America?) *Radical America Komics, Big Ass, Hydrogen Bomb, God Nose, Armadillo, Conspiracy Capers, Captain Guts, Mom's Home-made Comics, The Adventures of Jesus, Slow Death, Despair,* women's lib-uplifting *It Ain't Me, Babe,* and perhaps thirty other titles—but the original impetus to the movement was definitely through the underground papers.

For example, some late 1960s issues of Seattle's *The Helix* were little more than comix and ads, and any one strip originating in an underground paper might appear, via syndication, in scores of other papers. The *East Village Other,* flagship of the underground press movement, was a virtual fountainhead for comix as it attracted a regular group of artists to its pages. These included: of course, Robert Crumb, who is at once the Lenny Bruce and W. C. Fields and Marx Brothers of the field; Spain Rodrigues, whose creation, *Trashman,* features a Che-like, street-fighting "agent" of the 6th Internat'l" who usually won't take leave of his machine gun even to indulge in some nonpartisan sex 'n violence, although some of the other characters in the strip have no such compunctions; Kim Deitch, whose choice of weekly titles for his page in the paper—*Kryptic Kapers, Cul de Sac Comics, Scarey Comix*— do not do justice to a truly uninhibited imagination (Waldo is a super-hip Felix the Cat and Uncle Ed [The India Rubber Man] is a dirty old man worthy of Nabokov); Art Spiegelman, whose *Adventures of Jolly Jack Off, the Masturbating Fiend,* raise the world's least honored but also least expensive sport to new heights; Roger Brand, whose title character, Strawbrick, would have made Candide look like a functioning super-hero and whose collective neuroses

("WHY was I born different. . . ?") would have turned Freud to a different line of work; and Vaughn Bode, a highly gifted, astonishingly prolific artist whose mind turns to fantasy worlds both long ago and long off —machines battle mutants in a world of post-atomic madness, a caveman ponders the wonders of the universe with his best friend (a spear), and talking lizards are warriors in the most bestial human tradition unless confronted with nubile maidens chock full of humanistic sexual responses—and whose draftsmanship already far exceeds most workers in the comics field, whether underground-bound or nationally syndicated.

On the other side of Middle America, another band of drawing renegades were initiating underground comix in their own fashion. (It used to be that San Francisco reflected New York; now there is a cross-cultural, cross-continental transference.) In the Bay City, the peripatetic Robert Crumb—who by virtue of his very large talent, constant output, and widespread syndication throughout the underground press had become the Johnny Appleseed of underground comix—created *Zap Comix* at the same time he was contributing the antic-heroic, pro-hedonistic adventures of fritz the cat to *Cavalier* Magazine (then a very lively and provocative magazine of the *Playboy* genre) and also producing deliberately pornographic comix books (*Reader's Digest*-sized at that) which unfortunately were more distinguished for their arrests record than for their contents. Crumb soon became associated with the Print Mint, a Berkeley hostel for underground culture. Its owner, Don Shenker, became at age forty the Instant Grand Old Man of Underground Comix. He not only distributed subsequent *Zaps* but published a tabloid comix paper called *Yellow Dog* (later to switch to comic-book format) that ran not only strips but contributors' sketches and drawings as well, and this latter was some of the more interesting work in the field.

"*Yellow Dog* got started," Shenker wrote me at the end of 1968, "because, partly, interest in posters lagged. We were in the poster business from its inception and when it waned, I turned to comix because the almost violent young public desire which produced the poster boom needed in some way to keep being turned on. For the second part, the artists were present. Here in the Bay Area. Joe Beck (who, I suppose, you might call the father of 'underground' comix; he started with the University of California *Pelican* back in the days of the FSM), John Thompson and, finally, the giant of them all, R. Crumb. *Yellow Dog* is a pun and switch of many other things. An American title, out of The Yellow Kid of Pulitzer, out of a nitty gritty dog pissing upon the deepest symbol of the American subconsciousness, Capt. Ahab, who searched and still searches for the White Whale (who, too, pissed on all his black masses and soul-selling.) If Melville was right when he said, about *Moby Dick,* I have written a naughty book, then *Yellow Dog* was designed to be a naughty paper.

"Underground comix," he continued, "definitely represent a reaction away from the current comix the same way a loving child leaves home or rots. In the movies the kid sees this chick with her face painted and her tits all trussed up so's they'll look pointy and 'sexxy.' Well, if you consider this (somewhat like D. H. Lawrence did) with a mind either turned on or fresh in some other way, it's pornographic, and the little books you buy about Popeye and Dick Tracy—'hot books'—are, at least, honest, direct, and done with considerable talent. All of the artists in *Zap, Dog,* etc., pay homage to the old comix you used to buy for 12¢. Harvey Kurtzman is their idol, but they are not tongue-tied before him. They feel his equals. Both Crumb and Gil Shelton *(Feds 'n Heads)* both worked with him before he went to *Playboy.* He himself admires them. But from our correspondence, Kurtzman must, I feel, think of himself now as an old man."

Kurtzman's "prime target in his original *Mad Comics,*" Shenker subsequently pointed out in an article written for *The Daily Californian's Weekly Magazine,* "was the institutionalization of the funnies . . . Where there had been a marvelous, disgruntled quality to the pronouncements of cartoonists, a delightfully anti-usual air, a sourly fantastic and individualistic series of styles and manners before the war, there began to appear a shift. Comics . . . became propagandistic. In short, establishmentarian." Well, it may be argued, I suppose, that the characters of the comic strips had been mobilized in a Great Cause—the defense of democracy and the defeat of fascism—but it is certainly true that after the war the new strips tended toward adventure or soap opera rather than the human comedy. For almost a decade after the war, *Beetle Bailey, Pogo,* and *Peanuts* were the sole distinguished exceptions to the "realistic" turn the postwar strips had taken.

For their part, the contributors to *Yellow Dog* owed no allegiance to comic-strip tradition—except to kid it—and toward American institutions there was scarcely a bugle call except for an occasional cacophonic rendition of *Taps.* Crumb of course was a regular participant—kidding God and man, kidding the State versus man, kidding man versus man, kidding the estate of man, kidding self-knowledge as religion, kidding sex and sexiness, spiritual acne and *angst,* to mention but a few of his comic concerns—as was Gilbert Shelton, who ranks perhaps next to Crumb as the seminal figure of the movement. An émigré from Austin, Texas, Shelton had spent much of the past decade either as student or satirist, or both, and his Wonder Wart-Hog—"the hog of steel"—is unquestionably the ugliest undergrowth super-hero of recent centuries, and properly so. More recently he has concentrated on the Freak Brothers, now appearing under the banner of *The Fabulous Furry Freak Brothers,* not super-heroes but super-"heads" who always keep a huge stash of dope and sometimes get to enjoy it without governmental interdiction. Not necessarily a strip for the "high"-minded only, Shelton's creation may well represents the comic apotheosis of the drug culture in America. Like Crumb, and a few others in the comix field, Shelton can generally be expected to tell a funny story and there exists in his work a sense of broad comedy that is itself a kind of maturity, and evidence that an artist not only is enjoying what he is doing, but is reasonably certain of his achievement.

This is not to say, for a moment, that Crumb and Shelton were the only talents associated with *Yellow Dog* worth a bit of critical howling about, one way or the other. Joel Beck, a former Berkeley student who had already published two books—*The Profit,* a mixed bag of clever and under-realized satire, and *Lenny of Laredo,* good fun, a bit obvious, but, happily, no part of the Lenny Bruce industry that emerged after the comedian's death—continued his acerbic spoofs of American society in the comix paper (first of its kind, it was followed by *Gothic Blimp Works,* originally edited by Vaughn Bode, then by *East Village Other* editors, but now defunct). Ron White, who appears a Beck disciple, did a nice turn on the comic-strip medium itself (and its Pleistocene Era rules) via his B. Bear character whose specialty is getting arrested "for appearing in a comic strip without a morality card." And John Thompson's *The Spiritual Stag Film,* never to be an art director's delight, was nonetheless refreshingly irreverent because of its ofttimes sly and/or cranky lead character, Sam God, who concedes without too much rancor that "all prayers have two parts: one: butter him up [and] two: ask for something." There was also frequently arresting visual material by a variety of artists, including Franz Cilensek and Buckwheat Florida, Jr.—who owns the grandest name in underground comix—which suffered somewhat because of the newsprint on which *Yellow Dog* was then printed (and on which the capricious canine, with undisguised glee, always pisses).

There are also four other artists who contributed to the early issues of *Zap* and *Yellow Dog* whose work—if one is going to apply serious standards to underground comix—requires more extensive analysis. Three of them are demonstrably among the half-dozen or so finest draftsmen in the field. The exception to this is S. Clay Wilson, a transplanted Kansan who is easily the most violent artist in the comix field, and so all enjoy distinction.

Robert Crumb has credited Wilson with inaugurating the "sex revolution" in comix, and this is a little bit like Washington crediting Jefferson for the whole Revolution bit. Still, no one in the comix field has utilized sex and bloodshed to such a degree as has Wilson—and what Crumb refers to is Wilson's apparent refusal from the beginning to accede to any self-censorship. His plots are usually short on narrative and his visual center-piece is frequently an orgiastic clash between various adversaries (pirates, both sides mostly homosexual; motorcycle gangs, both

sides in part homosexual; monsters and people, the sexual climate confusing, but predictably violent; pirates and their modern counterparts,
Hell's Angels, with a time warp providing the drama) that culminates in
a literal or metaphorical ship's hold of sperm and gore. Wilson's work is
generally too non-stop violent to be very pornographic, sometimes too
pornographic to be entertaining, and depressingly restrictive in terms of
the characters he depicts—all are physically repulsive and treacherous if
not evil incarnate. Yet there is a raw power and compelling quality to his
work—in particular the group clashes—and a legitimate exploitation of
the grim strain of violence in American life that make him an artist if not
worthy of the associations with Hieronymus Bosch that have cropped up
in some writings about him—then at least one well worth a continuing
critical attention. If nothing else, it makes for good reading—and can be
just as deliciously cultist as the writing about films these days.

For example, in the Summer 1970 (No. 12) issue of *Funnyworld,* an excellent comics fanzine—fan magazine devoted to a certain field, in this
instance comic strips and books and animated cartoons—Bob Follett, a
veteran observer of the comic art field, responded to the sharp criticism
of Wilson made by Mike Barrier, *Funnyworld's* editor, in a previous issue.
"I can't really write a rebuttal to your comments on Wilson," he wrote,
doing just that. "Your argument used the premise that there are subjects
and styles which should be closed to the cartoonist for reasons of
propriety. Wilson fails, in your opinion, because his characters, draped
in an abundance of warts and a paucity of clothing, are invariably involved in pastimes that will never make it to the late late show."

Follett goes on to say that this sort of criticism is useless to the
underground comix reader "since he generally doesn't share your
aversions," and an examination of Wilson's techniques and achievements
as a cartoonist—not "the moral suitability of his subjects"—is a more
legitimate measure of his work. "Wilson's pluses are as magnificent as
his failings," Follett continues his auteuristic style-before-substance argument. "I would imagine that he fails as a cartoonist in the normal sense.
There is little if any coherence to a Wilson's 'story line.' Wilson produces
images—vivid, vivid images . . . the major fault in Wilson's work and one
which may relegate him forever to the group of also-rans—given the
absence of a story line and limiting himself to 'meth' freaks, motorcycle
bandits, dyke queens, and tide monsters—give or take a wall-eyed professor of two—Wilson can only come up with a certain very finite number
of combinations for his drawings. The 'meth' freaks can only meet so
many 'Screaming Gypsy Bandits' before the work loses its charm. But
Wilson will answer this question for us in the next couple of years."

Writing in that same issue, Barrier, who publishes *Funnyworld*—now a
magazine grown from its mimeographed days to one professional in
looks as well as contents—as a sidelight to his columnist job at the

Arkansas Gazette, returned to his criticism of Wilson in an article which deals, among other things, with what he feels is a sex obsession among underground cartoonists. "There can be no valid 'moral' objection to Wilson's work," he wrote, apparently utilizing editor's prerogative in responding to material elsewhere in the magazine, "even though every imaginable sexual practice takes place in his strips. No girl is ever going to be seduced in an underground comic book. My basic complaint about Wilson's work is that it *is* moral, in the narrowest, nastiest sense. I said back in *Funnyworld* No. 10 that S. Clay Wilson impressed me as an uptight little old lady in disguise. By that I mean that he seemed to share an attitude common to many little old ladies, that sex—and, by implication, life itself—is dirty and disgusting. It is in his strips, certainly. His people are all warts, moles, sweat, flab, and body hair (he can make any part of the human anatomy unappealing) and all freaks in one way or another. However there's no indication that 'normal people' would come out looking any better. He looks at humans as a Houyhnhnm might. Wilson refuses to see human beings as a whole; rather, he seizes on physical imperfections and magnifies them. This may be preferable to what happens in syndicate comic strips and traditional comic books, where everyone seems to have been photographed through those Doris Day gauzes, but it's still a distorted and limited way of looking at things."

Now whereas Wilson—and it may be fairly argued, I think, that his distortions of behavior as well as physiognomy are precisely what make his work distinctive (and of course could make it ultimately repetitious and boring)—is among the best known, and easily the most controversial artist in the field, another West Coast artist, Andy Martin, is hardly known, apart from readers of *Yellow Dog,* yet his is a talent that is all the more remarkable for being unique in the field. Martin does not draw comix— he draws political cartoons utilizing the strip form. His line is extremely fine—one is reminded of Lyonel Feininger, the artist who also drew comic strips in the first part of the century, and certain German expressionists—and it is applied to truly savage caricature that builds its effects through distorted bodies with recognizable faces and arresting compositions within the individual panels. His is an inside-out Alice in Wonderlandish trip—picture Alice high on LSD—sounding as though it must be written, though the dialogue is sparse, simultaneously by Thomas Pynchon, Paul Kassner, Timothy Leary, the late Dr. Eric Berne, and Gene Shepherd, with walk-ons by Norman Mailer and Jules Feiffer. Yet it is more the surreal art that makes Martin's work so different. There is nothing like it in comix, comics, or political cartooning in this country.

For example, an early *Yellow Dog* cover depicted Lyndon Johnson defecating on top of a toilet bowl that bore the features of the 1968 Democratic candidate for President—surely a vulgar comic conceit—but the meaning behind the image made this a powerful cartoon and one that many readers might find more telling than, say, a caricature of Johnson by David Levine or one by England's Gerald Scarfe, whose distortions always go for the jugular and thus have become somewhat predictable. Martin's satiric world is one in convoluted progress: His *Hop-Frogian Bible,* "Featuring Dr. Caligari as gynecologist," and dealing with the adventures of Prof. Murayev, Mr. Pueno, Ave, Trippeta, Ahab, and of course Hop-Frog himself (partial cast of characters at that) practically requires a magnifying glass to read because so much is going on. But it is worth the effort because what's there is a visual looney tune deliberately playing against our notions of expectation and order. It is at once chaotic and richly entertaining: Nothing is resolved except our desire to see what happens next. And in that regard, the observations of Don Shenker, who, after all, published Martin, are particularly relevant. Shenker points out that Martin's characters "dwell in a machinistic landscape: they are twisted and crippled by the horror of steel bulkheads which end in vanishing points. Also they are extraordinarily literate. It is not enough that they leer and wring their hands in expectation of imminent catastrophe, but they fly to and fro about it, packing machines like 'fallacy filters' and screaming, 'Dissect the political animal!' " Martin, Shenker adds, agonizes over his work and I doubt if his total published output would consume one issue of *Yellow Dog,* but he is an artist whose promise is not merely looming—it is here with us now, exciting and significant—and whose future work should provide additional reason for our admiration.

The question of what is and what is not estimable in the comix field now logically leads us to consider the cases of Rick Griffin and Victor Moscoso, whose published fantasies are much admired in the field and much emulated. Picture the entire Walt Disney Studios high on something or other and you perhaps may then be able to conjure up a vision of Griffith's and Moscoso's work, which seems at once so private— seemingly drawn while on drugs and probably best enjoyed in the same state—and yet so adroitly drawn that it represents a wing of underground comix that is both fascinating and more or less inaccessible. Here I omit Moscoso's delightful on-going orgy in *Zap* No. 4, in which comic strip and movie cartoon characters as well as a variety of other creatures —most notably Mr. Peanuts of candybar face—participate for several pages in what must be comix' most densely-populated orgy to date, but it is hardly a generalization to regard these two gentlemen as deliberate (though not necessarily self-conscious) proponents of something avant- garde in the comix field. And, as I say, they have their followers.

For what it is worth, and I do not mean to be snide when I say that I am not at all certain *what* it is worth, I offer Jacob Brackman's explanation in *Playboy* as to what Griffin and Moscoso are up to: "Much as experimental playwrights pare theater back to basics, Griffin and Moscoso break down comics into their fundamental integers, toy with reassembling them in slow motion, at odd moments freezing transformations midway. Griffin uses words nonsensically. Moscoso hardly uses them at all. Both are fascinated with speech and thought balloons, floating exclamation points, idea bulbs—all of which gain a third dimension, open to reveal their innards, interact with characters and landscapes. The continual flux of their worlds, in which every element is equally animate, achieves the obliviousness of pure play—suggesting true liberation from the old necessity for significance, from any obligation to one's readers."

Anyone familiar with the bulk of Brackman's writing knows him to be a writer of intelligence, but one has to question the true significance of a comic artist's not wishing to communicate. And if "pure play" is a virtue, it should be fun to witness. Saul Steinberg, for instance, makes no concessions to easy comprehension of his work and the greatest accomplishments in comic strips have been creations that manage to communicate on a multitude of levels. It's a silly business to over-intellectualize the funnies, but *Krazy Kat* provided more visual pleasure than just the business of seeing Krazy get hit in the head with a brick thrown by Ignatz (George Herriman's shifting backgrounds, best seen in the Sunday colored pages, and his use of phonetic language were both things of joy), and Walt Kelly's *Pogo* has provided some of the more salient political satire of the past two decades. Being syndicated and being "something else"—both in the usual and hip senses of the term—is what divides the best of popular art from the packaged goods. Brackman rightly observes that Griffin and Moscoso share with other underground artists a fascination with comic strips' past, but their is a psychedelic vision, and not a shared vision, and I fail to see—which may be *my* failing, of course—that it affords much pleasure. Neither artist is under any obligation to do other kinds of drawing, but one suspects that they will find their present mode of expression rather constricting and it will surely be interesting to see where their sense of playfulness may lead them. This observer, at least, would welcome a de-Disneyizied comic world in which Snow White ravishes the Seven Dwarfs, and Minnie Mouse and Donald Duck are guilty of miscegenation.

Turning away from the San Francisco area, which is unquestionably the hot center of underground comix these days, we head eastward toward the Bijou Publishing Empire, which appears on no map of Chicago. *Bijou Funnies,* one of the best of the underground comix magazines, is the co-conception of a pair of energetic artists, Skip Williamson and Jay Lynch, whose comix capers are the core of *Bijou Funnies.* The magazine itself represents the happy end product of a lifetime interest in comic art. Throughout their teens both Lynch and Williamson had edited and contributed to numerous fanzines and their mimeographed columns of disputation, worship, and scholarship, and it is worth a lengthy examination of the role of fanzines in leading artists to the comix field for the simple reason that so many underground artists *have* followed this route. Moreover, for purposes of authenticity, we may look to Lynch himself, who offers a highly personable and informative story of his (and Williamson's) odyssey into the underground.

Lynch writes (and his letter is reproduced more or less in the free-form style in which it was written): "In 1960, when normal teens were going to sock hops and doing th' stroll and stuff, Skip Williamson, Artie Spiegelman and I were involved in producing cartoons for what was and still is known as 'fandom.' I was living with my parents in Miami, Fla., and was going to high school. Skip was living in Canton, Missouri, and going to high school. Artie was living in Rego Park, N.Y., and going to junior high school. Then somehow the three of us started doing cartoons for fanzines. Fanzines are little mimeographed or hectographed magazines that deal with a specific topic. There are science fiction fanzines, classical music fanzines, there are even fanzines that just ramble on for entire issues about how they went about putting out each issue of the previous fanzine. We were into what was called satire fandom. We did cartoons for satire fanzines, which would try to imitate old *Mad* comics. The first satire fanzine we were exposed to was *Smudge,* which was edited by Joe Pilati, who is now a columnist for the *Village Voice*. *Smudge* had a circulation of eighty. Soon other satire fanzines began to appear. *Wild* and *Jack High* were two of the ones to come out immediately after *Smudge*. *Wild* lasted ten issues, more than any satire fanzine of the early sixties. After a while Skip started his own fanzine called *Squire* and Spiegelman started one called *Blasé*. We all contributed to each other's fanzines, and everything went along pretty much the same till 1963. So for three years the three of us were into fandom. Robert Crumb was doing a fanzine called *Foo* around this time, but none of us paid much attention to it. Robert was into what was known as funny animal fandom. Walt Bowart of the *East Village Other* (formerly editor and publisher) was doing a science fiction fanzine in the early sixties. Harvey Ovshinsky, who now edits *The Fifth Estate,* which is Detroit's underground newspaper, did a fanzine then called *Transylvanian Newsletter*. Harvey was into monster fandom. Fanzines were not only the original underground press, but many underground cartoonists started out in fandom as well. Trina, a girl cartoonist who does these art nouveau comics for *E.V.O.* was into what is called *femmefandom*. Trina was a femfan. Femfans just put out magazines about how neet it is to be a girl.

"Fanzines were good because doing stuff for fanzines taught me to discipline myself. For three years I turned out at least ten pages a month of comic strips."

It wasn't, of course, merely the discipline of fanzine cartooning which profited Lynch and the others, but also the camaraderie of the thing.

Recalls Lynch: "In 1961, Spiegelman and his parents visited Miami. I got together with Artie and we talked about what the cartoonists we admired were up to and stuff. I used to correspond with Skip and Artie, and it was very good that we did this. We'd share all the knowledge that we were gaining by writing each other and telling the other guy what was happening. Artie would write to tell me of a new comic book that came out. He'd send the address, and I'd mail away for a copy. If it weren't for this correspondence network we had I'd have missed a lot of good stuff. We really dug the work of Jack Davis, Basil Wolverton, Wally Wood, all the old comic book guys."

"In 1962 I contributed to *Cracked,* an imitation of *Mad; PREP;* a teen age mag for which I did a regular comic strip about an Archie-type guy called *Hoagie.* Hoagie was hip and neet and sharp. He had a hot rod with twelve cams and he could do the twist. I also did some cartoons for *Zig Zag Libre,* a Cuban exile newspaper in Miami. Everybody must have a cause, so I began to identify with the Cuban exiles. Nobody would print intergration cartoons then, especially in Miami."

At some point in the narrative, Lynch has moved to Chicago, a move which augers all kinds of big-time possibilities.

Canton, Missouri, where Skip lived, is only 250 miles from Chicago," Lynch continues. "Skip came to visit me, and I went to visit Skip, and soon we were planning stupendous feats of cartooning together. The first thing we did was to visit the cartoon editor at *Playboy,* a fruitless pursuit which we had repeated every six months for several years. *Playboy* doesn't use new cartoonists. The cartoon editor has all these really nice cartoons on the wall of her office—great stuff by dynamic new guys —but, alas, they'll never see print. 1963 was a year when *Playboy* was going through a fantastic rate of growth—not wanting to risk their reputations, they decided to use only the cartoonists which they'd been using before. *Playboy* hasn't had a new cartoonist for six years. [Author's note: This communication from Lynch reached me in early 1969]. Eventually Skip and I got sick of going to *Playboy*—we realized that there was no hope of getting into the magazine at this point.

"Skip and I took to sending gag cartoons through the mail to magazines in other cities. I appeared in Harvey Kurtzman's *Help* then, and Skip did, too. Soon we had stuff in *The Realist* and many other mags, but it got to the point where more stuff was lost by the various editors than was printed.

"Now the year is 1965. College mags were going out and underground newspapers were starting up. The first underground comic strip that I saw was a thing called 'Captain High' in an early issue of the *East Village Other.* This was about a guy who would take LSD and turn into a super hero. It was really crude. The art was poor. Soon Gilbert Shelton had a thing in *EVO* called 'Clang Honk.' By this time I had started doing surrealist comic strips. I don't know why. I hadn't taken acid yet. I hadn't seen anybody else doing surrealist strips, but everybody started doing them in '65. For me it was a Bob Dylan influence—I was trying to do the same thing in comic strips that Dylan was doing in music. Some early surrealist strips that Skip and I did are in the *Chicago Mirror.* We did them two years before the *Mirror,* came out, though. The early surrealist strips that I did were printed in *Nexus,* a San Francisco literary magazine, and in *Oyez,* the literary magazine at Culver Stockton College which Skip edited. I was working nights as a short order cook in a restaurant. Soon I started doing cartoons for the *Chicago Seed,* the local flower kids' newspaper. In 1966 I took LSD and didn't draw anything but paisleys for the *Seed* for six months.

"So now it's 1967 and Skip, who has moved to Chicago, and I are doing things for the *Seed,* but the paper is not printing our stuff well. As soon as we give the *Seed* a cartoon, they photostat it so someone can take home the original art to hang on their wall. Then they make a reduction of the photostat and make an offset negative from that, so by the time it gets printed it's fourth generation instead of second, and it's all blurry and illegible. So Skip and I decide to do our own magazine.

"We did the *Chicago Mirror,* which we published quarterly for three-fourths of a year—1967–68—we called it the *Mirror* because we couldn't think of anything better. We decided that if a better title came up, we'd just change it. So I wanted to call it *Bijou* Magazine. Then we realized that we're cartoonists and we really wanted to do a comic book anyway. *Zap Comix,* Crumb's thing, partially inspired *Bijou,* but not totally, since some of the stuff in *Bijou* No. 1 was done before *Zap* came out. It's kind of a spontaneous generation thing—comix are happening all over the place. But without Crumb's breakthrough with the first *Zap,* nobody would have done any one hundred percent comix magazine. I can't really say that, though—underground comix have always been around. Jack Jaxon in Austin, Texas, did one called *God Nose* in 1963. It was a great comic book about God and his magical nose. . . .

"The other day Skip said to me, 'You know, if there ever *is* a revolution, we'll be big folk heroes after it's over.' But the thing is that there *is* a revolution going on right now! It's a revolution of the mind—of perception and sanity. The sanity of mankind is changing, and a whole new anti-intellectual generation of kids is growing up. Comix books will fill the space that the death of newspapers will leave. Comix will be an integral part of the life of humans in the future. This is why old ladies are down on comic books—they *know* what it's all about. The very old and the very young know. People's opinions were formed by comic books they read in the first seven years of their lives. Now a new wave of adult comix books comes along and changes their opinions. It's the ultimate medium! No question about it."

On this question, Lynch might get some argument from authorities who have busted bookstores selling underground comix in at least two cities—in particular *Zap* #4, with its chronicle of good-natured incest among members of the Joe Blow Family—but among comix artists in general there does exist a carryover of youthful interest in comics that has now matured into white heat enthusiasm for the new strips *they* are now creating.

Vaughn Bode: "I started drawing when I was six, and by the time I was in college I had 1,500 named cartoon characters—recorded in a book. It became a fetish to invent and invent—out-invent everyone on earth . . . I built my own planets—I believe in those planets—and most of the equipment I use in the strips (fighting machines with the worst of human traits), I've designed," he says, adding with a small smile the information that his "Hypocket Infantry Machines, Model 1940" have "developed a disease—empathy—they cry." Bode does elaborate model sheets for his "machines" before putting them into action, and if all this begins to sound a bit compulsive, he'd probably be the last one to deny it. The important thing, of course, is that the work is so well-drawn, genuinely offbeat and often highly perceptive in its analysis of mankind's foibles. "I need to express myself," says Bode. "The work is me. I can't be at ease—all my emotions go into my work. I think Kim Deitch is the same. I know Crumb is the same."

Peter Bramley (who is both underground cartoonist and above-ground commercial artist): "I've been interested in doing comics, literally, all my life. I think the strongest thing about the cartoon is the vulgarity of the drawing—the whole lack of subtlety is what visually happens . . . when you see a Japanese or Chinese comic book, you realize you don't *need* writing."

Art Spiegelman: "You're very aware you're working in the comic book form . . . We've all gone through a phase of treating comics as art instead of comics—then after a certain phase, you *know* they're art and treat them like comics again . . . It *is* a groovy form—you do the words *and* the art."

Moreover, as in any other field, there are both the broad general influences and the private jokes, as it were, which really turn on an artist.

Peter Bramley: "I'm into *Smokey Stover* and *Krazy Kat,* and I'm into mouses a lot—I really love mouses!"

Art Spiegelman: "I'm into Winsor McCay (creator of a fabulously drawn comic strip of yesteryear called *Little Nemo in Slumberland*) and Jay Lynch is into funny animal comics and Crumb is into Rube Goldberg." (Apparently there is a subdivision of underground comix entirely given to assigning influences to Robert Crumb. The artist himself told an interviewer that he had been influenced by Jules Feiffer, Chester Gould [*Dick Tracy*], Harold Gray [*Little Orphan Annie*], Elzie Segar [*Popeye*] and

Harvey Kurtzman. Roger Brand allows Crumb Elzie Segar, adds Billy DeBeck [*Barney Google*], then insists "it's quite obvious his biggest influence is Basil Wolverton." Mike Barrier observed in *Funnyworld* No. 12 that Crumb's work "looks 'old-fashioned' but no one agrees on which 'old-fashioned' cartoonists had the most to do with shaping his style. Billy DeBeck, Elzie Segar, Carl Barks, Basil Wolverton, John Stanley . . . the list is a long one. Anyone whose style seems to reflect that many influences . . . and yet is clearly in thrall to no one of them . . . has to be a good cartoonist, and a supreme synthesizer.")

Kim Deitch: "I was a painter—I *came* to New York to be a painter—and Winsor McCay really snapped my mind. Then, during the winter of '66, I started getting interested in *Marvel Comics* and my paintings started to look like comics. I just fell into the *EVO* thing. The first thing I brought there wasn't accepted by Walter Bowart because he wanted something psychedelic, but when I came back with *Sunshine Girl,* Walter thought it was a real underground character. To me, *Sunshine Girl* was about the most organic thing possible, but I guess it was a case of being in the right place at the right time."

Interestingly enough, the emergence of underground comix—it is surely propitious timing, as Deitch infers, that the underground papers were there to provide a forum for artists whose material wouldn't stand much chance of exposure in the professional cartoon field—has happened at the *same* time that professional cartoonists have also been raising fandom to a new level. Some working cartoonists, weary of following the commercial formulas of the marketplace, have been contributing more personal—and frequently more imaginative—efforts to various magazines which exist for just that purpose. *Star-Studded Comics,* published by two Carrollton, Texas, comics buffs named Howard Keltner and Buddy Saunders, is actually pretty conventional comic book stuff with its *Xal-kor, the Human Cat, Doctor Weird,* and *Powerman,* but *Nick Fury, Agent of S.H.I.E.L.D.* is, at the least, graphically impressive. More significant to our examination of the underground comix phenomenon, however, are two publications, *Graphic Story Magazine* and *witzend,* where both underground artists and professionals have been—let the phrase be forever buried after this one, last, dastardly usage—doing their thing.

Graphic Story Magazine, formerly *Fantasy Illustrated,* is edited and published by a Los Angeles gentleman named Bill Spicer, and he does nice work. The magazine, printed on heavy stock, serves as a forum for comic book buffs to indulge in scholarly critiques and launch broadsides at one another, but its more arresting function for the outsider is to publish innovative graphic material. Issue Number Nine, for instance, had an engrossing twenty-one-page rendering of a story by Robert Sheckley, the noted science fiction writer, drawn by Vincent Davis, which found three criminal entrepreneurs searching on a deserted Mars for the ultimate weapon that had destroyed the inhabitants there. It turns out to be a genie-like creature—if that is the term for it—with a voracious appetite for protoplasm. End of Mars, it is explained, and end of the explorers from Earth. *Graphic Story* has also been running the work of George Metzger, whose *Kaleida Smith* and *Master Tyme and Mobius Tripp* represent a level of intricacy and sophistication of story that I strongly doubt is matched anywhere in the commercial comic-book field. Metzger's exciting—an interesting head in action. He's also damn hard to read and could stand an art editor who would make his work even more provocative—science fiction come to startling graphic realization.

Issue Number Ten ran featured two Vaugh Bode sections—*The Man,* an early caveman series, and *The Machines,* another Bode World War III-plus projection—that seemed to split *Graphic Story* readers almost diametrically (it's nice they react). The more recent issues of *Graphic Story* seem to be devoting proportionally more space to long interviews with veteran artists from the comics field, which, while certainly a valuable service, is not likely to have much influence on young cartoonists whose only artistic theory seems to be that radical culture at first borrows freely from the past, then rapidly creates its own cultural antecedents. It would be too bad if Spicer cannot afford both to honor the past and provide a proving ground for the future. But this is observation, not criticism, because without a doubt the work Spicer and the editors of other fanzines are doing will be of more than passing interest to libraries and future historians of comic art.

Witzend is another matter, entirely. True, both magazines, professional as they are, avoid the marketplace entirely and are only available by subscription. Even getting back issues can be a problem. Still, *witzend* started off with a specific future cast—the cultivation of a sophisticated audience and the utilization of the magazine as a sounding board and preview theater for artists.

Wallace Wood, whose parodies of comic strips are delightfully familiar to anyone who read the first decade of *Mad,* founded *witzend* in 1967 as an occasional "public service." Wood wrote in the second issue of *witzend* that he regards the magazine as a "unique publication comprised of *editorless* [emphasis added] artistic creations from the minds and hands of some very talented people. It is a place to experiment, as well as to display some previously unpublished work done by professional artists for their own enjoyment. And to establish copyrights on properties which may have commercial possibilities." He also noted that the magazine "does not and will not seek general distribution by diluting any contribution to suit the preconditioned tastes of a mass audience."

Given these bold words, it's only fair to apply them, as a critical frame of reference, to what *witzend* has published to date. The magazine has featured, among others, Vaughn Bode, Roger Brand, and Art Spiegelman, plus such well-known "pros" as Harvey Kurtzan, *Mad's* Don Martin, Jeff Jones, and Steve Ditko—the latter two comic-book artists—and of course Wood himself. Perhaps the most experimental element, at least in contrast to comics published under the Comics Code, has been a fondness for drawing bare breasts. Since the artists supplying these works of art are good-to-excellent draftsmen, this has not been an unpleasant surprise —there are tons of tits in underground comix, but, taken as a group, the artists are not superior draftsmen and, indeed, would seem to prefer drawing grotesque creatures—and the breasts have helped decorate some interesting science fiction and fantasy material.

However, the best of these strips has been Jones' outer space tale, entitled *Alien,* in *witzend* No. Six, which relied on breastworks not at all, instead utilizing extremely fine graphics to tell a story with almost no reliance on dialogue. *Alien* is an example of the service the magazine can provide its readers, but some of the other professional artists have merely given *witzend* more extreme versions of what they regularly produce for the comic-book racks. The most controversial of these artists has been Ditko, whose *Mr. A.* and *The Avenging World* (this a visual lecture rather than a strip) depict a moral universe strictly divided by an East Berlin Wall of good versus bad. Ditko's work has prompted one reader to cite the artist's "small-minded, arrogant ignorance . . . this piece is a total failure in its blind hatred," and in *witzend* No. Seven, Bill Pearson, now editor of the magazine, and artist Tim Brent parodied Mr. A. with their Mr. E., a "crusading moralist and amateur economist of the quid pro quo" whose "rigid, stony facemask [conceals] the rigid, stony face beneath." By my lights, *Mr. E.* was the most interesting thing in this issue, but the issue was hardly a milestone in *witzend's* first four years of publishing.

The contributions of underground artists to *witzend* have also been uneven in roughly the same scale that *witzend* has been uneven. I enjoyed Brand's *Homesick,* a time-travel fantasy set in Atlantis and in the here and now, but Bode's brutal salute to war, *The Junkwaffel Invasion of Kruppeny Island* was cruelly crowded on four pages and far too text-heavy. Ironically enough, the most admirable work to date has been Wood's delightful on-going "fairy tale," *Pipsqueak Papers,* but the artist is no longer formally associated with the magazine, having sold it, after four issues, to the Wonderful Publishing Company for the vast sum of one dollar. The only proviso to the purchase, apart from the selling price, was that *witzend* publish at least four more issues in an attempt to achieve artistic, if not financial, solvency.

In 1970 Bill Pearson, who is both editor and publisher, moved his home and the magazine to Arizona, where he hopes to continue publishing it. He recognizes that there must be far more to *witzend* than merely providing a showcase for unpublished commercial material. On the other hand, he doesn't expect to find salvation emanating solely from the underground activity. "It's a great personal artform," he observes, "and you can do things with it. But not enough of the guys have, yet. You have to have a theme."

Thematic direction, of course, usually implies firm editorial direction, and my equally firm suspicion is that underground comix magazines will most prosper when they either are drawn by one person (Crumb has done several entire magazines) or else are run by a strong editor, one kicking the amateurism and self-indulgence out. But this is precisely *not* the way most underground comix are being published—usually they are happening, not being published—and the artists *are* right when they say that the most important aspect to the field is a freedom of expression which would be virtually impossible to attain in the commercial world.

Just as important, this freedom takes many forms. For Jay Lynch, whose *Nard n' Pat* is one of the most "traditional"-looking strips, the fun and charm (rare commodity in the comix field as yet) of his work may simply be the reversal of roles whereby his human character, the chinless, and feckless, Nard has to play foil to Pat th' Cat, a lascivious-minded "kitty-kat" who places ads in the underground press ("Chicks, howdjya' like ta' share my pad? I'm a groovie cat with a way-out mustache.") and who will good-naturedly seduce the "Avon calling" lady at the ring of a doorbell. Lynch's drawing calls up a host of influences (would you believe *Andy Gump*?) but his dialogue and writing are more irreverent and far more playful than will be found in all but a few syndicated comic strips. And, like Crumb, his strips often kid the comic strip medium itself, and in general break all the rules with which above-ground art cartoonists have to live.

Lynch's *Bijou* buddy, Skip Williamson, draws terrific covers and his continuing strip, *Snappy Sammy Smoot,* is one of the more highly stylized in the field—(there is more cross-hatching in some individual panels than there is artwork in some of the cruder comix strips). But what is even more interesting about *Snappy Sammy Smoot* is that it manages to be politically radical at the same time it is satirical and funny and looks like nothing else in the field. Sammy is a well-meaning *nebish* to whom things happen and this strip and others of Williamson's often take the logic of Establishment dicta to their painfully logical consequences—flower power is no match for police power. However, in a marvelous one-page strip in *Bijou* No. Three entitled *Class War Comics,* a hairy revolutionary echoes the "BRA DAP! FOOM!" of his machine gun with this roar: "EAT LEADEN DEATH IMPERIALISTIC REACTIONARY BUSINESS ADMINISTRATION MAJORS!!" And in the last panel, he reminds us: "An' when yer smashing th' state, kids . . . don't fergit t' keep a smile on yer lips an' a song in yer heart!" Williamson may not be working to overthrow "the System" in some secret revolutionary cell (indeed, now that he is a parent he holds down a day job at *Playboy,* that formerly unhospitable corporation), but his strips slyly, and not so slyly, get a lot of ideas out. "For me," Williamson explains, "it's like an absurd reflection of what happens to me personally. I don't write a script—I work from panel to panel—it's sort of a stream of consciousness comic strip."

Not sex or politics or Mom or any of our hallowed notions but censorship itself may be the only taboo in the comix field, and so for many of the young artists there is a rite of passage equivalent to masturbating in public. Hopefully this is simply a growth point, since most of this work is neither very erotic nor very funny. In any case, S. Clay Wilson and Robert Crumb got there first, although my own feeling about Crumb is that he always tries to be funny and therefore will always manage to produce a kind of smut rather than pornography because there is too much joy and fun in his work to allow prurient interest, his *or* ours, to become dominant in his work. He has already created the largest and most memorable cast of characters in the field: fritz the cat, Mr. Natural, Flakey Foont, Whiteman (I'm an AMERICAN! . . . A real hard charger! . . . A Citizen on the go!"), Schuman the Human, Angel Food McSpade, Edgar and Mary Jane Crump, Lenore Goldberg (and her Girl Commandos), plus that epitome of slobdom, Bo Bo Bolinski. His comedy, taken as a body of work, has been the most ebullient force in the comix field. As Don Shenker has written of him, "Nothing is sacred except talent; that is life. Nothing is forbidden except not exercising talent/life," and when I spoke to Crumb some months back and mentioned that *Snatch Comics* ("Are you tired of sex books that promise but never deliver? Tired of looking for the good stuff? Search no further, Bud!") had seemed to zap (yes! an underground pun) all taboos in a single outing, his response was spontaneous: "If taboos were broken by *Snatch Comics*—groovy? Then we can move on to something else. There are millions of other ideas—I've got so many ideas for comix I wish I had more time to draw!" Similarly, Art Spiegelman, whose work has been both lyrically psychedelic and cheerfully scatological, points out that an artist's kicks derived from violating taboos can be simply another form of conformity. "Professionals think it's a big thing to draw a bare tit," he says. "I'll only transgress them [taboos] when I've something to say. Originally I was going to take a book by Dave Breger called *How to Draw and Sell Cartoons* and violate each taboo he listed. Sex, nudity, religion, motherhood, the whole lot. Hell, then I decided not to bother."

Vaughn Bode is an artist whose industry and commitment to comix represents a slightly astonishing level of dedication. He believes that the freedom allowed him by *Cavalier,* where his *Deadbone Erotica* strips are a regular three-page feature, has helped him to grow not only as an artist, but as a human being as well. "As I have changed, so have the creatures in *Deadbone* (or vice versa!), since I don't know where I end and where the creatures begin," he said recently. "When I first started the series, I was so inhibited that I couldn't draw women, even though I'd taken years of life drawing at school, and now, look at the chicks! Even my lizards were sexless, but now they're all hung. It's been very good therapy for me—very cathartic." Bode's catharsis aside, his work has clearly improved. There is less of the "dis-da" dialogue and text-heavy strips of which Mike Barrier has rightly complained in *Funnyworld,* and his women *do* look delicious. There is more attempt at political and social satire, this reflecting his need to have his work "endure and not become dated." Perhaps reflecting his lack of admiration for most professional comics toilers, he now labels his work "pictography"—picture-writing ("I write and then illustrate what I write"). Whether or not this is more pretentious than portentous, there is simply no doubting his sincerity. "I would like to be a good part of the underground thing and mold it for the future," says Bode, speaking with a strange mixture of boyishness and intensity which somehow *does* come out as a kind of super-sincerity. "What they're all trying to do, I'm *sure,* is express themselves, and this is the only place they can do it. There are so many facets to what they're trying to do—their work is maybe going to have rejuvenated cartooning in this country, loosened it up—they're going to be important people."

Naturally enough, the progress and future importance of comix do rest with its artists, but much also rests with the future of America. There are no nice, benevolent cops in comix, no Presidents en route to sanity, no authority figures who aren't the enemy—representatives of a nation in which reality imitates satire, as witnessed by the front pages of our newspapers, a nation at once in a high state of stasis and frenetic *angst.* The American Dream has become polluted by real life, *has* become a psychedelic nightmare, and at least some of the underground artists recognize, as Don Shenker has pointed out, that the language itself "has been fragmented into a host of rhetorics, most of them authoritarian and totalitarian. Americans are talked at, talked down to, and not with." In his view, the underground comix "undermine by simply being true." Just as the best of the posters have done, he observes, "so are the underground comix providing the place in life and the language which is spoken there, depicting the new country to which so many of us have an earnest desire to be deported. Comix, posters—these are the media of the new poetry, and this is why the police bust them."

If Shenker is right, and unless he is speaking of "dropping out," it is difficult to fault *his* rhetoric, we may reasonably anticipate more suppression of comix as the artists mature and really begin doing that important subversive work of which Shenker and Bode and others speak. But it is still too early to tell if this is going to happen. Thus far the only arrests have been made because the police were afraid someone would get horny by looking at a comix book. The only trend discernible at this writing is a depressing number of "horror comix" that usually just extend what is already admissible in the commercial titles. On the other hand, there are intriguing new artists, for example, Dave Sheridan, Greg Irons, Fred Schrier, "Foolbert Sturgeon" (pseudonym for a college professor who is the creator of *The New Adventures of Jesus* and *Jesus Meets the Armed Forces*), and Jack Jaxon. The last two are making a return debut, as it were, since they each produced one of the earliest comix while living in Texas. The work of these artists is provocative both in terms of graphics and writing. Also, a number of new comix publishing enterprises have been formed (usually in San Francisco) for the dual purpose of maintaining artistic freedom and getting a larger hunk of the cover price, so presumably outlets for comix are expanding into more bookstores, "head shops," and other underground chambers of commerce. This should mean wider distribution for comix and an increased ability to defend themselves should any kind of suppression occur. But whether or not they will become a vital part of America's radical youth subculture and politics strictly remains to be seen. If no girl has ever been seduced by an underground comix book, it may be too much to hope for something along those lines for our political system.

Still, underground comix are exciting because some of them have been clever and funny and have made telling points about America in a new way, and because the times have called them forth. Thus, if it is true, as has been observed, that America without its comic strips would not *be* America, then America with its new comix would be a much more somber America. I think we're witnessing the mere beginnings of a cultural kick with real kick in it.

Imagine. . . .

S. Clay Wilson becoming political, versus the American involvement in Latin America!

Vaughn Bode intercepting our egocentric probes of outer space! !

Gilbert Shelton outwitting the entire Narcotics Bureau by implanting an entire kilo of grass in Bugs Bunny's ears! ! !

Jay Lynch's Pat th' Cat practicing whatever Masters and Johnson have preached! ! ! !

Robert Crumb versus Spiro Agnew! ! ! ! !

Robert Crumb versus Spiro Agnew! ! ! ! ! ?

I *like*—no, I'm afraid I relish—the match-up. After all, it'll only be satire imitating reality once again.

Who Put the Bomp in the Bomp De-Bomp De-Bomp*

By Greil Marcus

It was at the Avalon Ballroom in San Francisco. Lead guitarist Barry Melton was introducing the next tune by Country Joe and the Fish: "This song is dedicated to all the teenyboppers . . . and (casting an eye at a huge chick dancing on the stage) to all the big boppers too . . . yes, we all remember the Big Bopper, and Richie Valens and Buddy Holly, who all went down that day over Missouri or something in their Lear Jet, who've gone away to Juke Box Heaven . . ."

"You know, they should teach a course in rock 'n' roll."

"Yeah, it'd be a lotta fun."

"There'd be problems . . . it'd have to be a year, maybe a two year course."

"Come on . . . they teach the whole history of European intellectual thought or political theory in one year—that's 2500 years of material! Rock's fifteen, at the most."

"Well, seventeen, if you count *Sixty Minute Man* by the Dominoes, in 1951. But the thing is, people really *care* about rock 'n' roll, it's part of them, even if they only know it subconsciously, or when it hits them. I mean, who really cares if you leave out Marsilius of Padua. But everyone had their greatest song, and they'd scream if you left it out, and they should. Two years."

"D'you read *Silver Screen* and *Photoplay* and stuff like that for stories about rock stars?"

"Yeah . . . isn't it strange . . . we'll even go through *Peyton Place* to get to one good picture of John Lennon. You know, Dylan said a lot of

---

people are afraid of the bomb, but more are afraid to be seen carrying a *Modern Screen* magazine . . . maybe rock's important enough to overcome the fear . . ."

"KFRC is coming out with a Top 300 survey. Everyone's supposed to send in a postcard with their all-time top ten on it, and then they count it up. Hey, we've got to offset the teenybopper vote. Get the postcards . . . my top ten's *Like A Rolling Stone, Eight Days a Week,* and *Money* by the Beatles, *Play With Fire* and *Tell Me* by the Stones, *Little Darlin'* by the Diamonds, *Johnny B. Goode* by Chuck Berry, *The Kids Are Alright,* by the Who, *One Fine Day* by the *Chiffons, Da Do Ron Ron* by the Crystals."

"That's great. But mine's *Like A Rolling Stone, Like A Rolling Stone, Like A Rolling Stone, Like A Rolling Stone . . .*"

So a few weeks later, six of us . . .

"It's incredible, the top songs are all great, and *Like A Rolling Stone* was number eight, fantastic . . . only two to go. Bet you five bucks the number one is *Lovin' Feeling* by the Righteous Brothers."

"You're on."

"And now, here it is, the number *two* hit of all time—*You've Lost That Lovin' Feeling,* by the Righteous Brothers!"

"Shit."

"AND NOW, THE ALL-TIME, ALL-TIME HIT, NUMBER ONE! IT'S *SATISFACTION* BY THE ROLLING STONES! ! !"

We all won.

"Remember the Nutmegs?"

"*Story Untold,* 1956. Remember when Chuck Berry got sent to prison for taking a fifteen-year-old chick across state lines?"

"Yeah—like when Jerry Lee Lewis married his thirteen-year-old cousin and got his records banned from the radio stations . . ."

*   *   *

Two Berkeley professors, writing in the *New York Review of Books* about the student strike which broke out two years after the climactic sit-in of the Free Speech Movement, stated that the remark most often heard around campus during the crisis was that of Marx, from *The 18th Brumaire of Louis Napoleon:*

Hegel remarks somewhere that all facts of great importance in world history occur twice. He forgot to add: the first time as tragedy, the second as farce.

Well, the remark may have held wide currency among some circles, but among students, it was another quote which provided the metaphor for our situation, from Bob Dylan's *Memphis Blues Again:*

And here I sit so patiently
Waiting to find out what price
You have to pay to get out of
Going through all these things twice

The differences in metaphors are important. One seeks an academic and intellectual conclusion, a truth that will last the ages; the other tries to establish and confirm the present moment, and in doing so, to save one from it. One metaphor structures time; the other tries to escape it. More important to me, though, is the fact that one statement is drawn from the vast stores of academic knowledge, the other from rock 'n' roll. The students can play the first game, if they want to, but the professors cannot play the second. This isn't simply because professors aren't in the habit of playing Dylan records; some are. It's because the ability to involve oneself with rock 'n' roll, to understand it instinctually, to know that any one piece of music is part of over ten years of experience, to be in tune with a medium, is not something one can pick up by a little attention or a casual listening.

Rock 'n' roll was, is, and will be a basic part of the experience, of the growing up years, of the present college or nonstudent generation. It will continue to be so for the generations that will follow. But rock 'n' roll has existed only since about 1954, and thus it's a sad fact that most of those over thirty cannot be a part of it, and it cannot be a part of them. I don't want to talk about the ability of adults to "enjoy the Beatles" or to "think Dylan has something to say," but about the rock 'n' roll era as the exclusive possession of our generation, about what our love for it and our immersion in it might imply for our consciousness and vision.

This essay will center on the "student"—in school or out of it, graduate or dropout—the person who reads, thinks about what he hears, who likes to talk with his friends about it. I'll look at what it meant for that kind of person to have grown up with rock 'n' roll in the fifties and early sixties, enjoying it; and what it meant for the same person, somewhat older, to discover, with the coming of the Beatles and the renaissance that followed, that he loved, rock 'n' roll, the old as well as the new, that this music was part of him, that he was interested in it, seriously, and with joy. I'll try to examine how ways of thinking and perceiving are formed; how people create the metaphors by which they interpret, consciously and unconsciously, the internal and external things that are important to them.

"Youth today lives mythically and in depth," wrote Marshall McLuhan. What this *means* is not important. What is, as with most metaphors, is how it works.

The old idea of popular music viewed the words as the essential basis for listening; the music, even with a catchy tune, was in the background. In Cole Porter songs, surely the best of old-time pop music, the instrumentation—watered-down swing or more sophisticated Broadway musical

—was so understated it was hardly there at all. The words were the thing, whether, as with Cole Porter, they were meaningful *(Miss Otis Regrets)*, or as was usual, trite *(Stardust)*. It was the old Hit Parade Show, with Snooky Lanson, Dorothy Collins, and the others. They really knew how to *enunciate*—otherwise we might have missed the tag line of *The Naughty Lady of Shady Lane.* This was a slick music, perfectly suited, words and all, to serve as background sounds for cocktail lounges and piano bars. Pop music, performed live, was an atmosphere for small talk. Remember "mood music"?

And then Chuck Berry was on stage, with his flashing electric guitar. Rock 'n' Roll had begun to come together, around 1954, from all kinds of sources, in all kinds of places: New York City, the West Coast, Nashville, Memphis. Roots? You could talk about Arthur "Big Boy" Crudup, a Negro bluesman who had a great influence on the early Elvis; you could get really academic and talk about the Mississippi Sheiks, a thirties group that sang the blues, a prototype of the black vocal groups of the late forties and early fifties like the Ravens, the Cardinals, the Orioles, and Billy Ward and the Dominoes. The Dominoes included Clyde McPhatter, who was to become the great lead singer for the Drifters, the best of the many groups attached to Atlantic Records, then a small new company in New York City. Atlantic introduced the Clovers and Ray Charles, and brought the fantastic Robins from the West Coast. With the help of Jerry Leiber and Mike Stoller, they turned the Robins into the Coasters. Leiber and Stoller were brilliant songwriters, responsible for *Hound Dog, Jailhouse Rock,* and all of the Coasters' hits. Along with Chuck Berry, they wrote the songs that expressed all the frustrations of white teenagers. They told us what our secret rebellions were all about.

Back in Los Angeles, the Coasters' home town, Dootsie Williams assembled more Negro vocal groups for his company, Dooto Records: Don Julian and the Meadowlarks, the Medallions, the Penguins. Drawing heavily on these early rhythm and blues records, on the blues, on country music, but still coming up with a tough, distinctive sound, was the Nashville-Memphis scene, centered around Sun Records; and out of those cities came rockabilly: Elvis, Roy Orbison, Carl Perkins, Johnny Cash, Jerry Lee Lewis. Bill Haley somehow caught the spirit of it all with *Rock Around the Clock,* a record that still hasn't stopped selling. Alan Freed, a New York disk jockey, brought Bill Haley to town for a great rock 'n' roll show, and as Bill Haley began playing, a rock 'n' roll riot got off the ground as well. There were too many tickets sold to too many kids, and they wanted to get in.

The stars began to emerge: Elvis, Little Richard, Chuck Berry, Fats Domino, Buddy Holly; and as the parental attack began—"How can you listen to that garbage?"—dozens of songs echoed the line, "Rock 'n' roll is here to stay . . ." Or the Coasters:

> In the beginning
> There was nothing but rock
> Then somebody invented the wheel
> And things just began to roll!
> You say that music's for the birds
> You say you can't understand the words
> Well baby if you did
> You'd really blow your lid
> Baby, that is rock and roll
>
> The Coasters: *That Is Rock and Roll*

Yeah, "you can't understand the words." We all heard that one. You could, of course, if you wanted to, but they were and still are unintelligible for the first few hearings, partly because the hypnotic music and the pounding beat caught your attention first, partly because white kids weren't used to hearing the voices of black people, and white parents weren't interested in trying. The beat and the "meaningless babble" guaranteed that rock 'n' roll would be our own exclusive property.

The songs gave us a complete experience in two minutes, fading out at the end so the disk jockey could start talking quicker, giving the impression that the song never stopped. It was the nonverbal incantations that were important:

> Da do ron ron ron!
> Da do ron ron!
> Da do ron ron!
> Da do ron ron ron!

The Crystals sang it. "What does that *mean?*" David Susskind asked Phil Spector, writer and producer of *Da Do Ron Ron*, the Crystals' million-seller, the creator of the most powerful and distinctive sound in rock 'n' roll. "It's not what *I say it means,*" Spector came back, "it's what it makes you *feel!* Can't you hear the *sound* of that record, can't you hear that?"

But the old lessons of pre-rock music held on, the sniveling sentiment of entertainers not interested in making music, just interested in doing what their managers told them to do. The music became quieter, softer, less "obtrusive"; and the singers, even the great Sam Cooke, began to use proper grammar, instead of the phrases and expressions that came naturally. Rock 'n' roll had always been the place where a kid could sneak off and say "ain't," and that was fading too.

The ancient hit, *I am the Japanese Sandman* by the Chellos, had a typical rock 'n' roll chorus of odd sounds, and in the middle of the song one of the back-up singers breaks in on the leader, and complains:

> All you guys say the big things
> All I get to say is:
> Ah he goes rang tang ding dong
> Ranky sanky . . .

We thought rock 'n' roll had gotten over its inferiority complex; that it had brushed off the jibes and taunts at a spirit that told us that words were sounds we could feel before they were statements to understand. But no one was going to catch Bobby Vee singing "ranky sanky." For by the early sixties the burst of creation that exploded in the fifties was drying up. In the words of a time-honored litany, Chuck Berry was in prison, Buddy Holly was dead, Little Richard had decided to become a preacher, and Fats Domino was back playing bars and dives. The great groups that were still around, like the Coasters and the Drifters, were eclipsed by the clean, sugary rock 'n' roll of Bobby Vinton and Annette Funicello, even though the music of the originals was as great as ever. Rock 'n' roll was going straight. Only Phil Spector, in his twenties, who'd grown up with rock 'n' roll, preserved the spirit of our music. He set up his own record company in Hollywood, and created a full, crashing sound for the singers he made into stars—the Crystals, the Ronettes, Darlene Love, the Righteous Brothers. Spector wrote the songs, coached the singers, arranged the instruments, and brought us records that were the quintessence of rock 'n' roll. Words screamed, saxophone blaring, double pianos jingling, what seemed like a thousand voices singing over it all. You strained your radio dial to wring one of Spector's songs out of the disk jockey. *That* was rock 'n' roll.

But that was about all that was left of true rock by the end of 1963. There was only one million-seller that year, an insipid ditty called *Sugar Shack* by Jimmy Gilmore. I remember New Year's Eve, listening to the radio's review of the top songs of the year. The disk jockey played the number one song, Gilmore's atrocity, and he said with disgust, "That's *their* number one. Here's mine—enjoy it while you can." He played *On Broadway* by the Drifters, a dramatic song that sold far below its worth. Later that night, about five A.M., we heard *Some of Your Loving,* a great song by a forgotten group, something we hadn't heard for years, a song I've never heard again. It was thrilling, exciting—and scary, because we couldn't possess it when we wanted to. That power belonged to the radio, and to the failing taste of the record-buying public. We had grown up with rock 'n' roll; it had been our music, and there wasn't much of it left. In that music was a place of joy, a nonverbal celebration of all the senses, of hanging on chords and notes, anticipating a sax or guitar solo, smashing the sound up on a car radio. A good part of the joy of those years came from the radio and its music. Once, overcome by the Drifters' *There Goes My Baby,* we stopped our car and pulled over, just to listen. Four friends drove by while the song was on, and all did the same thing, as five radios blasted out the same song. But it was 1963, and rock 'n' roll was slipping away from us.

Within one month the Beatles hit America, took over the number one, two, three, four, and five spots on the charts at the same time, and opened the door to a score of previously unheard British groups—the

Rolling Stones, Them, the Kinks, the Swingin' Blue-jeans, the Animals, the Nashville Teens, the Zombies—all of which affirmed their devotion to early rock 'n' roll and "race" (black) music. In doing so, they opened another door all the way, this one to the acceptance of rhythm and blues and nonverbal rock by white teenagers and students who'd forgotten where it all came from. Coming into true prominence about the same time as the Beatles was Motown Records, a black company from Detroit, with its stable of the Supremes, Martha and the Vandellas, the Four Tops, the Temptations, and Smokey Robinson and the Miracles. As Motown was aided by the Beatles' popularization of their hits, the Rolling Stones, with a much tougher sound, helped make possible the Top Forty success of truly uncompromising black artists like Solomon Burke, Wilson Pickett, and the greatest of them all, the late Otis Redding, a musical descendant of Little Richard and Sam Cooke who before his death surpassed them both.

What was happening was that the people who had grown up with rock 'n' roll were taking over. These people understood rock, loved it, and they knew that for them to be able to play and sing, to produce records and manage bands, meant that they could join the greats of the past that they'd idolized in their youth. The renaissance of rock 'n' roll was a continuing celebration that has not ended. As the Beatles and the Stones re-created rock in 1964, Dylan changed everything in 1965. San Francisco began it again in 1966; and in 1967, the Beatles and the Stones once more pushed on farther than anyone else. Nineteen sixty-eight belongs to Bob Dylan, with his perfect *John Wesley Harding,* and to his band as well. Today, Chuck Berry is back at the Fillmore Auditorium, with San Francisco's Steve Miller Band backing him up. The Coasters and the Drifters and Bill Haley play at the Avalon Ballroom across town; Little Richard's back on the road; Fats Domino has released a new record, with Beatle tunes, taking something back from those who took so much from him. Rock belongs to those whose first musical memories are of Chuck Berry and the Five Satins.

Thus, a brief personal history of rock 'n' roll. What does this have to do with our "consciousness and vision"? Quite a bit, I think. To find out, we have to look at the myths and depths of rock, today's music as formed by yesterday's, and probe the dynamic of our music.

The Beatles revolutionized rock 'n' roll by bringing it back to its sources and traditions. The new era, in America, began with a song, a joyous song, which had what one friend of mine calls the "takeover sound"—music that breaks from the radio and is impossible to resist. The first notes of *I Want To Hold Your Hand* were there, day after day. Everyone knew something different had happened. For months, every new Beatles song had part of that first record in it—that was just the way you had to hear it; that's what a new beginning, a sense of a new beginning means. All the rules were changing, as they'd changed in the fifties. Like the Beatles, groups had to write their own lyrics and music, and play their own instruments—they had to be as involved as possible. With the coming of the Rolling Stones, a new pattern was set; for the first time in the entertainment world, singers and musicians would appear, in photographs and on stage, in the clothes they wore every day. The music and the mystique were coming closer and closer to life as we lived it. For the new groups and for those of us who listened, rock 'n' roll became more a way of life than a sideshow. There was a hint that those stars up on stage might even be the same kind of people as the ones in the audience. Rock became more comfortable and more exciting at the same time.

Rock 'n' roll seeks to do something that earlier popular music had always denied—to establish and confirm, to heighten and deepen, to create and re-create the present moment. Rock, as a medium, knows that it is only up to a certain point that this can be done. To keep a moment of time alive it's necessary to make a song new every time it's performed, every time it's played, every time it's heard. When a song gets stale it only fills time, marks time, expends itself over two or three or ten minutes, but it doesn't *obliterate* time and allow you to move freely in the space that the music can give you. When a song is alive, the mind and the body respond—they race, merge with the music, find an idea or an emotion, and return. When a song is dead, the mind only waits for it to be over, hoping that something living will follow.

Judy Garland has sung *Over the Rainbow* some thousands of times; there's a man who keeps count. The tally is published in the newspapers occasionally, like the Gross National Product, which is really what it is: Judy Garland's GNP. You measure her progress that way. The same kind of mentality that demands this tune from Judy Garland, the same kind of mentality that makes her want to sing it, made a Santa Monica grandmother watch *The Sound of Music* over seven hundred times, once a day, at five o'clock. Listening to a rock song over and over, seeing *A Hard Day's Night* a dozen times, isn't the same—with that you participate when you must, stay away when you desire. The mind is free to remake the experience, but it isn't a prisoner. You don't demand the same songs from Bob Dylan every time he gives a concert—you understand that he's a human being, a changing person, and you try to translate his newness into your own.

This movement of the re-creation of the moment, with the constant changing of the dynamic, is mostly the result of the radio, the way it gives one music. When a song is new, and you like it, when it possesses that intangible grace that makes it part of you, you wait and hope all day that it will come out of the radio and into your ears. You listen, stop what you're doing, and participate. Finally, you'll get tired of it, ignoring the song when it comes on. Months or years later, when it returns as an oldie, the initial experience will be repeated, but with understanding, with a sense of how it all happened. You can't pretend that grace is there when it's not. When *Like A Rolling Stone* was released, I liked it, but I got tired of it pretty quickly. A few months later I put it on the phonograph and it jumped out and claimed me. I think it's the greatest rock 'n' roll record ever made—but I didn't decide that, I accepted it.

An incredible number of songs provide this sort of experience. Because of this, because of the way songs are heard, with an intensity that one provides for himself, they become part of one's mind, one's thought and subconscious, and they shape one's mental patterns. People sense this: there is a conscious effort by the members of the generation I'm talking about to preserve and heighten the experiences of rock 'n' roll, to intensify the connection between the individual and his music, between one's group of friends and the music they share. That effort takes the form of games and contests. These games reinforce the knowledge that this music is ours, that it doesn't and can't belong to anyone else. The kids who'll follow us will have a lot of it, but they can never really know the absolute beginnings of rock 'n' roll—that's our treasure. The generations that came before us are simply somewhere else. In a strange, protective way, people who are now in middle age aren't *allowed* to possess the music we have. When the Beatles were becoming acceptable, listenable for adults, with *Michelle* and *Yesterday,* the foursome responded with hard rock and experimental music, with sitars and tape machines and driving guitars. *Day Tripper* and *Strawberry Fields Forever* blasted the Beatles back home to students, kids, intellectuals, dropouts. The exclusiveness of rock 'n' roll is well-guarded. If the adults can take it, we'll probably reject it. In a way we want to share it, but in the end, it's better that we can't. If we're to be different, we'd best protect the sources of our differences, whenever they are re-created. That is what the Beatles did when they sang *I'm Down,* the toughest rock 'n' roll since Little Richard—they returned to the beginnings, even as they stayed far ahead of everyone else.

And we preserve our possession with games. As small boys quiz each other on baseball statistics, young people today are constantly renewing each other's memories of rock 'n' roll. If you can't identify an old song by the first few bars, something's wrong. "Who did *Come Go With Me?*" "The Del-Vikings, 1957." That's a conversation between Yale and Harvard football players, caught on the field. Once, in an elevator on the Berkeley campus, a friend and I were singing "Who put the bomp in the bomp de-bomp de-bomp, who put the dang in the rama lamma ding dang, who was . . ." ". . . that man, I'd like to shake his hand . . ." joined in another passenger. "He made my baby fall in love with me!" sang a girl entering the elevator, completing the verse. Another friend of mine once made a list of all the Beatle songs released up to the time, about eighty then, identifying the songs only by the first letter of each word in the title. He quizzed everyone on it. Two years later I asked him about the list— he remembered, and started the game all over again. Then there was the guy who, when about twelve, set up an incredible routine for responding to the current hits. He'd budget enough money to buy five records a week, and he'd buy the ones he dug the most. Then, when he got them home, having also picked up a copy of the most recent Top Forty survey, the ritual would begin: he'd draw elaborate tables, as he correlated his taste with that of the record-buying public, redrawing the graphs each week as a song moved up or down the charts; and he had elaborate sets of figures establishing and revising the position of his all-time favorites on the same sort of scale. The next week would bring more new songs, adding to his mathematical history of his love for rock 'n' roll. And then there was the disk jockey on an FM rock show who played some records, and then announced: "You've just heard *Since I Don't Have You* by the Skyliners, and *Ain't That Just Like Me* by the Searchers, both of which formerly tied for the all-time record in repetitions of a final rock 'n' roll chorus, and *A Quick One While He's Away*, by the Who, a song that *destroyed* that record by going over *thirty!*" In live performance, the Who have taken *A Quick One* past one hundred. Anyone who's seen them do it knows why that's important.

Rock 'n' roll has always had an awareness of its music as a special thing, reserved for a certain audience. There are dozens of songs *about* rock 'n' roll, a game within a game. There's *Roll Over Beethoven* and *Rock and Roll Music* by Chuck Berry, Little Richard's *All Around the World (Rock 'n' Roll Is All They Play)*, the magnificent *Do You Believe in Magic* by the Lovin' Spoonful, and the classic *It Will Stand* by the Showmen, released at a time when it looked as if rock and roll might not:

> They're always trying to ruin
> Forgive them, for they know not what they're doin'
> Cause rock and roll forever will stand . . .

The vitality and determination of these songs, that consciousness of rock as a special thing, something to be cherished, has reached the listener, who might have come to it on his own anyway, and helped him into the greatest game of all, the use of lyrics and phrases, verbal, "nonsense," and musical, as metaphors to describe and enclose situations, events, and ideas. " 'Da do ron ron' to you too," wrote a reader in the letters column of a rock newspaper, responding to an offensive article on Phil Spector's Ronettes, and revealing at the same time the wealth of undefined and undefinable meaning possessed by that phrase David Susskind just couldn't understand.

This is a great game that never stops; and it's more than a game, it's a way of responding to life. Situations are "set"; one puts himself down; reveals an irony; takes comfort in the knowledge that someone has been there before him. There is a feeling that if we could only hear enough, and remember all we hear, that the answers would be there on the thousands of rock 'n' roll records that have brought us to the present. It is the intensity of this game of metaphors that allows one to feel this way, to have this kind of innocent confidence. It's not that people haven't used metaphors before; "metaphors," as opposed to "explanations," have been drawn from all of literature and art for the same kinds of reasons. What is different is that rock 'n' roll is a medium that is ever-present, thanks to the radio, and repetitive, thanks to Top Forty and oldies and record players, so that the habit of using metaphors in this way comes so naturally it is a characteristic of how the more articulate part of this generation thinks at any time and responds to any situation. The fact that rock 'n' roll is a body of myths private to this generation only heightens the fact.

People quote lines and phrases from songs to their elders, who can't possibly have any idea of what they're talking about; they quote them to friends, who do know. A line from Dylan can stop whatever action is in progress and return the group to the warmth of a mental community. Since the renaissance of rock 'n' roll, people are finding out that what they thought was their private fetish is the style of a generation. There is a shared body of myths, a common style of feeling and responding, a love of a music that allows one to feel the totality of an experience without missing the nuances and secrets—and as we become aware of our myths we deepen them and practice our own mythmaking. The metaphors drawn from these myths aren't just a matter of fitting the proper words to the proper situation, but of knowing the music is there, somehow, in the same place that the idea is, that somewhere the two have met, and that you have been allowed to see the connection. It is a way of thinking that allows one to give mood and emotion the force of fact, to believe one's instinctual reaction more than someone else's statistical analysis or logical argument.

The music is all around. There's a radio in every car, at least one in every apartment. They are on much of the time—maybe all day. There's a record player, more and more, as people become aware of their music, finding "Oldies But Goodies" and "Greatest Hits" albums on it, as it also plays today's music. A hit song, one you like, is heard at least a hundred times. For the month or so it's popular, it becomes part of the day's experience. If it's on a record you buy, you have control over that part of your experience, instead of receiving it as a surprise from the radio. But playing a favorite song on your own record player lacks the grateful thrill of hearing it cascade from the radio as a gift of smoky airwaves. Rock exists—something makes one want not to control it, but to accept and experience it as it comes. After a record has passed from the charts, it will come back, as an oldie, every once in a while. You only need the rarity of renewal. It's like the surprise of hearing the Beatles' *All You Need Is Love* for the first time, with all those old songs, some virtually legends, jumping and twisting in and out of the chorus: *Greensleeves, In the Mood,* and a line from *She Loves You* with just a hint of *Yesterday.*

The incessant, happy repetition of words and music that is provided when a song is a hit on the radio or a favorite on the record player makes the song part of one's mind. The musical patterns and lyrics become second nature, as they merge and separate. The fact and experience of repetition, a song half-heard, half-enjoyed, a quick turning up the sound when a favorite chord comes, then withdrawal—this makes a difference as to how one thinks or subconsciously reacts to a situation. Once a song becomes part of you it is accepted. Then you are more naturally inclined to take that song, or any song, as a metaphor, to "name" the place you're in, and leave it at that. A person who feels this wouldn't employ *For What It's Worth* by the Buffalo Springfield to help explain the Sunset Strip riots, as did two writers in the *New York Review of Books;* he'd just say, "Listen to *For What It's Worth*—it's all there." The habit and facility of taking metaphors from music, taking music *as* metaphor, and even more important, using these metaphors in a simple and absolute way, is, I think, the result of the musical experiences I've tried to describe. The metaphor isn't even principally the "meaning" of the words to a song; more often it is that the music, or a phrase, or two words heard, jumping out as the rest are lost, seem to fit one's emotional perception of a situation, event, or idea. A pattern of notes or the way in which a few words happen to fit together hit a chord of memory and a perception takes place, a perception which structures and "rationalizes" itself into a metaphor, not on the basis of a "logical" relationship, but because of the power of music and song to reach into the patterns of memory and response. "If you could just listen to it, you'd know what I mean, competely. It's all there."

"It's all there" is an expression used so often in the making of a song or a musical experience into a metaphor that it's as if some members of this generation had a secret language, with this phrase as the signal that an exclusive kind of discourse is about to begin. But no two people ever hear the same song in the same way, or connect the song with the same things. An organ movement in the "live" recording of Dylan's *Just Like Tom Thumb's Blues* is to me the terrifying presence of an evil serpent, swallowing the singer; to someone else, that part of the music slips by unheard, and the notes of the guitar become tears.

What this means is that a strange kind of communication must take place. In one sense, the communication is perfect—one person has complete trust in the other when he is told that a song holds all the truth of a moment or an experience. They both know it; they both accept the validity of the metaphor. Thus, on a nonverbal, nonvisual level, they understand each other and the way in which they both think, and they share the knowledge that only certain people can understand them. They realize the privacy and the publicness of their communication. The repetition, over and over, of a two or three minute musical experience has given them an effortless metaphorical consciousness. One knows what the other is talking about. There is an identification and a sharing. It is the language of people who comprehend instinctually and immediately. To know "where it's at" isn't rational, it's automatic. "You can't talk about it, you have to groove with it." Of course that can be valid. Two people may try to talk about it, perhaps; but they'll get closer to the truth by placing the experience in front of them, starting with a shared understanding of a common purpose and an unspoken language of intuition and emotion, ending with a respect for the experience as well as for each other. Thus the communication is perfect, among those lucky enough to be a part of it.

But on another level, communication is impossibly difficult and confused. One person will not hear what another has heard in a song. It is hard, and wrong, to force another to put specific meanings on music he can hear for himself. It will bring forth associations for him as well. They both know the truth is there; that is not in doubt. What's there? Who can tell? I know, you know—what else matters? What is vital is that the situation has been captured, probed, made livable by understanding, a mythical understanding with a depth that is private and public, perfectly and impossibly communicable. Perfectly communicable in that there is mutual trust that the situation is *ours,* that we have each and together made it our own; it can't destroy us; it can only be relived and reexperienced with each hearing of our metaphor. Impossibly communicable in that we never know exactly what our friend *is* experiencing. But that can be accepted, when one can create or be given metaphors—imperfect knowledge that is perfect understanding, our kind of roots to joy and tragedy. In John Barth's *Giles Goat-Boy,* the various characters of the novel all go to the theatre, where the Barthian paraphrase of *Oedipus Rex* ("Taliped Decanus") is presented. All know that the drama has affected them profoundly, but none knows just how, for himself or for the others. Yet all trust the play to give them the metaphors by which they will shape and interpret their lives, their actions, and the actions of the others. Each knows, by grace of the gift of art, that they will accept, instinctually and nonrationally, the validity of the others' pictures. All trust the play, as we trust our music. The Greeks perhaps lived with this kind of depth, within this pattern of myth. The same treasure the Greeks of the tragic era possessed is, in some prosaic way, ours again.

Out of the experience of growing up with rock 'n' roll, we have found out that rock has more to give us than we ever knew. With a joyful immediacy, it has taught us to participate with ourselves, and with each other. A repetitive history of songs and secrets has given us a memory patterned by games, within a consciousness of a shared experience, exclusive to our generation. Fifteen years of a beat, and thousands of songs that had just enough humor in those words that are so hard to hear, have brought us a style of thought that allows ideas to create themselves out of feeling and emotion, a style of thought that accepts metaphors as myths. Those myths, when we find them, are strong enough to sustain belief and action, strong enough to allow us to fashion a sense of reality out of those things that are important to us. This is not an attempt to "justify" rock 'n' roll by linking it to something "bigger" than itself—we have nothing bigger than rock 'n' roll, and nothing more is needed to "justify" it than a good song.

The kind of thinking I've tried to describe, the manner of response, the consciousness and unconsciousness of metaphor, the subtle confidence of mystique that leads to the permanence of myth—such an intellectual mood, I think, will have a deep and lasting effect on the vision and the style of the "students" of this generation. They will, and already do, embrace an instinctual kind of knowledge. This is partly a reaction against a programmed, technological culture—but so is rock 'n' roll, a dynamic kaleidoscope of sound that constantly invents new contexts within which to celebrate its own exhilarating power to create a language of emotional communication, sending messages to the body as well as to the mind, reaching the soul in the end.

What rock 'n' roll has done to us won't leave us. Faced with the bleakness of social and political life in America, we will return again and again to rock 'n' roll, as a place of creativity and renewal, to return from it with a strange, media-enforced consciousness increasingly a part of our thinking and our emotions, two elements of life that we will less and less trouble to separate.

This is a kind of freedom we are learning about. Affecting our own perspectives—artistic, social, and political—it makes the tangible and the factual that much more reprehensible, that much more deadening. The intellectual leap, the habit of free association, the facility of making a single rock 'n' roll metaphor the defining idea for a situation or a time of one's life—that is the kind of thinking that makes sense. It is the factual made mystical, with a mythic consciousness given the force of fact, that is our translation of society's messages. It's the elusive situation or idea that fascinates, not the weight of proof or conclusion, and that fascination, captured by metaphor, will be, I think, our kind of knowledge, leading to our kind of vision.

The isolation that is already ours will be increased, of course; but that isolation, as politics and as art, is here now. If it isn't comfortable, there is at least a kind of fraternity to be discovered within its limits.

Chuck Berry has been out of jail for a long time, the Stones for just a little while, and we're not going to let anyone put them back in.

Rock on the Rocks or Bubblegum, Anybody?*

By Irving Louis Horowitz

> *I don't care what people say*
> *Rock 'n' roll is here to stay.*
> —Danny and the Juniors

A year ago there were three AM radio stations in New York City that played only rock music. Now there is one. Four years ago dozens of discotheques and clubs featured rock music in New York. Now most of them are out of business.

Rock 'n' roll is dying. It is now going through the terminal symptoms that jazz went through in the forties and early fifties. And it will die the same way jazz did—by growing up, by being transformed.

Jazz picked up most of its fans during its dance stage. Post-World-War-I flappers and Post-World-War-II beboppers crowded into ballrooms across the country to hear the new music and dance the night away to toe-tapping rhythms.

> *It's got a good beat. You can dance to it.*

RAPPORT

For many years there was a close mutual appreciation between performer and audience. But as the art form matured, so did the musicians. They came to know much more about jazz than their audiences did. The fans knew nothing of the notation system, complex rhythms, time signatures. They just wanted to hear *Caravan* or *One O'clock Jump.* A professional distance began to develop between artist and listener—some musicians looked on their audiences with contempt and took few pains to conceal it.

Distance from the general audience was reinforced by the appearance in the late thirties of a new type of fan. In the slang of the day these jazz followers were known as alligators. Like the groupies of the late sixties, they didn't dance—they stood in front of the bandstand all night and listened. Alligators understood. They knew the music. They knew

---

* Reprinted from *Psychology Today,* Jan. 1971, by permission of the author and copyright holder, Communications/Research/Machines, Inc.

the instruments and the soloists and they appreciated what they heard.

In this context many musicians came to define their own worth not in terms of the mass audience and the hit record, but in terms of peer approval. If the guys in the band and a few sophisticated fans appreciated what one was doing musically, then he was a success—and the rest of the audience be damned. Before they would play, the Modern Jazz Quartet and the Charlie Mingus Quartet often made outrageous demands for concert-hall levels of silence in their audiences. The jazz musician came to expect a nonemotional response to emotion. In some sense this is what the rock culture was originally in rebellion against.

The transition from get-up-and-dance music to sit-down-and-listen music took several years, but it was discernible in many later jazz bands —Cab Calloway's and Duke Ellington's, for example—and in the swing orchestras of Harry James and Benny Goodman.

PACKAGE

Finally, jazz moved from the dance floor to the concert hall. Norman Granz, the Billy Graham of his day, collected the biggest stars into one-nighter packages—Jazz at the Philharmonic—that toured the largest auditoriums in the country. These packaged performances stifled the creativity of many brilliant musicians, but there was big money in them. As Granz's malignant concerts spread through the land, jazz began to die.

The big bands acknowledged their mass audiences and, when pressed, they would play their familiar, danceable hits. But to maintain their self-esteem and professional integrity many artists sought other outlets. Small groups began to develop within the larger bands. The big band was for mass appeal— the small group was for displaying musical expertise and for building personal satisfaction. From Artie Shaw's orchestra came the Gramercy Five, and from Benny Goodman's big outfit came the Benny Goodman Trio. Instead of dancing, audiences were expected to sit and listen to Teddy Wilson's educated piano or to the cascading vibes of Lionel Hampton.

Thelonious Monk and Dizzy Gillespie achieved results similar to those of Bartok and Stravinsky—by innovating and creatively extending their traditions. The soloist became king, and Charlie Parker and, later, John Coltrane were canonized.

As the musicians grew older, so did their fans. Young, unsophisticated ears didn't know enough about the music to appreciate a good tenor-sax solo by Lester Young or Ben Webster. Artists became intraprofessional. Financial success ceased to be a criterion for musical esteem. The musicians who did reach mass audiences had by definition "sold out," and their sounds were disdained—they were "commercial" and "Tin-Pan Alley."

And then came rock 'n' roll.

It's got a good beat. You can dance to it.

The emphasis again was mass appeal. There were few intraprofessional standards, so an artist's worth was defined in the simplest, most obvious way—in terms of how many records he could sell. The focus was on the 45 rpm single, and the Top 40 list was updated every week.

Every music reflects the society in which it flourished. In the Renaissance new needs for humanistic expression gave birth to tonal music which rejected the previous ecclesiastical doxology of the Medieval period. The ideals of freedom in the French Revolution gave rise to the chromatics and the gradual development from the sonata to the cyclical form of the Romantic Movement. Jazz itself, inherently an interracial music, represented a mixture of polyphonic African rhythms and modes with the tonal homophony of the European colonizers.

And rock music, a child of the technological age, reflects its parentage in every aspect. Each year amplifiers and preamplifiers get more sophisticated and more powerful, speaker systems get larger and louder, and new electronic gimmicks alter the sound or become part of it (feedback, cross-phasing, fuzz tones, wah-wah).

The contemporary recording process is so complex that a new group cannot make an album without sophisticated knowledge of electronics—mikeing, mixing, and mastering. Since *Sergeant Pepper,* the multitrack tape recorder has taken over. Voices and instruments are cut onto separate tracks so that the producer can make the piano louder than the bass on one chorus, or add echo to one voice but not another. Six months later, if he feels like it he can add a background of violins or cricket chirps.

Electronic experimentation has taken rock artists away from their roots —the song and the beat. To hear the Beatles as a group one must return to *Revolver,* vintage 1966.

Today's young take all the gadgetry for granted—they are not alienated by technological innovation, nor are they particularly impressed. Jazz musicians, on the other hand—especially followers of Gillespie and Monk —tend to resist technological innovation. Some, like Freddie Hubbard and Ornette Coleman, openly state their opposition to electronic music. They tend to think that any device not to be found in a 19th-Century symphony orchestra is by definition not a musical instrument.

HIT

As rock has matured it has gone through many of the self-conscious changes that marked the rise and fall of jazz. In the first place musicians have changed their definition of success. The hit single is no longer necessary. A group can have a successful album without the support of a Top-40 single (for example, Jefferson Airplane, Jimi Hendrix, Country Joe and the Fish). And if an artist is respected by his fellow musicians, finds approval from a devoted circle of sophisticated fans, and is certified by a semiprofessional publication like *Rolling Stone,* he can maintain high self-esteem even while remaining relatively unknown (for example, Van Dyke Parks, Randy Newman, Captain Beefheart).

Some artists at their pinnacles—Bob Dylan, for example—have turned their backs on their audiences and retreated into seclusion. They may need to do this to preserve their sanity, but the effect is to increase the separation between artist and audience. The Beatles swore off personal appearances in 1966; Dylan retired to his Woodstock home after his motorcycle accident in 1966 and has made few public appearance since then; Elvis retreated from public appearances and holed up in his Tennessee mansion for nine years before his recent comeback at the International Hotel in Las Vegas.

Rock music has just entered the sit-and-listen stage. Even five years ago one could see the young dancing wildly to the omnipresent beat at San Francisco's Fillmore Auditorium. Now the fans don't dance—they sit, they concentrate, they get close to the stage so they can watch the guitarist move his fingers. They know rock music; they know the electric guitar; and they can tell immediately whether their favorite soloist is in peak improvisational form.

SUPER-GROUPS

Just as the stars of yesterday's big bands sought professional recognition and creative opportunities by splitting off to form their own trios and quartets, the most talented musicians today look to each other for support in super-groups.

Many rock musicians have begun to look down on the mass audience. The leader of a top English group said after a recent U.S. tour that American audiences are indiscriminately appreciative—they applaud and yell for more, whether the performance is inspired or inept. This instills in the rock artist the same disrespect and contempt for the audience that the jazz musician felt when he finally gave in to a half-dozen requests for *Tico Tico.* Frank Zappa, on the first dissolution of the Mothers of Invention, complained that most audiences "wouldn't know music if it came up and bit 'em on the ass."

Rock is dying because it has matured and its fans have become self-selective. They sit intently and listen to complex guitar arrangements and improvisations. Eric Clapton, Mike Bloomfield, and Frank Zappa are being hailed as the greatest guitarists and rock musicians of our age.

Their fans are devoted, musically sophisticated, and old. Young teenagers find it very difficult to follow this improvisational music because they do not have background experience with rock. Their ears are not yet equipped to understand or appreciate complexity and innovation. Innovation is a break with tradition, and a thirteen-year-old has no tradition by which he can judge the improvisational forms being explored by many rock musicians.

BUBBLEGUM

Young teenagers don't like to sit and listen anyway. They want to move. And so they turn to the simpler, more danceable music that has come to be known as *bubblegum.*

> *It's got a good beat. You can dance to it.*

To the disbelief and dismay or rock fans, bubblegum music has scored tremendous financial successes. *Sugar, Sugar* sold six million copies, making it the fifth largest-selling record in history. It is the Archies, Tommy Roe, and Bobby Sherman who get the golden records—not Traffic, not Leon Russell, and not Delaney and Bonnie.

Rock fans speak of bubblegum in a tone usually reserved for words like *excreta.* They look down on the 1910 Fruitgum Company with the same distaste that their parents reserved for Chuck Berry and Danny and the Juniors: *How can you listen to that garbage over and over? It's so simple, so repetitious, so childish.* Is this observation any more true of *Sugar, Sugar* than it was of *At the Hop?*

Different types of music appeal to different types of persons, yet there are always artists at the interface who want to reconcile the generations. Thus, in the midfifties white artists came out with cover versions of black rhythm-and-blues songs. In the early sixties rock songs became legitimate when they were set to the schmaltzy arrangements of Percy Faith, Ray Conniff, and the Hollyridge Strings. These albums catered to the older audience. The younger generation snickered as they would at a fifty-year-old housewife who wore a miniskirt and headband. Staying young beyond one's chronology is a complex and often painful undertaking. As Jefferson Airplane explains: "One generation got old/One generation got soul."

Today there are fewer gap-bridging acts. This is partly because groups are providing their own nostalgic ties with older musical styles. A Mantovani version isn't needed any more—one can get lush, syrupy strings on the Beatles' last album, *Let It Be;* and on *Self Portrait,* Bob Dylan provides his own undercover versions of *Blue Moon* and *I Forgot More Than You'll Ever Know About Love.*

VOLTAGE

In the search for new identity and innovation it was inevitable that rock would reiterate jazz. New bands don't feature just the electric guitar—trumpets, flutes, violins, and other traditional instruments are accepted in the contemporary rock band, as long as they are electric. Many recent bands (Blood, Sweat and Tears, Chicago, and Cold Blood, for example) are highly reminiscent in their instrumentation of such earlier groups as Miles Davis' Tentet in the late forties. And the loud brassy arrangements are direct descendants of Count Basie. A promising new group, Ten Wheel Drive, provides a mixture of Big Mama Thornton blues and a tenor sax reminiscent of Coltrane, all set to tight arrangements that remind one of The Jazz Messengers with Art Blakey and Horace Silver.

Other rock artists are reviving traditional jazz forms—on piano, Leon Russell sounds like Jelly Roll Morton, and Janis Joplin was certainly the best jazz singer since Ma Rainey and Bessie Smith.

With other artists—Miles Davis, Don Ellis, and Gary Burton, for example—the cross-fertilization between musical forms is so complete that classification becomes meaningless, or at least tedious.

TRACKS

Other events in the evolution of jazz give hints of the future development of rock. For a brief period jazz found acceptance as background music in movies *(East of Eden, The Man With The Golden Arm),* and later served a similar function on action TV shows *(Peter Gunn, Richard Diamond).* Similarly, rock has recently found its way onto the sound tracks of dramatic movies *(Easy Rider, Zabriskie Point),* and we can expect that soon TV shows will feature rock 'n' roll theme music. After the extended stay of The Who at the Metropolitan Opera, anything can happen.

The musical statements that rock will make in its final years can only be guessed at. Innovation in style and song is essential in recent rock music—any group that fails to innovate does not attract a mass audience. No modern artist becomes popular on someone else's songs, unless he has arranged unique interpretations (e.g., Janis Joplin, Joe Cocker).

When any music reaches the sit-and-listen phase, it becomes a different music—jazz becomes *modern* jazz, rock becomes *hard* or *acid* rock. The music fails to pick up a new, young audience and it begins to die. Perhaps twenty years from now we will look back on Woodstock as the beginning of the end—similar to Benny Goodman's famous Paramount Theater and Carnegie Hall engagements of 1938. It may have marked the crystalization of the sit-and-listen phase, and therefore the imminent death of rock 'n' roll.

Perhaps fifteen years from now there will be a bubblegum revival, the Archies will be likened to Bill Haley and the Comets, and Bobby Sherman will be called the musical genius of his time who broke away from tradition and forged the new music.

Sociological speculations are many and fascinating. But when some new musical form sweeps the mass audience out from under the aging bubblegum musicians, the young fans will have a clear and classic reason for liking the new music:

It's got a good beat. You can dance to it.

Alternatives*

By Richard Todd

According to Robert Glessing's recent book, *The Underground Press in America,* some 400 newspapers and magazines now serve the counter culture. There are probably as many like-minded radio stations; and more than one underground "wire service" exists, along with radical film and video-tape studios and street theater troupes and poster artists. The preferred name for this considerable activity is "alternative media."

Alternative in more senses than one: the other media offer one of the few opportunities for a radical occupation, and for some the underground is a place of corporate drama. *Rolling Stone,* the most successful of the underground papers, has a circulation of 200,000 and has started a book publishing division, headed by an editor hired away from Holt, Rinehart and Winston (though at last report the paper had run into trouble owing to overexpansion). But commercial success is abnormal and not wholly relevant: what counts, of course, is the alternative media's vision of who, and why, they are.

Speaking to this question recently, Paul Krassner said, "We want a chance to do some distortion of our own." But he was mostly kidding. Krassner, the founder of *The Realist* and ideologue for the Yippies, was addressing a group of fellow workers in the underground press, talking to several hundred of them sprawled on a sunny Vermont hillside this past summer. The occasion was the first of what may, or may not, be an annual conference sponsored by the Alternative Media Project. It was an alternative to the straight world's convention; problems of identity, not profits, occupied most minds. The four-day conference, at Goddard College, attracted 300 broadcasters, representatives of such papers as *The Liberated Guardian* and *Rat,* and such philosophers of the counter-culture

---

as Krassner and Baba Ram Dass (the former Richard Alpert). Every sort of communicator not associated with the "straight media" was welcome and was there (and several straight personalities, especially record company men, were there too, if not wholly welcome): about 2000 people at the peak. A chartered-plane-load flew in from California, an apparently marvelous journey of which Krassner said fondly: "I don't know if you've ever been on a flight where the stewardess was turning on . . . and the captain pointed out some lightning in the sky and said, 'That's God's own light show.' "

I had arrived at the conference simultaneously with a truck that said on the outside, in NASA-style lettering, "Cosmic Labs." (The driver of the truck wanted to know the way to Montpelier. The girl at the registration booth told him to take a right on the first "real road." "You mean the others aren't real? Oh, far out.") Inside, I moved across the campus and sought the crowd's flow. Goddard College is set in a high valley and surrounded by pinewoods; architecturally it is an uneasy mixture, brown-shingled, summer-place buildings amidst several small, pastel structures, which serve as dormitories. The crowd was heading through the campus and down a pine-bordered road to a field where a contingent from the New Mexican commune, the Hog Farm, had an encampment.

You might object that the Hog Farm and its many followers in the meadow (which had been provided with sanitation and water, courtesy of the college) had little to do with the "media," but perhaps this is placing too narrow a construction on the word. One way to see the Hog Farm is as a sort of ambulatory magazine: clear instructions in how-to-live come with the commune's festival services. They provided a great circus tent and food: garbage-can-sized containers of peanut butter, bread, brown rice, and a black kettle full of soup made from lettuce, carrots, and onions. To drink, electric lemonade in gallon jugs. Everyone who received some of the Hog Farmers' free LSD was painted with a bright red dot on the forehead, or occasionally treated more elaborately to warpath streaks.

The Hog Farm's buses and those of others were drawn up in a circle at noon on Friday, and in the midst of them, barebacked communicants were swigging acid from gallon jugs. A man lay spread-eagled on his back. A girl stroked his throat. He stared at the sky. His stomach, shallowly heaving, was rippled with tremors. In a moment of quiet you could hear his breath and then a choked bellow: "Hap-py! Hap-py!" he yelled.

A crew with a Sony video-tape outfit moved through the scene, shooting and taping voices, and for a while I followed them. They were Fobile Muck, a free-lance organization devoted to traveling around the country and making tapes, with which they hope to "explain the alternative world to the straight world and the other way around." I sat with them under the Hog Farm's circus tent and listened to their tapes. Nearby an entangled couple moved in languid copulation. On the machine, sounds of swigging, as the jug of electric lemonade went around, and a recorded voice said, "This is *really* alternative media."

Meanwhile, up the hill, "workshops" were in session under such headings as "Multi-image Stereo Environment Newsletter," "The Spiritual Responsibility of the Alternative Media," "Capitalism and Alternative Media," "Radical Software." Competing with the Hog Farm's encampment and swims in the college pond, the workshops were often sparsely attended, but they had their moments. At a discussion of "Free Enterprise and the Cultural Revolution" a man brandished a gun ("This may turn into a workshop on killing people"), and the workshop leader was assaulted by some of the audience at his workshop, carried bodily away, and rolled down a hill; ceremonial copulation was used at another to demonstrate the uselessness of words.

I have no adequate record of the ideas generated by the conference, but a random few of them follow. An intercommune linkup of ham radio operators is proposed; already the Aquarian Family of San Jose has such a rig. And techniques of guerrilla radio (broadcasting from the back of a moving truck on unused frequencies) are discussed. A revolutionary magazine aimed at radicalizing straight society is planned: *America Now.* Liberation News Service, the underground AP, now mails its stories; the possibilities of a genuine wire service are explored. (Ken Kesey would reportedly do the job with trucks full of Pranksters, serving as town criers.) Plans are formed to share radio tapes, and three video tape makers in New York—Video Freex, Raindance, and Global Village—discuss a national data bank of tapes: "radical software." (Not clear how the tapes will be used—until video recorders become widely available and cable television opens the airways.) Practical information is sought: a man from a New Haven radio station has broadcast an unexpurgated Jerry Rubin speech. Does anyone know how to fight an FCC complaint? And forward-looking advice is proffered: the Penguin book *Civilian Resistance As a National Defense* will be useful in the days of repression sure soon to come.

At the outdoor meeting, Paul Krassner surveys the crowd and says, "Blah, Blah, Blah, Blah, Blah. I'm just trying to articulate the consciousness of the group." And defining the consciousness of the group is a problem. Has Goddard been transformed into "a fantastic energy center"? Is what is really being born here "an alternate circulatory system for information"? "A fantastic alternative to Time Inc."? Maybe, but obstacles intrude. Women's Lib is angry over a male-sponsored orgy the day before: "We'll call our own." And several speakers want to remind others not to be deceived by the green hills and sunshine. (Frank Oliver, counsel for the Chicago 15, says in a thick, deep voice, "Does any prudent person believe that a meeting like this one will be possible one year from now?"

And unavoidable schismatic questions arise. Flowers or guns? Confrontation or counterinstitutions? Politics or transcendence?

Alternative media men, like virtually everyone else, find it easier to say who they are not than who they are; perhaps this is the chief reason that the journal I heard mentioned most often was not *A Different Drummer* or the *Berkeley Barb,* but the New York *Times.* Even at one of the Hog Farm's luncheons a girl with bare, tanned breasts stirred the soup in the iron kettle, and another girl chewed up carrots and spit them into the broth, remarking: "Tomorrow the New York *Times* will say 'Hog Farm Poisons Hundreds With Regurgitated Carrots.' "

One organization at the conference was devoted to specifying the differences between alternative and straight, and to offering regular criticism of the aboveground press, and to making gestures, at least, at subverting them. This is the "Media Project" (distinct from the Alternative Media Project), a New York-based coalition of people from various papers and from such nonprint media as Newsreel (the film-makers) and Radio Free People (producers of political radio tapes). The MP publishes a paper of its own called *Pac-O-Lies,* which includes occasional unbylined pieces by straight media people.

I talked with one MP member, a man of thirty-five, who had worked in commercial television, but now is with Blue Bus, a film-making company that lives and works in a blue bus. "I was making $20,000 a year," he said. "I had a house on Cape Ann. I had everything. I had *nothing.* I realized one day: I was shelling out $5000 a year to kill people."

The man (who did not want to be identified) accompanied almost everything he said with a kind of incredulous laugh, a sound that seemed to express gratitude at being the survivor of an accident that might have been fatal. He said that he contrasted his action with those of many of his relatives who were victims of the Nazis in Germany. "Fifty-four people in my family went right into the gas chambers thinking everything would be all right if they just kept their mouths shut."

I promised him that if I quoted anything I would quote the Media Project's statement on the occasion of the conference. ("I trust you as a person," he had said, "but I don't trust the place you work for.") The statement appeared with a drawing of the RCA Victor logotype ("His Master's Voice"):

This is a conference about alternative media.

We are participants in the conference who are part of the media of the political left.

We feel that for media to be a true alternative, they must be tools to build and struggle toward an alternative society. The struggle is for a society in which power is in the hands of the people. Media which create that society must also be in the hands of the people.

All media are political. The same forces control the media that control all other institutions. True alternative media do not undermine the people's culture by making the culture a commodity. True alternative media undermine the institutions of oppression.

The Media Project published a critique of *Newsweek's* cover story, early this year, on the Black Panthers. The text of the article is reproduced on the page and a running commentary follows it, in the manner of a gloss to a page of poetry. It is an interesting document, though it demands some complicated quoting.

The *Newsweek* piece begins: "They were the Bad Niggers of white America's nightmares come chillingly to life—a black-bereted, black-jacketed cadre of street bloods risen up in arms against the established order."

The MP responds: "This article reduces serious political movements to theatrical productions produced solely for the benefit of the media."

Newsweek: "They are guerrilla theater masterfully done. . . ."

The MP: ". . . everything is transformed into a matter of style."

Newsweek: "It matters little to the national imagination that there are fewer than 1,000 of them or that their gift for getting shot considerably exceeds their gift for shooting."

The MP: "BULLSHIT."

Newsweek: "If the Panthers survive as a party, they will be powerfully indebted to the police. The Panthers have fared best when they have had a martyr—a Newton bound for prison, a Cleaver in flight—and Fred Hampton's death in bed in Chicago gave them the best martyr they have ever had."

The MP: "Read: If the Kennedys survive as a dynasty, they will be powerfully indebted to political assassins. The Kennedys have fared best when they have had a martyr—a Joe Kennedy Jr. killed in flight, a Joe Kennedy Sr. disabled by a stroke, a Jack Kennedy murdered in Dallas—and Bobby gave them the best martyr they have ever had. . . .
"If you reacted to this as being in bad taste, and you didn't react to the parallel Panther paragraph, then you begin to understand the depths of your white supremacy."

Newsweek: [citing a Panther's remark] " 'I refer to crime as being the exploitation of poor people by filthy rich, money-mad, avaricious capitalist pigs. . . .' Tabor had mastered his catechism well."

The MP: "Political analysis is called a catechism, an attempt to depoliticize the content of the Panther's program. . . . The black community has been raped by this country for 200 years. . . ."

What to make of this exchange? All that seems truly clear is that no one—quoted Panthers or *Newsweek* or the Media Project—is engaging in something that ought to be called "political analysis." I don't want to enlarge that vacuum, except to admit for the record that *Newsweek's* political assumptions seem defensible to me (though they ought to be made explicit), and that the Media Project's position (though it has the virtue of candor) seems to me simplistic at its best.

There are real issues here. One can feel several ways about the Panthers, and some of those ways allow for genuine outrage on hearing, for example, *Newsweek's* ironic remark that the Panthers have "a gift for getting shot." And yet, I think there is a useful way to read the Media Project's critique that has not much to do with politics (though I hear the MP calling this approach evil or naïve), except in the broadest sense of that term.

At least this much is true: reading the article, even as I cannot swallow the MP's ideology, I want to object, at virtually every moment they do, to *Newsweek's* treatment of the subject. Assuming one is less than outraged, what is it that is troublesome? What goes wrong, for instance, at that moment when *Newsweek* remarks on the Panther's lucklessness at gun-fighting? As it happens, the sentence is one on which the article turns. In a short space the Panthers have been reduced from a "black-jacketed cadre of street bloods risen up . . . against the established order," to performers of "guerrilla-theater," to bumblers. The progression intro-duces *Newsweek's* unstartling argument: that the Panthers are something less than a menace, and that the police must share in the responsibility for the violence between them. But the menace that *Newsweek* debunks seems in some measure to have been invented by the magazine: those elab-orately dressed Panthers at the start were made out of straw. It is true enough, as the MP charges, that *Newsweek* is preoccupied with the Panthers' style. And whether or not this amounts to "depoliticization," it is certainly a kind of gratuitous diminishment.

The nettling thing (whether or not you are a Panther devotee) is *Newsweek's* pretense at certainty. It is a pretense only, I think; sounds of stifled doubt recur in the piece, as in the edgy overkill of he "had mas-tered his catechism well." But the magazine speaks as if it were addressing an audience that will find nothing to argue about, that needs no per-suasion. The reader is supposed to believe what the magazine believes; indeed, is supposed to know what the magazine knows. (Thus *News-week's* references to "bloods" and "Bad Niggers," which say to the reader, "We are all very familiar with this scene.") In fact, of course, many readers don't know, and are unsure of what they believe. The func-tion of the article is to provide minimal information, and a way-to-think about the Panthers, but under the guise of stating what is obvious to thoughtful men. The method works against exploration and complication: the magazine is not unwrapping but packaging the Panthers.

But of course in its melancholic way the Media Project is doing much the same thing. Seeing the magazine and the MP at loggerheads (and yet with more in common than either would like to admit), it is interesting to wonder if only ideology separates alternative from straight. Could the underground press have flourished these past years without the political provocations that are its central subject? My point is that it *should* have flourished; there are reasons for its existence that are more complex than "capitalism" or "racism," and that will no doubt remain when Vietnam and the Panthers are memories.

One reason is that we lack a common voice. It is true that phrases move from NBC to Wyoming with unprecedented speed, become universal clichés, and evanesce ("Would you believe . . . ?" "Middle America"). But who has hold of a way of speaking that begins to be adequate even to the daily experience of the society? You can hear *Newsweek* struggling to speak in a tongue shared by all who listen; you can hear an allied attempt on the objective pages of the New York *Times,* or on these pages. "We" live in a world where the only true sentence seems to begin with "I." I once heard a reporter for the *Times* defending the integrity of his job to a New York magazine editor. "I'll believe you," the editor said, "when they let you write in the first person." In this situation, the alternative media's opportunity is to allow the private voice to prosper and reinvigorate the larger language. Occasionally it does, and the MP should not, perhaps, be made to symbolize its brothers: its rhetoric (like the newsmagazines') only illustrates a characteristic snare, the temptation to create a set of beliefs, and ways of expression, that are all too symmetrically a "counter culture." While *Newsweek* cajoles, the MP throttles the reader; an alternative only in the sense that the other side of the coin is.

". . . some distortion of our own," Paul Krassner had said at the mass meeting, and lightly enough. Then, with what seemed to me sincerity, he offered a vision of communication in the longed-for future. He was taking off after some radicals who had played along with the system, made some money at it: the new media should be noncompetitive, and not personal showplaces; they are not for profit or ego-tripping, but all and only for the good of the movement. "What the revolution is all about," he said, "is making no distinction between your private and your public life."

Whatever "the revolution" may gain from our loyalty, who cannot hear the personal invitation of that remark, who has not felt a longing for the condition it implies? Freedom from compromise, from mincing distinctions, from a life lived in compartments; a wholeness of mind and purpose; *authenticity.* There is, though, a distance to go between here and authenticity, and questions about the route: Is, say, the Media Project's orthodoxy freedom enough for you? And can you lose your self in confidence that there's another waiting to be found? Well, no need to be abstract: consider the last event of the conference.

Held in Goddard's rather opulent library, a multilevel structure with stark stone walls and plush, bright-colored carpets, the last session is a workshop on "Cartoons and the Mass Consciousness": in the nature of things that the final meeting should not be planned as a summary, but natural too that it should, in a way, take on that function. The discussion ranges far.

—It is pointed out that radical art may be pasted irremovably onto glass windows with a concoction made of Carnation milk.

—A boy leaps into the center of the rough circle of participants, screaming, at first incoherently, until he yells in explanation: "I am the freak man! I am the freak man!" He is wrestled to the ground. A girl says afterward, "I love you for doing your own thing."

—Clapping, in an approximation of their rhythm, occurs as two couples make love in the center of the discussion Later, one of them explains that an invasion was once headed off somewhere, China perhaps, when the women gave themselves to the attacking army.

—Capitalism may be *used* to the advantage of the revolution, it is argued. "To say 'use capitalism' is to extend a logic that doesn't work," it is countered. "What do you want? Nam in Day-glo?"

—A considerable debate occurs on whether to cover the walls of the new library with graffiti. Only the cleaning ladies will suffer, someone says. "Hip the ladies, off the school," a voice responds . . .

At moments like this the mind often turns into a camera, saving judgment for later. Had I been doing a film of the couple who, toward the end of the workshop, were making love on the floor, I think I would have resorted to a lot of stylized editing—perhaps beginning the sequence with the girl's blond head flung sideways, her gasps, her partner's twitching, thrusting buttocks; and back then to the unhasty preparations and to the friend of the couple who bent over to talk to them as they began; and finally to the girl's face as she stood, still naked, afterward (though it would have been right to prepare for this with the quickest cut), her lips tremulously holding a cigarette, her face abruptly uncertain and inward. The point of all this, I guess, would have been to suggest that the distinction between public and private life is not often a thing to surrender.